Baroque *Classical*

Heinrich Schütz (1585–1672)

Giacomo Carissimi (1605–74)

Jean-Baptiste Lully (1632–87)

Arcangelo Corelli (1653–1713)

Henry Purcell (1659–95)

François Couperin (1668–1733)

Antonio Vivaldi (1678–1741)

Georg Phillip Telemann (1681–1767)

Jean-Philippe Rameau (1683–1764)

Johann Sebastian Bach (1685–1750)

Domenico Scarlatti (1685–1757)

George Frideric Handel (1685–1759)

Giovanni Battista Pergolesi (1710–36)

Christoph Willibald Gluck (1714–87)

Joseph Haydn (1732–1809)

William Billings (1746–1800)

Wolfgang Amadeus Mozart (1756–91)

Ludwig van Beethoven (1770–1827)

The Enjoyment of Music

27.95

BY THE AUTHOR

Introduction to Contemporary Music, Second Edition
Music: Adventures in Listening
OPERAS IN ENGLISH *(singing versions)*
Beethoven: *Fidelio*
Falla: *Atlantida*
Leoncavallo: *Pagliacci*
Mascagni: *Cavalleria rusticana*
Montemezzi: *L'Amore dei tre re* (The Loves of Three Kings)
Musorgsky: *Boris Godunov*
Poulenc: *Dialogues des Carmélites; La Voix humaine* (The Human Voice)
Prokofiev: *The Flaming Angel; War and Peace*
Puccini: *La Bohème; Il Tabarro* (The Cloak); *Tosca*
Tcherepnin: *The Farmer and the Nymph*
Verdi: *Rigoletto; La Traviata*

JOSEPH MACHLIS
Professor of Music, Queens College of the City University of New York

FIFTH EDITION

The Enjoyment of Music

An Introduction to Perceptive Listening

W · W · NORTON & COMPANY · NEW YORK · LONDON

Acknowledgments

PHOTOGRAPHS:

F. A. Ackermanns Kunstverlag: pp. 79, 112.
Alte Pinakothek, Munich: p. 361.
Aston Magna Foundation: p. 365.
Austrian National Library: p. 249.
Bayerische Staatsbibliothek: p. 343.
The Bettman Archive: pp. 100, 531, 534.
Bert Bial: p. 587.
BMI Archive: p. 503.
Boston Symphony Orchestra: p. 3.
Photographie Bulloz: pp. 94, 99, 427.
Margaret Carson: pp. 31, 34.
CBS Records: p. 34.
Veste Coburg: p. 319.
Colbert Artists Management, Inc.: p. 31.
Columbia Artists Management, Inc.: p. 39.
Columbia-Princeton Electronic Music Center, New York: p. 572 (photo by Manny Warman).
Bob van Dantzig: p. 582.
Defense Department Photo (Marine Corps): p. 532.
Deutsche Gramophone: p. 559.
Lee Edmundson: p. 36.
Embassy of the Polish People's Republic: p. 581.
G. S. Fraenkel: p. 475.
Alison Frantz: p. 223.
Galerie der Stadt Stuttgart, Stuttgart, Germany: p. 476.
German Tourist Information Office: p. 363.
Casa di Goldino, Museo Theatrale, Venice: p. 379.
Henry Goodman: p. 590.
Mrs. Toni Greenberg: p. 323.
Jane Hamborsky: p. 34.
Historischen Museums der Stadt Wien: p. 69.
ICM Artists, Ltd.: pp. 28, 31.
Jenco, Decatur, Illinois: p. 36.
Alexander Jolas Gallery: p. 460.
John F. Kennedy Center for the Performing Arts: p. 5.
Lincoln Center for the Performing Arts: p. 39.
Ludwig Industries: p. 36.
Mariedi Anders Artist Management, Inc.: p. 28.
Collection André Meyer, Paris: pp. 369, 482.
Moderna Museet, Stockholm: p. 566.
Mozart Museum, Salzburg: p. 247.
Joseph Muller Collection, Music Division, The New York Public Library, Astor, Lenox and Tilden Foundations: p. 403.
Musical America: pp. 89, 172, 454, 553.
Musser, Division of Ludwig Industries: p. 36.
C. F. Peters Corporation: p. 584.
The Philadelphia Orchestra: p. 31.
Research Center for Musical Iconography, C.U.N.Y.: p. 545.
William H. Scheide, Library, Princeton: p. 382.
Schubert-Museum: p. 70.
Ulli Seltzer: p. 477.
Edwin Smith: p. 352.
Sovfoto: p. 181.
Staatliche Museum zu Berlin, Hauptstadt der DDR, Nationalgalerie, p. 104.
Theatermuseum, Munich: p. 426.
United Press International Photo: p. 48.

MUSIC:

Jacob Arcadelt, *Il bianco cigno*: Copyrighted by American Institute of Musicology/Hänssler-Verlag, Neuhausen-Stuttgart, W. Germany. All rights reserved. Used by permission only. p. 347.

Allan Berg, *Wozzeck*: Reprinted through the courtesy of London Records, a Division of PolyGram Classics, Inc. pp. 505–508.

Acknowledgments continued on p. vi.

Cover illustration by Reginald Pollack. Cover design by Antler & Baldwin Design Group.

The text of this book is composed in Times Roman, with display type set in Caslon. Composition by Penn Set. Manufacturing by The Murray Printing Company. Book design by Antonina Krass. Layout by Ben Gamit.

ISBN 0-393-95297-5

W. W. Norton & Company, Inc., 500 Fifth Avenue, New York, N. Y. 10110
W. W. Norton & Company Ltd., 37 Great Russell Street, London WC1B 3NU

4 5 6 7 8 9 0

For Earle Fenton Palmer

Acknowledgments (continued from p. iv)

Béla Bartók, *Concerto for Orchestra*: © Copyright 1946 by Hawkes & Son (London) Ltd; Renewed 1973. Reprinted by permission of Boosey & Hawkes, Inc. pp. 491–93.

Aaron Copland, *Hoe-Down* from *Rodeo*: © Copyright 1946 by Aaron Copland, Renewed 1973. Reprinted by permission of Aaron Copland, Copyright Owner, and Boosey & Hawkes, Inc., Sole Licensees. pp. 551–52.

Guillaume Dufay, *Navré je suis*: Copyrighted by American Institute of Musicology/Hänssler-Verlag, Neuhausen-Stuttgart, W. Germany. All rights reserved. Used by permission only. p. 320.

George Gershwin, *Rhapsody in Blue*: © 1924 (renewed) NEW WORLD MUSIC CORPORATION. All rights reserved. Used by permission of Warner Bros. Music. pp. 547–48.

Philip Glass, *Floe* from *Glassworks*: © 1982 by Dunvagen Music Publishers, Inc. p. 603.

Philip Glass, *Music in Fifths*: © Philip Glass 1973. p. 601.

Clément Janequin, *Les Cris de Paris*: © Editions de L'Oiseau-Lyre, Les Remparts, Monaco. p. 338.

György Ligeti, *Atmosphères*: © 1963 by Universal Editions A. G., Wien. Used by permission of European American Music Distributors Corporation, Sole U.S. Agent for Universal Editions. p. 583.

Guillaume de Machaut, *Hareu!—Helas!—Obediens* and *Rose, liz*: © Editions de L'Oiseau-Lyre, Les Remparts, Monaco. pp. 315 and 316.

Konrad Paumann, *Elend, du hast umfangen mich*: From *Geschichte der Musik in Beispielen* by Arnold Schering, used by permission of Breitkopf & Härtel, Wiesbaden. p. 326.

Igor Stravinsky, *Le Sacre du Printemps*: © Copyright 1921 by Edition Russe de Musique. Copyright assigned 1947 to Boosey & Hawkes, Inc. Reprinted by permission. pp. 480–83.

Stravinsky, *Symphony of Psalms*: © Copyright 1931 by Edition Russe de Musique; Renewed 1958. Copyright and Renewal assigned to Boosey & Hawkes, Inc. Revised Edition Copyright by Boosey & Hawkes, Inc. Renewed 1975. Reprinted by permission. pp. 484–86.

Anton Webern, *Pieces for Orchestra*, Op. 10, Nos. 3 and 4: Copyright 1923 by Universal Edition A. G., Wien; Copyright renewed 1951; Used by permission of European American Music Distributors Corporation, Sole U. S. agent for Universal Edition. p. 514.

TRANSLATIONS:

Excerpt from *Aïda* by Giuseppe Verdi, pp. 158–162, translation from *Seven Verdi Librettos* by William Weaver. Copyright © 1963 by William Weaver. Reprinted by permission of Doubleday & Company, Inc.

Excerpt from *Tristan und Isolde* by Richard Wagner, pp. 169–70, translation by David Hamilton.

Excerpt from *Don Giovanni* by W. A. Mozart, pp. 253–57, translation by Andrew Porter.

Translations of *Les Cris de Paris*, p. 337, *Reis Glorios*, p. 306, *Rose Liz*, p. 316, *Navré je suis*, p. 319, by Dr. Yvette Louria.

Text translation of Jacob Arcadelt, *Il bianco cigno*, from *Arcadelt Opera Omnia* vol. 2, by Albert Seay, p. 346.

Excerpt from *Wozzeck*, Act III, scenes 4 & 5, pp. 509–11, translation London 1981 Sarah E. Soulsby.

Poetry on pp. 585–86 (Nos. 1, 2, 4) from Federico García Lorca, *Selected Poems*. Copyright 1955 by New Directions Publishing Corporation. Reprinted by permission of New Directions Publishing Corporation.

Poetry on pp. 585–86 (Nos. 3, 5) from J. L. Gili, *Lorca*. Copyright © J. L. Gili, 1960. Reprinted by permission of New Directions Publishing Corporation. Poetry translation on p. 588 courtesy Columbia Records.

Contents

TWO Nineteenth-Century Romanticism 57

FIVE *Medieval, Renaissance, and Baroque Music* *293*

Preface to the Fifth Edition

In preparing this new edition of *The Enjoyment of Music*, I pondered the question of whether the philosophy of the original book was still valid for students today. Had the unprecedented dissemination of music—made possible by all the recent technological advances—altered my conviction that teaching a student how to enjoy an art is not quite the same as teaching its history? After much thought, I decided that the order in which the material is presented should still be determined by psychological rather than purely chronological considerations. Supporting this decision is the thought that, if I wanted to introduce a young person today to the joys of English literature, I would begin with the great novels of the nineteenth century or the works of Norman Mailer and Kurt Vonnegut before tackling Beowulf or *The Faerie Queene*. Similarly, once the basic elements of music have been explained, I discuss composers such as Schubert, Tchaikovsky, and Brahms, Verdi, Wagner, and their contemporaries, whose harmonic and melodic language is most accessible to students today; then I move back to the late-eighteenth-century Classicism of Haydn, Mozart, and Beethoven, from there to the older music of Gregorian chant to Bach and Handel; and finally, to the twentieth century. I am delighted that so many teachers have found this to be a convincing way to approach the world of Western art music. There are those, of course, who would rather follow a chronological approach; some have found the Baroque period to be an excellent point of entry; others prefer to start with the present and move backwards from the familiar to the unfamiliar. Since each section of my book is a self-contained unit, teachers can rearrange the order of the text to achieve the sequence they prefer.

A number of changes were made in the light of recent classroom experience and shifting tastes. The first two chapters of the fourth edition are here replaced with a new one titled *Music in the Modern World*, designed to stimulate class discussion about the role of music in our lives today. In the section on nineteenth-century Romanticism, I dropped several minor works, replaced Dvořák's beautiful but idiosyncratic *New World Symphony* with Tchaikovsky's *Pathétique*, and shifted from Brahms's *Third* to his somewhat more accessible *Second Symphony*. Schumann's *Piano Concerto* now represents that genre for the period, and *Aïda* has replaced

La traviata. Among the songs, *Die beiden Grenadiere* has given way to the more personal *Ich grolle nicht*, and Brahms's *A German Requiem* is studied along with Verdi's *Requiem*, to round out the discussion of choral music. In the section on the Classical era, Haydn's *Symphony No. 104* has replaced his *Surprise Symphony*. In addition, I dropped Mozart's *Symphony No. 40*, since teaching it seemed to present certain analytical difficulties.

In recognition of the growing popularity of old music, I have included several accessible secular and instrumental works from the Middle Ages and Renaissance—all of them available in lively performance on records. Given the wide variations among performances of music from these periods, I have, in the discussions of these works, referred to specific interpretations (which are included in the Norton recordings). Among the new works are a beautiful troubadour song, *Reis glorios* by Guiraut de Bornelh; two love songs by Machaut replacing the Kyrie from his *Messe de Notre Dame*; Dufay's charming chanson *Navré je sui*; Janequin's colorful *Les Cris de Paris*; and three examples of late-Medieval instrumental music: an anonymous *Saltarello* from the fourteenth century; Paumann's *Elend, du hast umfangen mich*; and an anonymous basse danse from the fifteenth century, *Il Re de Spagna.*

Current interest in Baroque music will be well served by the replacement of the Vivaldi *Concerto Grosso* with his popular work *The Four Seasons.* New among the Bach works is Cantata No. 80, *Ein feste Burg,* based on the most celebrated of all Lutheran hymns. Domenico Scarlatti is now represented by his brilliant *Sonata in E major.*

In the material on the twentieth century, I retained most of the considerably enlarged section prepared for the fourth edition, deleting only a few works to keep the book from becoming unwieldy. But Britten's *Four Sea Episodes* from *Peter Grimes* has been added, a fitting tribute to the late English master. The American section is now prefaced by an introductory chapter that traces the development of a musical style unique to this country. In addition, Copland's *Rodeo* replaces his *Billy the Kid*, and the treatment of George Gershwin's *Rhapsody in Blue* is greatly expanded. To the concluding part of the book, *The New Music*, I've added discussions of Ligeti and Philip Glass.

The appendices have been revised, especially the *Suggested Reading* list, which emphasizes recent and easily available books on all areas touched upon in the text; also, the *Chronological List* has been brought up to date, and new end papers designed to provide an instantaneous historical perspective. I hope that these and similar changes will make the text more useful for both student and teacher.

After serious reflection, I decided to drop the chapters on jazz that were written by Martin Williams for the fourth edition, since their presence in the book was wholly inconsistent with my stated objectives, and the subject is worthy of a course of its own. Instead, I discuss jazz, rock, folk, and popular music in the context of their influence on art music, rather than as separate entities. And I have not wavered in my rejection of the practice, currently the fashion in books of this nature, of devoting a token chapter or two to non-Western music. The musics of Asia and Africa represent a diversity of ancient cultures with an extraordinarily rich and complex literature, any adequate discussion of which would carry us far beyond the confines of this book. To attempt to cover so vast a subject in a few pages is as pointless as it would be, in a book on African or Asian music, for the author to dismiss the musical heritage of the West in a chapter or two. Such a procedure can have no educational or intellectual validity whatever.

For those who are using the Norton recordings that go with the book, references in the margin point to the location in the set of the particular work being discussed. In acknowledgment of the increasing number of cassette machines currently in use, the recordings are now available in both disc and cassette form. It is not suggested that the text cannot be taught with other recordings of the same work, if the instructor so prefers. The sole advantage of the Norton recordings is convenience: they bring together the most important works discussed in the text. Whatever recordings are used, the text should serve only as an introduction to the music itself.

I am heavily indebted to David Hamilton and Claire Brook for their devoted reading of the manuscript, and to Kathleen Wilson Spillane for her care in preparing it for publication. I very much want to thank the many colleagues who were sufficiently interested in this revision to share with me their suggestions for making this a better book.

The text, naturally, covers a much wider field than the course, but it is designed to achieve the same goal: to create music lovers. In this connection, it is well to recall Stravinsky's wonderful remark, "The trouble with music appreciation in general is that people are taught to have too much respect for music; they should be taught to love it instead."

JOSEPH MACHLIS

PART ONE

The Materials of Music

"There are only twelve tones. You must treat them carefully." — PAUL HINDEMITH

1

Music in the Modern World

"The artist speaks to our capacity for delight and wonder, to the sense of mystery surrounding our lives, to our sense of pity, and beauty, and pain." — JOSEPH CONRAD

We live surrounded by music. From the moment we wake up, the radio provides us with a musical background for our activities throughout the day. We can hear music while we eat our breakfast, in the car on our way to work or school, in hotel lobbies and elevators, restaurants and cafeterias, shops and trains and planes. At home, if the radio is resting, its place may be taken by the record or tape player. Music is very much in evidence in the movies, theater, and television. We can carry it with us when we move around, thanks to the personal stereo. We can listen to it "live" at concerts, outdoor festivals, the opera house, or the ballet, and we can even make it ourselves by singing or playing an instrument.

What is more, modern technology has placed at our disposal every kind of music, from virtually every period in history and every corner of the globe. We can hear an African drummer playing in a tribal ritual, a Wag-

Listening to music "live" on a Sunday afternoon at Tanglewood, summer home of the Boston Symphony Orchestra. (Photo by Lincoln Russell.)

A standing ovation for the legendary Artur Rubinstein at Carnegie Hall. (Photo by Eva Rubinstein.)

ner opera performed in the theater in Bayreuth that Wagner himself designed and built, a jazz improvisation by Louis Armstrong, or a Medieval Mass from a cathedral in France. We can enjoy in turn a new piece played at an avant-garde festival in Chicago, a Broadway musical as performed by the original cast forty years ago, an eighteenth-century concerto played on instruments of its own period, or an aria from a Puccini opera sung by the singer, long since dead, who first performed it under the composer's supervision. So, too, we can turn from an old English ballad as handed down by generations of folk singers in the Appalachian mountains to the song hits of the Beatles in the '60s or a Stravinsky ballet conducted by the composer. There is simply no end to the variety of musical experiences we can choose from, according to our taste and mood.

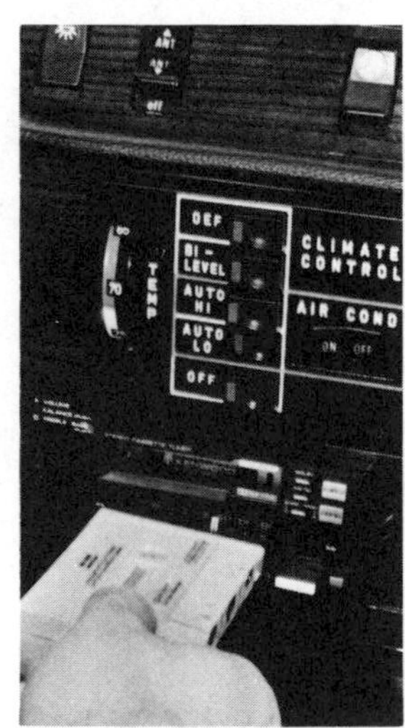

Modern technology allows us to listen to our favorite music while driving to work or school. (Photo by Robert Curtis.)

Only in the twentieth century has such a wealth and variety of musical experience been available to one person. This is a direct consequence of a century of technological developments, beginning with the invention of the phonograph by Thomas Edison in 1875, and continuing with radio broadcasting, tape recording, television, the miniaturization of electronic equipment and, most recently, digital recording methods. These have revolutionized the place of music in our lives.

It may even be difficult for us today to imagine a world in which all music had to be "hand-made," so to speak, where sounds, once uttered, could not be recaptured but had to be made again from scratch. In that world, music almost always served a specific purpose or occasion. From the songs and dances of the peasantry to the art music of the aristocracy, it accompanied every important ceremony of public and private life, whether

A free concert in the Grand Foyer of the Kennedy Center. (Photo by Richard Braaten.)

wedding or funeral, military triumph, or religious rite, theatrical entertainment or the expression of personal feeling. Different countries and ethnic groups developed their own kinds of music, each distinct from the other, conditioned by their social life, the sounds and rhythms of their languages, the rituals of their religions. Within each society, a variety of musical types and styles arose to fulfill the different needs of the palace and the church, the townspeople and the countryside, of farmhands, stevedores, drivers, shepherds. Thus the music of each society mirrored the life of which it was a part, and as society developed through history, music changed with it.

There was always a distinction made between "popular" and "classical," between the indigenous music of the folk and the art music of the court or cathedral. Frequently, there was an active interchange between the two types, so that each vastly enriched the other. During the Middle Ages and Renaissance, a Catholic Mass might be based upon a popular, even frivolous, song. Later on, popular dances such as the gavotte or jig found their way into the suites of Handel and Bach. Similarly, a stylized form of the minuet became a standard feature of the symphonies of Haydn and Mozart. This interchange continues into modern times. Composers such as Stravinsky and Milhaud in Europe, Copland and Thomson in the United States, were strongly influenced by jazz. George Gershwin successfully bridged the gap between Tin Pan Alley and Carnegie Hall. Today composers like Steve Reich and Philip Glass introduce elements that originated with rock into their concert works, while a rock musician such as Frank Zappa has been influenced by the music of Edgard Varèse.

Much of the music we encounter in daily life does not require formal study; its impact is direct and immediate, for it uses familiar sounds in familiar patterns. Popular music today, as in every age, is intended to be immediately accessible, to speak to its audience directly, without the need of intermediaries to explain its forms and meanings. But our modern world of music also brings us into contact with music that is not always so quickly grasped. It may use unfamiliar sound materials, or familiar ones in unfamiliar ways. It may have been written in a time and place far removed from our own, or for situations that are no longer part of our lives; therefore its full meaning is not immediately apparent to us. We may enjoy listening to such music, simply basking in the sheer novelty, even the beauty, of the unfamiliar sounds. We may, with repeated hearings, begin to understand the ways in which the composer has arranged these sounds into interesting patterns. Eventually, we will probably feel the urge to study further, to learn more about some of these unfamiliar kinds of music. And that is the main purpose of a book such as this: to broaden the reader's experience into kinds of music hitherto unfamiliar.

The language of music cannot be translated into the language of words. You cannot deduce the actual sound of a piece of music from anything written about it; the ultimate meaning lies in the sounds themselves. What, you will wonder, can be said to prepare the nonmusician for those sounds? A great deal. We can discuss the social and historical context in which a work developed. We can learn about the characteristic features of the various style-periods in music history, so that we are able to relate the music to parallel developments in literature and the fine arts. We can read about the lives and thoughts of the composers who left us so rich a heritage, and take note of what they said about their art. We can acquaint ourselves with the elements out of which music is made, and discover how these are combined in the particular work we are studying. All this knowledge—social, historical and biographical, technical and analytical—can be interrelated. What will emerge is a total picture of the work that will clarify, in far greater degree than you may have thought possible, the form and meaning of the piece.

No music exists in a vacuum. In discussing the tradition of Western art music, we will touch briefly upon other types of music as they have interacted with that tradition. The varied musics of Africa and Asia, the worlds of European and American folk music, the remarkable flowering of American jazz in the twentieth century, the vibrant history of popular and theatrical music—each of these is in itself a subject worthy of serious study. (The bibliography, p. 609, lists some books treating these special areas in detail.) But in this book we will concentrate on the main currents in Western art music, out of which grew the repertory on which our concert life depends.

There are people who tell you that they prefer not to know anything about the music they hear. Technical information, they claim, spoils their enjoyment. Yet they would never suggest that the best way to enjoy a football game is to know nothing about the rules of the game. What they really fear, one suspects, is that knowledge of any kind will interfere with their daydreams while they are listening. Intelligent music lovers have no such fear of knowledge. They realize that the true source of the musical experience is not in themselves but in the sounds. Consequently, they are curious to know how these sounds are put together, why one thing happens rather than another. The closer listeners come to the sounds, the more they hear and the more they comprehend.

"To understand," said the painter Raphael, "is to equal." When we fully understand a great musical work we grasp the "moment of truth" that gave it birth. For a moment we become, if not the equal of the master who created it, at least worthy to sit in his company. We receive his message, we fathom his intention. In effect, we listen perceptively—and that is the one sure road to the enjoyment of music.

2

Melody: Musical Line

"It is the melody which is the charm of music, and it is that which is most difficult to produce. The invention of a fine melody is a work of genius." — JOSEPH HAYDN

Melody is that element of music which makes the widest and most direct appeal. It has been called the soul of music. It is generally what we remember and whistle and hum. We know a good melody when we hear it and we recognize its unique power to move us, although we might be hard put to explain wherein its power lies. The melody is the musical line—or curve, if you prefer—that guides our ear through a composition. The melody is the plot, the theme of a musical work, the thread upon which hangs the tale. As Aaron Copland aptly put it, "The melody is generally what the piece is about."

A *melody* is a succession of single tones perceived by the mind as a unity. In order to perceive a melody as a unity, we must find a significant relationship among its constituent tones. We must derive from them an impression of a conscious arrangement: the sense of a beginning, a middle, and an end. We hear the words of a sentence not singly but in relation to the thought as a whole. So too we perceive tones not separately but in relation to each other within a pattern. A melody seems to move up and down, its individual tones being higher or lower than each other. It also moves forward in time, one tone claiming our attention for a longer or shorter duration than another. From the interaction of the two dimensions emerges the total unit which is melody.

Melodic range

In addition, a melody may move stepwise along the scale or it may leap to a tone several degrees away. The leap may be narrow or wide, as may be the *range* of the melody (the distance from its lowest to highest tone). Compare the narrow range and stepwise movement of *America* with the bold leaps and far-flung activity of *The Star-Spangled Banner*. Clearly *The Star-Spangled Banner* is the more vigorous melody. A melody may be fast or slow, loud or soft. A loud and fast tune such as *Dixie* creates the atmosphere of jaunty activity proper to a marching song as surely as a soft, slow melody like *Silent Night* suggests a hymnlike serenity and peace. In short, the character of a melody is determined by its overall pattern of movement.

The Structure of Melody

Let us examine the pattern of a well-known tune.

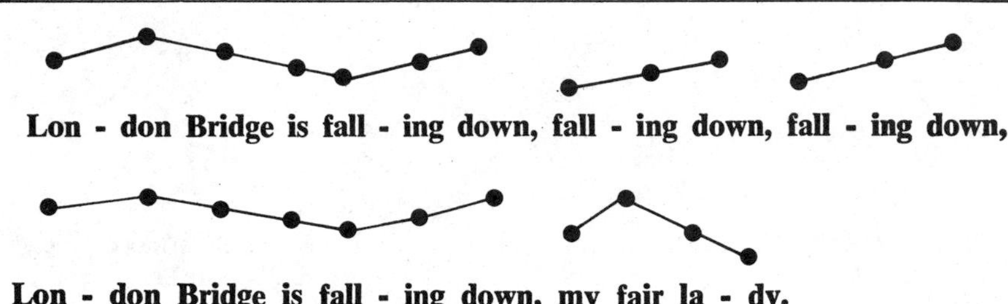

The phrase

You will notice that this melody divides itself into two halves. Such symmetry is found frequently in melodies dating from the eighteenth and nineteenth centuries. Each of these halves is called a *phrase*. In music, as in language, a phrase denotes a unit of meaning within a larger structure. Two phrases together form a musical *period*.

Each phrase ends in a kind of resting place that punctuates the flow of the music. Such a resting place is known as a *cadence*. The first phrase of *London Bridge* ends in an upward inflection, like a question. This is an inconclusive type of cadence, indicating, like a comma in punctuation, that more is to come. The second phrase ends in a full cadence that creates a sense of conclusion. The vigorous downward inflection on the word "la-dy" contributes to this decisive ending. (It should be pointed out, however, that not all final cadences move downward.) Both phrases of *London Bridge* combine in a question-and-answer formation: the second phrase grows out of the first and completes its meaning. We find here the quality of organic unity that is of prime importance in art.

The composer unifies his structure by repeating some of his musical ideas. Thus both phrases of *London Bridge* begin in identical fashion. The necessary contrast is supplied by fresh material, which in our example comes on the words "my fair lady." Through repetition and contrast the composer achieves both unity and variety. This combination of traits is basic to musical architecture, for without unity there is chaos, without variety—boredom.

The melodic line does not leave off haphazardly, as if it suddenly found something better to do. On the contrary, it gives the impression of having reached its goal. If you will hum the last phrase of several well-known tunes such as *The Star-Spangled Banner, America,* and *Auld Lang Syne,* you will notice they all end on a tone that produces this effect of finality. We encounter here what for centuries has been a basic principle in our music: one tone is singled out as the center of the group and serves as a landmark for the others. This central tone is the one to which, in most cases, the melody ultimately returns.

Melodic shape

The phrase as a whole may trace an upward or downward curve. Not infrequently, the one is balanced by the other. *The Farmer in the Dell* presents an ascending first phrase which is answered by a descending second phrase:

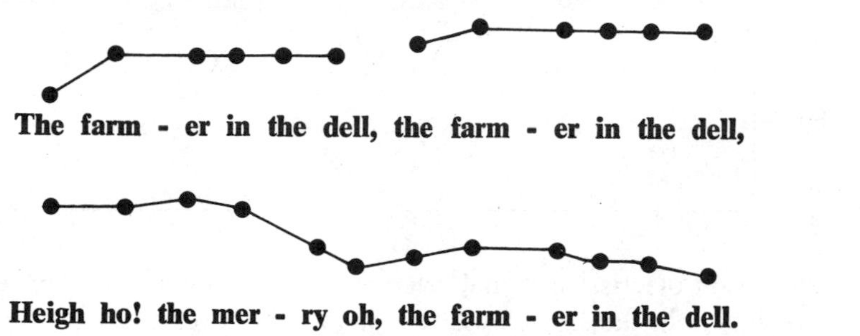

The melody moves forward in time, now faster, now slower, in a rhythmic pattern that holds our attention even as does its up and down movement. Without the rhythm the melody loses its aliveness. Try singing *London Bridge* or *The Farmer in the Dell* in tones of equal duration, and see how much is lost of the quality of the pattern. Without rhythm, the melody could not be organized into clear-cut phrases and cadences.

Our gestures when we speak are purely physical movements, yet they carry emotional meaning. In the same way, the physical facts that make up a melody take on psychological implications. The melodic line may be described as angular or smooth, tense or relaxed, energetic or languid. Above all, the melody must be interesting. We say of a painter that he has a sense of line, meaning that he is able to sustain movement over the whole of his canvas. The same holds for the unfolding melodic line with its rising and falling, its peaks and valleys. A melody has to have what musicians call the "long line." It must build tension as it rises from one level to the next, and must retain its drive until the final note.

What makes a striking effect on the listener is the climax, the high point in the melodic line that usually represents the peak of intensity. The climax gives purpose and direction to the melodic line. It creates the

The undulating line in a painting or a melody sustains movement. A drawing by Pablo Picasso (1881–1973), **Four Ballet Dancers.** (Collection, The Museum of Modern Art, New York; Gift of Abby Aldrich Rockefeller.)

impression of crisis met and overcome. Our national anthem contains a fine climax in the last phrase, on the words "O'er the land of the free." There can be no doubt in anybody's mind that this song is about freedom. Clearly, too, freedom must be striven for, to judge from the effort we have to make to get up to the crucial tone.

The principles we have touched upon are to be found in the melodies of the masters. Let us take some familiar examples. Brahms's popular *Hungarian Dance No. 5* opens with vigorous upward leaps. The impression of energy is reinforced by the lively rhythm. As is often the case with dance tunes, the phrases are symmetrical, with a clearly marked cadence at the end of each. The activity of this melodic line contrasts with the gentle flow of the Air from Bach's *Suite No. 3* for orchestra, which moves at a much slower pace. So too the soaring line of the March from *Aïda* contrasts with the restricted activity of Chopin's *Prelude in E minor,* which moves mostly stepwise and within a narrow range. However, this melody ascends to a dramatic climax in the final section, whence it subsides to a serene final cadence.

Chopin's *Mazurka in B flat,* Opus 7, No. 1, exemplifies a type of melody that, because of its wide range and leaps, is more suitable for an instrument than for the voice. (*Opus,* abbreviated Op., the Latin for "work," is used together with a number to indicate the chronological position of a piece–or a group of pieces–in a composer's output. The opus number may refer to either the order of composition or the order of publication.)

The lively rhythm of Chopin's *Mazurka* underlines the dance character of this piece. A fine example of how rhythm can make a melody memorable is offered by the *Hallelujah Chorus* from Handel's *Messiah.* The sharply defined rhythm on the word "Hallelujah," repeated again and again in the course of the piece, stamps itself unforgettably on the mind.

"Melody," writes the composer Paul Hindemith, "is the element in which the personal characteristics of the composer are most clearly and most obviously revealed." For melody is the essential unit of communication in music: the direct bearer of meaning from composer to listener.

3

Harmony: Musical Space

"Music, to create harmony, must investigate discord." — PLUTARCH

We are accustomed to hearing melodies against a background of harmony. To the movement of the melody, harmony adds another dimension —depth. Harmony is to music what perspective is to painting. It introduces the impression of musical space. The supporting role of harmony is apparent when a singer accompanies his melody with chords on the guitar or banjo, or when a pianist plays the melody with his right hand while the left strikes the chords. We are jolted if the wrong chord is sounded, for at that point we become aware that the necessary unity of melody and harmony has been broken.

Interval and chord

Harmony pertains to the movement and relationship of intervals and chords. An *interval* may be defined as the distance—and relationship— between two tones. In the familiar *do-re-mi-fa-sol-la-ti-do* scale, the interval *do-re* is a second, *do-mi* is a third, *do-fa* a fourth, *do-sol* a fifth, *do-la* a sixth, *do-ti* a seventh, and from one *do* to the next is an octave. The tones of the interval may be sounded in succession or simultaneously.

A *chord* may be defined as a combination of three or more tones that constitutes a single unit of harmony. Just as the vaulting arch rests upon columns, so melody unfolds above the supporting chords, the harmony. The melodic line constitutes the horizontal aspect of music; the harmony, consisting of blocks of tones (chords), constitutes the vertical:

The Function of Harmony

Chords have meaning only in relation to other chords: that is, only as each leads into the next. Harmony therefore implies movement and progression. In the larger sense, harmony denotes the overall organization of tones in a musical work in such a way as to achieve order and unity.

The triad

The most common chord in our music is a certain combination of three tones known as a *triad.* Such a chord may be built by combining the first, third, and fifth degrees of the *do-re-mi-fa-sol-la-ti-do* scale: *do-mi-sol.* A triad may be built on the second degree (steps 2–4–6 or *re-fa-la*); on the third degree (steps 3–5–7 or *mi-sol-ti*); and similarly on each of the other degrees of the scale. The triad is a basic formation in our music. "In the world of tones," observes one authority, "the triad corresponds to the force of gravity. It serves as our constant guiding point, our unit of measure, and our goal."

Although the triad is a vertical block of sound, its three tones often appear horizontally as a melody. The first three tones of the *Blue Danube Waltz* form a triad, as do the first three of our national anthem (on the words "O-oh-say"). When the lowest tone (or root) of the chord is duplicated an octave above, we have a four-tone version of the triad. This happens at the beginning of *The Star-Spangled Banner,* on the words "say can you see." It is apparent that melody and harmony do not function independently of one another. On the contrary, the melody implies the harmony that goes with it, and each constantly influences the other.

Active and Rest Chords

Music is an art of movement. Movement to be purposeful must have a goal. In the course of centuries musicians have tried to make the progression of chords meaningful by providing such a goal.

Tonic and Dominant

We noticed, in the previous chapter, that a number of melodies ended —that is, came to rest—on a central tone. This is the *do* which comes both first and last in the *do-re-mi-fa-sol-la-ti-do* scale. The triad on *do* (*do-mi-sol*) is the I chord or *Tonic,* which serves as the chord of rest. But rest has meaning only in relation to activity. The chord of rest is counterposed to other chords which are active. The active chords seek to be completed, or *resolved,* in the rest chord. This striving for resolution is the dynamic force in our music. It shapes the forward movement, imparting direction and goal.

The fifth step of the *do-re-mi-fa-sol-la-ti-do* scale is the chief representative of the active principle. We therefore obtain two focal points: the active triad on *sol* (*sol-ti-re*), the V chord or *Dominant,* which seeks to be resolved to the restful triad on *do.* Dominant moving to Tonic constitutes a compact formula of activity completed, of movement come to rest.

The cadence

We saw that the cadence is a point of rest in the melody. This point of rest is underlined by the harmony. For example, Dominant resolving to Tonic is the most common final cadence in our music. We hear it asserted over and over again at the end of many compositions dating from the eighteenth and nineteenth centuries. After generations of conditioning we feel a decided expectation that an active chord will resolve to the chord of rest.

Following is the harmonic structure of *Down in the Valley,* involving a simple progression from Tonic to Dominant and back.

Down in the valley,	**valley so low,**
I ______	**V** ______
Hang your head over,	**hear the wind blow.**
V ______	**V** ______ **I** ___

The Subdominant

The triad built on the fourth scale step *fa* (*fa-la-do*) is known as the IV chord or *Subdominant*. This too is an active chord, but less so than the Dominant. The progression IV—I creates a less decisive cadence than the other. It is familiar to us from the two chords associated with the Amen often sung at the end of hymns.

These three triads, the basic ones of our system, suffice to harmonize many a famous tune.

Silent night!	**Holy night!**	**All is calm,**	**all is bright,**
I ______	**I** ______	**V** ______	**I** ______
Round yon Virgin	**Mother and Child!**	**Holy Infant, so**	**tender and mild,**
IV ______	**I** ______	**IV** ______	**I** ______
Sleep in heavenly	**peace,**	**Sleep in heavenly**	**peace.**
V ______	**I** ______	**I** ______ **V** ___	**I** ______

Consonance and Dissonance

Harmonic movement, we saw, is generated by the tendency of active chords to be resolved to chords of rest. This movement receives its maximum impetus from the dissonance. *Dissonance* is restlessness and activity, *consonance* is relaxation and fulfillment. The dissonant chord creates tension. The consonant chord resolves it.

Dissonance introduces the necessary tension into music. Without it, a work would be intolerably dull and insipid. What suspense and conflict are to the drama, dissonance is to music. It creates the areas of tension

Harmony lends a sense of depth to music, as perspective does to painting. Meindert Hobbema (1638–1709), **The Avenue, Middleharnis.** (Courtesy of the Trustees, The National Gallery, London.)

without which the areas of relaxation would have no meaning. Each complements the other; both are a necessary part of the artistic whole.

In general, music has grown more dissonant through the ages. It is easy to understand why. A combination of tones that sounded extremely harsh when first introduced began to seem less so as the sound became increasingly familiar. As a result, a later generation of composers had to find ever more dissonant tone-combinations in order to produce the same amount of tension as their predecessors. This process has extended across the centuries, as is apparent if we listen in succession to music of different epochs. For example, the Kyrie from the *Mass for Pope Marcellus* by Palestrina, (1567), has all the seraphic calm we associate with the sacred music of that composer; yet it must have sounded considerably less consonant to Palestrina's contemporaries than it does to us. Next, listen to the first movement of Mozart's *Eine kleine Nachtmusik* or the duet *Là ci darem la mano* from his opera *Don Giovanni:* both works date from 1787. The harmony will strike you as predominantly consonant, although less so than the Palestrina piece. In the Prelude to his most romantic music drama, Wagner tried to express the unfulfilled yearning of Tristan for Isolde (1859). There is a markedly higher level of dissonance tension here than in the music of Mozart. Finally, for an example of twentieth-century dissonance, listen to Arnold Schoenberg's *Vorgefühle* (Premonition), Opus 16, No. 1 (1909). This piece will suggest to you the distance that separates the music of our century, in regard to dissonance tension, from the music of earlier times.

Harmony is a much more sophisticated phenomenon than melody. Historically it appeared much later, about a thousand years ago. Its real development took place only in the West. The music of the Orient to this day is largely melodic. Indeed, we may consider the great achievement of Western music to be harmony (hearing in depth), even as in painting it is perspective (seeing in depth). Our harmonic system has advanced steadily over the past ten centuries. Today it is adjusting to new needs. These constitute the latest chapter in man's age-old attempt to impose law and order upon the raw material of sound; to organize tones in such a way that they will manifest a unifying idea, a selective imagination, a reasoning will.

4

Rhythm: Musical Time

"In the beginning was rhythm." — HANS VON BÜLOW

Rhythm—the word means "flow" in Greek—is the term we use to refer to the controlled movement of music in time. The duration of the tones, their frequency, and the regularity or irregularity with which they are sounded determine the rhythm of a musical passage. Rhythm is the element of music most closely allied to body movement, to physical action. Its simpler patterns when repeated over and over can have a hypnotic effect on us. For this reason rhythm has been called the heartbeat of music, the pulse that betokens life. It is this aspect of rhythm that people have in mind when they say of a musician that "he's got rhythm," meaning an electrifying quality, an aliveness almost independent of the notes. Yet, since music is an art that exists solely in time, rhythm in the larger sense controls all the relationships within a composition, down to the minutest detail. Hence Roger Sessions's remark that "an adequate definition of rhythm comes close to defining music itself."

The Nature of Rhythm

It is rhythm that causes people to fall in step when the band plays, to nod or tap with the beat. Rhythm releases our motor reflexes even if we do not respond with actual physical movement. We feel it in ourselves as a kind of ideal motion; we seem to dance without leaving our chairs.

Rhythm springs from the need for order inherent in the human mind. Upon the tick-tock of the clock or the clacking of train wheels we automatically impose a pattern. We hear the sounds as a regular pulsation of strong and weak beats. In brief, we organize our perception of time by means of rhythm.

In architecture, symmetry and repetition of elements are expressions of rhythm. The interior of the Guggenheim Museum, New York City. (Ezra Stoller, © Esto.)

The ancients discerned in rhythm the creative principle of the universe manifested alike in the regular movement of planets, the cycle of seasons and tides, of night and day, desire and appeasement, life and death. Yet these rhythms framed an existence that all too often lacked design and meaning. Rivers overflowed for no good reason, lightning struck, enemies pillaged. Exposed to the caprice of a merciless destiny, man fashioned for himself an ideal universe where the unforeseen was excluded and divine order reigned. This universe was art; and its controlling principle was rhythm. The symmetrical proportions of architecture, the balanced groupings of painting and sculpture, the patterns of the dance, the regular meters of poetry—each in its own sphere represents man's deep-seated need for rhythmical arrangement. But it is in music, the art of ideal movement, that rhythm finds its richest expression.

Meter

If we are to grasp the flow of music through time, time must be organized. Musical time is usually organized in terms of a basic unit of length, known as a *beat*—the regular pulsation to which we may tap our feet. Some beats are stronger than others—these are known as *accented* or *strong* beats. In much of the music we hear, these strong beats occur at regular intervals—every other beat, every third beat, every fourth, and so on—and thus we perceive the beats in groups of two, three, four, or more. These groups are known as *measures,* each containing a fixed number of beats. The first beat of the measure generally receives the strongest accent.

Meter, therefore, denotes the fixed time patterns within which musical events take place. Within the underlying metrical framework, the rhythm flows freely. In a dance band, the drummer will beat a regular pattern, with an accent on the first beat of every measure, while the trumpeter or another soloist will play a melody, containing many notes of different lengths, flowing freely over the regular pattern. Together, both of them articulate the rhythm or overall flow of the music. We may say that all waltzes have the same meter: ONE-two-three ONE-two-three. Within that meter, however, each waltz follows its own rhythmic pattern.

Although meter is one element of rhythm, it is possible to draw a subtle distinction between them. This may be noted in the domain of poetry. A metrical reading of a poem—such as these lines by Robert Frost—will bring out the regular pattern of accented and unaccented syllables:

The wóods are lóve-ly, dárk and déep.
But Í have próm-is-és to kéep,

When we read rhythmically, on the other hand, we bring out the natural flow of the language within the basic meter and, more important, the expressive meaning of the words. It is this distinction that the English critic Fox-Strangways has in mind when he observes: "A melody—an Irish reel perhaps—is in strict time, or people could not dance to it correctly; but if it had not also rhythm, they would not dance to it passionately."

Metrical Patterns

The simpler metrical patterns, in music as in poetry, depend on the regular recurrence of accent. Simplest of all is a succession of beats in which a strong alternates with a weak: ONE-two ONE-two—or in marching, LEFT-right LEFT-right. This is known as duple meter and is often encountered as two-four time ($\frac{2}{4}$). The pattern occurs in many nursery rhymes and marching songs.

Twín - kle	**twín - kle**	**lít - tle**	**stár———,**
ONE - two	**ONE - two**	**ONE - two**	**ONE - two**
Hów I	**wón - der**	**whát you**	**áre———.**
ONE - two	**ONE - two**	**ONE - two**	**ONE - two**

The best way to perceive rhythm is through physical response. The above tune can be accompanied, while singing, with a downward movement of the hand on ONE and an upward movement on *two*.

Duple meter

Duple meter, then, contains two beats to the measure, with the accent generally falling on the first beat. Within this meter a tune such as *Yankee Doodle* presents a somewhat more active rhythmic pattern than the above example. That is, in *Twinkle, twinkle, little star* there is mostly one melody note to a beat. *Yankee Doodle* contains, for the most part, two melody notes to a beat. Here the meter is the steady ONE-two ONE-two that constitutes the underlying beat, above which flows the rhythmic pattern of the melody.

Yánkee Doodle	**wént to town**	**Ríding on a**	**pó - ny**
ONE - two	**ONE - two**	**ONE - two**	**ONE - two**

Triple meter

Another basic metrical pattern is that of three beats to the measure, or *triple meter,* with the accent normally falling on the first beat. This is the pattern of three-four time (¾) traditionally associated with the waltz and minuet.

Three celebrated examples of triple meter are *Down in the Valley*, *America* and *Home on the Range*.

Mýy coun - try	**'tís——of thee,**
ONE - two - three	**ONE - two - three**
Sweet land of	**líí——ber - ty**
ONE - two - three	**ONE - two - three**
Óf thee I	**síng————**
ONE - two - three	**ONE - two - three**

Oh	**gíve me a**	**hóme————**
three	**ONE - two - three**	**ONE - two -**
where the	**búf - fal - lo**	**róam————**
three	**ONE - two - three**	**ONE - two -**

Quadruple meter

Quadruple meter, also known as *common time,* contains four beats to the measure. The primary accent falls on the first beat of the measure, with a secondary accent on the third: ONE-two-THREE-four. Quadruple meter, generally encountered as four-four time (4/4), is found in some of our most widely sung melodies: *Good Night Ladies, Annie Laurie,* the *Battle Hymn of the Republic, Long, Long Ago, Auld Lang Syne,* and a host of others.

Compound meters

Duple, triple, and quadruple meter are regarded as the *simple meters.* The *compound meters* contain five, six, seven, or more beats to the mea-

Gόod night, lá-dies!——	**Gόod night, lá-dies!——**
ONE - two - Three - four	**ONE - two - Three - four**
Gόod night, lá-dies!—— We're	**going to leave you nów——.**
ONE - two - Three - four	**ONE - two - Three - four**

Should	**aúld—— ac - quáin - tance**	**bé——**	**for - gót,**
four	**ONE - two - Three - four**	**ONE - two - Three**	
and	**né——ver bróught to**	**mínd——,**	
four	**ONE - two - Three - four**	**ONE - two - Three**	

sure, with primary and secondary accents marking the metrical pattern. Most frequently encountered among the compound meters is *sextuple meter:* six-four or six-eight time. This is often marked by a gently flowing effect. Popular examples are *Silent Night, Believe Me if All Those Endearing Young Charms, Drink to Me Only with Thine Eyes.*

Drínk to me ón——ly	**with——thine éyes——and**
ONE - two - three - Four - five - six	**ONE - two - three - Four - five - six**
Í——will plédge——with	**míne——**
ONE - two - three - Four - five - six	**ONE - two - three - Four - five - six**

You may hear examples of duple meter in the Gavotte from Bach's *Suite No. 3,* Schubert's *Marche militaire* and the *Hungarian Dance No. 5* of Brahms. Three-four time is exemplified by the Minuet from Mozart's *Eine kleine Nachtmusik,* Chopin's *Mazurka in B flat,* Opus 7, No. 1, and the *Emperor Waltz* of Johann Strauss. The *Triumphal March* from Verdi's *Aïda* is a good example of $\frac{4}{4}$ time, as is the March from Prokofiev's *The Love for Three Oranges.* For examples of $\frac{6}{8}$ time listen to *Morning* from *Peer Gynt Suite No. 1* by Grieg or Mendelssohn's *Venetian Boat Song.* When $\frac{6}{8}$ time is taken at a rapid pace the ear hears the six beats in two groups of three, so that the effect is akin to that of duple meter. An example is the Gigue from Bach's *Suite No. 3.*

The four meters just mentioned are the ones most frequently encountered in folk music and in the art music of the eighteenth and nineteenth centuries.

Syncopation

In music based on dance rhythm the meter has to be very clearly defined. This accounts for the decisive accents in a piece such as Brahms's *Hungarian Dance No. 5* or Chopin's *Mazurka in B flat.* Lyric pieces, on the other hand, achieve a more flowing effect by not emphasizing the accent so strongly, as in *Morning* or the *Venetian Boat Song*. In Debussy's popular piece *Clair de lune* (Moonlight) there is hardly any accent at all, so that the meter flows dreamily from one measure to the next.

Composers devised a number of ways to keep the recurrent accent from becoming monotonous. They used ever more complex rhythmic patterns within the measure, and learned how to vary the underlying beat in many subtle ways. The most common of these procedures is *syncopation*. This term denotes a deliberate upsetting of the normal accent. The accent, instead of falling on a strong beat of the measure, is shifted to a weak beat, or to an *offbeat* (between the beats), as in *Good Night, Ladies,* on the second syllables of *ladies*. Through this irregularity the accent is made to conflict with the pattern that has been set up in the listener's mind. The pleasure of satisfying his expectations is abandoned for the equally important pleasure of surprise. Syncopation has figured in European art music for centuries, and was used by the masters with great subtlety. It is associated in the popular mind with the Afro-American dance rhythms out of which modern jazz developed.

To sum up: music is an art of movement in time. Rhythm, the artistic organization of musical movement, permeates every aspect of the musical process. It shapes the melody and harmony, and binds together the parts within the whole: the notes within the measure, the measures within the phrase, the phrases within the period. Through the power of rhythm the composer achieves a dimension in time comparable to what painter, sculptor, and architect achieve in space.

Time is the crucial dimension in music. And its first law is rhythm.

5

Tempo: Musical Pace

"The whole duty of a conductor is comprised in his ability to indicate the right tempo."
— RICHARD WAGNER

Meter tells us how many beats there are in the measure, but it does not tell us whether these beats occur slowly or rapidly. The *tempo,* by which we mean the rate of speed, the pace of the music, provides the answer to this vital matter. Consequently the flow of the music in time involves both the meter and the tempo.

Tempo carries emotional implications. We hurry our speech in moments of agitation. Our bodies press forward in eagerness, hold back in lassitude. Vigor and gaiety are associated with a brisk gait as surely as despair demands a slow one. In an art of movement such as music, the rate of movement is of prime importance. We respond to musical tempo physically and psychologically. Our pulse, our breathing, our entire being adjusts to the rate of movement and to the feeling engendered thereby on the conscious and subconscious levels.

Because of the close connection between tempo and mood, tempo markings indicate the character of the music as well as the pace. The tempo terms are generally given in Italian, a survival from the time when the opera of that nation dominated the European scene. In the following table, *andante* (literally, "going," from the Italian *andare,* to go) indicates the speed of a normal walking pace. With this term as a midpoint, the table gives the most common Italian markings for the various tempos:

solemn (very, very slow):	*grave*
broad (very slow):	*largo*
quite slow:	*adagio*
slow:	*lento*
a walking pace:	*andante*
somewhat faster than andante:	*andantino*
moderate:	*moderato*
moderately fast:	*allegretto*
fast (cheerful):	*allegro*
lively:	*vivace*
very fast:	*presto*
very, very fast:	*prestissimo*

(For the pronunciation of these and other terms see the Index.) Frequently encountered too are modifying adverbs such as *molto* (very), *meno* (less), *poco* (a little), and *non troppo* (not too much). It should be noted that andante, which in the eighteenth century indicated a "going" pace, in the nineteenth came to mean "fairly slow."

Of great importance are the terms indicating a change of tempo. The principal ones are *accelerando* (getting faster) and *ritardando* (holding back, getting slower); *a tempo* (in time) indicates a return to the original pace.

For examples of the various tempos, listen to the opening section of the following works:

largo	Chopin, *Prelude in E minor*
adagio	Beethoven, *Sonata pathétique*, second movement
lento	Chopin, *Etude in A minor*, Op. 25, No. 11, introduction
andante	Bach, *Brandenburg Concerto No. 2*, second movement
	Mozart, *Là ci darem la mano* from *Don Giovanni*
andantino	Schubert, *Trout Quintet*, theme of the fourth movement
allegretto	Mozart, *Eine kleine Nachtmusik*, third movement
	Tchaikovsky, *Arabian Dance* from *Nutcracker Suite*
allegro	Mozart, *Eine kleine Nachtmusik*, first movement
	Beethoven, *Sonata pathétique*, third movement

Wagner's statement about tempo, quoted at the head of this chapter, is of course an exaggeration; the conductor has many other duties besides setting the tempo. It does make clear, however, that when a conductor hits on "the right tempo" he has correctly gauged the meaning and intent of the music.

6

Dynamics: Musical Volume

"The player must be guided by the passion. Sometimes a note requires a rather vigorous attack, at other times a moderate one, at still other times one that is barely audible." — LEOPOLD MOZART (1756)

Dynamics denotes the degree of loudness or softness at which the music is played. In this area, as in that of tempo, certain responses seem to be rooted in the nature of our emotions. Mystery and fear call for a whisper, even as jubilation and vigorous activity go with full resonance. A lullaby or love song moves in another dynamic range than a triumphal march. Modern instruments place a wide gamut of dynamic effects at the composer's disposal.

The principal dynamic indications are:

very soft:	*pianissimo (pp)*
soft:	*piano (p)*
moderately soft:	*mezzo piano (mp)*
moderately loud:	*mezzo forte (mf)*
loud:	*forte (f)*
very loud:	*fortissimo (ff)*

Of special importance are the directions to change the dynamics. Such changes are indicated by words or signs. Among the commonest are:

growing louder:	*crescendo* (<)
growing softer:	*decrescendo* or *diminuendo* (>)
sudden stress:	*sforzando* (*sf*, forced)—accent on a single note or chord

As the orchestra increased in size and precision, composers extended the range of dynamic markings in both directions, so that we find *ppp* and *fff*. Ultimately four and even five *p*'s or *f*'s were used.

The markings for tempo and dynamics are so many clues to the expressive content of a piece of music. These so-called "expression marks" steadily increased in number during the late eighteenth century and during the nineteenth, as composers tried to indicate their intentions ever more precisely. In this regard it is instructive to compare a page of Bach (early eighteenth century) with one of Tchaikovsky (late nineteenth century; see pp. 24–25).

Tempo and Dynamics as Elements of Musical Expression

Crescendo and diminuendo are among the important expressive effects available to the composer. Through the gradual swelling and diminishing of the tone volume, the illusion of distance enters music. It is as if the source of sound were approaching us and then receding. As orchestral style developed, composers quickly learned to take advantage of this procedure. Rossini, for example, was so addicted to employing a long-drawn-out swell of tone for the sake of dramatic effect that he was caricatured in Paris as "Monsieur Crescendo." The impact of such a crescendo can be little short of electrifying, as is apparent from the closing section of his Overture to *The Barber of Seville.* A similar effect is to be observed in Ravel's *Bolero,* in which an extended melody is repeated over and over while the music grows steadily louder. The crescendo is achieved, first, by piling on instruments one after the other; second, by causing the various instruments to play progressively louder.

Wagner's Prelude to *Lohengrin* is intended to depict the descent from heaven of the Holy Grail. The image of a band of angels approaching from the distance and then receding is translated into what has become a basic pattern in music, the crescendo-and-decrescendo (< >).

Dynamic contrasts in music are analogous to light and shade in painting. **Christ at Emmaus** *by Rembrandt van Rijn (1606–69).* (Musée Jacquemart-André, Paris.)

A page from the score of Bach's Brandenburg Concerto No. 2. *(Note the lack of expression marks.)*

A page from the score of Tchaikovsky's Pathétique Symphony. *(Observe the profusion of expression marks.)*

Other striking examples of this dynamic scheme are to be found in the second half of Debussy's nocturne for orchestra, *Fêtes* (Festivals), and in the first movement of Bartók's *Music for Strings, Percussion, and Celesta.*

Crescendo in conjunction with accelerando (louder and faster) creates excitement as surely as decrescendo together with ritardando (softer and slower) slackens it. The effect of an intensification of volume and pace is exemplified in Honegger's *Pacific 231,* in which the composer tries to suggest the sense of power conjured up by a locomotive as it gradually builds up momentum and tears through the night. Here crescendo and accelerando are translated into the imagery of motion, as is the case in the finale of Tchaikovsky's *Waltz of the Flowers,* which is designed to build up to a rousing curtain for the *Nutcracker Ballet.* In the Tchaikovsky piece the music climbs steadily from the middle register to the bright and nervous high, so that the three elements—acceleration of pace, increase in volume, and rise in pitch—reinforce one another to create the climax.

Devices of this kind never fail in their effect upon audiences, which would seem to indicate that they are not the arbitrary procedures of a single imagination but are rooted in certain basic responses inherent in our nature.

7

Instruments of the Orchestra (I)

"With these artificial voices we sing in a manner such as our natural voices would never permit." — JOHN REDFIELD: *Music—A Science and an Art*

Properties of Musical Sound

A note played on a trumpet will sound altogether different from the same note played on a violin or a flute. The difference lies in the tone-color characteristic of each instrument, its *timbre.* (The word retains its French pronunciation, *tám'br.*)

Timbre

The composer has at his disposal two basic media—human voices and musical instruments. He may write for either or both, according to his purpose. If he is writing for a group of instruments, he tries to make each instrument do the things for which it is best suited, taking into account its capacities and limitations. There are, to begin with, the limits of each instrument's range—the distance from its lowest to its highest tone, beyond which it cannot go. There are also the limits of dynamics—the degree of softness or loudness beyond which it cannot be played. There are technical peculiarities native to its low, middle, and high register, as a result of which a certain formation of notes will be executed more easily on one instrument than another. (By *register* we mean a specific area in the range of an instrument or voice, such as low, middle, or high.) These and a host of similar considerations determine the composer's choice as he clothes his ideas in their instrumental garb.

An *instrument* is a mechanism that is able to generate musical vibrations and launch them into the air. Each instrument, according to its capacities, enables us to control the four properties of musical sound: pitch, duration, volume, and color.

Pitch

By *pitch* we mean the location of a tone in the musical scale in relation to high or low. The pitch is determined by the rate of vibration, which to a large extent depends on the length of the vibrating body. Other conditions being equal, the shorter a string or column of air, the more rapidly it vibrates and the higher the pitch. The longer a string or column of air, the fewer the vibrations per second and the lower the pitch. The width, thickness, density, and tension of the vibrating body also affect the outcome.

Duration

Duration depends on the length of time over which vibration is maintained. We hear tones as being not only high or low but also short or long.

Volume

Volume (dynamics) depends on the degree of force of the vibrations, as a result of which the tone strikes us as being loud or soft. As for the *timbre* or tone color, that is influenced by a number of factors, such as the size, shape, and proportions of the instrument, the material of which it is made, and the manner in which vibration is set up.

Instruments figure in our music singly; in small groups (chamber music); and as part of that most spectacular of ensembles, the orchestra. In the orchestra they are divided into four sections (or choirs): string, woodwind, brass, and percussion.

The String Section

The string section of the orchestra includes four instruments—violin, viola, violoncello, and double bass. These have four strings, which are set vibrating by either drawing a bow across them or plucking them. The hair of the bow is rubbed with rosin so that it will "grip" the strings. The player holds the bow in his right hand. He *stops* the string by pressing down a finger of his left hand at a particular point on the fingerboard, thereby leaving a certain portion of the string free to vibrate. By stopping the string at another point he changes the length of the vibrating portion, and with it the rate of vibration and the pitch.

Violin

The *violin* was brought to its present form by the brilliant instrument makers who flourished in Italy from around 1600 to 1750. Most famous among them were the Amati and Guarneri families—in these dynasties the secrets of the craft were transmitted from father to son—and the master builder of them all, Antonio Stradivari (c. 1644–1737).

Violinist Itzhak Perlman.

Double-bass player Gary Karr.

Pinchas Zukerman playing the viola. (Photo by Bruce Goldstein.)

Yo-Yo Ma, cellist. (Photo by Bill King.)

The violin, the highest-pitched of the string choir, is universally admired for its singing tone, which brings it of all instruments closest to the human voice. Pre-eminent in lyric melody, the violin is also capable of brilliance and dramatic effect, of subtle nuances from soft to loud, of the utmost rhythmic precision and great agility in rapid passages. It has an extremely wide range. (For the comparative range of the instruments and the tuning of the strings, see Appendix II.)

Viola

The *viola* is somewhat larger than the violin, and is lower in range. Its strings are longer, thicker, heavier. The tone is husky in the low register, somber and penetrating in the high. The viola is an effective melody instrument, and often serves as a foil for the more brilliant violin by playing a secondary melody. It usually fills in the harmony, or may *double* another part; that is, reinforce it by playing the same notes an octave higher or lower.

Violoncello

The *violoncello,* popularly known as *cello,* is lower in range than the viola and is notable for its lyric quality, which takes on a dark resonance in the low register. Composers value highly its expressive tone. In the orchestra the cellos perform functions similar to those of the violins and violas. They often carry the melody. They enrich the sonority with their full-throated songfulness. They accentuate the rhythm. And together with the basses they supply the foundation for the harmony of the string choir.

Double bass

The *double bass,* known also as *contrabass* or *bass viol,* is the lowest in range of the string section. Accordingly, it plays the bass part—that is, the foundation of the harmony. Its deep indistinct tones come into focus when they are duplicated (doubled) an octave higher, usually by the cello. When this is done, the double bass assumes great carrying power and furnishes basic support for the entire orchestra. In more recent music, the dark timbre of the instrument has also been much used to achieve special color effects.

The string instruments are pre-eminent in playing *legato* (smooth and connected), though they are capable too of the opposite quality of tone, *staccato* (short and detached). A special effect, *pizzicato* (plucked), is executed by the performer's plucking the string with his finger instead of using the bow. *Vibrato* denotes a throbbing effect achieved by a rapid wrist-and-finger movement that slightly alters the pitch. In *glissando* the player moves a finger of his left hand rapidly along the string while the right hand draws the bow, thereby sounding all the pitches of the scale. *Tremolo,* the rapid repetition of a tone through a quick up-and-down movement of the bow, is associated in the popular mind with suspense and excitement. No less important is the *trill,* a rapid alternation between a tone and its neighbor. *Double-stopping* involves playing two strings simultaneously; when three or four strings are played simultaneously, it is called *triple-* or *quadruple-stopping.* Thereby the members of the violin family, essentially melodic instruments, became capable of harmony. The *mute* is a small attachment that fits over the bridge, muffling (and changing) the sound. *Harmonics* are crystalline tones in the very high register.

They are produced by lightly touching the string at certain points while the bow is drawn across the string. (For an explanation of harmonics, see Appendix V.)

The string section has come to be known as "the heart of the orchestra." This term indicates the versatility and general usefulness of this choir. The strings also figure prominently as solo instruments and in chamber music: in duets, trios, quartets, quintets, and the like.

The Woodwind Section

In the woodwind instruments the tone is produced by a column of air vibrating within a pipe that has little holes in its side. When one or another of these holes is opened or closed, the length of the vibrating air column within the pipe is changed. The woodwind instruments are capable of remarkable agility by means of an intricate mechanism of keys arranged so as to suit the natural position of the fingers.

The woodwinds are a less homogeneous group than the strings. Nowadays they are not necessarily made of wood, and they represent several methods of setting up vibration: by blowing across a mouth hole (flute family); by blowing into a mouthpiece that has a single reed (clarinet and saxophone families); by blowing into a mouthpiece fitted with a double reed (oboe and bassoon families). They do, however, have one important feature in common: the holes in the side of the pipes. In addition, their timbres are such that composers think of them and write for them as a group.

Flute

The *flute* is the soprano voice of the woodwind choir. Its timbre ranges from the poetic to the brilliant. Its tone is cool and velvety in the expressive low register, and smooth in the middle. In the upper part of the range the timbre is bright, birdlike, and stands out against the orchestral mass. The present-day flute, made of a silver alloy rather than wood, is a cylindrical tube that is held horizontally. It is closed at one end. The player positions his lips (*embouchure*), blowing across a mouth hole cut in the side of the pipe at the other end. The flute is much prized as a melody instrument and offers the player complete freedom in playing rapid repeated notes, scales, and trills.

Piccolo

The *piccolo* (from the Italian *flauto piccolo,* "little flute") has a piercing tone that produces the highest notes in the orchestra. In its upper register it takes on a shrillness that is easily heard even when the orchestra is playing fortissimo. For this reason the instrument contributes to many an orchestral climax. On the other hand, composers are coming more and more to make use of the limpid singing quality of its lower register.

Oboe

The *oboe* is made of wood. Its mouthpiece is a double reed consisting of two slips of cane bound together so as to leave between them an extremely small passage for air. Because of this compression, the tone is

James Galway, flute virtuoso.

Heinz Holliger playing the oboe. (Photo by Mike Evans.)

Bernard Garfield, principal bassoonist of The Philadelphia Orchestra.

Benny Goodman, master of the clarinet.

Wendy Rolfe studies the piccolo at the Manhattan School of Music. (Photo by Ken Howard.)

focused and intense in all registers. Oboe timbre is generally described as plaintive, nasal, reedy. The instrument is associated with pastoral effects and with nostalgic moods. The pitch of the oboe is not readily subject to change, for which reason it is chosen to sound the A for the other instruments when the orchestra is tuning up.

English horn

The *English horn* is an alto oboe. Its wooden tube is wider and longer than that of the oboe and ends in a pear-shaped bell, which largely accounts for its soft, somewhat mournful timbre. The instrument would be well named were it not for the fact that it is neither English nor a horn. Its expressive, gently poignant tone has made it a favorite with composers.

Clarinet

The *clarinet* has a single reed, a small flexible piece of cane fastened against its chisel-shaped mouthpiece. The instrument possesses a beautiful liquid tone, clear and powerful in the high register, relaxed in the middle, cool and almost spectral in the low. It has a remarkably wide range from low to high and from soft to loud. The clarinet is a favorite instrument when it comes to playing melody. Almost as agile as the flute, it has an easy command of rapid scales, trills, and repeated notes.

Bass clarinet

The *bass clarinet* is one octave lower in range than the clarinet. Its rich singing tone, flexibility, and wide dynamic range make it an invaluable member of the orchestral community.

Bassoon

The *bassoon* belongs to the double-reed family. Its tone is weighty and thick in the low register, dry and sonorous in the middle, reedy and intense in the upper. Capable of a hollow-sounding staccato and wide leaps that create a humorous effect, it is at the same time a highly expressive instrument.

Contra-bassoon

The *contrabassoon,* known also as double bassoon, produces the lowest tone in the orchestra. Its tube, over sixteen feet in length, is folded four times around to make it less unwieldly. Its function in the woodwind section may be compared to that of the double bass among the strings, in that it supplies a foundation for the harmony.

Saxophone

The *saxophone* is of more recent origin, having been invented by Adolphe Sax of Brussels in 1840. It was created by combining the features of several other instruments–the single reed of the clarinet, the conical tube of the oboe, and the metal body of the brass instruments. The saxophone blends well with either woodwinds or brass. In the 1920s it became the characteristic instrument of the jazz band. Although it figures prominently in a number of important modern scores, it has not yet established itself as a permanent member of the orchestra.

8

Instruments of the Orchestra (II)

"Lucidity is the first purpose of color in music." — ARNOLD SCHOENBERG

The Brass Section

The brass section consists of the French horn, trumpet, trombone, and tuba. These instruments have cup-shaped mouthpieces (except for the horn, whose mouthpiece is shaped like a funnel). The tube flares at the end into an opening known as a *bell.* The column of air within the tube is set vibrating by the tightly stretched lips of the player, which act as a kind of double reed. To go from one pitch to another involves not only mechanical means, such as a slide or valves, but also variation in the pressure of the lips and breath. This demands great muscular control.

Horns and trumpets were widely used in the ancient world. The primitive instruments were fashioned from the horns and tusks of animals, which at a more advanced stage of civilization were reproduced in metal. They were used chiefly in religious ceremonies and for military signals. Their tone was on the terrifying side, as is evidenced by what happened to the walls of Jericho.

French horn

The *French horn*—generally referred to simply as horn—is descended from the ancient hunting horn. Its golden resonance lends itself to a variety of uses: it can be mysteriously remote in soft passages, and nobly sonorous in loud. The timbre of the horn blends equally well with woodwinds, brass, and strings, for which reason it serves as the connecting link among them. Although capable of considerable agility, the horn is at its best in sustained utterance; for sheer majesty, nothing rivals the sound of several horns intoning a broadly flowing theme in unison. The muted horn has a poetic faraway sound; if the muted tone is forced, however, the result is an ominous rasping quality.

Trumpet

The *trumpet,* highest in pitch of the brass choir, possesses a firm, brilliant timbre that lends radiance to the orchestral mass. It is associated with martial pomp and vigor. Played softly, the instrument commands a lovely round tone. The muted trumpet is much used; the mute, a pear-shaped device of metal or cardboard, is inserted in the bell. When the muted tone is forced, a harsh snarling sound results that is not soon forgotten. Jazz trumpet players have experimented with various kinds of mutes, and these are gradually finding their way into the symphony orchestra.

Trombone

The *trombone*—the Italian word means "large trumpet"—has a grand sonorousness that combines the brilliance of the trumpet with the majesty

Steven Johns playing the tuba.

Barry Tuckwell plays the French Horn. (Photo by Richard Holt/EMI.)

Trombonist J. J. Johnson.

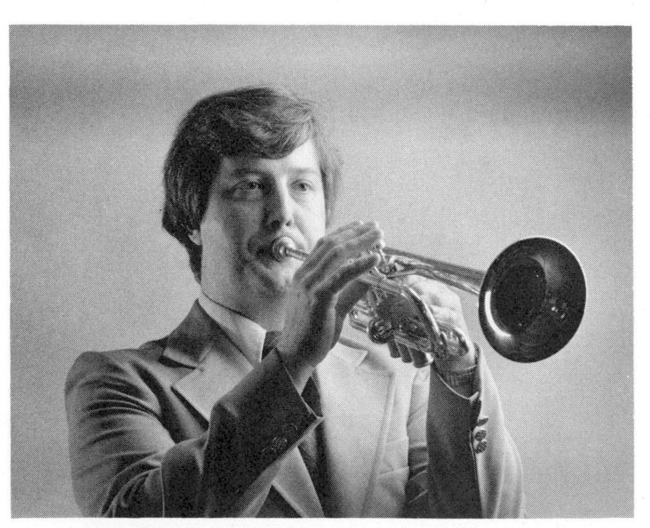

Dale Fredericks studies the trumpet at the Manhattan School of Music. (Photo by Ken Howard.)

of the horn. In place of valves it has a movable U-shaped slide that alters the length of the vibrating air column in the tube. (There is a valve trombone that is used occasionally, but it lacks the rich tone of the slide trombone.) Composers consistently avail themselves of the trombone to achieve effects of nobility and grandeur.

Tuba

The *tuba* is the bass of the brass choir. Like the string bass and contrabassoon, it furnishes the foundation for the harmonic fabric. It is surprisingly responsive for so unwieldly an instrument. To play it requires—among other things—good teeth and plenty of wind. The tuba adds body to the orchestral tone, and a dark resonance ranging from velvety softness to a growl.

Mention should be made, too, of the brass instruments used in military and outdoor bands. Most important of these is the *cornet,* which was developed early in the nineteenth century from the posthorn. The cornet has a shorter body than the trumpet and possesses greater agility. (It is basically an instrument of conical shape, whereas the body of the trumpet is cylindrical for the greater part of its length.) The tone of the cornet is rounder but less brilliant than that of the trumpet. Because of the comparative ease with which it is played, the cornet has become the mainstay of school and municipal bands. Among the brass-band instruments are the *flügelhorn,* which is similar in shape to the cornet but wider; the *baritone* and *euphonium,* which are tenor tubas; and the *helicon,* which is a double-bass tuba, circular in form so that the player is able to carry the instrument over his shoulder. (An American type of helicon is the *sousaphone,* named after John Philip Sousa, who suggested its specially designed bell.) The *bugle,* originally a hunter's horn, has a powerful tone that carries in the open air. Since it is not equipped with valves, it is able to sound only certain tones of the scale, which accounts for the familiar pattern of duty calls in the army.

The Percussion Instruments

The percussion section comprises a variety of instruments that are made to sound by striking or shaking. Certain ones are made of metal or wood. In others, such as the drums, vibration is set up by striking a stretched skin.

The percussion section of the orchestra is sometimes referred to as "the battery." Its members accentuate the rhythm, generate excitement at the climaxes, and inject splashes of color into the orchestral sound. Like seasoning in food, they are most effective when used sparingly.

Tuned percussion

The percussion instruments fall into two categories: those which are capable of being tuned to definite pitches, and those which produce a single sound in the borderland between music and noise (instruments of indefinite pitch). In the former class are the *kettledrums,* or *timpani,* which are generally used in sets of two or three. The kettledrum is a hemispheric

Chimes.

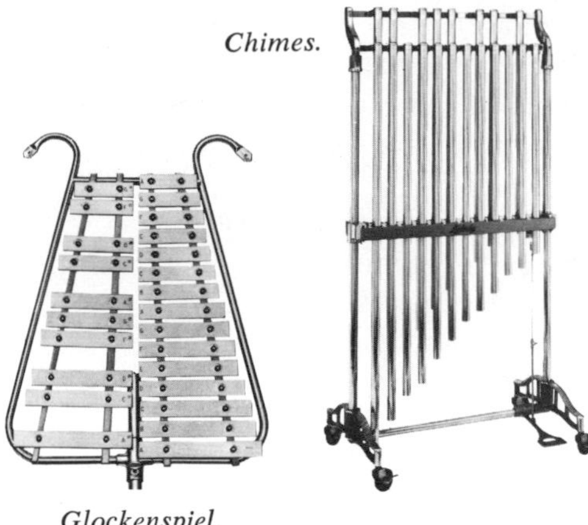

Glockenspiel.

Bobby Christian playing the timpani.

Al Payson with the snare drum.

The bass drum is played by Jacqueline Meyer.

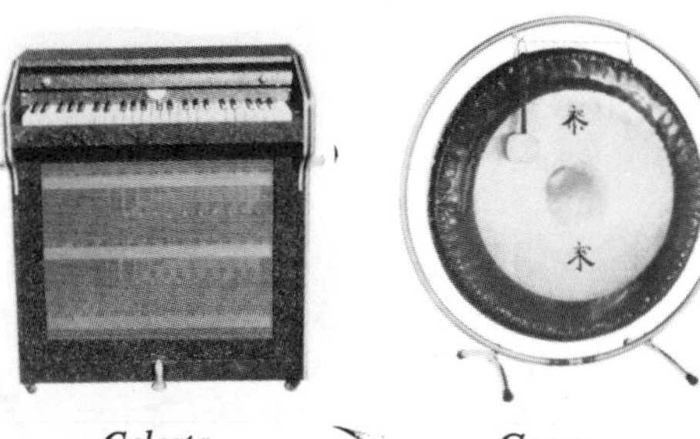

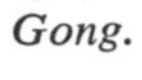

Celesta.

Gong.

copper shell across which is stretched a "head" of calfskin held in place by a metal ring. Adjustable screws or a pedal mechanism enable the player to change the tension of the calfskin head, and with it the pitch. The instrument is played with two padded sticks, which may be either soft or hard. Its dynamic range extends from a mysterious rumble to a thunderous roll. The muffled drum frequently figures in passages that seek to evoke an atmosphere of mystery or mourning. The *glockenspiel* (German for "set of bells") consists of a series of horizontal tuned plates of various sizes, made of steel. The player strikes these with mallets, producing a bright metallic sound. The *celesta,* which in appearance resembles a miniature upright piano, is a kind of glockenspiel that is operated by a keyboard: the steel plates are struck by small hammers and produce an ethereal sound. The *xylophone* consists of tuned blocks of wood laid out in the shape of a keyboard. Struck with mallets with hard heads, the instrument produces a dry, crisp timbre. If mallets with soft heads are used, the tone is warmer and mellower. Expert xylophone players attain dazzling speed and accuracy. The *marimba* is a more mellow xylophone of African and South American origin, pitched an octave lower. The *vibraphone* combines the principle of the glockenspiel with resonators, each containing revolving disks operated by electric motors. Its highly unusual tone is marked by an exaggerated vibrato, which can be controlled by changing the speed of the motor. Also known as a *vibraharp,* this instrument plays a prominent part in jazz, and has been used by a number of contemporary composers. *Chimes* consist of a set of tuned metal tubes of various lengths suspended from a frame and struck with a hammer. They have a broad dynamic range, from a metallic tinkle to a sonorous clang, and are frequently called upon to simulate church bells.

Unpitched percussion

In the other group are the percussion instruments that do not produce a definite pitch. The *side drum* or *snare drum* (also known as *military drum*) is a small cylindrical drum with two heads stretched over a shell of metal. It is played with two drumsticks, and owes its brilliant tone to the vibrations of the lower head against taut snares (strings). The *tenor drum* is larger in size, with a wooden shell, and has no snares. The *bass drum,* played with a large soft-headed stick, produces a low heavy sound. It is much used in dance bands. The *tom-tom* is a name given to American Indian or Oriental drums of indefinite pitch, imitations of which are often used in dance bands. The *tambourine* is a small round drum with "jingles"–little metal plates–inserted in its rim. It is played by striking the drum with the fingers or elbow, by shaking, or by passing the hand over the jingles. The tambourine is much used in the folk dances of Italy. *Castanets* are widely used in Spain. They consist of little wooden clappers moved by the thumb and forefinger of the player. The *triangle* is a small round bar of steel bent in the shape of a triangle. It is open at the upper end and, when struck with a steel beater, gives off a bright tinkling sound. *Cymbals* are two large circular brass plates of equal size. When struck sidewise against each other, they produce a shattering sound. A suspended cymbal, when struck lightly with a drumstick, produces a mysterious sound. The *gong,* or *tam-tam,* is a broad circular disk of metal, suspended in a frame so as to hang freely. When struck with a heavy drumstick, it produces a deep roar. If a soft stick is used the effect can be ghostly, even terrifying.

Other Instruments

Besides the instruments just discussed, several are occasionally used in the orchestra without being an integral part of it. Among these are the harp, piano, and organ.

Harp

The *harp* is one of the oldest of musical instruments. It appears in its earliest form on Babylonian inscriptions of over four thousand years ago. It was the traditional instrument of the bards of ancient Britain and Ireland, and became the national emblem of the latter country. Its strings are played by plucking and produce a crystalline tone that sounds lovely, both alone and in combination with other instruments. The pedals are used to tighten the strings, hence to raise the pitch. Chords on the harp are frequently played in broken form; that is, the tones are sounded one after another instead of simultaneously. From this circumstance comes the term *arpeggio,* which means a broken chord (*arpa* is the Italian for "harp"). Arpeggios occur in a variety of forms on many instruments.

Piano

The *piano* was originally known as the *pianoforte,* the Italian for "soft-loud," which indicates its wide dynamic range and its capacity for nuance. Its strings are struck with little hammers controlled by a keyboard mechanism. The piano cannot sustain tone as well as the string and wind instruments, but in the hands of a fine performer it is capable nonetheless of singing melody. Each string (except in the highest register) is covered by a damper that stops the sound when the finger releases the key. There are three pedals. If the one on the right is pressed down, all the dampers are raised, so that the strings continue to vibrate, producing that luminous haze of sound which the great piano composers used to such advantage. The pedal on the left shifts the hammers to reduce the area of impact on the strings, thereby inhibiting the volume of sound; hence it is known as the "soft pedal." The middle pedal (lacking on upright pianos) is the sustaining pedal, which sustains only the tones held down at the moment the pedal is depressed. The piano is pre-eminent for brilliant scales, arpeggios and trills, rapid passages and octaves. It has a wide range from lowest to highest tone and commands great rhythmic vitality.

Organ

The *organ,* once regarded as "the king of instruments," is a wind instrument; air is fed to its pipes by mechanical means. The pipes are controlled by two or more keyboards and a set of pedals. Gradations in the volume of tone are made possible on the modern organ by means of swell boxes. The organ possesses a multicolored sonority and majestic harmonies that fill a huge space. Nowadays the electronic organ is coming into use. Here the sound is produced not by wind but by electrical oscillators.

Harp.

André Watts at the piano. (Photo by James J. Kriegsmann.)

André Marchal playing the great tracker organ in Alice Tully Hall, New York.

The instruments described in this chapter form a vivid and diversified group. To composer, performer, and listener alike they offer an endless variety of colors and shades of expression.

9

The Orchestra

"Orchestration is part of the very soul of the work. A work is thought out in terms of the orchestra, certain tone-colors being inseparable from it in the mind of its creator and native to it from the hour of its birth." — NIKOLAI RIMSKY-KORSAKOV

From the group of approximately twenty instruments that Bach had at his disposal or the forty-odd that Mozart knew, the modern orchestra has grown into an ensemble that may call for more than a hundred players. These musicians, many of artist stature, give their full time to rehearsal and performance, achieving a precision unknown in former times.

The orchestra is constituted with a view to securing the best balance of tone. The performers are divided into the four sections we have described. In large orchestras approximately two thirds are string players, one fourth are wind players. From three to five players take care of the percusssion. The following distribution is typical of the orchestras of our largest cities:

strings:	18 first violins 15 second violins 12 violas 12 violoncellos 9 double basses
woodwinds:	3 flutes, 1 piccolo 3 oboes, 1 English horn 3 clarinets, 1 bass clarinet 3 bassoons, 1 double bassoon
brass:	4–6 horns 4 trumpets 3 trombones 1 tuba
percussion:	1 kettledrum player 2–4 performers for bass and side drum, glockenspiel, celesta, xylophone, triangle, cymbals, tambourine, etc.

It will be noticed that the violins are divided into two groups, first and second. Each group functions as a unit and plays a separate part. In general, the size of the orchestra varies according to the demands of the music. Included in the largest ensembles are two harps and, for certain works, a piano or organ.

The instruments are arranged so as to secure the best balance of tone. Most of the strings are up front. Brass and percussion are at the back. A characteristic seating plan is shown below; this arrangement varies somewhat from one orchestra to the next.

The ensemble is directed by the conductor, who beats time and indicates the entrances of the various instruments, the shadings in the volume

The Chicago Symphony Orchestra with its conductor, Sir Georg Solti.

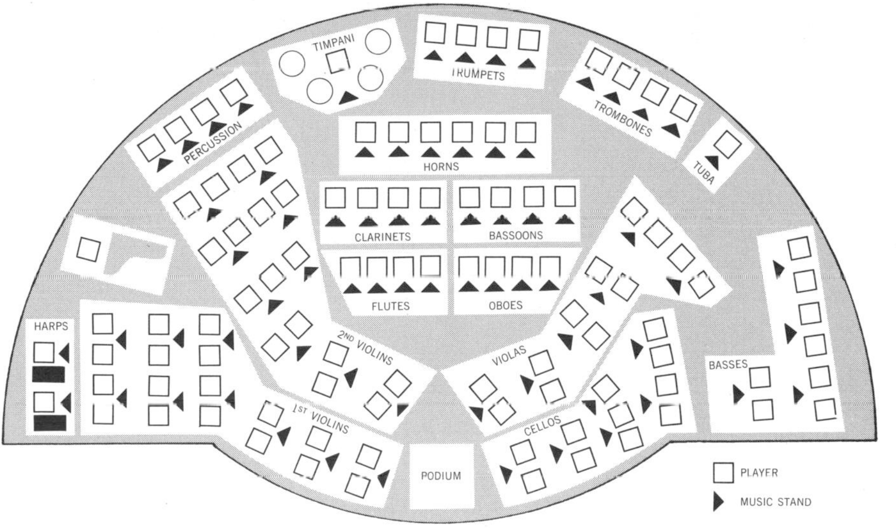

The seating plan of the Chicago Symphony Orchestra.

The conductor

of tone, the principal and subordinate lines, and a host of related details that serve to make clear the structure of the work. Beyond that, like any performing artist, he presents his personal interpretation of what the composer has written. He has before him the *score* of the work. This consists of from a few to as many as twenty-five or more staves (staffs), each representing one or more instrumental parts. All the staffs together comprise a single composite line. What is going on at any moment in the orchestra is indicated at any given point straight down the page. It will be observed from the illustration on p. 43 that the instruments are grouped in families, woodwinds on top, then brass, percussion, and strings.

The Art of Orchestration

The composer bent over a page of score paper envisions the colors in his imagination as he blends and contrasts the timbres. He judges accurately the kind of sound he desires, be it powerful, caressing, or delicate; and he uses color to highlight the rhythmic patterns and the architectural design, to set off the principal ideas from the subordinate, and to weld the innumerable details into a whole.

The foregoing should dispel the widespread misconception that one person writes the music while another orchestrates it. This is true of most popular music, the score of a musical comedy, and the movie industry. But in art music, as the quotation from Rimsky-Korsakov makes clear, the two functions cannot be separated. What the composer says and how he says it are part and parcel of his individual manner of conceiving sound.

Erroneous too is the notion that the composer first writes his orchestral piece for the piano and then arranges it for instruments. An orchestral work, from its inception, is conceived in terms of the orchestra. If many composers like to have a piano in the room while writing, it is primarily because this gives them contact with the living sound. But the piano is no more able to render a symphonic piece than a black-and-white reproduction can reveal the colors of a Raphael or a Titian.

Listening to the orchestra is a favorite pastime of the musical public today. Most of this listening is done via recordings, radio, and television, so that many listeners never come in contact with the living orchestral sound. A pity, for the best way to become familiar with the orchestral instruments is to be in the concert hall, where one can see as well as hear them. Recorded music plays a vital role in our musical life, but it should be regarded as a preparation for the live performance, not as a substitute.

The Orchestra in Action: Tchaikovsky's Nutcracker Suite

We shall in the course of this book have ample occasion to comment on how various composers wrote for the orchestra. At this point, however, the reader may find a helpful introduction to the orchestra in a work such as

A page from Schumann's Fourth Symphony, *showing the arrangement of instrumental parts.*

Tchaikovsky's *Nutcracker Suite,* which is a particularly fine example of vivid orchestral sonorities. The word *suite* indicates an instrumental work consisting of a number of short pieces (*movements*) related to a central idea. The suite may be either an independent work or a set of pieces drawn from a larger work. The *Nutcracker Suite* was drawn from a Christmas Eve ballet concerning a little girl who dreams that the nutcracker she received as a gift has turned into a handsome prince. Russian nutcrackers are often shaped like a human head, hence the transformation. The fairy-tale atmosphere impelled Tchaikovsky to some enchanting music.

Miniature Overture

The *Miniature Overture* sets the mood. It is in $2/4$ time, marked Allegro giusto (fairly fast), and begins pianissimo. To achieve an effect of lightness, Tchaikovsky omitted most of the bass instruments—cellos, double basses, trombones, tuba—as well as trumpets. The percussion section is represented only by the triangle. The dainty effect is enhanced by the use of staccato and the prevalence of the upper register. The sense of climax at the end is achieved through a crescendo—the music moves from pianissimo to fortissimo—as well as a rise in pitch.

March
SIDE 1/1
(E II AND S)*

There follows the *March,* in a lively 4/4 time. The characteristic march rhythm is set forth by clarinets, horns, and trumpets. Winds are answered by strings—a widely used orchestral device. Worthy of note is the filigree work in the accompaniment, in this case presented by the cellos and double basses pizzicato, an effect dear to Tchaikovsky's heart. In the middle section a staccato theme in high register is presented by three flutes and clarinet, mezzo forte, and vividly conveys a suggestion of ballet movement. The first part is repeated and the piece ends fortissimo.

Dance of the Sugar-Plum Fairy

"I have discovered a new instrument in Paris, something between a piano and a glockenspiel, with a divinely beautiful tone," wrote Tchaikovsky to his publisher in 1891. "I want to introduce this into the ballet." The instrument was the celesta, whose ethereal sound pervades the *Dance of the Sugar-Plum Fairy.* The piece, marked Andante non troppo (fairly slow, not too much so) is in 2/4 time. It opens with four bars of pizzicato introduction, pianissimo; soon the celesta tone is effectively contrasted with that of the bass clarinet. There is a passage for celesta alone, after which the opening theme is repeated. The piece ends with a pizzicato chord marked forte.

Trepak

The *Trepak* or *Russian Dance,* marked Molto vivace (very lively), is in 2/4 time. The fast tempo, active rhythm, and heavy accents create the suggestion of vigorous movement proper to a peasant dance. The orchestral sonority is enlivened by the presence of the tambourine. Tchaikovsky, at the end, achieves a climax through a crescendo and an accelerando; the final measures are played fortissimo.

Arab Dance
SIDE 1/2
(E II AND S)

The little girl and her prince are entertained by various sweetmeats in the castle of the Sugar-Plum Fairy. The character representing Coffee dances the *Arab Dance,* a subdued number marked Allegretto that forms an effective contrast with the *Trepak* that preceded. It is in 3/8 time. Muted violas and cellos set up a *rhythmic ostinato*—that is, an "obstinate" rhythm repeated over and over with an almost hypnotic insistence. Against this dark curtain of sound, after introductory chords in the woodwinds, the muted violins unfold an oriental-sounding melody. Striking is the long-drawn-out Oriental wail of the oboe, in the upper register, over the quiet movement of the melody and harmony in the strings below. The music dies away at the end.

* For all selections included in the Recordings that accompany this text, references have been provided to the specific sides and bands. Thus, the *March* from *The Nutcracker* may be found on Side 1, Band 1 of both the Standard (*S*) version of the Recordings and the Expanded (*E*) version, volume II.

Chinese Dance

Not to be outdone, the character representing Tea presents the *Chinese Dance,* an Allegro moderato in 4/4 time. The piece begins mezzo forte. Bassoons, playing staccato, establish a rhythmic ostinato against which flute and piccolo trace a somewhat shrill melody. Whether this music bears any resemblance to that heard in Peking is beside the point. It is sufficiently close to what Western ears have come popularly to regard as Chinese—which means that it is pleasantly exotic and colorful. This dance closes with a crescendo and a chord played fortissimo.

Dance of the Toy Flutes
SIDE 1/3
(E II AND S)

The *Dance of the Toy Flutes,* marked Moderato assai (very moderate) and in 2/4 time, has always been a favorite with devotees of Tchaikovsky. Against a pizzicato accompaniment of violas, cellos, and double basses, three flutes outline a suave and beguiling melody. A short solo on the English horn arrests the ear, after which the opening theme returns. The middle section of the piece is devoted to a telling idea presented by the trumpets against a background of brass and percussion sounds, with a slight crescendo as the melodie line ascends and a decrescendo as it moves downward. After this the gracious melody of the flutes is heard again.

Waltz of the Flowers

The *Waltz of the Flowers* that closes this suite displays to the full Tchaikovsky's gift as a composer of ballet music. It is marked Tempo di Valse and is, of course, in 3/4 time. Flowing melody and brilliancy of color are here associated with that sense of movement and gesture which are of the essence in the dance theater. The introduction alternates chords in the woodwinds and horns with arpeggios on the harp. The harp has a striking *cadenza* (a solo passage frequently introduced into an orchestral work in order to display the virtuosity of the performer and the capacities of the instrument). After four bars of an "oom-pah-pah" introduction, the waltz proper begins with a phrase for the horns marked piano, alternating with one for the solo clarinet. A contrasting melody emerges on the strings, punctuated by a measure on the woodwinds—always an effective orchestral procedure. Both melodies are repeated; the first is set off by ornamentation on the flutes. The middle section presents a second waltz, also consisting of two tunes. The first is sung by the flutes and oboes, piano; the second is a full-throated melody presented by the violas and cellos, forte. The first waltz is repeated and works up to a climax through a steady crescendo, accelerando, and rise to the brilliant upper register; the final measures are marked *fff.* With its suggestion of swirling ballerinas, this music conjures up everything we have come to associate with the romantic ballet.

The modern orchestra, with its amplitude of tonal resources, its range of dynamics and infinite variety of color, offers a memorable experience both to the musician and the music lover. There is good reason for the widespread conviction that it is one of the wonders of our musical culture.

10

Form: Musical Structure and Design

"The principal function of form is to advance our understanding. It is the organization of a piece which helps the listener to keep the idea in mind, to follow its development, its growth, its elaboration, its fate." — ARNOLD SCHOENBERG

Form is that quality in a work of art which presents to the mind of the beholder an impression of conscious choice and judicious arrangement. It represents clarity and order in art. It shows itself in the selection of certain details and the rejection of others. Form is manifest too in the relationship of the parts to the whole. It helps us to grasp the work of art as a unity. It can be as potent a source of beauty as the content itself.

Whether in the domestic arts—the setting of a table, the weaving of a basket—or in the loftier ones, a balance is required between unity and variety, between symmetry and asymmetry, activity and repose. Nor is this balance confined to art. Nature has embodied it in the forms of plant and animal life and in what man likes to think of as her supreme handiwork—his own form.

Form in Music

Repetition and contrast

Our lives are composed of sameness and differentness: certain details are repeated again and again, others are new. Music mirrors this dualism. Its basic law of structure is *repetition* and *contrast*—unity and variety. Repetition fixes the material in our minds and ministers to our need for the familiar. Contrast sustains our interest and feeds our love of change. From the interaction of the familiar and the new, the repeated elements and the contrasting ones, result the lineaments of musical form. These are to be found in every type of musical organism, from the nursery rhyme to the symphony.

The principle of form is embodied in a variety of musical forms. These utilize procedures worked out by generations of composers. No matter how diverse, they are based in one way or another on repetition and contrast. The forms, however, are not fixed molds into which the composer pours his material. What gives a piece of music its aliveness is the fact that it adapts a general plan to its own requirements. All faces have two eyes, a nose, and a mouth. In each face, though, these features are to be found in a wholly individual combination. The forms that students in composition follow are ready-made formulas set up for their guidance. The forms of the masters are living organisms in which external organization is delicately adjusted to inner content. No two symphonies of Haydn or Mozart, no two sonatas of Beethoven are exactly alike. Each is a fresh and unique solution to the problem of fashioning musical material into a logical and coherent form.

Three-Part or Ternary Form (A-B-A)

A basic pattern in music is *three-part* or *ternary form.* Here the composer presents a musical idea, next presents a contrasting idea, and then repeats the first. Hence this type of structure embodies the principle of "statement-departure-return" **(a-b-a)**. The repetition safeguards the unity, while variety is supplied by the middle section.

This principle is manifest in its simplest form in a nursery song such as *Twinkle, Twinkle, Little Star:*

a—Twinkle, twinkle, little star, how I wonder what you are.
b—Up above the world so high, like a diamond in the sky!
a—Twinkle, twinkle, little star, how I wonder what you are.

Often the first phrase is immediately repeated, so as to engrave it on the mind. This **a-(a)-b-a** structure is to be found in many melodies such as *Believe Me If All Those Endearing Young Charms; Maryland, My Maryland*; and *Old Man River*. It is the standard formula for the tunes of Tin Pan Alley. Our need for security is so great that, in a song consisting of four phrases, we are quite content to hear the opening phrase three times.

The four phrases in the **a-a-b-a** structure make up a unit that corresponds roughly to a paragraph in prose. Such a unit may be built up into a larger formation. For instance, a contrasting unit may be fashioned from new material (melodies **c** and **d**), after which the composer repeats the first unit, either as before or with some variation. There results a large **A-B-A** structure, each section of which is itself a three-part form or some variant thereof. (Notice that we use capital letters for the overall sections and small letters for the components within the section.) Tchaikovsky's *Waltz of the Flowers* (after the introduction) is a good example of this kind of formation:

A	B	A	
a-b-a-b	c-d-c	a-b-a-b	Coda

Coda, the Italian word for "tail," indicates the concluding section of a composition, which is added to the form proper to round it off.

Left: The facade of St. Paul's Cathedral in London (1675–1710), the work of Sir Christopher Wren, illustrates that three-part (A-B-A) form is as appealing to the eye as it is to the ear. Right: The Trylon and Perisphere, symbol of the New York World's Fair of 1939, is a visual realization of binary (A-B) form.

Three-part form became the standard pattern for innumerable short pieces of a simple song or dance type. This pattern is clear in several of the compositions mentioned in the preceding chapters. You will have no difficulty in recognizing the basic pattern of statement-departure-return in such pieces as the minuets from Mozart's *Eine kleine Nachtmusik* and *Symphony in G minor,* or Chopin's *Etude in E major* and the *Dance of the Toy Flutes* from Tchaikovsky's *Nutcracker Suite*.

With its attractive symmetry and its balancing of the outer sections against the contrasting middle one, the three-part or ternary form constitutes a simple, clear-cut formation that is a favorite in painting and architecture no less than in music.

The statement-departure-return principle is presented most effectively when there is a real departure; that is to say, when the middle section offers a decided contrast to the first and third parts. This contrast may show itself in a number of ways. An agitated first section may be opposed to a lyric middle part. The first part may lie in the dark lower register, the second in the middle or upper range. The contrast may be further underlined by opposing loud to soft, fast to slow, staccato to legato, strings to woodwinds and/or brass. These and similar ways serve to emphasize the contrast between the first and second sections as well as between the second section and the return of the first. Thus, in Chopin's celebrated *Fantasie-Impromptu* for piano, the first section is based on an impetuous running melody that extends across the keyboard, while the middle part presents a serenely songlike idea in the treble register.

 *Two-Part or Binary Form (A-B)*

Two-part or *binary form* is based on a statement and a departure, without a return to the opening section. This type of structure can be observed in the question-and-answer formation of a tune like *America*. A similar structure is to be observed in the Italian folksong *Santa Lucia* and in Brahms's *Lullaby*. Binary form is much in evidence in the short pieces that made up the suite of the seventeenth and eighteenth centuries, a period of lively experimentation in the realm of musical structure. Since each section generally is repeated, two-part form is not quite as apparent to the ear as is the three-part pattern. You will hear examples of **A-B** form in Scarlatti's *Sonata in E major*, K. 46 and the Gigue from Bach's *Suite No. 3*.

We will examine in subsequent chapters the great forms of Western music. No matter how imposing their dimensions, they all show the principle of repetition and contrast, of unity and variety, that we have traced here. In all its manifestations our music displays the striving for organic form that binds together the individual tones within the phrase, the phrases within the musical period, the periods within the section, the sections within the movement, and the movements within the work as a whole; even as, in a novel, the individual words are bound together in phrases, sentences, paragraphs, sections, chapters, and parts.

It has been said that architecture is frozen music. By the same token, music is floating architecture. Form is the structural principle in music. It distributes the areas of activity and repose, tension and relaxation, light and shade, and integrates the multitudinous details, large and small, into the spacious structures that are the glory of Western music.

11

Musical Style

"A good style should show no sign of effort. What is written should seem a happy accident." — SOMERSET MAUGHAM

Style may be defined as the characteristic manner of presentation in any art. The word may refer to the element of fitness that shapes each type of art work to its function. We distinguish between the style of the novel and that of the essay, between the style of the cathedral and that of the palace. The word may also indicate an artist's personal manner of expression, i.e., the distinctive flavor that sets him apart from all others. Thus we speak of the style of Dickens or Thackeray, or Raphael or Michelangelo, of Wagner or Brahms. In a larger sense we often identify style with national culture, as when we speak of French, Italian, or German style; or with an entire civilization, as when we contrast the musical style of the West with that of the Orient.

Style periods

Since all the arts change from one age to the next, one very important use of the word is in connection with the various historical periods. Here the concept of style enables us to draw the proper connection between the artist and his time, so that the art work is placed in its socio-historical frame. No matter how greatly the artists of a particular era may vary in personality and outlook, when seen in the perspective of time they turn out to have certain qualities in common. The age has put its stamp upon all. Because of this we can tell at once that a work of art—whether music, poetry, painting, or architecture—dates from the Middle Ages or the Renaissance, from the eighteenth century or the nineteenth. The style of a period, then, is the total art-language of all its artists as they react to the forces—artistic, political, economic, religious, philosophic—that shape their environment.

Scholars will always disagree as to precisely where one style period ends and the next begins. Each period leads by imperceptible degrees into the following one, dates and labels being merely convenient signposts. The following outline shows the main style periods in the history of Western music. Each represents a conception of form and technique, an ideal of beauty, a manner of expression and performance attuned to the cultural climate of the period; in a word—a style! (The dates, naturally, are approximate.)

350–600 A.D.	Period of the Church Fathers
600–850	Early Middle Ages. Gregorian Chant
850–1150	Romanesque. Development of the staff in musical notation, about 1000
1150–1450	Gothic
1450–1600	Renaissance
1600–1750	Baroque
1725–1775	Rococo
1775–1825	Classical
1820–1900	Romantic
1890–1915	Post-Romantic, including Impressionism
1910–	Twentieth century

12

Musical Notation

"Musical notation is so familiar to us that few are aware of the difficulty of the problems which had to be solved, and the innumerable experiments undertaken for the invention and perfection of a satisfactory method of recording musical sounds."

— SYLVIA TOWNSEND WARNER

Our musical notation is the result of an evolution that reaches back to antiquity. It has adapted itself to successive systems of musical thought, and continues to do so. It is by no means a perfect tool, but it has proved adequate to the constantly new demands made upon it.

The Notation of Pitch

Staff

Musical notation presents a kind of graph of the sounds with regard to their duration and pitch. These are indicated by symbols called *notes,* which are written on the *staff,* a series of five parallel lines with four spaces between:

The position of the notes on the staff indicates the pitches, each line and space representing a different degree of pitch.

Clefs

A symbol known as a *clef* is placed at the left end of the staff, and determines the group of pitches to which that staff refers. The *treble clef* (𝄞) is used for pitches within the range of the female singing voices, and the *bass clef* (𝄢) for a lower group of pitches, within the range of the male singing voices.

Pitch names

Pitches are named after the first seven letters of the alphabet, from A to G; the lines and spaces are named accordingly. (From one note named A to the next is the interval of an octave, which—as we have seen—is the distance from one *do* to the next in the *do-re-mi-fa-sol-la-ti-do* scale). The pitches on the treble staff are named as follows:

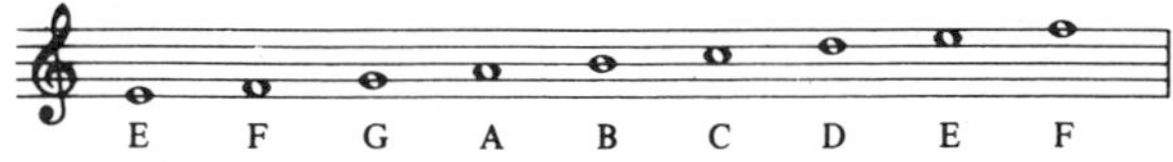

And those on the bass staff:

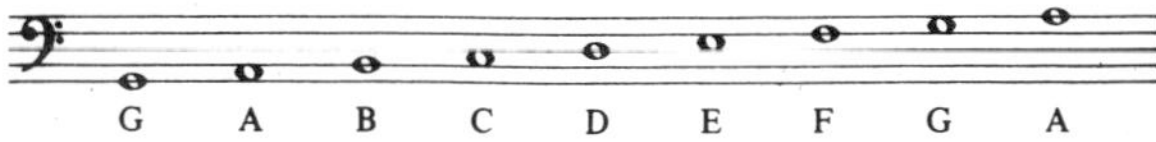

For pitches above and below these, short extra lines called *ledger lines* can be added:

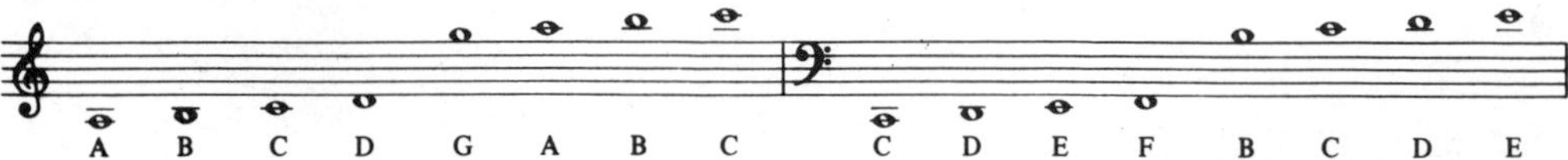

Middle C—the C that, on the piano, is situated approximately in the center of the keyboard—comes between the treble and bass staffs. It is represented by either the first ledger line above the bass staff or the first ledger line below the treble staff, as the following example, makes clear. This combination of the two staffs is called the *great staff* or *grand staff:*

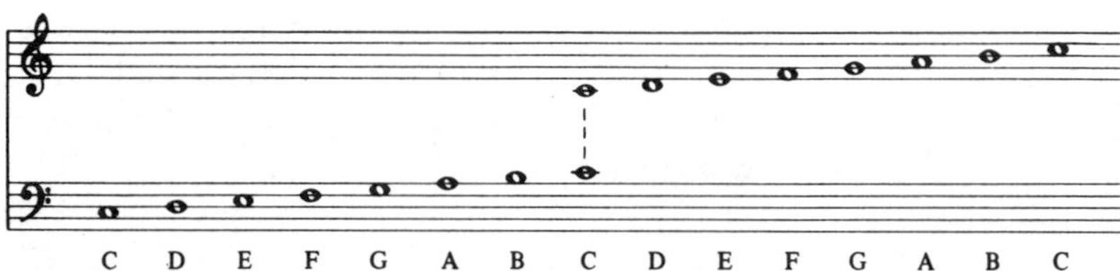

Accidentals

There are also signs known as *accidentals,* which are used to alter the pitch of a written note. A *sharp* (♯) before the note indicates the pitch a semitone above; a *flat* (♭) indicates the pitch a semitone below. A *natural* (♮) cancels a sharp or flat. Also used are the *double sharp* (𝄪) and *double flat* (♭♭), which respectively raise and lower the pitch by two half-tones—that is, a whole tone.

Semitones

The piano keyboard exemplifies this arrangement of whole and half tones. The distance from one piano key to its nearest neighbor is a *semitone* (also called a *half tone,* or *half step.*) This is true whether the adjacent keys are both white, or one white and the other black: thus, from E to F is a semitone, also from C to C♯.

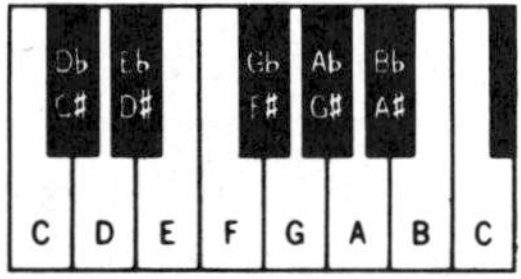

Each of the black keys has two names, depending on whether it is considered in relation to its upper or lower neighbor. For example, the black key between C and D can be called either C♯ or D♭. Similarly, D♯ is the same as E♭, F♯ as G♭, G♯ as A♭, and A♯ as B♭.

In many pieces of music, where certain sharped or flatted notes are used consistently throughout the piece, the necessary sharps or flats are written at the beginning of each line of music, in order to save repetition. This may be seen in the following example of piano music. Notice that piano music is written on the great staff, with the right hand usually playing the notes written on the upper staff and the left hand usually playing the notes written on the lower:

The Notation of Rhythm

The duration of tones is indicated by the appearance of the notes placed on the staff. These use a system of relative values. For example, in the following table each note represents a duration half as long as the preceding one:

Note values

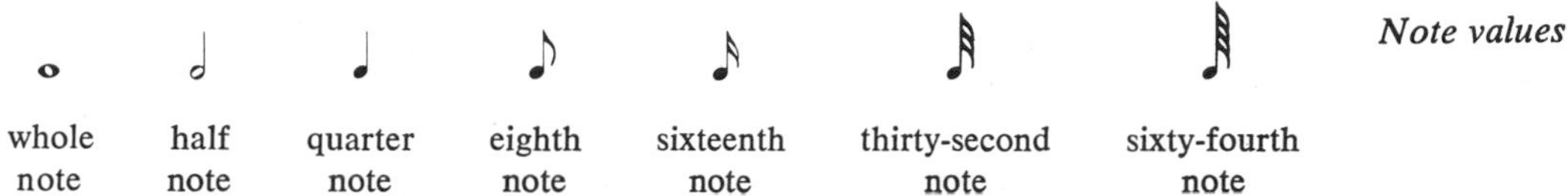

whole note · half note · quarter note · eighth note · sixteenth note · thirty-second note · sixty-fourth note

In any particular piece of music, these note values are related to the beat of the music. If the quarter note represents one beat, then a half note lasts for two beats, a whole note for four, with two eighth notes on one beat, or four sixteenths. The following chart makes this clear:

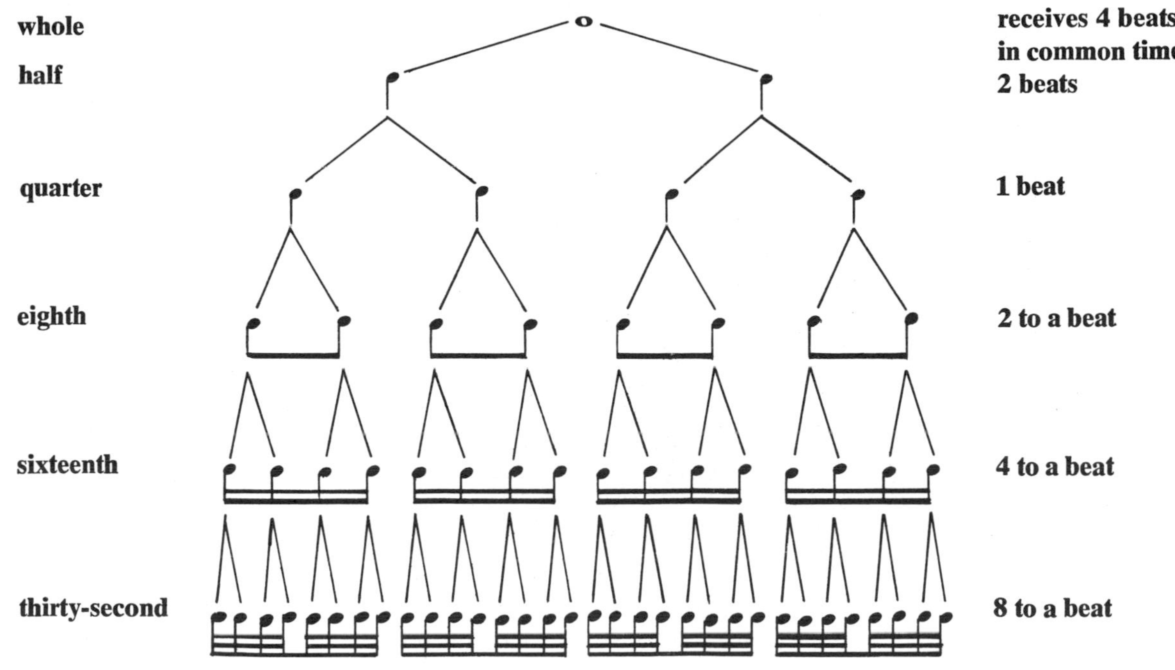

Triplet

When a group of three notes is to be played in the time normally taken up by only two of the same kind, we have a *triplet:*

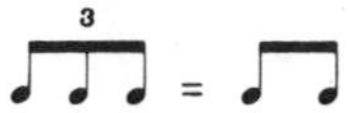

3

=

Tie

It is possible to combine successive notes of the same pitch, using a curved line known as a *tie:*

beats: 4 + 4 = 8 2 + 4 = 6 1 + ½ = 1½

Augmentation dot

A *dot* after a note extends its value by half:

beats: 4 + 2 = 6 2 + 1 = 3 1 + ½ = 1½ ½ + ¼ = ¾

Rests

Time never stops in music, even when there is no sound. Silence is indicated by symbols known as *rests,* which correspond in time value to the notes:

whole rest	half rest	quarter rest	eighth rest	sixteenth rest	thirty-second rest	sixty-fourth rest

Time signature

The metrical organization of a piece of music is indicated by the *time signature,* which specifies the meter. This consists of two numbers, written one above the other. The upper numeral indicates the number of beats within the measure; the lower one shows which unit of value equals one beat. Thus, the time signature 3/4 means that there are three beats to a measure, with the quarter note equal to one beat. In 6/8 time there are six beats in the measure, each eighth note receiving one beat. Following are the most frequently encountered time signatures:

duple meter	2/2	2/4	2/8	
triple meter	3/2	3/4	3/8	3/16
quadruple meter		4/4	4/8	
sextuple meter		6/4	6/8	

Also in use are 9/8 (3 groups of 3) and 12/8 (4 groups of 3). Contemporary music shows a wide use of nonsymmetrical patterns such as 5/4 or 5/8 (3 + 2 or 2 + 3) and 7/4 or 7/8 (4 + 3, 3+ 4, 2 + 3 + 2, etc.).

Four-four (4/4) is known as *common time* and is often indicated by the sign **C**. A vertical line drawn through this sign (**¢**) indicates *alla breve* or *cut time,* generally quick, with the half note receiving one beat instead of the quarter; in other words, two-two (2/2).

The following examples show how the system works. It will be noticed that the measures are separated by a vertical line known as a *barline;* hence a measure is often referred to as a *bar*. As a rule, the barline is followed by the most strongly accented beat, the ONE.

PART TWO

Nineteenth-Century Romanticism

"Music is the most romantic of all the arts—one might almost say, the only genuinely romantic one—for its sole subject is the infinite. Music discloses to man an unknown realm, a world in which he leaves behind him all definite feelings to surrender himself to an inexpressible longing." — E. T. A. HOFFMANN (1776–1822)

13

The Romantic Movement

"Romanticism is beauty without bounds—the beautiful infinite."

— JEAN PAUL RICHTER (1763–1825)

Historians observe that style in art moves between two poles, the classic and the romantic. Both the classic artist and the romantic strive to express significant emotions, and to achieve that expression within beautiful forms. Where they differ is in their point of view. The classical spirit seeks order, poise, and serenity as surely as the romantic longs for strangeness, wonder, and ecstasy. The classic artist is apt to be more objective in his approach to art and to life. He tries to view life sanely and "to see it whole." The romantic, on the other hand, is apt to be intensely subjective, and views the world in terms of his personal feelings. The German philosopher Friedrich Nietzsche, in his writings on art, dramatized the contrast between the two through the symbol of Apollo, god of light and measure, as opposed to Dionysus, god of intoxication and passion. Classic and romantic have alternated and even existed side by side from the beginning of time, for they correspond to two basic impulses in man's nature: on the one hand his need for moderation, his desire to have emotion purged and controlled; on the other, his desire for uninhibited emotional expression, his longing for the unknown and the unattainable.

Specifically, the classic and romantic labels are attached to two important periods in European art. The one held the stage in the last quarter of the eighteenth century and the early decades of the nineteenth. The other, stemming out of the social and political upheavals that followed in the wake of the French Revolution, came to the fore in the second quarter of the nineteenth century.

Romanticism in the Nineteenth Century

The French Revolution was the outcome of momentous social forces. It signalized the transfer of power from a hereditary feudal-agricultural aristocracy to the middle class, whose position depended on commerce and industry. As in the case of the American Revolution, this upheaval heralded a social order shaped by the technological advances of the In-

Revolutionary ardor was one of the mainsprings of the Romantic period, as can be seen in this massive sculptural group by François Rude (1784–1855), **La Marseillaise** *(The Departure of the Volunteers in 1792). Arc de Triomphe, Paris.*

dustrial Revolution. The new society, based on free enterprise, emphasized the individual as never before. Freedom—political, economic, religious, personal—was its watchword. On the artistic front this urge for individualism found expression in the Romantic movement.

The slogan of "Liberty, Equality, Fraternity" inspired hopes and visions to which few artists failed to respond. Sympathy for the oppressed, interest in simple folk and in children, faith in man and his destiny—all these, so intimately associated with the time, point to the democratic character of the Romantic movement. Whereas the eighteenth century had found inspiration in the art of ancient Greece, the Romantics discovered the so-called Dark Ages. King Arthur and Siegfried, fairy tale and medieval saga usurped the place formerly held by the gods and heroes of antiquity. Romantic architecture fell under the spell of the Gothic revival. So too, the formal gardens of the eighteenth century, with their spacious symmetries, were supplanted in public favor by picturesque grottoes and mysterious bowers. The Romantics became intensely aware of nature, but nature as a backdrop for the inner conflicts of man. When the heroine of a Romantic novel felt sad, it rained.

The Romantic poets rebelled against the conventional form and matter of their Classical predecessors; they leaned toward the fanciful, the picturesque, and the passionate. In Germany a group of young writers, following in the footsteps of Goethe and Schiller, created a new kind of lyric poetry that culminated in the art of Heinrich Heine; he became one of the favorite poets of the Romantic composers. A similar movement in France was led by Victor Hugo, its greatest prose writer, and Alphonse Lamartine, its greatest poet. In England the revolt against the formalism of the Classical age numbered among its adherents a line of lyric poets such as Gray, Cowper and Burns, Wordsworth and Coleridge, Byron, Shelley, and Keats. The new spirit of individualism expressed itself in the Romantic artist's sense of his uniqueness, his heightened awareness of himself as an individual apart from all others. "I am different from all the men I have seen," proclaimed Jean Jacques Rousseau. "If I am not better, at least I am different."

Thus, one of the prime traits of Romantic art was its emphasis on an intensely emotional type of expression. It has been well said that with Romanticism the pronoun "I" made its appearance in poetry. Gone were the elegantly abstract couplets of the eighteenth-century Classicists. The new age found expression in the passionate lyricism of such lines as Shelley's—

> Oh! lift me as a wave, a leaf, a cloud!
> I fall upon the thorns of life! I bleed!

or Keats's—

> When I have fears that I may cease to be
> Before my pen has gleaned my teeming brain . . .

The newly won freedom of the artist proved a not unmixed blessing. He confronted a philistine world from which he felt himself more and

A prime trait of Romantic art was its emphasis on an intensely emotional type of expression. **The Sleep of Reason** *from* **Los Caprichos** *by Francisco Goya (1746–1828), whose passionate realism anticipated a later age.* (Courtesy, Philadelphia Museum of Art, Ars Medica Collection.)

more cut off. A new type emerged—the artist as bohemian, the rejected dreamer who starved in an attic and through peculiarities of dress and behavior "shocked the bourgeois." This was the sensitive individual who was both too good for the moneyed world about him and not good enough. Increasingly the Romantic artist found himself arrayed against the established order. He was free from the social restraints imposed by court life; but he paid dearly for his freedom in loneliness, in knowing himself apart from his fellows. Withdrawal from the world brought a preoccupation with inner problems. Eternal longing, regret for the lost happiness of childhood, an indefinable discontent that gnawed at the soul—these were the ingredients of the Romantic mood. Yet the artist's pessimism was not without its basis in external reality. It became apparent that the high hopes fostered by the Revolution were not to be realized overnight. Despite the brave slogans, men were not yet equal or free. Inevitably optimism gave way to doubt and disenchantment—"the illness of the century."

This malaise was reflected in the art of the time. Thus, Balzac's *Human Comedy* depicted the warping of human relationships in the new society. Hugo dedicated *Les Misérables* "to the unhappy ones of the earth." The nineteenth-century novel found its great theme in the conflict between the individual and society. Jean Valjean and Heathcliff, Madame Bovary and Anna Karenina, Oliver Twist, Tess of the d'Urbervilles, and the Karamazovs—a varied company rises from those impassioned pages to point up the frustrations and guilts of the nineteenth-century world.

Hardly less persuasive was the art of those who sought escape. Some glamorized the past, as did Walter Scott and Alexandre Dumas. Longing for far-off lands inspired the exotic scenes that glow on the canvases of Turner and Delacroix. The Romantic poets and painters showed a remarkable fondness for the picturesque, the fantastic, and the macabre. Theirs was a world of "strangeness and wonder": the eerie landscape we encounter in the writings of a Coleridge, a Hawthorne, or a Poe.

Romanticism, in fine, dominated the art output of the nineteenth century. It gave its name to a movement and an era, and created a multitude of colorful works that still hold millions in thrall.

14

Romanticism in Music

"Music is the melody whose text is the world." — SCHOPENHAUER

Great changes in the moral, political, and social climate of an epoch seek to be expressed also in the art of that epoch. But they cannot be unless the new age places in the artist's hand the means of giving expression to new ideas. This was precisely the achievement of the Romantic movement in music—that it gave composers the means of expressing what the age demanded of them.

Improvements in instruments

In the first place, the Industrial Revolution brought with it not only the production of cheaper and more responsive instruments, but also introduced important improvements in the wind instruments that strongly influenced the sound of Romantic music. For example, the addition of valves to the brass instruments made them much more maneuverable, so that composers like Wagner and Tchaikovsky could assign melodies to the horn that would have been unplayable in the time of Haydn and Mozart. So too, as a result of improved manufacturing techniques, the piano acquired a cast-iron frame and thicker strings that gave it a deeper and more brilliant tone. If the impassioned *Sonata* of Liszt sounds different from a sonata of Mozart it is not only because Liszt's time demanded of him a different kind of expression, but also because it put at his disposal a piano capable of effects that were neither available nor necessary in the earlier period.

Secondly, the gradual democratization of society brought with it a broadening of educational opportunities. Conservatories that trained more and better musicians than formerly were established in the chief cities of Europe. As a result, nineteenth-century composers could count on instru-

The nineteenth-century orchestra offered the composer increased range and variety. Contemporary woodcut of an orchestral concert at the Covent Garden Theater, London, 1846.

mental performers whose skill was considerably in advance of what it had been in former times. As music moved from palace and church to the public concert hall, orchestras increased in size and efficiency, and gave the composer a means of expression more varied and colorful than he had ever had before. This naturally had a direct influence upon the sound. For example, where most eighteenth-century music ranged in dynamic level from piano to forte, the dynamic range of the orchestra in the nineteenth century was far greater. Now came into fashion the heaven-storming crescendos, the violent contrasts of loud and soft that lend such drama to the music of the Romantics. As orchestral music became more and more important, the technique of writing for orchestra—that is, orchestration—became almost an art in itself. At last the musician had a palette comparable to the painter's, and used it as the painter did—to conjure up sensuous beauty and enchantment, to create mood and atmosphere, to suggest nature scenes and calm or stormy seascapes.

The public concert hall

Increased expressiveness

The desire for direct communication led composers to use a large number of expressive terms intended to serve as clues to the mood of the music, with the result that a highly characteristic vocabulary sprang up. Among the directions frequently encountered in nineteenth-century scores are *dolce* (sweetly), *cantabile* (songful), *dolente* (weeping), *mesto* (sad), *maestoso* (majestic), *gioioso* (joyous), *con amore* (with love, tenderly), *con fuoco* (with fire), *con passione, espressivo, pastorale, agitato, misterioso, lamentoso, trionfale*. These suggest not only the character of the music but the frame of mind behind it.

Use of folklore

The interest in folklore and the rising tide of nationalism impelled the Romantic musicians to make use of the folk songs and dances of their native lands. As a result, a number of national idioms—Hungarian, Polish, Russian, Bohemian, Scandinavian—came to the fore and opened up new areas to European music, greatly enriching its melody, harmony, and rhythm.

Romantic melody

Even when written for instruments, Romantic melody was easy to sing and hum. The nineteenth century above all was the period when musicians tried to make their instruments "sing." It is no accident that the themes from Romantic symphonies, concertos, and other instrumental works have been transformed into popular songs; for Romantic melody was marked by a lyricism that gave it an immediate emotional appeal, as is evidenced by the enduring popularity of the tunes of Schubert, Chopin, Verdi, and their fellows. Through innumerable songs and operas as well as instrumental pieces, Romantic melody appealed to a wider audience than had ever existed before.

Chromatic harmony

Nineteenth-century music strove for a harmony that was highly emotional and expressive. Under the impact of the Romantic movement composers sought tone combinations that were more dissonant than what their forbears had been accustomed to. Richard Wagner was a leader in the trend towards what we shall come to know as *chromatic harmony* (a type of harmony in which chords based on the tones that belong to the key are made more colorful through the addition of tones that do not). The poignant dissonances through which he expressed the yearning of the lovers in *Tristan und Isolde* voiced the longing of an era. The tendency towards chromatic harmony became one of the important characteristics of musical Romanticism.

Expanded forms

The composers of the nineteenth century gradually expanded the instrumental forms they had inherited from the eighteenth. These musicians needed more time to say what they had to say. A symphony of Haydn or Mozart is apt to take about twenty minutes; one by Tchaikovsky, Brahms, or Dvořák lasts at least twice that long. As public concert life developed, the symphony became the most important form of orchestral music, comparable to the most spacious form in Romantic literature—the novel. As a result, the nineteenth-century composer approached the writing of a symphony with greater deliberation—some would say trepidation—than his predecessors. Where Haydn wrote over a hundred symphonies and Mozart more than forty, Schubert, Bruckner, and Dvořák (following the example of Beethoven) wrote nine; Tchaikovsky, six; Schumann and Brahms, four; César Franck, one. As the Romantics well realized, it was not easy to write a symphony after Beethoven.

Romantic man desired to taste all experience at its maximum intensity. He was enchanted in turn by literature, music, painting. How much more intoxicating, he reasoned, would be a "union of the arts" that combined all three. Music in the nineteenth century drew steadily closer to literature and painting—that is, to elements that lay outside the realm of sound. The connection with Romantic poetry and drama is most obvious, of course, in the case of music with words. However, even in their purely orchestral music the Romantic composers responded to the mood of the time and captured with remarkable vividness the emotional atmosphere that surrounded nineteenth-century poetry and painting.

The result of all these tendencies was to make Romanticism as potent a force in music as it was in the other arts. Nineteenth-century music was linked to dreams and passions, to profound meditations on life and death, man's destiny, God and nature, pride in one's country, desire for freedom, the political struggles of the age, and the ultimate triumph of good over evil. These intellectual and emotional associations, nurtured by the Romantic movement, enabled music to achieve a commanding position in the nineteenth century as a moral force, a vision of man's greatness, and a direct link between his inner life and the world around him.

15

The Short Lyric Forms as an Expression of Romanticism

"Out of my great sorrows I make my little songs." — HEINRICH HEINE

Through the short lyric forms the Romantic movement satisfied its need for intimate personal expression. Coming into prominence in the early decades of the century, the song and piano piece emerged as particularly attractive examples of the new lyricism.

The Song

The repertory of song–folk, popular, and art–is more extensive than that of all other types of music. For song combines two musical elements of universal appeal–melody and the human voice. A *song* is a short lyric composition for solo voice based on a poetic text. The vocal melody is presented as a rule with an instrumental accompaniment that gives it harmonic background and support.

A great poem is complete in itself and needs nothing more to enhance it. A melody, too, is a thing complete in itself. To blend the two into an artistic whole requires imagination of the highest order. The creators of the Romantic art song were so successful in combining words and music that many of the lyric poems they used have survived mainly in their musical settings.

Types of Song Structure

Strophic song

We distinguish between two main types of song structure. In *strophic form* the same melody is repeated with every stanza, or strophe, of the poem. This formation, which occurs very frequently in folk and popular song, permits of no great closeness between words and music. Instead it sets up a general atmosphere that accommodates itself equally well to all the stanzas. The first may tell of the lover's expectancy, the second of his joy at seeing his beloved, the third of her father's harshness in separating them, and the fourth of her sad death, all these being sung to the same tune. The prevalence of strophic song throughout the ages points to one conclusion: the folk learned early that a lovely tune is a joy in itself, and that it heightens emotion no matter what the content of a particular stanza.

Through-composed song

The other type is what the Germans call *durchkomponiert,* literally "through-composed"—that is, composed from beginning to end, without repetitions of whole sections. Here the music follows the story line, changing with each stanza according to the text. This makes it possible for the composer to mirror every shade of meaning in the words.

There is also an intermediate type that combines the repetition of the strophic song with the freedom of the song that is through-composed. The same melody may be repeated for two or three stanzas, with new material introduced when the poem seems to require it, generally at the climax. Schubert's celebrated *Ständchen* (Serenade) is a fine example of this structure.

The Art Song in the Romantic Period

Lied

Despite the prominence of song throughout the ages, the art song as we know it today was a product of the Romantic era. It was created by the union of poetry and music in the early nineteenth century. This union was consummated with such artistry by Franz Schubert and his successors, notably Robert Schumann and Johannes Brahms, that the new genre came to be known all over Europe by the German word for song—*Lied* (plural, *Lieder*).

The immense popularity of the Romantic art song was due in part to the emergence of the piano as the universal household instrument. A drawing by Ferdinand Walmüller, **House Music,** *1827.* (Albertina Museum, Vienna.)

The lied depended for its flowering on the upsurge of lyric poetry that marked the rise of German Romanticism. Goethe (1749–1832) and Heine (1797–1856) are the two leading figures among a group of poets who, like Wordsworth and Byron, Shelley and Keats in English literature, cultivated a subjective mode of expression through the short lyric poem. The lied brought to flower the desire of the Romantic era for the union of music and poetry, ranging from tender sentiment to dramatic balladry. Its favorite themes were love and longing, the beauty of nature, the transience of human happiness.

The triumph of the Romantic art song was made possible by the emergence of the piano as the universal household instrument of the nineteenth century. The piano accompaniment translated the poetic images into musical ones. Voice and piano together created a short lyric form charged with feeling, suited alike for amateurs and artists, for the home as for the concert room. Within a short time the lied achieved immense popularity and made a durable contribution to world art.

The Piano Piece

The short lyric piano piece was the instrumental equivalent of the song in its projection of lyric and dramatic moods within a compact frame. Among the titles most frequently used for it are *bagatelle* (literally, "a trifle"), *impromptu* ("on the spur of the moment"), *intermezzo* (interlude), *nocturne* (night song), *novelette* (short story), *moment musical, song without words, album leaf, prelude, romance, capriccio* (caprice); and, of larger dimensions, the *rhapsody* and *ballade.* In the dance category are the *waltz, mazurka, polka, écossaise* (Scottish dance), *polonaise* (Polish dance), *march,* and *country dance.* Composers also used titles of a fanciful and descriptive nature. Typical are Schumann's *In the Night, Soaring,* and *Whims;* Liszt's *Forest Murmurs* and *Fireflies.* The nineteenth-century masters of the short piano piece—Schubert, Chopin and Liszt, Mendelssohn, Schumann and Brahms, and their fellows—showed inexhaustible ingenuity in exploiting the technical resources of the instrument and its capacities for lyric-dramatic expression.

The short lyric form became one of the most popular types of music in the output of the Romantic era. Yet even here we find the urge to achieve large-scale structure. This expressed itself in the cycle of songs or piano pieces joined together by a literary or musical idea, as in Schubert's *Die schöne Müllerin* (The Lovely Maid of the Mill) and Schumann's *Carnaval.* Such cycles may be compared to the series of short stories within a frame, such as *The Canterbury Tales* or *The Decameron,* that had been popular in European literature for centuries.

In any case, the short lyric forms sprang out of the composer's realization that size is no criterion in art, and that an exquisitely wrought miniature may contain as much beauty as a symphony. In the song and piano piece, nineteenth-century Romanticism found one of its most characteristic means of expression.

16

Franz Schubert

"When I wished to sing of love it turned to sorrow. And when I wished to sing of sorrow it was transformed for me into love."

Franz Schubert

In the popular mind Franz Schubert's life has become a romantic symbol of the artist's fate. He suffered poverty and was neglected during his lifetime. He died young. And after his death he was enshrined among the immortals.

His Life

He was born in 1797 in a suburb of Vienna, the son of a schoolmaster. The boy learned the violin from his father, piano from an elder brother; his beautiful soprano voice gained him admittance to the imperial chapel and school where the court singers were trained. His teachers were duly astonished at the musicality of the shy, dreamy lad. One of them remarked that Franz seemed to learn "straight from Heaven."

His schooldays over, young Schubert tried to follow in his father's footsteps, but he was not cut out for the routine of the classroom. He found escape in the solitude of his attic, immersing himself in the lyric poets who were the first voices of German Romanticism. As one of his friends said, "Everything he touched turned to song." With a spontaneity comparable to Mozart's, the melodies took shape that gave to the new Romantic lyricism its ideal expression. *Gretchen at the Spinning Wheel,* to Goethe's verses, was written in a single afternoon—when he was seventeen. A year later came his setting of the same poet's *Erlking.* One of his greatest songs, it was the work of a few hours.

Schubert's talent for friendship attracted to him a little band of followers. Their appreciation of his genius comforted him for the neglect and incomprehension of the world. With their encouragement Schubert, not yet twenty, broke with the drudgery of his father's school. In the eleven years that were left him he occupied no official position (although he occasionally made half-hearted attempts to obtain one). He lived with one or another of his friends in a mixture of poverty and camaraderie, hope and despair. And steadily, with an almost self-devouring intensity, the music poured from the bespectacled young man. "How do you compose?" he was asked. "I finish one piece," was the answer, "and begin the next."

Schubert was singularly unable to stand up to the world. Songs that in time sold in the hundreds of thousands he surrendered literally for the

A Schubert Evening at Joseph Von Spaun's. *In this unfinished oil sketch by Moritz von Schwind (1804–71), we see Schubert at the piano, surrounded by his friends.*

price of a meal. As the years passed, the buoyancy of youth gave way to a sense of loneliness, the tragic loneliness of the Romantic artist. "No one feels another's grief," he wrote, "no one understands another's joy. People imagine that they can reach one another. In reality they only pass each other by." Yet he comprehended–and in this he was the Romantic–that his very suffering must open to his art new layers of awareness. "My music is the product of my talent and my misery. And that which I have written in my greatest distress is what the world seems to like best."

He still yielded to flurries of optimism when success appeared to lie within his grasp, but eventually there came to him an intimation that the struggle had been decided against him. "It seems to me at times that I no longer belong to this world." This was the emotional climate of the magnificent song cycle *Die Winterreise* (The Winter Journey), in which he struck a note of somber lyricism new to music. Depressed by illness and poverty, he abandoned himself to the mournful images of Wilhelm Müller's poems. The long, dark journey–was it not the symbol of his own life? Overcoming his discouragement, he embarked on his last effort. To the earlier masterpieces was added, in that final year, an amazing list that includes the *Mass in E flat*, the *String Quintet in C*, the three posthumous piano sonatas, and thirteen of his finest songs, among them the ever-popular *Serenade*.

Despite the magnitude of these achievements, he made arrangements to study counterpoint. "I see now how much I still have to learn." Ill with typhus, he managed to correct the proofs of the last part of *Die Winterreise*. The sense of defeat accompanied him through the final delirium; he fancied that he was being buried alive. "Do I not deserve a place above the ground?" His last wish was to be buried near the master he worshiped above all others—Beethoven.

He was thirty-one years old when he died in 1828. His possessions consisted of his clothing, his bedding, and "a pile of old music valued at ten florins": his unpublished manuscripts. In the memorable words of Sir George Grove, "There never has been one like him, and there never will be another."

His Music

Schubert stood at the confluence of the Classic and Romantic eras. His symphonic style bespeaks the heir of the Classical tradition; but in his songs and piano pieces he was wholly the Romantic, an artist whose magical lyricism impelled Liszt to call him "the most poetic musician that ever was." Like every composer of the nineteenth century, he was weighed down by the greatness of his predecessors. "Who can do anything more after Beethoven?" he complained. Yet within the orbit of that towering figure he developed a symphonic idiom of his own. His symphonies, for all their Romantic ardor, are Classical in their dramatic momentum and continuity. They rank with the finest since Beethoven.

Chamber music was Schubert's birthright as a Viennese. To the tradition of intimate social music he brought his own inwardness of spirit. The string quartets (1812–26), the *Trout Quintet* (1819), the two trios for piano, violin, and cello (1826–27), and the transcendent *Quintet in C* (1828) bear the true Schubertian stamp. They end the line of Viennese Classicism.

In the *Impromptus* and *Moments musicaux* (Musical Moments) the piano sings the new lyricism. Caprice, spontaneity, and the charm of the unexpected take their place as elements of Romantic art. Of comparable freshness is the popular tone of the dance pieces, waltzes, *ländlers* (Austrian peasant dances), and écossaises. His piano sonatas were neglected for years, but have now found their rightful place in the repertory. Schubert's broadly flowing lyricism expanded the form he inherited from his predecessors.

Finally there are the songs, more than six hundred of them. Many were written down at white heat, sometimes five, six, seven in a single morning. Certain of his melodies achieve the universality of folk song, others display the highest sophistication. In either case they issue directly from the heart of the poem. Their eloquence and freshness of feeling have never been surpassed. Of special moment are the accompaniments: a measure or two, and the rustling brook is conjured up, the dilapidated hurdy-gurdy, or the lark "at heaven's gate." Of Schubert's songs may be said what Schumann remarked about the *Symphony No. 9 in C major:* "This music transports us to a region where we cannot remember ever to have been before."

Erlkönig

SIDE 1/4
(E II AND S)

This masterpiece of Schubert's youth (1815) captures the Romantic "strangeness and wonder" of Goethe's celebrated ballad. *Erlkönig* (the Erlking) is based on the legend that whoever is touched by the King of the Elves must die. The poem has four characters: the narrator, the father, the child, and the seductive Elf.

NARRATOR

Wer reitet so spät durch Nacht und Wind?
Es ist der Vater mit seinem Kind;
er hat den Knaben wohl in dem Arm,
er fasst ihn sicher, er hält ihn warm.

Who rides so late through the night and the wind?
It is the father with his child;
he folds the boy close in his arms,
he clasps him securely, he holds him warmly.

FATHER

"Mein Sohn, was birgst du so bang dein
Gesicht?"

"My son, why hide your face so anxiously?"

SON

"Siehst, Vater, du den Erlkönig nicht?
den Erlenkönig mit Kron' und Schweif?"

"Father, don't you see the Erlking?
The Erlking with his crown and his train?"

FATHER

"Mein Sohn, es ist ein Nebelstreif."

"My son, it is a streak of mist."

ERLKING

"Du liebes Kind, komm, geh mit mir!
gar schöne Spiele spiel' ich mit dir;
manch bunte Blumen sind an dem Strand;
meine Mutter hat manch' gülden Gewand."

"Dear child, come, go with me!
I'll play the prettiest games with you.
Many colored flowers grow along the shore,
My mother has many golden garments."

SON

"Mein Vater, mein Vater, und hörest du
nicht,
was Erlenkönig mir leise verspricht?"

"My father, my father, and don't you hear
The Erlking whispering promises to me?"

FATHER

"Sei ruhig, bleibe ruhig, mein Kind;
in dürren Blättern säuselt der Wind."

"Be quiet, stay quiet, my child;
The wind is rustling in the dead leaves."

ERLKING

"Willst, feiner Knabe, du mit mir gehn?
meine Töchter sollen dich warten schön;
mein Töchter führen den nächtlichen Reihn
und wiegen und tanzen und singen dich ein."

"My handsome boy, will you come with me?
My daughters shall wait upon you;
my daughters lead off in the dance every night,
and cradle and dance and sing you to sleep."

SON

"Mein Vater, mein Vater, und siehst du nicht dort
Erlkönigs Töchter am düstern Ort?"

"My father, my father, and don't you see there
The Erlking's daughters in the shadows?"

FATHER

"Mein Sohn, mein Sohn, ich seh' es genau,
es scheinen die alten Weiden so grau."

"My son, my son, I see it clearly;
The old willows look so gray."

ERLKING

"Ich liebe dich, mich reizt deine schöne Gestalt,
und bist du nicht willig, so brauch' ich Gewalt."

"I love you, your beautiful figure delights me!
And if you're not willing, then I shall use force!"

SON

"Mein Vater, mein Vater, jetzt fasst er mich an!
Erlkönig hat mir ein Leids gethan!"

"My father, my father, now he is taking hold of me!
The Erlking has hurt me!"

NARRATOR

Dem Vater grauset's, er reitet geschwind,
er hält in Armen das ächzende Kind,
erreicht den Hof mit Müh' und Noth:
in seinen Armen das Kind war todt.

The father shudders, he rides swiftly on;
He holds in his arms the groaning child,
He reaches the courtyard weary and anxious:
In his arms the child was dead.

The eerie atmosphere of the poem is established by the piano part. Galloping triplets are heard against a rumbling figure in the bass. This motive, so Romantic in tone, pervades the canvas and imparts to it an astonishing unity.

The characters are vividly differentiated through changes in the melody, harmony, rhythm, and type of accompaniment. The child's terror is suggested by clashing dissonance. The father, allaying his son's fears, is represented by a more rounded vocal line. As for the Erlking, his cajoling is given in suavely melodious phrases.

The song is through-composed; the music follows the unfolding of the narrative with a steady rise in tension—and pitch—that builds to the climax. Abruptly the obsessive triplet rhythm lets up, giving way to a ritard as horse and rider reach home. "In his arms the child"—a dramatic pause precedes the two final words—"lay dead."

The thing seems strangely simple, inevitable. The doing of it by a marvelous boy of eighteen was a milestone in the history of Romanticism.

Impromptu in A flat

A Viennese publisher hit on the title "Impromptu," the French word for "on the spur of the moment." The name accorded with the Romantic notion that music came in a flash of inspiration. The *Impromptu in A flat,* Opus 90, No. 4, one of Schubert's most widely played piano pieces, was written in 1827. It is an **A-B-A** form, with each section subdividing into symmetrical smaller sections. The piece is an Allegretto in ¾ time. The principal idea involves arpeggios that sweep down gently in a broad arc, beneath which an upward thrusting melody presently emerges in the bass.

The middle part presents an effective contrast to the opening sections. A somber melody, consisting of sustained legato tones, is heard over an accompaniment of repeated chords. Tension builds in a steady line to a fortissimo climax; the emotion is direct, concentrated, inescapable. Then the first section is repeated, rounding off the form.

In this enchanting piece are manifest the qualities that set Schubert apart: his charm of melody, his tenderness, and an ineffably romantic longing that can only be described as Schubertian.

17

Robert Schumann

"Music is to me the perfect expression of the soul."

Robert Schumann.

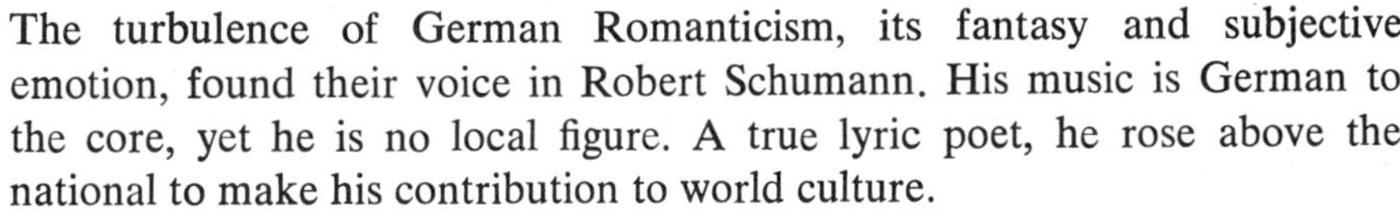
The turbulence of German Romanticism, its fantasy and subjective emotion, found their voice in Robert Schumann. His music is German to the core, yet he is no local figure. A true lyric poet, he rose above the national to make his contribution to world culture.

His Life

Robert Schumann (1810–56) was born in Zwickau, a town in Saxony, son of a bookseller whose love of literature was reflected in the boy. At his mother's insistence he undertook the study of law, first at the University of Leipzig, then at Heidelberg. The youth daydreamed at the piano, steeped himself in Goethe and Byron, and attended an occasional lecture. His aversion to the law kept pace with his passion for music; it was his ambition to become a pianist. At last he won his mother's consent and returned to Leipzig to study with Friedrich Wieck, one of the foremost pedagogues of the day. "I am so fresh in soul and spirit," he exulted, "that life gushes and bubbles around me in a thousand springs."

The young man practiced intensively to make up for his late start. In his eagerness to perfect his technique he devised a contrivance that held the fourth finger immobile while the others exercised. The gadget was so effective that he permanently injured the fourth finger of his right hand. The end of his hopes as a pianist turned his interest to composing. In a burst of creative energy he produced, while still in his twenties, his most important works for the piano.

The spontaneity of his production astonished him. "Everything comes to me of itself," he wrote, "and indeed, it sometimes seems as if I could play on eternally and never come to an end." Such intensity—the prime quality of the lyricist—carried with it a premonition of early doom. "Oh I cannot help it, I should like to sing myself to death like a nightingale. . . ."

He was engaged concurrently in an important literary venture. With a group of like-minded enthusiasts he founded a journal named *The New Magazine for Music*. Schumann threw himself into his editorial activities as impetuously as he had into composing. Under his direction the periodical became one of the most important music journals in Europe. Schumann's critical essays revealed the composer as a gifted literary man. Cast in the form of prose poems, imaginary dialogues, or letters, they were as personal as his music. He fought the taste of the bourgeois—the Philistines, as he liked to call them—and agitated for the great works of the past as well as the new Romanticism.

The hectic quality of this decade was intensified by his courtship of the gifted pianist Clara Wieck. When he first came to study with her father she was an eleven-year-old prodigy. She was about sixteen when Robert realized he loved her. Wieck's opposition to the marriage bordered on the psychopathic. Clara was the supreme achievement of his life and he refused to surrender her to another. For several years she was cruelly torn between the father she revered and the man she loved. At length, since she was not yet of age, the couple was forced to appeal to the courts against Wieck. The marriage took place in 1840, when Clara was twenty-one and Robert thirty. His happiness overflowed into a medium more personal even than the piano. This was his "year of song," when he produced over a hundred of the lieder that represent his lyric gift at its purest.

The two artists settled in Leipzig, pursuing their careers side by side. Clara became the first interpreter of Robert's piano works and in the ensuing decade contributed substantially to the spreading of his fame. Yet neither her love nor that of their children could ward off his increasing withdrawal from the world. Moodiness and nervous exhaustion culminated, in 1844, in a severe breakdown. The doctors counseled a change of scene. The couple moved to Dresden, where Schumann seemingly made a full recovery. But the periods of depression returned ever more frequently.

In 1850 Schumann was appointed music director at Düsseldorf. But he was ill-suited for public life; he could neither organize music festivals nor deal with masses of men, and was forced to relinquish the post. During a tour of Holland, where Clara and he were warmly received, he began to complain of "unnatural noises" in his head. His last letter to the violinist Joachim, two weeks before the final breakdown, is a farewell to his art. "The music is silent now . . . I will close. Already it grows dark."

He fell prey to auditory hallucinations. Once he rose in the middle of the night to write down a theme that he imagined had been brought him by the spirits of Schubert and Mendelssohn. It was his last melody. A week later, in a fit of melancholia, he threw himself into the Rhine. He was rescued by fishermen and placed in a private asylum near Bonn. Despite occasional flashes of lucidity, the darkness did not lift. He died two years later at the age of forty-six.

His Music

As a piano composer Schumann was one of the most original figures of the century. Whimsy and ardent expressiveness pervade his miniatures, which brim over with impassioned melody, novel harmonies, and vigorous rhythms. The titles of the collections strike the Romantic note; among them we find *Fantasy Pieces, Papillons* (Butterflies), *Romances, Scenes from Childhood.* Among his large piano works are three *Sonatas,* the *Fantasy in C,* the *Symphonic Etudes,* and the *Piano Concerto in A minor.*

As a composer of lieder he ranks second only to Schubert. His songs are finely wrought and rich in poetic suggestion. His favorite theme is love, particularly from the woman's point of view. His favored poet was Heine, for whom he had an affinity like that of Schubert for Goethe.

Thoroughly Romantic in feeling are the four symphonies. Schumann has been taken to task for his inability to develop thematic material and for his occasional awkwardness in orchestration. Yet the best of his symphonies, the first and fourth, communicate a lyric freshness that has kept them alive long after many more adroitly fashioned works have fallen by the way. What could be closer to the essence of German Romanticism than the "nature sound" of the horns and trumpets at the opening of the *Spring Symphony,* his first? "Could you infuse into the orchestra," he wrote the conductor, "a kind of longing for spring? At the first entrance of the trumpets I should like them to sound as from on high, like a call to awakening."

Ich grolle nicht

The introspective side of Schumann's lyricism predominates in what is probably his most powerful love song. Heine's lines fired the composer to a lied of brooding intensity.

Ich grolle nicht, und wenn das Herz auch bricht,
Ewig verlornes Lieb! ich grolle nicht.
Wie du auch strahlst in Diamantenpracht,

Es fällt kein Strahl in deines Herzensnacht.

Das weiss ich längst. Ich sah dich ja im Traum,
Und sah die Nacht in deines Herzens Raum,
Und sah die Schlang', die dir am Herzen frisst,
Ich sah, mein Lieb, wie sehr du elend bist.

I bear no grudge, even though my heart may break,
eternally lost love! I bear no grudge.
However you may shine in the splendor of your diamonds,
no ray of light falls in the darkness of your heart.

I have long known this. I saw you in a dream,
and saw the night within the void of your heart,
and saw the serpent that is eating your heart—
I saw, my love, how very miserable you are.

Schumann here achieves the supreme aim of the Romantic lied—to give utterance to a state of soul. The repetitions of Heine's opening line later in the song produce a spontaneous-sounding irregularity. The soaring melody becomes a kind of graph that follows sensitively the rise and fall of emotion. Sustained dissonances in the accompaniment build harmonic and psychological tension. The song falls into two halves, both of which begin identically.

SIDE 1/5 (E II AND S)

Ich grolle nicht stands between the strophic song and the through-composed type. Schumann repeats material from the first half of the song in the second, and also introduces new material that builds relentlessly to the tragic chords of the climax: "And saw the snake that eats at your heart . . ."

This song–both words and music–is a perfect embodiment of the Romantic spirit.

Aufschwung

Schumann's piano pieces exhibit his mastery of the miniature. Within the pattern of statement-departure-return **(A-B-A)** he found an ideal frame for what he had to say.

SIDE 1/6 (E II)

Aufschwung (Soaring) is the second of the *Phantasiestücke,* Opus 12 (Fantasy Pieces; 1837). Bold rhythmic patterns and a flow of melodic ideas made this piece precisely what its name implies: a soaring, an upsurge of spirit. The meter is $^6/_8$, the tempo lively. The mood is fiery, as indicated by Schumann's marking Sehr rasch (very spirited). The main idea shows the exuberant side of his Romantic nature:

This alternates with two lyrical melodies in the pattern **A-B-A-C-A-B-A.** The second theme flows in a legato line that moves within a narrow range by half step or narrow leap. It offers a perfect contrast to the first:

The impetuous first theme returns. Then the third idea **(C)** offers a serene contrast:

The different sections are linked by transitional passages that lead the listener from one mood to the next; they serve also to unify the structure. For example, in the transition from the third theme back to the first, a bass line associated with the **B** melody is gradually combined with a foreshadowing of the **A** theme. These measures therefore are both a remembrance and an anticipation. As a result of procedures such as this, *Aufschwung* is a tightly-knit composition that, in both its boisterous and lyrical moments, exemplifies the Romantic piano piece at its best and shows off Schumann's highly individual manner of writing for the instrument.

"Music still devours me. I must often tear myself from it by violence." This remark indicates the passionate creativity of the decade-and-a-half in which he was at his peak. His peak was the spring tide of German Romanticism, during which he nobly discharged what he conceived to be the artist's mission: "To send light into the depths of the human heart!"

Romantics such as J. M. W. Turner (1775–1851) used nature as a backdrop for the inner conflicts of man.
The Slave Ship. (Henry Lillie Pierce Fund. Courtesy, Museum of Fine Arts, Boston.)

*Romanticism seized on themes of passionate intensity. This is clearly demonstrated in the famous painting **The Raft of the "Medusa"** by Théodore Géricault (1791–1824).* (Clichés des Musées Nationaux.)

18

Frédéric François Chopin

"My life . . . an episode without a beginning and with a sad end."

Frédéric François Chopin.

In the annals of his century Chopin (1810–49) is known as the "Poet of the Piano." The title is a valid one. His art, issuing from the heart of Romanticism, constitutes the golden age of that instrument.

His Life

The national composer of Poland was half French. His father emigrated to Warsaw, where he married a lady-in-waiting to a countess and taught French to the sons of the nobility. Frédéric, who displayed his musical gift in childhood, was educated at the newly-founded Conservatory of Warsaw. His student years were climaxed by a mild infatuation with a young singer, Constantia Gladkowska, who inspired him with sighs and tears in the best nineteenth-century manner. "It was with thoughts of this beautiful creature that I composed the Adagio of my new concerto." The concerto was the one in F minor. Frédéric was nineteen.

When the young artist set forth to make a name in the world, his comrades sang a farewell cantata in his honor. Frédéric wept, convinced he would never see his homeland again. In Vienna the news reached him that Warsaw had risen in revolt against the Tsar. Gloomy visions tormented him; he saw his family and friends massacred. He left Vienna in the summer. On reaching Stuttgart he learned that the Polish capital had been captured by the Russians. The tidings precipitated a torrent of grief, and the flaming defiance that found expression in the *Revolutionary Etude*.

In September, 1831, the young man reached Paris. He thought of continuing to London, even to America. But he was introduced by his countryman, Prince Radziwill, into the aristocratic salons and there created a sensation. His decision was made, and the rest of his career was linked to the artistic life of his adopted city. Paris in the 1830s was the center of the new Romanticism. The circle in which Chopin moved included as brilliant a galaxy of artists as ever gathered anywhere. Among the musicians were Liszt and Berlioz, Rossini and Meyerbeer. The literary figures included Victor Hugo, Balzac, Lamartine, George Sand, de Musset, and Alexandre Dumas. Heinrich Heine was his friend, as was the painter Delacroix. Although Chopin was a man of emotions rather than ideas, he could not but be stimulated by his contact with the leading intellectuals of France.

Through Liszt he met Mme. Aurore Dudevant, "the lady with the somber eye," known to the world as the novelist George Sand. She was thirty-four, Chopin twenty-eight when the famous friendship began. Mme. Sand was brilliant and domineering; her need to dominate found its counterpart in Chopin's need to be ruled. She left a memorable account of this fastidious artist at work: "His creative power was spontaneous, miraculous. It came to him without effort or warning . . . But then began the most heartrending labor I have ever witnessed. It was a series of attempts, of fits of irresolution and impatience to recover certain details. He would shut himself in his room for days, pacing up and down, breaking his pens, repeating and modifying one bar a hundred times . . . He would spend six weeks over a page, only to end by writing it out finally just as he had sketched it in the original draft."

For the next eight years Chopin spent his summers at Mme. Sand's chateau at Nohant, where she entertained the cream of France's intelligentsia. These were productive years for him, although his health grew progressively worse and his relationship with Mme. Sand ran its course from love to conflict, from jealousy to hostility. They parted in bitterness.

According to his friend Liszt, "Chopin felt and often repeated that in breaking this long affection, this powerful bond, he had broken his life." Chopin's creative energy, which had lost its momentum in his middle thirties, came to an end. The "illness of the century," the lonely despair of the Romantic artist pervades his last letters. "What has become of my art?" he writes during a visit to Scotland. "And my heart, where have I wasted it? I scarce remember any more how they sing at home. That world slips away from me somehow. I forget. I have no strength. If I rise a little I fall again, lower than ever."

He returned to Paris suffering from tuberculosis and died some months later, at the age of thirty-nine. His funeral was his greatest triumph. Princesses and artists joined to pay him homage. Meyerbeer, Berlioz, and Delacroix were among the mourners. George Sand stayed away. His heart was returned to Poland, the rest of him remained in Paris. And on his grave a friendly hand scattered a gobletful of Polish earth.

His Music

Chopin was one of the most original artists of the Romantic era. His idiom is so entirely his own there is no mistaking it for any other. He was the only master of first rank whose creative life centered about the piano. From the first, his imagination was wedded to the keyboard, to create a universe within that narrow frame. His genius transformed even the limitations of the instrument into sources of beauty. (The prime limitation, of course, is the piano's inability to sustain tone for any length of time.) Chopin overcame these with such ingenuity that to him as much as to any individual is due the modern piano style. The widely spaced chords in the bass, sustained by pedal, set up masses of tone that wreathe the melody in enchantment. "Everything must be made to sing," he told his pupils. The delicate ornaments in his music–trills, grace notes, runs of gossamer lightness–seem magically to prolong the single tones. And all this generally lies so well for the hand that the music seems almost to play itself.

It is remarkable that so many of his works have remained in the pianist's repertory. His Nocturnes–night songs, as the name implies–are tinged with varying shades of melancholy. They are usually in three-part form. The Preludes are visionary fragments; some are only a page in length, several consist of two or three lines. The Etudes crown the literature of the study piece. Here piano technique is transformed into poetry. The Impromptus are fanciful, capricious, yet they have a curious rightness about them. The Waltzes capture the brilliance and coquetry of the salon. They are veritable dances of the spirit. The Mazurkas, derived from a Polish peasant dance, evoke the idealized landscape of his youth.

Among the larger forms are the four Ballades. These are epic poems of spacious structure, like sagas related by a bard. The Polonaises revive the stately processional dance in which Poland's nobles were wont to hail their kings. Heroic in tone, they resound with the clangor of battle and brave deeds. In reminding his countrymen of their ancient glory the national poet strengthens their will to freedom. The *Berceuse* (Cradle Song), the *Barcarolle* (Boat Song), the *Fantasy in F minor,* and the dramatic Scherzos reveal the composer at the summit of his art. The *Sonatas in B minor* and *B-flat minor* are thoroughly Romantic in spirit as are the *Piano Concertos in E minor* and *F minor.*

Chopin's style emerged fully formed when he was twenty. It was not the result of an extended intellectual development, as was the case with masters like Beethoven or Wagner. In this he was the true lyricist, along with his contemporaries Schumann and Mendelssohn. All three died young, and all three reached their peak through the spontaneous lyricism of youth. In them the first period of Romanticism found its finest expression.

Etude in A minor

SIDE 2/1 (E II)
SIDE 1/6 (S)

An *etude* is a study piece that deals with a specific technical problem, such as rapid scales, arpeggios, octaves, and the like. Every instrumentalist has to spend hours practicing such study pieces which, apart from their use as exercises, have either very little or no musical value.

It was Chopin's achievement to lift the study piece from its purely utilitarian level into the high realm of art. His Etudes are little tone poems suffused with all the glow of his creative imagination. At the same time they approach the technical problems of a new style of Romantic piano playing with an inventiveness that had never been envisaged before.

Typical is the *Etude in A minor,* Opus 25, No. 11. The technical problem here is one that the pianist encounters fairly frequently: a melody in the left hand articulated against rapid passages in the right. To meet these requirements Chopin created one of his most tumultuous tone paintings. The right hand alone, then both together announce the brief theme on which the piece is based—a solemn melody, like a summons, marked Lento:

This motto gives rise to a theme that shapes the piece, projected at first in tumultuous, quasi heroic accents. The tension abates for an instant when the melody is switched to the right hand while the left takes over the passage work. Eventually both hands play the rapid passages simultaneously, building a tremendous climax. Throughout, the piece demands from the pianist the utmost accuracy, speed and endurance. Finally the motto thunders from the bass, then in massive chords. A sweeping scale in both hands concludes this tonal epic.

One is swept along by the tremendous drive, the almost explosive force of the music. This Etude is popularly known as the *Winter Wind,* one of a series of fanciful titles that affixed themselves to various works of Chopin long after he had written them.

Prelude in E minor

SIDE 1/7
(E II AND S)

The *Prelude in E minor,* Opus 28, No. 4 (1839) reveals Chopin's uncanny power to achieve the utmost expressiveness with the simplest means. The melody hardly moves, unfolding in sustained tones over a succession of chords that change very subtly, usually one note at a time:

The music strikes a gently mournful mood that is of the essence of Romanticism. Tension gathers slowly; there is something inevitable about the rise to the climax, where the melody, advancing in bold leaps, takes on the character of a passionate outcry that subsides to a sorrowful pianissimo ending. Rarely has so much been said in a single page. Schumann did not exaggerate when he said of the Preludes, "In each piece we find in his own hand, 'Frédéric Chopin wrote it!' He is the boldest, the proudest poet of his time."

Rubato

Important here, as in all of Chopin's music, is the *tempo rubato*—the "robbed time" (better, "borrowed time") that is so characteristic of the Romantic style. In tempo rubato, certain liberties can be taken with the rhythm without upsetting the basic beat. As Chopin taught it, the accompaniment—say, the left hand—played in strict time while above it the right hand, as it sang the melody, might hesitate a little here or hurry forward there. In either case, the "borrowing" had to be repaid before the end of the phrase. Rubato, like any seasoning, has to be used sparingly. But when it is done well it imparts to the music a waywardness, a quality of caprice that can be enchanting. And it remains an essential ingredient of the true Chopin style.

Polonaise in A flat

SIDE 1/8 (E II AND S)

The heroic side of Chopin's art shows itself in the most popular of his Polonaises, the one in A flat, Opus 53 (1842). The opening theme is

proud and chivalric. The octaves for the left hand in the following section approach the limits of what the piano can do. The emotional temperature drops perceptibly after the octave episode, which is Chopin's way of building up tension against the return of the theme. In the hands of a virtuoso this Polonaise takes on surpassing brilliance; it is the epitome of the grand style.

His countrymen have enshrined Chopin as the national composer of Poland. Withal he is a spokesman of European culture. It is not without significance that despite his homesickness he spent the whole of his adult life in Paris. Thus Poland was idealized in his imagination as the symbol of that unappeasable longing which every Romantic artist carries in his heart: the longing for the lost land of happiness that may never be found again. Heine, himself an expatriate, divined this when he wrote that Chopin is "neither a Pole, a Frenchman, nor a German. He reveals a higher origin. He comes from the land of Mozart, Raphael, Goethe. His true country is the land of poetry."

19

Other Short Lyric Works

"Is not music the mysterious language of a faraway spirit world whose wondrous accents awaken us to a higher, more intense life? — FRANZ LISZT

Liszt: Sonetto 104 del Petrarca

SIDE 3/1 (E II)

Franz Liszt (1811–86) stands alongside Chopin as one of the creators of modern piano technique. He exploited resources of the instrument—octaves, trills, rapid runs, arpeggios—with the utmost ingenuity; in his hands the piano became an orchestra capable of the most varied colors and sonorities.

Typical of Liszt's poetic lyricism is the piece, composed in 1848, that was inspired by the 104th Sonnet of Petrarch, in which the fourteenth-century Italian poet gave utterance to a lover's anguish:

> Warfare I cannot wage, yet know not peace;
> I fear, I hope, I burn, I freeze again;
> Mount to the skies, then bow to earth my face;
> Grasp the whole world, yet nothing can obtain . . .
>
> Death I despise, and life alike I hate:
> Such, lady, dost thou make my wayward state!

The piece opens Agitato assai with a series of *sequences* (a sequence is a melodic or harmonic pattern that is duplicated at a higher or lower pitch) that leads into an Adagio marked molto espressivo (very expressively). Here is presented a heartfelt melody supported by arpeggios. In the answering phrase the melody is heard in the bass, played by the left hand while the right plays arpeggios above it. Now Liszt repeats the melody in high register against a running accompaniment in the bass; it is marked Cantabile con passione (singing, with passion):

The music evokes the sighs and tears of Petrarch's sonnet. Technically the piece displays several of Liszt's favorite procedures, such as articulating a melody in the middle register while the left hand wreathes it in arpeggios both above and below (this involves crossing the hands). In a more elaborate version heard later on, the single notes in the melody are transformed into octaves, the arpeggios in the bass become a series of double notes, and the melody itself is embellished with rapid runs that envelop it in a magical mist. The music ends on a simple triad that is sustained until the sound dies away.

Brahms: Vergebliches Ständchen

SIDE 2/2 (E II)

From Schubert and Schumann the leadership in the realm of the art song passed to Johannes Brahms (1833–97). He handled the short form with consummate ease and craftsmanship, bringing to his songs an inwardness of feeling both deep and restrained. The extrovert side of Brahms's personality—robust, delighting in broad humor—is to be observed in the *Vergebliches Ständchen* (Futile Serenade; 1881). It is his version of a lusty folk song from the Lower Rhineland.

Guten Abend, mein Schatz, Guten Abend, mein Kind! Ich komm' aus Lieb' zu dir, Ach, mach' mir auf die Tür! Mach' mir auf die Tür!	HE	Good evening, my dear, Good evening, my child! I come out of love for you, Ah, open the door for me! Open the door for me!
Meine Tür ist verschlossen, Ich lass dich nicht ein; Mutter die rät' mir klug, Wär'st du herein mit Fug, Wär's mit mir vorbei!	SHE	My door is locked, I will not let you in. Mother warned me That if I let you in willingly All would be over with me!
So kalt ist die Nacht, So eisig der Wind, Dass mir das Herz erfriert, Mein' Lieb' erlöschen wird; Öffne mir, mein Kind!	HE	The night is so cold, The wind is so icy, That my heart is freezing. My love will be extinguished, Open up for me, child!
Löschet dein Lieb' Lass sie löschen nur! Löschet sie immer zu, Geh' heim zu Bett zur Ruh', Gute Nacht, mein Knab'!	SHE	If your love is extinguished, Just let it go out! Just keep on extinguishing it; Go home to bed, to rest! Good night, my boy!

The four stanzas call forth a modified strophic form. Following a short introduction, the melody outlines the common triads and moves in an animated $\frac{3}{4}$ time, achieving the simplicity and naturalness of the folk mood. The opening phrase contains the same little figure repeated three times, each time from a lower note—in a word, a sequence. The melody is marked Lebhaft und gut gelaunt (lively and good-humored).

The relationship of folk song to the dance is underlined by the regularity of structure: four measures to the phrase, four phrases to the stanza. Yet Brahms introduces a charming asymmetry: the usual four-bar phrase is extended for two bars by repeating the words "mach' mir auf" (let me in). This extension is repeated in every stanza, the momentary waywardness setting off the symmetry of the rest.

Charming too is the sudden change of color at the third stanza. The melody takes on a plaintive tone as the lover beseeches: "The night is so cold, so icy the wind!" This is achieved by flatting certain tones (a change from major to minor—a procedure we will discuss in a later chapter). The light-fingered accompaniment, which grows more elaborate with each stanza, keeps the song moving and creates an admirable frame for the spirited dialogue. Here is the thoroughly German aspect of Brahms—the soil from which flowered the more cultivated blossoms of his art.

Nineteenth-century song and piano piece have maintained their popularity to this day. These short forms filled an important need for intimate lyricism and spontaneous expression. They stand as one of the most attractive manifestations of the Romantic style.

20

The Nature of Program Music

". . . The renewal of music through its inner connection with poetry." — FRANZ LISZT

Program music is instrumental music endowed with literary or pictorial associations; the nature of these associations is indicated by the title of the piece or by an explanatory note—the "program"—supplied by the composer. Program music is distinguished from *absolute* or *pure music,* which consists of musical patterns devoid of literary or pictorial connotations.

Program music was of special importance in a period like the nineteenth century when musicians became sharply conscious of the connection between their art and the world about them. It helped them to bring music closer to poetry and painting, and to relate their work to the moral and political issues of their time. It also helped them to approach the forms of absolute music in a new way. All the same, the distinction between absolute and program music is not as rigid as many suppose. A work entitled *Symphony No. 1* or *Third String Quartet* falls into the former category. Yet the composer in the course of writing it may very well have had in mind specific images and associations that he has not seen fit to divulge. Beethoven, whom we think of as the master of absolute music, confessed to a friend, "I have always a picture in my thoughts when I am composing, and work to it." Conversely, a piece called *Romeo and Juliet Overture* comes under the heading of program music. Yet if we were not told the title we would listen to it as a piece of absolute music. This is what we are apt to do in any case once we get to know the work. What concerns us ultimately is the destiny not of the lovers but of the themes.

Varieties of Program Music

The concert overture

A primary impulse toward program music derived from the opera house, where the overture was a rousing orchestral piece in one movement designed to serve as an introduction to an opera (or a play). Many operatic overtures achieved independent popularity as concert pieces. This pointed the way to a new type of overture not associated with an opera: a single-movement concert piece for orchestra, based on a striking literary idea, such as Tchaikovsky's *Romeo and Juliet.* This type of composition, the *concert overture,* might be descriptive, like Mendelssohn's seascape *Hebrides* (*Fingal's Cave*); or it could embody a patriotic idea, as does Tchaikovsky's *1812 Overture.*

The concert overture, despite its literary program, retained the design traditionally associated with the first movement of a symphony (what will be discussed in a later chapter as *sonata-allegro form*). This consists of three sections—the *Exposition* (or *Statement*), in which the themes are presented; the *Development;* and the *Recapitulation* (or *Restatement*). In other words, the concert overture retained a form associated with absolute music, but combined it with the poetic or pictorial ideas associated with program music. Thus, it offered composers a single-movement form of orchestral music which they were able to invest with the imagery of a romantic story or scene.

Incidental music

An engaging species of program music is that written for plays, generally consisting of an overture and a series of pieces to be performed between the acts and during the important scenes, known as *incidental music.* Nineteenth-century composers produced a number of works of this type that were notable for tone painting, characterization, and theater atmosphere.

The most successful pieces were generally arranged into suites, a number of which became vastly popular. Mendelssohn's music for *A Midsummer Night's Dream* is one of the most successful works in this category. Hardly less appealing are the two suites from Bizet's music for Alphonse Daudet's play *L'Arlésienne* (The Woman of Arles) and the two from Grieg's music for Henrik Ibsen's poetic drama *Peer Gynt*. Incidental music is still used today, and has spawned two very important offshoots: film music, which plays an important role in, as Aaron Copland put it, "warning the screen," and background music for television drama.

The program symphony

The impulse toward program music was so strong that it invaded even the hallowed form of absolute music—the symphony. Composers tried to retain the grand form of Beethoven and at the same time to associate it with a literary theme. Thus came into being the *program symphony*. The best known examples are three program symphonies of Berlioz—*Symphonie fantastique, Harold in Italy, Romeo and Juliet*—and two of Liszt, the *Faust* and *Dante* symphonies.

The symphonic poem

As the nineteenth century wore on, the need was felt more and more for a large form of orchestral music that would serve the Romantic era as well as the symphony had served the Classical. Toward the middle of the century the long-awaited step was taken with the creation of the symphonic poem. This was the nineteenth century's one original contribution to the large forms. It was the achievement of Franz Liszt, who first used the term in 1848. His *Les Préludes* is among the best known examples of this type of music.

A *symphonic poem* is a piece of program music for orchestra, in one movement, which in the course of contrasting sections develops a poetic idea, suggests a scene, or creates a mood. It differs from the concert overture in one important respect: whereas the concert overture generally retains one of the traditional Classical designs, the symphonic poem is much freer in form. The name is used interchangeably with *tone poem*. The symphonic poem as cultivated by Liszt and his disciples was an immensely flexible form that permitted its course to be shaped by the literary idea. The programs were drawn from poets and painters dear to the Romantic temperament: Shakespeare, Dante, Petrarch; Goethe and Schiller; Michelangelo and Raphael; Byron and Victor Hugo. A strong influence was the "return to nature" that had been advocated by Rousseau. The symphonic poem gave composers the canvas they needed for a big single-movement form. It became the most widely cultivated type of orchestral program music throughout the second half of the century.

The varieties of program music just described—concert overture, incidental music, program symphony, and symphonic poem—comprise one of the striking manifestations of nineteenth-century Romanticism. This type of music emphasized the descriptive element; it impelled composers to try to express specific feelings; and it proclaimed the direct relationship of music to life.

21

Felix Mendelssohn

Felix Mendelssohn.

"People often complain that music is too ambiguous; that what they should think when they hear it is so unclear, whereas everyone understands words. With me it is exactly the opposite, and not only with regard to an entire speech but also with individual words. These too seem to me so ambiguous, so vague, so easily misunderstood in comparison to genuine music, which fills the soul with a thousand things better than words."

Felix Mendelssohn stands out in the roster of musicians for the fortunate circumstances that attended his career: he was born to wealth; he found personal happiness; and he was the idol of a vast public, not only in his German homeland, but also in England.

His Life

Felix Mendelssohn (1809–47) was the grandson of Moses Mendelssohn, the Jewish philosopher who expounded Plato to the eighteenth century. His father was an art-loving banker; his mother read Homer in the original. They joined the Protestant faith when Felix was still a child. The Mendelssohn home was a meeting place for the wit and intellect of Berlin. The garden house, seating several hundred guests, was the scene of memorable musicales where an orchestra under the boy's direction performed his numerous compositions. Here, when he was seventeen, his Overture to *A Midsummer Night's Dream* was presented to an enraptured audience.

The youth's education was thorough and well-rounded. He visited the venerable Goethe at Weimar and attended Hegel's lectures at the University of Berlin. He worshiped Bach, Mozart, and Beethoven. In 1829 the twenty-year-old enthusiast organized a performance of Bach's *St. Matthew Passion,* which had lain neglected since the death of its composer. The event proved to be a turning point in the nineteenth-century revival of that master.

Mendelssohn's misfortune was that he excelled in a number of roles—as pianist, conductor, organizer of musical events, and educator. For the last fifteen years of his life his composing was carried on amid the distractions of a public career that taxed his energies and caused his early death even as poverty and neglect might have done. At twenty-six he was conductor of the Gewandhaus Orchestra at Leipzig, which he transformed into the finest in Europe. He was summoned to Berlin by Frederick William IV to carry out that monarch's plans for an Academy of Music. Later he founded the Conservatory of Leipzig, which raised the standards for the training of musicians. He made ten visits to England, where his appearances elicited a frenzy of enthusiasm. All this in addition to directing one or another of the provincial festivals that formed the backbone of musical life in Germany. Mendelssohn composed with a speed and facility that invite comparison with Mozart or Schubert, but he seldom allowed himself the inner repose that might have imparted profundity to much of his music.

His last major composition, the oratorio *Elijah,* was produced in 1846 at the Birmingham Festival and "touched off the emotional spring of Victorian religious respectability as no other work had done." The following year he won fresh triumphs in England, appearing as pianist and conductor of his works. He returned to Germany in a state of nervous exhaustion. The happiness he found in the company of his wife and children was shattered by a severe blow—the death of his sister Fanny, to whom he was deeply attached. Six months later, at the age of thirty-eight, he succumbed to a stroke. Huge throngs followed his bier. Condolences came from all over Europe. A world figure had died.

His Music

Mendelssohn was dedicated to a mission: to preserve the tradition of the Classical forms in an age that was turning from them. His fastidious craftsmanship links him to the great tradition. Serene and elegant expression was the characteristic trait of a mind as orderly as it was conservative. Mendelssohn represents the Classicist trend within the Romantic movement. But it should not be supposed that he was untouched by Romanticism. In his early works he is the ardent poet of nature, a landscape painter of gossamer brush. Tenderness and manly fervor breathe from his music, and a gentle melancholy that is very much of the age.

Of his symphonies the best known are the third, the *Scotch,* and the fourth, the *Italian*—mementos of his youthful travels. Both works were begun in 1830, when he was twenty-one. The *Reformation Symphony,* his fifth, also dates from his early twenties. The *Concerto for Violin and Orchestra* (1844) retains its position as one of the most popular ever written. The *Octet for Strings,* which he wrote when he was sixteen, is much admired, as are the *Songs without Words* (1829–42), a collection of short piano pieces. Mendelssohn was a prolific writer for the voice. The oratorio *Elijah* represents the peak of his achievement in this category.

In England Mendelssohn was admired as no composer had been since Handel and Haydn. The first edition of Grove's Dictionary, which appeared in 1880, devoted its longest article to him—sixty-eight pages. Bach received eight.

A scene from the New York Shakespeare Festival production of Shakespeare's **A Midsummer Night's Dream.** (Photo by George E. Joseph.)

A Midsummer Night's Dream: *Overture and Incidental Music*

SIDE 3/2 (E II)

The Overture (1826) to Shakespeare's fairy play is in Mendelssohn's happiest vein. The mood of elfin enchantment that the seventeen-year-old composer here achieved was to return again and again in his later music, but nowhere more felicitously. Four prolonged chords in the woodwinds and horns open the portals to the realm of Oberon and Titania. The Exposition begins with the fairy music, which is introduced by the violins in high register, Allegro di molto (very lively) and very softly. The dots over the notes indicate that they are to be played staccato (short and detached).

The fairy music is expanded. Presently the violins introduce, *ff*, an energetic melody that serves as a bridge between the first and second theme:

The second theme evokes the young lovers in the play. It is a lyric idea, legato and flowing, presented expressively by the strings, and provides an effective contrast with the rhythmic theme of the opening:

The third idea is the boisterous dance of the clowns. Energetic rhythm and wide leaps set the character of this theme, which is presented by the violins against a background of wind tone. The last four notes (under the bracket) suggest the "Hee-haw" of a donkey, since in the play Puck's magic spell fastens an ass's head on Bottom the Weaver.

Now that the themes have been "exposed," there follows the middle section of the overture, the Development, which is an extended fantasy on the first theme. The composer gives free rein to his imagination in exploring a mood close to his heart; an atmosphere of mystery is sustained throughout. He changes the melody slightly; or presents it in a new light, developing it through imitation:

and through expansion:

When the development of the idea has run its course, the four mystic chords are heard again, introducing the Recapitulation, in which the material is restated more or less as we heard it before. A coda extends the donkey theme, and the piece ends on a note of quiet farewell. (A coda, you will recall, is a concluding section that rounds off a musical work and brings it to its appointed end.) This coda emphasizes the energetic theme that served as a bridge in the Exposition; finally the violins play it in a gentle pianissimo:

As the youthful composer explained, "After everything has been satisfactorily settled and the principal players have joyfully left the stage, the elves follow them, bless the house and disappear with the dawn. So ends the play, and my overture too."

In 1842 Frederick William IV of Prussia decided on a production of Shakespeare's comedy at the royal theater and suggested to Mendelssohn that he write incidental music for the play. The composer added twelve numbers for this occasion, in which he recaptured the spirit of the Overture he had written sixteen years before. Several of the pieces—the Scherzo, Nocturne, and *Wedding March*—have achieved worldwide popularity and are frequently performed together with the Overture as a suite.

Incidental music

The Scherzo serves to launch Act II. To Puck's query, "How now, spirit? Whither wander you?" the Elf makes his famous reply: "Over hill, over dale, thorough bush, thorough brier. . . ."

The *scherzo*—the Italian word meaning "jest," "joke"—as cultivated by Mendelssohn, was an instrumental piece compounded of elfin grace and humor. The Scherzo from *A Midsummer Night's Dream,* in 3/8 time, is an Allegro vivace. The first idea is a rhythmic pattern introduced by the

Scherzo

woodwinds staccato and softly in the upper register. A contrasting second theme is presented pianissimo, in a low register, by the strings. The two ideas alternate throughout the work. This Scherzo is remarkable for its continuity of fabric. Tension is sustained from first note to last. Characteristic is the pianissimo ending in which an agile run on the flute leads to a final statement of the first theme.

The Nocturne is played while the lovers, lost in the enchanted wood, sleep. Here Mendelssohn is the poet of nature. The beauty of the forest is evoked by the French horn in a serenely tender melody.

Nocturne

The play ends happily with the marriage of the Duke. A fanfare on the trumpets introduces the famous *Wedding March*. The movement is an Allegro vivace in 4/4 time, for the most part forte. The main theme **(A)** is a three-part form **(a-b-a)** in which the sections are repeated.

Two sections of quieter character supply the necessary contrast to the recurrent festive theme. The result is a well-rounded form—**A(||a:||:ba:||)-B-A-C-A-Coda**—with an abundance of melody right on to the ceremonious flourishes at the end.

Mendelssohn has always been extremely popular with the public. His elegant workmanship, melodious charm, and refinement of feeling are qualities that wear well.

22

Hector Berlioz

Hector Berlioz. Portrait by Gustave Courbet (1819–77).

"The prevailing characteristics of my music are passionate expression, intense ardor, rhythmic animation, and unexpected turns. To render my works properly requires a combination of extreme precision and irresistible verve, a regulated vehemence, a dreamy tenderness, and an almost morbid melancholy."

His Life

Hector Berlioz (1803–69) was born in France in a small town near Grenoble. His father, a well-to-do physician, expected him to follow in his footsteps, and at eighteen Hector was dispatched to the medical school in Paris. The Conservatory and the Opéra, however, exercised an infinitely greater attraction than the dissecting room. The following year the fiery youth made a decision that horrified his upper-middle-class family: he gave up medicine for music.

The Romantic revolution was brewing in Paris. Berlioz, along with Victor Hugo and the painter Delacroix, found himself in the camp of "young France." Having been cut off by his parents, he gave lessons, sang in a theater chorus, and turned to various musical chores. He fell under the spell of Beethoven; hardly less powerful was the impact of Shakespeare, to whose art he was introduced by a visiting English troupe. For the actress whose Ophelia and Juliet excited the admiration of the Parisians, young Berlioz conceived an overwhelming passion. In his *Memoirs,* which read like a Romantic novel, he describes his infatuation for Harriet Smithson: "I became obsessed by an intense, overpowering sense of sadness. I could not sleep, I could not work, and I spent my time wandering aimlessly about Paris and its environs."

In 1830 came the first official recognition of Berlioz's gifts. He was awarded the coveted Prix de Rome, which gave him a stipend and an opportunity to live and work in the Eternal City. That year also saw the composition of what has remained his most celebrated work, the *Symphonie fantastique.* Upon his return from Rome a hectic courtship of Miss Smithson ensued. There were strenuous objections on the part of both their families and violent scenes, during one of which the excitable Hector attempted suicide. He was revived. They were married.

Now that the unattainable ideal had become his wife, his ardor cooled. It was Shakespeare he had loved rather than Harriet, and in time he sought the ideal elsewhere. All the same, the first years of his marriage were the most fruitful of his life. By the time he was forty he had produced most of the works on which his fame rests.

To earn money he turned to music criticism, producing a stream of reviews and articles. His literary labors were a necessary part of his musical activity; he had to propagandize for his works and create an audience capable of understanding them. In the latter part of his life he conducted his music in all the capitals of Europe. But Paris resisted him to the end. Year after year he dissipated his energies in reviewing the works of nonentities while his own were neglected. Disgust and misanthropy settled upon him. His last major work was the opera *Béatrice et Bénédict,* on his own libretto after Shakespeare's *Much Ado about Nothing.* After this effort the flame was spent, and for the last seven years of his life the embittered master wrote no more. He died at sixty-six, tormented to the end. "Some day," wrote Richard Wagner, "a grateful France will raise a proud monument on his tomb." The prophecy has been fulfilled.

His Music

Berlioz was one of the boldest innovators of the nineteenth century. His approach to music was wholly original, his sense of sound unique. From the start he had an affinity—where orchestral music was concerned—for the vividly dramatic or pictorial program.

His works exemplify the favorite literary influences of the Romantic period. The overtures *Waverley* (c. 1827) and *Rob Roy* (1832) were inspired by novels of Walter Scott, *The Damnation of Faust* (1846) by Goethe. *Harold in Italy,* a program symphony with viola solo (1834) and *The Corsair,* an overture (final version, 1855), are after Byron. Shakespeare is the source for the overture *King Lear* (1831) and for the dramatic symphony for orchestra, soloists, and chorus, *Romeo and Juliet* (1839).

Berlioz's most important opera, *Les Troyens* (The Trojans), on his own libretto based on Vergil, has been successfully revived in recent years. The *Requiem* (Mass for the Dead; 1837) and the *Te Deum* (Hymn of Praise; 1849) are conceived on a grandiose scale. This love of huge orchestral and choral forces represents only one aspect of Berlioz's personality. No less characteristic is the tenderness that finds expression in the oratorio *L'Enfance du Christ* (Childhood of Christ; 1854); the finespun lyricism that wells up in his songs; the sensibility that fills his orchestra with Gallic clarity and grace.

It was in the domain of orchestration that Berlioz's genius asserted itself most fully. His daring originality in handling the instruments opened up a new world of Romantic sonority. Until his time, as Aaron Copland pointed out, "composers used instruments in order to make them sound like themselves; the mixing of colors so as to produce a new result was his achievement." His scores abound in novel effects and discoveries that served as models to all who came after him. Indeed, the conductor Felix Weingartner called Berlioz "the creator of the modern orchestra."

Symphonie fantastique

Berlioz's best-known symphony was written at the height of his infatuation with Harriet Smithson, when he was twenty-seven years old. It is hardly to be believed that this remarkable "novel in tones" was conceived by a young man only three years after the death of Beethoven. Extraordinary is the fact that he not only attached a program to a symphony, but that he drew the program from his personal life. In this autobiographical approach to his art Berlioz is a true Romantic. "A young musician of morbid sensibility and ardent imagination in a paroxysm of lovesick despair has poisoned himself with opium. The drug, too weak to kill, plunges him into a heavy sleep accompanied by strange visions. His sensations, feelings, and memories are translated in his sick brain into musical images and ideas. The beloved one herself becomes for him a melody, a recurrent theme [*idée fixe*] that haunts him everywhere."

The "fixed idea" that symbolizes the beloved–the basic theme of the symphony–is subjected to variation in harmony, rhythm, meter, and tempo; dynamics, register, and instrumental color. These transformations take on literary as well as musical significance. Thus the basic motive, recurring by virtue of the literary program, becomes a musical thread unifying five movements that are diverse in mood and character.

First movement

Reveries, Passions. "He remembers the weariness of soul, the indefinable yearning he knew before meeting his beloved. Then, the volcanic love with which she at once inspired him, his delirious suffering . . . his religious consolation."

A spacious introduction marked Largo establishes the atmosphere of reverie. It establishes, too, the luminous resonance of Berlioz's orchestra. The movement proper is marked Allegro agitato e appassionato assai (lively, agitated, and very impassioned). Solo flute and first violins announce a soaring melody—the "fixed idea":

Characteristic is Berlioz's frequent use of the orchestral crescendo. At the climax of the movement the "fixed idea" is recapitulated by full orchestra *ff*. The last bars, consisting of sustained chords and marked religiosamente, suggest what Berlioz's program refers to as "his religious consolation."

Second movement

A Ball. "Amid the tumult and excitement of a brilliant ball he glimpses the loved one again." The dance movement of the symphony is marked Valse Allegro non troppo (Waltz, not too fast). The introduction presents arpeggios on the harp against a string tremolo—an enchanting sonority. The Waltz proper begins "sweet and tender."

The movement is in ternary or three-part form. In the middle section the "fixed idea" reappears in waltz time, introduced by flute and oboe.

Notable is the climax at the end, which is built up through a crescendo, an accelerando, and a rise in pitch.

Third movement

Scene in the Fields. "On a summer evening in the country he hears two shepherds piping. The pastoral duet, the quiet surroundings . . . all unite to fill his heart with a long absent calm. But *she* appears again. His heart contracts. Painful forebodings fill his soul. . . . The sun sets—the distant rumble of thunder—solitude—silence . . ."

The movement, marked Adagio, is an **A-B-A** form in 6/8 time. Berlioz's comment on the orchestration shows his emotional attitude toward the instruments. "The English horn repeats the phrases of the oboe in the lower octave, like the voice of a youth replying to a girl in a pastoral dialogue." His aim, he wrote, was a mood "of sorrowful loneliness."

There follows a broadly spun melody for flute and violins that breathes a pastoral quiet. The "fixed idea" appears in the middle section in a new version in 6/8 time, introduced into this idyllic setting by solo flute and oboe in octaves. The "distant rumble of thunder" is given on the kettledrums, while the English horn suggests the solitude of the unhappy lover.

Fourth movement

March to the Scaffold. "He dreams that he has killed his beloved, that he has been condemned to die and is being led to the scaffold. The procession moves to the sounds of a march now somber and wild, now brilliant and solemn. . . . At the very end the 'fixed idea' reappears for an instant, like a last thought of love interrupted by the fall of the axe."

Marked Allegretto non troppo in 4/4, the march movement exemplifies the nineteenth-century love of the fantastic. Not easily forgotten is the sound of the opening: muted horns, timpani, pizzicato chords on cellos and double basses. The lower strings play an energetic theme that strides down the scale:

After this idea is given to the violins, the diabolical march emerges in the woodwinds and brass:

The theme of the beloved appears at the very end, on the clarinet, and is cut off by a grim fortissimo chord. The effect ("a last thought of love interrupted by the fall of the axe") has been much criticized as being too realistic. One must remember, however, that when Berlioz wrote it he was opening up new fields of expression for his art.

Fifth movement

SIDE 3/3 (E II)

SIDE 3/1 (S)

Dream of a Witches' Sabbath. "He sees himself at a witches' sabbath surrounded by a host of fearsome specters who have gathered for his funeral. Unearthly sounds, groans, shrieks of laughter. . . . The melody of his beloved is heard, but it has lost its noble and reserved character. It has become a vulgar tune, trivial and grotesque. It is she who comes to the infernal orgy. A howl of joy greets her arrival. She joins the diabolical dance. Bells toll for the dead. A burlesque of the *Dies Irae.* Dance of the witches. The dance and the *Dies Irae* combined."

The movement opens with a Larghetto (not quite as slow as largo). Berlioz here exploits a vein that nourished a century of satanic operas, ballets, and symphonic poems. Flickering chromatic scales, *ppp,* on muted violins and violas create the properly infernal atmosphere. In the Allegro that follows, the theme of the beloved is transformed into a "vulgar dance

tune" played by a high-pitched clarinet. The traditional religious melody *Dies irae* (Day of Wrath), from the ancient *Mass for the Dead,* is given out by bassoons and tubas in a section in 6/8 time marked Lontano (dis-

tant). It is caricatured in shorter note values. In the *Ronde du sabbat* (Witches' Dance), a driving 6/8 rhythm is heard in the cellos and basses, after which it is taken up in turn by various instrumental groups. The interweaving of the various lines makes for an intricate orchestral fabric.

Berlioz points out in the score the combining of the dance theme and the *Dies irae*, not that anybody would miss it. This passage, of which he was so proud, leads to a rousingly theatrical ending for his theatrical subject.

There is a bigness of line and gesture about the music of Berlioz, an overflow of vitality and inventiveness. He is one of the major prophets in the Romantic era.

23

Franz Liszt

Franz Liszt.

"Sorrowful and great is the artist's destiny."

As composer and conductor, teacher, and organizer of musical events, Franz Liszt (1811–86) occupied a central position in the artistic life of the nineteenth century. Yet this fabulously successful artist did not escape the Romantic melancholy. "To die and die young—" he once exclaimed, "—what happiness!"

His Life

Liszt was born in Hungary, son of a steward in the employ of a wealthy family. A stipend from a group of Hungarian noblemen enabled him to pursue his musical studies in Paris. There he came under the spell of French Romanticism, with whose leaders—Victor Hugo, Delacroix, George Sand, Berlioz—he formed close friendships.

The appearance in Paris of the sensational violinist Paganini, in 1831, made Liszt aware of the possibilities of virtuoso playing. The new mass public required spectacular soloists. Liszt met the need. He was one of the greatest of pianists—and showmen. An actor to his fingertips, he possessed the personal magnetism of which legends are made. Instead of sitting with his back to the audience or facing it, as had been the custom hitherto, he introduced the more effective arrangement that prevails today. It showed off his chiseled profile, which reminded people of Dante's. He crouched over the keys, he thundered, he caressed. Countesses swooned. Ladies less exalted fought for his snuffbox and tore his handkerchief to shreds. Liszt encouraged these antics as a necessary part of the legend. But behind the façade was a true musician. For his friends and disciples he played the last sonatas of Beethoven; they never forgot the experience.

Inseparable from the legend of the pianist was that of the lover. Liszt never married. His path for the better part of fifty years led through a thicket of sighs, tears, and threats of suicide. Among those briefly smitten were George Sand—they toured Switzerland for a summer—Lola Montez, and Marie Duplessis, the original of Dumas's Lady of the Camellias. More

Liszt represented the apotheosis of Romanticism in his time. In this portrait by Joseph Dannhauser, he is seated at the piano gazing at a bust of Beethoven. Kneeling beside him is Madame D'Agoult; seated behind him, George Sand and Alexandre Dumas, père.

important in his intellectual development was his relationship with Countess Marie d'Agoult, who wrote novels under the name of Daniel Stern. They eloped to an idyllic interlude in Switzerland that lasted for a number of years. Of their three children, Cosima subsequently became the wife of Wagner. Liszt and the Countess parted in bitterness. She satirized him in her novels.

He withdrew from the concert stage at the height of his fame in order to devote himself to composing. In 1848 he settled in Weimar, where he became court conductor to the Grand Duke. The Weimar period (1848–61) saw the production of his chief orchestral works. As director of the ducal opera house he was in a position to mold public taste. He used his influence unremittingly on behalf of the "Music of the Future," as he and Wagner named the type of program music, both dramatic and symphonic, that they, along with Berlioz, advocated. At Weimar Liszt directed the first performances of Wagner's *Lohengrin,* Berlioz's *Benvenuto Cellini*, and many other contemporary works. History records few instances of an artist so generous, so free from envy in his dealings with his fellow artists.

The Weimar period saw his association with the woman who most decisively influenced his life. Princess Carolyne Sayn-Wittgenstein, wife of a powerful noble at the court of the Tsar, fell in love with Liszt during his last concert tour of Russia. Shortly thereafter she came to Weimar to unite her life with his. For years their home, the Altenburg, was a center of artistic activity. A woman of domineering will and intellect, the Princess assisted Liszt in his later literary efforts. These include a book on Gypsy music and a *Life of Chopin*. Both are eloquent and inaccurate.

In his last years Liszt sought peace by entering the Church. He took minor orders and was known as Abbé Liszt. This was the period of his major religious works. He divided his time between Rome, Weimar, and Budapest, the friend of princes and cardinals. The gloom of old age was dispelled by fresh triumphs. At seventy-five he was received with enthusiasm in England, which had always been reluctant to recognize him as a composer. He journeyed to Bayreuth to visit the widowed Cosima and died during the festival of Wagner's works, naming with his last breath the masterpiece of the "Music of the Future"–Wagner's *Tristan*.

His Music

Liszt's goal was pure lyric expression, the projecting of a state of soul through what he called "the mysterious language of tone." To give his lyricism free scope he created the symphonic poem. The form was held together by the continuous transformation of a few basic themes. By varying the melodic outline, harmony, or rhythm of a theme, by shifting it from soft to loud, from slow to fast, from low to high register, from strings to woodwinds or brass, he found it possible to transform its character so that it might suggest romantic love in one section, a pastoral scene in another, tension and conflict in a third, and triumph in the last.

His thirteen symphonic poems (1848–58 and 1882) exercised incalculable influence on the nineteenth century and were responsible for many a work that is still popular. His masterpiece for orchestra is the *Symphony after Goethe's Faust* (1854–57), comprising three portraits: *Faust, Gretchen, Mephistopheles*. A companion work is the *Symphony to Dante's Divine Comedy* (1855–56), also in three movements: *Inferno, Purgatory,* and *Vision of Paradise*. In these program symphonies he honored his companions in arms. The *Faust* is dedicated to Berlioz, the *Dante* to Wagner.

Liszt, we saw, was one of the creators of modern piano technique. The best of his piano pieces, like his songs, are in the vein of true Romantic lyricism. Characteristic are *Sonetto 104 del Petrarca,* which we discussed in Chapter 19, the colorful *Hungarian Rhapsodies,* the vastly popular *Liebestraum* (Love Dream; c. 1850), and the first *Mephisto Waltz* (1860). In a class apart are his chief works for the piano, the *Sonata in B minor* and the two piano concertos that date from the 1850s. Here is the Liszt of impassioned rhetoric, the contemporary in every sense of Victor Hugo, Byron, and Delacroix.

Liszt injected the picturesque personality—embodiment of Romantic individualism—into the concert hall, where it has remained ever since. A great teacher, he raised a generation of giants of the keyboard. His easily accessible music helped create the modern mass public, and he influenced composers from Wagner and César Franck to Ravel and George Gershwin.

Les Préludes

SIDE 4/1 (E II)
SIDE 2/1 (S)

The most famous of the symphonic poems, *Les Préludes* (The Preludes), was written in 1854. It served conductors as a showpiece for several generations and remains a basic document in any study of the Romantic movement. Liszt appended to the score a program note of his own devising that had some connection in his mind with one of the *Méditations poétiques* of the mystical poet Alphonse de Lamartine. "What is our life but a series of preludes to that unknown song whose first solemn note is tolled by Death? The enchanted dawn of every life is love. But where is the destiny on whose first delicious joys some storm does not break? . . . And what soul thus cruelly bruised, when the tempest rolls away, seeks not to rest its memories in the pleasant calm of pastoral life? Yet man does not long permit himself to taste the kindly quiet that first attracted him to Nature's lap. For when the trumpet sounds he hastens to danger's post, that in the struggle he may once more regain full knowledge of himself and his strength." Such a program related the music to one of the favorite themes of the age—the image of man pitted against Fate—unfolding a series of moods, dramatic, lyric, pastoral, triumphal, that appealed immensely to the Romantic mentality.

The work is fashioned from a basic motive of three notes presented by the strings. The ascending interval of a fourth imparts to the motive a questioning upward inflection. This becomes a characteristic feature of the melodic material.

There follows a passage for full orchestra, Andante maestoso (fairly slow, majestic), the "prelude to that unknown song." Notice that the characteristic upward leap of a fourth is present both in the melody and the accompaniment (under the bracket):

Two themes in Liszt's suavest manner evoke the image of love that he calls "the enchanted dawn of every life." The first, espressivo cantando (expressively, in singing style), is assigned to the second violins and cellos. The germ motive (under bracket) is embedded in the melody. The second

amorous theme is played by muted violas and a quartet of horns, espressivo ma tranquillo (expressive but tranquil). This melody contrasts with the preceding. On closer examination, however, it too turns out to be an ingenious expansion of the basic motive (notes marked ×).

Thus, behind all talk of the program and its literary associations we see the mind of the musician at work. What the piece is about, quite apart from love, nature, and destiny, is a three-note motive that contains an ascending leap. Out of these three notes is woven the musical tissue, by a process of continuous transformation.

The tempo quickens, tension mounts. The basic material is presented Allegro tempestoso. The atmosphere of struggle is associated with chromatic scales. (The *chromatic scale* takes in all twelve tones within the octave. On the piano it includes the seven white and five black keys. Chromatic scales become a favorite device of the Romantics for whipping up excitement.) Naturally the tempestuous passage features the brass.

An area of relaxation ensues. There follows an Allegretto pastorale, a peaceful nature scene that features the woodwinds. The motive is now transformed into a pastoral theme scored for woodwinds and horn. The

return to the fray is marked by an Allegro marziale animato (fast, martial, animated). Through changes in pace, register, dynamics, and color, the two love themes are transformed into rousing battle calls—the second one marked "march tempo."

Finally the mood of exaltation returns, to round off the action with the grandiose ending so dear to the Romantics. The basic motive has triumphed along with Man.

Today, the "Music of the Future" has become that of the past. Yet Liszt remains—man and musician—the voice of an era. "In art," he said, "one must work on a grand scale." This he did.

Richard Strauss. Portrait by Max Liebermann.

24

Richard Strauss

"I work very long on melodies. The important thing is not the beginning of the melody but its continuation, its development into a fully completed artistic form."

Among the composers who inherited the symphonic poem of Liszt, Richard Strauss (1864–1949) occupied a leading place. Although he lived well into the twentieth century, the symphonic poems he wrote during the last years of the nineteenth century came out of and belong to the Romantic tradition.

His Life

Strauss was born in Munich. His father was a virtuoso horn player who belonged to the court orchestra. His mother was the daughter of a successful Munich brewer. In this solid middle-class environment, made familiar to American readers by the novels of Thomas Mann, a high value was placed on music and money. These remained Strauss's twin passions throughout his life.

His first works were in the Classical forms. At twenty-one he found his true style in the writing of vivid program music, setting himself to develop what he called "the poetic, the expressive in music." *Macbeth* (1886–90), his first tone poem, was followed by *Don Juan* (1888), an extraordinary achievement for a young man of twenty-four. Then came the series of tone poems that blazed his name throughout the civilized world: *Tod und Verklärung* (Death and Transfiguration; 1889), *Till Eulenspiegels lustige Streiche* (Till Eulenspiegel's Merry Pranks; 1894–95), *Also sprach Zarathustra* (Thus Spake Zarathustra; 1896), *Don Quixote* (1897), *Ein Heldenleben* (A Hero's Life; 1898), and two program symphonies, the *Domestic* and the *Alpine*. These works shocked the conservatives and secured Strauss's position, around the turn of the century, as the *enfant terrible* of modern music, a role he thoroughly enjoyed.

In the early years of the twentieth century Strauss conquered the operatic stage with *Salome* (1906), *Elektra* (1909), and *Der Rosenkavalier* (The Knight of the Rose; 1911). The international triumph of the last-named on the eve of the First World War marked the summit of his career. He collected unprecedented fees and royalties for his scores. Strauss was eager to dispel the romantic notion that the artist is better off starving in a garret. On the contrary, he insisted that "worry alone is enough to kill a sensitive man, and all thoroughly artistic natures are sensitive."

Strauss's collaboration with Hugo von Hofmannsthal, the librettist of *Elektra* and *Rosenkavalier,* continued until the latter's death in 1929. By this time, new conceptions of modernism had come to the fore; the one-time bad boy of music, now entrenched as a conservative, was inevitably left behind. The coming to power of the Nazis in 1933 confronted Strauss with a challenge and an opportunity. He was by no means reactionary in his political thinking; his daughter-in-law was Jewish, and the cosmopolitan circles in which he traveled were not susceptible to Hitler's ideology. Hence the challenge to speak out against the Third Reich—or to leave Germany as Thomas Mann, Hindemith, and other intellectuals were doing. On the other hand the new regime was courting men of arts and letters. Strauss saw the road open to supreme power, and took the opportunity. In 1933, on the threshold of seventy, he was elevated to the official hierarchy as president of the Reichsmusikkammer (State Chamber of Music). His reign was brief and uneasy. He declined to support the move to ban Mendelssohn's music from Teutonic ears. His opera *Die schweigsame Frau* (The Silent Woman; 1935) was withdrawn after its premiere because the librettist, Stefan Zweig, was non-Aryan; whereupon Strauss resigned.

The war's end found the eighty-one-year-old composer the victim of a curious irony. He was living in near-poverty because the huge sums owing him for performances of his works in England and America had been impounded as war reparations. He was permitted to return to his villa at Garmisch, in the Bavarian Alps. To his friends Strauss explained that he had remained in Nazi Germany because someone had to protect culture from Hitler's barbarians. Perhaps he even believed it.

There were speeches at the Bavarian Academy of Arts on the occasion of his eighty-fifth birthday. Shortly thereafter he died.

His Music

Strauss carried to its extreme limit the nineteenth-century appetite for story-and-picture music. His tone poems are a treasury of orchestral discoveries. In some he anticipates modern sound effects—the clatter of pots and pans, the bleating of sheep, the gabble of geese, hoofbeats, wind, thunder, storm. Much more important, these works are packed with movement and gesture, with the sound and fury of an imperious temperament. His scores show the most intricate interweaving of the separate instrumental parts; page after page is strewn with notes that the ear cannot possibly unravel. When chided for his complexity he would exclaim, "The devil! I cannot express it more simply."

Strauss's operas continue to be widely performed. *Salome,* to Oscar Wilde's famous play, and *Elektra,* based on Hofmannsthal's version of the Greek tragedy, are long one-act operas. Swiftly paced, moving relentlessly to their climax, they are superb theater. *Der Rosenkavalier* has a wealth of sensuous lyricism and some entrancing waltzes. The scene is Vienna in the reign of Maria Theresa. The theme is eternal: the fading of youth and beauty. The aging Marschallin, waging her losing battle with time; the disreputable Baron Ochs; Sophie and Octavian awaking to the wonder of

Alfred Roller's stage design contributed to the immediate success of **Der Rosenkavalier** *in Vienna (1911) on the eve of the First World War.* (Reproduced by Permission of Boosey & Hawkes, Inc.)

young love—they ring true in the theater, they come alive through music. Strauss here summoned all his wizardry of orchestral color, his mastery of the stage, his knowledge of the human heart. There comes a time, alas, when *Rosenkavalier* seems a trifle long. It is a sign that one's youth is over.

Don Juan

The figure of Don Juan has attracted artists for hundreds of years, from Molière in the seventeenth century to Bernard Shaw in the twentieth. (We will discuss Mozart's handling of the legend in Chapter 51.) It is a mistake to regard the Don as a great lover. Actually he is incapable of love; what drives him is the need for conquest. Oblivious of other human beings, he cannot relate to anyone outside himself. This condemns him to the loneliness that is his real punishment, a loneliness he forever seeks to escape. Strauss, on the score of his symphonic poem, quoted excerpts from *Don Juan* by the Austrian Romantic poet Nicolaus Lenau (1802–50). Lenau's Don seeks the ideal woman, hoping through her to enjoy all women. Because he cannot find her he reels from one to another, eaten by boredom and satiety. In a duel with the son of a man he has killed he drops his sword and lets his enemy kill him, thus ending a life that has brought him only self-disgust.

Strauss's symphonic poem suggests the fiery ardor with which Don Juan pursues his ideal, the charm of the women who lure him on, and the selfish idealist's ultimate disappointment and atonement by death. This involves, in purely musical terms, the sharpest possible contrast between aggressively rhythmic themes and romantically lyrical ones—the contrast between the masculine and the eternal feminine that so strongly appealed to the Romantic era. The symphonic poem, marked Allegro molto con brio (very fast, with vigor) opens with one of those upward-sweeping gestures of which Strauss knew the secret. (He once said that it was of the utmost importance to capture the audience's attention at the outset. Once that was accomplished, the composer could do as he liked.) Then we hear the theme of Don Juan, a brusque, impetuous melody whose tension is underlined by dotted rhythm, wide leaps, and a wide span:

Notice the syncopation in the second phrase (measures 5 and 7) where the accent falls after the first beat. This theme expands into a section of enormous vitality. There can be no question that the Don is an arresting personality.

The excitement dies down, a solo violin soars high above the orchestra. The melody representing the feminine ideal, marked tranquillo and espressivo (expressive), is a songful tune filled with romantic longing. Notice the upward leap at the beginning and the triplet rhythm in the second measure:

This section reaches a climax in a passage marked molto appassionato (very impassioned). After a calming episode, the opening theme returns fortissimo, sounding more impetuous than ever. Another lyric melody appears to evoke the eternal feminine, a full-throated song for violas and cellos, whose dark coloring gives it a somber cast.

After repetition and expansion of this theme, the scene is set for the third theme that symbolizes the feminine ideal: the love song of Don Juan. Intoned "in a sustained and expressive manner" by the oboe, this soulful melody unfolds in a broad arc and eloquently suggests the Don's unattainable ideal:

Again there is a change of mood. Horns introduce the second theme of the Don, a gallant tune that evokes the chivalric side of his nature. Notice, in the eleventh bar, the bold ascent of the melody in triplets:

One more episode furnishes the last of the thematic material. Marked giocoso (playful), this suggests a scene of merrymaking. The descending grace-note figure in the first two measures, which gives the theme a puckish character, is balanced by the ascending triplets in the following measures:

Strauss weaves a colorful fabric out of his themes, pitting one against the other, combining them, transforming them. He builds up to a *fff* marked sempre molto agitato (always very agitated). A diminuendo leads into a saddened version of the first "feminine ideal" theme, introduced by English horn and bassoon. The music gathers strength with the return of the opening theme (the Don's) which may be regarded as the basic idea of the piece. The final buildup expatiates on both themes of the Don, in a section notable for its sweep and passion, carrying the listener along on a current of glorious sound. An ominous silence, and the epilogue unfolds briefly in shuddering tremolos in the strings that descend from high to low register and lead to the pianissimo ending. Don Juan's hectic life is over.

A world figure, Strauss dominated his era as few artists have done. He may have suspected toward the end that the world had been too much with him. "We are all of us children of our time," he said, "and can never leap over its shadows." He was one of the major artists of our century.

25

Nationalism and the Romantic Movement

"I grew up in a quiet spot and was saturated from earliest childhood with the wonderful beauty of Russian popular song. I am therefore passionately devoted to every expression of the Russian spirit. In short, I am a Russian through and through!"

— PETER ILYICH TCHAIKOVSKY

The Rise of Musical Nationalism

In giving voice to his personal view of life the artist also expresses the hopes and dreams of the group with which he is identified. It is this identification, seeping through from the most profound layers of the unconscious, that makes Shakespeare and Dickens so English, Dostoevsky so Russian, Proust so French. Yet this national quality does not cut the artist off from other peoples. Shakespeare, Dostoevsky, and Proust belong not only to their own nations but to all mankind. In depicting the life they knew they expressed what all men feel.

Alongside the national artist stands the nationalist, who affirms his national heritage in a more conscious way. Needless to say, the two categories overlap. This was especially true in nineteenth-century Europe, where political conditions encouraged the growth of nationalism to such a degree that it became a decisive force within the Romantic movement. National tensions on the Continent—the pride of the conquering nations and the struggle for freedom of the subjugated ones—gave rise to emotions that found an ideal expression in music. The Romantic composers expressed their nationalism in a number of ways. Several based their music on the songs and dances of their people: Chopin in his Mazurkas, Liszt in his *Hungarian Rhapsodies,* Dvořák in the *Slavonic Dances,* Grieg in the *Norwegian Dances.* A number wrote dramatic works based on folklore or the life of the peasantry. Examples are the German folk opera *Der Freischütz* by Carl Maria von Weber, the Czech national opera *The Bartered Bride* by Bedřich Smetana, as well as the Russian fairy-tale operas and ballets of Tchaikovsky and Rimsky-Korsakov. Some wrote symphonic poems and operas celebrating the exploits of a national hero, a historic event, or the scenic beauty of their country. Tchaikovsky's *1812 Overture* and Smetana's *The Moldau* exemplify this trend, as does the glorification of the gods and heroes of German myth and legend in Richard Wagner's music dramas, especially *The Ring of the Nibelung,* a vast epic centering about the life and death of Siegfried. The nationalist composer might unite his music with the verses of a national poet or dramatist. Schubert's settings of Goethe fall into this category; also Grieg's music for Ibsen's *Peer Gynt* and Tchaikovsky's operas based on the dramas of Alexander Pushkin, the Russian national poet who also inspired Rimsky-Korsakov and Musorgsky. Of special significance was the role of music in periods of political turmoil, when the nationalist composer was able to give emotional expression to the aspirations of his people, as Verdi did when Italy was striving for unification, or Sibelius did when Finland struggled against its Russian rulers at the end of the century.

The political implications of musical nationalism were not lost upon the authorities. Verdi's operas had to be altered again and again to suit the Austrian censor. Sibelius's tone poem *Finlandia* with its rousing trumpet calls was forbidden by the tsarist police when Finland was demanding her independence at the turn of the century. During World War II the Nazis forbade the playing of *The Moldau* in Prague and of Chopin's Polonaises in Warsaw because of the powerful symbolism residing in these works.

Nationalism added to the language of European music a variety of national idioms of great charm and vivacity. By associating music with the love of homeland, nationalism enabled composers to give expression to the cherished aspirations of millions of people. In short, national consciousness pervaded every aspect of the European spirit in the nineteenth century. The Romantic movement is unthinkable without it.

Exoticism

Exoticism in music, painting, and literature evokes the picturesque atmosphere and color of far-off lands. The trend, needless to say, was strongly

Eugène Delacroix (1798–1863) brought the glorious spirit of his time to incandescent expression in his canvas ***Liberty Leading the People, 1830.*** (Scala/Art Resource.)

The rise of nationalism is reflected in this heroic painting by Jacques Louis David (1748–1825), titled ***Bonaparte Crossing the Alps.*** (Giraudon/Art Resource.)

The Royal Pavilion at Brighton (1815–18), built for the prince regent, later George IV, by John Nash (1752–1835), is a confection of Islamic domes, minarets, and screens that reflect the nineteenth-century longing for the exotic splendors of the Orient.

encouraged by the Romantic movement. Nineteenth-century exoticism manifested itself, in the first place, as a longing of the northern nations for the warmth and color of the south; in the second, as a longing of the West for the fairy-tale splendors of the Orient. The former impulse found expression in the works of German, French, and Russian composers who turned for inspiration to Italy and Spain. The long list includes several well-known works by Russian composers: Glinka's two *Spanish Overtures,* Tchaikovsky's *Capriccio italien,* and Rimsky-Korsakov's *Capriccio on Spanish Themes.* The German contribution includes Mendelssohn's *Italian Symphony,* Hugo Wolf's *Italian Serenade,* and Richard Strauss's *Aus Italien.* Among the French works are Chabrier's *España* and Lalo's *Symphonie espagnole.* The masterpiece in this category is, of course, Bizet's *Carmen.*

Russian national school

The glamor of the East was brought to international prominence by the Russian national school. In an empire that stretched to the borders of Persia, exoticism was really a form of nationalism. The fairy-tale background of Asia pervades Russian music. Rimsky-Korsakov's orchestrally resplendent *Scheherazade* and his opera *Sadko,* Alexander Borodin's opera *Prince Igor* and symphonic poem *In the Steppes of Central Asia,* and Ippolitov-Ivanov's *Caucasian Sketches* are among the many orientally inspired works that for a time found favor throughout the world. A number of French and Italian composers also utilized exotic themes: Saint-Saëns in *Samson and Delilah,* Delibes in *Lakmé,* Massenet in *Thaïs,* Verdi in *Aïda,* and Puccini in his operas *Madame Butterfly* and *Turandot.*

26

Nationalism and the Symphonic Poem

Bedřich Smetana.

Smetana: The Moldau

"I try to write only as I feel in myself."

The Czech national school was founded by Bedřich Smetana (1824–84). As in the case of several nationalist composers, Smetana's career unfolded against a background of political agitation. Bohemia stirred restlessly under Austrian rule, caught up in a surge of nationalist fervor that culminated in the uprisings of 1848. Young Smetana aligned himself with the patriotic cause. After the revolution was crushed, the atmosphere in Prague was oppressive for those suspected of sympathy with the nationalists. In 1856 Smetana accepted a post as conductor in Sweden. By this time, as a fervent admirer of Liszt, he had espoused the cause of program music. "I cannot describe to you," he wrote the master, "the soul-stirring impression your music has made on me. Art as taught by you has become my credo. Please regard me as one of the most zealous disciples of your artistic school of thought, who will champion its sacred truth in word and deed." Henceforth he devoted his career to creating operas and symphonic poems with a nationalistic content. He became convinced that the forms of the past were finished. "Absolute music," he declared, "is quite impossible for me."

On his return to Bohemia in 1861, he resumed his career as a national artist and worked for the establishment of a theater in Prague where the performances would be given in the native tongue. Of his eight operas on patriotic themes, several still hold the boards in the theaters of his native land. One—*The Bartered Bride*—attained worldwide fame. Hardly less important in the establishing of Smetana's reputation was the cycle of six symphonic poems entitled *My Country*, which occupied him from 1874 to 1879. These works are steeped in the beauty of Bohemia's countryside, the rhythm of her folk songs and dances, the pomp and pageantry of her legends. Best known of the series is the second, *Vltava* (The Moldau), Smetana's finest achievement in the field of orchestral music.

In this tone poem the famous river becomes a poetic symbol that suffuses the musical imagery with patriotic associations. The program appended to the score explains the composer's intention. "Two springs pour forth in the shade of the Bohemian forest, one warm and gushing, the other cold and peaceful." These join in a brook that becomes the river Moldau. "Coursing through Bohemia's valleys, it grows into a mighty stream. Through thick woods its flows as the gay sounds of the hunt and the notes of the

The Moldau flows in majestic peace through Prague.

hunter's horn are heard ever closer. It flows through grass-grown pastures and lowlands where a wedding feast is being celebrated with song and dance. At night, wood and water nymphs revel in its sparkling waves. Reflected on its surface are fortresses and castles—witnesses of bygone days of knightly splendor and the vanished glory of martial times." The stream races ahead through the Rapids of St. John, "finally flowing on in majestic peace toward Prague and welcomed by historic Vysehrad"—the legendary site of the castle of the ancient Bohemian kings. "Then it vanishes far beyond the poet's gaze."

SIDE 4/2 (E II)
SIDE 2/2 (S)

The opening is marked Allegro commodo non agitato (moderately fast, not agitated). A rippling figure is heard as a dialogue between two flutes against a pizzicato accompaniment by violins and harp. From this emerges a broadly flowing melody played by oboe and violins—the theme of the river—that describes a broad arc in its stepwise movement along the scale. Smetana adapted his melody from a Czech folk song.

This theme subsequently is heard with the G raised to G sharp, which subtly alters the effect:

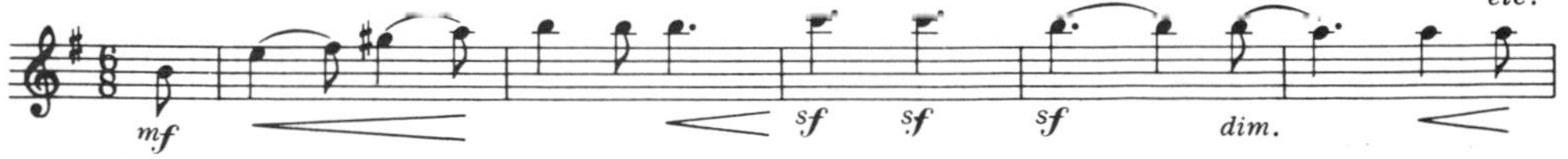

After a repetition of this idea, horns, woodwinds, and trumpets evoke a hunting scene. A fanfare such as the following not only creates an outdoor atmosphere but also underlines the descent of the modern French horn from the old hunting horn:

The section labeled *Peasant Wedding* is in the spirit of a rustic dance. Presented by clarinets and first violins against a staccato accompaniment, the melody has the stepwise movement, narrow skips within a narrow range, and repeated-note figures that we associate with folk song and dance:

Where the score is marked *Moonlight–Nymphs' Revels,* the mood changes to one of mystery. An atmosphere of woodland enchantment is evoked by the muted strings against a background of flute, clarinet, horn, and harp.

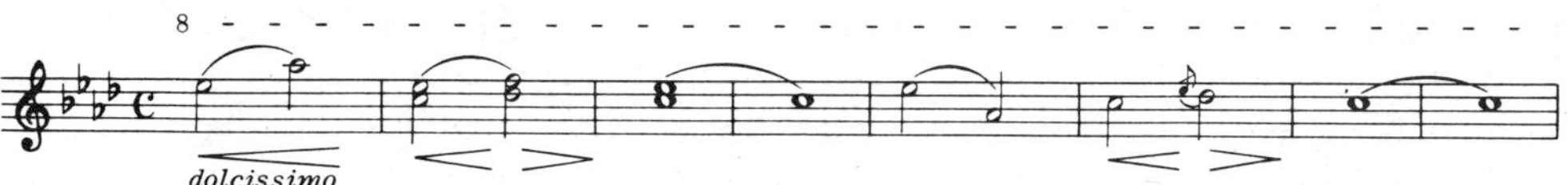

A gradual crescendo leads to the return of the principal melody. The pace quickens as the music graphically depicts the Rapids of St. John, with full use of the brass choir against the rippling of the strings. As the river approaches the ancient site of the royal castle, the principal melody returns in an exultant mood with certain tones (G and C) raised a half step to G sharp and C sharp. The result, as we shall learn in a later chapter, is to shift the tune from minor to major. This is taken care of by the change in key signature, which becomes four sharps:

Now the brass and woodwinds intone a triumphal chorale, as though the composer were promising his countrymen that their former glory will return.

There is a diminuendo to the end as the river "vanishes far beyond the poet's gaze."

The Czechs regard this symphonic landscape as a national tone poem that mirrors the very soul of their land. The rest of the world sees in it one of the more attractive examples of late Romantic tone painting.

Other Nationalists

Dvořák

Antonín Dvořák (1841–1904) stands alongside Bedřich Smetana as a founder of the Czech national school. His art was rooted in the songs and dances of Bohemia. He was born in a village near Prague and never lost touch with the soil that was the source of his strength. His father kept an inn and butcher shop; poverty for a time threatened to rule out a musical career. However, the boy managed to get to Prague when he was sixteen, and became a viola player in the orchestra of the Czech National Theater. Success as a composer came slowly, but by the time he was forty he was able to resign his post and devote himself to his art. The spontaneity and melodiousness of his music assured its popularity. When the last decade of the century arrived, Dvořák was famous throughout Europe. His large output covered all branches of music: opera, choral works, symphonies, concertos, chamber music, overtures, rhapsodies, symphonic poems, songs, and piano pieces.

In 1892 he was invited to become director of the National Conservatory of Music in New York City, where he was paid fifteen thousand dollars a year—a fabulous sum in those days—as compared with the six hundred dollars he received annually as a professor in Prague. His stay in the United States was fruitful. He produced what has remained his most important symphony, *From the New World*; a number of chamber works, among them the *American Quartet*; and the *Concerto for Cello and Orchestra.* Although every effort was made to induce him to continue at the Conservatory, his homesickness overrode all other considerations. After three years he returned to his beloved Bohemia, and spent his remaining years in Prague.

Coming to the United States as one of the leading nationalists of Europe, Dvořák tried to influence his American pupils toward a native art. One of his students was Henry T. Burleigh, the black baritone and arranger of spirituals. The melodies he heard from Burleigh stirred the folk poet in Dvořák and strengthened his conviction that American composers would find themselves only when they had thrown off the European past and drew inspiration from the Indian, Negro, and cowboy songs of their own country. The time was not ripe for his advice to be heeded; yet his instinct did not mislead him concerning the future of American music. One has but to consider the rich harvest of modern American works based on folklore to realize how fruitful was his view.

Grieg

To the international music public, Edvard Grieg (1843–1907) came to represent "the voice of Norway." The nationalist movement of which his music was an expression had a political background. Agitation for independence from Sweden came to a head during the last quarter of the nineteenth century. This cause, to which Grieg was devoted with all his heart, was crowned with success not long before his final illness. "What has happened in our country this year," he wrote, "seems like a fairy tale. The hopes and longings of my youth have been fulfilled. I am deeply grateful that I was privileged to live to see this." His songs and piano pieces attained enormous popularity during his lifetime, and are still current. To the concert public he is best known for his ever popular *Piano Concerto*, the incidental music for Ibsen's *Peer Gynt*, and three sonatas for violin and piano.

Glinka

It was Mikhail Ivanovich Glinka (1804–57) who laid the foundation for the Russian national school. His two operas, *A Life for the Tsar* (1836) and *Russlan and Ludmila* (1842), prepared the way for later developments. His dream of a Russian music was taken over by a group of young musicians whom an admiring critic named "The Mighty Five." Their leader was Mily Balakirev (1837–1910), a self-taught composer who persuaded his four disciples—Alexander Borodin (1833–87), César Cui (1835–1918), Nikolai Rimsky-Korsakov (1844–1908) and Modest Musorgsky (1839–81)—that they would have to free themselves from the influence of German symphony, Italian opera and French ballet if they wanted to express the Russian soul. Their colleague Peter Ilyich Tchaikovsky (1840–93) was more amenable to European influences. We will study works by Russia's two greatest composers, Tchaikovsky and Musorgsky, in later chapters. Of the others, Cui and Balakirev are all but forgotton outside their native land. The works of Glinka, Borodin and Rimsky-Korsakov, on the other hand, are still very much with us.

The Mighty Five

Sibelius

As in the case of Smetana and Grieg, the career of Jean Sibelius (1865–1957) unfolded against a struggle for national independence. In the final decades of the nineteenth century, Finland tried to free itself from the yoke of tsarist Russia. Out of this ferment flowered the art of Sibelius, which served notice to the world that his country—musically—had come of age. Sibelius's reputation rests mainly upon his seven symphonies, in which he discoursed upon the great themes of nineteenth-century music—nature, man, destiny. "I love the mysterious sounds of the fields and forests, rivers, and mountains," he wrote. "It pleases me greatly to be called a poet of nature, for nature has been the book of books for me." Sibelius was most explicitly nationalist in the orchestral and choral works of his first period. During the 1890s he produced a series of symphonic poems that captured the spirit of Finnish legends and myths. Best known of these is *Finlandia* (1899), which occupies the same position in Finland as *The Moldau* does in Czechoslovakia. In his native land Sibelius continues to be regarded with the special reverence that a small nation lavishes on the favorite son who becomes an international figure. The rest of the world remembers him as a high-minded musician who is assured an honorable place in the annals of his art.

Toward the end of the century, national schools appeared in England and Spain, to be followed some years later by the rise of an American school. Thus nationalism continued to be a seminal force in music beyond the nineteenth century and into our own time.

27

The Symphony

"A great symphony is a man-made Mississippi down which we irresistibly flow from the instant of our leave-taking to a long foreseen destination." — AARON COPLAND

Absolute music is music for which the composer has not indicated to us any nonmusical associations, whether of story, scene, or mood. Here the musical ideas are organized in such a way that, without any aid from external images, they give the listener a satisfying sense of order and continuity.

The Nature of the Symphony

A *symphony* is a large-scale work for orchestra, in several parts or movements. These generally are three or four in number, in the sequence fast-slow-fast or fast-slow-moderately fast-fast. (There are many exceptions to this pattern.) The movements contrast in character and mood. Taken together they form an architectural entity and establish the symphony as the most exalted type of absolute music. (By a *movement* we mean a complete and comparatively independent part of a larger musical work.)

First movement

We will postpone a detailed discussion of symphonic structure to a later part of this book. It will suffice for the present to establish the character of the first movement of the cycle as a large form based on three sections—Exposition (Statement), Development, and Recapitulation (or Restatement). Sometimes a slow introduction leads into the movement proper. The Exposition usually presents two contrasting themes—one strongly rhythmic, the other lyric—which expand into contrasting sections. There is a bridge or transitional passage that leads from the first theme group to the second. A *codetta* (little coda) completes the Exposition. The Development is marked by a tremendous increase in tension. Here the composer may break the themes into fragments, recombining them in fresh patterns and revealing them in a new light. As he does so he explores the possibilities of the material for dynamic growth and development. Conflict and drama are of the essence in the Development. In the Recapitulation we hear again the themes of the Exposition more or less in their original guise, but with the wealth of new meaning that these have taken on in the course of the movement. There follows the coda, whose function is to round off the action and to bring the movement to its appointed conclusion.

The first movement is generally the most dramatic of the cycle. It is written in what is known as *sonata form, sonata-allegro form* (because the tempo of this movement is almost always allegro), or *first-movement form.* This form may also be used for an independent piece such as the overture. We encountered sonata-allegro form in the *Midsummer Night's Dream Overture*.

Second movement

In contrast to the first movement, the second—in the nineteenth-century symphony—is generally a slow movement of tenderly lyric nature. It may, however, vary in mood from the whimsical, even playful, to the tragic and passionate. The tempo marking in most cases is andante, adagio, or largo. This movement may be in three-part (**A-B-A**) form; sometimes it is a theme and variations. (Other possibilities are indicated in later chapters.)

Third movement

Third in the cycle, in the symphonies of the Romantic period, is the strongly rhythmic and impetuous scherzo, with overtones of humor, surprise, whimsy, or folk dance. You may recall that *scherzo* is the Italian word for "jest"; but the mood may range from elfin lightness to demonic energy. The tempo marking indicates a lively pace—allegro, allegro molto, vivace, or the like. The form is usually a large **A-B-A**; the middle section, known as the *trio,* is of a somewhat quieter nature. In some symphonies the scherzo comes second.

Fourth movement

The fourth and last member of the cycle is of a dimension and character to balance the first. It may bring the symphony to a close on a note of triumph. The movement is generally a spirited allegro. In most of the Romantic symphonies to be discussed in the next chapters the final movement, like the first, is based on sonata-allegro form.

We have here given the barest outline of symphonic form, not attempting a complete picture until after we shall have heard several representative symphonies. What is important at this point is to understand that the symphony is a drama whose several movements are concerned with the presentation of abstract musical ideas. These ideas unfold in such a way as to give each movement a quality of logical continuity. The essence of symphonic style is dramatic contrast and development. It arouses emotion in the listener, but emotion not directed to any specific image.

Themes

The word *theme* figures prominently in any serious discussion of musical form. By a theme we mean a distinctive musical idea that serves as a building block, a germinating element in a large musical work. The theme may be a fully rounded melody or it may be a compact melodic-harmonic-rhythmic kernel that is capable of further growth and flowering. The theme may be broken down into its constituent fragments, which are known as *motives*. For example, the melody of *Down in the Valley* might serve as a theme in a large work. The first five notes (on the words "Down in the

Motives

Valley") could constitute one motive, the next five notes (on the words "the valley so low"), another. In the unfolding of a work this theme and its motives might undergo continual development, in the course of which their capacity for growth would be explored. We shall have more to say on theme and motive when we discuss the Classical form in detail.

The nineteenth-century symphony holds a place of honor in the output of the Romantic era. It retains its hold on the public, and remains one of the striking manifestations of the spirit of musical Romanticism.

28

Mendelssohn: Italian Symphony

"The *Italian Symphony* is getting on well. It is becoming the merriest piece I have yet composed." (1831)

The *Italian Symphony* dates from the "grand tour" that Mendelssohn undertook in his early twenties, in the course of which he visited England, Scotland, Italy, and France. Like most visitors from northern Europe he was enchanted by Italy, its sunny skies and exuberant people. He recorded his impressions in one of his most widely loved works, the first version of which occupied him from 1831 to 1833. Despite the success of the symphony it failed to satisfy him; he kept revising the piece for a number of years.

First movement

The first movement is a dynamic Allegro vivace (fast and lively) whose headlong pace never slackens. Its main theme is a dancelike tune of boundless energy:

The opening notes of this theme serve as an easily recognized motive that dominates the movement:

The drive and vigor of this music are not to be resisted. The strings are clearly the heart of Mendelssohn's orchestra; woodwinds and brass are set off against them with capital effect. The orchestral sound is transparent—everything is clear and bright, with much staccato in the graceful manner associated with this composer.

The second theme contrasts with the first. Less active, it is a gracious idea that begins with an ascending arpeggio scored for clarinets and bassoons:

A codetta based on the first theme rounds off the opening section of the movement, the exposition. Mendelssohn, in accordance with Classical procedure, indicates that this is to be repeated.

The development refashions both themes into fresh patterns. It also presents a striking new motive that is bandied about by various instruments.

Some idea of how a composer develops his material may be gleaned from the following examples.

1. Expansion of the principal theme:

2. Expansion of the new motive:

3. Combination of both:

An exciting crescendo leads into the final section of the movement, the Recapitulation. The material is restated in shortened form. The coda is marked Più animato poco a poco (more animated, little by little) and provides a fitting climax to this truly sunny Allegro.

Second movement

The second movement is an Andante con moto (moderately slow, with motion). The form is a modified sonata-allegro, consisting of an Exposition and Recapitulation without a Development—what is known as a *sonatina* ("little sonata"). Nineteenth-century commentators associated this movement with a religious procession. After a brief introduction the oboe, supported by "dark" instruments—two bassoons and violas—introduces a sedate melody. Cellos and double basses supply a soft staccato background

to this theme, which is then presented in octaves by the violins. Both here and in the contrasting material Mendelssohn reveals his gift for lyricism of a subdued, somewhat elegiac cast. The first section is recapitulated and a feelingful coda rounds off the movement.

Third movement

Third is a lyrical movement that stands closer to the graceful minuet than to the boisterous scherzo. The first violins present a broadly designed melody, marked "with moderate motion."

The emotional temperature rises a little as this idea is expanded. The Trio features wind instruments; the prominence of horn sound imparts to this music a suggestion of the outdoors. Bassoons and horns announce a relaxed theme against which the first violins play a gracefully ascending scale that is continued by the flutes:

The opening section is repeated, and the coda ingeniously combines a motive from the Scherzo with one from the Trio. The movement ends pianissimo.

Fourth movement

The final movement is a Presto based on the popular Italian "jumping dance" known as the *saltarello*. Its rhythm is marked by triplets in a rapid 4/4 time:

This Saltarello was inspired by a visit to a Roman carnival. In a letter to his family the young composer described how he was pelted with confetti. "Amid a thousand jokes and jeers and the most extravagant masks, the day ended with races." The movement evokes a scene of tumultuous merry-making, with crowds dancing wildly in the streets. Of special note are the slowly gathering crescendos that propel the music forward. The overall effect of this hard-driving finale is one of unflagging vitality.

The *Italian Symphony* embodies the urge toward exoticism that was to occupy an important place in nineteenth-century music. Beyond that it combines the Classical impulse toward clarity of form with the Romantic fondness for picturesque mood and atmosphere.

29

Peter Ilyich Tchaikovsky

"Truly there would be reason to go mad were it not for music."

Peter Ilyich Tchaikovsky.

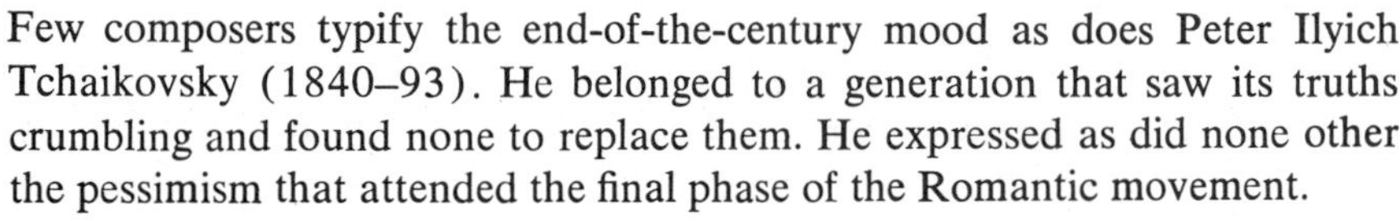

Few composers typify the end-of-the-century mood as does Peter Ilyich Tchaikovsky (1840–93). He belonged to a generation that saw its truths crumbling and found none to replace them. He expressed as did none other the pessimism that attended the final phase of the Romantic movement.

His Life

Tchaikovsky was born at Votinsk in a distant province of Russia, son of a government official. His family intended him for a career in the government. He graduated at nineteen from the artistocratic School of Jurisprudence at St. Petersburg and obtained a minor post in the Ministry of Justice. Not till he was twenty-three did he reach the decision to resign his post and enter the newly founded Conservatory of St. Petersburg. "To be a good musician and earn my daily bread"–his was a modest goal.

He completed the course in three years and was immediately recommended by Anton Rubinstein, director of the school, for a teaching post at the new Conservatory of Moscow. Despite the long hours and large classes, the young professor of harmony applied himself assiduously to composition. His twelve years at Moscow saw the production of some of his most successful works.

Extremely sensitive by nature, Tchaikovsky was subject to attacks of depression aggravated by his irregular personal life. In the hope of achieving some degree of stability, he entered into an ill-starred marriage with a student of the Conservatory, Antonina Miliukov, who was hopelessly in love with him. His sympathy for Antonina soon turned into uncontrollable aversion, and in a fit of despair he wandered into the icy waters of the

Moscow River. Some days later he fled, on the verge of a serious breakdown, to his brothers in St. Petersburg.

In this desperate hour, as in one of the fairy tales he liked to turn into ballets, there appeared the kind benefactress who enabled him to go abroad until he had recovered his health, freed him from the demands of a teaching post, and launched him on the most productive period of his career. Nadezhda von Meck, widow of an industrialist, was an imperious and emotional woman. She lived the life of a recluse in her mansion in Moscow, from which she ran her railroads, her estates, and the lives of her eleven children. Her passion was music, especially Tchaikovsky's. Bound by the rigid conventions of her time and her class, she had to be certain that her enthusiasm was for the artist, not the man; hence she stipulated that she was never to meet the recipient of her bounty.

Thus began the famous friendship by letter which soon assumed a tone of passionate attachment. For the next thirteen years Mme. von Meck made Tchaikovsky's career the focal point of her life, providing for his needs with exquisite devotion and tact. Save for an accidental glimpse of one another at the opera or during a drive, they never met.

The correspondence gives us an insight into Tchaikovsky's method of work. "You ask me how I manage the instrumentation. I never compose in the abstract. I invent the musical idea and its instrumentation simultaneously." Mme. von Meck inquires if the *Fourth Symphony* (which he dedicated to her) has a definite meaning. Tchaikovsky replies, "How can one express the indefinable sensations that one experiences while writing an instrumental composition that has no definite subject? It is a purely lyrical process. It is a musical confession of the soul, which unburdens itself through sounds just as a lyric poet expresses himself through poetry. The difference lies in the fact that music has far richer resources of expression and is a more subtle medium. . . . As Heine said, 'Where words leave off music begins.' "

The years covered by the correspondence saw the spread of Tchaikovsky's fame. He was the first Russian whose music appealed to Western tastes, and in 1891 he was invited to come to America to participate in the ceremonies that marked the opening of Carnegie Hall. From New York he wrote, "These Americans strike me as very remarkable. In this country the honesty, sincerity, generosity, cordiality, and readiness to help you without a second thought are extremely pleasant. . . . The houses downtown are simply colossal. I cannot understand how anyone can live on the thirteenth floor. I went out on the roof of one such house. The view was splendid, but I felt quite giddy when I looked down on Broadway. . . . I am convinced that I am ten times more famous in America than in Europe."

The letters of his final years breathe disenchantment and the suspicion that he had nothing more to say. "Is it possible that I have completely written myself out? I have neither ideas nor inclinations!" But ahead of him lay his two finest symphonies.

Immediately after finishing his *Sixth Symphony,* the *Pathétique,* he went to St. Petersburg to conduct it. The work met with a lukewarm reception, due in part to the fact that Tchaikovsky, painfully shy in public, conducted his music without any semblance of conviction. Some days later, although he had been warned of the prevalence of cholera in the capital, he carelessly drank a glass of unboiled water and contracted the disease. He died within the week, at the age of fifty-three. The suddenness of his death and the tragic tone of his last work led to rumors that he had committed suicide. Almost immediately there accrued to the *Symphonie pathétique* the sensational popularity it has enjoyed ever since.

His Music

"He was the most Russian of us all!" said Stravinsky. In the eyes of his countrymen Tchaikovsky is a national artist. He himself laid great weight on the Russian element in his music. "Why is it that the simple Russian landscape, a walk in summer through Russian fields and forest or on the steppes at evening can affect me so that I have lain on the ground numb, overcome by a wave of love for nature." At the same time, in the putting together of his music Tchaikovsky was a cosmopolite. He came under the spell of Italian opera, French ballet, German symphony and song. These he assimilated to the strain of folk melody that was his heritage as a Russian, setting upon the mixture the stamp of a sharply defined personality.

Tchaikovsky cultivated all branches of music. Of prime importance are his last symphonies, the *Fourth* (1877), the *Fifth* (1888), and the *Sixth* (1893). They abound in spectacular climaxes that endear them to the virtuoso conductor. In the domain of program music two arresting works continue to be played: the overture-fantasy *Romeo and Juliet* and the symphonic fantasy *Francesca da Rimini* (1876). Hardly less popular is the colorful *Capriccio italien* (1880). Of his eight operas, two hold the international stage: *Eugene Onegin* (1877–78) and *Pique Dame* (Queen of Spades, 1890). Based on librettos derived from the national poet Pushkin, both are essentially lyric in character. Tchaikovsky's ballets enjoy immense popularity. *Swan Lake* (1876), *The Sleeping Beauty* (1889), and *The Nutcracker* (1892) are appreciated both in the ballet theater and in the concert hall.

The *Piano Concerto in B-flat minor* (1875) and the *Violin Concerto in D major* (1878) are staple display pieces of the virtuoso. His songs too—he wrote more than a hundred, many of them in his favorite vein of Slavic melancholy—figure prominently on recital programs.

Symphony No. 6 (Pathétique)

"I have put my whole soul into this work," Tchaikovsky wrote to his nephew in the last year of his life. His new symphony, he stated, had a program, "but a program of the kind that will remain an enigma to all. Let them guess it who can." He intended to call the piece *A Program Symphony*; his brother Modest suggested the title *Pathétique*. The program, Tchaikovsky wrote, was penetrated with subjective sentiment. "During my journey, while composing it in my mind, I frequently shed tears."

He wrote down the first movement in less than four days. "There will be much in this work," he pointed out, "that is novel as regards form. The finale, for example, will not be a great allegro but an adagio of considerable dimensions." He finally shook off the fear of having outlived his creativeness. "You cannot imagine what joy I feel at the thought that my day is not yet over and that I may still accomplish much."

First movement
SIDE 5/2 (E II)
SIDE 4/2 (S)

The symphony opens with a brief introduction, marked Adagio, that is somber in color and establishes a mood of brooding intensity. A solo bassoon in low register moves sluggishly along the scale, outlining a four-note motive that is heard three times, each time a step higher. (A pattern repeated in this manner at a higher or lower pitch is known as a *sequence*, and this is an ascending sequence.)

This motive, which is then presented by the violas, becomes the germinating idea of an expressive sonata-allegro form marked Allegro non troppo (not too fast).

Notice that it is immediately repeated in a slightly altered form. The answering phrase heightens the agitation. It, too, consists of a pattern repeated in sequence at various pitch levels.

It will be instructive to observe some of the transformations of the basic motive, for the procedures Tchaikovsky follows give us some insight into the way a composer's mind works. In the next example the motive is speeded up through the use of shorter notes. This, combined with a rise in pitch, produces an effect of intensification:

Now the basic motive gives rise to a new sequence that carries the music to a high point:

During the expansion of the first idea, the basic motive appears with mounting urgency in the brass, in a new guise:

The transition to the lyric second theme requires a relaxation of tension. Tchaikovsky achieves this by moving from the tense high register to middle ground, from a dramatic Allegro to a gentle Andante. In the final measures of the transitional passage, the rhythm is slackened by a gradual progression from sixteenth notes to triplets, eighths, quarters, and halves. This change in rhythm is reinforced by a retard in tempo and a diminuendo to *ppp* (pianississimo):

The great lyric theme, in Tchaikovsky's most romantic style, is sung by muted violins and cellos, Andante. He wanted the passage to be played "tenderly, very songful, expansively." The opening motive is repeated, a new idea appears, and is followed by a return to the first, giving the phrase structure an **A-A-B-A** form:

Notice that in Phrase 3, the first half of the phrase is repeated in sequence a step lower.

This theme is answered by a contrasting melody in the flutes. It is imitated a measure later by the bassoon, which makes for a striking dialogue:

This theme, too, shows Tchaikovsky's fondness for repeating a fragment of melody in sequence. After a suitable expansion of this idea, the lyric theme returns, forming a clearcut **A-B-A** within the Exposition. This section is rounded off with a serene codetta marked "as sweetly as possible."

An explosive fortissimo chord ushers in the Development section, which is based chiefly on the germinal motive. In a passage that Tchaikovsky wanted played "with fierce vehemence," he expanded the motive in an extended ascending sequence:

The excitement mounts steadily to a passage in high register marked *fff* (fortissississimo). Tension is maintained at fever pitch as the brass and woodwinds hurl clangorous chords against great arcs of sound in the strings. The basic motive is expanded in new and ingenious ways as the movement surges forward relentlessly from one climax to the next. There is a simmering down of excitement as the Recapitulation approaches; the first theme returns and is worked up with even greater intensity than before. Before the lyric theme reappears, Tchaikovsky introduces one of his most spectacular ideas—a dramatic confrontation between strings allied with woodwinds against the brass:

Tchaikovsky knew when he had a great tune. The movement reaches its emotional high point with the reappearance of the lyric theme, which is now heard against an ascending line in the bass that sheds a new light upon it. The coda strikes a tragic note; it unfolds against a descending scale played pizzicato by the strings, which is repeated again and again. To nineteenth-century commentators the sound invariably conjured up the footfalls of fate. The final markings are pianissimo and "dying away."

Second movement
SIDE 6/1 (E II)
SIDE 5/1 (S)

Next is the Allegro con grazia (lively, with grace), an **A-B-A** movement of dancelike character in 5/4 (2 + 3), which in the 1890s was a most unusual meter. The alternation of groups of two and three beats gives the music its wayward charm. This Allegro is a large **A-B-A** in which each of the three sections is itself a three-part form, with a transition or *bridge* connecting the parts. We have here a fine example of how a movement can be built up into a large cohesive form through the repetition and expansion of little phrases, as is made clear by the following outline.

A	bridge	**B**	bridge	**A**	Coda
a-a-b-b-a-a		**c-c-d-d-c**		**a-b-b-a-a**	on motives from **a** and **c**

When Tchaikovsky repeats material, he sometimes changes register, dynamics, orchestration, or type of accompaniment to present it in a fresh light.

The opening melody (**a**), introduced by the cellos and taken over by woodwinds, contains patterns in sequence. The first two measures (x) are repeated at a higher pitch in measures 3–4 (x′); measures 5–6 (y) are repeated a step lower in measures 7–8 (y′):

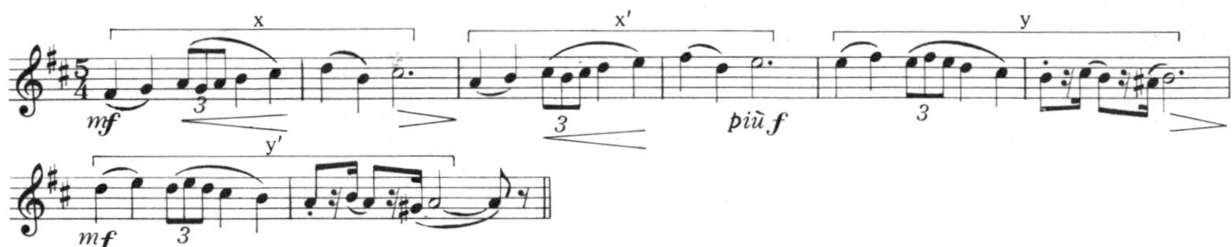

The answering phrase (**b**) begins with a downward leap and makes a good foil for the first:

When theme **a** returns it is heard against a background of running scales, which makes a capital effect. The bridge to section **B** is based on a motive drawn from theme **a.** The section ends forte.

By contrast, the middle section (**B**) begins piano. It is based on an idea (**c**) that contrasts with the first. Where the first moves in a generally upward direction, this one moves downward and is far less active:

As you can see, the pattern of the first measure is repeated in subsequent measures, either exactly or in a modified form. Tchaikovsky's direction for this theme is "with sweetness and plaintive." It unfolds over a low D that is reiterated by bassoons, kettledrums, and double basses. Such a tone, sustained or repeated in one part while the harmonies change in the other parts, is known as a *pedal point* or *organ point* (from the fact that it occurs frequently in organ music as a note held or repeated by one of the pedal keys). The **d** phrase makes a lovely curve, growing a little louder on the way up and softer on the way down. Notice the sequence:

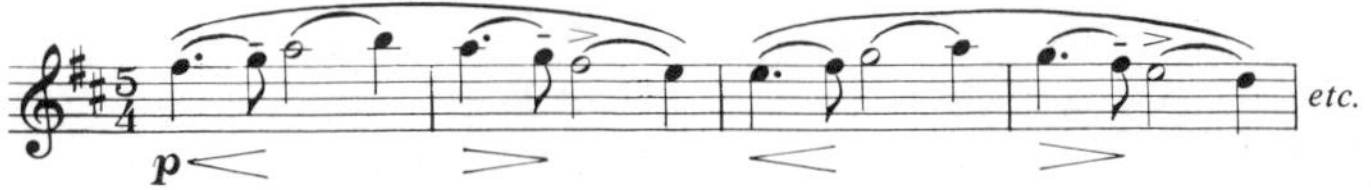

A bridge leads back to the lighter mood of the **A** section, which is shorn of its repeat and leads into the coda.

An extraordinarily exciting scherzo-march follows, marked Allegro molto vivace (very fast and lively). The opening theme consists of very fast staccato triplets, of a lightness and grace that suggest Tchaikovsky's affinity for the ballet:

Third movement
SIDE 6/2 (E II)
SIDE 5/2 (S)

The march theme that will dominate the movement later on is heard for an instant and disappears. The twittering of strings and woodwinds prevails. Out of it emerges a dancelike idea in the first violins, marked piano and *leggiero* (lightly):

Akin to it in spirit is another idea that takes shape against the triplet rhythm. It is played pizzicato by the first violins, reinforced by the flutes:

The music gathers momentum in a long drawn-out crescendo, setting the stage for the appearance of the second theme. This turns out to be an imperious march tune marked by incisive rhythm, with a syncopated "snap" in the second measure consisting of a short note on the beat followed by an accented longer one on the offbeat (at *):

While Tchaikovsky gives this arresting idea a suitable expansion, he avoids building it up into a fortissimo. He is saving this effect for the grand climax at the end of the movement.

The scherzo is repeated, as is the march. However, the movement differs in form from a simple **A-B-A-B** because of relationships among its elements that we will explore in later chapters. It is more accurately described as an Exposition and Recapitulation without a Development section between them. Several procedures prepare us for the triumphal reappearance of the march theme. Most striking is the expansion of its opening motive (the first seven notes) by repetition through overlapping—that is, one instrument takes up the motive before another has finished it:

Characteristic, too, is the heightened tension achieved by expanding the last three notes of the motive, E-A-D:

After sweeping scales, ascending and descending, by strings and woodwinds—a dramatic device much favored by Tchaikovsky—the march melody makes its appearance in full orchestral panoply, *fff*. From that point on the movement surges forward to one of the most electrifying climaxes in symphonic literature. A fine example of Tchaikovsky's way of achieving tension is the following expansion of a three-note motive drawn from the theme:

A grandiose coda rounds off the movement.

Fourth movement
SIDE 6/3 (E II)
SIDE 5/3 (S)

Nothing could be farther in spirit from this ending than the Adagio lamentoso (very slow, lamenting) that follows. In Chekhov's moving play *The Sea Gull*, Masha is asked why she wears black and replies, "I am in mourning for my life." Here Tchaikovsky is garbed in black. The sorrowful opening theme is presented by the violins. Notice that the first motive (under the bracket) is immediately repeated, but with the addition of one note in measure 4, which makes a difference:

The first section unfolds in a great outpouring that becomes an outcry and then subsides to a pianissimo. Anguish is dispelled for a space by the consoling second theme, a tightly knit melody that Tchaikovsky wanted played "with gentleness and devotion." The opening motive (under the bracket) is immediately repeated, then its first three notes are heard three times in an ascending sequence:

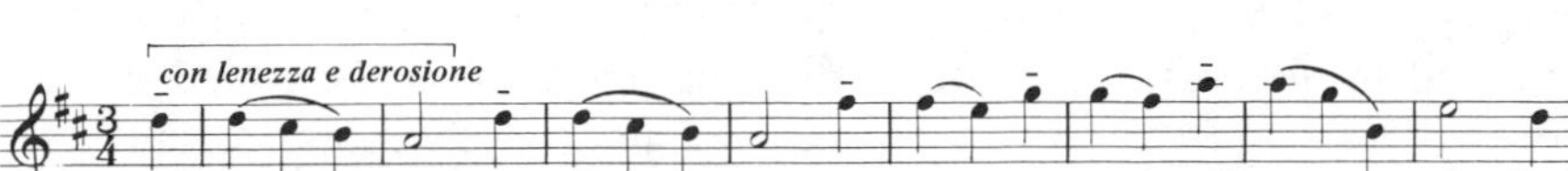

This theme, which is first heard against a pedal point in the horns, unfolds in a great arc of melody that works up to a magnificent climax. The following example shows how Tchaikovsky builds a climax in this movement by moving ever so gradually to a high point and then descending:

He achieves a comparable intensification in the following passage through the use of ever shorter—that is, ever more rapid—notes, first a dotted half, then two, three, four, six, and seven notes to a beat:

The theme of the lament returns, given a more tragic import through the upward sweeping figure in the strings that serves to introduce it. Here, too, Tchaikovsky uses his favorite device of ascending sequence in conjunction with ever shorter notes and ever shorter units of the motive:

The coda is based on the second theme. Tchaikovsky alters it so that it loses the serene quality it had earlier in the movement and takes on the sorrowing mood of the first theme. In the final measures we hear a combination of bassoon and string tone similar to that with which the symphony opened; the music fades to a *pppp* and descends into the dark abyss whence it issued.

Through his art, Tchaikovsky conquered the forces of disunity within himself, lifted himself above despair, and won his place in history. He captured in his music the mood of a time and a place, endowed it with artistic form, and, by an act of will and imagination, gave it universal significance.

30

Johannes Brahms

Johannes Brahms.

"It is not hard to compose, but it is wonderfully hard to let the superfluous notes fall under the table."

Against the colorful program art of Berlioz, Liszt, and Wagner there arose an austere, high-minded musician dedicated to the purity of the Classical style. His veneration for the past and his mastery of the architecture of absolute music brought him closer to the spirit of Beethoven than were any of his contemporaries.

His Life

Johannes Brahms (1833–97) was born in Hamburg, son of a double-bass player whose love of music was greater than his attainments. As a youngster of ten Johannes helped increase the family income by playing the piano in the dance halls of the slum district where he grew up. By the time he was twenty he had acquired sufficient reputation as a pianist to accompany the Hungarian violinist Eduard Reményi on a concert tour.

His first compositions made an impression on Joseph Joachim, leading violinist of the day, who made possible a visit to Robert Schumann at Düsseldorf. Schumann recognized in the shy young composer a future leader of the camp dedicated to absolute music. He published in his journal the famous essay entitled "New Paths," in which he named the twenty-year-old "young eagle" as the one who "was called forth to give us the highest ideal expression of our time." Brahms awoke to find himself famous.

Robert and Clara took the fair-haired youth into their home. Their friendship opened up new horizons for him. Five months later came the tragedy of Schumann's mental collapse. With a tenderness and strength he had not suspected in himself, Brahms tided Clara over the ordeal of Robert's illness.

The older man lingered for two years while the younger was shaken by the great love of his life. Fourteen years his senior and the mother of seven children, Clara Schumann appeared to young Brahms as the ideal of womanly and artistic perfection. What had begun as filial devotion ripened into romantic passion. She for her part found a necessary source of strength in the loyalty of the "young eagle." For Johannes this was the period of storm and stress, as his letters to her reveal. "You have taught me and every day teach me more and more to marvel at the nature of love, affection, and self-denial. I can do nothing but think of you." At the same time he was rent by feelings of guilt, for he loved and revered Schumann, his friend and benefactor, above all others. He thought of suicide and spoke of himself, as one may at twenty-two, as "a man for whom nothing is left."

This conflict was resolved the following year by Schumann's death; but another conflict took its place. Now that Clara was no longer the unattainable ideal, Brahms was faced with the choice between love and freedom. Time and again in the course of his life he was torn between the two, with the decision going always to freedom. His ardor subsided into a lifelong friendship. Two decades later he could still write her, "I love you more than myself and more than anybody and anything on earth."

His appointment as musician to the Prince of Detmold inaugurated his professional career. After four years at this post he returned to Hamburg to devote himself to composition. But he failed to obtain an official appointment in his native city—the directors of the Philharmonic never forgot that Johannes came from the slums—and settled in Vienna, which remained the center of his activities for thirty-five years. In the stronghold of the Classical masters he found a favorable soil for his art, his northern seriousness refined by the grace and congeniality of the South. The time was ripe for him. His fame filled the world and he became the acknowledged heir of the Viennese masters.

This exacting artist had a curiously dual nature. He could be morose and withdrawn, yet he loved rough humor. A bohemian at heart, he craved bourgeois respectability. Behind a rough exterior he hid the tenderness that found expression in his music and his love of children. He fought the softness in himself and came to be feared for his caustic wit. To a musician fishing for compliments he remarked, "Yes, you have talent. But very little!" The elderly ladies whom he was rehearsing in *The Creation* were admonished: "Why do you drag it so? Surely you took this much faster under Haydn." When a renowned quartet played his work the viola player inquired if he was satisfied with the tempo. Brahms snapped, "Yes—especially yours!" Thus the crotchety bachelor went his way through the middle-class circles of Vienna, the center of an adoring coterie. Although he complained of loneliness and on occasion fell in love, he was unable to accept the responsibility of a sustained relationship. His motto was *Free—*

but happy! "It would be as difficult for me to marry," he explained, "as to write an opera. But after the first experience I should probably undertake a second!"

Just as in early manhood his mother's death had impelled him to complete *A German Requiem,* so the final illness of Clara Schumann in 1896 gave rise to the *Four Serious Songs.* Her death profoundly affected the composer, already ill with cancer. He died ten months later, at the age of sixty-four, and was buried not far from Beethoven and Schubert.

His Music

Brahms was a traditionalist. His gaze was directed back to the Classical era whose splendor it was no longer possible to resurrect. This sense of being a latecomer imparts to his music its gently retrospective flavor, its autumnal resignation. Endowed with the historic sense, Brahms looked upon himself as a preserver of the great tradition. His aim was to show that new and important things could still be said in the tradition of the Classical masters. In this he differed from avowed innovators such as Berlioz, Liszt, and Wagner.

Symphonies

Brahms's four symphonies (1876, 1877, 1883, 1885) are unsurpassed in the late Romantic period for breadth of conception and design. Best known of the other orchestral works are the *Variations on a Theme by Haydn* (1873) and the concert overtures—the *Academic Festival* and the *Tragic* (1880). In the two concertos for piano and orchestra (1858, 1881) and the one for violin (1878), the solo instrument is integrated into a full-scale symphonic structure. The *Double Concerto for Violin and Cello* (1887) draws its inspiration from the age of Bach.

Chamber music

In greater degree than any of his contemporaries Brahms captured the tone of intimate communion that is the essence of chamber-music style. The duo sonatas, trios, quartets, quintets, and sextets for string and wind instruments, with and without piano, comprise a body of works marked by lyricism and a quality of introspection peculiarly his own. He is an important figure too in piano music. The three sonatas (1852–53) are works of his youth. The *Variations and Fugue on a Theme by Handel* (1861) represents his top achievement in this field. A favorite with concert performers is the set of *Variations on a Theme by Paganini* (1863), a composition that requires supreme virtuoso playing. The Romantic in Brahms also found expression in short lyric pieces; the Rhapsodies, Ballades, Capriccios, and lyrical meditations known as Intermezzi are among the treasures of the literature. On the popular level are the *Hungarian Dances* and the set of sixteen Waltzes for piano duet.

Songs

As a song writer Brahms stands in the direct line of succession to Schubert and Schumann. His output includes about two hundred solo songs and an almost equal number for two, three, and four voices. The favorite themes are love, nature, death. His finest choral work is the *German*

Requiem (1857–68), written to texts from the Bible selected by himself. A song of acceptance of death, this work more than any other spread his fame during his lifetime.

The nationalist in Brahms—he spoke of himself as *echt deutsch* (truly German)—inspired his arrangements of German folk and children's songs as well as the popular tone of many of his art songs. In his waltzes he paid tribute to the popular dance of his beloved Vienna, but he knew he was too much the north German to capture the real Viennese flavor. When he gave his autograph to Johann Strauss's daughter—composers customarily inscribed a few bars of their music—he wrote the opening measures of the *Blue Danube Waltz* and noted beneath it, "Not, alas, by Johannes Brahms."

Symphony No. 2

The *Symphony No. 2 in D major*, Opus 73, was composed in 1877. Brahms found it "so merry and tender" that he thought it could have been written especially for a newly wedded couple—a rather arch description from so crusty a bachelor. The piece abounds in true Brahmsian lyricism. Characteristic is the subdued orchestral color: woodwinds and brass in low register, blending with the strings in a silver-gray sonority, warmed by the mellifluous sound of the horn. This is a lovely work.

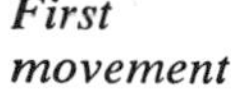
First movement

The first movement is a spacious sonata-allegro form. Its opening idea, shared by horns, woodwinds, and lower strings (cellos and double basses), contains three motives that assume increasing importance. The first of these (**a**) may be regarded as a kind of basic motive that in one shape or another pervades the piece. Notice that the first three notes of motive **c** follow the pattern of motive **a** upside down—that is, in inversion.

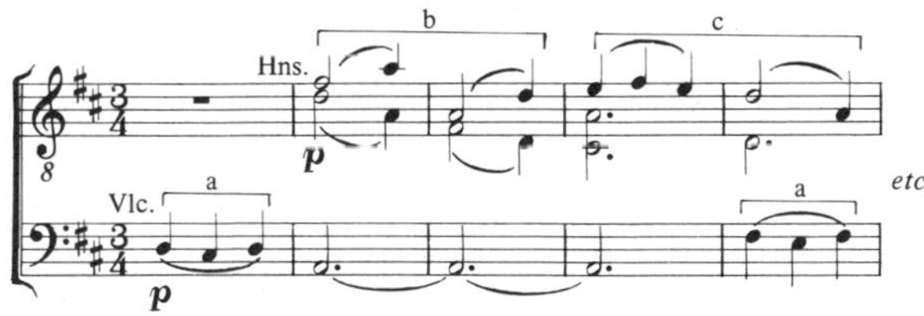

This material expands into a mysterious passage that serves as introduction. Now motive **a** blossoms into the first theme of the movement. It is marked *p* dolce (soft and sweetly):

This idea is developed into a vigorous passage with emphasis on motive **a**, which is heard against an accompaniment of motive **b** in shorter notes—that is, in *diminution*:

A transition leads into the second theme. In this passage motives **a** and **b** are both heard in diminution:

The second theme, marked *cantando* (singing), introduced by violas and cellos, is one of those heart-warming Brahmsian tunes that, once heard, engrave themselves indelibly on the mind:

This melody is accompanied by motive **b** in diminution, and is expanded. Presently an episode takes shape marked by vigorous dotted rhythms and syncopated accents. The theme strides across a remarkably broad range:

Motive **a** now takes on a strongly rhythmic form:

We hear an extended dialogue between upper and lower strings—first and second violins ranged against cellos and double basses, with woodwinds and brass in the background. The second theme returns against a new countermelody in triplets. (A *countermelody* is a melody heard against another. It serves as accompaniment to the main melody, but has a shape and character of its own.) The melody is played by the strings as the flute presents the countermelody. Then the roles are reversed—the melody passes to flutes and oboes while the first violins take over the countermelody. A brief codetta brings the Exposition to a quiet conclusion.

In the Development section Brahms follows the procedure that is at the heart of classical symphony. He breaks down the themes into their component motives and recombines them into ever fresh patterns. As a result, the motives take on new and fanciful forms. In the following example the first three notes of motive **c** are transformed into a new idea by being repeated in a descending sequence:

The basic motive **a** is imitated by various instruments on different beats within the measure:

The basic motive gives rise to a new pattern in diminution, eighth notes being used instead of quarters, followed by the motive in its original rhythm:

Motive **b** is expanded through repetition at different octaves:

The material is heard again in the Recapitulation, but in somewhat abbreviated form and with significant changes in orchestration and accompaniment. A serene tenderness breathes through these wonderful measures. Motives **a** and **b** are combined to create a new melody:

In the coda, marked "In Tempo" and "always tranquil," the basic motive is heard in syncopation as the strings play it pizzicato on the offbeat:

The movement ends, as it began, with the basic motive uttered in a mysterious whisper.

Second movement

The second movement, Adagio non troppo (not too slow), is a lyric meditation in Brahms's most introspective manner. Its principal theme, a long-breathed melody presented by the cellos, derives its serious character from the downward inflection of the opening measures. It contains three motives that take on structural importance:

This melody is given an extended orchestral treatment, with much interplay among the instruments as one imitates the other. The contrasting second theme makes a graceful ascending-descending curve. The main melody notes, somewhat lighter in character, fall before the beat instead of on it, resulting in a gently flowing motion of singular charm:

These two ideas are rounded out by subordinate themes and connective material. When the principal idea returns, it is subjected to elaborate variation in the course of which its $\frac{4}{4}$ time is made to conform with the $\frac{12}{8}$ pattern of the middle section. This procedure is not as complicated as it sounds, since a measure of $\frac{12}{8}$ consists of four triplets. In any case, you will need more than one hearing to appreciate fully this searching orchestral song.

Third movement

The scherzo, a gracious Allegretto, offers pleasant relief from the seriousness of the Adagio. Its principal theme, introduced by the oboe, is a delightful tune in which, if you look closely, you will find embedded the basic motive, in inversion:

There is a gentle lilt to the rhythm of this section that is most engaging. Notice the syncopated accent on the offbeat in measures 1 and 2 (indicated by a little arrow above the note).

Presently the meter changes to $\frac{2}{4}$, the tempo marking is Presto; the music takes on a different mood. Yet the new melody, introduced by the violins staccato and leggiero, turns out to be a variation of the first tune. As you can see, it uses almost the same notes:

The music takes on momentum, what with forceful dotted rhythms and syncopated accents. Yet despite the difference between Allegretto and Presto, the change from one section to the other is not as abrupt as it may seem, since in this movement one measure of the Presto is regarded as equivalent to one beat of the Allegretto. As a result, the underlying pulse remains the same.

The original tune returns, marked Tempo I. A new variation emerges as a Presto in $\frac{3}{8}$. In the transition back to Tempo I, Brahms underlines the steadfastness of the underlying pulse by combining the end of the Presto theme with the beginning of the Allegretto theme. A brief coda brings the movement to a quiet ending.

Fourth movement
SIDE 7/1 (E II)
SIDE 3/2 (S)

The finale is a tumultuous Allegro con spirito in which Brahms marshals all the resources of his orchestra. The movement is remarkable for the wealth of its thematic material and the inexhaustible invention with which the composer treats the themes and motives. The principal theme is a sinuous melody that is first presented by the strings. It contains two motives that soon take on structural significance.

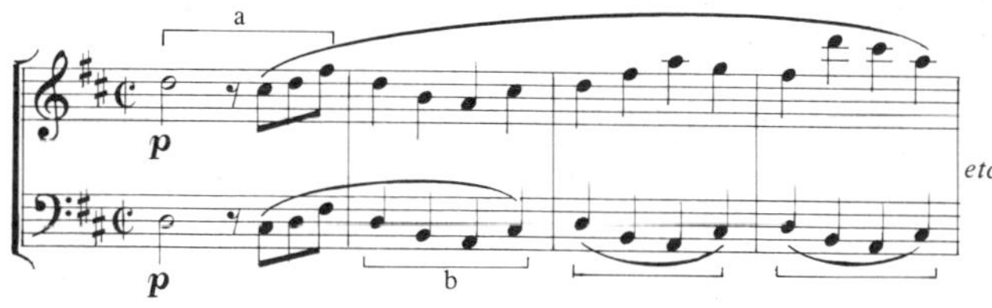

Motive **b** is immediately repeated in the bass as an accompaniment to the melody above it. A motive repeated over and over in this fashion is known as an *ostinato*, or obstinate figure.

The answer has a similar flow:

The opening melody returns, expanded and varied in the following fashion:

The first theme is taken up by the orchestra and expanded in a brilliant tutti. A transitional passage based on motive **a** leads into the second theme, one of those broadly flowing, noble tunes of which Brahms possessed the secret. It is introduced by the first violins:

From this melody are derived several accessory themes that complete the Exposition.

In the Development section, Brahms breaks up the themes into their component motives. The material is brought back in the Recapitulation, but in somewhat abbreviated form, constantly varied and with fascinating changes in the scoring. In one of the most striking transformations of the first theme, Brahms presents it in a triplet rhythm:

The passage is marked Tranquillo and has the tender, searching quality that Brahms associated with this term.

A remarkable moment comes when the first theme, in its triplet version, is combined with the second:

Brahms is not a composer usually cited in connection with brilliant orchestration, yet nothing could be more exciting than his handling of the orchestra in this movement. Tension mounts steadily until the climactic passage when trumpets and horns proclaim the second theme in a grand flourish, and the movement rushes headlong to its triumphal close.

The sonata-allegro form of this movement can be summed up as follows:

Exposition	Development	Recapitulation
Theme 1 bridge Theme 2 codetta	Themes broken up into their constituent motives and recombined into fresh patterns.	Themes 1 and 2 varied and restated in abbreviated form.

The art of Brahms—tender, searching, retrospective—marks the end not only of a century but of a cultural epoch. This lonely rhapsodist remains an impressive figure, one of the last representatives of nineteenth-century German idealism.

31

The Concerto

"We are so made that we can derive intense enjoyment only from a contrast."
— SIGMUND FREUD

The Nature of the Concerto

A *concerto* is a large-scale work in several movements for solo instrument and orchestra. (Occasionally, more than one soloist is involved.) Here the attention is focused upon the solo performer. This circumstance helps determine the style. The dramatic tension between soloist and orchestra is analogous to that between protagonist and chorus in Greek tragedy. The massive sonorities of the piano, the sweetness of the violin, or the dark resonance of the cello may be pitted against the orchestra. This opposition of forces constitutes the essential nature of the concerto.

Form

In its dimensions the concerto is comparable to a symphony. Most concertos are in three movements: a dramatic allegro, usually in sonata form, is followed by a songful slow movement and a brilliant finale. In the opening movement, as in the first movement of a symphony, contrasting themes are stated ("exposed"), developed, and restated. In this case, however, the tension is twofold: not only between the contrasting ideas but also between the opposing forces–that is, the solo instrument against the group. Each of the basic themes may be announced by the *tutti* (literally, "all"; i.e., the orchestra as a whole) and then taken up by the solo part. Or the latter may introduce the ideas and the orchestra expatiate upon them.

Cadenza

A characteristic feature of the concerto is the cadenza which, you will recall, is a fanciful solo passage in the manner of an improvisation that is interpolated into the movement. The cadenza came out of a time when improvisation was an important element in art music, as it still is today in jazz. Taken over into the solo concerto, the cadenza made a dramatic effect: the orchestra fell silent and the soloist launched into a free play of fantasy on one or more themes of the movement. Before the nineteenth century the performer was usually the composer; consequently the improvisation was apt to be of the highest caliber. With the rise of a class of professional players who interpreted the music of others but did not invent their own, the art of improvisation declined. Thus the cadenza came to be composed beforehand, either by the composer or the performer.

The concerto has to be a "grateful" vehicle that will enable the performing artist to exhibit his gifts as well as the capacities of the instrument. This element of technical display, combined with appealing melodies, has helped to make the concerto one of the most widely appreciated types of concert music.

32

Mendelssohn: Violin Concerto

"I should like to write a violin concerto for you next winter. One in E minor is running through my head, and the beginning does not leave me in peace." (Letter to Ferdinand David)

First movement
SIDE 5/1 (E II)
SIDE 4/1 (S)

The *Violin Concerto in E minor* (1844), a staple of the repertory, dates from the latter part of Mendelssohn's career. The work reveals his special gifts: clarity of form and grace of utterance, a subtle orchestral palette, and a vein of sentiment that is tender but reserved. The first movement, Allegro molto appassionato (very fast and impassioned), is a shapely example of sonata-allegro form. The customary orchestral introduction is omitted; the violin announces the main theme of the movement almost immediately. This is a resilient and active melody in the upper register, marked by decisive rhythm and a broad arch that unfolds in symmetrical phrases.

The expansion of this theme gives the violinist opportunity for brilliant passage work, much of it in triplets. These serve as a unifying element throughout the movement. The theme is then proclaimed by full orchestra (tutti).

The main function of the bridge is to lead from the first theme to the second. Sometimes, however, this transition is made so attractive that it takes on the character of a new idea. Such is the case with this energetic melody of wide range:

The contrasting second theme is narrow of range and characterized by stepwise movement and narrow leaps. It is introduced by clarinets and flutes, tranquillo and pianissimo over a sustained tone on the open G string of the solo instrument. (Such a sustained tone in one part while the harmonies change in the other parts, as we have seen, is known as a *pedal point.*) The lyric theme provides an area of relaxation in the precipitous forward drive of the movement.

The development section explores motives of the principal theme and the transitional idea. It is marked by genuine symphonic momentum, culminating in the cadenza which, instead of coming at the end of the movement as is customary, serves as a link between the Development and a shortened Recapitulation. Under a curtain of widely spaced arpeggios on the violin the opening theme emerges in the orchestra. From here to the coda the movement gains steadily in power.

A violin concerto performed in the Hall of the Paris Conservatory, 1843. From a contemporary woodcut after a sketch by P.-S. Germain.

A brief transitional passage is in the 6/8 meter of the Andante that follows. This is a large **A-B-A** form. The opening theme is calm and meditative:

Second movement

The middle section, somber and elegiac, shows Mendelssohn in his most romantic mood; after which the serene opening melody returns.

An interlude in 4/4 marked Allegretto non troppo (fairly fast, not too much so) leads into the next movement. The customary pauses between movements are omitted in this concerto, exemplifying the Romantic desire to bind together the movements of a large work. The finale, an Allegro molto vivace (very fast and lively) in 4/4 time, is introduced by brave flourishes scored for oboes, bassoons, horns, and trumpets, *ff*. It is a sonata-allegro form in the light breezy manner that is Mendelssohn's most

Third movement

characteristic vein. The movement demands agile fingers and high spirits, a crisp staccato and brilliance of tone. The second theme continues in the light-hearted manner of the first, but is a much less active melody:

Mendelssohn elaborates on the chief theme and, in the Recapitulation, combines it with a singing melody in the orchestra:

Excitement builds steadily to the dazzling virtuosity of the coda.

Felicitous in melody and graceful in form, the Concerto displays the tender sentiment and Classic moderation that are so typical of Mendelssohn's style.

33

Schumann: Piano Concerto

"In these years I have been very industrious. One must work as long as the day lasts."

The first movement of Schumann's celebrated *Piano Concerto in A minor* was written in 1841 as an independent *Phantasie for Piano and Orchestra.* The second and third movements were added four years later.

First movement

The Allegro affettuoso (lively and with feeling) opens with an imperious sequence of chords in dotted rhythms on the piano. The oboe announces the lyric theme from which the movement germinates. The piano answers. The first half of the melody for the most part moves stepwise along the scale. The leap of an octave to the topmost note (at ×) makes an arresting climax, from which the melodic curve gently subsides. Two motives (**a** and **b**) are to be distinguished, which assume importance not only in this but also in the subsequent movements.

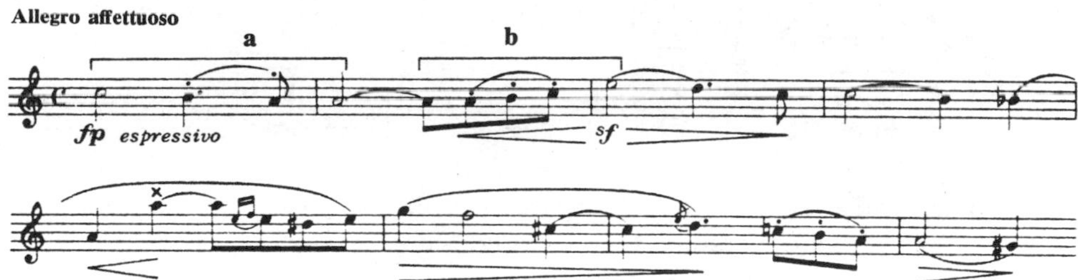

A somber melody in the violins, in the nature of a transition, ends in a third motive (**c**) which assumes great structural significance in the course of the movement. Notice that this motive is immediately repeated at a higher pitch (ascending sequence):

The second theme of the movement is not a new idea at all, but an imaginative transformation of the first theme. It is played by the clarinet against impetuous descending arpeggios on the piano. After a triumphal *tutti* (the entire orchestra), the principal theme is heard in a new transformation, as a

tender dialogue between piano and clarinet in 6/4 time, Andante espressivo. The fantasy-like character of the movement permits the composer to achieve an effect of spontaneity and caprice within the frame of sonata-allegro form, which he handles with the freedom of a poet. The thematic material is stated, developed, and restated. There is a steady drive to the rhapsodic cadenza, which is woven in whole out of the germinal theme. The latter appears in a new transformation in the coda, as a vigorous march in 2/4 time.

Second movement

Schumann called the slow movement an Intermezzo (Interlude). It is marked Andantino grazioso (at a going pace, gracefully). This meditative song starts out as a gracious colloquy between piano and orchestra. Notice that the material is derived from the **b** motive of the first movement and is repeated in sequence:

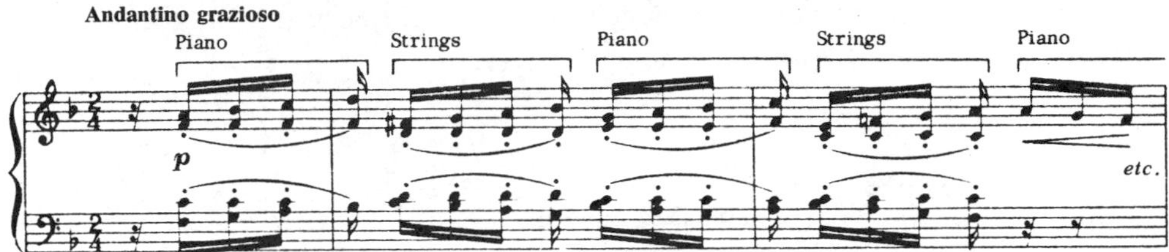

The middle section is based on a broadly flowing melody in the cellos, to which the piano responds with decorative patterns spun out in true Schumannesque manner. The opening section returns to round out the **A-B-A** form, and a fleeting reference to the first movement acts as a transition to the third.

Third movement

The finale is an Allegro vivace in 3/4 time. A vigorous theme on the piano is seconded by the orchestra. The **b** motive of the germinal theme

appears in a new context. This Allegro gives the listener a sense of vigorous movement and abounds in elaborate passagework for the solo instrument. A contrasting theme appears which, through clever shifting of accent, creates a phrase of slower motion without actually changing either the meter or the tempo:

In this concerto Schumann achieved the perfect fusion of dramatic and lyric elements. The work is universally regarded as his masterpiece.

34

Sergei Rachmaninoff

"Light, gay colors do not come easily to me."

Sergei Rachmaninoff. (Photo by Eric Schaal.)

His Life

Although Sergei Rachmaninoff lived well into the twentieth century (his dates are 1873–1943), he was a traditionalist whose gaze was fixed on the Romantic past. His was the heritage of Tchaikovsky. His music is marked by long soulful melodies of an exuberant lyricism, dramatic climaxes, and colorful sonorities. One of the great concert pianists of his time, he wrote for his chosen instrument with great facility and flair. Within the late Romantic style he created several works of enormous popular appeal.

During his middle twenties he went through an inner crisis of self-doubt. He lost confidence in his gifts and fell into a deep depression. Psychoanalysis had not yet made its mark. The doctor who helped him overcome his despondency practiced a form of autosuggestion. "I heard the same hypnotic formula repeated day after day while I lay half asleep in an armchair in Dr. Dahl's study. 'You will begin to write your Concerto . . . You will work with great facility . . . The Concerto will be of an excellent quality . . .' It was always the same, without interruption. Although it may sound incredible, this cure really helped me." Out of this experience came the *Piano Concerto No. 2,* which he finished in 1901, when he was twenty-eight, and dedicated to Dr. Dahl. It launched the young composer on an international career.

Piano Concerto No. 2

First movement

The work owes its popularity to its soaring melodies and intensely personal sentiment. The first movement, marked Moderato, follows the three-section pattern we noted in the first movement of the symphonies we studied: Exposition-Development-Recapitulation. Eight bars of chords on the piano lead into the first theme, a broadly flowing melody presented by violins, violas, and clarinets against tumultuous arpeggios on the piano. The composer's marking is "with passion."

This idea broadens into a lyric expansion of great surge and power, in the course of which the piano takes over the melody. The pace quickens. A *transition* (bridge) leads into the second theme, a romantic melody that for several seasons—fitted out with appropriate words—was on the Hit Parade. It is introduced by the piano:

Noteworthy is Rachmaninoff's ability to spin out a tune in a broad arc, rising higher and higher to its peak and then subsiding. This is a technique he inherited from Tchaikovsky.

A brief codetta rounds out the Exposition. The Development is an exciting section. It presents the first theme and a subsidiary idea that will take on greater importance as the movement unfolds. Rachmaninoff refashions his material into fresh patterns. He highlights the piano part and builds tension in a great crescendo up to the Recapitulation. The first theme returns in the orchestra while high above it the piano plays the subsidiary idea in a series of powerful chords. The passage is marked Maestoso, Alla marcia (majestic, like a march), and makes a dramatic effect. The second theme returns in a romantic setting–solo horn against tremolos in the strings marked *ppp*. Rachmaninoff here is at his most introspective. The final passage gets faster and louder as it prepares for the fortissimo ending.

Second movement

Rachmaninoff belonged to a generation more cosmopolitan in outlook than the Russian nationalists who preceded him. Folk song played a far less important role in his music than it did in the music of Tchaikovsky, Musorgsky, or Rimsky-Korsakov. Indeed, the slow movement of the Concerto stands closer to the spirit of German Romanticism—the tradition, that is, of Schubert, Schumann, and Brahms. Marked Adagio sostenuto (very slow and sustained), this is a lyric meditation of ample proportions. Slow chords in the low winds and muted strings introduce, first, a contemplative mood on the piano and then a tender melody on the flute:

This passes to the clarinet and then to the piano, in a continually expanding lyric song, gradually building to a climax, a cadenza, and a return of the main theme. The mood is somber and contemplative.

Third movement

The final movement, Allegro scherzando (fast and playful), derives its momentum from the opposition between two contrasting ideas—the first rhythmically propulsive, the second appealingly melodious. The basic rhythm, established in the opening measures, leads into a cadenza and is

then fleshed out by the piano. After a suitable expansion, oboe and viola bring in the melody, which is Rachmaninoff at his most expansive. Taken over by the piano, it unfolds in an extremely broad span, an undulating line of sensuous appeal sung over expressive harmonies. Rachmaninoff here revels in his favorite device: chords and octaves in the right hand over broadly spaced arpeggios in the left:

The rhythmic idea is now developed at length, and then the melody returns. After a buildup and another cadenza, we reach the romantic "apotheosis" in a passage marked Maestoso (majestic). The orchestra sings forth the melody in triumph while the piano embellishes it with clangorous chords.

This movement amply confirms Rachmaninoff as the legitimate heir of Tchaikovsky. He was a fervent spokesman for Romanticism in an anti-romantic age.

35

The Nature of Opera

"It is better to invent reality than to copy it." — GIUSEPPE VERDI

For well over three hundred years the opera has been one of the most alluring forms of musical entertainment. A special glamor is attached to everything connected with it–its arias, singers, and roles, not to mention its opening nights. Carmen, Mimi, Violetta, Tristan–what character in fact or fiction can claim, generation after generation, so constant a public?

An *opera* is a drama that is sung. It combines the resources of vocal and instrumental music–soloists, ensembles, chorus, orchestra and ballet–with poetry and drama, acting and pantomime, scenery and costumes. To weld the diverse elements into a unity is a problem that has exercised some of the best minds in the history of music.

At first glance opera would seem to make impossible demands on the credulity of the spectator. It presents us with human beings caught up in dramatic situations, who sing to each other instead of speaking. The reasonable question is (and it was asked most pointedly throughout the history of opera by literary men): how can an art form based on so unnatural a procedure be convincing? The question ignores what must always remain the fundamental aspiration of art: not to copy nature but to heighten our awareness of it. True enough, people in real life do not sing to each other. Neither do they converse in blank verse, as Shakespeare's characters do; nor live in rooms of which one wall is conveniently missing so that the audience may look in. All the arts employ conventions that are accepted both by the artist and his audience. The conventions of opera are more in evidence than those of poetry, painting, drama, or film, but they are not different in kind. Once we have accepted the fact that the carpet can fly, how simple to believe that it is also capable of carrying the prince's luggage.

Some of the allure of an opera performance may be glimpsed in this photograph of the interior of the Cuvilliés Theater in Munich, one of the world's most beautiful opera houses, during a performance of Wagner's Das Rheingold.

Opera functions in the domain of poetic drama. It uses the human voice to impinge upon the spectator the basic emotions—love, hate, jealousy, joy, grief—with an elemental force possible only to itself. The logic of reality gives way on the operatic stage to the transcendent logic of art, and to the power of music over the life of the heart.

The Components of Opera

Recitative

In the classic type of opera the explanations necessary to plot and action are presented in a kind of musical declamation known as *recitative.* This vocal style imitates the natural inflections of speech; its rhythm is curved to the rhythm of the language. Instead of a purely musical line, recitative is often characterized by a rapid patter and "talky" repetition of the same note; also by rapid question-and-answer dialogue that builds dramatic tension in the theater.

Aria

Recitative gives way at the lyric moments to the *aria,* which releases the emotional tension accumulated in the course of the action. The aria is a song, generally of a highly emotional kind. It is what audiences wait for, what they cheer, and what they remember. An aria, because of its beauty, may be effective even when removed from its context. Many arias are familiar to multitudes who never heard the operas from which they are excerpts.

Opera types

Grand opera is sung throughout. In opera of the more popular variety, the recitative is generally replaced by spoken dialogue. This is the type known among us as *operetta* or *musical comedy,* which has its counterpart in the French *opéra-comique* and German *Singspiel.* Interestingly enough, in Italy–the home of opera–even the comic variety, the *opera buffa,* is sung throughout.

The emotional conflicts in opera are linked to universal types and projected through the contrasting voices. Soprano, mezzo-soprano, and contralto are counterposed to tenor, baritone, and bass. The coloratura soprano has the highest range and greatest agility in the execution of trills and rapid passages. The dramatic soprano is preferred for dynamic range and striking characterization, the lyric for gentler types. If the heroine is a soprano, her rival for the hero's love will often be a contralto. The tenor may be lyric or dramatic. German opera has popularized the *Heldentenor* (heroic tenor) who, whether as Siegfried or Tristan, is required to display endurance, brilliance, and expressive power.

Voice classifications

Ensembles

An opera may contain ensemble numbers–trios, quartets, quintets, sextets, septets–in which the characters pour out their respective feelings. The unique quality of an ensemble number lies in its ability to project several contrasting emotions at the same time, the music binding these together into an artistic whole.

Chorus

The chorus is used in conjunction with the solo voices or it may function independently in the mass scenes. It may comment and reflect upon the action, in the manner of the chorus in Greek tragedy. Or it may be integrated into the action. In either case choral song offers the composer rich opportunities for varied musical-dramatic effects.

Orchestra and ballet

The orchestra provides the accompaniment. It sets the mood and creates the atmosphere for the different scenes. It also functions independently, in the overture, preludes to the acts, interludes, and postludes. Sometimes the ballet provides an eye-filling diversion in the scenes of pageantry that are an essential feature of grand opera. In the folk operas of the nineteenth century the ballet was used to present peasant and national dances.

Libretto

The *libretto,* or text, of an opera must be devised so as to give the composer an opportunity for the set numbers—the arias, duets, ensembles, choruses, marches, ballets, and finales–that are the traditional features of this art form. The librettist must not only create characters and plot with some semblance of dramatic insight, but he also has to fashion situations that justify the use of music and could not be fully realized without it.

Opera appeals primarily to those composers and music lovers who are given to the magic of the theater. It exerts its fascination upon those who love to hear singing. Thousands who do not feel at home with the abstract instrumental forms warm to opera, finding there a graphic kind of music linked to action and dialogue, whose meaning it is impossible to mistake. Countless others are attracted for the very good reason that opera contains some of the grandest music ever written.

36

Giuseppe Verdi

"Success is impossible for me if I cannot write as my heart dictates!"

Giuseppe Verdi.

In the case of Giuseppe Verdi (1813–1901), the most widely loved of operatic composers, it happened that the time, the place, and the personality were happily met. He inherited a rich tradition, his capacity for growth was matched by masterful energy and will, and he was granted a long span of life in which his gifts attained their full flower.

His Life

Born in a hamlet in northern Italy where his father kept a little inn, the shy, taciturn lad grew up amid the poverty of village life. His talent attracted the attention of a prosperous merchant in the neighboring town of Busseto, a music lover who made it possible for the youth to pursue his studies. After two years in Milan he returned to Busseto to fill a post as organist. When he fell in love with his benefactor's daughter, the merchant in wholly untraditional fashion accepted the penniless young musician as his son-in-law. Verdi was twenty-three, Margherita sixteen.

Three years later he returned to the conquest of Milan with the manuscript of an opera. *Oberto, Count of San Bonifacio* was produced at La Scala in 1839 with fair success. The work brought him a commission to write three others. Shortly after, Verdi faced the first crisis of his career. He had lost his first child, a daughter, before coming to Milan. The second, a baby boy, was carried off by fever, a catastrophe followed several weeks later by the death of his young wife. "My family had been destroyed, and in the midst of these trials I had to fulfill my engagement and write a comic opera!" *Un giorno di regno* (King for a Day) failed miserably. "In a sudden moment of despondency I despaired of finding any comfort in my art and resolved to give up composing."

The months passed; the distraught young composer adhered to his decision. One night he happened to meet the impresario of La Scala, who forced him to take home the libretto of *Nabucco* (Nebuchadnezzar, King of Babylon). "I came into my room and, throwing the manuscript angrily on the writing table, I stood for a moment motionless before it. The book opened as I threw it down. My eyes fell on the page and I read the line *Va pensiero sull' ali dorate* (Go, my thought, on golden wings—first line of the chorus of captive Jews who by the waters of Babylon mourn their ravished land). Resolved as I was never to write again, I stifled my emotion, shut the book, went to bed, and put out the candle. I tried to sleep, but *Nabucco* was running a mad course through my brain." In this fashion the musician was restored to his art. *Nabucco,* presented at La Scala in 1842, was a triumph for the twenty-nine-year-old composer and launched him on a spectacular career.

Italy at this time was in the process of birth as a nation. The patriotic party aimed at liberation from the Hapsburg yoke and the establishment of a united kingdom under the House of Savoy. Verdi from the beginning identified himself with the national cause. "I am first of all an Italian!" In this charged atmosphere his works took on special meaning for his countrymen. No matter in what time or place the opera was laid, they interpreted it as an allegory of their plight. The chorus of exiled Jews from *Nabucco* became a patriotic song. As the revolutionary year 1848 approached, Verdi's works–despite the precautions of the Austrian censor –continued to nourish the zeal of the nationalists. In *Attila* the line of the Roman envoy to the leader of the Huns, "Take thou the universe–but leave me Italy!" provoked frenzied demonstrations. When, in *The Battle of Legnano,* a chorus of medieval Italian knights vowed to drive the German invaders beyond the Alps, audiences were aroused to indescribable enthusiasm.

But the impact of Verdi's operas went deeper than the implications of the plot. The music itself had a dynamic force, a virility that was new in the Italian theater. This was truly, as one writer called it, "agitator's music." It happened too that the letters of Verdi's name coincided with the initials of the nationalist slogan–*V*ittorio *E*mmanuele *R*e *d'I*talia (Victor Emmanuel King of Italy). The cries of *Viva Verdi* that rang through Italian theaters not only hailed the composer but voiced the national dream. Rarely has a musician more ideally filled the role of a people's artist.

Although he was now a world-renowned figure, Verdi retained the simplicity that was at the core both of the artist and man. He returned to his roots, acquiring an estate at Busseto where he settled with his second wife, the singer Giuseppina Strepponi. She was a sensitive and intelligent woman who had created the leading roles in his early operas and who was his devoted companion for half a century. After Italy had won independence, he was urged to stand for election to the first parliament because of the prestige his name would bring the new state. The task conformed neither to his talents nor inclinations, but he accepted and sat in the chamber of deputies for some years.

The outer activities of this upright man framed an inner life of extraordinary richness. It was this that enabled him to move with unflagging creative tension from one masterpiece to the next. He was fifty-seven when he wrote *Aïda.* At seventy-three he completed *Otello,* his greatest lyric tragedy. In 1893, on the threshold of eighty, he astonished the world with *Falstaff*. Such sustained productivity invites comparison with the old masters, with a Monteverdi, Michelangelo, or Titian.

His death at eighty-seven was mourned throughout the world. He bequeathed the bulk of his fortune to a home for aged musicians founded by him in Milan. Italy accorded him the rites reserved for a national hero. From the thousands who followed his bier there sprang up a melody—*Va pensiero sull' ali dorate*. It was the chorus from *Nabucco* that he had given his countrymen as a song of solace sixty years before.

His Music

Verdi's music struck his contemporaries as the epitome of dramatic energy and passion. Endowed with an imagination that saw all emotion in terms of action and conflict—that is, in terms of the theater—he was able to imbue a dramatic situation with shattering expressiveness. Again and again he demanded of his librettists "a short drama, swift-moving and full of passion . . . Passions above all!" True Italian that he was, he based his art on melody, which to him was the most immediate expression of human feeling. "Art without spontaneity, naturalness, and simplicity," he maintained, "is no art."

Early period

Of his first fifteen operas the most important is *Macbeth* (1847), in which for the first time he derived his story material from Shakespeare, whom he called "the great searcher of the human heart." There followed in close succession the three operas that established his international fame: *Rigoletto* in 1851, based on Victor Hugo's drama *Le Roi s'amuse* (The King is Amused); *Il trovatore* (The Troubadour) in 1853, derived from a fanciful Spanish play; and *La traviata* (The Lost One), also produced in 1853, which he adapted from the younger Dumas's play *La Dame aux camélias* (The Lady of the Camellias). In these works of sustained pathos the musical dramatist stands before us in full stature.

Middle period

The operas of the middle period are on a more ambitious scale, showing Verdi's attempt to assimilate elements of the French grand opera. The three most important are *Un ballo in maschera* (A Masked Ball; 1859), *La forza del destino* (The Force of Destiny; 1862), and *Don Carlos* (1867). In these the master fought his way to a higher conception of dramatic unity. "After *La traviata,*" he declared, "I could have taken things easy and written an opera every year on the tried and true model. But I had other artistic aims."

Final period

These aims came to fruition in *Aïda,* the work that ushers in his final period (1870–93). *Aïda* was commissioned in 1870 by the Khedive of Egypt to mark the opening of the Suez Canal. Delayed by the outbreak of the Franco-Prussian War, the production was mounted with great splendor in Cairo the following year. In 1874 came the *Requiem Mass* in memory of Alessandro Manzoni, the novelist and patriot whom Verdi revered as a national artist.

Verdi found his ideal librettist in Arrigo Boito (1842–1918), himself a composer whose opera *Mefistofele* was popular in Italy for years. For their first collaboration they turned to Shakespeare. The result was *Otello* (1887), the apex of three hundred years of Italian lyric tragedy. After its opening night the seventy-four-year-old composer declared, "I feel as if I had fired my last cartridge. Music needs youthfulness of the senses, impetuous blood, fullness of life." He disproved his words when six years later, again with Boito, he completed *Falstaff* (1893). Fitting crown to the labors of a lifetime, this luminous comic opera ranks with Mozart's *Figaro,* Rossini's *Barber of Seville,* and Wagner's *Meistersinger.*

Aïda

In plot and music, grand opera strives for a style of lofty pathos, and exploits all the possibilities of the opera house for spectacular display. In *Aïda* Verdi produced what has been called "the perfect grand opera." The libretto by Antonio Ghislanzoni gives ample opportunity for picturesque scenery, ballets, processionals, and mass scenes; the exotic setting admirably frames the inner experiences of the protagonists. Character and situation are conceived in the grand manner.

The action is laid in Egypt in the time of the Pharaohs during a war with the Ethiopians. Aïda, princess of Ethiopia, has been captured and is slave to Amneris, the Egyptian princess. The latter is in love with the conquering general Radamès but rightly suspects that he loves Aïda rather than herself. Aïda's father Amonasro, the Ethiopian king, is brought into captivity, his identity unknown to his enemies. He still hopes to break the Egyptian power. Radamès, torn between his passion for the enemy princess

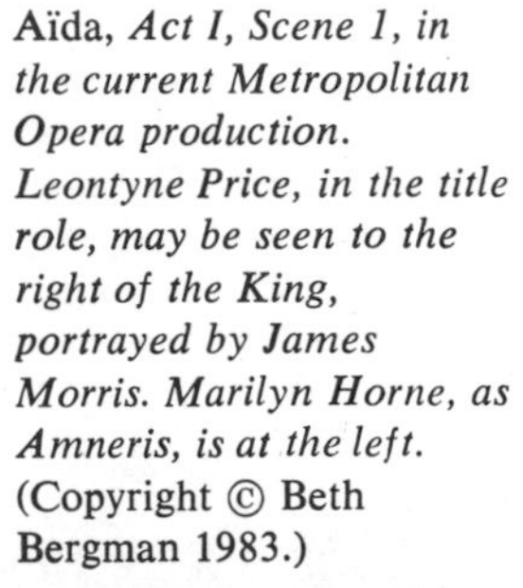

Aïda, *Act I, Scene 1, in the current Metropolitan Opera production. Leontyne Price, in the title role, may be seen to the right of the King, portrayed by James Morris. Marilyn Horne, as Amneris, is at the left.* (Copyright © Beth Bergman 1983.)

and devotion to his country, is induced to flee with Aïda and her father, but the plan is foiled by the jealous Amneris. Aïda and Amonasro make their escape, Radamès surrenders to the High Priest. He is sentenced to die by being entombed in a subterranean vault. Amonasro having been killed while leading the revolt, Aïda returns in time to make her way into the crypt. The lovers die together.

Act I

The Prelude is evolved from the lyrical phrase associated with Aïda throughout the opera. Act I is in two scenes, the first of which is laid in the

palace of the Pharaohs at Memphis. Radamès reveals his love in the famous aria *Celeste Aïda:*

The basic conflict is established in a dramatic trio in which Amneris voices her jealousy, Radamès fears she suspects the truth, and Aïda wavers between love and her devotion to the Ethiopian cause. The entrance of the King and court introduces the note of pomp that alternates throughout the play with the expression of personal emotion. Radamès is appointed leader of the Egyptian forces against the Ethiopians. Aïda, alone, echoes the words with which the Egyptians acclaimed Radamès, *Ritorna vincitor!* (Return a conqueror!), but realizes that his victory would spell her father's defeat and is cruelly torn between both loyalties.

The second scene takes place in the temple at Memphis. Priests pray to

the god Phtah. The music assumes an oriental coloring as priestesses perform a sacred dance. Radamès receives the consecrated arms and is blessed by the High Priest.

Act II

Act II opens in the royal palace. Moorish slaves perform a lively dance to distract the Princess. Aïda enters. A tense scene ensues between both women, at the climax of which Amneris in a jealous rage threatens to destroy her rival.

There follows the great scene at the gates of Thebes where the returning hero is welcomed by King, court, and populace. Trumpets sound the theme of the Triumphal March.

Ablaze with color and movement, this grand finale of Act II culminates in a stirring sextet. Amneris and the High Priest demand death for the prisoners. Amonasro, in chains, begs for mercy. The King, in a magnanimous mood, releases all the prisoners except Amonasro, and bestows the hand of his daughter upon the victorious general. Radamès and Aïda hide their consternation. This mass scene, with its interplay of personal drama and regal splendor, has come to represent everything we associate with grand opera.

Act III
SIDE 7/2 (E II)
SIDE 6/1 (S)

Act III is packed with action of the kind that Verdi needed for the full deployment of his powers. The scene—"Night: stars and a bright moon"—is on the banks of the Nile, unforgettably painted by a texture combining violin arpeggios and tremelos, pizzicatos, harmonics in the lower strings, and an exotic flute melody. We hear the voices of the priests in the temple of Isis: Amneris, accompanied by the High Priest, arrives to pray on the eve of her marriage.

CHORUS (*in the temple*)

O tu che sei d'Osiride Madre immortale e sposa, Diva che i casti palpiti Desti agli umani in cor: Soccorri a noi pietosa, Madre d'immenso amor. Soccorri a noi, soccorri a noi.	O thou who are the immortal Mother and bride of Osiris, Goddess who wakest the chaste Beating of human hearts; Succor us pityingly, Mother of immense love. Succor us, succor us. *From a boat that draws up to the bank, Amneris steps out, followed by Ramfis, some heavily veiled women, and guards.*

RAMFIS (*to Amneris*)

Vieni d'Iside al tempio: alla vigilia Delle tue nozze invoca Della Diva il favore. Iside legge de' mortali nel core; Ogni mistero degli umani A lei è noto.	Come to the Temple of Isis: on the eve Of your marriage implore The Goddess's favor. Isis reads the hearts of mortals; Every human mystery Is known to her.

AMNERIS

Sì, io pregherò che Radamès Mi doni tutto il suo cor, Come il mio cor a lui Sacro è per sempre . . .	Yes, I will pray that Radamès Give me all of his heart, As my heart is consecrated To him forever . . .

RAMFIS

Andiamo. Pregherai fino all'alba; Io sarò teco.	Let us go. You will pray until dawn; I will be with you.

They disappear within the temple; Aïda's theme in the orchestra announces her arrival. In an extended aria, *O patria mia,* into which an oboe interjects sorrowful phrases, she bemoans the fact that she will never see her native land again.

AÏDA

Qui Radamès verrà! . . .
Che vorrà dirmi? Io tremo! . . .
Ah! se tu vieni a recarmi,
O crudel, l'ultimo addio,
Del Nilo i cupi vortici
Mi daran tomba . . . e pace forse . . .
E pace forse e oblio.
Oh, patria mia, mai più,
Mai più ti rivedrò!
O cieli azzurri, a dolci aure native,
Dove sereno il mio mattin brillò . . .
O verdi colli . . . o profumate rive . . .
O patria mia, mai più ti rivedrò!
No . . . no . . . mai più, mai più!
O fresche valli, o queto asil beato
Che un dì promesso dall'amor mi fu . . .
Or che d'amore il sogno è dileguato . . .
O patria mia, non ti vedrò mai più!

Radamès will come here! . . .
What can he want to say to me? I tremble! . . .
Ah! If you are coming,
O cruel one, to bid me a last farewell,
The dark eddies of the Nile
Will give me a grave . . . and perhaps peace . . .
And perhaps peace and forgetfulness.
O my country, never,
Never shall I see you again!
O blue skies, O gentle native breezes,
Where the morning of my life serenely shone . . .
O green hills . . . O perfumed shores . . .
O my country, never shall I see you again!
No . . . no . . . never, never again!
O cool valleys, O calm, happy refuge
That love promised me one day . . .
Now that the dream of love has vanished . . .
O my country, I'll never see you again!

This aria is in two stanzas, the second ascending in a passionate phrase to the high C.

There follows a dramatic encounter with her father.

AÏDA

Ciel! mio padre!

Heaven! My father!

AMONASRO

A te grave cagion
M'adduce, Aïda.
Nulla sfugge al mio sguardo.
D'amor ti struggi per Radamès . . .
Ei t'ama . . . qui lo attendi.
Dei Faraon la figlia è tua rivale . . .
Razza infame, abborrita
E a noi fatale!

A serious matter brings me
To you, Aïda.
Nothing escapes my eyes.
You are consumed with love for Radamès . . .
He loves you . . . you are waiting for him here.
The daughter of the Pharaohs is your rival . . .
Infamous, detested race,
And fatal to us!

AÏDA

E in suo potere io sto! . . .
Io, d'Amonasro figlia! . . .

And I am in her power! . . .
I, daughter of Amonasro! . . .

AMONASRO

In poter di lei! . . . No! . . . se lo brami
La possente rival tu vincerai,
E patria, e trono, e amor,
Tutto tu avrai.

In her power! . . . No! . . . If you wish it
You will defeat your powerful rival,
And homeland, throne, love,
You will have them all.

Amonasro recalls the beauties of their homeland—one of the most expansive melodies in the opera:

AMONASRO

Rivedrai le foreste imbalsamate,
Le fresche valli, i nostri templi d'ôr! . . .

You will see again the aromatic forests,
The cool valleys, our golden temples! . . .

AÏDA *(ecstatic)*

Rivedrò le foreste imbalsamate! . . .
Le fresche valli . . . i nostri templi d'ôr!

I'll see again the aromatic forests! . . .
The cool valleys . . . our golden temples!

AMONASRO

Sposa felice a lui che amasti tanto,
Tripudii immensi ivi potrai gioir . . .

The happy bride of the man you love so,
Great bliss you will enjoy there . . .

AÏDA *(opening her heart)*

Un giorno solo di sì dolce incanto . . .
Un'ora, un'ora di tal gioia, e poi morir!

A single day of such sweet enchantment . . .
An hour, an hour of such joy, and then to die!

AMONASRO

Pur rammenti che a noi l'Egizio immite
Le case, i templi e l'are profanò . . .
Trasse in ceppi le vergini rapite . . .
Madri . . . vecchi . . . fanciulli ei trucidò.

Remember, then, that the cruel Egyptian
Profaned our houses, temples, and altars . . .
Dragged off in chains the captured maidens . . .
He slaughtered mothers . . . old men . . . children.

AÏDA

Ah! ben rammento quegl'infausti giorni
Rammento i lutti che il mio cor soffrì!
Deh! fate, o Numi, che per noi ritorni
L'alba invocata de' sereni dì.

Ah! Well I remember those unhappy days!
I remember the mourning my heart suffered!
Ah! Grant, O Gods, that the prayed-for dawn
Of peaceful days return to us.

Aïda echoes his nostalgic phrases. When she has been thoroughly beguiled by the vision of returning home, Amonasro reveals how it is to be realized: he orders her to find out from Radamès the plan of the forthcoming Egyptian campaign. He curses her when she refuses and his rage breaks her will. Amonasro conceals himself at the approach of Radamès.

AMONASRO

Non fia che tardi. In armi ora si desta
Il popol nostro; tutto è pronto già . . .
Vittoria avrem . . . Solo a saper mi resta
Qual sentier il nemico seguirà . . .

Let it not delay. Our people are rising
In arms now; now everything is ready . . .
We'll win the victory . . . I have only to learn
What road the enemy will take . . .

AÏDA

Chi scoprirlo potria? Chi mai?

Who could ever discover that? Who?

AMONASRO

Tu stessa!

You yourself!

AÏDA

Io? . . .

I? . . .

AMONASRO

Radamès so che qui attendi . . .

Ei t'ama . . . ei conduce gli Egizii . . .
Intendi? . . .

I know you are waiting here for Radamès . . .
(meaningfully)
He loves you . . . He is leading the Egyptians . . .
You understand? . . .

AÏDA

Orrore! Che mi consigli tu?
No! no! giammai!

Horror! What are you suggesting to me?
No! No! Never!

AMONASRO *(with savage vehemence)*

Su, dunque, sorgete,
Egizie coorti!
Col fuoco struggete
Le nostre città . . .
Spargete il terrore,
Le stragi, le morti . . .
Al vostro furore
Più freno non v'ha.

On, then! Arise,
Egyptian cohorts!
With fire destroy
Our cities . . .
Sow terror,
Slaughter, death . . .
There is no obstacle
To your fury now.

AÏDA

Ah! padre! . . . padre! . . .

Ah, Father! . . . Father! . . .

AMONASRO *(thrusting her away)*

Mia figlia ti chiami!

You call yourself my daughter!

AÏDA *(terrified and pleading)*

Pietà! pietà! pietà!

Have pity! Pity Pity!

AMONASRO

Flutti di sangue scorrono
Sulle città dei vinti . . .
Vedi? . . . dai negri vortici
Si levano gli estinti . . .
Ti additan essi e gridano:
"Per te la patria muor!"

Rivers of blood flow
Over the cities of the defeated . . .
You see? . . . From their black eddies
Rise the dead . . .
They point to you and shout:
"Because of you, the fatherland dies!"

AÏDA

Pietà! pietà! padre, pietà!

Pity! Pity! Father, have pity!

AMONASRO

Una larva orribile
Fra l'ombre a noi s'affaccia . . .
Trema! le scarni braccia
Sul capo tuo levò . . .

A horrible form
Comes toward us from the shadows . . .
Tremble! Its wasted arms
Are raised toward your head . . .

AÏDA

Ah! padre! . . . No! . . . Ah! . . .

Ah, father! . . . No! . . . Ah! . . .

AMONASRO

Tua madre ell'è . . . ravvisala . . .
Ti maledice . . .

It is your mother . . . recognize her . . .
She curses you . . .

AÏDA *(filled with terror)*

Ah, no! ah, no! . . . padre, pietà, pietà!	Ah, no! Ah, no! . . . Father, pity, pity!

AMONASRO *(rejecting her)*

Non sei mia figlia . . . Dei Faraoni tu sei la schiava!	You are not my daughter . . . You are the slave of the Pharaohs!

AÏDA *(with a cry)*

Ah, pietà! pietà!	Ah, pity! Pity! *(dragging herself painfully to her father's feet)*
Padre! . . . a costoro . . . schiava . . . non sor Non maledirmi . . . non imprecarmi . . . Ancor tua figlia potrai chiamarmi . . . Della mia patria degna sarò.	Father! . . . I am not . . . their . . . slave . . . Don't curse me . . . don't revile me . . . You can still call me your daughter . . . I shall be worthy of my country.

AMONASRO

Pensa che un popolo, vinto, straziato Per te soltanto risorger può . . .	Think, a martyred, defeated people Can rise again only through you . . .

AÏDA

Oh patria! oh patria . . . Quanto mi costi!	Oh, fatherland! . . . Fatherland . . . What you are costing me!

AMONASRO

Coraggio! ei giunge . . . Là tutto udrò . . .	Be brave! He is coming . . . There I will hear everything . . .

In the rapturous duet of the lovers, Aïda persuades Radamès that they can never find happiness within reach of the vengeful Amneris. He consents to flee with her, and divulges the plan of attack against Ethiopia. Amonasro appears and reveals himself as the enemy king; Radamès realizes that he has betrayed his country. At this point Amneris, who has come out of the temple, grasps the situation and accuses Radamès of treason. Amonasro, drawing his knife, rushes upon her, but Radamès interposes and saves her life. He implores Aïda and her father to save themselves. Soldiers appear before the temple and give pursuit. Radamès, lost, surrenders to the implacable High Priest.

Act IV

Act IV opens in a hall in the palace. Amneris orders Radamès to be brought before her. She tells him she can save him if he will renounce Aïda. He spurns her offer and is led back to his cell. Overcome with remorse, the Princess curses the jealousy that has brought ruin to her beloved and endless misery to herself. The priests are heard pronouncing the death sentence.

In the final scene we see the subterranean vault and the temple above it. As the fatal stone is lowered Radamès voices his hope that Aïda will never learn his fate. Then he discovers her in the crypt. Against the chorus of the priests in the temple above, the eerie chant of the priestesses, and the lamenting of Amneris, the lovers sing their final duet, a farewell to earth, a vision of eternal bliss to come:

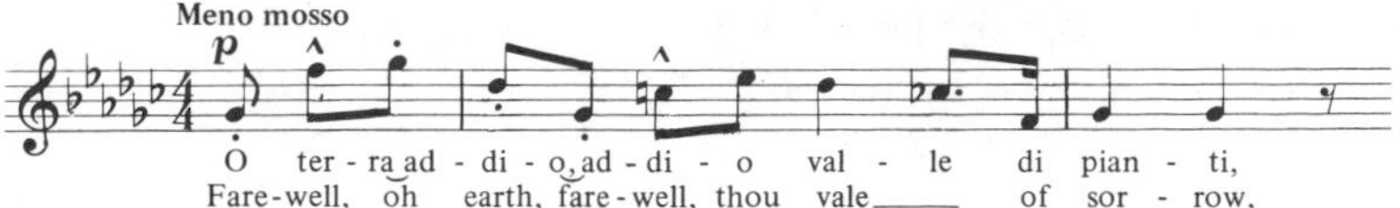

The creator of this majestic drama incarnated the soul of his nation. Boito recognized this when he saluted in Verdi "the genius of our race. He revealed to the world the ardor, the dash, the affection, the force of the Italian spirit."

37

Richard Wagner

"The error in the art genre of opera consists in the fact that a means of expression—music—has been made the object, while the object of expression—the drama—has been made the means."

Richard Wagner.

Richard Wagner (1813–83) looms as probably the single most important phenomenon in the artistic life of the latter half of the nineteenth century. Historians, not without justice, divide the period into "Before" and "After" Wagner. The course of post-Romantic music is unthinkable without the impact of this complex and fascinating figure.

His Life

Early years

He was born in Leipzig, son of a minor police official who died when Richard was still an infant. A year later the widow married Ludwig Geyer, a talented actor, playwright, and painter, who encouraged the artistic inclinations of his little stepson. The future composer was almost entirely self-taught; he had in all about six months of instruction in music theory. At twenty he abandoned his academic studies at the University of Leipzig and obtained a post as chorus master in a small opera house. In the next six years he gained practical experience conducting in provincial theaters. He married the actress Minna Planer when he was twenty-three, and produced his first operas—*Die Feen* (The Fairies; 1834) and *Das Liebesverbot* (The Ban on Love, after Shakespeare's *Measure for Measure;* 1836). As with all his later works, he wrote the librettos himself. He was in this way able to achieve a unity of the musical-dramatic conception beyond anything that had been known before.

While conducting at the theater in Riga he began a grand opera based on Bulwer-Lytton's historical novel *Rienzi, Last of the Tribunes*. This dealt with the heroic figure who in the fourteenth century led the Roman populace against the tyrannical nobles and perished in the struggle. With the first two acts of *Rienzi* under his arm he set out with Minna to conquer the world. His destination was Paris. But the world, then as now, was not easily conquered; Wagner failed to gain a foothold at the Paris Opéra.

The two and a half years spent in Paris (1839–42) were fruitful nevertheless. He completed *Rienzi* and produced *A Faust Overture,* the first works that bear the imprint of his genius. To keep alive he did hack work such as arranging popular arias for the cornet, and turned out a number of articles, essays, and semifictional sketches. He also wrote the poem and music of *The Flying Dutchman* (1841). All this despite poverty and daily discouragement.

Just as the harassed young musician was beginning to lose heart, a lucky turn rescued him from his plight: *Rienzi* was accepted by the Dresden Opera. Suddenly his native land was wreathed in the same rosy mist as had formerly enveloped Paris. He started for Dresden, gazed on the Rhine for the first time, and "with great tears in his eyes swore eternal fidelity to the German fatherland." *Rienzi,* which satisfied the taste of the public for historical grand opera, was extremely successful. As a result, its composer in his thirtieth year found himself appointed conductor to the King of Saxony.

With *The Flying Dutchman* Wagner had taken an important step from the drama of historical intrigue to the idealized folk legend. He continued on this path with the two dramas of the Dresden period–*Tannhäuser* (1843–45) and *Lohengrin* (1846–48)–which bring to its peak the German Romantic opera as established by his revered model, Carl Maria von Weber (1786–1826). The operas use subjects derived from medieval German epics, display a profound feeling for nature, employ the supernatural as an element of the drama, and glorify the German land and people. But the Dresden public was not prepared for *Tannhäuser.* They had come to see another *Rienzi* and were disappointed.

Wagner the revolutionary

A dedicated artist who made no concessions to popular taste, Wagner dreamed of achieving for opera something of the grandeur that had characterized the ancient Greek tragedy. To this task he addressed himself with the fanaticism of the born reformer. He was increasingly alienated from a frivolous court that regarded opera as an amusement; from the bureaucrats in control of the royal theaters, who thwarted his plans; and from Minna, his wife, who was delighted with their social position in Dresden and had no patience with what she considered his utopian schemes. He was persuaded that the theater was corrupt because the society around it was corrupt. His beliefs as an artist led him into the camp of those who, as the fateful year 1848 approached, dreamed of a revolution in Europe that would end the power of the reactionary rulers.

With reckless disregard of the consequences, Wagner appeared as speaker at a club of radical workingmen, and published two articles in an anarchist journal: "Man and Existing Society" and "The Revolution." "The present order," he wrote, "is inimical to the destiny and the rights of man. The old world is crumbling to ruin. A new world will be born from it!"

The revolution broke out in Dresden in May 1849. King and court fled. Troops dispatched by the King of Prussia crushed the insurrection. Wagner escaped to his friend Liszt at Weimar, where he learned that a warrant had been issued for his arrest. With the aid of Liszt he was spirited across the border and found refuge in Switzerland.

The Zurich years

In the eyes of the world—and of Minna—he was a ruined man; but Wagner did not in the least share this opinion. "It is impossible to describe my delight when I felt free at last—free from the world of torturing and ever unsatisfied desires, free from the distressing surroundings that had called forth such desires." He settled in Zurich and entered on the most productive period of his career. He had first to clarify his ideas to himself, and to prepare the public for the novel conceptions toward which he was finding his way. For four years he wrote no music, producing instead his most important literary works, *Art and Revolution, The Art Work of the Future,* and the two-volume *Opera and Drama* which sets forth his theories of the *music drama,* as he named his type of opera. He next proceeded to put theory into practice in the cycle of music dramas called *The Ring of the Nibelung.* He began with the poem on Siegfried's death that came to be known as *Götterdämmerung* (Dusk of the Gods). Realizing that the circumstances prior to this action required explaining, he added the drama on the hero's youth, *Siegfried.* The need for still further background led to a poetic drama concerning the hero's parents, *Die Walküre* (The Valkyrie). Finally, the trilogy was prefaced with *Das Rheingold* (The Rhinegold), a drama revolving about the curse of gold out of which the action stems.

The Ring

Although he wrote the four librettos in reverse order, he composed the operas in sequence. When he reached the second act of *Siegfried* he grew tired, as he said, "of heaping one silent score upon the other," and laid aside the gigantic task. There followed his two finest works—*Tristan und Isolde* (1857–59) and *Die Meistersinger von Nürnberg* (The Mastersingers of Nuremberg; 1862–67). The years following the completion of *Tristan* were the darkest of his life. The mighty scores accumulated in his drawer without hope of performance: Europe contained neither theater nor singers capable of presenting them. Wagner succumbed to Schopenhauer's philosophy of pessimism and renunciation—he who could never renounce anything. He was estranged from Minna, who failed utterly to understand his artistic aims. His involvement with a series of women who did understand him—but whose husbands objected—obtruded the *Tristan* situation into his own life and catapulted him into lonely despair. As he passed his fiftieth year, his indomitable will was broken at last. He contemplated in turn suicide, emigration to America, escape to the East.

At this juncture intervened a miraculous turn of events. An eighteen-year-old boy who was a passionate admirer of his music ascended the throne of Bavaria as Ludwig II. One of the young monarch's first acts was to summon the composer to Munich, where *Tristan* and *Meistersinger* were performed at last. The King commissioned him to complete the *Ring*, and Wagner took up the second act of *Siegfried* where he had left off a number of years before. A theater was planned especially for the presentation of his music dramas, which ultimately resulted in the festival playhouse at Bayreuth. And to crown his happiness he found, to share his empire, a woman equal to him in will and courage—Cosima, the daughter of his old friend Liszt. For the last time the *Tristan* pattern thrust itself upon him. Cosima was the wife of his fervent disciple, the conductor Hans von Bülow. She left her husband and children in order to join her life with Wagner's. They were married some years later, after Minna's death.

Bayreuth

The Wagnerian gospel spread across Europe, a new art-religion. Wagner societies throughout the world gathered funds to raise the temple at Bayreuth. The radical of 1848 found himself, after the Franco-Prussian War, the national artist of Bismarck's German Empire. The *Ring* cycle was completed in 1874, twenty-six years after Wagner had begun it, and the four dramas were presented to worshipful audiences at the first Bayreuth festival in 1876.

One task remained. To make good the financial deficit of the festival the master undertook his last work, *Parsifal* (1877–82), a "consecrational festival drama" based on the legend of the Holy Grail. He finished it as he approached seventy. He died shortly after, in every sense a conqueror, and was buried at Bayreuth.

His Music

Wagner gave shape to the desire of the Romantic era for the closest possible connection between music and dramatic expression; and beyond that, for the closest connection between music and life. "Every bar of dramatic music," he maintained, "is justified only by the fact that it explains something in the action or in the character of the actor."

He did away with the old "number" opera with its arias, duets, ensembles, choruses, and ballets. His aim was a continuous tissue of melody that would never allow the emotions to cool. This meant abandoning the old distinction between recitative and aria. He evolved instead an "endless melody" that was molded to the natural inflections of the German language, more melodious than traditional recitative, more flexible and free than traditional aria.

The focal point of Wagnerian music drama, however, is not the melody but the orchestra. Here is the nub of his operatic reform. He developed a type of symphonic opera as native to the German genius as vocal opera is to the Italian. The orchestra is the unifying principle of his music drama. It is both participant and ideal spectator; it remembers, prophesies, reveals, comments. The orchestra floods the action, the characters, and the audience in a torrent of sound that incarnates the sensuous ideal of the Romantic era.

Leitmotifs

The orchestral tissue is fashioned out of concise themes, the *leitmotifs,* or "leading motives"–Wagner called them basic themes–that recur throughout the work, undergoing variation and development even as the themes and motives of a symphony. The leitmotifs carry specific meanings, like the "fixed idea" of Berlioz or the germ theme in a symphonic poem of Liszt. They have an uncanny power of suggesting in a few strokes a person, an emotion, or an idea; an object–the gold, the ring, the sword; or a landscape–the Rhine, Valhalla, the lonely shore of Tristan's home. Through a process of continual transformation the leitmotifs trace the course of the drama, the changes in the characters, their experiences and memories, their thoughts and hidden desires. As the leitmotifs accumulate layer upon layer of meaning, they themselves become characters in the drama, symbols of the relentless process of growth and decay that rules the destinies of gods and heroes.

Harmonic innovations

Wagner's musical language was based on chromatic harmony, which he pushed to its then farthermost limits. Chromatic dissonance imparts to Wagner's music its restless, intensely emotional quality. Never before had the unstable tone combinations been used so eloquently to portray states of soul. The active chord (Dominant) seeking resolution in the chord of rest (Tonic) became in Wagner's hands the most romantic of symbols: the lonely man–Flying Dutchman, Lohengrin, Siegmund, Tristan–seeking redemption through love, the love of the ideal woman, whether Senta or Elsa, Sieglinde or Isolde.

Tristan und Isolde

For unity of mood, sustained inspiration, and intensity of feeling *Tristan und Isolde* is the most perfectly realized of Wagner's lyric tragedies. Certainly no more eloquent tribute has ever been offered to consuming passion.

Isolde, proud princess of Ireland, has been promised in marriage to the elderly King Mark of Cornwall. Tristan, the King's nephew and first knight of his court, is sent to bring her to her new home. They had met before when Tristan fought against her country. What had begun as hate, wounded pride, and desire for revenge turns to overpowering love.

Prelude
SIDE 8/1 (E II)

The Prelude to the drama depicts the passion that enmeshes them. This extraordinary tone poem evolves from a leitmotif that recurs throughout the opera. Used always to suggest the yearning, tenderness, and rapture of the lovers, the famous progression is the epitome of chromatic–that is, romantic–harmony. Notice how the voices move by half step along the chromatic scale:

The arrival of Tristan. Act I of the current Metropolitan Opera production of Tristan und Isolde. (Copyright © Beth Bergman 1983.)

Prelude, in Wagner's use of the term, indicates a freer and more flexible form than overture. It is more in the character of a fantasy, lyric rather than dramatic, contemplative rather than narrative. This Prelude comes as close as any piece ever did to those twin goals of musical Romanticism: intoxication and ecstasy.

Love Duet
SIDE 8/2 (E II)
SIDE 6/2 (S)

The *Love Duet* is from Act II, which takes place outside King Mark's castle. The King has left, ostensibly on a hunt. Tristan and Isolde meet in the garden, while her confidante Brangäne stands watch in the tower. The scene between them is one of the high points of Wagnerian drama. The lovers hymn the night:

TRISTAN AND ISOLDE

O sink' hernieder,	Descend upon us,
Nacht der Liebe,	night of love,
gib Vergessen,	let me forget
dass ich lebe;	that I still live;
nimm mich auf	take me up
in deinen Schoss,	into your womb,
löse von	release me
der Welt mich los!	from the world!
Verloschen nun	Extinguished now is
die letzte Leuchte;	the last glimmer;
was wir dachten,	what we thought
was uns deuchte,	and what we imagined,
all' Gedenken,	all remembering,
all' Gemahnen,	all reminding,
heil'ger Dämm'rung	holy twilight's
hehres Ahnen	brightest omen
löscht des Wähnens Graus	quenches delusion's terror,
welterlösend aus.	redeeming the world.
Barg im Busen	In our breasts
uns sich die Sonne,	the sun is hidden,
leuchten lachend	smilingly shine
Sterne der Wonne.	stars of wonder.
Von deinem Zauber	By your magic
sanft umsponnen,	gently enwrapped,
vor deinen Augen	before your eyes
süss zerronnen,	sweetly melting,
Herz an Herz dir,	heart to your heart,
Mund an Mund,	mouth to mouth,
Eines Atems	from single breaths
einzger Bund;—	bound into one;
bricht mein Blick sich	my sight gives way
wonnerblindet,	blinded by wonder,
erbleicht die Welt	the world fades away
mit ihrem Blenden:	with its deception;

die uns der Tag
trügend erhellt,
zu täuschendem Wahn
entgegengestellt,
selbst—dann
bin ich die Welt,
wonne-hehrstes Weben,
liebe-heiligstes Leben,
nie-wieder-Erwachens
wahnlos
hold bewusster Wünsch.

to all that the day
deceitfully lit for us,
to cheating madness
defiantly opposed,
myself, then,
I am the world,
wonder-exalted weaving,
love-holiest living,
never-again-to-awaken,
free from illusion,
sweetly conscious desire.

From the tower, the warning voice of Brangäne floats down:

BRANGÄNE

Einsam wachend
in der Nacht,
wem der Traum
der Liebe lacht,
hab' der Einen
Ruf in Acht,
die den Schläfern
Schlimmes ahnt,
bange zum
Erwachen mahnt.
Habet acht!
Habet acht!
Bald entweicht die Nacht.

Alone I watch
in the night,
you on whom
love's dream smiles,
attend to the call
of one who
foresees ill
for the sleepers,
and anxiously
warns them to awake.
Take care!
Take care!
Soon the night will pass.

Day represents the loathed reality that stands between them, the pretense and hopelessness of their worldly existence. Night is the symbol of their inner life—the real life. In this scene is consummated the great romantic theme of the individual estranged from society. Love is the dream and the search, the longing for oblivion. Since happiness is not to be attained in life, love leads beyond its confines, becoming the ultimate escape. Thus the impulse that generates life is transformed, by a magnificently romantic gesture, into the self-destroying passion whose fulfillment is death.

At the high point of the Duet, King and retinue burst in upon the lovers. Tristan has been betrayed by his false friend Melot. He takes leave of Isolde and in the ensuing scuffle is mortally wounded. The doom they knew was inescapable is now upon them.

Act III

Act III is laid before Tristan's castle in Brittany, where he has been brought by his faithful servant Kurvenal. In his delirium he fancies himself back in the garden with Isolde. She arrives in time to see him die. The opera culminates in her hymn to love and death, the *Liebestod*. She envisions herself united with Tristan, the obstacles that kept them apart in life surmounted at last. Transfigured, she sinks lifeless on Tristan's body.

A painting by Max Brückner of his stage design for Act III of the 1886 production of Tristan und Isolde. (Richard Wagner-Gedenkstätte, Bayreuth.)

The *Love Death* follows a basic design in music. Beginning softly and from a low pitch, it builds up in a steadily mounting line to the torrential

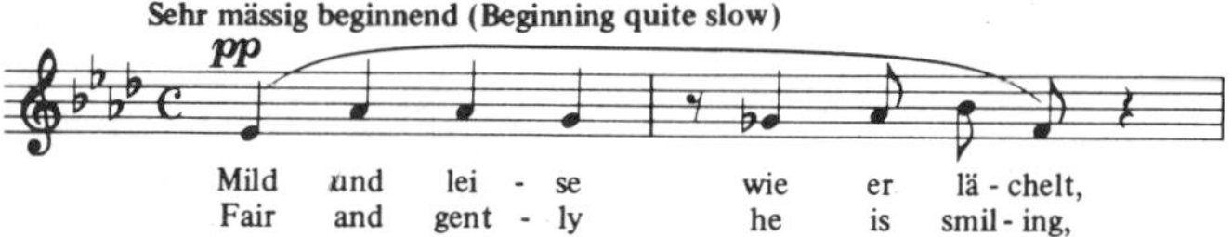

climax, whence it subsides. The aria is fashioned from a motive first heard during the love scene in Act II. There it was cruelly interrupted by the arrival of the King. Now, ascending wave upon wave, it achieves its final resolution.

Wagner satisfied the need of an era for sensuous beauty, for the heroic, the mystical, the grandiose. He takes his place in history as the most commanding figure of the Romantic period: a master whose achievements have become part and parcel of our musical heritage.

38

Georges Bizet

"The composer gives the best of himself to the making of a work. He believes, doubts, enthuses, despairs, rejoices, and suffers in turn."

Blazing with color and passion, *Carmen* is one of those rare works which enjoy the admiration of musicians no less than that of a worldwide public. It exemplifies the Gallic genius at its best.

His Life

Georges Bizet.

Georges Bizet (1838–75) was born and raised in Paris. A student at the Conservatory, in his twentieth year he won the highest award of the school, the Prix de Rome, which made possible a three-year stay in the Italian capital. The rest of his career was passed in his native city. The works of his youth were followed by three operas that display the composer's power of evoking exotic atmosphere. *Les Pêcheurs de perles* (The Pearl Fishers; 1863) is a drama of love and ritual in Ceylon. Four years later came *La Jolie Fille de Perth* (The Fair Maid of Perth, after Walter Scott's novel), which takes place in a romanticized Scotland. *Djamileh* (1872) is laid in Cairo. Although none of these was an overwhelming success, they established Bizet's reputation as a composer to be reckoned with.

The greater Bizet emerges in the incidental music to Alphonse Daudet's somber drama *L'Arlésienne* (The Woman of Arles; 1872). He revealed himself here as the master of a limpid style with a tenderness all his own. Bizet was now offered the libretto that Meilhac and Halévy had fashioned from Prosper Mérimée's celebrated story of Gypsy life and love. He was ready for his appointed task. There resulted the greatest French opera of the century.

Mérimée's tale belonged to a new type of literature dealing with elemental beings and passions, seeking to bring literature closer to the realities of life. Mérimée's Gypsies, smugglers, and brigands were depicted with an honesty that heralded the new realism. The opera softened the naked fury of the original story. But enough remained to disturb the audience that assembled for the opening night on the third of March, 1875. The Opéra-Comique was a "family theater" where the bourgeois of Paris brought their wives and marriageable daughters. Passion on the stage was acceptable if it concerned kings and duchesses long dead; Carmen and her unsavory companions were too close for comfort.

The opera was not the fiasco that popular legend makes it out to have been. It did fail, incomprehensibly, to conquer its first audience. However, the rumor that the piece was not quite respectable helped give it a run of thirty-seven performances in the next three months, an average of three a week. In addition the manager offered the composer and his liberettists a contract for their next work. The failure of *Carmen* was only in Bizet's mind. He had put every ounce of his genius into the score. Its reception was a bitter disappointment. His delicate constitution, worn out by months of rehearsals and by the emotional tension that had attended the production, was ill-prepared to take the blow. Exactly three months after the premiere he succumbed to a heart-attack, at the age of thirty-seven. His death came just when he had found his mature style.

The work was immediately dropped by the Opéra-Comique. Yet within three years it had made its way to Vienna and Brussels, London and New York. Five years later it returned to Paris, was received rapturously, and embarked on its fabulously successful career. Today it is one of the best-loved operas of the world.

Carmen

The power of this lyric drama stems from the impact with which it projects love, hate, desire. The story line follows one of the most compelling themes literature has to offer—the disintegration of a personality. The action is swift and unfaltering as the characters are carried step by step to their doom. The libretto is a tightly knit affair revolving around a few key words—love, fate, death, nevermore—all of them eminently singable. Carmen dominates the action, by turn tender, cruel, seductive, imperious, sensual, arch. She remains one of the great characters of opera. As for Don José, the simple soldier who is brought to ruin through his obsessive love, he is caught in a web not of his making, in which he is held by the deepest forces of his nature. Escamillo, the bullfighter who supplants José in Carmen's fickle affections, is properly vain and swaggering. Micaela, José's childhood sweetheart who seeks in vain to lead him back to the wholesome life of his village, is the incarnation of goodness and devotion. (As frequently happens, she comes off less vividly than the questionable characters.) These personages and their conflicts are realized on the highest level of operatic art. They come to life through the music; they are unthinkable without it.

Prelude

The Prelude foreshadows the contrasting moods of the opera. The opening theme is the one that returns in the final scene outside the bull ring at Seville: a melody gay, external, charged with excitement and pleasure-seeking, its character accentuated by the pounding rhythm and the bright orchestration.

There follows the suave melody of the *Toreador Song*.

Against this is posed the motive of Fate. Beneath a tremolo on the strings is heard the ominous phrase, played by clarinet, bassoon, trumpet, and cellos, that runs like a dark thread through the score:

The curtain rises on a square in Seville. Soldiers loiter before the guard house. Micaela appears, inquiring for Don José. Abashed by the flirtatious young men, she withdraws. A trumpet in the distance announces the changing of the guard. The relieving company, led by Lieutenant

Act I

Zuniga and Corporal Don José, is preceded by a crowd of urchins who enter to the strains of a captivating march. The clock strikes twelve. The girls emerge from the cigarette factory, which attracts the young blades of Seville. Carmen's entrance is heralded by a rhythmic transformation of the Fate motive.

Her character is established at once by the *Habanera,* based on a teasing tango rhythm. Bizet rewrote it thirteen times before he was satisfied. "Love is fickle and wild and free, A bird that none may ever tame. . . . If you love me not, I love you. And if I love–beware!" The refrain is enhanced by the emphasis of the chorus on the crucial word–"l'amour."

Don José, waiting for Micaela to return, is absorbed in his thoughts. Piqued by his indifference, Carmen takes the flower from her dress and throws it to him. José, bewildered, picks it up. The orchestra sounds the motive of Fate. Meanwhile, the clock having struck in the factory, the girls withdraw. Micaela enters with a letter from José's mother. The ensuing duet establishes José and Micaela as the "good people" in the play.

Micaela's exit is followed by a quarrel in the factory between Carmen and another girl. At once the stage is filled with two factions of chattering women. Carmen is led in, insolent, self-assured. She tries to strike one of the women who demands that she be sent to jail. Zuniga and his men go off to obtain an order for her arrest. Carmen, hands tied behind her back, is left in the custody of José.

She loses no time in exerting her wiles. "Near the ramparts of Seville, at the inn of my friend Lillas Pastia, I shall soon dance the gay seguidilla."

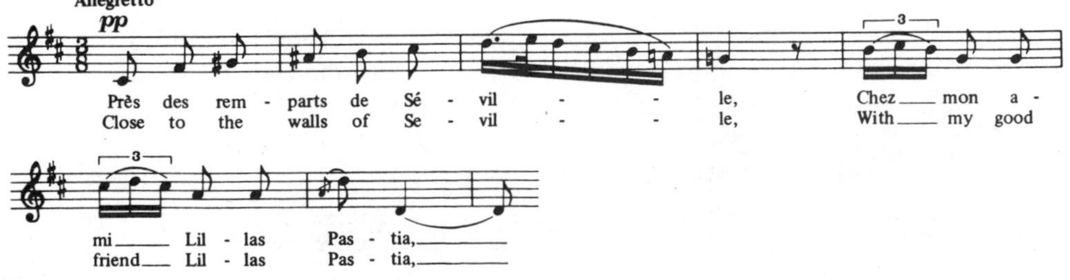

Carmen, *Act II. In Lillas Pastia's tavern, Carmen (Grace Bumbry) celebrates the joys of gypsy life.*

What is more, she will dance it with him. Only two steps are necessary for them to achieve this delightful prospect: that he set her free and that he join her there. José manfully resists her allurements, but the outcome is assured. By the time the lieutenant returns, the rope around Carmen's wrists has been loosened. She is marched off to jail guarded by José. At the bridge, as prearranged, she knocks him down and escapes.

Act II

The Entr'acte (Prelude to the second act) opens with a lonely melody, Moorish in coloring, played by two bassoons accompanied by strings and drum. The curtain rises on Lillas Pastia's tavern. Carmen's song celebrates the joys of Gypsy life. She is joined in the refrain by her friends Mercedes and Frasquita.

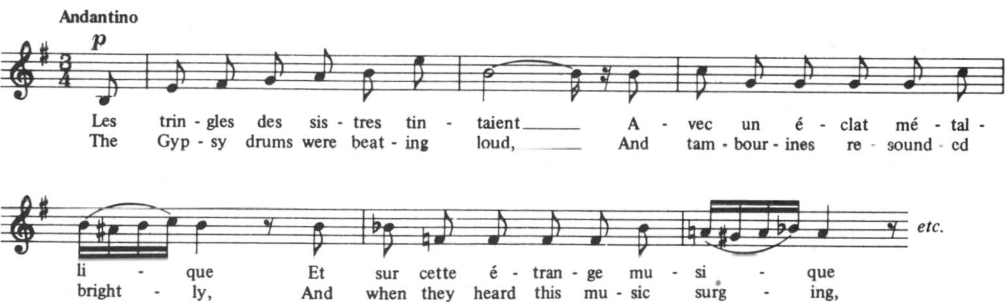

Lieutenant Zuniga presses his attentions on Carmen. She learns from him that José, who received two months in jail for helping her escape, has just been set free. Escamillo arrives, his musical portrait being given by the swaggering opening of the *Toreador Song*.

He is taken with Carmen, which does not in the slightest please Lieutenant Zuniga. Both men leave, the lieutenant promising to return.

The Quintet follows, a brilliant ensemble number in which two of the smugglers invite Carmen and her friends to join them in a little matter of contraband that evening. Mercedes and Frasquita accept with delight. Carmen declines. Her reason? She awaits Don José. His voice is heard in the distance, singing the plaintive melody of the Entr'acte. The Gypsies leave, suggesting that Carmen recruit her new lover into the smugglers' band.

The scene between her and José covers a wide range of emotions. She begins by dancing for him, accompanying herself on the castanets. José is enchanted. When the retreat sounds from the distant barracks he prepares to leave. Carmen, infuriated at a lover who puts duty above her, mocks him as a dullard and bids him go. José, sadly drawing from his pocket the flower he has treasured these many weeks, sings an aria that is a favorite: "Here is the flower that you threw me, I kept it still in my dark cell. In dead of night I saw your face. I had but one desire, one hope—to see you once again."

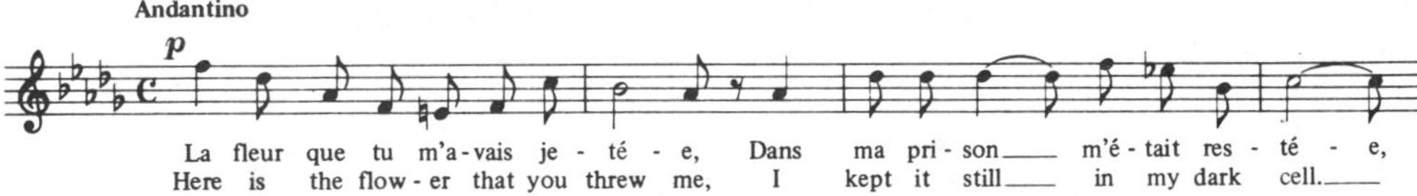

Carmen, realizing her power over him, decides to lure José into the smugglers' band. She holds out to him the attractions of a life of freedom. José implores her not to tempt him. He begins to realize that he must renounce her. At this point there is a knocking at the door. Lieutenant Zuniga demands admittance, breaks in, and scoffs at Carmen for taking a common solider when she can have an officer. He orders José to leave. The latter, mad with jealousy, draws his saber. The two men fight and are separated by the Gypsies. Zuniga is hustled out by Carmen's friends. For José the die is cast: he has attacked an officer and may return no more to the life he knew. The smugglers welcome the deserter into their midst with a rousing finale that hails the freedom of their lawless life.

Act III

The Prelude to the third act affords a breathing spell in the unfolding tragedy. A flute solo over harp accompaniment evokes the quietude of a mountain fastness. The curtain rises on the hideout of the smugglers, who enter to an eerie march. Don José gloomily reflects on his situation. His mother still thinks him an honest man. If she but knew. Carmen, already tired of him, suggests that perhaps he had better return to his village. They quarrel. The orchestra comments with the motive of Fate.

The *Card Trio* is one of the highlights of the opera. Frasquita and Mercedes tell their fortunes. The cards promise each what her heart desires—to Frasquita a handsome young lover, to Mercedes a rich old husband who will die and leave her his money. Carmen cuts the cards and draws the ace of spades. "Death! I've read it well. First I, then he." In a monologue of great pathos she accepts her fate. "In vain you shun the answer that you dread, in vain you cut the cards. To no avail—the cards remain sincere. . . . Though you try twenty times, the pitiless cards repeat—Death!" One must hear it in the opera house to realize the explosive power of that word "mort."

There follows the famous aria of Micaela, who comes seeking José hoping still to rescue him from his madness. The horn adds romantic luster to the melody.

Escamillo arrives, eager to join Carmen. A fight develops between him and the jealous José. The men draw knives but are separated. José learns from Micaela that his mother is dying and is persuaded to leave with her. "We will meet again!" he warns Carmen as the motive of Fate is heard.

Act IV

The Prelude to the last act, with its somber melody on the oboe above an accompaniment of pizzicato strings and tambourine, has a quality of foreboding. The curtain goes up on a brilliant scene outside the arena in Seville. The crowd hails the various groups of bullfighters who march in to the blatant tune of the Overture. Finally Escamillo enters, with a radiant Carmen on his arm. There is a tender exchange between them. The crowd accompanies him into the ring. Carmen remains to face José.

The encounter is taut, volcanic. Each is driven by the basic law of his nature: José cannot give up his love, she cannot surrender her freedom. He entreats her to go with him—there is still time to begin anew. She refuses. "Then you love me no more?" "No, I love you no more." "But I, Carmen, I love you still!" He reaches the breaking point against the jubilant strains of the chorus in the arena. "For the last time, you fiend, will you come with me?" "No!" He stabs her as the *Toreador Song* rises from the crowd pouring out of the arena. José, dazed, kneels beside her body. The orchestra sounds the motive of Fate.

It was a German philosopher who, awakening from the intoxication of Wagnerian music drama, discovered in *Carmen* the ideal lyric tragedy. "It is necessary to Mediterraneanize music!" Nietzsche declared in one of the most eloquent tributes ever penned to a work of art. "I envy Bizet for having had the courage of this sensitiveness–this southern, tawny, sunburnt sensitiveness–which hitherto in the music of European culture had found no means of expression. I know of no case in which the tragic irony that constitutes the kernel of love is expressed with such severity or in so terrible a formula as in the last cry of Don José: 'Yes, it is I who killed her–Ah, my adored Carmen!' "

39

Modest Musorgsky

"The artist believes in the future because he lives in it."

Modest Musorgsky. Portrait by Ilya Repin.

His Life

The most unmistakably Russian of composers, Modest Musorgsky (1839–81) was born in the town of Karevo in the province of Pskov. He prepared for a military career, in accordance with the family tradition, and was commissioned an officer in a fashionable regiment of Guards. At eighteen he came under the influence of a group of young musicians whose dream it was to found a Russian national school. With him as one of their number they formed "The Mighty Five," as an admiring critic named them. Their leader was Mily Balakirev (1837–1910), a self-taught composer who persuaded his four disciples–Alexander Borodin (1834–87), *César Cui* (1835–1918), Nikolai Rimsky-Korsakov (1844–1908), and Musorgsky–that they had no need of exercises in German counterpoint to give expression to the Russian soul.

As his talents developed, the young officer found his duties irksome and decided to withdraw from the military so that he could devote his life to music. His young friends had not yet accepted music as a full-time profession; Borodin was studying medicine, Cui was preparing for his later career as an expert on military fortification, and Rimsky-Korsakov was being trained as a naval officer. They counseled prudence. But Musorgsky, an ardent youth confident of his powers, was not to be dissuaded. At the age of twenty-two he resigned his commission.

History intervened at this point. The emancipation of the serfs in 1861 proved disastrous to the smaller landowners. Instead of being free to devote himself to art, the young aristocrat was obliged to seek employment. He established himself in St. Petersburg, where a post at the Ministry of Transport gave him a modest subsistence. Evenings were devoted to reading, musical sessions with his four comrades, and his first attempts at composition.

There asserted itself almost immediately a personality that would accept neither tradition nor guidance. He was one of those who must find their own path. His path led to an uncompromisingly realistic approach to life and art: "To trace the finest traits in man's nature and in the mass of humanity, digging resolutely through these unexplored regions and conquering them—that is the true mission of the artist!" How close in spirit to the credo of Dostoevsky, that other interpreter of "the insulted and the injured": "My function is to portray the soul of man in all its profundity."

The background of Boris Godunov

Musorgsky at twenty-nine was ready for the great task of his life. In *Boris Godunov* he found a worthy theme out of his country's past. He fashioned the libretto himself, after Pushkin's drama and the old chronicles. The years spent in the composition of this drama were the happiest he was ever to know. He was sustained by the fellowship of the "Mighty Five" and was especially close to Rimsky-Korsakov. When *Boris* was submitted to the Imperial Opera, it was rejected on the ground that it lacked a leading woman's part. Musorgsky revised the work, adding the role of Marina. Finally all obstacles were overcome and the opera was presented in 1874. The critics damned it but the public was impressed. Nor were its political implications lost on the young intelligentsia, at that time seething with unrest under the tsarist regime. The choruses depicting the revolt against Tsar Boris were soon heard on the streets of St. Petersburg. Despite its success—or because of it—the opera was regarded with suspicion by the censor and, it was rumored, aroused the displeasure of the imperial family. In the following season it was presented with drastic cuts and ultimately dropped from the repertory.

The withdrawal of *Boris* ushered in the bitter period of Musorgsky's life. In the six years that remained to him he moved ever further from his comrades of the "Five." He had outgrown his admiration for Balakirev. Cui, by now an influential critic, had betrayed him by attacking *Boris*. Rimsky and Borodin, he felt, had sold out for success, capitulating to the academic spirit which he regarded as the enemy of true art. He remained alone, a rebel to the end.

But the lonely struggle demanded sterner stuff than he was made of. Moods of exuberant belief in himself alternated with periods of depression. Poverty, lack of recognition, and the drudgery of his clerical post played their part. His need for escape revived a craving for stimulants that he had kept more or less under control since early manhood. Increasingly his life lost its direction and followed the erratic course of the alcoholic.

To these years of despair belong his greatest songs, the cycles *Sunless* and the *Songs and Dances of Death.* The major work of this period was the national opera *Khovanshtchina,* on his own libretto, dealing with the revolt of the imperial bodyguard against Peter the Great. But the creative force that had carried him through *Boris* was spent. He worked at this somber drama until his death, refashioning it again and again, but left it unfinished.

As his former comrades rose higher in the social scale, Musorgsky sank lower. He who since childhood had identified himself with the humble of the earth now joined their ranks. The arc was complete, from the debonair young officer of the Guards to the slovenly tragic figure of Repin's famous portrait. Yet the spirit of the fighter remained with him to the end. In the last year of his life, when his friends had abandoned all hope of saving him, he still was able to write, "My motto remains unchanged. 'Boldly on! Forward to new shores!' . . . To seek untiringly, fearlessly, and without confusion, and to enter with firm step into the promised land–there's a great and beautiful task! One must give oneself wholly to mankind."

To give himself wholly he left his post and tried to support himself by accompanying singers. He was soon destitute. While attending a musical evening he collapsed and was placed in a hospital, suffering from delirium tremens. His comrades rallied to his side. But he died–as he had lived–alone, on his forty-second birthday, crying out, "All is ended. Ah, how wretched I am!"

Boris Godunov

In *Boris Godunov* (first version 1868–69, second version 1871–72) Musorgsky gave his country its great national drama. It has been said that the real hero of the opera is the Russian people. In the magnificent choral tableaux we encounter, instead of the conventional operatic chorus, vivid types drawn from the peasantry. The drama (in four acts with a prologue), which covers the years 1598–1605, centers about the guilt of a usurper. Boris Godunov, having contrived the murder of the young Tsarevich Dmitri, rightful heir to the throne, has himself proclaimed Tsar. As the years pass he is tormented by remorse. An adventurous young monk named Gregory resolves to pass himself off as the murdered Dmitri. He escapes to the Lithuanian frontier and proclaims himself heir to the throne. Welcomed by the Polish nobility who are opposed to Boris, he falls in love with the haughty Marina, daughter of the noble house of Mnishek. Marina knows that his claims are false, but she sees in him a means of becoming Empress and encourages him to aspire to her hand. The Pretender, back in Russia, rallies to his standard all who are discontented with Boris's rule. Boris, a prey to his guilt, is obsessed by hallucinations in which he sees the ghost of the murdered

The Coronation Scene from Boris Godunov, *in which the majesty of tone and movement appropriate to a national drama is captured. Bolshoi Theater production.*

boy advancing toward him. He dies as the victorious Gregory-Dmitri marches on the Kremlin.

The Prologue, which takes place some years before the drama proper, consists of two great choral scenes. In the first the people gather before a monastery outside Moscow imploring Boris to accept the crown. They are egged on by a police officer who threatens them for not evincing sufficient enthusiasm. There follows the *Coronation Scene,* in which Musorgsky captures the majesty of tone and movement appropriate to a national drama. The bells of the Kremlin peal as the boyars proceed into the cathedral. The people sing a hymn of praise based on an ancient folk tune.

Act I Scene 1

In the first scene of Act I the aged monk Pimen, alone in his cell, works through the night on his chronicle, "that future generations of the Faithful may know the fateful story of their land." (This line was chosen by Musorgsky's friends to be carved on his tomb.) Gregory, awaking from a troubled dream in which he saw himself raised above all the world, muses on the usurper in the Kremlin. None dares remind Boris of the murdered child, yet in this cell an unknown hermit records the terrible truth. The powerful archaic harmonies that Musorgsky loved evoke a distant, troubled time.

Scene 2

The second scene takes place in an inn on the Lithuanian frontier. Song is interspersed with action. The proprietress of the inn, as she darns, sings the *Song of the Drake*. Missail and Varlaam, two vagabonds masquerading as mendicant friars, arrive at the inn. With them is Gregory, anxious to cross the frontier. Warmed by the good woman's wine, Varlaam sings a ballad in old folk style of how Tsar Ivan smote the Tartars at Kazan. When the patrol arrives seeking the runaway monk, Gregory manages to divert their suspicion to Varlaam and makes his escape.

Act II

The second act, laid in the royal apartment in the Kremlin, sets off lyric song forms against dramatic recitative. Xenia, daughter of Boris, mourns her betrothed who has fallen in battle. To distract her the old nurse—the familiar Mamka of Russian tradition—sings the *Song of the Gnat*. Boris's young son Feodor responds with a "clapping song"—a worthy companion to Musorgsky's *Songs of Childhood*. Counterposed to these is the great monologue of the guilt-ridden Tsar. "I am supreme in power . . . and yet all happiness eludes my tortured soul."

The scene in which the agonized Tsar struggles with his hallucination is on the level of Shakespearean tragedy. "O conscience, thou art cruel. . . ." In his horror Boris becomes aware of the supreme irony: he, the all-powerful, is helpless against his fears.

Act III
Scene 1

Act III opens in the castle of the Mnisheks in Poland. Marina is characterized from the start—beautiful, proud, calculating. She dismisses the song of her maidens in praise of her beauty; for her, only songs of brave deeds. The rhythms of mazurka and polonaise are associated with the princess throughout. She has a short and violent encounter with the Jesuit Rangoni, who orders her to gain the throne through the Pretender in order to lead Russia back to the true faith.

Scene 2

The second scene takes place in the garden where Gregory, tormented by love, awaits her. Marina and her guests issue from the castle to the strains of a spirited polonaise. The ensuing love scene is admirable for its

characterization of Gregory and Marina, the dramatic interplay between them, and the love melody—which makes a capital effect in the theater:

Act IV
Scene 1

Act IV opens outside a convent near Moscow. The people await Boris and his retinue. They entreat the Tsar for bread; his boyars distribute alms. The village idiot, tormented by boys, appeals to Boris: "These boys took my only coin away. Why don't you have them murdered, as long ago you murdered our Tsarevich!" The courtiers would arrest the simpleton; but Boris, shaken, restrains them. "Go, pray for your Tsar, poor idiot. . . ." The second scene takes place in the throne room of the Kremlin. Boris, half crazed by guilt, appears before the Council of Boyars. The old monk Pimen tells of a vision in which he heard the voice of the murdered Dmitri. Boris, overcome, falls into the arms of the boyars. Feeling his end approach, he calls for his son. The boyars coldly eye the dying monarch as he takes leave of the boy. Musorgsky's recitative rises to the heights of lyric tragedy. "O bitter death! How cruel is thy clutch. Not yet, not yet–I still am Tsar! Death, be merciful. . . ."

Scene 2

Scene 3

The closing scene is set in a forest clearing. Peasants revolting against Boris's authority bind one of his noblemen and make sport of him. The Pretender appears at the head of his army and is acclaimed by the people. All leave save the village idiot who, seated on a stone, sings to himself. "Flow, silent tears, flow, bitter tears . . . Weep, Russian folk. Weep, hungry folk." It is a surpassingly eloquent ending. The curtain falls as Musorgsky–crowning audacity!–ends his work on an incomplete cadence.

The creator of this profound drama of conscience was forgotten by his countrymen for several decades after his death. It was in the Paris of the nineties that his work first came to be understood. Musicians of a new generation, among them Debussy and Ravel, discovered in him the first exponent of the modern temper, and found in his audacious harmonies an inspiration for their own.

The twentieth century has made amends for the incomprehension of the nineteenth. He who died so abjectly is recognized today as one of the towering figures of the late Romantic period. As far as certain contemporary musicians are concerned, he is Russia's greatest composer.

40

Giacomo Puccini

"Almighty God touched me with his little finger and said, 'Write for the theater—mind you, only for the theater!' And I have obeyed the supreme command."

The Italian operatic tradition was carried on, in the post-Romantic era, by a group of composers led by Giacomo Puccini (1858–1924). His generation included Ruggiero Leoncavallo, remembered for *I pagliacci* (The Clowns; 1892), and Pietro Mascagni, whose reputation likewise

Giacomo Puccini.

rests on a single success, *Cavalleria rusticana* (Rustic Chivalry; 1890). These Italians were associated with the movement known as *verismo* (realism), which tried to bring into the lyric theater the naturalism of Zola, Ibsen, and their contemporaries. Instead of choosing historical or mythological themes, they picked subjects from everyday life and treated them in down-to-earth fashion. Puccini was strongly influenced by this trend towards operatic realism.

His Life

He was born in 1858 in Lucca, son of a church organist in whose footsteps he expected to follow. It was at Milan, where he went to complete his studies, that his true bent came to the fore. He studied at the Conservatory with Amilcare Ponchielli, composer of *La gioconda*. The ambitious young musician did not have to wait long for success. His first opera, *Le villi* (The Spirits; 1884), produced when he was twenty-six, was received with enthusiasm. *Manon Lescaut* (1893), based on the novel of Abbé Prévost, established him as the most promising among the rising generation of Italian composers. In Luigi Illica and Giuseppe Giacosa he found an ideal pair of librettists, and with this writing team he produced the three most successful operas of the early twentieth century: *La bohème* in 1896; *Tosca* in 1900; and *Madame Butterfly,* after a play by David Belasco, in 1904. The dates should dispel the popular notion of Puccini as a facile melodist who tossed off one score after another. Each of his operas represented years of detailed work involving ceaseless changes until he was satisfied.

The Girl of the Golden West (1910) was based, like its predecessor, on a play by Belasco. The world premiere at the Metropolitan Opera House was a major event. A more substantial achievement was the trio of one-act operas: *Il tabarro* (The Cloak), *Suor Angelica* (Sister Angelica), and the comic opera *Gianni Schicchi* (1918). The first two are not heard frequently. The third is a masterpiece.

Handsome and magnetic, Puccini was idolized and feted wherever he went. His wife was jealous, not without reason. "I am always falling in love," he confessed. "When I no longer am, make my funeral." As he entered middle age this singer of youth and love began to feel that his time was running out. "I am growing old and that disgusts me. I am burning to start work but have no libretto and am in a state of torment. I need work just as I need food." After much seeking he found a story that released the music in him and embarked on his final task–*Turandot*. He labored for four years on this fairy-tale opera about the beautiful and cruel princess of China. A work of consummate artistry, it is his most polished score. Puccini, ill with cancer, pushed ahead with increasing urgency. "If I do not succeed in finishing the opera someone will come to the front of the stage and say, 'Puccini composed as far as this, then he died.' "

He was sent to Brussels for treatment, accompanied by his son and the rough draft of the final scene. He died in 1924, following an operation, at the age of sixty-six. *Turandot* was completed from his sketches by his friend Franco Alfano. However, at the first performance at La Scala on April 25, 1926, the composer's wish was fulfilled. Arturo Toscanini, his greatest interpreter, laid down the baton during the lament over the body of Liù. Turning to the audience he said in a choking voice, "Here ends the master's work."

La bohème

Puccini's best-loved work is based on Henri Murger's *La Vie de bohème* (Bohemian Life). The novel depicts the joys and sorrows of the young artists who flock to Paris in search of fame and fortune, congregating in the Latin Quarter on the Left Bank of the Seine. "A gay life yet a terrible one," Murger called their precarious existence woven of bold dreams and bitter realities. Puccini's music was peculiarly suited to this atmosphere of "laughter through tears." Remembering his own life as a struggling young musician in Milan, he recaptured its wistfulness and charm.

Act I

The Bohemian mood is set by the exuberantly rhythmic motive with which the opera opens.

The curtain rises at once, disclosing the attic in which live Rodolfo the poet, Marcello the painter, and their two comrades-in-arms, the young philosopher Colline and the musician Schaunard. Rodolfo's first arietta, *Nei cieli bigi,* is associated with him throughout the work. Its mixture of ardor and dreaminess well characterizes the young poet.

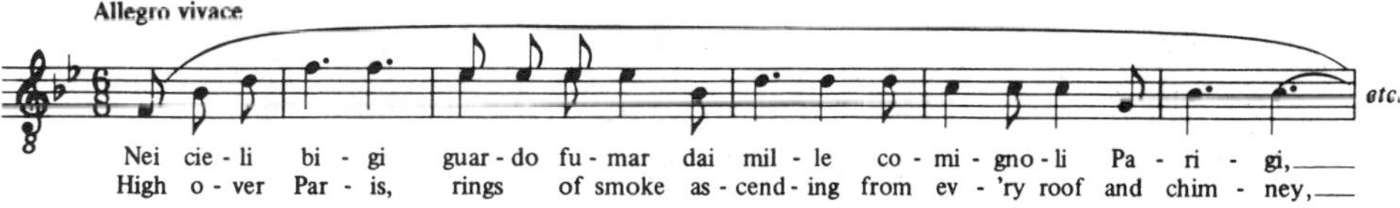

Marcello and Rodolfo try to work, but can think of nothing but the cold. They are presently joined, first by Colline, then by Schaunard, who by a stroke of luck has come on some money. The landlord arrives with a nasty word—rent!—and is gotten rid of. The young men go off to the

La bohème, *Act I: Rodolfo (José Carreras) and Mimi (Teresa Stratas) touch hands in the Metropolitan Opera production.* (Copyright © Beth Bergman 1983.)

Café Momus to celebrate Christmas Eve, Rodolfo remaining behind to finish an article he is writing.

There is a knock on the door. Enter Mimi and romance. Her arrival is heralded in this act as in later ones by a poignant phrase in the orchestra. Her candle has gone out. Will Rodolfo light it? Their dialogue, bathed by the orchestra in a current of emotion, exemplifies the spell that Puccini casts over the homeliest sentiments. "A little wine? . . . Thank you . . . Here it is . . . Not so much . . . Like this? . . . Thank you."

Mimi returns, having lost her key. Their candles are extinguished by a gust of wind; they search for the key on the floor, in the dark. Rodolfo, finding it, has the presence of mind to slip it into his pocket. Their hands touch and Rodolfo sings his aria *Che gelida manina* (How cold your little hand, let me warm it here in mine). Here is the Italian cantabile, the melody gliding along the scale and rising in a broad golden curve to its crest. Three centuries of operatic tradition stand behind an aria such as this.

Rodolfo asks who she is. Mimi replies with the aria *Mi chiamano Mimi:*

There follows a duet, based on a phrase from Rodolfo's aria, which now becomes the love theme of the opera.

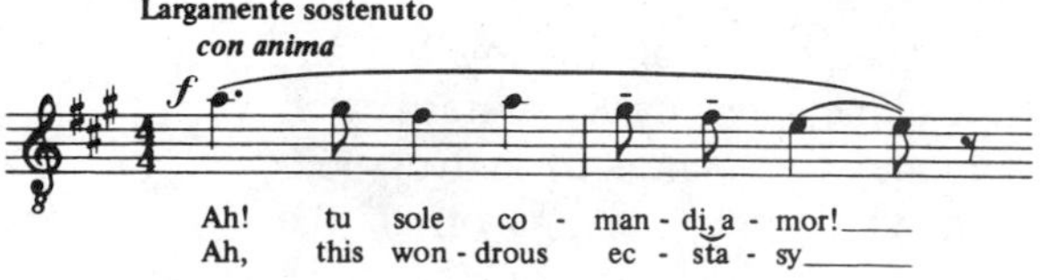

Rodolfo, smitten, invites her to the café, to phrases that have become part of the Italian folklore of flirtation. "Give me your arm, my little one. . . . I obey you, signor." The act ends, as it should, with a high C on the word "amor."

Act II

Christmas Eve in the Latin Quarter: a festive street scene opens Act II, in which Puccini's Italian sensibility blends with the Parisian setting. His feeling for atmosphere is manifest in the bright, brassy parallel chords with which the act opens. Rodolfo, having bought his new flame a rose-colored bonnet, brings her to the table where his friends are waiting. The appearance of Musetta causes a stir, proving especially agitating to her former love Marcello. This pert young lady is accompanied by an elderly dandy named Alcindoro, whom she persists in calling, in the tone of addressing a pet dog, Lulù. Marcello's agitation increases visibly as she sings her coquettish waltz song *Quando me'n vo'*.

Having decided to get rid of "the old boy," she sends him on an errand. A grand reconciliation ensues between her and Marcello. The waiter brings the bill. The young men realize to their dismay that they haven't enough to pay it, whereupon the resourceful Musetta instructs the waiter to add it to Alcindoro's and present it to that gentleman upon his return. The young people disappear in the crowd as the act ends in the liveliest fashion.

Act III

In dramatic contrast, Act III opens in a pallid wintry dawn. We see a toll gate outside Paris. Peasant women enter bringing butter and eggs. From the tavern sound the voices of the last carousers, including Musetta's. Mimi appears, seeking Marcello. She confides to him her difficulties with Rodolfo, who is insanely jealous and makes their life unbearable. In this dialogue and the next the voices occasionally move in a free plastic declamation while the orchestra sings the melody. It is a favorite device with Puccini, and one that he uses with infallible effectiveness.

Rodolfo awakes within. To avoid a scene Mimi hides to one side behind some trees. Rodolfo appears and pours out his heart to Marcello; he is helpless against his jealousy and fears. Mimi is ill, she is dying; he is too poor to provide her with the care she needs. Mimi's tears and coughing reveal her presence. She bids farewell to Rodolfo in a touching aria, *Addio, senza rancor* (Goodbye, without bitterness).

The peak of the act is the Quartet—better, double duet—at the close. Mimi and Rodolfo melodiously resign themselves to the parting they dread, while Marcello and Musetta quarrel violently, he accusing her of flirting, she retaliating with lively epithets. This Puccinian blend of pathos and comedy offers an excellent example of how an ensemble number may project the conflicting emotions of several characters. Marcello and Musetta run off in fury, leaving Mimi and Rodolfo to conclude their melancholy farewell.

Act IV

The Bohemian motive of the opening introduces Act IV. We are back in the attic. Marcello and Rodolfo try to work, as they did in the opening scene; but their thoughts revert to their lost loves. Schaunard and Colline arrive with four rolls and a herring for their scanty meal. The young men indulge in horseplay that comes to an abrupt halt with the entrance of Musetta. In great agitation she tells them that Mimi is below, too weak to climb the stairs. They help her in.

The friends depart on various errands to lighten Mimi's last moments. Now the lovers are alone. "Ah, my lovely Mimi" . . . "You still think me pretty?" . . . "Lovely as the sunrise" . . . "You've made the wrong comparison; you should have said, 'Lovely as the sunset . . .' " They recollect the night they met. The scene derives its impact from Puccini's masterful use of reminiscence. How better underline their blasted hopes than by quoting the music of that first encounter?

The others return, Marcello with medicine, Musetta with a muff to warm Mimi's hands. Rodolfo weeps. Mimi comforts him. "Why do you cry so? Here . . . love . . . always with you! My hands . . . warm . . . and . . . to sleep . . ." Musetta prays. Schaunard whispers to Marcello that Mimi is dead. Rodolfo's outcry "Mimi . . . Mimi!" is heard against the brief and terrible postlude of the orchestra. Puccini wrote the final scene with tears in his eyes. It has been listened to in like fashion.

La bohème has retained its freshness for more than half a century. Within its genre it is a masterpiece.

41

The Nature of Choral Music

"In a sense no one is ignorant of the material from which choral music springs. For this material is, in large measure, the epitomized thought, feeling, aspiration of a community rather than an individual." — PERCY M. YOUNG: *The Choral Tradition*

By *choral music* we mean music performed by many voices—a chorus, a choir, or a glee club. A *chorus* is a fairly large body of singers, generally consisting of both men and women. (The term also refers to the pieces that such a group sings.) A *choir* is a smaller group, usually connected with a church. A *glee club* functions as a rule in a college and performs popular music and college songs along with more serious works.

The chorus consists of four groups, corresponding to the principal vocal ranges: sopranos, altos, tenors, and basses. Choral music therefore is usually arranged in four parts. The groups may be subdivided into first and second sopranos, first and second altos, and so on, so that the music may unfold in from five to eight or more parts. But four parts is the standard arrangement. Choral music consequently differs in one important respect from most of the instrumental and vocal music we have discussed thus far. There the ear followed a single melody line that was supported by a background of harmony. In choral music, on the other hand, the ear is aware of several voice parts. These unfold like so many threads that interweave in an ever changing pattern. Often an idea is presented in one voice and imitated in turn by each of the other voices. The result is a different kind of musical texture.

In earlier times choral music was often performed without accompaniment. By the eighteenth century the orchestra had firmly established itself as a partner of the chorus. This trend continued throughout the nineteenth century. Choral music consequently offered the composer exciting opportunities for contrast: between voices and orchestra, between men's and women's voices, between high and low voices, between solo voices and chorus, as well as all possible combinations of these. Small wonder that works for soloists, chorus, and orchestra challenged the imagination of composers and brought forth some of their finest efforts.

In many performances today, strict attention is paid to replicating the vocal and instrumental forces for which a piece of music was written. Here, in concert, the chorus and orchestra of Musica Sacra perform an eighteenth-century work with the group's director, Richard Westenburg, at the harpsichord. (Photo by John Fell.)

Choral Music in the Nineteenth Century

The nineteenth century, we found, witnessed a broadening of the democratic ideal and an enormous expansion of the musical public. This climate was uniquely favorable to choral music, which flowered as an enjoyable group activity involving increasing numbers of music lovers. As a result, choral music came to play an important part in the musical life of the Romantic era.

Amateur choral groups

Singing in a chorus required less skill than playing in an orchestra. It attracted many music lovers who had never learned to play an instrument, or who could not afford to buy one. With a modest amount of rehearsal (and a modest amount of voice), they could learn to take part in the performance of great choral works. The music they sang, being allied to words, was somewhat easier to understand than absolute music, both for the performers and the listeners. The members of the chorus not only enjoyed a pleasant social evening once or twice a week but also, if their group was good enough, became a source of pride to their community.

This development was encouraged by several circumstances. The growth of the music-publishing industry made available editions of choral masterpieces at cheaper prices. The growth of music education produced large numbers of amateurs who, under the guidance of professionals, were able to achieve impressive results. Choral groups sprang up all over Europe, especially in England and Germany, for the express purpose of studying and performing the great works of Bach and Handel, Haydn, Mozart, and Beethoven. Their efforts could not but contribute materially to nineteenth-century musical life.

In the nineteenth century, enormous choral and orchestral forces were the order of the day. A contemporary engraving depicting the opening concert at St. Martin's Hall, London, 1850.

Under the impact of the French Revolution, music festivals had taken place in Paris at which huge choruses hailed the new rule of liberty, fraternity, and equality. The decades that followed saw the development of even larger festivals throughout England and Germany, at which choral music played the dominant role. These were organized in such a way as to reach ever larger masses of people. Composers took a leading part in these activities, both as conductors and organizers of musical events. Mendelssohn was pre-eminent in this field. A number of other composers—among them Schumann and Brahms, Liszt and Berlioz, Smetana and Dvořák—did their stint as choral conductors.

Choral festivals

The middle class was the backbone of the great choral festivals. However, they were joined by increasing segments of the working class, especially since a developing capitalism was able to give its workers more leisure. Choral music offered the masses an ideal outlet for their artistic energies. It served to alleviate the drabness of life in the English factory towns of the early Victorian period. And it had the solid support of the authorities, who felt that an interest in music would protect the lower orders from dangerous new ideas that were floating around. This aspect of the situation is amusingly illustrated in the constitution of the Huddersfield Choral Society (1836), which stipulated that "No person shall be a member of this Society who frequents the 'Hall of Science' or any of the 'Socialist Meetings', nor shall the Librarian be allowed to lend any copies of music (knowingly) belonging to this society to any Socialist, upon pain of expulsion." England was approaching the ferment of the Chartist uprisings, and one had to be careful.

The repertory centered about the great choral heritage of the past. Nevertheless, if choral music was to remain a vital force, its literature had to be enriched by new works that would reflect the spirit of the time. The list of composers active in this area includes some of the most important names of the nineteenth century: Schubert, Berlioz, Mendelssohn, Schumann, Liszt, Verdi, Gounod, Bruckner, Franck, Brahms, Dvořák. Out of their efforts came a body of choral music that forms a delightful enclave in the output of the Romantic period.

Choral forms

Among the main forms of choral music in the nineteenth century were the Mass, Requiem, and oratorio. We will discuss these in detail in later chapters. It will suffice at this point to define them briefly. A *Mass* is a musical setting of the most solemn service of the Roman Catholic Church. A *Requiem* is a musical setting of the Mass for the Dead. It takes its name from the opening line of the text: "Requiem aeternam dona eis Domine" (Give them eternal rest, O Lord). An *oratorio* is a dramatic composition based on a text of religious or serious character, performed by solo voices, chorus, and orchestra. All three forms were originally intended to be performed in church. By the nineteenth century they had found a wider audience in the concert hall.

In addition, a vast literature sprang up of secular choral pieces. These were settings for chorus of lyric poems in a variety of moods and styles.

They were known as *part songs*—that is, songs in three or four voice parts. Most of them were short melodious works, not too difficult for amateurs. They gave pleasure both to the singers and their listeners, and played an important role in developing the new mass audience of the nineteenth century.

The text

It is important to remember that in choral music the text is related to the music in a different way than in solo song. The words are not as easy to grasp when a multitude of voices project them. In addition, the four groups in the chorus may be singing different words at the same time. Most important of all, music needs more time to establish a mood than words do. For these reasons the practice arose of repeating a line, a phrase, or an individual word over and over again instead of introducing new words all the time. This principle is well illustrated by both choral works discussed in the next chapter.

42

Two Choral Masterpieces

Verdi: Messa da Requiem

"I am not a learned composer, but I am a very experienced one."

Verdi's *Requiem* (1874) was written in memory of Alessandro Manzoni, the poet-novelist who was the leading Italian writer during the mid-nineteenth century. In a larger sense the *Requiem* was a tribute to the Italian genius. As Verdi put it, "It was a crying need of my heart to do all in my power to honor this great spirit, whom I valued so highly as a writer and revered as a man—the true pattern of patriotic virtue."

Like many liberals of his time, Verdi was a free-thinker; his wife called him "a man of little faith." Nonetheless the Catholic tradition of his childhood retained its hold upon him, as is evident from the many religious episodes in his operas. He approached the supreme liturgy of the Church with utter assurance. The old masters did not draw an artificial distinction between sacred and secular music. When they wished to honor God they spoke the living musical language of their time. Verdi did likewise. His natural language was Italian opera, and this became the language of his *Requiem Mass.* (More than a century earlier, even Bach had been accused of being too "operatic" in the *St. Matthew Passion.*) Verdi saw the text of the *Requiem* as a great spiritual drama, a conflict between man's fear of death and his hope for salvation in the hereafter. He treated this conflict with the dramatic power that was uniquely his. There resulted a work of shattering force and sensuous lyricism. His vision of the Last Judgment—the central fresco of the Requiem—has been compared not inappropriately to Michelangelo's.

The work is in seven movements:

First movement

I. *Requiem and Kyrie.* Andante, 4/4, for the four soloists—soprano, alto, tenor, bass—and chorus. Muted cellos play a descending phrase, *pp,* in low register. They sound a note of solemn supplication that reflects the opening line of the text: "Requiem aeternam dona eis, Domine, et lux perpetua luceat eis." (Eternal rest grant them, Lord, and let eternal light shine upon them.) The sweetness of the muted violins above the voices reflects Verdi's indications: con espressione, dolcissimo (with expression, very sweetly), and *ppp.*

The music gathers momentum with the next thought: "Te decet hymnus, Deus, in Sion" (A hymn is fitting to Thee, God, in Zion). We hear again the opening section. Now the soloists take over in a lyrical expansion of four basic words: "Kyrie eleison, Christe eleison" (Lord have mercy on us, Christ have mercy on us). Their voices interweave, now imitating one another, now blending in a melodious flow. Notice the dramatic contrasts between loud and soft. The movement ends *ppp.*

Second movement
SIDE 9/1 (E II)
SIDE 13/7 (S)

II. *Dies irae.* This, the central movement of the work, is in nine sections:

1. *Dies irae.* Allegro agitato, alla breve, for chorus. Crashing chords in the orchestra and headlong descending scales suggest the awesome terror of Judgment Day. The fury and tension anticipate the storm scene in *Otello,* which Verdi wrote a decade later. The chorus hurls out the text like an imprecation: "Dies irae, dies illa, solvet saeclum in favilla, teste David cum Sibylla." (That day of wrath, that day of anger will dissolve the world

in ashes, as David prophesied, and the Sybil.) The next verse describes the trembling when the Judge appears to weigh their deeds. Tremolos in the string instruments vividly suggest the shuddering of the sinners. Trumpets "from afar and invisible"—that is, backstage—are echoed by trumpets in the main orchestra. There is a tremendous upsurge of sound as the brass and drums take over, preparing for the next section.

2. *Tuba mirum.* Allegro sostenuto, 4/4, for chorus. The music is a powerful evocation of the text: "Tuba mirum spargens sonum per sepulcra regionum, coget omnes ante thronum" (The trumpet, hurling its wondrous sound over the graves of the world, will summon all before the throne). Fanfares and mighty strokes on the kettledrum convey the terror of that awesome moment. The next verse, for the solo bass, describes how Déath and Nature alike will be astounded when all creation rises again to answer

the Judge. The key word, "mors" (death), is repeated with chilling impact. The section ends *pppp*.

3. *Liber Scriptus.* Allegro molto sostenuto (very fast, sustained), 4/4, for alto and chorus. The text tells how the written record will be brought forth in which all men's deeds are entered. "Everything will be revealed, none shall go unpunished." The alto traces a long lyric line while the chorus, in the background, mutters repeatedly "Dies irae." Verdi's indication here is "with subdued and very sad voices." Here too the central word "nil" (none) is repeated with intensely dramatic effect. There is a great crescendo, and the chorus repeats a phrase from the *Dies irae* that runs like a unifying thread through the work.

4. *Quid sum, miser.* Adagio, 6/8, for soprano, alto, and tenor. "What shall a wretch such as I say, of what protector ask help when the righteous are scarcely secure?" The flowing 6/8 meter relaxes the tension. The three solo voices echo one another in a melodious phrase that might have come out of *La traviata.* Extremely affecting are the groups of two or three notes, always descending, that express human despair. Notice how Verdi uses the dark sound of a solo bassoon to underline the mood.

5. *Rex tremendae majestatis.* Adagio maestoso, 4/4, for chorus and four soloists. Berlioz, in his setting of this text (King of Terrible Majesty, who freely saves those worthy of salvation, save me, Fount of Mercy) as part of his imposing *Requiem Mass*, based his conception on the contrast between God the Merciful Father and God the Judge. Verdi combines the two ideas, building to a climax with all his forces, much as in his operatic ensembles. The plea for mercy is continued in the last four sections of the *Dies irae.*

6. *Recordare, Jesu pie.* Adagio maestoso, 4/4, for soprano and alto. "Remember, merciful Jesus, that I am the cause of Thy journey on earth; let me not be lost on that day." The two women's voices are heard first in succession, then overlapping, then in close harmony.

7. *Ingemisco, tamquam reus.* Poco meno mosso (a little slower), 4/4, for tenor. "I moan as one accused; my countenance flushes with guilt; O God, spare the suppliant." The solo voice is pitted against various woodwinds and strings. Here Verdi recalls the heroic sound of the tenors in his operas.

8. *Confutatis maledictis.* Andante, 4/4, for bass. "When the cursed are confounded and assigned to bitter flames, call me among the blessed." The accursed souls, in the opening lines, are contrasted with the penitent, who appeal for forgiveness in an eloquent melody.

8A. *Allegro come prima* (Fast, as at first). A return to the opening section of the *Dies irae,* with its crashing chords, headlong descending scales, and exciting choral sound.

9. *Lacrymosa dies illa.* Largo, 4/4, for the four soloists and chorus. "That day will be one of weeping, on which accused man shall rise again from the ashes to be judged; therefore spare him, O Lord." A lament that Verdi marked con molto espressione (with much expression). Its broad melody

is sung first by the alto soloist, then the bass, and developed by the entire ensemble. This section brings the *Dies irae* to a solemn close, *ppp,* on the words "Pie Jesu Domine, dona eis requiem" (Merciful Jesus, grant them rest).

The great choral works of the past had consisted of a series of contrasting numbers that were fairly short. In the *Dies irae* Verdi instead linked a succession of contrasting sections into a single movement. He thereby created a structural span of enormous breadth and substance, a kind of vaulting arch that rested at either end on the stirring sound of his main section. This architecture was of a spaciousness hitherto uncommon in choral music.

Third movement

III. *Domine Jesu.* Andante mosso (fairly slow, with movement), 6/8, for the quartet of soloists. "Lord Jesus Christ, King of Glory, deliver the souls of all the faithful." A tranquil prayer, almost pastoral in style. There is a change of meter to 4/4 when the text recalls the forgiveness that God promised Abraham and his seed, with a quickening of pace and a rise in tension.

Fourth movement

IV. *Sanctus.* Allegro, 4/4, for double chorus. Verdi here writes for two choral groups—that is, eight parts instead of four. The result is an intricate texture of interweaving lines that reflects the joyous text: "Holy, holy, holy, Lord God of Hosts. Heaven and earth are full of Thy glory. Hosanna in the highest. Blessed is he that cometh in the name of the Lord."

Fugue

This type of texture is known as a *fugue,* which we will discuss in detail in a later chapter. The term comes from the Latin *fugere,* to flee, suggesting the flight of a basic theme from one voice to another. In effect, the different voice parts take turns in presenting the basic idea or *subject* of the fugue. The subject of this fugue leaps up boldly along the tones of the chord before it gradually descends:

Fifth movement

V. *Agnus Dei.* Andante, 4/4, for soprano, alto, and chorus. The two women's voices move in unison as they implore the Lamb of God, who washes away the sins of the world. Their opening phrase is repeated in unison by chorus and orchestra. The movement broadens into harmonies of a tenderly expressive kind.

Sixth movement

VI. *Lux aeterna.* Allegro moderato, 4/4, for alto, tenor, and bass. "Let eternal light shine upon them, Lord, and on Thy saints forever, for Thou art merciful." Verdi omits soprano and chorus; he is saving these for the final movement. The plea for everlasting light is accompanied by flickering colors in the orchestra—woodwinds and strings in the upper register. The effect is magical.

Seventh movement

VII. *Libera me.* Moderato, 4/4, for soprano and chorus. The soprano's plea for salvation is echoed by the chorus: "Deliver me, O Lord, from eternal death, on that awesome day when the heavens shall be moved, and the earth." Her solo leads into the thunderous chords and precipitous scales of the *Dies irae,* which is now heard for the last time. The soprano resumes, her voice soaring above the chorus into celestial regions, in a melody from the opening movement. Unforgettable is the effect of the upward octave leap in her part on the word "Requiem," *pppp,* against wraithlike chords whispered by the chorus.

The movement works up to a tremendous choral fugue whose subject leaps downward as decisively as the subject of the previous fugue leaped upward:

The soprano ends with an ecstatic invocation to hope and faith: "Libera me, Domine, de morte aeterna in die illa tremenda" (Deliver me, Lord, from eternal death on that great Judgment Day). And the chorus intones the final words *pppp:* "Libera me, libera me."

Brahms: A German Requiem

"I had the whole of humanity in mind."

If the purpose of the Catholic Mass for the Dead was to pray for the souls that must face Judgment Day, Brahms's *A German Requiem* (1866) had a simpler goal—to console the living, and lead them to a serene acceptance of death as an inevitable part of life. Hence its prevailing mood of gentle lyricism is at the opposite pole from the shattering dramaticism of the work we have just discussed. This Requiem issued from the heart of the Protestant tradition into which Brahms was born; unlike Verdi's, it is not a liturgical piece. Brahms chose his text from the Old as well as New Testament, from the Psalms, Proverbs, Isaiah, and Ecclesiastes as well as from Paul, Matthew, Peter, John, and Revelation. He was not a religious man in the conventional sense, nor was he affiliated with any particular church;

significantly, Christ's name is never mentioned. He was impelled to compose the *Requiem* by the death, first, of his benefactor and friend Robert Schumann, then of his mother, whom he idolized; but the piece transcends the personal and endures as a song of mourning for all mankind.

Fourth movement

Written for soloists, four-part chorus and orchestra, the *Requiem* is in seven movements arranged in a formation resembling an arch. There are connections between the first and last movements, between the second and sixth, and between the third and fifth; which leaves the fourth movement, the widely sung chorus *How Lovely Is Thy Dwelling Place*, as the centerpiece of the arch. This is a lyrical meditation akin in mood to the gently flowing, melodious movements that Brahms, in his symphonies, substituted for the scherzo. The verse is from the eighty-fourth Psalm:

Wie lieblich sind deine Wohnungen,	How lovely is Thy dwelling place,
Herr Zabaoth!	O Lord of hosts!
Meine Seele verlanget und sehnet sich	My soul longs and even faints
nach den Vorhofen des Herrn;	for the courts of the Lord;
mein Leib und Seele freuen sich	my flesh and soul rejoice
in dem lebendigen Gott.	in the living God.
Wohl denen, die in deinem Hause wohnen,	Blessed are they that dwell in Thy house,
die loben dich immerdar!	that praise Thee evermore!

Flutes and clarinets present a brief introductory phrase that is an upside-down version (inversion) of the phrase with which the chorus begins: it moves up where the other moves down and vice versa, as is apparent from a comparison of both:

The relationship between vocal parts and orchestral accompaniment resembles that between voice and piano in a Brahms song. At times the accompaniment duplicates the soprano melody, at times it goes its own way and presents a countermelody.

The movement is in rondo form: **A-B-A-C-A.** The **A** section is a setting of the first two lines, which are heard again with each return of this section. The **B** section presents the next four lines, and the **C** section focuses on the last two. As is usual in choral works, there is much repetition of text. In certain passages the voice parts move together in harmony. In others, the four groups imitate each other. For example, a phrase introduced by the tenors will be repeated by the sopranos. The most emotional word in a line is generally set as the high point of the vocal phrase: in the **A** section *Herr Zebaoth* (Lord God of Hosts), in the **B** section *sehnet* (faints) and *lebendigen* (living), and in **C** *loben* (praise). The first two sections for the most part move in quarter notes. With the third section **(C)** eighth notes come to the fore in a more vigorous rhythm, as befits the line *that praise*

Thee evermore, with much expansion on *evermore*. With the final reappearance of the **A** section the quarter notes return. This section, marked *p* and dolce (soft, sweet) serves as a coda that brings the piece to its gentle close.

First movement

The opening movement of the *German Requiem* is marked *Ziemlich langsam und mit Ausdruk* (fairly slow and with expression). It is an **A-B-A** form that moves from despair to acceptance, from darkness to light. "Blessed are they that mourn, for they shall be comforted. They that sow in tears shall reap in joy." Brahms sought a dark sound in this movement and omitted the brighter instruments—violins, clarinets, trumpets. The **A** section hovers between the low and middle register, piano. The **B** section unfolds a crescendo to a more robust sound, and lies somewhat higher in pitch; now piano gives way to forte. When the **A** section returns, with a lovely passage for harp toward the end, it does so in a spirit of consolation.

Second movement

The second movement, marked *Langsam, marschmässig* (slow, in the manner of a march), is a march in ¾ time that begins in a spectral pianissimo, with the violins and violas muted. "Behold, all flesh is as the grass, and all the goodliness of man is as the flower of grass. For lo, the grass withers and the flower thereof decays." To some nineteenth-century listeners these measures conjured up the image of *Danse macabre*, the grisly dance of death that haunted the imagination of so many medieval painters. This part of the movement is in **A-B-A** form, with a middle section marked *Etwas bewegter* (a little more animated) that strikes a more cheerful note. Notable is the evocative pitter-patter in the flutes and harp when the text speaks of the morning and evening rain.

A brief *transition* or bridge leads to an Allegro non troppo (not too fast) in 4/4. The basses announce the subject of an energetic fugue that fits the more positive thought: "The redeemed of the Lord shall return, and come to Zion with shouts of joy."

This is worked up into a fortissimo climax with much repetition of the key word *Freude* (joy). But in the final passage Brahms allows this burst of energy to simmer down and brings the movement to a quiet ending, as though beyond the shouting and joy were an inner quietude of spirit that was even more precious.

Third movement

Third is an Andante moderato (the German marking is *mässig bewegt*) for baritone solo. "Lord, teach me that my life has to end and I must leave it." The chorus repeats the suppliant's broadly curved melody as he reflects on the vanity of life. Brahms indulges his fondness for "two against three," the chorus singing in half notes, quarters, and eighths against a background of triplets in the orchestra. Here, too, the movement surges forward from doubt and entreaty to an affirmation of faith on the thought, "The souls of the righteous are in the hand of God, no pain nor grief shall touch them." Again we hear a fugue, its subject presented by the tenors:

*Here the cut time symbol ₵ applies to four half-notes to the measure rather than the more usual four quarter-notes to the measure.

Meanwhile the orchestra presents a fugue of its own on what sounds like another theme, so that we really hear a double fugue. However, this new melody is a cleverly disguised version of the other, as becomes apparent if we compare the two. You can see that most of its notes are drawn from the first subject:

This double fugue unfolds over a protracted pedal point on a low D held by the bass instruments—trombone, tuba, kettledrums, and double basses—which becomes like a bedrock of faith supporting the mighty structure. Building to a triumphal close, this section represents a unique amalgam of technique and imagination.

Fifth movement

The fifth movement, with its soprano solo, is the counterpart of the third. The baritone's outpouring of grief in the third movement is answered by the soprano's promise of solace in the fifth. Added by the composer after the death of his mother, the movement contains a setting of the poignant line from Isaiah, "I will comfort you as one whom his mother comforts." Muted strings and woodwinds prepare the way for the soprano voice; the interchange between soloist and chorus is more intimate than in the third movement. Notable is the passage that presents one of Brahms's favorite devices: the soprano sings a tune in eighth notes while the tenors duplicate it in quarter notes:

Sixth movement

The sixth movement sings the final victory over death. From its uncertain beginning—"For here we have no continuing place, but we seek one in the future"—the music advances inexorably to the promise that when the last trumpet sounds, the dead will arise. Brahms resisted the temptation to bring the trumpet to the fore; the fortissimo chords that greet the vision of Resurrection resound throughout the whole orchestra. "O death, where is your sting?" the chorus exults. "O grave, where is your victory?" This vision of a Last Judgment stripped of all its terror culminates in a powerful double fugue whose exaltation balances the spirit of the fugue in the second movement, but on a higher plane. The subject is presented by the altos and works up to a climax worthy of the power and glory mentioned in the text:

Seventh movement

The opening line of the seventh movement—"Blessed are the dead which die in the Lord henceforth"—is akin in mood to the opening line of the work. The music accordingly recaptures the gentle flow and serenity of the first movement. But the relationship of last to first goes deeper. In the final measures of the *Requiem*, Brahms returns to the passage that ended the first movement. Therewith the circle is closed, and the listener is left with a wonderful sense of completion.

PART THREE

More Materials of Music

"In any narrative—epic, dramatic or musical—every word or tone should be like a soldier marching towards the one, common, final goal: conquest of the material. The way the artist makes every phrase of his story such a soldier, serving to unfold it, to support its structure and development, to build plot and counterplot, to distribute light and shade, to point incessantly and lead up gradually to the climax—in short, the way every fragment is impregnated with its mission towards the whole, makes up this delicate and so essential objective which we call FORM." — ERNST TOCH

43

The Organization of Musical Sounds: Key and Scale

"All music is nothing more than a succession of impulses that converge towards a definite point of repose." — IGOR STRAVINSKY

At the beginning of this book we discussed various elements of music. Now that we have had occasion to hear how these are interwoven in a number of works, we are ready to consider the materials of music on a more advanced level, particularly as they relate to the organization of the large Classical forms.

Tonality

A system of music must have set procedures for organizing tones into intelligible relationships. One of the first steps in this direction is to select certain tones and arrange them in a family or group. In such a group one tone assumes greater importance than the rest. This is the *do,* the Tonic or keynote around which the others revolve and to which they ultimately gravitate.

Key

By a *key* we mean a group of related tones with a common center or Tonic. The tones of the key serve as basic material for a given composition. When we listen to a composition in the key of A we hear a piece based in large part upon the family of tones that revolve around and gravitate to the common center A.

This "loyalty to the Tonic" is inculcated in us by most of the music we hear. It is the unifying force in the *do-re-mi-fa-sol-la-ti-do* scale that was taught us in our childhood. You can test for yourself how strong is the pull to the Tonic by singing the first seven tones of this pattern, stopping on *ti.* You will experience an almost physical compulsion to resolve the *ti* up to *do.*

The sense of relatedness to a central tone is known as *tonality.* This sense, needless to say, resides in our minds rather than in the tones themselves. Tonality underlies the whole system of relationships among tones as embodied in keys, scales, and the harmonies based on those, such relationships converging upon the "definite point of repose." Specifically, tonality refers to those relationships as they were manifest in Western music from around 1600 to 1900.

The "Miracle of the Octave"

A string of a certain length, when set in motion, vibrates at a certain rate per second and produces a certain pitch. Given the same conditions, a string half as long will vibrate twice as fast and sound an octave above. A string twice as long will vibrate half as fast and sound an octave below. When we sound together on the piano two tones other than an octave, such as C–D or C–F, the ear distinctly hears two different tones. But when we strike an octave such as C–C or D–D, the ear recognizes a very strong similarity between the two tones. Indeed, if one were not listening carefully one would almost believe that he was hearing a single tone. This "miracle of the octave" was observed at an early stage in all musical cultures, with the result that the octave became the basic interval in music. (An interval, we saw, is the distance and relationship between two tones.)

Division of the octave

The method of dividing the octave determines the scales and the character of a musical system. It is precisely in this particular that one system differs from another. In Western music the octave is divided into twelve equal intervals. The fact is apparent from the look of the piano keyboard, where counting from any tone to its octave we find twelve keys—seven white and five black. These twelve tones are a half tone (semitone) apart. That is, from C to C sharp is a half step, as is from C sharp to D. The half step is the smallest unit of distance in our musical system. From C to D is a distance of two semitones, or a whole tone.

Oriental music is based on other units. In India, for example, quarter-tone scales are used. The Javanese divide the octave into five nearly equal parts. Arabic music contains a scale that divides the octave into seventeen parts. We are not able to play Oriental music on the piano, which is tuned in semitones. Nor could we readily sing it, since we have been trained to think in terms of the whole- and half-tone intervals of our system.

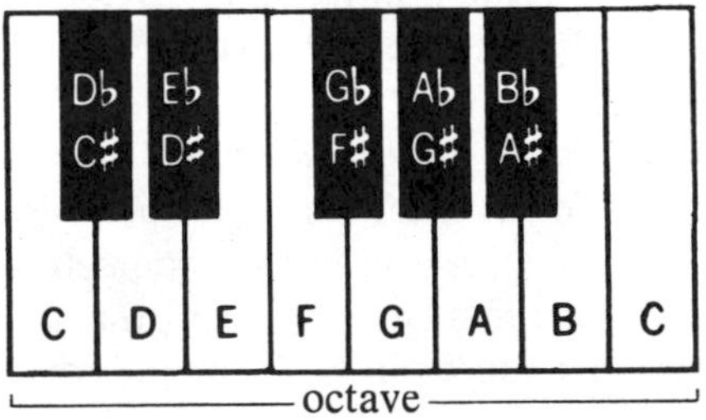

Note: The black keys are named in relation to their white neighbors. When the black key between C and D is thought of as a semitone higher than C, it is known as C sharp. When it is regarded as a semitone lower than D, the same key is called D flat. Thus D sharp is the same tone as E flat, F sharp is the same tone as G flat, and G sharp is the same tone as A flat. Which of these names is used depends upon the scale and key in which a particular sharp or flat appears.

The twelve semitones into which Western music divides the octave constitute what is known as the *chromatic scale*. They are duplicated in higher and lower octaves. No matter how vast and intricate a musical work, it is made up of the twelve basic tones and their higher and lower duplications.

The Major Scale

The scale

A *scale* is a series of tones arranged in consecutive order, ascending or descending. Specifically, a scale presents the tones of a key. The word is derived from the Italian *scala,* "ladder." In the widest sense a scale is a musical alphabet revealing at a glance the principle whereby tones are selected and related to one another in a given system.

The music of the Classic-Romantic period is based on two contrasting scales, the *major* and the *minor*. These consist of seven different tones, with the octave *do* added at the end of the series. The major scale has the familiar *do-re-mi-fa-sol-la-ti-do* pattern. Its seven tones are picked out of the possible twelve in order to form a centralized family or key out of which musical compositions may be fashioned. It becomes clear that compositions based on the major scale represent a "seven out of twelve" way of hearing music.

The major scale

If you play the white keys on the piano from C to C you will hear the familiar *do-re-mi-fa-sol-la-ti-do* series; in other words, the major scale. Let us examine this series a little more closely.

We notice that there is no black key on the piano between E–F (*mi-fa*) and B–C (*ti-do*). These tones, therefore, are a semitone apart, while the others are a whole tone apart. Consequently, when we sing the *do-re-mi-fa-sol-la-ti-do* sequence we are measuring off a pattern of eight tones that are a whole tone apart except steps 3–4 (*mi-fa*) and 7–8 (*ti-do*). In other words, we are singing the pattern *do,* whole step, whole step, half step, whole step, whole step, whole step, half step. You will find it instructive to sing this scale trying to distinguish between the half- and whole-tone distances as you sing.

This scale implies certain relationships based upon tension and resolution. We have already indicated one of the most important of these—the thrust of the seventh step to the eighth (*ti* seeking to be resolved to *do*). There are others: if we sing *do-re* we are left with a sense of incompleteness that is resolved when *re* moves back to *do; fa* gravitates to *mi; la* descends to *sol*. These tendencies, we saw, reside not in the tones but in our minds. They are the meanings attached by our musical culture to the raw material of nature.

Most important of all, the major scale defines the two poles of Classical harmony: the *do* or Tonic, the point of ultimate rest; and the *sol* or Dominant, representative of the active harmony. Upon the trackless sea of sound this relationship imposes direction and goal. Tonic going to Dominant and returning to Tonic becomes a basic progression of Classical harmony. It will also serve, we shall find, as a basic principle of Classical form.

The Key as an Area in Musical Space

The major scale, we said, is a "ladder" of whole and half tones.

8	do	C
7	ti	B
6	la	A
5	sol	G
4	fa	F
3	mi	E
2	re	D
1	do	C

A ladder may be placed on high ground or low, but the distance between its steps remains the same. So too the major scale may be measured off from one starting point or another without affecting the sequence of whole and half steps within the pattern.

The Tonic

Any one of the twelve tones of our octave may serve as starting point for the scale. Whichever it is, that tone at once assumes the function of the Tonic or key center. The other tones are chosen according to the pattern of the ladder. They immediately assume the functions of activity and rest implicit in the major scale. Most important, they all take on the impulse of gravitating more or less directly to the Tonic.

With each different Tonic we get another group of seven tones out of the possible twelve. In other words, every major scale has a different number of sharps or flats. The scale of C major is the only one that has no sharps or flats. If we build the major scale from G we must include an F sharp in order to conform to the pattern of whole and half steps. (Try building the pattern whole step, whole step, half step, whole step, whole step, whole step, half step, from G. You will find that F natural does not fit this pattern.) If we build the major-scale pattern from D, we get a group of seven that includes two sharps. If F is our starting point the scale includes B flat. (The twelve major scales are listed in Appendix III.) When we play a tune like *America* on the piano with C as keynote–that is, in the key of C major–we use only the white keys. Should we play it with G as a keynote –that is, in the key of G major–we should in the course of it have to sound F sharp, not F natural. Were we to play F natural we would be off key.

Tonal position and function

It becomes clear that the meaning of a tone, its direction and drive, are determined not by its intrinsic nature but by its position in the scale. The tone C may be the Tonic or point of rest in one scale. In another it may be the seventh step seeking to be resolved by ascending to the eighth. In still another it may be the second step thrusting down to the first. In any case its impulse of activity or rest depends not on its character as the tone C but on its function as the *do,* the *ti,* or the *re*—the 1, 7, or 2—of that particular key and scale. The Classical system is based on the eminently social doctrine that the significance of a tone depends not upon itself but upon its relationship to other tones.

The key serves as a means of identification. The title *Symphony in A major* refers to a work based in large measure upon the tones of the A-major scale and the harmonies fashioned from those, with the keynote A serving as the central tone to which the others gravitate. This group is the one that includes three sharps.

The Minor Scale

Whether the major scale begins on C, D, E, or any other tone, it follows the same pattern in the arrangement of the whole and half steps. Such a pattern is known as a *mode.* Thus, all the major scales exemplify the major mode of arranging whole and half steps.

The natural minor

There is also a *minor mode,* which complements and serves as a foil to the major. It differs primarily from the major in that its third degree is lowered a half step; that is, the scale of C minor has E flat instead of E. In the pure or *natural minor scale* the sixth and seventh steps are also lowered: C–D–E♭–F–G–A♭–B♭–C.. (For two other versions of the minor scale—*harmonic* and *melodic*—see Appendix III.) The minor is pronouncedly different from the major in mood and coloring. *Minor,* the Latin word for "smaller," refers to the fact that the distinguishing interval C–E♭ is smaller than the corresponding interval C–E in the major ("larger") scale.

Like the major, the pattern of the minor scale may begin on each of the twelve tones of the octave. In each case there will be a different group of seven tones out of twelve; that is, each scale will include a different number of sharps or flats. It becomes clear that every tone in the octave may serve as starting point or keynote for a major and a minor scale. This gives us twelve keys according to the major mode and twelve keys according to the minor mode. If the mode of a work is not specified, the major is implied, as when we speak of the *Melody in F, Minuet in G,* or *Symphony in A.* The minor is always specified, as in the case of Schubert's *Symphony in B minor* or Mendelssohn's *Violin Concerto in E minor.*

Music in the minor modes

Is the minor "sadder" than the major? Such connotations exist only in reference to the music of a particular time and place. The nineteenth century seems to have regarded the minor as more somber than the major. The funeral music of Beethoven, Mendelssohn, Chopin, Wagner, and Grieg is conspicuously in the minor, while the triumphal finales of a number of symphonies and overtures of the same period are as conspicuously in the major.

The minor mode has a certain exotic ring to Western ears and is associated in the popular view with Oriental and east European music. This aspect of the minor is prominent in such works as the *Turkish Rondo* of Mozart; in a number of pieces in Hungarian style by Schubert, Liszt, and Brahms; in the main theme of Rimsky-Korsakov's *Scheherazade,* César Cui's *Orientale,* and similar exotica. The folk songs of certain regions appear to incline to the major while others lean toward the minor. There are, however, so many exceptions that such a generalization must be viewed with caution.

The contrast between minor and major became an element of musical structure during the Classic-Romantic period. For example, in A-B-A form, the outer sections might be in one mode and the contrasting middle section in the other. Or a symphony might start out in the minor and shift to the major in an access of triumph, as in Beethoven's *Fifth,* Franck's *D minor,* and Tchaikovsky's *Fifth.* Thus the distinction between major and minor lent itself to contrasts of color, mood, and emotional intensity.

Key signatures

The key signature at the head of a piece announces the number of sharps or flats that prevail in that particular composition. Notice that beneath each major key in the example is listed the minor key with the same number of sharps or flats. This is known as its *relative minor.*

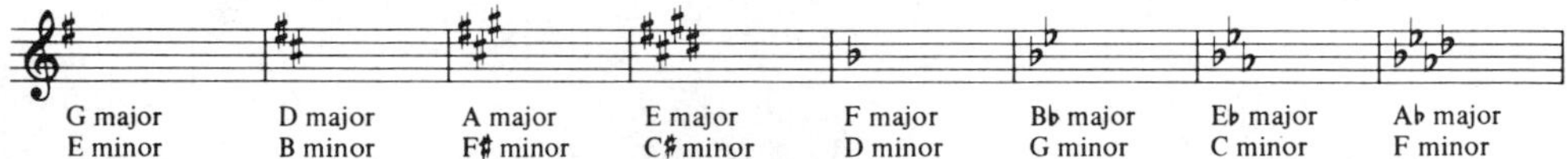

The twelve major and twelve minor keys make up the harmonic system of the Classical period. There had to come into existence an art form that would mobilize the resources of this system, that would bring into focus its capacities for dramatic conflict and architectural expanse. It was the great achievement of the eighteenth century to evolve and perfect this form.

44

The Major-Minor System

"Form follows function." — LOUIS SULLIVAN

Transposition

Suppose a certain melody begins on G. If one felt that the song lay a little too high for his voice, he might begin on F instead of G and shift all the tones of the melody one step lower. Someone else might find that the song lay too low for his voice. He would begin on A and sing each tone of the melody one step higher than it was written. The act of shifting all the tones of a musical composition a uniform distance to a higher or lower level of pitch is called *transposition.*

When we transpose a piece we shift it to another key. We change the level of pitch, the keynote, and the number of sharps or flats. But the melody line remains the same because the pattern of its whole and half steps has been retained in the new key as in the old. That is why the same song can be published in various keys for soprano, alto, tenor, and bass.

We have all transposed melodies without being aware of it. For example, a group of children will begin a song from a certain note. If the melody moves too high or too low for comfort, their teacher will stop them and have them begin again from another tone. On an instrument, transposing is a more complicated matter. The player must adjust his fingers to another arrangement of sharps or flats. If he is a pianist or organist he must shift not only the melody but the harmonies as well. The ability to transpose a piece at sight is a skill that musicians regard with respect. It is a necessity for professional accompanists, who are constantly required to transpose songs to higher or lower keys to suit the range of singers.

Choice of key

Why does a composer choose one key rather than another for his piece? In former times external factors strongly influenced this choice. Up to the time of Beethoven, for example, the brass instruments were not able to change keys as readily as they are now. In writing for the string instruments composers considered the fact that certain effects, such as playing on the open strings, could be achieved in one key rather than another. Several composers of the Romantic period seemed to associate a certain emotional atmosphere or color with various keys. Characteristic was Mendelssohn's fondness for E minor, Chopin's for C-sharp minor.

Modulation

If a piece of music can be played in one key as in another, why not put all music in the key of C and be done with it? Because the contrast between keys and the movement from one key to another is an essential element of musical structure. We have seen that the tones of the key form a group of "seven out of twelve," which imparts coherence and focus to the music. But this closed group may be opened up, in which case we are shifted—either gently or abruptly—to another area centering about another keynote. Such a change gives us a heightened sense of activity. It is an expressive gesture of prime importance.

The process of passing from one key to another is known as *modulation.* There is no way to describe in words something that can be experienced only in the domain of sound. Suffice it to say that the composer has at his disposal a number of ways of modulating; therewith he "lifts" the listener from one tonal area to another. As Arnold Schoenberg put it, "Modulation is like a change of scenery."

The twelve major and twelve minor keys may be compared to so many rooms in a house, with the modulations equivalent to corridors leading from one to the other. The eighteenth-century composer as a rule established the home key, shaped the passage of modulation—the "corridor"—in a clear-cut manner, and usually passed to a key area that was not too far away from his starting point. There resulted a spaciousness of structure that was the musical counterpart of the rolling sentences of the eighteenth-century novel and the balanced façades of eighteenth-century architecture.

Nineteenth-century Romanticism, on the other hand, demanded a whipping-up of emotions, an intensifying of all musical processes. In the Romantic era modulations were ever more frequent and abrupt. There came into being a hyperemotional music that wandered restlessly from key to key in accord with the need for excitement of the mid- and late-Romantic era. By the same token, the balanced structure of the Classical system, with its key areas neatly marked off one from the other, began to disintegrate.

Chromaticism

When seven tones out of twelve are selected to form a major or minor key, the other five become extraneous in relation to that particular Tonic. They enter the composition as transients, mainly to embellish the melody or harmony. If the piece is to sound firmly rooted in the key, the seven tones that belong to the key must prevail. Should the composer allow the five foreign tones to become too prominent in his melody and harmony, the relationship to the key center would be weakened and the key feeling become ambiguous. The distinction between the tones that do not belong within the key area and those that do is made explicit in the contrasting terms *chromatic* and *diatonic*. Chromatic, as we saw, refers to the twelve-tone scale including all the semitones of the octave. Chromatic melody or harmony moves by half steps, taking in the tones extraneous to the key. The word comes from the Greek *chroma,* which means "color." Diatonic, on the other hand, refers to musical progression based on the seven tones of a major or minor scale, and to harmonies that are firmly rooted in the key.

Diatonic vs. chromatic harmony

Diatonic harmony went hand in hand with the clear-cut key feeling that marked the late-eighteenth-century style. We may say that the music of Haydn, Mozart, and Beethoven tends to be diatonic. (There are of course many passages in their music, especially in their late works, that belie this generalization.) Chromatic harmony, on the other hand, characterized the ceaseless modulation and surcharged emotional atmosphere of nineteenth-century music. The Romantic composers, from Schubert to Wagner and his followers, indefatigably explored the possibilities of chromaticism. In an earlier section of this book we described the Romantic movement in music.

We may now establish, as one of its important characteristics, a tendency toward chromatic harmony.

The Key as a Form-Building Element

By marking off an area in musical space with a fixed center, the key provides the framework within which musical growth and development take place. The three main harmonies of the key–Tonic (I), Dominant (V), and Subdominant (IV)–become the focal points over which melodies and chord progressions unfold. In brief, the key is the neighborhood inhabited by a tune and its harmonies. Thus the key becomes a prime factor for musical unity.

At the same time the contrast between keys may further the cause of variety. The Classical composer pitted one key against another, thereby achieving a dramatic opposition between them. He began by establishing the home key. Presently he modulated to a related key, generally that of the Dominant (for example, from C major with no sharps or flats to G major, one sharp; or from G major to D major, two sharps). In so doing he established a tension, since the Dominant key was unstable compared to the tonic. This tension required resolution, which was provided by the return to the home key.

The progression from home key to contrasting key and back outlined the basic musical pattern of statement-departure-return. The home key was the anchorage, the safe harbor; the foreign key represented adventure. The home key was the symbol of unity; the foreign key ensured variety and contrast.

The tension between two keys and their ultimate reconciliation became the motive power of the music of the Classical era. This conflict-and resolution found its frame in the grand form of the latter half of the eighteenth century–the ideal tone-drama known as the sonata.

45

The Development of Themes: Musical Logic

"I alter some things, eliminate and try again until I am satisfied. Then begins the mental working out of this material in its breadth, its narrowness, its height and depth."

— LUDWIG VAN BEETHOVEN

Thinking, whether in words or tones, demands continuity and sequence. Every thought must flow out of the one before and lead logically into the next. In this way is created a sense of steady progression toward a goal. If we were to join the beginning of one sentence to the end of another, it would not make any more sense than if we united the first phrase of one melody and the second of another. In our discussion of melody (pages 7–11) we compared the two phrases of *London Bridge* to a question-and-answer formation. A similar impression of cause and effect, of natural flow and continuity, must pervade the whole musical fabric.

Theme

When a melodic idea, we noted, is used as a building block in the construction of a musical work it is known as a theme or subject. The theme is the first in a chain of musical situations, all of which must grow out of the basic idea as naturally as does the plant from the seed. The process of spinning out a theme, of weaving and reweaving the threads of which it is composed, is the essence of musical thinking. This process of expansion has its parallel in prose writing, where an idea stated at the beginning of a paragraph is embroidered and enlarged upon until all its aspects appear in view. Each sentence leads smoothly into the one that follows. In similar fashion, every measure takes up where the one before left off and brings us inexorably to the next.

Thematic development

The most tightly knit kind of expansion in our music is known as *thematic development.* To develop a theme means to unfold its latent energies, to search out its capacities for growth and bring them to fruition. Thematic development represents the constructional element in music. It is one of the most important techniques in musical composition, demanding of the composer imagination, master craftsmanship, and intellectual power.

In the process of development, certain procedures have proved to be particularly effective. The simplest is repetition, which may be either exact or varied; or the idea may be restated at another pitch. For example, in *America,* the melodic idea on the words "Land where my fathers died" is restated immediately, but a tone lower, on the words "Land of the pilgrims' pride." Such a restatement at a higher or lower pitch level is known, we saw, as a sequence. The original idea may also be varied in regard to melody, harmony, rhythm, timbre, dynamics, and register. It may be attended by expansion or contraction of the note values as well as by bold and frequent changes of key.

Sequence

Motive

A basic technique in thematic development is the breaking up of the theme into its constituent motives. A motive, we found, is the smallest fragment of a theme that forms a melodic-rhythmic unit. The motives are the cells of musical growth. Through fragmentation of themes, through repeating and varying the motives and combining them in ever fresh patterns the composer imparts to the musical organism the quality of dynamic evolution and growth.

Thematic development is too complex a technique to appear to advantage in short lyric pieces, songs, or dances. In such compositions a simple contrast between sections and a modest expansion within each section supplies the necessary continuity. By the same token, thematic development finds its proper frame in the large forms of music. To those forms it imparts an epic-dramatic quality, along with the clarity, coherence, and logic that are the indispensable attributes of this most advanced type of musical thinking.

46

The Sonata: The First Movement

"The history of the sonata is the history of an attempt to cope with one of the most singular problems ever presented to the mind of man, and its solution is one of the most successful achievements of his artistic instincts." — HUBERT PARRY

The name sonata comes from the Italian *suonare,* "to sound," indicating a piece to be sounded on instruments, as distinct from cantata, a piece to be sung. A *sonata* (as Haydn, Mozart, and their successors understood the term) is an instrumental work consisting of a series of contrasting movements, generally three or four in number. The name sonata is used when the piece is intended for one or two instruments. If more than two are involved the work is called, as the case may be, a trio, quartet, quintet, sextet, septet, octet, or nonet. A sonata for solo instrument and orchestra is called a concerto; a sonata for the whole orchestra, a symphony. The sonata, clearly, accounts for a large part of the instrumental music we hear.

Sonata-Allegro Form

The most highly organized and characteristic member of the several movements that make up the sonata cycle is the opening movement. This is what is variously known as *first-movement form, sonata-allegro form,* or *sonata form.* Each of these names is useful but somewhat misleading. "First-movement form" is good provided we remember that this form may also be used for the other movements, and also for single-movement works. "Sonata-allegro form" is appropriate, since this type of movement is at its most characteristic in a lively or allegro movement. Unfortunately, the name fails to take into account that slow movements were sometimes cast in this form, especially in the eighteenth century. "Sonata form" is correct, and is much used by modern writers; but it is too easily confused with the term "sonata," which includes all the movements.

A movement in sonata-allegro form is based on two assumptions. The first is that a musical movement takes on direction and goal if, after establishing itself in the home key, it modulates to other areas and ultimately returns to the home key. We may therefore regard sonata form as a drama between two contrasting key areas. The "plot," the action, and the tension derive from this contrast. Sonata-allegro form, in brief, is an artistic embodiment of the principles underlying the major-minor system—the establishment, that is, of different key areas which serve as points of reference for a statement, a departure, and a return.

Second is the assumption that a theme may have its latent energies released through the development of its constituent motives. Most useful for this purpose is a brief, incisive theme, one that has momentum and tension, and that promises more than at first sight it reveals. The themes will be stated or "exposed" in the first section; developed in the second; and restated or "recapitulated" in the third.

The Exposition (Statement)

The opening section, the Exposition or Statement, sets forth the two opposing keys and their respective themes. (A theme may consist of several related ideas, in which case we speak of it as a theme group.) The first theme and its expansion establish the home key. A transition or bridge leads into a contrasting key; in other words, the function of the bridge is to modulate. The second theme and its expansion establish the contrasting key. A closing section or codetta rounds off the Exposition in the contrasting key. In the Classical sonata form the Exposition is repeated. The adventurous quality of the Exposition derives in no small measure from the fact that it brings us from the home key to the contrasting key.

The Development

The Development wanders further through a series of foreign keys, building up tension against the inevitable return home. Temperature is kept at fever pitch through frequent modulation, resulting in a sense of breathless activity and excitement.

At the same time the composer proceeds to reveal the potentialities of his themes. He breaks them into their component motives; recombines them into fresh patterns; and releases their latent energies, their explosive force. Conflict and action are the essence of drama. In the development section the conflict erupts, the action reaches maximum intensity. The protagonists of the drama are hurled one against another; their worlds collide. Emotion is transformed into motion. The theme may be modified or varied, turned upside down (*inversion*), expanded to longer note values (*augmentation*), contracted into shorter note values (*diminution*), combined with other motives or even with new material. If the sonata is for orchestra—that is, a symphony—a fragment of the theme may be presented by one group of instruments and imitated by another. Now it appears in the upper register, now deep in the bass. Each measure seems to grow out of the preceding by an inescapable law of cause and effect. Each adds to the drive and the momentum. Unity and diversity, logic and passion fuse at white heat to create much out of little.

When the developmental surge has run its course, the tension abates. A transition passage leads back to the home key. The beginning of the third section, the Recapitulation or Restatement, is in a sense the psychological climax of sonata form, just as the peak of many a journey is the return home. The first theme appears as we first heard it, in the home key, proclaiming the victory of unity over diversity, of continuity over change.

The Recapitulation (Restatement)

The Recapitulation follows the general path of the Exposition, restating the first and second themes more or less in their original form, but with the wealth of additional meaning that these have taken on in the course of their wanderings. Most important of all, in the Recapitulation the opposing elements are reconciled, the home key emerges triumphant. For this reason, the third section differs in one important detail from the Exposition: the composer now remains in the home key. He generally shifts the second theme, which was originally in a contrasting key, to the home area. In other words, although the second theme and its expansion unfold in substantially the same way as before, we now hear this material transposed into the home key. There follows the final pronouncement, the coda, in the home key. This is fashioned from material previously heard in the codetta, to which new matter is sometimes added. The coda rounds off the movement and asserts the victory of the home key with a vigorous final cadence.

Coda

The procedure just described is summed up in the following outline:

Sonata-Allegro Form (Sonata Form)

Exposition * (or Statement)	Development	Recapitulation (or Restatement)
First theme (or theme group) and its expansion in home key	Builds up tension against the return to home key by	First theme (or theme group) and its expansion in home key
Bridge–modulates	1. Frequent modulation to foreign keys	Bridge
Second theme (or theme group) and its expansion in contrasting key	2. Fragmentation and manipulation of themes and motives	Second theme (or theme group) and its expansion transposed to home area
Codetta. Cadence in contrasting key	Transition back to home key	Coda. Cadence in home key

* Note: The Exposition may be preceded by a slow introduction. Also, certain Classical masters, especially Haydn, occasionally based the sonata-allegro movement on a single theme, which appeared first in the home key, then in the contrasting key. However, as time went on composers preferred a movement based on contrasting themes.

The main features of the outline above are present in one shape or another in innumerable sonata-allegro movements, yet no two are exactly alike in their disposition of the material. Each constitutes a unique solution of the problem in terms of character, mood, and relation of forces, for the true artist—and it is his work alone that endures—shapes the form according to what he desires to express; so that what looks on paper like a fixed plan becomes, when transformed into living sound, a supple framework for infinite variety.

Thematic opposition

Even as the dramatist creates opposing personalities as the chief characters of his work, so the composer achieves a vivid contrast between the musical ideas that form the basis of the movement. The opposition between two themes may be underlined in a number of ways. Through a contrast in dynamics—loud against soft; in register—low against high; in timbre—strings against winds, one instrumental combination against another; in rhythm and tempo—an animated pattern against one that is sustained; in tone production—legato against staccato; in type of melody—an active melody line with wide range and leaps against one that moves quietly along the scale; in type of harmony—consonance against dissonance, diatonic harmony against chromatic; in type of accompaniment—quietly moving chords against extended arpeggios. Not all of these may appear in a given work. One contrast, however, is required, being the basis of the form: the contrast of key. And the opposition may be further intensified by putting one theme in the major and the other in minor.

The reader should be cautioned, in conclusion, against a widespread misconception. The conventional description of sonata-allegro form, by its emphasis upon the few themes that serve as building blocks for an instrumental movement, seems to imply that everything between these themes is in the nature of filling-in or transitional material. Unfortunately many people listen in precisely this way to a symphonic movement, waiting for the themes—that is, the melodies they recognize—just as, in another context, they wait for the arias in an opera. But from everything we have said it is clear that the sonata-allegro movement is an organic unity in which the growth, the development, the destiny of a theme is no less important than the theme itself (just as, in assessing a human action, we consider its consequences no less than the deed proper). The music examples in the past chapters and in those to come represent what is generally regarded as "Theme 1," "Theme 2," or "Theme 3" of a sonata movement. They are actually only the kernels, the beginnings of themes. The theme, in the profoundly musical sense, must be considered to include not only the few notes in the example but also the "etc."—that is, the passage or section that constitutes the flowering of the idea. It is only when we take this larger view of the theme (or theme group) that we come to understand the symphonic movement for what it is: a continuous expansion and growth of musical ideas from first note to last, from which not a measure may be omitted without disturbing the equilibrium and the organic oneness of the whole. Only by listening to the movement in this way do we apprehend the essential qualities of sonata style, its concentration, its continuity, its unflagging dynamism. It should be added that sonata-allegro form is the representative form of the Classical period.

47

The Sonata, Continued: The Other Movements

"To write a symphony means, to me, to construct a world." — GUSTAV MAHLER

We now consider the other types of musical structure that came to be included in the sonata cycle.

Theme and Variations

We found that repetition is a basic element of musical structure. This being so, composers devised ways of varying an idea when they restated it. Variation is an important procedure that is to be found in every species of music. But there is one type of piece in which it constitutes the ruling principle—the *theme and variations*. The theme is stated at the outset, so that the audience will know the basic idea that serves as the point of departure. The melody may be of the composer's invention, as in the second movement of Beethoven's *Fifth Symphony;* or one that he has borrowed from another, as in the case of Brahms's *Variations on a Theme of Haydn*. The theme is apt to be a small two- or three-part form, simple in character so as to allow room for elaboration. There follows a series of variations in which certain features of the original idea are retained while others are altered. Each variation sets forth the idea with some new modification—one might say in a new disguise—through which the listener glimpses something of the original theme.

Melodic variations

To the process of variation the composer brings all the techniques of musical embellishment. He may, to begin with, vary the melody. To indicate the simplest way that this is done, suppose a melodic line moves C–D–E. One may ornament it by including intermediate notes, transforming the melodic progression into C–D–D♯–E or C–C♯–D–E, or C–C♯–D–D♯–E. In this way a more florid line results, although the melody is not fundamentally changed. Conversely, one may omit certain notes and thereby reduce the melody to its skeletal outline: C–E. Or one may shift the melody to another key, thereby throwing new light upon it. Melodic variation is a favorite procedure in the jazz band and rock group, where the solo player embellishes a popular tune with a series of arabesques.

Harmonic variation

In harmonic variation the chords that accompany a melody are replaced by others. Diatonic harmonies may give way to chromatic, simple triads to complex dissonances. Or the melody may be entirely omitted, the variation being based on the harmonic skeleton. The type of accompaniment may be changed; for example, from chords in block formation to decorative broken chords (arpeggios). Or the melody may be shifted to a lower register with new harmonies sounding above it.

Rhythmic variation

So too the rhythm, meter, and tempo may be varied, with interesting changes in the nature of the tune. This may take on the guise of a waltz, a polka, a minuet, a march. The texture may be enriched by interweaving the melody with new themes. Or the original theme may itself become an accompaniment for a new melody. By combining these methods with changes in dynamics and tone color, the expressive content of the theme may be changed, so that it is presented now as a funeral march, now as a serenade, folk dance, caprice, or boat song. This type of character variation was much in favor in the Romantic era.

The theme with variations challenges the composer's inventiveness and enables him to achieve a high degree of unity in diversity. One therefore understands why variation form has attracted composers for more than three hundred years, both as an independent piece and as one of the movements of the sonata.

Minuet and Trio

The *minuet* originated in the French court in the mid-seventeenth century; its stately ¾ time embodied the ideal of grace of an aristocratic age. In the eighteenth century the minuet was taken over into the sonata, where it served as the third movement, occasionally the second.

Since dance music lends itself to symmetrical construction, we often find in the minuet a clear-cut structure based on phrases of four and eight measures. (All the same, the minuets of Haydn and Mozart reveal an abundance of nonsymmetrical phrases.) In tempo the minuet ranges from stateliness to a lively pace and whimsical character. As a matter of fact, certain of Haydn's minuets are closer in spirit to the village green than to the palace ballroom.

The custom prevailed of presenting two dances as a group, the first being repeated at the end of the second **(A-B-A)**. The one in the middle was frequently arranged for only three instruments; hence the name *trio,* which persisted even after the customary setting for three was abandoned. The trio as a rule is lighter in texture and quieter of gait. Frequently woodwind tone figures prominently in this section, creating an out-of-doors atmosphere that lends it a special charm. At the end of the trio we find *da capo* or D.C. ("from the beginning"), signifying that the first section is to be played over again. Minuet-trio-minuet is a symmetrical three-part structure in which each part in turn is a small two-part or three-part form:

Minuet (A)	**Trio (B)**	**Minuet (A)**
a-b-a	**c-d-c**	**a-b-a**
or	**or**	**or**
a-b	**c-d**	**a-b**

This structure is elaborated through repetition of the subsections, a procedure that the composer indicates with a *repeat sign* (:||:). However, when the minuet returns after the trio the repeat signs are customarily ignored. A codetta may round off each section.

Minuet (A)	**Trio (B)**	**Minuet (A)**
‖: a :‖: b-a(codetta) :‖	**‖: c :‖: d-c :‖**	**a-b-a (codetta)**
or	**or**	**or**
‖: a :‖ b(codetta) :‖	**‖: c :‖: d :‖**	**a-b (codetta)**

Scherzo

In the nineteenth-century symphony the minuet was displaced by the scherzo. This is generally the third movement, occasionally the second. It is usually in $\frac{3}{4}$ time. Like the minuet, it is a three-part form (scherzo-trio-scherzo), the first section being repeated after the middle part. But it differs from the minuet in its faster pace and vigorous rhythm. The scherzo—the name, as you will recall, is the Italian word for "jest"—is marked by abrupt changes of mood ranging from the humorous or the whimsical to the mysterious and even demonic. In the hands of Beethoven the scherzo became a movement of great rhythmic drive.

The Rondo

The *rondo* is a lively movement suffused with the spirit of the dance. Its distinguishing characteristic is the recurrence of a central idea—the rondo theme—in alternation with contrasting elements. Its symmetrical sections create a balanced architecture that is satisfying esthetically and easy to grasp. In its simplest form, **A-B-A-B-A,** the rondo is an extension of three-part form. If there are two contrasting themes the sections may follow an **A-B-A-C-A** or similar pattern.

The true rondo as developed by the Classical masters was more ambitious in scope. Characteristic was the formation **A-B-A-C-A-B-A.** The first **A-B-A** was in the nature of an Exposition and the corresponding **A-B-A** at the end was a Recapitulation. Between them was the **C** section, which served as a kind of Development. What with contrasts of key and elaborate transitional passages, this type of rondo took on the spaciousness of sonata from and came to be known as a *rondo-sonata.*

Actually one may speak of rondo style as well as rondo form, for the essence of the rondo—at any rate as Haydn and Mozart cultivated it—is its vivacity and good humor. Because the theme is to be heard over and over again it must be catchy and relaxing. One should point out, however, that not every movement that follows the rondo form has the spirit of the gay Classical rondo. The rondo figured in eighteenth- and nineteenth-century music both as an independent piece and as a member of the sonata cycle. In the sonata it often served as the final movement.

The Sonata Cycle as a Whole

The four-movement cycle of the Classical masters, as found in their symphonies, concertos, sonatas, string quartets, and other types of chamber music, became the vehicle for their most important instrumental music. The following outline sums up the common practice of the Classic-Romantic era. It will be helpful to the reader, provided he remembers that it is no more than a general scheme and does not necessarily apply to all works of this kind. In Beethoven's *Ninth Symphony,* for example, the scherzo is the second movement while the Adagio comes third.

Movement	Character	Form	Tempo
First	Epic-dramatic	Sonata-allegro	Allegro
Second	Slow and lyrical	Theme and variations Sonata form A-B-A	Andante, Adagio, Largo
Third	Dancelike: Minuet (18th century)	Minuet and trio	Allegretto
	Scherzo (19th century)	Scherzo and trio	Allegro
Fourth	Lively, "happy ending" (18th century) Epic-dramatic, with triumphal ending (19th century)	Sonata-allegro Rondo Rondo-sonata Theme and variations	Allegro, Vivace, Presto

The Classical masters of the sonata thought of the four movements of the cycle as self-contained entities connected by identity of key. First, third, and fourth movements were in the home key, with the second movement in a contrasting key. The nineteenth century sought a more obvious connection between movements—a thematic connection. This need was met by *cyclical structure,* in which a theme from the earlier movements appeared in the later ones as a kind of motto or unifying thread.

The sonata cycle satisfied the need of composers for an extended instrumental work of an abstract nature. It mobilized the contrasts of key and mode inherent in the major-minor system. With its fusion of sensuous, emotional, and intellectual elements, its intermingling of lyric contemplation and action, the sonata cycle may justly claim to be one of the most ingenious art forms ever devised by man.

PART FOUR

Eighteenth-Century Classicism

"When a nation brings its innermost nature to consummate expression in arts and letters we speak of its classic period. Classicism stands for experience, for spiritual and human maturity which has deep roots in the cultural soil of the nation, for the mastery of the means of expression in technique and form, and for a definite conception of the world and of life; the final compression of the artistic values of a people."

— PAUL HENRY LANG: *Music in Western Civilization*

48

The Classical Spirit

> " 'Tis more to guide, than spur the Muse's steed;
> Restrain his fury, than provoke his speed;
> The winged courser, like a gen'rous horse,
> Shows most true mettle when you check his course."
> — ALEXANDER POPE: *Essay on Criticism*

The dictionary defines Classicism in two ways: in general terms, as pertaining to the highest order of excellence in literature and art; specifically, pertaining to the culture of the ancient Greeks and Romans. Implicit in the Classical attitude is the notion that supreme excellence has been reached in the past and may be attained again through adherence to tradition.

Being part of a tradition implies a relationship to things outside oneself. The Classical artist neither glories in nor emphasizes his apartness from other men. He regards neither his individuality nor his personal experience as the primary material of his art. For him, therefore, the work of art exists in its own right rather than as an extension of his ego. Where the Romantic is inclined to regard art primarily as a means of self-expression, the Classicist stresses its powers as a means of communication. His atten-

The Parthenon, Athens. The art of ancient Greece embodied the ideals of order, stability, and harmonious proportion.

tion is directed to clarity of thought and beauty of form. In effect, he is considerably more objective in his approach than is the Romantic. For the extremely personal utterance of the Romantic, he substitutes symbols of universal validity. Classicism upholds the control and the discipline of art, its potentialities for rational expression and exquisite workmanship, its vision of an ideal beauty. This wholeness of view encourages the qualities of order, stability, and harmonious proportion that we associate with the Classical style.

As we pointed out in our discussion of Romanticism, neither the Classical nor the Romantic spirit is limited to any one time. Both have alternated throughout the history of culture. However, just as conditions in the nineteenth century gave rise to an extended period of Romanticism, so the social climate of the eighteenth century favored the emergence of the Classical spirit.

Eighteenth-Century Classicism

Aristocratic patronage

The culture of the eighteenth century was under the patronage of an aristocracy for whom the arts were a necessary adornment of life. Art was part of the elaborate ritual that surrounded the existence of princes. In such a society, where the ruling caste enjoys its power through hereditary right, tradition is apt to be prized and the past revered. The center of art life is the palace and the privileged minority residing therein. In these high places the emphasis is on elegance of manner and beauty of style.

The art of the eighteenth century bears the imprint of the spacious palaces and formal gardens, with their balanced proportions and finely wrought detail, that formed the setting for enlightened despotism. In the middle of the century, Louis XV presided over the extravagant fetes in Versailles (although he foresaw the deluge). Frederick the Great ruled in Prussia, Maria Theresa in Austria, Catherine the Great in Russia. Yet disruptive forces were swiftly gathering beneath the glittering surface. The American Revolution dealt a shattering blow to the doctrine of the divine right of kings. And before the century had ended, Europe was convulsed by the French Revolution.

Bourgeois revolution

The second half of the eighteenth century, consequently, witnessed both the twilight of the *ancien régime* and the dawn of a new political-economic alignment in Europe; specifically, the transfer of power from the aristocracy to the middle class, whose wealth was based on a rapidly expanding capitalism, on mines and factories, steam power and railroads. This shift was made possible by the Industrial Revolution, which gathered momentum in the mid-eighteenth century with a series of important inventions, from Watt's steam engine and Hargreaves's spinning jenny in the 1760s to Cartwright's power loom in 1785 and Eli Whitney's cotton gin in 1793.

These decades saw significant advances in science. Benjamin Franklin discovered electricity in 1752, Priestley discovered oxygen in 1774, Jenner

Eighteenth-century Classicism drew its inspiration from the art and culture of ancient Greece. A painting by Jacques Louis David (1748–1825). **The Death of Socrates.** (The Metropolitan Museum of Art, Wolfe Fund, 1931. Catherine Lorillard Wolfe Collection.)

perfected vaccination in 1796, Laplace advanced his mechanistic view of the universe and Volta invented the voltaic pile in 1800. There were important events in intellectual life, such as the publication of Winckelmann's *History of Ancient Art* (1764), of the French *Encyclopédie* (1751–72), and the first edition of the *Encyclopaedia Britannica* (1771). The final quarter of the century produced such landmarks as Adam Smith's *The Wealth of Nations,* Kant's *Critique of Pure Reason,* Rousseau's *Confessions,* Gibbon's *Decline and Fall of the Roman Empire,* Boswell's *Life of Johnson,* and Malthus's *Essay on Population.*

Intellectual dualism

The intellectual climate of the Classical era, consequently, was nourished by two opposing streams. On the one hand Classical art captured the exquisite refinement of a way of life that was drawing to a close. On the other it caught the intimations of a new way of life that was struggling to be born. This dualism is of the essence in the Classical era and pervades all its attitudes. For example, the eighteenth century has been called the Age of Reason; but the two opposing camps invoked reason in diametrically opposite ways. The apologists of the status quo appealed to reason in order to justify the existing order. Early in the century Leibnitz taught that this was "the best of all possible worlds," and Pope proclaimed that "Whatever is, is right." As the century wore on, however, this spurious optimism became ever more difficult to maintain. The opponents of the established order, the *philosophes* who created the *Grande Encyclopédie* as an instrument of the Enlightenment–Voltaire, Diderot, Rousseau, Condorcet, d'Alembert and their comrades–also invoked reason, but for the purpose of attacking the existing order. Therewith these spokesmen for the rising middle class became the prophets of the approaching upheaval.

The Romantics, we saw, idealized the Middle Ages. But to eighteenth-century thinkers the Medieval period represented a thousand years of bar-

barism—the Dark Ages. The term *Gothic* represented everything that was opposed to what they regarded as rational and cultivated. Their ideal was the civilization of ancient Greece and Rome. To the Gothic cathedral, with its stained-glass windows, its bizarre gargoyles, its ribbed columns soaring heavenward in passionate mysticism, they opposed the Greek temple, a thing of beauty, unity and proportion, lightness and grace.

Classical ideals

Yet here too the revival of interest in Classical Antiquity meant different things to the opposing camps. The aristocrats and their spokesmen exalted Hellenism as the symbol of a rational, objective attitude that guarded one against becoming too deeply involved with the issues of life. They saw the ancient gods, kings, and heroes as a reflection of themselves—themselves ennobled, transfigured. But to the protagonists of the middle class, Greece and Rome represented city-states that had rebelled against tyrants and thrown off despotism. It was in this spirit that the foremost painter of revolutionary France, Jacques Louis David, decked his canvases with the symbols of Athenian and Roman democracy. In this spirit, too, Thomas Jefferson praised David for having "ennobled the contemporary countenance with the classical quality of ancient republican virtue." Jefferson patterned both the Capitol and the University of Virginia after Greek and Roman temples, thereby giving strength to the Classic revival in this country, which made Ionic, Doric, and Corinthian columns an indispensable feature of our public buildings well into the twentieth century.

The Augustan Age

The Classical point of view held sway in English letters to such an extent that the mid-eighteenth century is known as the Augustan Age (after the Roman emperor Augustus, patron of the poet Vergil). Its arbiter was Samuel Johnson, whose position of leadership in literature was as undisputed as was that of his friend Sir Joshua Reynolds in painting. Both men

Thomas Jefferson expressed his admiration for the pure beauty of the Roman temple form in his design for the Virginia State Capitol in Richmond.

Sir Joshua Reynolds (1723–92) invested his subjects with qualities borrowed from a noble past. **Jane, Countess of Harrington.** (Henry E. Huntington Library and Art Gallery.)

upheld a highly formal, aristocratic type of art. Yet within the formal stream of Augustan Classicism we become aware of a current of tender sentiment that is an early sign of the Romantic spirit. The novels of Samuel Richardson, Henry Fielding, Laurence Sterne, and Tobias Smollett were suffused with homely bourgeois sentiment, as were the poems of Thomas Gray, Oliver Goldsmith, and William Cowper. For the Age of Reason was also, curiously, the Age of Sensibility, and the sensibility steadily broadens into a trend toward the Romantic.

The Age of Sensibility

Thus it is that the Age of Reason begins to give way to the Age of Romance considerably earlier than is commonly supposed. In the 1760s there already appeared a number of works—such as Percy's *Reliques of Ancient English Poetry*—that clearly indicate the new interest in a romantic medievalism. In the same decade Rousseau, the "father of Romanticism," produced some of his most significant writings. His celebrated dictum, "Man is born free and everywhere he is in chains," epitomizes the temper of the time. So too the first outcropping of the Romantic spirit in Germany, the movement known as *Sturm und Drang* (Storm and Stress), took shape in the 1770s, when it produced two characteristic works by its most significant young writers—the *Sorrows of Werther* by Goethe and *The Robbers* by Schiller. (Goethe, it will be remembered, became a favorite lyric poet of the Romantic composers.) By the end of the century the atmosphere had completely changed. The two most important English poets of the late eighteenth century—Robert Burns and William Blake—stand entirely outside the Classical stream, as does the greatest end-of-the-century painter, Goya, whose passionate realism anticipates a later age.

Sturm und Drang

Late eighteenth-century culture, therefore, is neither as exclusively aristocratic nor as exclusively Classical as we have been taught to believe. It assimilated and was nourished by both democratic and Romantic elements. Precisely its dual nature lends it its subtle charm.

The Artist under Patronage

The eighteenth-century artist generally functioned under the system of aristocratic patronage. He created for a public high above him in social rank; his patrons were interested in his product rather than in his personality. Inevitably he was directed toward a Classical objectivity and reserve.

The artist under patronage was a master craftsman, an artisan working on direct commission from his patron. He produced works for immediate use, sustained by daily contact with his public. It is true that in point of social status the artist in livery was little better than a servant. This was not quite as depressing as it sounds, for in that society virtually everybody was a servant of the prince save other princes. The patronage system gave the artist economic security and a social framework within which he could function. It offered important advantages to the great artists who successfully adjusted to its requirements, as the career of Haydn richly shows. On the other hand, Mozart's tragic end illustrates how heavy was the penalty exacted from those unable to make that adjustment.

Eighteenth-century Classicism, then, mirrored the unique moment in history when the old world was dying and the new was in process of being born. From the meeting of two historic forces emerged an art of noble simplicity whose achievement in music constitutes one of the pinnacles of Western culture.

49

Classicism in Music

"Ought not the musician, quite as much as the poet and painter, to study nature? In nature he can study man, its noblest creature." — JOHANN FRIEDRICH REICHARDT (1774)

The Classical period in music (c. 1775–1825) centers about the achievements of the four masters of the Viennese school—Haydn, Mozart, Beethoven, and Schubert—and their contemporaries. Their art reached its flowering in a time of great musical experimentation and discovery, when musicians were confronted by three challenging problems: first, to explore to the full the possibilities offered by the major-minor system; second, to perfect a large form of absolute instrumental music that would mobilize those possibilities to the fullest degree; and third, having found this ideal form in the sonata cycle, to differentiate between its various types—the solo and duo sonata, trio, quartet, and other kinds of chamber music, the concerto, and the symphony.

The Viennese school

If by Classicism we mean adherence to traditional forms we certainly cannot apply the term to the composers of the Viennese school. They experimented boldly and ceaselessly with the materials at their disposal. An enormous distance separates Haydn's early symphonies and string quartets from his later ones; the same is true of Mozart, Beethoven, and Schubert. Nor can we call these masters Classical if we mean that they—like the poets and painters of the mid-eighteenth century—subordinated emotional expression to accepted "rules" of form. The slow movements of Haydn and Mozart are filled with emotion of the profoundest kind. What could be more impassioned than Beethoven's music, or more suffused with lyric tenderness than Schubert's?

Even in point of time the Classical label does not fit music very well. The Classical era in literature and painting spread across the middle of the eighteenth century, whereas in music it appeared several decades later, in the last quarter of the eighteenth and the first quarter of the nineteenth centuries, when the forces of Romanticism already were coming to the fore. It should not surprise us that Romantic elements abound in the music of Haydn, Mozart, and Beethoven, especially in their late works. As for Schubert, although his symphonies and chamber music fall within the Classical orbit, his songs and piano pieces—as we saw in an earlier section of this book—stamp him a Romantic.

In consequence, the term Classicism applies to the art of the four Viennese masters in only one—but that one perhaps the most important—of its meanings: "as pertaining to the highest order of excellence." They and their contemporaries solved the problems presented to them so brilliantly that their symphonies and concertos, piano sonatas, duo sonatas, trios, string quartets, and similar works remained as unsurpassable models for all who came after. They evolved a dynamic instrumental language that was the perfect vehicle for the processes of thematic growth and development. They perfected spacious designs born of reason and logic, whose overall structure was flexible enough to allow for free expression of the most varied sentiments. And in doing so they created a new world of musical thought and sound.

Vocal Music in the Classical Period

Classical opera

The opera house was a center of experimentation in the Classical era. Opera was the most important branch of musical entertainment and the one that reached the widest public. Classical opera was based on principles directly opposite to those that prevailed in the Romantic music drama. The music was the point of departure and imposed its forms on the drama. Each scene was a closed musical unit. The separate numbers were conceived as parts of the whole and held together in a carefully planned framework. There was the greatest possible distinction between the rapid patter of recitative and the lyric curve of aria. The voice reigned supreme, yet the orchestra displayed all the vivacity of the Classical instrumental style.

Opera buffa

A significant development was the importance of Italian comic opera (opera buffa), which adopted certain features of the serious opera and in turn influenced the latter. Far from being an escapist form of entertainment, comic opera was directly related to the life of the time. Its emphasis was on the affairs of "little people," on swift action, pointed situations, spontaneous emotion, and sharpness of characterization. This popular lyric theater showed an abundance of racy melody, brilliant orchestration, and lively rhythms. Characteristic were the ensemble numbers at the end of the act, of a verve and drive that influenced all branches of music. From its cradle in Italy, Classical opera buffa spread all over Europe, steadily expanding its scope until it culminated in the works of the greatest musical dramatist of the eighteenth century—Mozart.

Liturgical music

As a center of music making, the Church retained its importance alongside opera house and aristocratic salon. Whereas the first half of the century had seen the high point of Protestant music in the art of Bach and his contemporaries, the Catholic countries now assumed first place, especially the Hapsburg domains. The masters of the Viennese Classical school produced a great deal of Catholic church music: Masses, vespers, litanies, and the like. They did as composers have always done: they used the living idiom of their day (an idiom based on opera and symphony) to express their faith in God and man.

Instrumental Music of the Classical Period

The Classical masters established the orchestra as we know it today. They based the ensemble on the blending of the four instrumental groups. The heart of this orchestra was the string choir. Woodwinds, used with great imagination, ably seconded the strings. The brass sustained the harmonies and contributed body to the tone mass, while the kettledrums supplied rhythmic life and vitality. The eighteenth-century orchestra numbered from thirty to forty players. The volume of sound was still considered in relation to the salon rather than the concert hall. (It was toward the end of the Classical period that musical life began to move from the one to the other.) Foreign to Classical art were the swollen sonorities of the late nineteenth century. The orchestra of Haydn and Mozart lent itself to delicate nuances in which each timbre stood out radiantly.

The 18th-century orchestra

It follows that the Classical masters conceived their works on a smaller scale than did their nineteenth-century successors. They created a dynamic style of orchestral writing in which all the instruments participated actively. The interchange and imitation of themes among the various instrumental groups assumed the excitement of a witty conversation. The

The chamber music of the eighteenth century was designed for the entertainment of the aristocracy. **The Concert,** *an engraving by Augustin de Saint Aubin (1736–1807).*

Classical orchestra brought to absolute music a number of effects long familiar in the opera house. The gradual crescendo and decrescendo established themselves as staples of the new symphonic style. Hardly less conspicuous were the abrupt alternations of soft and loud, sudden accents, dramatic pauses, the use of tremolo and pizzicato. These and similar devices of operatic music added drama and tension to the Classical orchestral style.

The symphony

The central place in Classical instrumental music was taken by the "sonata for orchestra"—the symphony. This grew rapidly in dimension and significance until, with the final works of Mozart and Haydn, it became the most important type of absolute music (which it remained throughout the Romantic period). Important, too, was the "sonata for solo instrument and orchestra"—the concerto, which combined a virtuoso part for the featured player with the resources of the orchestra. The piano concerto was the chief type, although other solo instruments were not neglected.

The concerto

Chamber music

Chamber music enjoyed a great flowering in the Classical era, as did a type of composition that stood midway between chamber music and symphony, known as *divertimento*. The title fixes the character of this category of music as sociable diversion or entertainment. Closely related were the serenade, the *notturno* (night piece), and the *cassation* (a term of obscure origin probably referring to something in the streets or out-of-doors). Contemporary acounts tell of groups of street musicians who performed these works—for strings, winds, or both—outside the homes of the wealthy or in a quiet square before an appreciative audience of their fellow townsmen. At this time, too, the piano came into favor, gradually supplanting harpsichord and clavichord as an instrument for the home. Its more powerful tone also made it popular in the concert hall, although it must be remembered that the piano of the late eighteenth century was less powerful than its modern equivalent. The piano sonata became the most ambitious form of solo music, in which composers worked out new conceptions of keyboard style and sonata structure, creating a rich literature for both the amateur and the virtuoso.

Sonata form

Classical sonata form was based upon a clear-cut opposition of keys. This demanded a harmony well rooted in the key. What gives certain works of Haydn and Mozart their pure, even chaste quality is the fact that their harmony is firmly diatonic, as distinct from the tendency toward chromaticism that gained strength throughout the nineteenth century.

Other Aspects of Musical Classicism

International style

The Classical era created a universal style disseminated through two international art forms—Italian opera and Viennese symphony. These represented an all-European culture that transcended national boundaries. In this regard Classicism reflected the international character of the two most powerful institutions in eighteenth-century society, the aristocracy and the Church. Indeed, the eighteenth century was the last stronghold of internationalism in art (until the twentieth began). German, French, and Italian influences intermingle in the art of Haydn and Mozart. These masters were not German in the way that Wagner was, or Schumann, or Brahms. Romantic nationalism, we saw, opened up new dialects to composers. By the same token something was lost of the breadth of view that made artists like Beethoven and Goethe citizens of the world in the highest sense.

The Classical composers were far less concerned with exotic atmosphere than the Romantics (in spite of the *Turkish Rondo* of Mozart and the *Turkish March* of Beethoven). They already were strongly influenced by the "return to nature," especially Haydn in *The Creation* and *The Seasons* and Beethoven in the *Pastoral Symphony;* these works foreshadowed the numerous landscapes and sea scenes that were to play such an important part in nineteenth-century music. Also, significantly, despite the aristocratic spirit of the late eighteenth century, folklore elements entered increasingly into the Classical style. Popular song and dance are manifest not only in the German dances, contradances, ländler, and waltzes of the Viennese masters but also in the allegros and rondos of their larger works.

Classicism, to sum up, achieved the final synthesis of the intellectual currents of eighteenth-century life. The great theme of this pure and serene art was man, the measure of all things: a rational creature working out his destiny in an ordered universe whose outer garment was the beauty of nature and whose inner law was the clarity of reason. The Classical masters struck a perfect balance between emotion and intellect, heart and mind. So delicate an equilibrium is as rare in art as in life.

We have made reference to Nietzsche's distinction between the Dionysian and the Apollonian. The Classical spirit finds a fit symbol in the god of light, whose harmonious proportions so eloquently proclaim the cult of ideal beauty.

50

Joseph Haydn

"I have only just learned in my old age how to use the wind instruments, and now that I do understand them I must leave the world."

Joseph Haydn. (Crown Collections, Copyright reserved to Her Majesty the Queen.)

The long career of Joseph Haydn (1732–1809) spanned the decades when the Classical style was being formed. He imprinted upon it the stamp of his personality, and made a contribution to music that in scope and significance was second to none.

His Life

He was born in Rohrau, a village in Lower Austria, son of a wheelwright. Folk song and dance were his natural heritage. Displaying uncommon musical aptitude as a child, he was taught the rudiments by a distant relative, a schoolmaster. The beauty of his voice secured him a place as chorister in St. Stephen's Cathedral in Vienna, where he remained till he was sixteen. With the breaking of his voice his day at the choir school came to an end. He established himself in an attic in Vienna, managed to obtain a dilapidated clavier, and set himself to master his craft. He eked out a living through teaching and accompanying, and often joined the roving bands of musicians who performed in the streets. In this way the popular Viennese idiom entered his style along with the folk idiom he had absorbed in childhood.

Haydn before long attracted the notice of the music-loving aristocracy of Vienna, and was invited to the country house of a nobleman who maintained a small group of musicians. His next patron kept a small orchestra, so that he was able to experiment with more ample resources. In 1761, when he was twenty-nine, he entered the service of the Esterházys, a family of enormously wealthy Hungarian princes famous for their patronage of the arts. He remained in their service for almost thirty years—that is, for the greater part of his creative career. The palace of the Esterházys was one of the most splendid in Europe, and music played a central part in the constant round of festivities there. The musical estab-

Esterházy patronage

lishment under Haydn's direction included an orchestra, an opera company, a marionette theater, and the chapel. The agreement between prince and composer sheds light on the social status of the eighteenth-century artist. Haydn is required to abstain "from undue familiarity and from vulgarity in eating, drinking, and conversation." He is enjoined to act uprightly and to influence his subordinates "to preserve such harmony as is becoming in them, remembering how displeasing any discord or dispute would be to His Serene Highness. . . . It is especially to be observed that when the orchestra shall be summoned to perform before company the said Joseph Heyden shall take care that he and all the members of his orchestra do follow the instructions given and appear in white stockings, white linen, powdered, and with a pigtail or tie-wig."

Haydn's life is the classic example of the patronage system operating at its best. Though he chafed occasionally at the restrictions imposed on him by court life, he inhabited a world that questioned neither the supremacy of princes nor the spectacle of a great artist in livery. His final estimate of his position in the Esterházy household was that the advantages outweighed the disadvantages. "My Prince was always satisfied with my works. I not only had the encouragement of constant approval but as conductor of an orchestra I could make experiments, observe what produced an effect and what weakened it, and was thus in a position to improve, alter, make additions or omissions, and be as bold as I pleased. I was cut off from the world, there was no one to confuse or torment me, and I was forced to become *original.*"

Later years

Haydn had married when still a young man, but did not get on with his wife. They ultimately separated, and he found consolation elsewhere. By the time he reached middle age his music had brought him fame throughout Europe. He was asked to appear at various capitals but accepted none of these invitations as long as his patron was alive. After the Prince's death he made two visits to England (1791–92, 1794–95), where he conducted his works with phenomenal success. He returned to his native Austria laden with honors and financially well off.

When he was seventy-six a memorable performance of *The Creation* was organized in his honor by the leading musicians of Vienna and members of the aristocracy. At the words "And there was light"—who that has heard it can forget the grandeur of the C-major chord on the word "light"? —the old man was deeply stirred. Pointing upward he exclaimed, "It came from there!" His agitation increased as the performance advanced, so that it was necessary to take him home at the end of the first part of the work. As he was carried out in his armchair his admirers thronged about him. Beethoven, who had briefly been his pupil, kissed his hands and forehead. At the door he turned around and lifted his hands as if in blessing. It was his farewell to the public.

He died a year later, revered by his countrymen and acknowledged throughout Europe as the premier musician of his time.

The performance of The Creation *in Haydn's honor at the University of Vienna one year before his death. From a contemporary engraving.*

His Music

It was Haydn's historic role to help perfect the new instrumental language of the late eighteenth century, a language based on the dynamic development of themes and motives. The mature Classical idiom seemed to be fully realized for the first time in his terse, highly personal style with its angular themes and nervous rhythms, its expressive harmony, structural logic, and endlessly varied moods.

Chamber music

The string quartet occupied a central position in Haydn's art. The sixty-eight quartets he left are an indispensable part of the repertory. The works of his middle and late years contain notable experiments in sonority and form. One understands Mozart's remark, "It was from Haydn that I first learned the true way to compose quartets."

Symphonies

Like the quartets, the symphonies—over a hundred in number—extend across the whole of Haydn's career. Especially popular are the twelve written in the 1790s, in two sets of six, for his appearances in England. Known as the "Salomon Symphonies," after the impresario who brought him to England and arranged the concerts, they abound in effects that the public associates with later composers: syncopation, sudden crescendos and accents, dramatic contrasts of soft and loud, daring modulation, and an imaginative color scheme in which each choir and instrument plays its allotted part. Of Haydn's symphonies it may be said, as it has been of his quartets, that they are the spiritual birthplace of Beethoven.

Church music

Haydn was a prolific composer of church music. His fourteen Masses form the chief item in this category. The prevailing cheerfulness of these works reflects a trusting faith undisturbed by inner travail or doubt. "At the thought of God," he said, "my heart leaps foı joy and I cannot help my music doing the same." Among his oratorios, *The Creation,* which we will discuss, attained a popularity second only to that of Handel's *Messiah.* Haydn followed it with another work based on English literature–*The Seasons* (1801), on a text drawn from James Thomson's celebrated poem. Completed when the composer was on the threshold of seventy, it was his last major composition.

Vocal music

Haydn's tonal imagery was instrumental in character. Yet he recognized that a good melody must be rooted in the nature oι the human voice. "If you want to know whether you have written anything worth preserving," he counseled, "sing it to yourself without any accompaniment." His attitude toward his work shows that the time was passing when pieces were written for a single occasion or season. "I never was a quick writer and always composed with care and deliberation. That alone is the way to compose works that will last." His ceaseless experimenting with form should dispel the notion that the Classicist adheres to tradition. On the contrary, he chafed against the arbitrary restrictions of the theorists. "What is the good of such rules? Art is free and should be fettered by no such mechanical regulations. The educated ear is the sole authority on all these questions, and I think I have as much right to lay down the law as anyone." He upheld the expressive power of music against all rules. "Supposing an idea struck me as good and thoroughly satisfactory both to the ear and the heart, I would far rather pass over some slight grammatical error than sacrifice what seemed to me beautiful to any mere pedantic trifling." So, too, when his attention was called to an unconventional passage in a string quartet of Mozart's, he retorted, "If Mozart wrote it so he must have had good reason."

Haydn enriched the literature of the divertimento, the concerto, and the song. His piano sonatas, of late years unjustly neglected, are returning to favor. His numerous operas and marionette plays were designed specifically for the entertainment needs of the Esterházy court. "My operas are calculated exclusively for our own company and would not produce their effect elsewhere." But several, revived in recent years, have given delight.

Symphony No. 104 (London)

First movement
SIDE 8/1 (E I)
SIDE 7/1 (S)

Haydn's last symphony is regarded by many as his greatest. The solemn introduction, marked Adagio, opens with a fanfare-like motive announced in unison by the whole orchestra. The atmosphere is one of "strangeness and wonder," akin to that of the scene in Mozart's opera where the statue of the Commendatore comes to punish Don Giovanni. (Both, incidentally, are in D minor.) It was because of passages such as these that Haydn and Mozart, in their day, were considered to be romantics.

The movement proper, an Allegro in sonata form, is launched by an irresistible tune that has all the energy and verve of Haydn's mature style. It contains, to boot, two motives that will lend themselves to development:

Notice that measures 5 and 6 duplicate the pattern of measure 4. The melody is symmetrical. Two phrases, each of four measures, form an eight-measure statement that is answered by another eight-bar period ending on a full cadence. This theme and those that follow are shaped out of a few basic intervals in such a way that, despite the variety of the ideas, they all hang together. There results the effortless continuity, the miraculous sense of rightness and inevitability that constitutes the essence of the high Classical style.

An episode follows in which one motive is repeated exactly:

Another is heard in a descending sequence:

These become part of a transition that presents motive **b** of the main theme in a new light:

The bridge modulates to A major, the key that lies five tones above D—or the key of the dominant. In the nineteenth-century symphonies we studied, the composer's arrival at the contrasting key was marked by the introduction of a second lyric theme that served as a foil to the first. Instead of doing this, Haydn repeats his opening theme in the new key:

This procedure underscores an important point about sonata-allegro form. Many people think that it is based on the opposition between two themes. Clearly, in Haydn's mind the opposition is between two keys.

A closing theme introduces two new motives. The first has a bouncy staccato quality:

The second will play an important part in the Development section. Notice that its first three notes present motive **a** in inversion:

A codetta rounds off the Exposition with a jovial cadence.

The Development section moves through a series of modulations that must have sounded altogether daring to late-eighteenth-century audiences. Motive **b** is expanded through repetition in sequence:

The second motive of the closing theme, shifted to minor, is heard in a descending sequence:

Motive **b** of the main theme in an ornamented version:

Motive **b** transformed into an ascending line leading to a climax:

The Development section is mostly in minor, which sets off the predominantly major character of the Exposition and Recapitulation. After it

The theme in the middle section, in G minor:

The theme in the middle section, in B-flat major:

First measure of the theme expanded into an ascending sequence:

A more ornate version of the theme, in the Restatement:

A new rhythmic variation:

First measure of the theme expanded, in a sort of cadenza:

The theme itself is an **a-b-a** form, rounded off by a codetta that admirably suggests the sense of farewell implicit in codas. This is expanded into a beautiful passage at the end of the movement.

Third movement
SIDE 8/3 (E I)
SIDE 7/3 (S)

Third is a *Minuet and Trio*—that is, an **A-B-A** form—in Haydn's most exuberant manner. The main theme consists of two symmetrical four-bar phrases that are announced forte and immediately repeated pianissimo. How genial is Haydn's way of throwing off the accent through sudden stresses on the offbeat (marked *sf*—sforzando—in the score):

It is fascinating to observe how Haydn upsets the four-bar symmetry of the Classical minuet by sneaking in a six-bar phrase every now and then. He was much more given to irregularity than most listeners realize. When the tune returns, it does so in a more elaborate version:

Characteristic, in the codetta that rounds off this section, is the syncopated accent followed by an abrupt pause. Perhaps no other composer in history understood so well the value of a sudden silence in music. The effect is unfailingly dramatic.

The Trio, in the contrasting key of B-flat major, is an **a-b-a** form, to which Haydn adds an exquisite passage modulating back to the home key of D. Brass, timpani, and clarinets are silent during this more lyrical episode.

Fourth movement
SIDE 8/4 (E I)
SIDE 7/4 (S)

The finale is an Allegro spiritoso in cut time. The theme has the high spirits that Haydn derived from his heritage of Croatian folk song and dance:

The effect of folk dance is heightened by the low D which is sustained as a pedal point by horns and cellos. This kind of drone bass has always been a feature of European folk instruments, whether of the bagpipe or accordion variety.

The music moves at a whirlwind pace through a shapely sonata-allegro form. The opening idea is answered by another that maintains its lilt and charm:

Connective tissue is woven out of motives that scurry along the scale at breakneck speed. Much is made of a jaunty transitional theme:

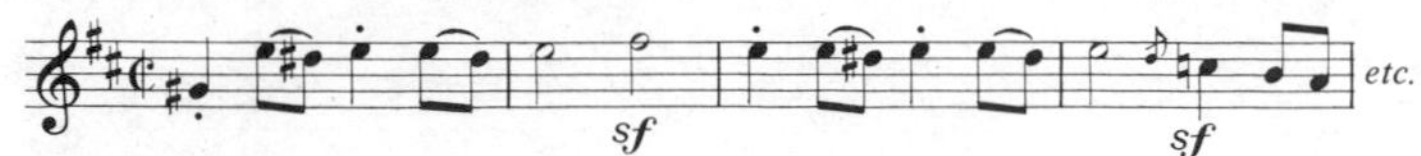

A special effect is provided by scales hurtling along in contrary motion, as the following two lines (first and second violins) demonstrate:

The first three notes of the theme are transformed into an exciting closing theme that moves in a descending sequence:

The Development manipulates these themes and their motives in ways akin to those we traced in our discussion of the first movement. Extraordinary is the unflagging momentum of this section. In the Recapitulation, theme 2 is transposed from A major to the tonic key of D. The brilliant coda brings a new version of the theme that changes the rhythm of the notes:

An energetic cadence in the home key of D ends this enchanting work that captured, for Haydn's aristocratic listeners, all the verve and humor of the folk.

The Creation

In this celebrated oratorio, the creation of the world and its creatures is described with that capacity for wonder which only children and artists know. (An oratorio, as we know, is a large-scale musical work for solo voices, chorus, and orchestra, set to a libretto of a sacred or serious character.) Due to reasons which we will examine when we discuss the life of Handel, the oratorio was extremely popular in England, with the result that during Haydn's two visits there he was made fully aware of the possibilities of this art-form. He wrote *The Creation* (1797–98) after his return to Vienna, when he was in his mid-sixties.

Libretto

The libretto is based on the biblical Book of Genesis and on Milton's *Paradise Lost*. Milton's majestic poem reached Haydn in a roundabout way; he wrote his music to a German translation prepared by his librettist, a Baron von Swieten; this was retranslated into English so as to fit the music he had composed. In this process the nobility of Milton's verse inevitably was lost, its place being taken by a text that is at its best when it quotes the Book of Genesis but leaves much to be desired everywhere else. Recently, new translations have begun to supplant the original version; most recordings are sung in German.

Recitative types

The recitatives, solos, and ensemble numbers are assigned to three archangels–Gabriel (soprano), Uriel (tenor), and Raphael (bass), and to Adam and Eve in Part III. The archangels' voices, whether singly or together, contrast with the chorus that represents the heavenly hosts. The *recitativo secco* (literally, "dry recitative"), in the older opera and oratorio, was a kind of musical declamation that followed the inflections of speech and was accompanied by the harpsichord. In contrast, the more expressive *recitativo accompagnato* (accompanied recitative) was supported by the orchestra and had a more melodious character.

Overture

The Overture, marked Largo, is a "Representation of Chaos" that begins with the emptiness of the octave, a sustained C held by the full orchestra. The eighteenth century, we have seen, moved toward law and order through tonality–that is, the system of the major-minor keys. Haydn's attempt to depict the null and void of pre-Creation inevitably led him to ambiguous tonality, dissonance, and chromatic harmonies. The music starts out uncertainly from C minor, drifts into the key of D flat and thence to E-flat major, but the feeling of a single key never lasts. Notable is Haydn's use of the motive of a descending scale step, which to his era suggested a sigh. The Overture reaches a climax on a fortissimo C repeated decisively by the orchestra. Haydn assigns a daring glissando-like run to the clarinet that is followed by a similar one on the flute–an effect without precedent. The final passage contains chromatic harmonics that are strangely prophetic of Wagner's. Compare, for example, the look (and sound) of the following measures with that of the opening of *Tristan* on p. 168. This is astonishing music to have been written in 1798!

Part I

The recitatives and the chorus that follows are based on the opening lines of Genesis:

Raphael (Recitative)

In the beginning God created the heaven and the earth; and the earth was without form, and void; and darkness was upon the face of the deep.

Chorus

And the Spirit of God moved upon the face of the waters. And God said, Let there be light, and there was light.

Uriel (Recitative)

And God saw the light, that it was good: and God divided the light from the darkness.

Raphael's recitative

Raphael's recitative sets out from C minor; touches briefly–between the void and the darkness–on E-flat major and minor; and makes a cadence in E flat. The chorus begins pianissimo. We have already alluded to the great moment here–the change from C minor to major on the word "light." At the end of Uriel's recitative, notice the two chords (what musicians recognize as a Dominant-seventh chord and its Tonic); they give the same effect of finality as a period at the end of a sentence. This underlining of the cadence at the end of a recitative is characteristic of eighteenth-century oratorio and opera.

Uriel's recitative and aria

The aria–the English call it *air*–and chorus that follow carry the action forward. Haydn shows great originality in the way he ends each day with choral passages.

Uriel (Aria)

Now vanish before the holy beams
The gloomy dismal shades of dark;
The first of days appears.
Now chaos ends and order fair prevails.
Aghast the fiends of hell confounded fly,
Down they sink in the deep abyss to endless night.

Chorus

Despairing, cursing rage attends their rapid fall;
A new-created world springs up at God's command.

Uriel's aria, in A major, depicts the end of chaos in a melodious Andante. A vivid contrast is provided by the agitated Allegro moderato in C minor that deals with the affrighted spirits of hell. Rapid chromatic scales, ascending and descending, suggest their agitation. This mood prevails throughout the section for chorus. The line "Despairing, cursing rage attends their rapid fall" is accompanied by chromatic scales, tumultuous harmonies, and modulation. Presently the commotion passes, the music returns to a serene A major to describe the new-created world. Both moods are repeated: Uriel's Allegro is heard again briefly, and the first day ends with a chorus in praise of the new world.

Repetition in choral music

You will notice the repetition of phrases and lines that is characteristic of choral music, especially in the eighteenth century. As we pointed out in the chapter on choral music, composers realized that music is slower than words in establishing a mood. They therefore repeated single words, phrases, and entire lines over and over again to give the music time to create the proper atmosphere. Such repetition also made it easier for the listener to catch the words. In this particular case it is interesting to observe that when Haydn restates the phrase "A new-created world," he changes the harmony.

Gabriel's recitative and aria

The first part of *The Creation* proceeds with the biblical narrative. A favorite number is Gabriel's recitative and aria describing the final event of the third day.

Recitative

And God said, let the earth bring forth grass, the herb yielding seed, and the fruit-tree yielding fruit after his kind, whose seed is in itself, upon the earth: and it was so.

Aria

O'er lofty hills majestic forests wave.
With verdure clad the fields appear,
Delighted to the ravished sense;
By flowers sweet and gay
Enhancèd is the charming sight.

Here perfumed herbs their fragrance shed,
Here grows the healing plant.
The heavy boughs with golden fruit abound,
The leafy arches twine in shady groves;

This aria, an Andante, is in Haydn's most melodious style. After a four-bar introduction we hear the melody:

The form rests firmly upon a structure of key relationships. The first four lines of text are set to music that establishes the home key of B-flat major. The middle section begins with the second stanza, and contains a modulation from B-flat major, which has two flats, to F major, which has one. Notice how the word "plant" is expanded to stretch over a whole line of florid melody. Such expansion of a single word is as characteristic of the Classical vocal style as is the repetition of lines and phrases.

The last three lines of text complete the middle part of this **A-B-A** aria. Here the music modulates frequently to build up tension for the inevitable return to the home key. When that is reached, the first section is repeated with two important modifications: first, the melody is subtly varied with an occasional embellishment; second, the vocal line changes its course to accommodate the fact that this time, instead of modulating, it must remain in the home key.

Part I; closing recitative and chorus

A high point of the work is the recitative and chorus that brings Part I to a close. Uriel's recitative—both *secco* and *accompagnato*—describes the creation of the sun, moon, and stars on the fourth day. It is followed by one of Haydn's most majestic choruses, *The Heavens Are Telling,* in which the choral passages are contrasted with two interjections by the trio of archangels, Gabriel, Uriel, and Raphael.

Uriel

In shining splendor, radiant now, the sun
Climbs in the sky; a joyful happy spouse,
A giant proud and glad to run his measur'd course.

With milder pace and gentle shimmer
Steals the silver moon through silent night;
The boundless vaults of Heav'n's domain
Shine with unnumber'd magnitude of stars.

And the sons of God rejoiced in the fourth day,
In chorus divine praising God's great might, singing:

Chorus

The heavens are telling the glory of God,
The wonder of His work displays the firmament;

Trio

Revealed are his ways by day unto day,
By the night that is gone to following night.

Chorus

The heavens are telling the glory of God,
The wonder of His work displays the firmament.

The orchestral introduction to Uriel's accompanied recitative, an Andante, depicts the sunrise. Beginning pianissimo, the melody climbs up the scale step by step. Meanwhile fresh instruments are added in almost every measure until the fortissimo climax on a repeated D-major chord makes it clear that the world is flooded with light. A passage marked Più adagio (slower) suggests the creation of the moon and stars.

The chorus, a vigorous Allegro in C major, opens with a full sound and moves forward with all the momentum of a steady rhythm. The music is based on contrasts: between wind and string tone in the orchestral background; between chorus and orchestra, which continually answer each other; above all, between the massive combination of chorus and orchestra and the lyrical passages of the three soloists. The music unfolds in symmetrical four-measure phrases. The flowing melodic line is based on movement mostly by step, enlivened by occasional narrow leaps. In the following example, notice how the stepwise movement and repeated notes in the first two measures are balanced by the narrow leaps in the third:

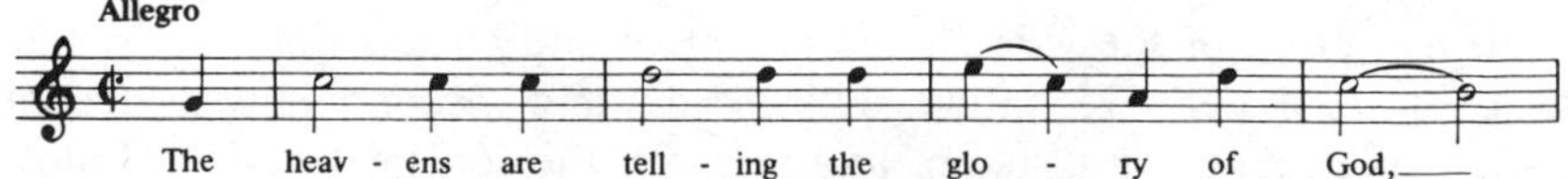

The chorus is in four parts: soprano, alto, tenor, bass. In a number of passages the voices sing the same words together; but this style alternates with another in which one section of the chorus enters alone and is imitated in turn by the other sections. The latter style, based on the interweaving of the voice parts, appears more and more in the second half of the piece. Text is repeated in order to give the music time to establish the mood. The sense of climax toward the end, achieved through crescendo and accelerando, is strengthened by vigorous movement in the orchestra. This closing section is marked Più allegro (faster). In the final phrase all the voices unite in massive chords for a majestic cadence.

Parts II and III

The second part of the oratorio begins with the fifth day of Creation, when the animals are created. Here Haydn's love of nature holds full sway; his impish humor illumines the description of the birds and beasts. A favorite number in the second part is the chorus *Achievèd Is the Glorious Work.* In the third part the human element enters the scene with Adam (bass) and Eve (soprano). Accompanied by the chorus, they praise the Creator. There is a love duet, and the work ends with a spacious chorus, *Sing the Lord, Ye Voices All.*

Haydn's is an optimistic music that even in its darker moments accepts life and finds it good. The nineteenth century, with its love of the grandiose, was not overly responsive to his wholesome discourse. Thus was created the stereotype of an amiable "Papa Haydn" in court dress and powdered wig who purveyed harmless pleasantries to the lords of the old regime. It has remained for the twentieth century to rescue this great musician from such incomprehension and to restore to its rightful place his deeply felt, finely wrought art—an art of moderation and humor, polished and lucid, profoundly human and unfadingly fresh.

51

Wolfgang Amadeus Mozart

"People make a mistake who think that my art has come easily to me. Nobody has devoted so much time and thought to composition as I. There is not a famous master whose music I have not studied over and over."

Wolfgang Amadeus Mozart.

Something of the miraculous hovers about the music of Mozart (1756–91). One sees how it is put together, whither it is bound, and how it gets there; but its beauty of sound and perfection of style, its poignancy and grace defy analysis and beggar description. For one moment in the history of music all opposites were reconciled, all tensions resolved. That luminous moment was Mozart.

His Life

He was born in Salzburg, son of Leopold Mozart, an esteemed composer-violinist attached to the court of the Archbishop. He began his career as the most extraordinarily gifted child in the history of art. He first started to compose before he was five, and performed at the court of the Empress Maria Theresa at the age of six. The following year his ambitious father organized a grand tour that included Paris, London, and Munich. By the time he was thirteen the boy had written sonatas, concertos, symphonies, religious works, an opera buffa, and the operetta *Bastien and Bastienne.*

Early works

He reached manhood having attained a mastery of all forms of his art. The speed and sureness of his creative power, unrivaled by any other composer, is best described by himself: "Though it be long, the work is complete and finished in my mind. I take out of the bag of my memory what has previously been collected into it. For this reason the committing to paper is done quickly enough. For everything is already finished, and it rarely differs on paper from what it was in my imagination. At this work I can therefore allow myself to be disturbed. Whatever may be going on about me, I write and even talk."

From patronage to free artist

His relations with his patron, Hieronymus von Colloredo, Prince-Archbishop of Salzburg, were most unhappy. The high-spirited young artist rebelled against the social restrictions imposed by the patronage system. At length he could endure his position no longer. He quarreled with the Archbishop, was dismissed, and at twenty-five established himself in Vienna to pursue the career of a free artist, the while he sought an official appointment. Ten years remained to him. These were spent in a tragic struggle to achieve financial security and to find again the lost serenity of his childhood. Worldly success depended on the protection of the court. But the Emperor Joseph II–who referred to him as "a decided talent"–either passed him by in favor of lesser men or, when he finally took Mozart into his service, assigned him to tasks unworthy of his genius such as composing dances for the court balls. Of his remuneration for this work Mozart remarked with bitterness, "Too much for what I do, too little for what I could do."

Marriage to Constanze

In 1782 he married Constanze Weber, against his father's wishes. The step signalized Mozart's liberation from the close ties that had bound him to the well-meaning but domineering parent who strove so futilely to ensure the happiness of the son. Constanze brought her husband neither the strength of character nor the wealth that might have protected him from a struggle with the world for which he was singularly unequipped. She was an undistinguished woman to whom Mozart, despite occasional lapses, was strongly attached. It was not till many years after his death that she appears to have realized, from the adulation of the world, the stature of her husband.

Mozart's birthplace in Salzburg as it looks today.

The da Ponte operas

With the opera *The Marriage of Figaro,* written in 1786 on a libretto by Lorenzo da Ponte, Mozart reached the peak of his career as far as success was concerned. The work made a sensation in Vienna and in Prague, and his letters from the latter city testify to his pleasure at its reception. He was commissioned to do another work for Prague the following year. With da Ponte again as librettist he produced *Don Giovanni.* But the opera baffled the Viennese. His vogue had passed. The composer whom we regard as the epitome of clarity and grace was, in the view of the frivolous public of his time, difficult to understand. His music, it was said, had to be heard several times in order to be grasped. What better proof of its inaccessibility? In truth, Mozart was entering regions beyond the aristocratic entertainment level of the day. He was straining toward an intensity of utterance that was new in the world. Of *Don Giovanni* Joseph II declared, "The opera is heavenly, perhaps even more beautiful than *Figaro.* But no food for the teeth of my Viennese." Upon which Mozart commented, "Then give them time to chew it." One publisher advised him to write in a more popular style. "In that case I can make no more by my pen," he answered. "I had better starve and die at once."

Late years

His final years were spent in growing want. The frequent appeals to his friends for aid mirror his despair and helplessness. He describes himself as "always hovering between hope and anxiety." He speaks of the black thoughts that he must "repel by a tremendous effort." The love of life that had sustained him through earlier disappointments began to desert him. Again and again he embarked on a journey that seemed to promise a solution to all his difficulties, only to return empty-handed.

In the last year of his life, after a falling off in his production, he nerved himself to the final effort. For the popular Viennese theater he wrote *The Magic Flute,* on a libretto by the actor-impresario-poetaster Emanuel Schikaneder. Then a flurry of hope sent him off to Prague for the coronation of the new Emperor, Leopold II, as King of Bohemia. The festival opera he composed for this event, *The Clemency of Titus,* failed to impress a court exhausted by the protracted ceremonies of the coronation. Mozart returned to Vienna broken in body and spirit. With a kind of fevered desperation he turned to his last task, the *Requiem.* It had been commissioned by a music-loving count who fancied himself a composer and intended to pass off the work as his own. Mozart in his overwrought state became obsessed with the notion that this *Mass for the Dead* was intended for himself and that he would not live to finish it. A tragic race with time began as he whipped his faculties to this masterwork steeped in visions of death.

He was cheered in his last days by the growing popularity of *The Magic Flute.* The gravely ill composer, watch in hand, would follow the performance in his mind. "Now the first act is over . . . Now comes the aria of the Queen of Night . . ." His premonition concerning the *Requiem* came true. He failed rapidly while in the midst of the work. His favorite pupil, Süssmayr, completed the Mass from the master's sketches, with some additions of his own.

Mozart died in 1791, shortly before his thirty-sixth birthday. In view of his debts he was given "the poorest class of funeral." His friends followed to the city gates; but the weather being inclement, they turned back, leaving the hearse to proceed alone. "Thus, without a note of music, forsaken by all he held dear, the remains of this prince of harmony were committed to the earth—not even in a grave of his own but in the common paupers' grave."

His Music

Many view Mozart as one in whom the elegance of court art reached its peak. To others he represents the spirit of artless youth untouched by life. Both views are equally far from the truth. Neither the simplicity of his forms nor the crystalline clarity of his texture can dispel the intensity of feeling that pervades the works of his maturity. Because of the mastery with which everything is carried out, the most complex operations of the musical mind are made to appear effortless. This deceptive simplicity is truly the art that conceals art.

It has been said that Mozart taught the instruments to sing. Into his exquisitely wrought instrumental forms he poured the lyricism of the great vocal art of the past. The peasant touch is missing from Mozart's music, which draws its inspiration neither from folk song nor nature. It is an indoor art, sophisticated, rooted in the culture of two musical cities—Salzburg and Vienna.

The Salzburg years saw the composition of a quantity of social music, divertimentos and serenades of great variety. In chamber music he favored the string quartet. His works in this form range in expression from the buoyantly songful to the austerely tragic. The last ten quartets rank with the finest specimens in the literature, among them being the set of six dedicated to Haydn, his "most celebrated and very dear friend." Worthy companions to these are the string quintets, in which he invariably used two violas. The somber *Quintet in G minor* represents the peak of his achievement in this medium.

Chamber music

One of the outstanding pianists of his time, Mozart wrote copiously for his favorite instrument. Among his finest solo works are the *Fantasia in C minor* and the *Sonata* in the same key, K. 475 and 457. (The K followed by a number refers to the catalogue of Mozart's works by Ludwig Koechel, who enumerated them all in what he took to be the order of their composition.) Mozart was less experimental than Haydn in regard to formal structure, yet he led the way in developing one important form: the concerto for piano and orchestra. He wrote more than twenty works for this medium. They established the piano concerto as one of the important types of the Classical era.

Piano works

The more than forty symphonies–their exact number has not been determined–that extend across his career tend toward ever greater richness of orchestration, freedom of part writing, and depth of emotion. The most important are the six written in the final decade of his life–the *Haffner*, in D (1782), the *Linz,* in C (1783), the *Prague,* in D (1786), and the three composed in 1788. With these works the symphony achieves its position as the most weighty form of abstract music. In an age when composers produced their works almost exclusively on commission, it is significant that Mozart's last three symphonies were probably never performed during his lifetime: he seems to have written them for no specific occasion but from inner necessity.

Symphonies

But the central current in Mozart's art that nourished all the others was opera. Here were embodied his joy in life, his melancholy, all the impulses of his many-faceted personality. None has ever surpassed his power to delineate character in music and to make his puppets come alive. His lyric gift, molded to the curve of the human voice, created a wealth of melody whose sensuous loveliness sets it apart in music. His orchestra, although it never obtrudes upon the voice, becomes the magical framework within which the action unfolds.

Operas

In Lorenzo da Ponte, an Italian-Jewish adventurer and poet who was one of the picturesque figures of the age, Mozart found a librettist whose dramatic vitality was akin to his own. (Da Ponte ultimately emigrated to America, operated a grocery store and sold illicit liquor on the side, taught Italian at Columbia College, was one of the first impresarios to bring Italian opera to New York, wrote a fascinating book of memoirs, and died in 1838.) The collaboration produced three works: *The Marriage of Figaro* (1786), which da Ponte adapted from the comedy of Beaumarchais satirizing the old regime; *Don Giovanni* (1787), "the opera of all operas"; and *Così fan tutte* (1790), which has been translated in a variety of ways from "So do all women" to "Girls will be girls!" These crown the history of Classical opera buffa, just as *The Abduction from the Seraglio* (1782) and *The Magic Flute* (1791), a gigantic fantasy steeped in the symbolism of Freemasonry, bring to its apex the German *Singspiel* (song-play). Abounding in irony and satire, these masterpieces reach beyond the world of satin and lace whence they issued. They achieve what da Ponte set forth as his and Mozart's intention: "To paint faithfully and in full color the divers passions."

Don Giovanni

Conceived in the tradition of the opera buffa, *Don Giovanni* oversteps that tradition into the realm covered by our term tragicomedy. Da Ponte called it a "jocose" or cheerful drama. The opera is unique for its range of emotions.

Da Ponte's Don heralds a new type in literature as in society: the supreme individualist who brooks no restraints and brushes aside every obstacle in the way of his self-realization. Don Juan is the eternal type of libertine for whom the pursuit of pleasure has become the final assertion of will. Mozart's music humanizes him, transforms him into one of the boldest conceptions in the entire range of the lyric theater.

Mozart put off writing the Overture until the last moment. He had to sit up the night before the dress rehearsal, Constanze telling him stories to keep him awake, in order to set it down. The parts were copied that day and read at sight by the orchestra. Mozart, who conducted, remarked that "plenty of notes fell under the table." From the statement quoted earlier in the chapter it is clear that we must amend this famous story in one detail. He did not compose the Overture that night; he committed to paper what was already finished in his mind.

Overture
Act I,
Scene 1
SIDE 10/1 (E I)

The Overture begins with an Andante in cut time that establishes the key of D minor. The opening measures are of an impressive dignity that will be associated at the climax of the work with the ghost of the Commandant. There follows a sonata-allegro movement in D major that serves to introduce the opera without being related to it by theme. The richness of sound and free interweaving of orchestral parts bespeak the high Classical style.

The curtain rises on Don Giovanni's servant Leporello, who is standing outside the residence of Donna Anna bemoaning his fate:

LEPORELLO

Notte e giorno faticar
Per chi nulla sà gradir,
Piòva e vento sopportar,
Mangiar male e mal dormir.
Voglio far il gentiluomo,
E non voglio più servir,
Nò, nò, nò, non voglio più servir.

Night and day, working away
For someone whom nothing pleases,
Putting up with rain and wind,
Eating badly and sleeping badly.
I want to live the life of a gentleman,
And I no longer want to serve,
No, no, no, I no longer want to serve.

Oh che caro galantuomo!
Voi star dentro colla bella,
Ed io far la sentinella!
Voglio far il gentiluomo . . . *etc.*

Oh, what a fine gallant!
You stay inside there with your beauty,
While I keep watch out here!
I want to live the life of a gentleman . . . *etc.*

Mammi par che venga gente,
Non mi voglio far sentir, Ah!

But I think that someone's coming,
I don't want to be found here, ah!

Don Giovanni, who had broken into Donna Anna's chamber, rushes out of the house struggling with her and concealing his face. Donna Anna, determined to discover the identity of her assailant, calls for help. Her father–the Commandant–appears, drawing his sword. Donna Anna withdraws into the house. The Don does not wish to fight the old man but is goaded into a duel in the course of which he mortally wounds the Commandant.

DONNA ANNA

Non sperar, se non m'uccidi,
Ch'io ti lasci fuggir mai!

Do not hope, unless you kill me
That I shall ever let you escape!

DON GIOVANNI

Donna folle! indarno gridi!
Chi son io tu non saprai.

Foolish woman! In vain you scream!
Who I am you shall not know.

LEPORELLO

(Che tumulto! Oh, ciel, che gridi!)
Il padron in nuovi guai!

(What a tumult! Oh heavens, what screaming!)
The master is in new trouble!

DON GIOVANNI

Taci, e trema al mio furore.

Quiet, and fear my anger.

DONNA ANNA

Scellerato!

Vile wretch!

DON GIOVANNI

Sconsigliata!

Ill-advised woman!

DONNA ANNA

Gente! servi!
Come furia disperata
Ti saprò perseguitar.

People! Servants!
Like a desperate fury
I intend to pursue you.

DON GIOVANNI

(Questa furia disperata
Mi vuol far precipitar.)

(Like a desperate fury
She wants to bring about my ruin.)

LEPORELLO

(Stà a veder ch'il libertino
Mi farà precipitar.)

(We shall see what the rascal
Will bring down upon my head.)

COMMENDATORE

Lasciala, indegno!
Battiti meco!

Unhand her, wretch!
Fight with me!

DON GIOVANNI

Va, non mi degno
Di pugnar teco.

Go, I disdain
To fight with you.

COMMENDATORE

Così pretendi
Da me fuggir?

On that pretext
You would escape?

LEPORELLO *(aside)*

(Potessi almeno
Di quà partir!)

(If I could only
Get out of here!)

COMMENDATORE

Battiti!

Fight!

DON GIOVANNI

Misero, Attendi,
Se vuoi morir!

Wretched man, Stay then
If you wish to die!

(They fight. The Commendatore falls.)

COMMENDATORE

Ah soccorso! Son tradito . . .
L'assassino m'ha ferito,
E dal seno palpitante
Sento l'anima partir.

Ah, help! I am betrayed . . .
The assassin has wounded me,
And from my throbbing breast
I feel my life departing.

DON GIOVANNI

Ah, già cade il sciagurato,
Affannosa e agonizzante
Già dal seno palpitante
Veggo l'anima partir.

Ah, the rash man has fallen,
In distress and agony
From his throbbing breast
I see his life departing.

LEPORELLO

(Qual misfatto! qual eccesso!
Entro il sen dallo spavento
Palpitar il cor mi sento,
Io non sò che far, che dir!)

(What a misdeed! What a crime!
I feel, within my breast,
My heart beating with terror.
I don't know what to do or say.)

The conversation between Don Giovanni and Leporello that follows establishes the moral climate they inhabit.

DON GIOVANNI

Leporello, ove sei?

(sotto voce)
Leporello, where are you?

LEPORELLO

Son quì per mia disgrazia; e voi?

I'm here, unfortunately; and you?

DON GIOVANNI

Son qui.

I'm here.

LEPORELLO

Chi è morto, voi, o il vecchio?

Who is dead, you, or the old boy?

DON GIOVANNI

Che domanda da bestia! Il vecchio.

What a stupid question! The old man.

LEPORELLO

Bravo! Due imprese leggiadre: sforzar la figlia ed ammazzar il padre.

Bravo! Two fine exploits: ravish the daughter and murder the father.

DON GIOVANNI

L'ha voluto, suo danno.

He asked for it, and he got it.

LEPORELLO

Mà Donn' Anna cos'ha voluto?

And Donna Anna, what did she ask for?

DON GIOVANNI

Taci! Non mi seccar, vien meco, se non vuoi qualche cosa ancor tu!

Quiet! Don't annoy me, come with me, unless you're asking for something too!

LEPORELLO

Non vuo'nulla Signor! Non parlo più.

I'm not asking for anything, sir. I'll say no more.

They escape. Donna Anna comes out of the house with Don Ottavio, her betrothed. She discovers her father's body and is overcome by grief. In the ensuing duet she and Don Ottavio swear to track down the murderer and make him pay for his crime.

As in *The Creation,* the recitative veers between the unadorned *secco* accompanied by harpsichord and the more expressive *accompagnato* supported by the orchestra. The dialogue between Don Giovanni and Leporello is given in *recitativo secco,* while the emotional interchange between Donna Anna and Don Ottavio has an orchestral background. Donna Anna is established forthwith as the great lady, noble of bearing and somewhat remote, who throughout the work represents the aristocracy, even as the middle station in life and the peasantry have their representatives. Conspicuous is the repetition of lines and phrases of the text, which allows space for the necessary expansion and repetition of musical material. This accords with Mozart's dictum that in opera the poetry must be the obedient daughter of the music. As in the symphony, large units are given shape and coherence through the unifying power of key. The opening scene ends in D minor, forming a musical entity that launches the dramatic-musical action.

Catalogue Aria
SIDE 10/2 (E I)
SIDE 9/5 (S)

Leporello's *Catalogue Aria,* which concludes the second scene, is sung to Donna Elvira, who has been abandoned by the Don but still loves him.

To persuade her of the futility of her passion Leporello reads her the list of his master's amours.

Madamina, Il catalogo è questo	Young lady, this is the catalogue
Delle belle, che amò il padron mio,	Of the beauties my master has loved,
Un catalogo egli è ch'ho fatto io;	It's a catalogue I've made myself;
Osservate, leggete con me!	Observe it, read it with me!
In Italia seicento e quaranta,	In Italy, six-hundred and forty,
In Alemagna duecento trent'una,	In Germany, two hundred and thirty-one,
Cento in Francia, in Turchia novant'una,	A hundred in France, in Turkey, ninety-one,
Mà, in Ispagna, son già mille e tre!	But in Spain, already a thousand and three!
V'han frà queste contadine,	Among them there are peasant girls,
Cameriere, cittadine,	Chambermaids and city girls,
V'han contesse, baronesse,	There are countesses, baronesses,
Marchesane, principesse,	Marchionesses, princesses,
E v'han donne d'ogni grado,	And there are women of every rank,
D'ogni forma, d'ogni età.	Every size, every age.
Nella bionda, egli ha l'usanza	With a blond, it's his custom
Di lodar la gentilezza,	To praise her kindness,
Nella bruna la costanza,	With a brunette, her constancy,
Nella bianca la dolcezza;	With a fair one, her sweetness;
Vuol d'inverno la grassotta,	In winter, he likes a plump one,
Vuol d'estate la magrotta;	In summer, a slim one;
E la grande, maestosa;	And the tall one is called stately;
La piccina è ognor vezzosa.	The tiny one is called charming.
Delle vecchie fa conquista	He conquers old ones
Per piacer di porle in lista;	For the pleasure of adding them to the list;
Sua passion predominante	But his chief passion
E la giovin pincipiante;	Is for the young beginner;
Non si pica se sia ricca,	He doesn't care if she's rich
Se sia brutta, se sia bella.	If she's ugly, if she's beautiful.
Purchè porti la gonnella,	Provided she wears a skirt,
Voi sapete quel che fà!	You know what he does!

What is left unsaid in the vocal line is filled in by the saucy accompaniment. This comic aria, in which the singer with a knowing wink takes the audience into his confidence, is in the great traditon of the theater of buffoons.

Duet
SIDE 10/3 (E I)
SIDE 9/6 (S)

In the next scene, *Là ci darem la mano*—a little duet, as Mozart called it—is sung by Don Giovanni and Zerlina, the artless peasant maid who has momentarily caught his fancy. He succeeds in detaching her from

her fiancé, the country bumpkin Masetto, assures her that he intends to marry her, and invites her to come with him to his villa.

DON GIOVANNI

Là ci darem la mano,	There, we will join our hands
Là mi dirai di sì;	There, you will say yes to me;
Vedi, non è lontano,	Look, it's not far away,
Partiam, ben mio, da qui!	Let's leave here, my treasure!

ZERLINA

Vorrei, e non vorrei; Mi trema un poco il cor; Felice, è ver sarei, Mà può burlarmi ancor!	I want to, and yet I don't want to, My heart trembles a little; I'd be happy, it's true Yet he might still deceive me!

DON GIOVANNI

Vieni mio bel diletto!	Come, my fair delight!

ZERLINA

Mi fà pietà Masetto.	I'm sorry for Masetto.

DON GIOVANNI

Io cangierò tua sorte.	I will change your destiny.

ZERLINA

Presto, non son più forte.	I will soon have no strength left.

DON GIOVANNI

Andiam,	Let's go,

ZERLINA

Andiam!	Let's go!

TOGETHER

Andiam, andiam, mio bene, A ristorar le pene D'un innocente amor.	Let's go, let's go, my treasure, To comfort the pangs Of an innocent love.

Don Giovanni, *Act I, scene 3: The Don (Sherrill Milnes) woos Zerlina (Teresa Stratas) in the duet* Là ci darem la mano. *Metropolitan Opera production.* (Copyright by Beth Bergman, 1974.)

The voices alternate, the phrases becoming ever shorter as he grows more ardent and she more amenable. The tempo changes from andante to allegro; 2/4 time gives way to 6/8 as she throws herself into his arms. There is much repetition of the key word "andiam" to allow for musical expansion. The melody is Mozart at his suavest.

In the course of the opera Donna Anna realizes that Don Giovanni is the man who broke into her room on the fatal night. She and Don Ottavio plan to deliver him to justice. Don Giovanni, meanwhile, during one of his escapades takes refuge in the dead of night in the cemetery where stands the statue of the Commandant. The stone figure chides Don Giovanni for disturbing the peace of the dead. Enjoying Leporello's terror, the Don now commits the crowning blasphemy: he invites the Statue to sup with him that evening. The stone figure nods acceptance.

Final scene

The final scene is the momentous supper in Don Giovanni's mansion. He directs his musicians to play while he eats. The entrance of the Commandant's statue is one of the supreme moments in opera. The music returns to the key in which the Overture began. Three trombones join the tutti to herald the entrance of the specter.

The awesome pronouncement is heard against the harmonies that opened the Overture. The melodic line, based on the downward leap of an octave, is of a supernatural dignity.

The Statue asks the Don to repay the visit and take supper with him. Leporello, shaking with fear, implores his master to decline. "He hasn't the time—please excuse him!" But the Don will not be accused of cowardice. "I have no fear. I'll come." "Give me your hand in pledge." "Take it!" He holds out his hand and feels the Statue's icy clasp. "Repent! Change your life before it is too late." The Don struggles to free himself, yet even now his courage does not desert him; he cannot renounce his destiny. "No, I will not repent, you old fool!" "Then it is too late." Flames shoot up. The demons of Hell rise to claim their prey. They drag the sinner to his doom.

The scene ends in D major, which prepares for the final sextet, in which Leporello describes Don Giovanni's fate to the interested parties—Donna Anna and Don Ottavio, Elvira, Zerlina and Masetto. This cheerful ending, implied in da Ponte's description of *Don Giovanni* as a "jocose drama," restores the opera buffa character of the work. It is heavenly music.

Piano Concerto in C major, *K. 467*

Mozart, we saw, played a crucial role in the development of the piano concerto. His concertos were written primarily as display pieces for his own public performances. They abound in the brilliant flourishes and ceremonious gestures characteristic of eighteenth-century social music.

The sunny *Piano Concerto in C major* (K. 467, 1785) belongs to one of Mozart's most productive periods. He is nothing short of prodigal with his tunes, and proceeds to weld them—with the firm hand of a master—into an architectural unity. The first movement is an Allegro maestoso whose opening pages show how richly Mozart's instrumental art was nourished by the opera house; the principal theme could have come straight out of a scene in an opera buffa. (Indeed, it bears a close resemblance to Leporello's opening aria in *Don Giovanni.*) More important, its first two measures constitute a motive wonderfully capable of growth. This motive dominates the movement. The theme is presented by the strings in unison. (We say that instruments are playing *in unison* when they are all playing the same notes.)

First movement
SIDE 9/1 (E I)
SIDE 8/1 (S)

In this movement we should speak of a theme group rather than a theme. The first of several subsidiary ideas is divided between brass and woodwinds:

Another subsidiary idea is no less appealing:

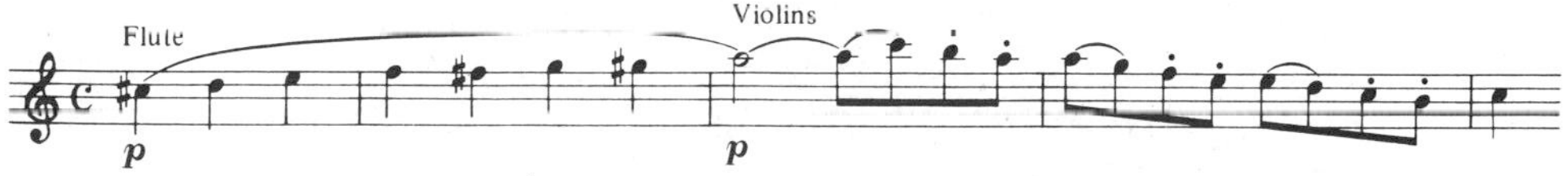

In his concertos Mozart uses the sonata-allegro form with infinite variety; no two first movements are alike. In this case, since the movement is fashioned out of flowing melodies, the result is an unusually spacious form. The orchestra gives the first theme-group in C; the piano enters with a series of flourishes and takes off from Theme 1 through a transitional passage that modulates to G. Although one expects a major tonality, Mozart surprises the hearer with a melody in G minor (which bears a startling resemblance to the opening theme of his famous *G-minor Symphony*). Moving though it is, the idea does not appear again.

The stage is now set for the appearance of the second theme in G major. It is introduced by the piano and repeated in the orchestra:

Brilliant passage-work by the piano rounds out the Exposition; the Development is ushered in by the whole orchestra. With such a wealth of material to draw upon, Mozart—astonishingly—still finds it necessary to introduce a new melody, in a passage in E minor that wreathes the music in a romantic glow:

The Development, despite its heightening of tension, never forfeits its melodious character. The virtuoso figuration in the solo instrument is heard against broadly spun phrases in the strings or woodwinds. Thus virtuosity never becomes an end in itself but remains a means of expression. The Recapitulation opens with the strings playing the main theme in the home key. This time the second theme follows immediately after the first. Where are the subsidiary themes? It turns out that Mozart is saving them for the coda, which rounds out the movement with all the courtly gestures of the eighteenth century. We unfortunately do not possess Mozart's cadenza; it is a wise artist who makes his own as short as possible. The basic motive returns in the final measures. One might have expected so bright an Allegro to have a brilliant ending. Mozart surprises us. The movement ends like one of those opera buffa scenes in which the characters tiptoe off stage.

Second movement
SIDE 9/2 (E I)
SIDE 8/2 (S)

The second movement is a serenely flowing Andante in F. Against a triplet rhythm in the strings, the muted first violins gravely unfold a melody that is taken over by the piano:

Its gentle poignancy explains why composers such as Chopin and Tchaikovsky worshipped Mozart above all others. The form unfolds freely, shaped by the material. Unity is provided by the ever-present triplets, diversity by the soaring melodic line. After a middle section that stresses D minor, the melody returns in the remote key of A-flat major—a procedure closer to the Romantic mind than the Classical. Mozart does not repeat the theme literally; he varies it with fanciful embellishments. The movement finds its way back to the home key, and the coda rounds it off with a pianissimo ending.

The gay finale is a rondo in C major, marked Allegro vivace assai (very fast and lively). The secret of such a piece lies in the impression it gives of effortless motion. It opens with an opera buffa tune in the violins that is taken over by the piano:

Third movement
SIDE 9/3 (E I)
SIDE 8/3 (S)

The second theme in G continues the mood of the opening idea, as does the codetta; then the main theme returns. This movement, in its vivacity and good humor, typifies the Classical rondo finale. But at this time the rondo was absorbing certain features of sonata-allegro form, especially the dynamic movement from key to key and—most important of all—the development of themes and motives. There resulted a form that may be considered a rondo-sonata, of which this Allegro is an example.

The filigree work on the piano demands nimble fingers. Clearly Mozart enjoyed displaying his prowess as a pianist. There is much lively interplay between piano and orchestra, both of which—after a brief cadenza that ushers in the final appearance of the theme—share in the brilliant C-major ending.

Eine kleine Nachtmusik

Mozartian elegance and delicacy of touch are embodied in this serenade for strings (K. 525, 1787), whose title means "A Little Night Music." Probably the work was intended for a double string quartet supported by a bass. The version we know has four movements, compact, intimate, and beautifully proportioned; originally there were five.

First movement
SIDE 7/3 (E I)
SIDE 9/1 (S)

The opening movement is a sonata-allegro form in $\frac{4}{4}$ time in G major. As was customary in music of this type, the first movement has a marchlike character—as if the musicians were arriving for their cheerful task. The main theme establishes the home key, G:

The second theme is in the key that lies five steps above G major—in the key of the dominant, D. The downward curve of its opening measure presents a graceful contrast with the upward-leaping character of the first theme:

A delightful closing theme rounds off the Exposition with a cadence in the contrasting key, D:

As befits the character of a serenade, which is less serious than a symphony or concerto, the Development section is brief. Woven out of the first and closing themes, it touches upon several keys before returning to G major. The Recapitulation follows the course of the Exposition, shifts the second theme into the home key, and expands the closing theme into a vigorous coda.

Second movement
SIDE 7/4 (E I)
SIDE 9/2 (S)

Second is the Romanza, an eighteenth-century Andante that maintains the balance between lyricism and a pleasant reserve. The key is C major, the meter cut time; symmetrical sections are arranged in an **A-B-A-C-A** structure. The **A** theme is utterly gracious:

The **B** theme maintains the mood of the first:

The **C** theme centers about C minor, and is heard against a restless background of sixteenth notes. The primacy of the C major tonality is reestablished with the return of the **A** theme.

Third movement
SIDE 7/5 (E I)
SIDE 9/3 (S)

The Minuet-and-Trio is an Allegretto in G major, marked by regular four-bar structure. It opens in a bright, decisive manner:

The Trio presents a lovely contrast with a soaring curve of truly Mozartian melody:

We then hear the Minuet da capo.

Fourth movement
SIDE 7/6 (E I)
SIDE 9/4 (S)

The rondo finale, Allegro, is in the home key of G. (The sign over the last note in measure 2 of the example indicates a *turn,* a type of ornament or embellishment.)

This alternates with an idea in the key of the dominant, D major. Here, too, there is a contrast of direction. The downward "dip" in the first measure of this tune stands out against the upward-skipping character of the principal theme.

Thenceforth the rondo pursues its merry course. The principal theme is shifted to D major and is then heard—a daring touch, this!—in E flat, whereupon the second theme is shifted to G. But all ends well with the rondo theme reestablishing itself firmly in the home key and wending its way into an assertive coda. We have said that there is a rondo style as well as a rondo form. This is the perfect example, bright, jovial, and—a trait inseparable from this master—stamped with an aristocratic refinement.

In the music of Mozart subjective emotion is elevated to the plane of the universal. The restlessness and the longing are exorcised by the ideal loveliness of Apollonian art. Mozart is one of the supreme artists of all time; the voice of pure beauty in music, and probably the most sheerly musical composer that ever lived.

52

Ludwig van Beethoven

Ludwig van Beethoven.

"Freedom above all!"

Beethoven (1770–1827) belonged to the generation that received the full impact of the French Revolution. He was nourished by its vision of the freedom and dignity of the individual. The time, the place, and the personality combined to produce an artist sensitive in the highest degree to the impulses of the new century. He created the music of a heroic age and, in accents never to be forgotten, proclaimed its faith in the power of man to shape his destiny.

His Life

The early years

He was born in Germany, in the city of Bonn in the Rhineland, where his father and grandfather were singers at the court of the local prince, the Elector Max Friedrich. The family situation was unhappy, the father being addicted to drink, and Ludwig at an early age was forced to take over the support of his mother and two younger brothers. At eleven and a half he was assistant organist in the court chapel. A year later he became harpsichordist in the court orchestra. A visit to Vienna in his seventeenth year enabled him to play for Mozart. The youth improvised so brilliantly on a theme given him by the master that the latter remarked to his friends, "Keep an eye on him–he will make a noise in the world some day."

Arrangements were made some years later for him to study with Haydn in Vienna at the Elector's expense. He left his native town when he was twenty-two, never to return. Unfortunately, the relationship between pupil and teacher left much to be desired. The aging Haydn was ruffled by the young man's volcanic temperament and independence of spirit. Beethoven worked with other masters, the most academic of whom declared that "he has learned nothing and will never do anything in decent style."

Meanwhile his powers as a pianist took the music-loving aristocracy by storm. He was welcomed in the great houses of Vienna by the powerful patrons whose names appear in the dedications of his works–Prince Lichnowsky, Prince Lobkowitz, Count Razumovsky, and the rest. Archduke Rudolph, brother of the Emperor, became his pupil and devoted friend. These connoisseurs, no less than the public, were transported by his highly personal style of improvisation, by the wealth of his ideas, the novelty of their treatment, and the surging emotion behind them.

The rebel

To this "princely rabble," as he called them, the young genius came—in an era of revolution—as a passionate rebel, forcing them to receive him as an equal and friend. "It is good to move among the aristocracy," he observed, "but it is first necessary to make them respect you." Beethoven, sensitive and irascible, stood up for his rights as an artist. When Prince Lichnowsky, during the Napoleonic invasion, insisted that he play for some French officers, Beethoven stormed out of the palace in a rage, demolished a bust of Lichnowsky that was in his possession, and wrote to his exalted friend: "Prince! what you are, you are through the accident of birth. What I am, I am through my own efforts. There have been many princes and there will be thousands more. But there is only one Beethoven!" Such was the force of his personality that he was able to make the aristocrats about him accept this novel idea. Beneath the rough exterior they recognized an elemental power akin to a force of nature.

Beethoven functioned under a modified form of the patronage system. He was not attached to the court of a prince. Instead, the music-loving aristocrats of Vienna helped him in various ways—by paying him handsomely for lessons, or through gifts. He was also aided by the emergence of a middle-class public and the growth of concert life and music publishing. At the age of thirty-one he was able to write, "I have six or seven publishers for each of my works and could have more if I chose. No more bargaining. I name my terms and they pay." A youthful exuberance pervades the first decade of his career, an almost arrogant consciousness of his strength. "Power is the morality of men who stand out from the mass, and it is also mine!" Thus spoke the individualist in the new era of individualism.

Deafness

Then, as the young eagle was spreading his wings, fate struck in a vulnerable spot: he began to lose his hearing. His helplessness in the face of this affliction dealt a shattering blow to his pride. "Ah, how could I possibly admit an infirmity in the one sense that should have been more perfect in me than in others. A sense I once possessed in highest perfection. Oh I cannot do it!" As his deafness closed in on him—the first symptoms appeared when he was in his late twenties—it became the symbol of his terrible sense of apartness from other men, of all the defiance and insecurity and hunger for love that had rent him for as long as he could remember. Upon the mistaken advice of his doctors he retired in 1802 to a summer resort outside Vienna called Heiligenstadt. A titanic struggle shook him, between the destructive forces in his soul and his desire to live and create. It was one of those searing experiences that either break a man or leave him stronger. "But little more and I would have put an end to my life. Only art it was that withheld me. Ah, it seemed impossible to leave the world until I had produced all that I felt called upon to produce, and so I endured this wretched existence."

It was slowly borne in on him that art must henceforth give him the happiness life withheld. Only through creation could he attain the victory of which fate had threatened to rob him. The will to struggle asserted itself; he fought his way back to health. "I am resolved to rise superior to every obstacle. With whom need I be afraid of measuring my strength? If possible I will bid defiance to my fate, although there will be moments in life when I will be the unhappiest of God's creatures . . . I will take Fate by the throat. It shall not overcome me. Oh how beautiful it is to be alive—would that I could live a thousand times!" He had stumbled on an idea that was to play a decisive part in nineteenth-century thought: the concept of art as refuge, as compensation for the shortcomings of reality; art as sublimation, atonement, faith—the idealized experience, the ultimate victory over life.

Having conquered the chaos within himself he came to believe that man could conquer chaos. This became the epic theme of his music: the progression from despair to conflict, from conflict to serenity, from serenity to triumph and joy. The revelation that had come to him through suffering was a welcome message to the world that was struggling to be born. The concept of man the master of his fate hit off the temper of the new middle-class society in its most dynamic phase. In giving expression to his personal faith Beethoven said what his generation needed to hear. He became the major prophet of the nineteenth century, the architect of its heroic vision of life. "I am the Bacchus who presses out the glorious wine for mankind. Whoever truly understands my music is freed thereby from the miseries that others carry about in them."

The final years

The remainder of his career was spent in an unremitting effort to subjugate the elements of his art to the expressive ideal he had set himself. Fellow musicians and critics might carp at the daring of his thoughts, but his victory was assured. A growing public, especially among the younger generation, responded to the powerful thrust of his music. His life was outwardly uneventful. There were the interminable quarrels with associates and friends—he grew increasingly suspicious and irritable, especially in his last years, when he became totally deaf. There were the complicated dealings with his publishers, in which he displayed an impressive shrewdness; his turbulent love affairs (he never married); his high-handed interference in the affairs of his brothers; his tortured relationship with his nephew Carl, an ordinary young man upon whom he fastened a tyrannical affection. All these framed an inner life of extraordinary intensity, an unceasing spiritual development that reached down to ever profounder levels of insight and opened up new domains to tonal art.

Biographers and painters have made familiar the squat, sturdy figure—he was five foot four, the same as that other conqueror of the age, Napoleon—walking hatless through the environs of Vienna, the bulging brow furrowed in thought, stopping now and again to jot down an idea in his sketchbook; an idea that, because he was forever deprived of its sonorous beauty, he envisioned all the more vividly in his mind. A ride in an open carriage in inclement weather brought on an attack of dropsy that proved fatal. He died in his fifty-seventh year, famous and revered.

His Music

Beethoven is the supreme architect in music. His genius found expression in the structural type of thinking embodied in the sonata-symphony. The sketchbooks in which he worked out his ideas show how gradually they reached their final shape and how painstakingly he molded the material into its one inevitable form. "I carry my thoughts within me long, often very long before I write them down. In doing this my memory stands me in such good stead that even years afterward I am sure not to forget a theme I have once grasped . . . As I know what I want, the fundamental idea never deserts me. It mounts, it grows in stature. I hear, I see the picture in its whole extent standing all of a piece before my spirit, and there remains for me only the task of writing it down."

Treatment of Classical forms

Inheriting the sonata form from Haydn and Mozart, he transformed it into a spacious frame for his ideas. He expanded the dimensions of the first movement, especially the coda. Like Haydn and Mozart, he treated the Development section as the dynamic center of sonata form. His short incisive themes offer limitless opportunity for expansion and development; they unfold with volcanic energy and momentum. The slow movement acquired in his hands a hymnic character, the embodiment of Beethovenian pathos. He transformed minuet into scherzo, making it a movement of rhythmic energy ranging from "cosmic laughter" to mystery and wonder. He enlarged the finale into a movement comparable in size and scope to the first, ending the symphony on a note of triumph.

Piano sonatas

The piano occupied a central position in Beethoven's art. His thirty-two sonatas are an indispensable part of its literature, whether for the amateur

The Theater an der Wien, shown here in a contemporary engraving, was the site of the first public performances of Fidelio *(1805), the* Eroica Symphony *(1805), the* Violin Concerto *(1806), and the* Pastoral Symphony *(1808).*

pianist or concert artist. They are well called the pianist's New Testament (the Old being the *Well-Tempered Clavier* of Bach). Dynamic contrasts, explosive accents, opposition of low and high register, syncopation, and powerful crescendos are essential features of his idiom. Characteristic is his fondness for the theme and variations. Here he becomes the master builder, marshaling his inexhaustible wealth of ideas to fashion out of the simplest material a towering edifice.

Symphonies

In the symphony Beethoven found the ideal medium wherein to address mankind. His nine symphonies are spiritual dramas of universal appeal. Their sweep and tumultuous affirmation of life mark them a pinnacle of the rising democratic art. They are conceived on a scale too grand for the aristocratic salon; they demand the amplitude of the concert hall. With his *Third Symphony,* the *Eroica* (1803–04), Beethoven achieved his mature style. The work was originally dedicated to Napoleon, First Consul of the Republic, in whom he saw incarnated the spirit of revolution and the freedom of man. When the news came that Napoleon had proclaimed himself Emperor, Beethoven was disenchanted. "He too is just like any other! Now he will trample on the rights of man and serve nothing but his own ambition." The embittered composer tore up the dedicatory page of the just-completed work and renamed it "Heroic Symphony to celebrate the memory of a great man."

The *Fifth Symphony* (1805–07) has fixed itself in the popular mind as the archetype of all that a symphony is. The *Seventh* (1812) rivals it in universal appeal. The *Ninth,* the *Choral Symphony* (1817–23), strikes the searching tone of Beethoven's last period. Its finale, in which soloists and chorus join with the orchestra, contains the famous line, "Be embraced, ye millions!" The choral movement is a setting of Schiller's *Ode to Joy,* a ringing prophecy of the time when "all men shall be brothers." In these works there sounds the rhetoric of the new century. Complementing them are the *Fourth* (1806) and *Eighth* (1812), two buoyant and serene symphonies; and the *Sixth,* the hymn to nature known as the *Pastorale* (1808).

Concertos and chamber music

The concerto offered Beethoven a congenial public form in which he combined virtuosity with symphonic architecture. Most popular of his works in this medium are the *Third Piano Concerto;* the *Fourth,* in G (1806); the *Fifth,* in E flat (the *Emperor,* 1809), which we will discuss; and the noble *Concerto for Violin,* in D (1806). He wrote much chamber music, the string quartet being closest to his heart. The six quartets Opus 18 are the first in a series that extended throughout the whole of his career. They were followed by the three of Opus 59 dedicated to Count Razumovsky, works pre-eminent for profundity of feeling and technical mastery. His supreme achievements in this area are the last five quartets, which, together with the *Grand Fugue,* Op. 133, occupied the final years of his life. In these, as in the last five piano sonatas, Beethoven found his way to a skeletal language from which all nonessentials had been rigidly pared—a language far transcending his time. The master's gaze is focused within, encompassing depths that music never before had plumbed.

Vocal music

Although his most important victories were won in the instrumental field, Beethoven enriched the main types of vocal music. Of his songs the best known is the cycle of six, *An die ferne Geliebte* (To the Distant Beloved). His sole opera *Fidelio* (originally called *Leonora,* completed in 1805) centers about wifely devotion, human freedom, and the defeat of those who would destroy it. There is much memorable music in it. All the same, Beethoven's imagination was hampered by the trappings of the stage; he is at his most dramatic in the abstract forms. Although the pious Haydn considered him an atheist, he hymned "Nature's God" through the traditional form of religious music. The *Missa solemnis* (Solemn Mass in D, 1818–23) ranks in importance with the *Ninth Symphony* and the final quartets. The work transcends the limits of any specific creed or dogma. Above the Kyrie of the Mass he wrote a sentence that applies to the whole of his music: "From the heart . . . may it find its way to the heart."

His creative activity, extending over a span of thirty-five years, bears witness to a ceaseless striving after perfection. "I feel as if I had written scarcely more than a few notes," he remarked at the end of his career. And a year before his death: "I hope still to bring a few great works into the world." Despite his faith in his destiny he knew the humility of the truly great. "The real artist has no pride. Unfortunately he sees that his art has no limits, he feels obscurely how far he is from the goal. And while he is perhaps being admired by others, he mourns the fact that he has not yet reached the point to which his better genius, like a distant sun, ever beckons him."

The Fifth Symphony

The most popular of all symphonies, Beethoven's *Fifth,* in C minor, Opus 67, is also the most concentrated expression of the frame of mind and spirit that we have come to call Beethovenian. It embodies in supreme degree the basic principle of symphonic thinking—the flowering of an extended composition from a kernel by a process of organic growth. The popular story that Beethoven, when asked for the meaning of the opening theme, replied, "Thus Fate knocks at the door," is probably not authentic. Such literalness seems unlikely in one who was so completely the tone-poet. If the work continues to be associated with Fate it is rather because of the inevitable, the relentless logic of its unfolding.

First movement
SIDE 12/1 (E I)
SIDE 10/1 (S)

The first movement, marked Allegro con brio (lively, with vigor), springs out of the rhythmic idea of "three shorts and a long" that dominates the symphony. Announced in unison by strings and clarinets (Beethoven holds his full forces in reserve), the motive establishes the home key of C minor. It is the most compact and commanding gesture in the whole symphonic literature.

Out of this motive flowers the first theme, which is a repetition, at different levels of the scale and with altered intervals, of the germinating rhythm.

a) The motive. b) Sequence, with smaller interval. c) Sequence. d) The motive with larger interval. e) Same as b. f) Sequence of motive. g) Motive with the interval filled in. h) Inversion (upside-down) of g.

The power of the movement springs from the almost terrifying single-mindedness with which the underlying idea is pursued. It is rhythm, torrential yet superbly controlled, that is the generating force behind this "storm and stress." Beethoven here achieved a vehemence that was new in music. The bridge to the related key of E-flat major is fashioned out of the basic motive. Notice how much more compact is this bridge than the transition in the first movement of Haydn's *Symphony No. 104* (*London*):

We reach an area of relaxation with the lyric second theme. Yet even here the headlong course of the movement does not slacken. As the violins, clarinet, and flute sound the gentle melody in turn, the basic rhythm of "three shorts and a long" persists in the cellos and double basses.

The Exposition is rounded off with a short section (codetta) reaffirming the basic rhythm.

The Development is dramatic, peremptory, compact. The following examples show how Beethoven weaves a tightly knit fabric out of the basic motive.

1. Motive with interval filled in. Expansion through a descending sequence:

2. Motive with interval filled in. Expansion through a descending sequence coupled with inversion (turning the motive upside-down):

3. Expansion through repetition. This passage leads into the Recapitulation:

No less characteristic of Beethoven's style are the powerful crescendos and the abrupt contrasts between soft and loud. The transition back to the home key culminates in a fortissimo proclamation of the underlying rhythm by full orchestra.

The Restatement is interrupted when an oboe solo introduces a note of pathos, momentarily slackening the tension. The second theme is transposed into C major. There is an extended coda in which the basic rhythm reveals a new fund of explosive energy.

Second movement
SIDE 12/2 (E I)
SIDE 10/2 (S)

Beethovenian serenity and strength imbue the second movement, Andante con moto (at a going pace, with movement). The key is A flat; the form, a theme and variations. There are two melodic ideas. The first is a broadly spun theme sung by violas and cellos. It is followed by one of

those hymnic upward-thrusting subjects so characteristic of the master, which echoes the basic rhythm—the "three shorts and a long" of the opening movement.

In the course of the movement Beethoven brings all the procedures of variation—changes in melodic outline, harmony, rhythm, tempo, dynamics, register, key, mode, and type of accompaniment—to bear upon his two themes. Here is how the first theme is embellished with running sixteenth notes in Variation 1:

In Variation 2 this melody is presented in thirty-second-note rhythm:

In the next Variation the melody is divided up among the various woodwind instruments:

Finally the melody is shifted into the minor:

The second theme undergoes analogous transformations, gathering strength until it is proclaimed by the full orchestra. The coda, marked Più mosso (faster), opens with a motive on the bassoon derived from Theme 1 against syncopated chords in the strings. A dynamic crescendo rounds off the movement.

Third movement
SIDE 12/3 (E I)
SIDE 10/3 (S)

Third in the cycle of movements is the Scherzo, which returns to the somber C minor that is the home key of the work. From the depths of the bass rises a characteristic subject, a rocket theme introduced by cellos and double basses.

The basic rhythm of the first movement reappears fortissimo in the horns. Nourished by dynamic changes and a crescendo, the movement steadily accumulates force and drive. The Trio shifts to C major. It is based on a gruffly humorous motive of running eighth notes stated by cellos and double basses and imitated in turn, in ever higher register, by violas, second violins, and first violins. The motive of the double basses

was described by Berlioz in a celebrated phrase as the "gambols of a frolicsome elephant." Here the term scherzo is applicable in its original meaning of "jest." Beethoven's cosmic laughter resounds through these measures: a laughter that shakes—and builds—a world.

This motive is expanded through repetition and sequence:

The Scherzo (section **A**) returns in a modified version, with changed orchestration. It is followed by a mysterious transitional passage that is spun out of the Scherzo theme and the basic rhythm, which is presented by various instruments and finally tapped out mysteriously by the kettledrums:

The Scherzo theme is developed through motivic expansion of its last three notes:

There is a steady accumulation of tension until the orchestra, in a blaze of light, surges into the triumphal Allegro in C major.

Beethoven achieves dramatic contrasts of color through his changes of mode. The first movement is in a somber minor. The second, with its Classical serenity, is in major. The third, save for the jovial Trio, returns to minor. Then the dark C minor is dispelled for good with the upsurge of the finale. At this point three instruments make their appearance for the first time in the symphonies of the Classical Viennese school—piccolo, double bassoon, and trombone, lending brilliance and body to the orchestral sound.

Fourth movement
SIDE 12/3 (E I)
SIDE 10/3 (S)

The fourth movement is a monumental sonata form in which Beethoven overcomes what would seem to be an insuperable difficulty: to fashion an ending that will sustain the tension of what has gone before. Rhythmic energy, bigness of conception, and orchestral sonority carry the work to its overpowering conclusion. Two themes in C major are opposed to one in G. The opening idea is based on a chord-and-scale pattern.

This is followed by a theme that serves as a bridge from C to G major.

The contrasting key of G major is represented by a vigorous theme containing triplets:

There follows a closing theme (codetta) played by clarinets and violas. It rounds off the Exposition with a decisive gesture:

The Development is marked by dynamic rhythm and free modulation. Then—an amazing stroke!—Beethoven brings back the "three shorts and a long" as they appeared in the third movement. This bringing back of material from an earlier movement gives the symphony its cyclical form. He deliberately allows the momentum to slacken so that he may build up tension against the upsurge of the Recapitulation, which is followed by an extensive coda fashioned from materials already heard. The pace accelerates steadily up to the concluding Presto. There is a final outcropping of the basic rhythm. The symphonic stream at the very end becomes an overwhelming torrent as the Tonic chord—source and goal of all activity—is hurled forth by the orchestra again and again.

The Pathétique Sonata

Unlike the case of the *Moonlight* and the *Appassionata,* the title of the *Piano Sonata in C minor,* Opus 13—*Pathétique*—was Beethoven's own, and certainly the quality of Beethovenian pathos is manifest from the first chords of the slow introduction. Marked Grave (solemn), this celebrated opening has something fantasy-like about it, as if Beethoven had captured here the passionate intensity that so affected his listeners when he improvised at the keyboard. Notice the dotted rhythm that contributes to the solemnity of these measures, and the contrary motion: when the melody ascends in the first measure, the bass line descends—and vice versa. The chord pattern is repeated at a higher level in measures 2 and 3 (ascending sequence):

First movement
SIDE 11/1 (E I AND S)

Striking, too, are the contrasts between forte and piano. This type of contrast, an essential feature of Beethoven's dynamism, is used with maximum effectiveness a little further on when it is combined with a change of register: fortissimo chords in the bass are contrasted with a softly expressive melody in the treble. All in all this introduction, written on the threshold of the nineteenth century (1799), speaks a powerful language new to piano music. It ends with a descending chromatic scale and the instruction "attacca subito il Allegro" (attack the Allegro immediately).

The movement proper, marked Allegro di molto e con brio (very fast and with vigor), opens in the home key—C minor—with an impetuous idea that climbs to its peak and descends, while the left hand maintains the rumble of a sustained tremolo in the bass.

A bridge passage modulates, leading to the second theme in E-flat minor, whose gentle lyricism offers an effective contrast to the first. This is a supplicating melody that leaps from the bass register to the treble, which involves crossing the hands.

A third theme in E flat, the relative major key, moves steadily upward in a gradual crescendo; a codetta rounds off the Exposition. Before proceeding with the next section Beethoven brings back the dramatic theme of the introduction, like a fleeting reminiscence. In the Development he skillfully combines the first theme of the Allegro with the theme of the introduction:

For a while the two hands reverse their roles as the left hand carries the melody while the right takes over the tremolo. A transitional passage that descends from high F to a low C leads back to the home key of C minor. In the Recapitulation the material is restated. The second theme is transposed not to the home key but to F minor. This makes possible an eftective return to the home key when the third theme appears in C minor. Very dramatic, just before the end of the movement, is a brief reminder of the slow introduction, followed by a precipitous cadence in the home key.

Throughout Beethoven uses the resources of the instrument most imaginatively. In addition to the contrasts we have mentioned between higher and lower register, as well as between soft and loud, he exploits the somber coloring of the bass, the rich sound of full chords, the brilliance of rapid scale passages, the excitement of a sustained tremolo, and the power of a slowly gathering crescendo allied with a gradual climb in pitch.

Second movement
SIDE 11/2
(E I AND S)

The second movement is the famous Adagio cantabile (slow and songful) which shows off the piano's ability to sing. A lyric melody is introduced in the middle register over a simple accompaniment. Here is the combination of inwardness and strength that impelled nineteenth-century writers to describe the Beethovenian slow movement as a "hymnic adagio":

This melody alternates with two contrasting sections, giving an **A-B-A-C-A** structure. Urgency is added to the third idea (**C**) by triplet rhythm, sudden accents, crescendos, and dramatic arpeggios deep in the bass. The principal melody is repeated with more elaborate figuration. A beautiful coda leads to the pianissimo ending.

Third movement
SIDE 11/3 (E I AND S)

Beethoven in this sonata abandons the usual four-movement scheme; the third is the final movement. This is a rondo, to whose principal theme the C-minor tonality imparts a darker coloring that sets it apart from the usually cheerful rondo-finales of Haydn and Mozart. With such a point

of departure Beethoven constructs a movement with more drama to it than had been customary in the rondo. The principal theme alternates with two other ideas in the pattern **A-B-A-C-A-B-A,** with a codetta after the **B** section and a coda at the end. The frame is spacious; within it, lyric episodes alternate with dramatic.

The *Pathétique* has been a favorite for generations. In the hands of a great artist it stands revealed as one of Beethoven's most personal sonatas.

Piano Concerto No. 5 (Emperor)

The term *Emperor* that attached itself to Beethoven's last piano concerto was not given by him. To the Viennese the word suggested all that was noble and great. The work is truly an emperor among concertos, but it hardly needs so conservative a label to affirm its greatness. Beethoven had completed six of his symphonies by the time he wrote this concerto. He here achieved a remarkable fusion of concerto style and symphonic form, projecting the tensions between piano and orchestra within a truly imposing architecture.

First movement

The Classical concerto, we saw, began with a long orchestral passage for orchestra. This built up suspense against the entrance of the soloist. In his last two piano concertos, Beethoven abandoned this procedure. He brought in the piano at once, creating thereby a dramatic confrontation between piano and orchestra. The *Emperor Concerto* opens with a majestic pronouncement of the three chords that served as the pillars of Classical harmonic architecture—the Tonic (I), Subdominant (IV), and Dominant (V). Each chord in turn is announced by the orchestra and expanded on the piano in a cadenza-like passage consisting of arpeggios, trills, broken octaves, and rapid scales. After this spectacular introduction, the orchestra sets forth the principal themes of the movement in a spacious Exposition. First is an imperious idea that establishes the home key of E flat. It contains two striking motives that will dominate the movement; the second is simply a dotted rhythm.

This theme is given a symphonic treatment. A short bridge passage leads into the mysterious second theme, pianissimo, in the key of E-flat minor:

It is immediately repeated in E-flat major by the horns, in which version it takes on a wonderfully serene quality.

Already in the Exposition Beethoven begins to develop motive **A,** as is evident from the following example:

In the Classical scheme, the codetta, we found, served to round off a section, striking a retrospective tone. Notice the rhythm of motive **B** at the end of this theme:

The piano enters boldly with an ascending chromatic scale followed by a trill. The themes take on a different quality when they are set forth by the piano in a second Exposition. We encounter here all the staples of piano virtuosity—rapid runs, scales and trills, brilliant octaves and arpeggios. Yet technique here is never an end in itself, but a means to musical expression.

Noteworthy are the daring modulations to distant keys. For example, the mysterious second theme now appears in the remote key of B minor:

There follows a beautiful epilogue, a kind of meditation—pianissimo—in the piano's upper register. It is in C-flat major, which is really B major:

The orchestra repeats the second theme in B-flat major, and the second Exposition closes with a virtuoso display.

The Development is ushered in by a chromatic scale on the piano followed by a trill. Motive **A** is bandied about by various instruments against passage work on the piano. Meanwhile the strings, in the background, remind us of motive **B** (the dotted rhythm). Motives from the Exposition are recombined in fresh patterns that derive their power from Beethoven's startling modulations through foreign keys.

At the end of the Development, Beethoven prepares for the Recapitulation by repeating the procedure he used at the beginning of the piece. The orchestra announces the three basic chords, each of which is expanded on the piano in a new cadenza-like passage. Again we hear an ascending chromatic scale, and the Recapitulation begins with the main idea in the home key. The subsidiary ideas are heard as before, but shifted to new keys. In the Classical concerto the orchestra was supposed to pause at a certain point and leave the soloist free to improvise a cadenza. Beethoven, in this work, opened a new chapter in the history of the piano concerto by writing out the cadenza. As though fearful that the earlier custom might prevail, he specified in the score: "Do not make a Cadenza, but quickly attack the following:" In other words, the time had passed when the composer could depend on the performer's ability to improvise a cadenza at the performance. Henceforth composers (with a few exceptions) followed Beethoven's example and wrote out the cadenza in advance.

The cadenza begins with the opening motive:

Soon the orchestra returns, and the cadenza turns into an extended fantasy on the basic themes of the movement. The dotted rhythm of motive **B** comes to the fore and leads to a powerful final cadence, *fff*.

Second movement

The slow movement is another example of what came to be called, in Beethoven literature, the "hymnic Adagio": a movement of profound serenity, inner strength and depth of feeling. Beethoven was influenced by the Deism that was fashionable after the French Revolution. His was an abiding belief in Nature's God rather than in a particular religious dogma. If certain of his Adagios have a hymnlike quality, it is because of the visionary quality, the sense of awe and wonder that emanates from them.

This movement is in **A-B-A** form. Muted strings introduce the chief idea **(A)** in the key of B major. The exploration of this thought con-

stitutes the first section. The piano enters with the second theme **(B)**, pianissimo and espressivo: a rhapsodical melody in the right hand and a

simple accompaniment of broken chords in the left, against sustained harmonies in the orchestra. This is repeated in another key, and the middle section ends with an ascending series of trills. The chief melody **(A)** returns pizzicato in the orchestra while the piano plays a more ornate version of it in triplet rhythm. The melody is repeated an octave higher while above it the piano quickens to a wavelike figure in sixteenth-note rhythm. This passage has the visionary quality to which we have alluded. The movement ends in a shadowy pianissimo that covers a modulation—very daring for its time—from B major (five sharps) to the home key of E-flat major (three flats). Out of it, like an upsurge of light, emerges the final movement, an energetic rondo.

Third movement

This rondo is dominated by its opening theme, a sturdy tune that leaps upward along the notes of the Tonic chord. Its rhythmic energy is powered by syncopation: groups of two instead of three eights in the first measure and a strongly accented chord on the offbeat in the second:

The combination of 6/8 meter with horn and trumpet calls creates a joyous outdoor atmosphere, of the kind traditionally associated in eighteenth-century music with hunting scenes. (Beethoven's hymn to Nature, the *Pastoral Symphony,* was composed a year before this concerto.) The opening passage on the piano is answered in kind by the orchestra. Notable is the theme that rounds off the opening section, an arresting idea in the violins that alternates with a dotted rhythm in the horns:

Two other themes should be noted, both cheerful melodies introduced by the piano:

The principle idea returns repeatedly, with interesting modulations to C major (no sharps or flats), A-flat major (4 flats) and E major (4 sharps). These divagations build up tension, naturally, against the final return to E-flat major. The material is recapitulated in the home key. Remarkable is the way Beethoven sustains the rhythmic vigor and emotional tension of the rondo until the affirmative final cadence.

The *Emperor* was a milestone in the history of the piano concerto. In it Beethoven looked beyond his time to the future. Since its full realization demands artistry of the highest order, it still—more than a century and a half later—poses a challenge to the concert pianist.

Overture to Egmont

Throughout his life Beethoven was preoccupied with the hero as representative of mankind's finest traits, especially the hero who led his fellow men in their struggle for freedom. He therefore responded with enthusiasm when asked, in 1808, to write the incidental music for a production of Goethe's tragedy *Egmont* at the Imperial Theater in Vienna. The hero of Goethe's drama was the Dutch soldier and diplomat Count Egmont, who in the sixteenth century played an important part in the struggle of the Netherlands against Spain. Egmont first fought for the Spanish Emperor Charles V and liberated Flanders from the French yoke. Charles was succeeded by Philip II, who decided to fasten his hold on the Netherlands. Egmont, in high favor with the Spanish authorities, at first hesitated to take a stand. Ultimately he cast his lot with his countrymen, was imprisoned, and sentenced to death for high treason. Visitors to Brussels can still see, on one of the magnificent old houses that line the town square, a plaque saying, "Near this spot, on June 4, 1568, Lamoral, Count of Egmont was beheaded, a victim of the implacable hate and tyranny of Philip II."

Goethe's drama

In writing the play Goethe added a love interest and took sundry liberties with history. When taken to task for this he replied, "Of what use would poets be if they only repeated what the historians said?" In any case, on the night before his execution Egmont, in chains, has a vision of the Goddess of Liberty who foretells the ultimate victory of his cause. Beethoven could not but be inspired by the hero's final words to his countrymen: "Fight for your hearths and homes and die joyfully—as I do—to save what you hold most dear."

In Classical tragedy the hero was torn between love and duty. In *Egmont* the struggle is on a more subtle level, springing from the hero's initial ambivalence: should he side with his Spanish patrons or with his countrymen? Beethoven's Overture gives a preview, as it were, of the drama and suggests the conflict in Egmont's soul. The slow introduction in F minor, marked Sostenuto ma non troppo (slow, but not too much) strikes a somber note. Strings in low register play the opening chords darkly:

The Overture: Introduction
SIDE 10/4 (E I)

This is answered by a phrase that presents a contrast on several levels: woodwinds against strings, upper register against lower, piano against forte, and a plaintive mood against the solemnity of the opening idea. A

dialogue develops between the two themes, at the end of which a transitional idea leads into the Allegro proper. This is in sonata-allegro form. Its main theme is a darkly turbulent melody sung by the cellos that moves downward over a wide range:

Allegro

This idea is expanded with steadily mounting tension until the whole orchestra hurls it out fortissimo in a powerful climax that projects the atmosphere of conflict.

A short bridge leads into the second theme. It is based on the opening idea but is now in A-flat major, is played in a faster tempo, and takes on a quality of bold resolution. A closing theme, consisting of upward-rushing scales, rounds off the Exposition.

The Development is brief and intense. It is based almost wholly on the opening notes of theme 1; that is, motive **A,** which is bandied about by various woodwind instruments and takes on new forms as it passes through a succession of foreign keys. The Recapitulation reviews the material, with Theme 2 transposed to D-flat major. This section is rounded off by a coda; the music proceeds from *ff* to a mournful *ppp*. Instead of ending on this sorrowful note, the Overture moves into an epilogue marked Allegro con brio (fast, with energy)—a "symphony of victory" that suggests Egmont's ecstatic vision in the final hours of his life, his—and Beethoven's—faith in the ultimate triumph of liberty and justice. Stirring trumpet calls help to project the heroic mood of this peroration, which is akin in spirit to the ending of the *Fifth Symphony*.

Chronologically Beethoven's life fell in almost equal parts in the eighteenth and nineteenth centuries. His career bridged the transition from the old society to the new. The sum of his message was freedom. By freedom, though, he understood not romantic revolt but the inner discipline that alone constitutes freedom. His music stems from a Promethean struggle for self-realization. It is the expression of a titanic force, the affirmation of an all-conquering will.

53

Classical Chamber Music

"No other form of music can delight our senses with such exquisite beauty of sound, or display so clearly to our intelligence the intricacies and adventures of its design."

— HENRY HADOW

By *chamber music* is meant ensemble music for from two to about eight or nine instruments with one player to the part, as distinct from orchestral music, in which a single instrumental part is presented by anywhere from two to eighteen players. The essential trait of chamber music is its intimacy

Chamber music is in the nature of a friendly conversation among equals. A painting by Jack Levine (b. 1915), **String Quartette.** (The Metropolitan Museum of Art, Arthur H. Hearn Fund, 1942.)

and refinement; its natural setting is the home. In this domain we find neither the surge and thunder of the symphony nor the grand gesture of the operatic stage. The drama is of an inward kind. Each instrument is expected to assert itself to the full, but the style of playing differs from that of the solo virtuoso. Where the virtuoso is encouraged to exalt his own personality, the chamber-music player functions as part of a team.

Instrumental combinations

The Classical era saw the golden age of chamber music. Haydn and Mozart, Beethoven, and Schubert established the true chamber-music style, which is in the nature of a friendly conversation among equals. The central position in Classical chamber music was held by the string quartet. Consisting of first and second violins, viola, and cello, this group came to represent the ideal type of happy comradeship among instruments, lending itself to music of exquisite detail and purity of style. Other favored combinations were the duo sonata–piano and violin or piano and cello; the trio–piano, violin, and cello; and the quintet, usually consisting of a combination of string or wind instruments, or a string quartet and solo instrument such as the piano or clarinet. The age produced, too, some memorable examples of chamber music for larger groups–sextet, septet, and octet.

Haydn: String Quartet in G, *Opus 64, No. 4*

Haydn's string quartets–he wrote nearly eighty–testify to a half-century of artistic growth. His mature works in this form served as a model for all who came after. The quartet style as he perfected it was one in which all four instruments shared equally. Goethe compared the string quartet to a conversation among four sensible people. He might have added that they were not only sensible but also sensitive and deeply feeling. This animated conversation was presented within the frame of sonata form, based on the dynamic development of short striking themes and motives within a continuous texture. Hand in hand with this went the exciting interaction of a home key and contrasting key, with modulation to foreign keys before the ultimate return to the home key.

First movement

Characteristic of Haydn's mature style is the *String Quartet in G major,* Opus 64, No. 4. The opening movement is a spirited sonata-allegro with all the bounce and vigor that have endeared Haydn to quartet players—both amateur and professional—the world over. The theme that dominates the movement is an upward-leaping rocket theme of the type we encountered in the finale of Mozart's *G-minor Symphony* and the Scherzo of Beethoven's *Fifth.* This seemingly simple tune is extraordinarily rich in motives that lend themselves to growth and development:

The second theme, which begins in D minor, contrasts with the first in the following ways:

Theme 1	*Theme 2*
Covers a wide range	Stays within a narrow range
Marked by wide leaps	Repeated notes and narrow leaps
Begins forte	Begins piano
Vigorous accents on the beat	Melody moves on the offbeat (syncopation)
Sharply defined tonality	Ambiguous tonality

The closing theme (codetta) is not only delightful in its own right but furnishes the motive that starts off the Development section. The opening measures of the Development show how each instrument presents this motive in turn:

The Development avoids the main theme, basing itself—in addition to the closing theme—on rapid figuration drawn from the Exposition and touching briefly on the second theme. The Recapitulation opens with a favorite device of the Classical era. The main theme, having been presented in the home key of G major, is shifted to G minor, a change that reveals it in a new light. The second theme is hinted at, the first theme is stated anew, and the closing theme (coda) decisively reaffirms the home key.

The Classical masters sometimes placed the minuet second and the slow movement third, instead of the other way around, which shifted the expressive center of the sonata cycle into the second half of the work. This quartet is a case in point. The Minuet, an Allegretto in G, is a sprightly **A-B-A** form. It has the urbanity of spirit and the flowing movement characteristic of Haydn's finest minuets. It consists of two concise sections, each of which is repeated.

Second movement: Minuet

Trio

The Trio or middle section **(B)** is based on arpeggio figures. Regular four-measure phrases suddenly give way to phrases of five measures—another example of Haydn's affinity for irregular structure. At the end of the Trio stands the direction da capo, indicating that the first section is to be played again, but this time without repeats.

Third movement

The Adagio is in C major. Marked cantabile sostenuto (songful and sustained), it is in the style of an aria sung by the first violin against a flowing accompaniment in the lower strings. The melody opens with a four-measure phrase answered by a phrase of five measures. This statement is set off by another, after which both are varied through increasingly elaborate ornamentation. You will get a good idea of Haydn's variation procedure by comparing the following three versions of the opening phrase. Notice that the third is in minor:

After the return to major, the ornamentation of the theme becomes still more elaborate. A brief coda relaxes the mood and leads to a pianissimo ending.

Fourth movement

The fourth movement is a Presto in 6/8 time, in the home key of G. This sonata-allegro skims along in the effortless manner that characterized so many finales of the Classical era. The contrast between the two basic

An evening of chamber music, Berlin, 1855. The elderly lady on the right is Bettina von Arnim, friend to Beethoven and Goethe, in this watercolor by Carl Johann Arnold (1829–1916). (Goethemuseum, Frankfurt.)

themes is carefully limited, so as not to disturb either the lighthearted mood or the forward momentum. Instead of the crescendo and fortissimo that usually accompanied a happy ending in the Classical style, Haydn surprises us by letting the music fade away.

Beethoven: String Quartet in F, *Opus 18, No. 1*

Beethoven did not undertake the writing of string quartets until he was almost thirty. The six quartets of Opus 18 date from the years 1798–1800. The *Quartet in F* (1799) was placed first when the set was published; actually it was written after the one now known as Opus 18, No. 3. Its opening movement, like that of the *Fifth Symphony,* is dominated by a rhythm as much as by a theme:

First movement
SIDE 11/4 (E I)

The notes under the bracket become the basic motive of the movement. Notice how subtly this motive is varied in measures 3–4 and 5–6.

There is another similarity here to the first movement of the *Fifth Symphony:* although the second theme is lyrical in nature, thereby contrasting with the first, Beethoven does not permit it to arrest the forward drive of the movement. An effective codetta reasserts the basic motive and brings the Exposition to a cadence in the related key of C major. Tension is heightened in the Development when the music modulates frequently as the basic motive is tossed about among the four instruments. The following example well illustrates Beethoven's developmental procedure. The motive is repeated in descending sequence in the first violin against repeated notes in the second violin and viola:

Then the second violin takes over the descending sequence while the first joins the viola in the repeated notes. Staccato scale passages, ascending and descending, lead into the Recapitulation. The principal theme is stated fortissimo in octaves; the lyrical second theme is transposed to the home key; and a sturdy coda brings the movement to a close.

Remaining movements

The remaining movements present no special problems to the listener. The slow movement, a lyric meditation in D minor in 9/8 time, is marked Adagio affettuoso ed appassionato (very slow, tender, and impassioned). Although *affettuoso* was frequently used in the eighteenth century, as was *appassionato* in the nineteenth, the combination of the two terms was most unusual at the time when this quartet was written. Sonata-allegro form gives this passionate lament its spacious architecture. The Scherzo, in F major, is marked Allegro molto and supplies the necessary contrast. The finale, an Allegro in 2/4 time, is a good-humored rondo that ends the work on a properly optimistic note.

Schubert: The Trout Quintet

One of the most popular of Schubert's chamber works, the *Trout Quintet* dates from 1819, when the composer was twenty-two. He had just completed a happy journey through upper Austria, whose landscape pervades this music. In the course of the trip he was asked to make his song *Die Forelle* (The Trout) available to players of chamber music. Schubert responded with the *Quintet in A major* for piano and strings, whose fourth movement consists of a set of variations on the melody of the song.

In a quintet for piano and strings, a natural opposition ensues between the piano sound and that of the string mass. Schubert, significantly, strengthened the string group. Instead of writing for the usual quartet he employed a violin, viola, cello, and double bass.

Fourth movement: Theme and Variations
SIDE 2/3 (E II)
SIDE 3/3 (S)

The most popular movement is the set of variations on *Die Forelle*. The theme is announced in D major by the first violin, against a background of the other string instruments:

Variation 1 assigns the melody to the piano against arpeggios in the strings. In Variation 2 the viola sings the tune against exciting arabesques in the upper register of the violin. Variation 3 shifts the melody to the double bass against elaborate running passages on the piano. In these three variations the melody remains unchanged. The next two variations present it with changes of register, dynamics, harmony, melodic outline, rhythm, and type of accompaniment. Variation 4 shifts to D minor and triplet rhythm, and is marked by some bewitching modulations, as is Variation 5, which begins in B-flat major. In the sixth and final variation Schubert returns to the mood of *Die Forelle* by using the rippling figure of the original piano accompaniment to the song.

Remaining movements

The other movements raise no issues that we have not already touched upon. The opening Allegro vivace in A, a cheerful movement in 4/4 time, is followed by an Andante in 3/4 in F that looks back to the quietude of the eighteenth-century slow movement and shows striking changes of key. The Scherzo is a Presto in A, in 3/4 time; it makes an effective contrast with the Theme and Variations that follow. The fifth movement is an Allegro giusto (fast, in strict time) in 2/4, in the home key of A: a beautiful rondo in Hungarian style. The prevailing optimism of Schubert's early twenties is reflected throughout the work.

Chamber music holds out to the listener a very special musical experience. It offers him delights that no other branch of music can duplicate.

54

From Classic to Romantic: Schubert's Unfinished Symphony

"I am very greatly obliged by the diploma of honorary membership you so kindly sent me. May it be the reward of my devotion to the art of music to become wholly worthy of such a distinction one day. In order to give musical expression to my sincere gratitude as well, I shall take the liberty before long of presenting your honorable Society with one of my symphonies in full score."

We discussed the songs and piano pieces of Franz Schubert in connection with the Romantic movement, whose first stirrings found in them so vivid an expression. In his symphonies, however, as in his chamber music, he was the heir of the Viennese Classical tradition.

The name *Unfinished* that has attached itself to Schubert's *Symphony No. 8,* in B minor, is unfortunate, suggesting as it does that the composer was snatched away by death before he could complete it. Actually the work was written when Schubert was twenty-five years old, in 1822, and was sent to the Styrian Musical Society in the town of Graz in fulfillment of the promise made in the letter just quoted. He completed two movements and sketched the opening measures of a scherzo. Given his facility, a work was no sooner conceived than written down; if he abandoned the task in this instance it was probably because he had said all that he had to say.

The work displays Schubert's radiant orchestral sonority, his power of making the instruments sing, his unique handling of woodwinds and brass. The wonder is all the greater when we remember that Schubert never heard his finest symphonic scores. The *B-minor Symphony,* for example, was never performed during his lifetime. The manuscript lay gathering dust for more than thirty-five years after his death.

First movement
SIDE 2/4 (E II)

The first movement, Allegro moderato, is based on three ideas. The first, in the nature of an introductory theme, establishes the home key of B minor. It emerges out of the lower register in a mysterious pianissimo, played by cellos and double basses. This is a simple yet memorable statement, not active rhythmically but containing three motives eminently capable of development. Melodic movement is by step and narrow leap:

There follows a broadly curved melody in the home key given out by an oboe and clarinet over the restless accompaniment of the strings. Notice how the downward leap in measures 1 and 3 is balanced by stepwise movement in measures 2 and 4 as well as in the second half of the phrase:

The bridge between the home key and the contrasting key consists of a sustained tone in the bassoon and horns, followed by three chords that modulate effectively from B minor into G major. Now is heard the great lyric subject sung by cellos against syncopated chords in the clarinets and violas. Extraordinary is the broad arch traced by the forward surge of this melody, yet how simple is its pattern:

The fragmenting of this theme into its motives begins already in the Exposition. Measure 6 is extracted and is bandied about by the upper and lower strings, one group imitating the other as the motive is repeated in sequence:

A serene codetta, fashioned from the same material in a new version, brings the Exposition to a close.

The Development section is remarkable for its architectonic force, its dramatic intensity and momentum. With sure symphonic instinct Schubert picks what seems like the least promising of his themes—the first—for expansion and working out. The idea reveals its latent energies in a symphonic fabric that grows steadily in power and impetus. Now it is presented by the lower strings and imitated in the upper; now a fragment flowers into new lines of thought. Here are several examples of Schubert's procedures:

Introductory theme in another key and with a new ending:

Introductory theme expanded by presenting the first two notes of motive **C** in ascending sequence:

Motive **A** of the introductory theme inverted and expanded, with each of its three notes falling in turn upon the accented (first) beat of the measure:

The Recapitulation restates the material of the first section. The lyric theme of the cellos is transposed to D major, the relative major of B minor.

The coda brings back the introductory theme, so that the movement ends in the home key with the idea out of which it flowered.

Second movement

The second movement in E major is marked Andante con moto (at a going pace, with motion). It is in abbreviated sonata form; that is, an Exposition and Recapitulation without a Development. How sheerly romantic is the sonority of the opening chords, played by bassoons and horns against a descending pizzicato on the double basses, out of which emerges the principal motive in the strings.

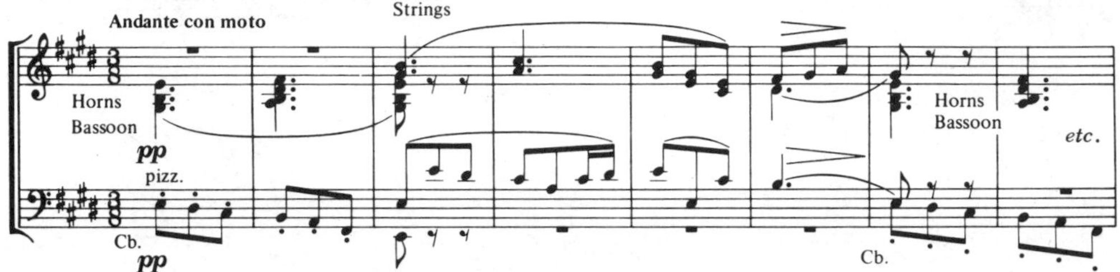

An orchestral crescendo leads to the second theme in the related key of C-sharp minor. This is a long-breathed song introduced by clarinet and answered by oboe against syncopated chords in the strings. The closing sec-

tion of the Exposition undergoes an animated symphonic expansion. Then the two ideas return in the Recapitulation, with subtle changes of color. This time, for example, it is the oboe that introduces the broadly curved second theme and the clarinet that answers. The coda looks back to the opening measures.

The creator of this music passed his uneventful life in the city of Beethoven; too diffident to approach the great man, he worshiped from afar. He could not know that of all the composers of his time, his name alone would be linked to that of his idol. They who far surpassed him in fame and worldly success are long forgotten. Today we speak of the four masters of the Viennese Classical school: Haydn, Mozart, Beethoven–and Schubert.

PART FIVE

Medieval, Renaissance, and Baroque Music

"Music was originally discreet, seemly, simple, masculine, and of good morals. Have not the moderns rendered it lascivious beyond measure?"

— JACOB OF LIÈGE (*fourteenth century*)

55

Harmony and Counterpoint: Musical Texture

"Ours is an age of texture." — GEORGE DYSON

In writings on music we encounter frequent references to the fabric or texture. Such comparisons between music and cloth are not as unreasonable as may at first appear, since the melodic lines may be thought of as so many threads that make up the musical fabric. This fabric may be one of several types.

Monophonic Texture

The simplest is *monophonic* or single-voice texture. ("Voice" refers to an individual part or line even when we speak of instrumental music, a reminder of the fact that all music stems from vocal origins.) Here the melody is heard without either a harmonic accompaniment or other vocal lines. Attention is focused on the single line. All music up to about a thousand years ago, of which we have any knowledge, was monophonic.

To this day the music of the Oriental world—of China, Japan, India, Java, Bali, and the Arab nations—is largely monophonic. The melody may be accompanied by a variety of rhythm and percussion instruments that embellish it, but there is no third dimension of depth or perspective such as harmony alone confers upon a melody. To make up for this lack the single line, being the sole bearer of musical meaning, takes on great complexity and finesse. The monophonic music of the Orient boasts subtleties of pitch and refinements of rhythm unknown in our music.

Polyphonic Texture

When two or more melodic lines are combined we have a *polyphonic* or many-voiced texture. Here the music derives its expressive power and its interest from the interplay of the several lines. Polyphonic texture is based on counterpoint. This term comes from the Latin *punctus contra punctum,* "point against point" or "note against note"—that is to say, one musical line against the other. *Counterpoint* is the art and science of combin-

Counterpoint

ing in a single texture two or more simultaneous melodic lines, each with a rhythmic life of its own.

It was a little over a thousand years ago that European musicians hit upon the device of combining two or more lines simultaneously. At this point Western art music parted company from the monophonic Orient. There ensued a magnificent flowering of polyphonic art that came to its high point in the fifteenth and sixteenth centuries. This development of counterpoint took place at a time when composers were mainly preoccupied with religious choral music, which by its very nature is many-voiced.

Homophonic Texture

In the third type of texture a single voice takes over the melodic interest while the accompanying voices surrender their individuality and become blocks of harmony, the chords that support, color, and enhance the principal part. Here we have a single-melody-with-chords or *homophonic* texture. Again the listener's interest is directed to a single line; but this line, unlike that of Oriental music, is conceived in relation to a harmonic background. Homophonic texture is familiar to all; we hear it when the pianist plays the melody with his right hand while the left sounds the chords, or when the singer or violinist carries the tune against a harmonic accompaniment on the piano. Homophonic texture, then, is based on harmony, just as polyphonic texture is based on counterpoint.

We have said that melody is the horizontal aspect of music while harmony is the vertical. The comparison with the warp and woof of a fabric consequently has real validity. The horizontal threads, the melodies, are held together by the vertical threads, the harmonies. Out of their interaction comes a weave that may be light or heavy, coarse or fine.

The three types of texture are apparent from the look of the music on the page:

HOMOPHONIC

A composition need not use one texture or another exclusively. For example, a symphonic movement may present a theme against a homophonic texture. In the development section, however, the texture is apt to become increasingly contrapuntal. So, too, in a homophonic piece the composer may enhance the effect of the principal melody through an interesting play of counterthemes and counterrhythms in the accompanying parts. This is the case in the best orchestral and piano music of the Classic-Romantic period.

The problem of texture is related too to the general style of an era. There was a great shifting of interest from polyphonic to homophonic music around the year 1600. Contrapuntal and harmonic texture existed side by side, the one influencing the other. After 1750 and throughout the Classic-Romantic period, composers emphasized the homophonic aspect of music over the contrapuntal. A reaction set in with the twentieth century, which turned back to independent part writing. We may sum up the various periods of music history, from the standpoint of texture, as follows:

Before the tenth century A.D.	monophonic
From around 1000 to 1600	polyphonic (contrapuntal)
1600–1750	polyphonic-homophonic
1750–1900	homophonic; contrapuntal procedures absorbed into orchestral and chamber music
Since 1900	revival of interest in polyphonic texture

We have studied the sonata-symphony and other forms that stemmed out of the homophonic-harmonic period. In subsequent chapters we will examine the great forms of polyphonic music.

Devices of Counterpoint

Imitation

When several independent lines are combined, composers try to give unity and shape to the texture. A basic procedure for achieving this end is *imitation,* in which a subject or motive is presented in one voice and then restated in another. While the imitating voice restates the theme, the first voice continues with counterpoint. This continuing repetition of an idea by all the voices is musically most effective. It is of the essence in contrapuntal thinking. We have spoken of the vertical and horizontal threads in musical texture. To these imitation adds a third, the diagonal, as is apparent from the following example:

How long is the statement that is to be imitated? This varies considerably. It may be the entire length of a melodic line that runs from the beginning to end of a piece. Or the imitation may occur intermittently. When the whole length of a melodic line is imitated, we have a strict type of composition known as a *canon*. The name comes from the Greek word for "law" or "order." Each phrase heard in the leading voice is repeated almost immediately in an imitating voice throughout the length of the work. The most popular form of canon is the round, in which each voice enters in succession with the same melody. A *round,* therefore, is a canon for voices at the unison or octave. Composers do not often cast an entire piece or movement in the shape of a canon. What they do is to use canonic devices as effects in all sorts of pieces. The example of diagonal texture just given shows canonic imitation as it occurs in the final movement of César Franck's *Sonata for Violin and Piano*. Since this canon is supported by harmonies in the piano part, it is obvious that Franck here combines contrapuntal and harmonic texture.

Canon

Contrapuntal writing is marked by a number of devices that have flourished for centuries. *Inversion* is a species of treatment in which the melody is turned upside down; that is, it follows the same intervals but in the opposite direction. Where the melody originally moved up by a third, the inversion moves down a third. Where it descended by a fourth, it now ascends a fourth. Thus, D–F–C (up a third, down a fourth), inverted

Inversion

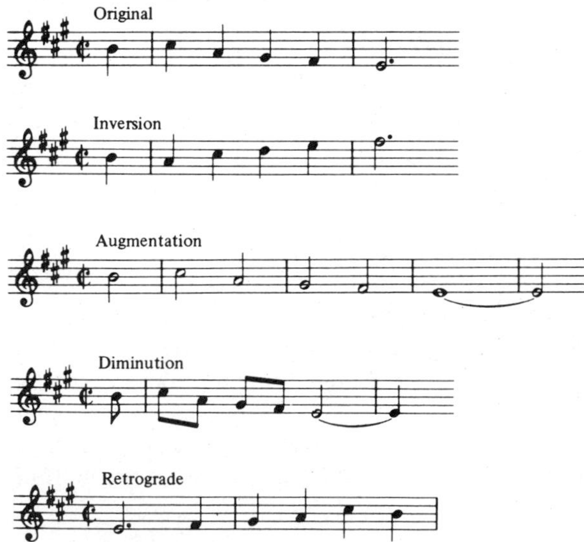

becomes D–B–E (down a third, up a fourth). *Augmentation* consists of presenting a theme in longer time values. A quarter note may become a half, a half note a whole, and so on. In consequence, if the tempo remains the same, the theme in its new version sounds slower. *Diminution* consists of presenting a theme in shorter time values. A whole note may become a half, a half note a quarter, which, at the same tempo, makes the theme sound faster. *Retrograde,* also known as *cancrizans* or *crab motion,* means to state the melody backwards. If the original sequence of notes reads B–D–G–F, the imitation reads F–G–D–B. Retrograde-and-inversion imitates the theme by turning it upside down and backwards at the same time. It should be added that, while imitation is an important element in contrapuntal writing, not all counterpoint is imitative.

Diminution

Retrograde

Musical Texture and the Listener

The different types of texture require different types of listening. Homophonic music poses no special problem to music lovers of today. They are able to differentiate between the principal melody and its attendant harmonies, and to follow the interrelation of the two. They are helped in this by the fact that most of the music they have heard since their childhood consists of melody and chords.

The case is different with polyphonic music, which is not apt to appeal to those who listen with half an ear. Here we must be aware of the independent lines as they flow alongside each other, each in its own rhythm. This requires much greater concentration on our part. Only by dint of repeated hearings do we learn to follow the individual voices and to separate each within the contrapuntal web.

As an exercise in listening contrapuntally, let us take a simple example: the second movement of Bach's cantata *Ein feste Burg ist unser Gott* (A Mighty Fortress Is Our God). The sopranos are singing the chorale melody, slightly ornamented, mostly in quarter notes. Below them, the bass sings a florid counterpoint of a livelier nature. The violins play another vigorous countermelody, with repeated notes. Below all this, the cellos and double basses carry the bass line, mostly in eighth notes. Thus the four lines are distinct not only in register but also in rhythm and color. It is well to listen to the piece several times, concentrating first on each voice alone, then on any two, any three, finally on all four. One becomes aware, in following the three planes of movement, of the illusion of space which it is the unique capacity of counterpoint to create; of the fascinating tensions, both musical and psychological, brought into being by the simultaneous unfolding of several lines.

SIDE 5/2 (E I)
SIDE 13/4 (S)

Contrapuntal music does not yield its secrets as readily as do the less complex kinds. By the same token it challenges our attention and holds our interest. With each rehearing we seem to discover another of its facets.

56

The Remote Past

"Nothing is more characteristic of human nature than to be soothed by sweet modes and stirred up by their opposites. Infants, youths, and old people as well are so naturally attuned to musical modes by a kind of spontaneous feeling that no age is without delight in sweet song." — BOETHIUS (c. 480–524)

The relics of the ancient civilizations—Sumer, Babylonia, Egypt—bear witness to a flourishing musical art. In the antique world, religious myth and tradition ascribed divine powers to music. The walls of Thebes rose and those of Jericho fell to the sound of music. David played his lyre to cure the melancholy of Saul. In the temple at Jerusalem the Levites, who were the musicians, "being arrayed in fine linen, having cymbals and psalteries and harps, stood at the east end of the altar, and with them an hundred and twenty priests sounding with trumpets."

Only a few fragments have descended to us of the music of antiquity. The centuries have forever silenced the sounds that echoed through the Athenian amphitheater and the Roman circus. Those sounds and the attitudes they reflected, in Greece and throughout the Mediterranean world, formed the subsoil out of which flowered the music of later ages. They became part of the heritage of the West.

Gregorian Chant

Music functioned in the Christian Church from its earliest days. St. Paul exhorted the Ephesians to be filled with the Spirit by "speaking to yourselves in psalms and hymns and spiritual songs, singing and making melody in your heart to the Lord." The music of the Church absorbed Greek, Hebrew, and Syrian influences. It became necessary in time to assemble the ever growing body of chants into an organized liturgy. The task extended over several generations but is traditionally associated with the name of Pope Gregory the Great, who reigned from 590 to 604.

Melody

Like the music of the Greeks and Hebrews from which it descended, *Gregorian chant* (also known as *plainchant* or *plainsong*) consists of a single-line melody. In other words, it is monophonic in texture and does not know the third dimension of harmony and counterpoint. Its freely flowing vocal line is subtly attuned to the inflections of the Latin text. Gregorian melody is free from regular accent. It embodies what may be called prose rhythm in music, or free-verse rhythm, as distinguished from metrical-poetry rhythm such as we find in the regularly accented measures of duple or triple meter. (Much of the liturgy was chanted in so-called

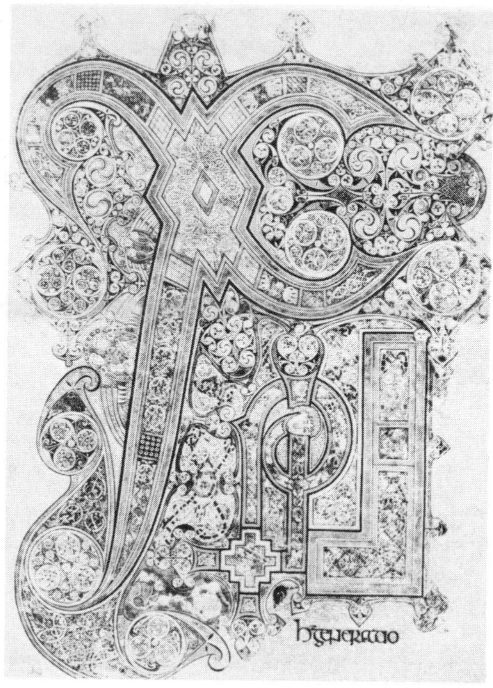

The continuous, undulating line of Gregorian chant parallels the curvilinear movement which animates early Romanesque art. A monogram page from the Book of Kells, *(c. 800* A.D.*).* (Trinity College Library, Dublin.)

recitation style, with many repeated notes. However, when we speak of Gregorian chant we generally mean the musically more interesting style of plainchant.)

The Gregorian melodies, numbering more than three thousand, were worked over in the course of generations until they took on their traditional shape. They formed a body of anonymous melody whose roots reached deep into the spiritual life of the folk; a treasure of religious song which, as someone well said, relates to "Everyman rather than Me." Gregorian chant avoids the excitement of wide leaps and dynamic contrasts. Its gentle rise and fall constitute a kind of disembodied musical speech, "a prayer on pitch." Free from the shackles of regular phrase structure, the continuous, undulating vocal line is the counterpart in sound of the sinuous traceries of Romanesque art and architecture.

Neumes

At first the Gregorian chants were handed down orally from one generation to the next. As the number of chants increased, singers needed to be reminded of the general outlines of the different melodies. Thus came into being the *neumes* (see p. 303), little ascending and descending signs that were written above the words to suggest the course of the melody.

Text settings

As far as the setting of text is concerned, the melodies fall into three main classes: *syllabic,* that is, one note to each syllable; *neumatic,* generally with groups of two to four notes to a syllable, each group represented by a single neume in the original notation; and *melismatic,* with a single syllable extending over longer groups of notes, as in the setting of the word *Alleluia.* The melismatic style, descended from the rhapsodic improvisations of the Orient, became a prominent feature of Gregorian chant and exerted a strong influence on subsequent Western music.

Modes

From Gregorian chant until the Baroque era, Western music used a variety of scale patterns or *modes*—including not only the major and minor modes familiar to us from later music, but also several other patterns. These were used freely rather than systematically, and did not have the strong sense of gravitation to a tonic note that marks our modern major-minor system. As a matter of fact, it was possible in plainchant to make the cadence on any one of several notes.

The modes served as the basis for European art music for a thousand years. With the development of polyphony, or many-voiced music, a harmonic system evolved, based on the modes. The adjective *modal* consequently refers to the type of melody and harmony that prevailed in the early and later Middle Ages. It is frequently used in opposition to *tonal*, which refers to the harmony based on the major-minor tonality that supplanted the modes.

A Gregorian Melody

SIDE 1/1 (E1)
SIDE 9/7 (S)

A beautiful example of Gregorian style is the Introit from the prayers for the Feast of the Assumption. (*Introit,* related to the Latin word for "entrance," was originally a chant accompanying the entrance of the priest to the altar.) The text of the Introit is four lines long:

Gaudeamus omnes in Domino,	Let us all rejoice in the Lord,
diem festum celebrantes sub honore Mariae Virginis:	Celebrating a feast-day in honor of the Blessed Virgin Mary,
de cujus Assumptione gaudent Angeli,	For whose Assumption the angels rejoice
et collaudant Filium Dei.	And give praise to the Son of God.

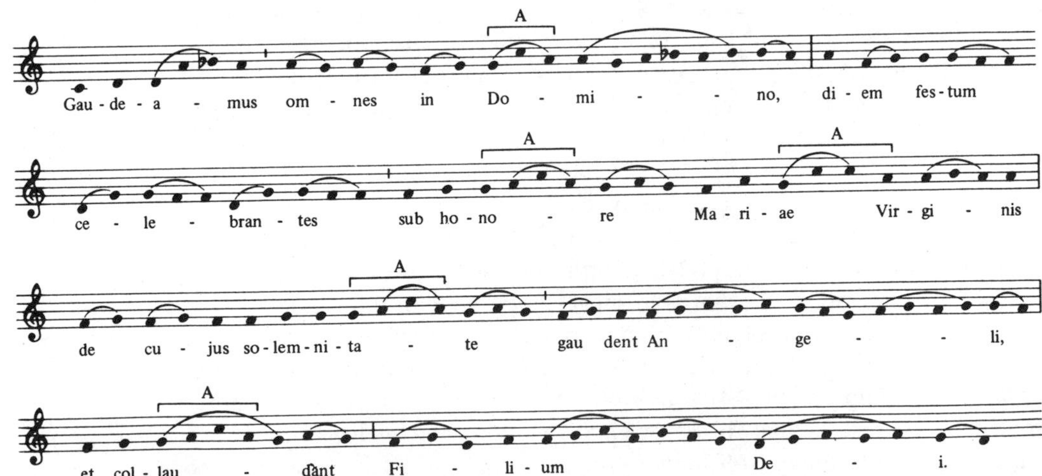

In liturgical use, the Introit is followed by a psalm verse:

Eructavit cor meum verbum bonum: dico ego opera mea regi.	My heart hath uttered a good word: I speak my words to the King.

Then the Doxology or *Gloria Patri* is sung to the same recitation tones as the psalm verse:

Gloria Patri, et Filio, et Spiritu Sancto. Sicut erat in principio, et nunc et semper, et in saecula saeculorum. Amen.	Glory be to the Father, Son, and Holy Ghost. As it was in the beginning, now, and forever, World without end. Amen.

The Introit is now repeated.

The melody lies within a narrow range and moves by step or narrow leap. It is more highly organized than is apparent at a first hearing, consisting of melodic cells that are repeated either exactly or somewhat varied. For example, the motive under the bracket (**A**) recurs in various guises on the words "Domino," "honore," and several others. As a result, the upward leap of a fourth common to all these becomes a distinguishing feature that imparts unity to the melodic line. Here is how this plainchant looks in Gregorian notation:

Motivic shape

Most of the text is set with one or two notes to a syllable. But key words are extended for several notes—for example, "Domino" (Lord), "Angeli" (angels) and "Filium Dei" (Son of God)—which serves to bring them into prominence. This melismatic style is a feature of the Introit, while the psalm verse and Doxology, by contrast, are chanted in recitative style, mostly one note to a syllable, and therefore sound less ornate, more direct. The return of the Introit rounds out the form as an **A-B-B-A,** achieving an effect of symmetry and balance.

Unmeasured rhythm

Throughout, the rhythm is unmeasured; it might be described as free rhythm, distinguished from its metrical counterpart as prose is from poetry. We do not normally think of prose in such terms, yet all good prose has rhythm, and the musical settings of Gregorian chant follow the natural flow of the Latin.

The note at the end of each text line is especially important since it serves as a resting-place or cadence. The four lines of the Introit end, respectively, on A, A, F, and D. These are the principal tones of this mode, and they also outline what we know as the D-minor chord. We can thus identify in Gregorian chant the beginnings of concepts about harmony and form that were not to mature until centuries later.

The Gregorian melodies are remarkable for their unhurried flow, their organic unity, and the way they mold themselves to the natural inflections of the text. Our richest legacy from the period of pure monophonic texture, they nourished fifteen hundred years of European folk, popular, and art music. They bring us as close as we shall ever come to the lost musical art of the ancient Mediterranean culture—the art of Greece, Syria, and Palestine.

Troubadours and Trouvères

The troubadours were Medieval poet-musicians who flourished in Provence, the region roughly equivalent to southern France, while the trouvères were active in the provinces to the north. Both terms mean the same thing—finders or inventors, implying that these musicians presented original material, as distinguished from the church musicians who based their art on melodies that had been handed down from the past. The troubadours wrote in Provençal, the *langue d'oc*, a Medieval language somewhere between French and Spanish, while the trouvères used the *langue d'oeil*, the dialect that evolved into modern French. (The two languages were easily distinguished by their words for "yes"—*oc* in Provençal, and *oeil*, which later became *oui.*) Some five hundred troubadours flourished in the twelfth and thirteenth centuries, and they set to music a wide variety of verse forms that ultimately served as the basis of modern European poetry. These poet-musicians flourished in aristocratic circles, numbering kings and princes among their ranks; but an artist of more humble birth might be accepted among them if his talent warranted it. They either sang their music themselves or entrusted its performance to a minstrel.

The texts

The poems ranged from simple ballads to love songs, political and moral ditties, war songs, laments, and dance songs. They exalted the virtues prized by the age of chivalry—valor, honor, nobility of character, devotion to an ideal, and the quest for perfect love. Like so many of our popular

songs today, many of them dealt with the subject of unrequited passion. The object of the poet's desire was generally unattainable, either because of her exalted rank or because she was already wed to another. Troubadour poetry, in short, dealt with love in its most idealized form. Significantly, the songs in praise of the Virgin Mary were cast in the same style and language, sometimes even to the same melodies, as served to express love of a more mundane kind.

The art of the troubadour flourished at the court of Alfonso the Wise, King of Castile (1252–84). In this manuscript illumination, the musicians may be seen with their instruments at both sides of the picture.

The music

The works of these knightly composers show that secular music was gradually taking over the more "learned" techniques of Church music, thereby acquiring a higher status. Understandably, the troubadours were strongly influenced by Gregorian chant. At the same time, both their poems and melodies bear the influence of Arab culture, indicating that artistic currents from north Africa and Moorish Spain were crossing the Pyrenees into the south of France.

Guiraut de Bornelh: Reis glorios

Alba

One of the most important types of troubadour song was the *alba* or dawn song. Dawn in this context signified the end of a night of love, as in the most famous example in English literature, Romeo's

> It was the herald of the morn,
> No nightingale; look, love, what envious streaks
> Do lace the severing clouds in yonder east:
> Night's candles are burnt out, and jocund day
> Stands tiptoe on the misty mountain tops . . .

The alba was usually sung by the friend who stood guard while the lovers met. As dawn approached, the danger increased that the lady's jealous husband might return. In Medieval legend, the prototype is Brangäne on watch in the tower while Tristan and Isolde are together in the garden below. Her aria in Wagner's opera is a direct descendant of the Medieval alba. The alba also symbolized the rebirth of the sun after the night had wiped him out, as well as the resumption of everyday life after the lovers had found fulfillment.

One of the best-known albas, *Reis glorios*, was composed by Guiraut de Bornelh, "the Master of the Troubadours." Very little is known about him except that he flourished in the years 1165–1215 and cultivated several genres of troubadour poetry. His poem is in four stanzas, each consisting of four lines followed by a refrain. The rhyme scheme is **a-a-b-b:**

Reis glorios, verais lums e clartatz,
Deus poderos, Senher, si a vos platz,
Al meu companh siatz fizels a juda;
Qu'eu no lo vi, pos la nochs fo venguda;
   Et ades sera l'alba!

Glorious King, light of truth and splendor,
Almighty God, Lord, if it please you,
Give faithful aid to my friend.
I have not seen him since night fell;
   And soon it will be dawn!

Bel companho, si dormetz o veillatz?
Non dormatz plus, suau vos ressidatz,
Qu'en orien vei l'estela creguda
Qu'amean-l jorn, qu'eu l'ai ben coneguda:
   Et ades sera l'alba!

Dear friend, are you asleep or awake?
Sleep no more, now you must rise,
For in the east the star grows bright
That heralds the day. I know it well:
   And soon it will be dawn!

Bel companho, en chantan vos apel:
Non dormatz plus, qu'eu aug chantar l'auzel,
Que vai queren la jorn per lo bocsatge;
Et ai paor que-l gilos vos assatge;
   Et ades sera l'alba!

Dear friend, my song is calling you.
Sleep no more, I hear a bird singing,
He goes seeking daylight through the woods.
I fear the jealous husband will catch you;
   And soon it will be dawn!

[The friend replies:]

Bel dous companh, tan soi en ric sojorn
Qu'eu no volgra mais fos alba ni jorn.
Car la gensor que anc nasques de naire,
Tenc e abras, per qu'en non prezi gaire
   Lo fol gelos ni l'alba.

My dear sweet friend, I am so happy where I am
That I wish for neither dawn nor day.
For the loveliest woman that ever was born
I hold in my arms. So I'm not going to worry
About the jealous fool or the dawn.

SIDE 1/2 (E I)
SIDE 11/4 (S)

When troubadour music was written down, only the intervals of the melody were indicated, as a kind of shorthand reminder for a singer. Here is the opening line:

The interval of the rising fifth at the beginning stands out prominently in a melody that otherwise moves mostly by step, sometimes circling around the pivotal notes D and A. The melody of the first line is repeated for the second, and there are other recurrent shapes: for example, the ascending phrase with which the refrain begins echoes the start of the fourth line.

What Medieval performers may have done in terms of rhythm, harmony, and accompaniment can only be conjectured from a careful study of the historical background. Modern scholars and performers usually base their guesses about rhythm on the accentuation of the words and on what is known of rhythmic procedures in other music of the period. In the recorded performance by Martin Best, for example, a relatively free triple time is adopted by the singer. But in the instrumental interludes between the stanzas, the melodic material is presented in a much stricter rhythm. In the final stanza, the reply of the lover, the stricter rhythm and more vigorous tempo of the interludes replace the freer declamation used earlier.

The accompaniment in Best's performance is given to several string instruments—the plucked lute (a relative of the guitar) and harp, the bowed *rebec* (an ancestor of the violin, popular in the Arabic lands and Spain)—and also a small organ known as a *regal*, and small kettledrums of Arabic origin called *nakers*. The resulting sound is distinctly Mediterranean in character, reflecting a view that the troubadours were influenced by the Moorish civilization of Spain—but an alternative and more austere interpretation, closer to the style of Gregorian chant, also has its partisans among scholars. Either way, Guiraut's alba crystallizes a compelling dramatic situation, which a performer, whether he be Medieval or modern, can use to enthrall an audience.

57

The Later Middle Ages

"There are many new things in music that will appear altogether plausible to our descendants." — JEAN DE MURIS (1319)

Towards the end of the Romanesque period (c. 850–1150) began the single most important development in the history of Western music: the emergence of polyphony as a stylistic factor of prime importance. This occurred at about the same time that European painting began developing the science of perspective. Thus hearing and seeing in depth came into European culture together, and must be accounted among its most significant products.

Once several melodic lines proceeded side by side, there could no longer be the flexible prose rhythms of single-line music. Polyphony brought about the emergence of regular meters that enabled the different voices to keep together. This music had to be written down in a way that would indicate precisely the rhythm and the pitch. In this way evolved our modern staff, whose lines and spaces made it possible to indicate the exact pitch, and whose notes, by their appearance, could indicate the duration of each sound.

Exact notation

Polyphony emerged as a stylistic factor of prime importance in Western music at about the same time that European painting began to reflect the science of perspective. Giotto *(c. 1267–1337),* **Lamentation.** *(Arena Chapel, Padua.)*

With the development of exact notation, music took a long step from being an art of improvisation and oral tradition to one that was carefully planned and that could be preserved accurately. Henceforth a musical work could be studied by many musicians; the creative experience of one could nourish all the rest. The period of anonymous creation characteristic of folk art drew to a close. The individual composer appeared upon the scene.

Gothic era

This development took shape during the Gothic era (c. 1150–1450). The period witnessed the rise of the cathedrals with their choirs and organs. The mastery of construction that made possible the building of those mighty edifices had its counterpart in music. The new science of counterpoint was brought to heights of virtuosity. The learned musicians, for the most part monks and priests, mastered the art of constructing extended musical works through the various devices of counterpoint. Their prime interest at this point was in the structural combining of musical elements, which explains the derivation of the word "composer" from the Latin *componere*, "to put together." The creative musician of the late Gothic period thought of himself primarily as a master builder.

The Notre Dame School

Organum

The earliest kind of polyphonic music was called *organum*. This developed when the custom arose of adding to the Gregorian melody a second or organal voice that ran parallel to the plainchant at the interval of a fifth or a fourth above or below. When these lines were duplicated an octave above, there resulted a piece of four voices that moved in parallel octaves, fifths, and fourths, as in the following example of ninth-century organum:

The way was now open for the development of a polyphonic art in which the individual voices moved with ever greater independence, not only in parallel but also in contrary motion. Leaders in this development were the composers whose center was the Cathedral of Notre Dame in Paris during the twelfth and thirteenth centuries. The two outstanding members of the Notre Dame school are the first composers of polyphonic music whose names are known to us: Leonin, who lived in the latter part of the twelfth century, and Perotin, who was active somewhere between 1180 and 1230.

It was self-evident to the Medieval mind that the new must be founded on the old. Therefore the composer of organum based his piece on a preexisting Gregorian chant. While the tenor sang the melody in enormously long notes, the upper voice moved freely above it. Here, for example, is an extensive melisma by Leonin over the first note of a Gregorian melody:

Leonin

Naturally, in this long-drawn-out version the Gregorian chant was no longer recognizable as a melody. Its presence was symbolic, anchoring the new in the old, inspiring and guiding the added voice.

Perotin

While Leonin limited himself to counterpoint in two parts, Perotin extended the technique by writing for three and four voices. His music shows a tendency toward shorter melodic phrases, clear-cut rhythms, at times even a vaguely "major" feeling (comparable to the "minor" atmosphere we noted in our example of Gregorian chant). His larger compositions take on a spacious resonance that evokes the echoing vaults of the Gothic cathedral. He is remembered today as the foremost member of a school that laid the foundation for a magnificent flowering of polyphonic art.

In both architecture and music, the Gothic period saw great advances in the techniques of construction. The Cathedral of Notre Dame, Paris (1163–1235).

A Thirteenth-Century Motet

The *motet* emerged as the most important form of early polyphonic music. This term is applied loosely to a vocal composition, sacred or secular, which may or may not have had instrumental accompaniment.

Cantus firmus

The early motet illustrates how the Medieval composer based his own work on what had been handed down from the past. He selected a fragment of Gregorian chant, and, keeping the notes intact, rearranged them in a rhythmic pattern, usually of very long notes that contrasted with the more active movement of the other parts. This served as the structural skeleton of the piece, and became known as the *cantus firmus* (fixed melody), to which the composer added one, two, or three countermelodies of his own. The cantus firmus therefore served him as a point of departure for his own creativity, and could be repeated as many times as he needed to fill out the length of the piece. The part containing the cantus firmus was called the *tenor*, from the Latin *tenere*, to hold, so called because the tenor "held" the long notes. (It should be noted that terms such as tenor, countertenor, alto, and bass did not signify specific ranges until a later time.) The second, third, and fourth parts were known respectively as *duplum, triplum,* and *quadruplum*. However, nomenclature in the Middle Ages was far from standardized. Different names were used at different times and places.

"Motet" derives from the French *mot* (word), referring to the words that were joined to the added parts. Duplum and triplum might sing two different Latin texts at the same time; or one might sing Latin words while another sang French. In this way a sacred text might be combined with a quite secular—even racy—one. The basic Gregorian theme, hidden among the voices and repeated over and over (like an ostinato in later music) fused these disparate elements into a unity—if not in the listener's ear, at least in the composer's mind.

SIDE 1/3 (E I)

This procedure is well illustrated by a typical French motet of the thirteenth century, the anonymous *O miranda Dei karitas,* in three voices. (The full title gives the opening words of all three parts: *O miranda Dei karitas—Salve mater salutifera—Kyrie.*) It is based on a cantus firmus drawn from the Gregorian melody *Kyrie XII*. This fragment of plainchant is altogether transformed when it becomes the tenor of the motet:

First we hear the cantus firmus with one added part (the duplum), then with both. The tenor repeats the single word "Kyrie," whose first syllable is extended for several measures. Meanwhile the duplum sings an eight-line stanza whose opening phrase is "Salve mater salutifera" (Hail, healing mother):

Salve, mater salutifera, Claritatis speculum, Tu cordis oculum Nostri considera, peccatorum sana vulnera. Virgo, salva seculum A morte populum eterna libera.	Hail, healing mother, mirror of clarity, consider the eye of our heart, heal the sinners' wounds. Virgin, deliver the world and free the people from eternal death.

Against it the triplum sings an eight-line stanza:

O miranda dei karitas! Per peccatum cecidit Homo quem condidit Sed eius bonitas Relaxavit penas debitas. Adam mundum perdidit, Sed vitam reddidit Christi nativitas.	O wondrous love of God! Through sin fell man whom He made but His goodness lightened the penalty owed. Adam destroyed the world, but life was restored to it through the birth of Christ.

When two texts are presented simultaneously they tend to cancel each other out. The listener is free to relegate them to the background and attend primarily to the music.

This motet is distinguished by lively movement and a clear-cut rhythmic structure based on triple meter. The cantus firmus consists of two phrases, one of five measures, the other of ten (see example above). These are

In this fourteenth-century Italian miniature, the central figure, Musica, *is playing a portative organ. Above her (left to right) are a fiddle, psaltery, and lute; beside her, tambourine and clappers; below her, bagpipes, shawm, nakers, and trumpets.*

Phrase structure

then repeated, giving the piece a symmetrical phrase structure. The melodies are simple, moving mostly stepwise and within a narrow range. The three vocal lines lie close together in the middle register and frequently cross. Each line seems to have been conceived with little concern for the others. Yet at the end of each phrase they show their interdependence, for the cadence chord always consists of the same tones, F–C–C, the open fifth and octave that figure so prominently in Medieval polyphony.

Instrumentation

The harmonies are based on these intervals, with passing dissonances that create a pleasantly pungent flavor, underlined by the ancient instruments that accompany the voices. The Medieval composer did not specify any instruments; the choice at any given performance depended largely on what was available. The piece has been recorded by the Munich Capella Antiqua with three instruments. The tenor part (cantus firmus) is supported by a *sackbut,* an early trombone with a narrow bore. The duplum is played by a *shawm,* a Medieval large oboe; and the triplum is accompanied by a *recorder,* a kind of flute that is held vertically, like a clarinet or oboe, and is made of wood. It is played by blowing into one end, the player's breath passing through a whistle mouthpiece and against the sharp edge of a side opening. It has a gentle, slightly reedy tone, became extremely popular in the sixteenth and seventeenth centuries, and has been revived in the twentieth.

The chord at the end of each cadence establishes F as the central tone. Indeed, the tenor part suggests the F-major scale. Because of its strong rhythmic impulse, the music does not in the slightest accord with our notion of Medieval religious feeling. If we disregard the text, this could easily be taken for a lively piece with the lilt of a folk song or dance. We see here how the motet, despite its religious origins, soon reached out toward the secular—a trend that was to shape its course increasingly as time went on.

Guillaume de Machaut

The breakup of the feudal social structure brought with it new concepts of life, art, and beauty. This ferment was reflected in the musical style that made its appearance at the beginning of the fourteenth century in France and somewhat later in Italy, known as *Ars Nova* (new art). The music of the French Ars Nova shows greater refinement than the *Ars Antiqua* (old art), which it displaced. Writers such as Petrarch, Boccaccio, and Chaucer were turning from the divine comedy to the human; painters would soon begin to discover the beauties of nature and the attractiveness of the human form. So, too, composers turned increasingly from religious to secular themes. The Ars Nova brought in changes in rhythm, meter, harmony, and counterpoint that transformed the art.

Its outstanding figure was the French composer-poet Guillaume de Machaut (c. 1300–77). He took holy orders at an early age, became secretary to John of Luxemburg, King of Bohemia, and was active at the court of Charles, Duke of Normandy, who subsequently became king of France. He spent his old age as a canon of Rheims, admired as the greatest musician of the time.

Machaut's double career as cleric and courtier impelled him to both religious and secular music. His poetic ballads reveal him as a proponent of the ideals of Medieval chivalry—a romantic who, like Sir Thomas Malory in his lament for King Arthur, exalted the moral and social code of an age that was already finished. We will study two examples of his varied output: a motet and a polyphonic song.

Hareu! hareu! le feu

The secular motet came to full flower in the art of Machaut. He expanded the form of the preceding century to incorporate the new developments made possible by the Ars Nova, especially the greater variety and flexibility of rhythm. Characteristic is the motet *Hareu! hareu! le feu/Helas! ou sera pris confors/Obediens usque ad mortem.* Since the three simultaneous parts have different texts, the listener is obviously expected to follow the general idea rather than the individual words.

SIDE 1/4 (E I)
SIDE 11/5 (S)

The top voice, the triplum, sings a poem on a favorite theme of fourteenth-century court verse—the suffering of the lover who is consumed by his desire. The poem is in four stanzas of six lines each, in the rhyme scheme **a-a-a-a-b-b**.

Hareu! hareu! le feu, le feu, le feu
D'ardant desir, qu'einc si ardant ne fu,
Qu'en mon cuer a espris et soustenu
Amours, et s'a la joie retenu
D'espoir qui doit attemprer telle ardure.

Las! se le feu qui ensement l'art dure,

Mes cuers sera tous bruis et esteins,
Qui de ce feu est ja nercis et teins,
Pour ce qu'il est fins, loyaus et certeins;
Si que j'espoir que deviez yert, eins
Que bonne Amour de merci l'asseure
Par la vertu d'esperance seure.

Car pour li seul, qui endure mal meint;
Pitié deffaut, ou toute biauté meint;
Durtés y regne et Dangiers y remeint,

Desdeins y vit et Loyautez s'i feint
Et Amours n'a de li ne de moy cure.
Joie le het, ma dame li est dure,

Et, pour croistre mes dolereus meschiés,
Met dedens moy Amours, qui est mes chiés,
Un desespoir qui si mal entechiés
Est quietous biens a de moy esrachiés,
Et en tous cas mon corps si desnature
Qu'il me convient morir malgré Nature.

Help! Help! Fire! Fire! Fire!
My heart is on fire with burning desire
Such as was never seen before.
Love, having started it, fans the flames,
Withholding all hope of joy which might put out
such a blaze.
Alas, if this fire keeps on burning,

My heart, already blackened and shrivelled.
Will be burnt to ashes.
For it is true, loyal, and sincere.
I expect I shall be mad with grief
Before gentle Love consoles it
With sound hope.

It alone, suffering much Hardship,
Is devoid of Pity, abode of all beauty.
Instead, Harshness rules over it and Haughtiness
flourishes.
Disdain dwells there, while Loyalty is a rare visitor
And Love pays no heed to it or to me.
Joy hates it, and my lady is cruel to it.

To complete my sad misfortune,
Love, my sovereign lord,
Fills me with such bitter despair
That I am left penniless,
And so wasted in body
That I shall surely die before my time.

At the same time, the middle voice, the duplum, sings a fifteen-line poem in a similar vein.

Helas! ou sera pris confors
Pour moy qui ne vail nés que mors?
Quant riens garentir ne me puet
Fors ma dame chiere qui wet
Qu'en desespoir muire, sans plus,
Pour ce que je l'aim plus que nulz,
Et Souvenir pour enasprir
L'ardour de mon triste desir
Me moustre adés sa grant bonté

Et sa fine vraie biauté
Qui doublement me fait ardoir.
Einssi sans cuer et sans espoir.
Ne puis pas vivre longuement,
N'en feu cuers humeins nullement
Ne puet longue duree avoir.

Alas, where can I find consolation
Who am as good as dead?
When my one salvation
Is my dear lady,
Who gladly lets me die in despair,
Simply because I love her as no other could.
And Memory, in order to keep
My unhappy desire alive,
Reminds me all the while of her great goodness

And her delicate beauty,
Thereby making me want her all the more.
Deprived thus of heart and hope
I cannot live for long.
No man's heart can long survive
When once aflame.

The tenor is taken from a plainsong gradual that refers to Christ, but Machaut chooses only the section that goes with the words *obediens usque ad mortem*—obedient unto death—a sentiment appropriate to the chivalric love described in the other poems. The notes of this cantus firmus are arranged in a repeated rhythmic pattern consisting of a shorter note, three longs and another short. When the notes of the chant are used up, six times through that pattern, they are then repeated twice as fast—that is, in diminution.

This procedure identifies ***Hareu! hareu! le feu*** as an example of the *isorthythmic motet* (*iso* means "the same"), based on the same rhythm repeated again and again—a device that in much later music would be known as an *ostinato*. Although the notes of this particular cantus firmus are not so long as to make it unsingable, it was probably played on an instrument, such as that slide trumpet (an early type of trumpet, with a slide like the trombone) used in David Munrow's recording.

The upper two voices move at a much faster rate, in a compound meter we could call 6/8 time. Though they occupy the same range, the triplum generally stays at the top of that range, the duplum near the bottom; both voices tend to rotate around the notes with which they begin: respectively, C-B-A and F-E-D.

Each six-line stanza of the upper voice coincides with ten notes of the cantus firmus, while the duplum gets through only three lines in the same time. Notice that the upper voices do not always sing or cadence simultaneously. Instead, they often overlap, so that the musical interest shifts from one line to another and an impression of continuous movement results.

In the last part of the motet, when the cantus firmus has doubled its speed, the upper voices also become more active, engaging in a favorite device of Medieval polyphony, known as *hocket:* each voice alternates notes and rests, but in opposite patterns, creating an exciting effect of exchange.

The intricate interplay of six-line stanzas, three-line stanzas, their respective rhyme schemes, and the isorhythmic pattern of the music is of a sort that delighted the Medieval mind. Such a highly stylized art may lack the directly emotional expressivity of some later music, but its delight in structural sophistication tells us something important about the society for which it was created.

Rose, liz

The polyphonic song, based upon the fixed forms of French lyric poetry, became the most important novelty of Machaut's generation. In his song *Rose, liz,* we again encounter the new flexibility of the Ars Nova. The poem is a *rondeau,* the most popular of the fixed forms; it comprises four stanzas, of which the words of the first return partly in the second and completely in the fourth:

Rose, liz, printemps, verdure, Fleur, baume et tres douce odour, Belle, passes en doucour.	Rose, lily, Spring, grass, Flower, balm and very sweet odor, Lovely one, whom you surpass in sweetness.
Et tous les biens de Nature, Avez dont je vous aour. Rose, liz, printemps, verdure, Fleur, baume et tres douce odour.	And all good things of Nature With which I endow you. Rose, lily, Spring, grass, Flower, balm, and very sweet odor.
Et quant toute creature Seurmonte vostre valour, Bien puis dire et par honnour:	And if any living thing Surpass your worth, Then can I say on my honor:
Rose, liz, printemps, verdure, Fleur, baume et tres douce odour, Belle, passes en doucour.	Rose, lily, Spring, grass, Flower, balm, and very sweet odor, Lovely one, whom you surpass in sweetness.

SIDE 1/5 (E I)

Machaut places the text in one voice, accompanied by another part in the same range, called triplum, and two lower parts, called tenor and contratenor. Although we don't know for certain how Machaut may have intended the piece to be performed (or, indeed, whether his ideas about instrumentation were anywhere near as specific as those of more recent composers), most modern performances present such songs as works for one voice with instrumental accompaniment. In one plausible realization of *Rose, liz,* by the Waverly Consort, plucked instruments (lute and harp) are used at first, with bowed strings (*vielles,* early ancestors of the violin family) added later on for contrast and balance. It is also possible, as in this performance, to vary some of the stanzas by omitting the contratenor part, since the harmonies are complete without it.

The melodic line features two main elements: gently rising phrases, as at the beginning, and more melismatic falling lines in shorter note values. The structure of the music reflects the pattern of the verse. The opening phrase—the music, that is, of the first line—rises from C, then falls and returns to its starting point:

The second line twice descends, and makes a cadence on D, with something of the effect of a dominant in later music. The third line begins with a striking B, and its final phrase repeats the final phrase of the previous line—but this time closes with a cadence on the "home" note of C.

In the second stanza, the first two lines are set like the first two of the opening stanza. This section of the melody is then repeated for the last two lines of the stanza. Thus each half of the stanza makes a cadence on D, but the striking B never returns. Its failure to do so sets up tension, a sense of incompletion, which is resolved in the third and fourth stanzas, since these duplicate the setting of the first. The rondeau, consequently, is marked by much repetition of material.

Although the lines of *Rose, liz* begin and end on consonant open fifths, some of Machaut's intervening harmonies may strike even twentieth-century ears as dissonant. We must remember that his original courtly audience was highly sophisticated. They were acutely sensitive to the nuances of his style—and also to the formal details of the rondeau, which occupied in its own time a place as prominent as that held by sonata form in the nineteenth century. With the increased familiarity made possible by recordings, modern listeners as well can attune their ears to the work of this refined and elegant master.

Guillaume Dufay

Guillaume Dufay (c. 1400–74) was one of the earliest composers from the Low Countries to make his career in Italy, where he spent nearly half his life and, as far as we can tell, wrote most of his finest music. He has been rediscovered by the twentieth century and is much admired by contemporary musicians.

Dufay was also active at the court of Philip the Good, Duke of Burgundy (1419–67), which for several decades rivaled that of the kings of France in the brilliance of its art. In the music of Dufay and his Burgundian colleague Gilles Binchois (c. 1400–60), the rhythmic complexities of fourteenth-century music were abandoned in favor of a simpler, more appealing style. The meandering vocal lines of the past were replaced by well-defined melodies and clear-cut rhythms, with something of the charm of folksong. Harmony grew simpler and more consonant, foreshadowing a language based on triads and sense of key. By placing the pre-existent cantus firmus in an upper part rather than the lowest voice, Dufay was free to compose his own bass line and control the harmonic motion. Eventually, Dufay would expand the standard musical texture from three voices to four.

Alma redemptoris mater

SIDE 1/6 (E I)
SIDE 11/6 (S)

Dufay's style is well exemplified by his motet *Alma redemptoris mater,* for three voices (which may have been doubled by instruments, as in the recording by the Capella Antiqua of Munich). Several important characteristics distinguish this music from Machaut's. To begin with, the cantus firmus, drawn from Gregorian chant, has been elevated to the highest part, where the listener can hear it. Instead of being a mystical symbol, it is now a graceful melody that delights the ear. As a result, this voice dominates the others. Also, instead of following the sacred chant slavishly, Dufay adapts it both rhythmically and melodically to his own expressive purpose, so that it takes on the quality of a popular tune. Compare his version with the original chant:

Equally significant, the open fifths and octaves that impart so harsh a color to Medieval harmony have been replaced in Dufay's music by the gentler thirds and sixths, reflecting the humanizing influence of Italy. As a result, Dufay's harmony impresses us as having moved a considerable distance away from the archaic sound of Machaut's.

Alma redemptoris mater, quae pervia caeli porta manes, et stella maris, succurre cadenti, surgere qui curat populo.	Gracious mother of the Redeemer, Abiding at the doors of Heaven, Star of the sea, aid the falling, Rescue the people who struggle.
Tu quae genuisti, natura mirante, tuum sanctum genitorem: Virgo prius ac posterius, Gabrielis ab ore sumens illud Ave, peccatorum miserere.	Thou who, astonishing nature, Hast borne thy holy Creator: Virgin before and after, Who heard the Ave from the mouth of Gabriel, Be merciful to sinners.

The motet opens with an extended melisma on the first vowel of "Alma." Throughout the piece, single words are sustained for series of notes. When words are dissolved in music this way, the composer is obviously using the text merely as scaffolding. Dufay's prime concern is the flow of the vocal lines.

Textual characteristics

The motet is in triple meter and in three sections. The first consists of a single melody, at first unaccompanied, repeated over supporting chords—that is, homophonic texture. The cadences fall on C- and G-major triads, giving the music—despite its modal inflection—a major-like ring. The second section has a fuller sound. The texture here is contrapuntal, with arresting imitations on the first lines of the second stanza. The third section, beginning with the word "Virgo," returns to the chordal texture of the first. Sustained chords, beginning with "sumens illud Ave," serve as a kind of codetta. The fact that his codetta begins in the middle of a sentence shows how much more preoccupied Dufay is with the music than with the text. The chords have three tones each, but in the final ones the sopranos divide, making four notes. In effect, harmony is moving towards the four-part layout that will become the norm, in which each of the four voices —soprano, alto, tenor, bass—occupies its respective register instead of crowding the others in the same range. This means, too, that the separate voices can take on greater definition and independence, with an attendant broadening of the musical space.

Navré je sui

The popular side of Dufay's art is well illustrated by his chanson *Navré je sui* (I have been wounded). It is in the same poetic and musical form as Machaut's *Rose, liz*—a rondeau. This, you will recall, is a poem of four stanzas in which the opening stanza returns partly in the second and completely in the fourth. In this case, the stanzas have four lines, with a rhyme scheme **a-b-b-a** (the second stanza differs, because of the text repetition).

SIDE 1/7 (E I)

Navré je sui d'un dart penetratif
qui m'a percié le cuer de part en part;
C'est ma dame qui par son doulx regart
Aimable me l'a point jusques au vif.

I have been wounded by a sharp arrow
That has pierced my heart through and through;
It is my lady who with her glance so sweet
And dear has stabbed me to the quick.

Tout souellement, se confort n'est actif,
En verité joye de moy depart.
Navré je sui d'un dart penetratif
Qui m'a percié le cuer de part en part.

All alone, if comfort come not soon,
In truth all joy will leave me.
I have been wounded by a sharp arrow
That has pierced my heart through and through.

Las, que feray se dangier m'est actif?
J'auray refus contre moy, main et tart,
Ne sçay qui puist la pointure du dart
En moy garir se non le vray motif.

Alas, what shall I do if the danger is real?
That I will be refused, early and late,
I know not who can heal me of the wound
Except the one who caused it.

Navré je sui d'un dart penetratif
Qui m'a percié le cuer de part en part;
C'est ma dame qui par son doulx regart
Aimable me l'a point jusques au vif.

I have been wounded by a sharp arrow
That has pierced my heart through and through;
It is my lady who with her glance so sweet
And dear has stabbed me to the quick.

The chanson enjoyed great popularity in courts throughout Europe in the late fifteenth century. An engraving by Israel von Meckenem (1450–1503), **Lutenist and Singer.**

The chanson is set for three voices of approximately the same range. In most modern performances, it is treated as a solo song, with the other parts played by instruments. (In the Pomerium Musices recording, a soprano sings with a lute and a vielle, while David Munrow's version offers a tenor with two wind instruments.) The stanzas are set to identical music—except for the second, in which the return of the opening lines brings the opening music again, instead of the contrast heard in the first stanza.

While some of Dufay's *chansons* (the French word for song) are marked by harmonic friction and rhythmic tension, this one, with its lilting melody and gentle triple meter, almost belies the unhappy love that it describes. But that light-hearted tone conceals contrapuntal subtleties that we associate with a more serious style. For example, the first four notes of the voice part are immediately imitated in the accompanying parts. In keeping with the light style of the music, the imitation is not continued.

The music for the third line of the poem begins with those same four notes turned upside down—that is, an inversion. Although the piece begins with a harmonic brightness that suggests C major to our ears, it is occasionally colored with touches of what sounds to us like the minor mode.

Dufay introduced a euphony and charm that were new to music. This was one of the signal achievements of his art—a deeply felt, serene art poised on the borderline between the Middle Ages and the Renaissance.

58

Early Instrumental Music

The fourteenth century witnessed a steady growth in the scope and importance of instrumental music. Though the central role in art music was still reserved for vocal works, instruments gradually found more and more uses. As we have seen, they could play a supporting role in vocal music, doubling or accompanying the singers. Instrumental arrangements of vocal works grew increasingly popular, filling a role similar to the piano transcriptions of songs made by Liszt and others during the nineteenth century. In dance music, where rhythm was the prime consideration (and where words might even be a distraction), instruments found early and abiding employment. And as players developed great virtuosity on their instruments, they created music that would show their powers to greatest advantage.

The "learned" vocal music of church and court was routinely written down, in part because its complexity made it difficult to remember, in part so that it could be carried from one place to another and even preserved for future generations. Much instrumental music, on the other hand, was improvised, like jazz, and never written down at all. (If it were not for recordings, we would know very little about jazz of the past—and, indeed, we only know indirectly what jazz was like before it was recorded.) We can therefore only speculate about the extent and variety of the instrumental repertory during the late Middle Ages. But our speculation can be guided by an ever-growing body of knowledge. Some of the instruments themselves survive, in museums and private collections. Paintings and sculpture contain many representations of instruments—not always reliable in detail, but informative about their use and playing technique. Literary descriptions are also helpful. Historical documents, such as court payrolls, tell us about the size and makeup of musical establishments. From these—and from such instrumental music as does survive—scholars have in recent years reconstructed a remarkable body of information about Medieval and Renaissance instruments.

Maximillian with his musicians, *(1505–16) woodcut by Hans Burkmair (1473–1531). On the left is a musician seated at a small positive organ; above him are four singers and a cornett player. In the center is a harpist and on the right, a keyboard instrument (probably a clavichord). On the table there is a viola da gamba, flute, recorders, cornet, and crumhorn. Piled up on the floor are a kettledrum, tabor, sackbut, and tromba marina.* (Austrian National Library, Vienna.)

These old instruments were naturally more limited in range and volume than their modern counterparts; yet today we have abandoned the notion that they were nothing more than primitive versions of their descendants. It has become increasingly clear that these instruments were perfectly suited to the purposes of the societies that devised them. There were no large concert halls to be filled; there was no need for the smoothly blended colors of the symphony orchestra. More delicate timbres were cultivated, and also saltier, more raucous ones; in fact, instruments were often divided into "indoor" and "outdoor" categories.

In those days, too, each individual instrument was a unique handcrafted item. The kind of standardization we take for granted today, the result of mass production, simply did not exist. No doubt this was one reason why composers do not seem to have been much concerned about which particular instruments were used in the performance of their music—after all, they could hardly be certain that any two instruments of a particular type would have the same range of notes, let alone the same tone color. In fact, the surviving sources of Medieval music contain no instrumental indications; it is only with the Renaissance that such things begin to be specified.

But there is also another reason, which lies in the essentially contrapuntal nature of most Medieval and Renaissance music. Counterpoint, we saw, was an art of line rather than color; of unfolding horizontal voices rather than vertical chordal masses. What was important to a composer of the time was not the specific color, but rather that each line be brought out distinctively. Otherwise, he seems to have regarded instruments as pretty much interchangeable. Therefore, modern performers have to make their own decisions about instrumentation, taking into consideration the layout of the music, its expressive character, and considerations of balance and proportion.

The revival of old instruments has burgeoned in recent decades, as scholars and performers have endeavored to reconstruct the appropriate performing conditions for early music. A growing number of ensembles specialize in this repertory, and their members have mastered the playing techniques of old instruments. Their concerts and recordings have made the public aware of the sound of old instruments to a degree that was undreamt of fifty years ago. What was once considered esoteric or "scholarly" has now become the regular fare of many music lovers.

Medieval and Renaissance Instruments

In recorded performances of Medieval vocal music, we have already encountered a number of instruments from the period. Although a complete survey is naturally beyond the compass of a book such as this (see the Bibliography for some specialized works on the subject), let us briefly mention some of the principal types.

The New York Pro Musica, founded and conducted by the late Noah Greenberg, was probably the first American ensemble to specialize in the performance of old music on old instruments. Here photographed in 1965, the group enjoyed an international reputation through their concert tours and recordings.

String instruments
SIDE 1/2, 5 (E I)
SIDE 11/4 (S)

Early instruments fall into the same categories as modern ones—that is, strings, winds, brass, percussion, and keyboard. String instruments further divide into plucked and bowed instruments. The elaborate concert *harp* of today has simpler ancestors going back to antiquity, in many shapes and sizes. Instruments with frets, like the guitar, are also very ancient; the *lute*, with a more rounded body than the guitar, is of Middle Eastern origin and apparently reached Europe around the thirteenth century. It became an instrument of high virtuosity in the Renaissance, and has been brilliantly revived in the twentieth century by artists such as Julian Bream.

SIDE 1/2, 5, 7 (E I)
SIDE 11/4 (S)

Playing on strings with a bow seems also to have come from the East. There were two principal types of bowed instruments in the Middle Ages: the pear-shaped *rebec* and the *vielle* or fiddle, whose figure-eight body proclaims it the ancestor of the violin. The rebec was particularly associated with popular song and dance, while the fiddle was primarily cultivated by the privileged classes.

SIDE 1/2 (E I)
SIDE 11/4 (S)
SIDE 1/5, 7 (E I)

Woodwind instruments
SIDE 1/3 (E I)

Among the woodwinds, today's transverse flute inherits a long tradition, although in earlier times it was made of wood rather than metal, and lacked the modern system of keys. There was also another type of flute, with a whistle mouthpiece, played vertically rather than horizontally, known as the *recorder*; its tone is more delicate and breathy than that of the transverse flute. Made in many sizes, the recorder remained in use until the eighteenth century, and has been widely revived in our own day. The other principal family of winds, you will recall, uses reeds to produce the sound. The *shawm*, the ancestor of the oboe, came in a variety of sizes, and still survives in many folk traditions of Europe, Africa, and Asia. Its buzzing, nasal tone color has been considerably domesticated in its art-music offspring. Less temperamental were instruments in which the reed was covered

SIDE 1/3, 8; 2/1 (E I)
SIDE 11/7 (S)

by a reed-cap, such as the *crumhorn*, the distinctive curve of which served only a decorative, not a musical purpose.

Brass instruments

SIDE 1/6; 2/1 (E I)
SIDE 11/6 (S)

SIDE 1/3, 6; 2/1 (E I)
SIDE 11/6 (S)

SIDE 1/4 (E I)
SIDE 11/5 (S)

SIDE 1/8 (E I)
SIDE 11/7 (S)

Medieval "brass" instruments were not always made from brass; other metals, ivory, horn, and wood were also used, especially before Renaissance advances in metalworking made greater precision possible in the shaping of brass. The *cornett* developed from the traditional cow horn, but was made of wood; its fingerholes made possible the playing of scales (valves for brass instruments were not invented until the nineteenth century). Another early method of filling in the notes not in the overtone series was the slide, as in the trombone; in the Middle Ages, besides the *sackbut,* the ancestor of the trombone, there was also a type of *slide trumpet.* Medieval *trumpets* were not always coiled in the modern fashion, and could be as much as six feet long—impressive to see as well as to hear at court ceremonials.

Keyboard instruments

SIDE 1/2 (E I)
SIDE 11/4 (S)

SIDE 1/9 (E I)

Mechanically speaking, keyboard instruments are among the most complex of musical devices, but several types and sizes of organ were already in use in the Middle Ages. There were large ones, requiring many men to pump their giant bellows and often several to manipulate the cumbersome slider mechanisms that opened and closed the pipes. At the other end of the scale were *portative* and *positive* organs, miniatures with keyboards and a few ranks of pipes. One type of small organ, the *regal,* took its name from one of the reedy stops of the larger organs.

An early ancestor of the piano was the *clavichord,* in which a keyboard was used to set strings in vibration; its very gentle tone was suitable only for private practice and intimate settings. Soon the harpsichord—and later the piano—would achieve greater carrying power, without superseding the charms of the smaller instrument.

Percussion instruments

SIDE 1/2, 8 (E I)
SIDE 11/4, 7 (S)

SIDE 1/8; 2/1 (E I)
SIDE 11/7 (S)

SIDE 1/8 (E I)
SIDE 11/7 (S)

Ample evidence indicates that many kinds of percussion instruments were common in the Middle Ages and Renaissance; what we don't know is how they were used musically. No doubt they marked the rhythm in a dance and set the pace for a march—but which instruments, and when? Here, modern performers are very much on their own. The small drums known as *nakers,* which usually came in pairs, are mentioned in Marco Polo's account of his travels in Asia. The *tabor* was a larger, cylindrical drum, while the *tambourine* is still used in Spanish and Italian music today. Many other familiar percussion instruments have existed for many centuries in some form or other.

Now we shall turn to three examples of instrumental music from this period. Characteristic of the fragmentary state in which this type of music has been handed down to us is the fact that the composers of two of them are unknown.

Anonymous: Saltarello

Professional instrumentalists of the Middle Ages must have been both skilled and sophisticated, since historical evidence indicates that their

In this fifteenth-century miniature, instrumental accompaniment is provided for an aristocratic group dancing in the garden. (Bibliothèque Nationale, Paris.)

earnings were often quite high. However, many of them did not read or write musical notation—they didn't need to, for most of their music-making was improvised—and so little of their music has survived. Some monophonic dance pieces were written down, however; this particular *Saltarello* dates from the fourteenth century, when it was among several tunes added to the end of a large manuscript of Italian vocal music.

SIDE 1/8 (E I)
SIDE 11/7 (S)

The saltarello, you will recall from the finale of Mendelssohn's *Italian Symphony*, is a lively Italian "jumping dance." This early example consists of short sections of varying lengths, alternating in the pattern **a-b-a-c-a-c-a.** Each section has two alternate endings, one a tone above the other. These were known as "open" and "closed"; the open ending leads back to a repetition, while the closed finishes that section and prepares the next, in a manner analogous to the "first" and "second" endings of later music. Each new section uses melodic figures from the preceding one. The chain-like construction obviously permits additional repetitions should the dancers have energy for more.

The wild, piercing sound of the shawm (used as the solo instrument in David Munrow's recording) seems quite appropriate for this energetic, even frenetic dance. Aside from the melody, everything about this performance is conjectural, resting upon the educated guesses of a knowledgeable and sensitive scholar-musician: the tempo, the phrasing, the freely improvisatory treatment of the written music, the rhythmic backing by nakers, tabor, and tambourine, the addition of a sustained single note (known as a *drone*, a common feature of folk music around the world) here played on a trumpet. But the results are musically convincing, breathing fresh life into music of which only the skeleton has survived the ravages of time.

Konrad Paumann: Elend, du hast umfangen mich

Early music for keyboard instruments is more extensively documented than other kinds of instrumental music. For one thing, the polyphonic music that was played on them was not easy to improvise, and so was more often written down. And counterpoint was the province of the trained musicians of the Church, who knew how to notate music. In fact, very little of the surviving keyboard music is sacred; most of it consists of arrangements of well-loved secular songs, like those for piano in the nineteenth century—a natural basis on which to build up a literature, relying on the popularity of the material to recommend the new medium.

SIDE 1/9 (E I)

A good example of this type of transcription is a keyboard version of the song *Elend, du hast umfangen mich* (Loneliness, you have embraced me), by the German organist and composer Konrad Paumann (c. 1410–73), who achieved a European reputation despite his having been born blind. Active in his native Nuremberg and, in the last years of his life, at the ducal court in Munich, Paumann travelled in France and Italy, where his brilliant playing astonished listeners. In addition to his more ambitious keyboard works, he wrote a number of fairly simple pieces, probably intended as studies for those learning to play. For these, as for his transcription, Paumann did not specify any particular instrument, and they can be played on any keyboard instrument—a clavichord, or some type of organ, or even on the harpsichord that was beginning to develop in the fifteenth century.

In his arrangement of *Elend, du hast umfangen mich*, Paumann puts the melody of the song in the left hand, while above it the right hand unfolds a counterpoint.

In triple meter, the piece alternates cadences on a D chord with several on G. At the beginning, the counterpoint might be sung as easily as played, but it becomes gradually more elaborate, with florid passages of rapid notes that fit easily under the fingers but would not be easy to sing. In other words, composers were beginning to find their way to an instrumental style that was distinct from the vocal.

Anonymous: Basse Danse, La Spagna

The *basse danse* (literally, low dance) was cultivated at the courts of Western Europe during the fifteenth century and became a more popular dance during the early sixteenth. The word "low" probably refers to the gliding or walking movements of the feet, in contrast to the more active steps of the saltarello, or "jumping dance"; in fact, the two dances were often paired.

SIDE 2/1 (E I)

Il Re de Spagna (The King of Spain) was a famous *basse danse* tune that in the fifteenth century found its way into literally scores of polyphonic compositions, used as a cantus firmus in the manner we observed earlier in vocal works. It strides along steadily in the bass while two other voices make florid (and frequently imitative) counterpoint above it.

As in the *Saltarello*, some aspects of a modern performance must be educated guesses rather than certainties. A typical *basse danse* band consisted of two shawms and a sackbut. In David Munrow's recording, a cornett is substituted for one of the shawms; a steady drumbeat is added, played on a tabor; and the piece is repeated with added ornamentation. The result has great vitality and drive.

The developments we have traced in this chapter set the stage for later composers to explore the possibilities of purely instrumental forms—works, that is, conceived and executed wholly in terms of what the instruments could do. From these humble beginnings sprang the mighty tradition of Western instrumental music.

59

The Renaissance

"I am not pleased with the Courtier if he be not also a musician, and besides his understanding and cunning [in singing] upon the book, have skill in like manner on sundry instruments." — BALDASSARE CASTIGLIONE: *The Courtier* (1528)

The Renaissance (c. 1450–1600) is one of the beautiful if misleading names in the history of culture: beautiful because it implies an awakening of intellectual awareness, misleading because it suggests a sudden rebirth of learning and art after the presumed stagnation of the Middle Ages. History moves continuously rather than by leaps and bounds. The Renaissance was the next phase of a cultural process that, under the leadership of the universities and princely courts, had begun long before.

Philosophical developments

What the Renaissance does mark is the passing of European society from an exclusively religious orientation to a secular; from an age of unquestioning faith and mysticism to one of belief in reason and scientific inquiry. The focus of man's destiny was seen to be his life on earth rather than in the hereafter. There was a new reliance on the evidence of the senses rather than on tradition and authority. Implied was a new confidence in man's ability to solve his problems and rationally order his world. This awakening found its symbol in the culture of Greek and Roman antiquity. The men of the Renaissance discovered the summit of human wisdom not only in the Church fathers and saints, as their ancestors had done, but also in Homer and Vergil and the ancient philosophers.

Historical developments

Historians used to date the Renaissance from the fall of Constantinople to the Turks in 1453 and the emigration of Greek scholars to the West. Today, we recognize that there are no such clear demarcations in history. But a series of momentous circumstances around this time help to set off the new era from the old. The introduction of gunpowder brought to an end the age of knighthood. The development of the compass made possible the voyages of discovery that opened up a new world and demolished old superstitions. The revival of ancient letters was associated with the humanists, and was spurred by the introduction of printing. This revival had its counterpart in architecture, painting, and sculpture. If the Romanesque found its grand architectural form in the monastery and the Gothic in the

The human form, denied for centuries, was revealed in the Renaissance as a thing of beauty. A statue by Donatello (c. 1386–1466), **David.** (Alinari/Art Resources.)

The Renaissance painter preferred realism to allegory and psychological characterizations to stylized stereotypes. These characteristics are exemplified in **The Virgin on the Rocks,** *by Leonardo da Vinci (1452–1519).* (Clichés des Musées Nationaux.)

cathedral, the Renaissance lavished its constructive energy upon palace and château. The gloomy fortified castles of the Medieval barons gave way to spacious edifices that displayed the harmonious proportions of the classical style. In effect, Renaissance architecture embodied the striving for a gracious and reasoned existence that was the great gesture of the age.

Artistic developments

So, too, the elongated saints and martyrs of Medieval painting and sculpture were replaced by the David of Donatello and the gentle Madonna of Da Vinci. Even where artists retained a religious atmosphere, the Mother of Sorrow and the symbols of grief gave way to smiling madonnas —often posed for by very secular ladies—and dimpled cherubs. The human form, denied for centuries, was revealed as a thing of beauty; also as an object of anatomical study. Nature entered painting along with the nude, and with it an intense preoccupation with the laws of perspective and composition. Medieval painting had presented life as an allegory; the Renaissance preferred realism. The Medieval painters posed their figures frontally, impersonally; the Renaissance developed psychological characterization and the art of portraiture. Medieval painting dealt in types; the Renaissance concerned itself with individuals. Space in Medieval painting was organized in a succession of planes over which the eye traveled as over a series of episodes. The Renaissance created unified space and the simultaneous seeing of the whole. It discovered the landscape, created the illusion of distance, and opened up endless vistas upon the physical loveliness of the world.

The Renaissance came to flower in the nation that stood closest to the classical Roman culture. Understandably the great names we associate with its painting and sculpture are predominantly Italian: Donatello (c. 1386–1466), Masaccio (1401–28), Botticelli (c.1444–1510), Leonardo da Vinci (1452–1519), Michelangelo (1475–1564), Raphael (1483–1520), and Titian (1488–1576). With the masters who lived in the second half of the century, such as Tintoretto (1518–94) and Veronese (1528–88), we approach the world of the early Baroque.

Intellectual developments

The Renaissance achieved a heightened awareness of the human personality. Its turbulence and dynamic force were in marked contrast to the static nature of Medieval society. It gave impetus to the twin currents of rationalism and realism that have prevailed in European culture ever since. Granted that its love of art and beauty existed side by side with tyranny, ignorance, superstition; that its humanism took shape in a scene dominated by treachery and lust. It is the noble usage of history to judge an age by its finest. By that measure this period ranks high. From the multicolored tapestry of Renaissance life emerge figures that have captured the imagination of the world: Lorenzo de' Medici and Ludovico Sforza, Benvenuto Cellini and Machiavelli, Pope Alexander VI and Sir Thomas More, Lucrezia Borgia and Beatrice d'Este. Few centuries can match the sixteenth for its galaxy of great names. The list includes Erasmus (1466–1536) and Martin Luther (1483–1546), Rabelais (1494?–1553) and Cervantes (1547–1616), Marlowe (1564–93) and Shakespeare (1564–1616).

With these people we find ourselves in a world that speaks our language. The Renaissance marks the birth of the modern European temper and of Western man as we have come to know him. In that turbulent time was shaped the moral and cultural climate we still inhabit.

Sixteenth-Century Music

The painting and poetry of the Renaissance abound in references to music. Nothing more clearly attests to the vast importance of the art in the cultural life of the time. The pageantry of the Renaissance unfolded to a momentous musical accompaniment. Throwing off its Medieval mysticism, music moved toward clarity, simplicity, and a frankly sensuous appeal.

A cappella music

The age achieved an exquisite appreciation of *a cappella* music. (Literally, "for the chapel." This term denotes a vocal work without instrumental accompaniment.) The sixteenth century has come to be regarded as the golden age of the a cappella style. Its polyphony was based on a principle called *continuous imitation*. The motives wandered from vocal line to vocal line within the texture, the voices imitating one another so that the same theme or motive was heard now in the soprano or alto, now in the tenor or bass. There resulted an extremely close-knit musical fabric that was capable of the most subtle and varied effects.

The composers of the Flemish school were pre-eminent in European music from around 1450 to the end of the sixteenth century. They came from the southern Lowlands, which is now Belgium, and from the adjoin-

The painting and poetry of the Renaissance abound in references to music. A painting by Jacopo Tintoretto (1518–94), **Ladies Making Music.** (Scala/Art Resource.)

ing provinces of northern France and Burgundy. In their number were several who wrote their names large in the history of music.

60

Josquin des Prez

"He is the master of the notes. They have to do as he bids them; other composers have to do as the notes will." — MARTIN LUTHER

Josquin des Prez.

With the Flemish master Josquin des Prez (c. 1450–1521), the transition is complete from the anonymous composer of the Middle Ages, through the shadowy figures of the late Gothic, to the highly individual artist of the Renaissance. He is the first composer who emerges from the mists of history as a fully rounded personality; the first musician, as one historian put it, "who impresses us as having genius."

Josquin studied with the Flemish master Johannes Ockeghem, who exerted a powerful influence on several generations of composers. His checkered career led him to Italy, where he served at several ducal courts—especially those of Galeazzo Sforza, Duke of Milan, and Ercole d'Este, Duke of Ferrara—as well as at the Sistine Chapel in Rome. During his stay in Italy his Northern art absorbed the classical virtues of balance and moderation, the sense of harmonious proportion and lucid form that found their archetype in the radiant art of Raphael. After leaving the Papal Chapel he appears to have been active for several years at the court of Louis XII of France. His last appointment was as a canon at the collegiate church of Condé; he was buried in the choir of this church.

His music

The older generation of musicians had been preoccupied with solving the technical problems of counterpoint—problems that fit the intellectual climate of the waning Middle Ages. Josquin appeared at a time when the humanizing influences of the Renaissance were wafting through Europe. The contrapuntal ingenuity that he inherited from Ockeghem he was able to harness to a higher end—the expression of emotion. The early years of his career were spent in achieving consummate mastery of canonic devices. Thenceforth he was able to advance to a free, continuous imitation of themes that left room for the imaginative development of musical ideas. His music is rich in feeling, in serenely beautiful melody and expressive harmony. Its clarity of structure and humanism bespeak the man of the Renaissance.

The Mass

The Mass is the most solemn ritual of the Roman Catholic Church. It constitutes a re-enactment of the sacrifice of Christ. The name is derived from the Latin *missa,* "dismissal" (of the congregation at the end of the service).

The aggregation of prayers that make up the Mass falls into two categories: those that vary from day to day throughout the church year, the *Proper;* and those that remain the same in every Mass, the *Ordinary.* The liturgy, which reached its present form about nine hundred years ago, provides Gregorian melodies for each item of the ceremony. With the rise of polyphony composers began to weave additional voices around the plainchant. They concentrated on the prayers that were an invariable part of the service rather than on the variable items that were heard only once during the liturgical year. Thus came into prominence the five sections that the public knows as the musical setting of the Mass: Kyrie, Gloria, Credo, Sanctus, and Agnus Dei. (Today these sections of the Mass are recited or sung in the language of the country.) The opening section, the Kyrie—a prayer for mercy—dates from the early centuries of Christianity, as its original Greek text attests. It is an **A-B-A** form that consists of nine invocations: three "Kyrie eleison" (Lord, have mercy), three "Christe eleison" (Christ, have mercy), and again three "Kyrie eleison." There follows the "Gloria in excelsis Deo" (Glory to God in the highest). This is a joyful hymn of praise which is omitted in the penitential seasons, Advent and Lent. The third movement is the confession of faith, "Credo in unum Deum, Patrem omnipotentem" (I believe in one God, the Father Almighty). It includes also the "Et incarnatus est" (And He became flesh), the "Crucifixus" (He was crucified), and the "Et resurrexit" (And He rose again). Fourth is "Sanctus, Sanctus, Sanctus" (Holy, Holy, Holy), which concludes with the "Hosanna in excelsis" (Hosanna in the highest) and the

Sections of the Mass

An engraving from the late sixteenth century depicting the celebration of the Mass. **A Religious Service,** *by Collaert after Stradanus.* (The Metropolitan Museum of Art, Whittelsey Fund.)

"Benedictus qui venit in nomine Domini" (Blessed is He who comes in the name of the Lord), after which the "Hosanna in excelsis" is repeated as a kind of refrain. The fifth and last part, "Agnus Dei, qui tollis peccata mundi" (Lamb of God, who takes away the sins of the world), is sung three times. Twice it concludes with "Miserere nobis" (Have mercy on us), and the third time with the prayer "Dona nobis pacem" (Grant us peace).

Cantus firmus

Like the motet, the polyphonic setting of the Mass was usually based on a fragment of Gregorian chant. This became the cantus firmus that served as the foundation of the work, supporting the florid patterns that the other voices wove around it. When used in all the movements of a Mass, the Gregorian cantus firmus helped to weld the work into a unity. As we noted in our discussion of organum and the motet, the combining of a composer's original creation with a pre-existing melody appealed to the Medieval mind and remained a traditional practice in the Renassiance. It provided him with the fixed element that he could embellish with all the resources of his artistry, somewhat as, centuries later, did the theme and variations.

Requiem

Of the Masses for special services the most important is the Mass for the Dead, the Requiem, which is sung at funeral and memorial services. We discussed Verdi's magnificent setting in Chapter 42. The name, you will recall, comes from the opening verse "Requiem aeternam dona eis, Domine" (Rest eternal grant unto them, O Lord). Included are prayers in keeping with the solemnity of the occasion, among them the awesome evocation of the Last Judgment, "Dies irae" (That Day of Wrath).

The history of the Mass as an art form extends over the better part of eight hundred years. In that time it garnered for itself some of the greatest music ever written.

Agnus Dei *from the* Missa L'homme armé (sexti toni)

In his Masses Josquin drew upon the rich polyphonic heritage of the Flemish School. Particularly attractive is the *Mass in the Sixth Mode,* based on a tune known as *L'homme armé* (The Armed Man) that was immensely popular in the fifteenth and sixteenth centuries. Originally, it will be recalled, composers drew the cantus firmus of a Mass from a portion of Gregorian chant. Gradually they turned to secular sources. There seemed to be something peculiarly challenging to them in basing the most sacred musical composition of the Church on a worldly—sometimes even vulgar—ditty. It enabled them to be naughty and, by and large, to get away with it. Naturally, by the time the tune was transformed into the long-drawn-out notes of the cantus firmus and buried in the counterpoint, it was hardly to be recognized. Its presence could be compared to that of homely, everyday objects in a religious painting. Still, one can understand why church authorities frowned upon this mixture of the sacred and the profane, and inveighed against it from one generation to the next.

SIDE 2/2 (E I)
SIDE 12/1 (S)

The Agnus Dei from the *Mass on L'homme armé* is a fine example of Josquin's older style, displaying as it does the wonderful flow of his polyphony. The cantus firmus is used in all the voices, so that it is given greater prominence than had been customary in earlier times. The movement demands virtuoso choral singing. The vocal lines move across a wide range, with frequent octave leaps and great rhythmic vitality. Here is how the popular tune is transformed into a cantus firmus, around which the other voices interweave in a texture of continuous imitation:

The Agnus Dei consists of three sections, each constituting another setting of the sacred text. The words are dissolved in music. Composers of Josquin's time felt free to do this, since they knew that their listeners were quite familiar with the prayers.

Gentile Bellini (c. 1429–1507), in his glorious painting ***Procession in Piazza San Marco,*** *captured the splendid pageantry of the city.* (Scala/Art Resource.)

The Renaissance painter developed psychological characterizations in portraiture, created unified space, and encouraged the simultaneous seeing of the whole. Paolo Veronese (1528–88), ***The Wedding at Cana.*** (Scala/Art Resource.)

Agnus Dei,	Lamb of God,
qui tollis peccata mundi,	Who takest away the sins of the world,
miserere nobis, [*first two times*]	Have mercy upon us,
dona nobis pacem. [*last time*]	Grant us peace.

The first section, which is set for four voices, would have been marked Adagio at a later time. Josquin uses short phrases in a descending sequence—that is, the same pattern is repeated again and again, each time a tone lower, giving the section a distinctive profile. Particularly beautiful is the flow of voices into the cadence.

In the second section the lines are reduced to three. This and the soloistic writing make for a more transparent texture. The vocal parts unfold in long, seamless phrases reminiscent of Josquin's forbears. The meter changes from triple to duple, the tempo from slow to moderate. This section is based on the second part of the cantus firmus.

The third Agnus Dei is a brilliant setting for six voices. Josquin here displays his mastery of canonic devices—the mastery of a virtuoso who glories in his virtuosity. (A canon, you will remember, is one of the strictest forms of counterpoint, in which one voice follows another in imitation throughout an extended passage.) The two lowest voices present the cantus firmus in long notes, one forward and the other backward simultaneously, while above them the other four voices in pairs weave a dazzling canonic tapestry. Upward leaps of an octave and successive runs along the scale add to the excitement. The movement builds steadily to a powerful cadence on the key word of every era—"pacem" (peace). It ends on a note of utter serenity.

61

Other Sixteenth-Century Masters

"It is impossible to find a man who is truly a musician and is vicious."
— VINCENZO GALILEI (father of the astronomer, 1581)

Janequin: Les Cris de Paris

Clément Janequin (c. 1485–1558) was mentioned by the poet Ronsard as being a disciple of Josquin. Rabelais pictured him among a merry company of musicians "in a private garden under an arbor and surrounded by a rampart of flagons, hams, pasties, and various sorts of tufted quails." He spent his last years in Paris as "composer in ordinary to the King." Not much is known about his life.

Janequin is remembered today as one of the masters of the French chanson, which he handled with a freedom and fluency that made it—alongside the Italian and English madrigal—one of the more attractive genres of the Renaissance. The use of short lyric poems of a secular nature, in the language of the composer instead of in liturgical Latin, inevitably brought with it a closer relationship between words and music, in a larger sense between music and life. Janequin's specialty was descriptive music that imitated the sounds and sights around him. His chansons evoked bird songs, battles, the excitement of the hunt, and the street cries of peddlers. In these works he captured the verve and tumult of the world he knew.

Such imitative pieces were popular in the Renaissance. The street music of a big city inspired not only Janequin; the English composers Weelkes and Gibbons wrote works based on the cries of London. The theme reappears in a literary form in Proust's *Remembrance of Things Past;* and in our time George Gershwin made a wonderful musical evocation, in his opera *Porgy and Bess*, of the peddlers of Catfish Row hawking their strawberries and devil crabs.

The chanson was an intimate form of vocal chamber music, intended for the private enjoyment of the singers and their friends rather than for public performance. The real theme of a chanson such as *Les Cris de Paris* was the witty interchange among the voices. Set for four singers, Janequin's chansons indicate the transition to four-part harmony. (The Medieval

This anonymous engraving, titled **Nicholas Houel's House of Christian Charity** *(1583), attests to the active Parisian music life in the sixteenth century.* (Bibliothèque Nationale, Paris.)

chansons we studied, you will recall, were for three voices.) Both syllabic and melismatic setting is used. The melodies are clearly defined, but they often overlap in the simple, fluent counterpoint, yielding a seamless flow that is marked by a charm and tunefulness we shall encounter again in the madrigal.

The text of *Les Cris de Paris* was doubtless based on the actual cries of peddlers that Janequin heard in the streets of Paris.

Voulez ouyr les cris de Paris?	Would you like to hear the cries of Paris?
Où sont ilz ces petiz pions?	Where's the crowd?
Pastez tres tous chaulx, qui l'aira?	The patés are very hot, who will buy them?
Vin blanc, vin cleret, vin vermeil, à six deniers.	White and red wine, claret at six sous.
Casse museaux tous chaulx,	Come and get your hot pies,
Je le vendz, je les donne pour ung petit blanc.	I sell them, I give them for a five-spot.
Tartelettes, friandes à la belle gauffre!	Delicious tarts like waffles,
Et est à l'enseigne du berseau	Fresh from the Sign of the Cradle
Qui est en la rue de la Harpe.	Which is on the Rue de la Harpe.
Sa à boyre, ça!	Who wants a tasty drink?
Aigre, vin aigre!	Vinegar, good and sharp!
Faut il point de saultce vert?	Anybody want green sauce?
Moustarde, moustarde fine!	Mustard, excellent mustard!
Harenc blanc, harenc de la nuyt!	White herring, delicious at night!
Cotrez secz, cotrez! Souliers vieux!	Cheap doublets! Old shoes!
Arde buche! Choux gelez!	Chewing tobacco! Cold cabbage!
Hault et bas rammonez les caminades!	Who needs a chimney sweep?
Qui veult du laict?	Anybody want milk?
C'est moy, c'est moy, je meurs de froit.	It's me, it's me, I'm dying of cold!
Poys vers! Mes belles lestues, mes beaulx cibotz!	Green peas! My beautiful lettuce! Onions!
Guigne, doulce guigne!	Cherries, sweet cherries!
Fault il point de sablon? Voire joly!	Anybody need soap? What a beauty!
Argent m'y duit, argent m'y fault.	I have money coming to me! I need it!
Gaigne petit! Lye! Alumet! Houseaux vieux!	Small earnings! Lye! Old boots!
Pruneaux de Saint Julien!	Prunes from St. Julien!
Febves de Maretz, febves! Je fais le coqu, moy!	Beans from Maretz! I make husbands jealous!
Ma belle porée, mon beau persin,	My beautiful leeks, lovely parsley!
Ma belle oseille, mes beaulx espinards!	Beautiful sorrel and spinach!
Peches de Corbeil! Orenge! Pignes vuidez!	Peaches from Corbeil! Oranges! Look at these combs!
Charlote m'amye! Apetit nouveau petit!	Charlotte, my darling! Makes your mouth water!
Amendez vous dames, amendez! Allemande nouvelle!	Make yourselves pretty, ladies! Something new from Germany!
Navetz! Mes beaux balais! Rave doulce, rave!	Turnips! My beautiful barley! Sweet radishes!
Feure, feure Brie! A ung tournoys le chapellet!	Wonderful Brie! Prayer beads, very cheap!
Marons de Lyon! Chervis! Mes beaulx pesons!	Chestnuts from Lyon! Limes! A pair of scales, the best!
Alumet, alumet, alumet, alumette seches! Vin nouveau!	Dry tinder wood! New wine!
Fault il point de grois? Choux, petit choux tous chaulx!	Anybody need lard? Sweet hotcakes!
Fault il point de gros boys? Choux gelez!	Anyone for tinderwood? Cold cabbage!
Et qui l'aura le moule de gros boys?	Anyone need a hamper for wood?
Eschaudez chaux! Seche bouree!	Plaster you can heat! Dry firewood!
Serceau, beau serceau! Arde chandelle! Palourde!	Hoops, lovely hoops! A candle that burns! Cockles!
A Paris sur petit point geline de feurre!	In Paris they scatter straw over the little bridge!
Si vous en voulez plus ouyr, allez les donc querre!	If you want to hear more, go ask them about it!

The opening section comes to a clear cadence on the C from which it started. All four voices sing the same text—the line—which is thus clearly audible.

SIDE 2/3 (E I)
SIDE 12/2 (S)

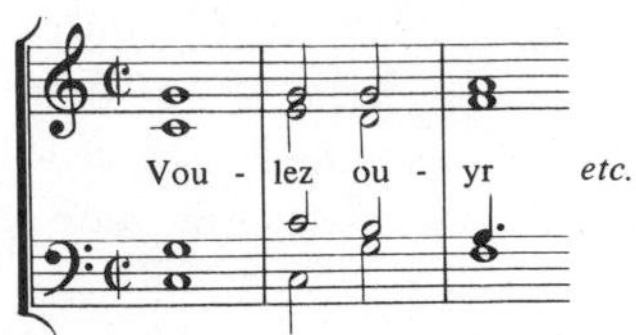

In what follows, however, Janequin recreates the hubbub of the streets: the four voices enter, one after the other, each with a different cry. Often they move at different rates: for a while, the bass can be heard hawking "moustarde" (mustard) in long notes while everybody else is moving rather faster. Sometimes the four voices all sing the same cry and make an intermediate cadence on it (as, for example, at "choux gelez"). In several episodes during the piece, contrast is provided by shifting from the prevailing duple meter into a swinging triple:

For all the tongue-in-cheek spirit of both text and music, *Les Cris de Paris* shows contrapuntal imitation and interplay handled with the lightness and grace that only a master can command. In the following passage, the same phrase passes in turn through each of the voices:

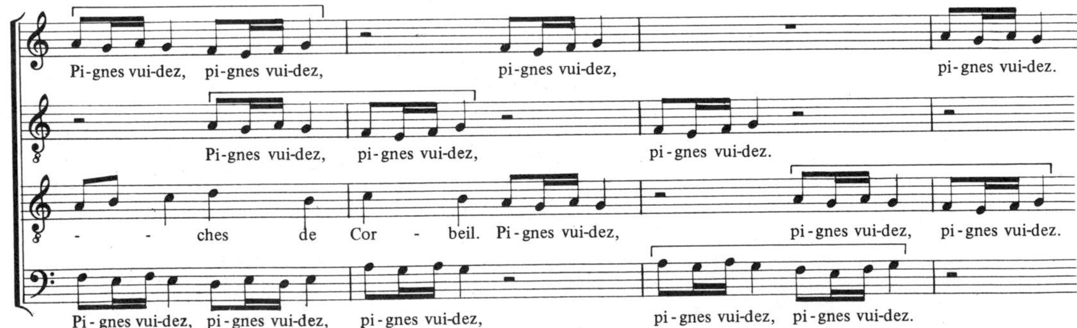

Although his introductory section was clearly centered around C, Janequin feels free to end his piece on G; the idea that a piece necessarily had to begin and end in the same place was still to come.

Especially attractive in *Les Cris de Paris* are the passages of running notes, the lively exchanges between upper and lower voices, the conversational air of the whole, and the insouciant charm that Paris seems to have imparted to all the artists who fell under its spell. Janequin's is a courtly art, subtle and highly civilized. He captured the elegance and refinement of the French spirit—that elusive quality which later generations came to admire as *l'esprit gaulois.*

Lassus: Prophetiae sibyllarum

The Flemish tradition culminates in the towering figure of Roland de Lassus (c. 1532–94). A citizen of the world (he was equally well known in Italy as Orlando di Lasso), Lassus absorbed into his art the main currents of Renaissance music—the elegance and wit of the French, the profundity and rich detail of the Germans, the sensuous beauty of the Italians. The greater part of his career was spent at the court of the Dukes of Bavaria in Munich, whence his fame spread all over Europe.

His works number over two thousand, from impetuous love songs (some with texts almost too erotic for the concert hall) to noble Masses, motets, and the profoundly felt *Penitential Psalms.* In his panoramic view of life, as in his feeling for vivid detail, Lassus elicits comparison with another great Fleming—his contemporary, Pieter Brueghel (c. 1525–69). His music is compounded of passion, tenderness, brilliance, humor, and—at the last—mysticism.

As with several other Flemish masters, Lassus spent his formative years in Italy. The *Prophetiae sibyllarum* (Prophecies of the Sibyls) belongs to

The earthy realism revealed by this Flemish master elicits comparison with his contemporary, Lassus. A painting by Pieter Bruegel (c. 1525–69), **The Harvesters.** (The Metropolitan Museum of Art, Rogers Fund, 1919.)

In this sixteenth-century miniature by Hans Muelich, **The Chapel Choir at Munich under the Direction of Roland de Lassus,** *the composer may be glimpsed in profile to the left of the podium.*

this early period; he was hardly out of his teens when he wrote it. This music has all the exuberance, the "storm and stress," of youth. It is characteristic of a strongly romantic trend within the classically oriented Renaissance—a trend that manifested itself in painting no less than in music. Here Lassus speaks to us across the centuries in accents peculiarly his own.

The sibyls were ancient prophetesses who were believed to have foretold the coming of Christ. Their cryptic utterances were preserved in fourteen books that combined Alexandrian Jewish and early Christian thought. These were written in Greek, in a rhapsodical style befitting divinely inspired revelations. The sibyls became a romantic image for the sixteenth century. They inspired a number of paintings, especially the group of five sibyls that Michelangelo painted in the Sistine Chapel and the cycle of twelve sibyls by Pinturicchio in the Borgia chambers in Rome. Lassus was living in Naples when he composed *Prophetiae sibyllarum,* not far from the Cumaean hills and caves where some of the sibyls were supposed to have lived.

Pinturicchio's paintings may have given him the idea of writing a cycle of twelve short motets, one for each sibyl. For his text he used a Latin translation of the *Prophecies*. The raw intensity of the poems, their fanciful imagery, abrupt transitions, and cryptic utterance were ideally suited to the kind of music the young composer wished to write. He clothed them in a musical language marked by boldly chromatic harmonies and emotional tension, a language that was utterly revolutionary for its time.

Introduction
SIDE 2/4 (E I)

Lassus added an introduction, with a text written by himself, that hailed the startling chromaticism of his harmony—a rare example of an artist writing a work of art about his art—much as, say, Keats did when he wrote a sonnet to the sonnet.

Carmina Chromatico,	Chromatic songs,
quae audis modulata tenore,	which you hear in artful modulation,
Haec sunt illa,	These are the ones
quibus nostrae olim arcana salutis	in which the secrets of our salvation
Bis senae intrepido,	With bold voices, long ago,
cecinerunt ore sibyllae.	were sung by the twelve sibyls.

The opening chords, with a startling progression on the key word "chromatico," reveal the intense expressivity that Lassus's chromatic harmony opened up to music:

The voices unfold in a texture that is predominantly homophonic. They move within a narrow range, mostly by step and narrow leap, crisscrossing frequently. The rhythm has the marvelous suppleness characteristic of Renaissance music, a suppleness that shapes itself to the natural inflection of the words rather than to a predetermined metrical scheme. Here, in all its purity, is the sixteenth-century a cappella style, yet imbued with a strange dramatic power. (A cappella, you will recall, denotes voices without instruments.) The emotional climax comes in the final line on the word "cecinerunt" (sung), which is given additional weight because it is repeated. From this peak the music subsides to the final cadence.

There follows the first motet—the prophecy of the Persian sibyl:

Virgine matre satus pando residebit aselli,	Born of a virgin, he will sit on the back of an ass,
Jucundus princeps unus qui ferre salutem	The joyous Prince who alone will bring happiness,
Rite queat lapsis tamen illis forte diebus.	He the mighty one, in days to come.
Multi multa ferent immensi fata laboris,	Many will bear the heavy burden of labor,
Solo sed satis est oracula prodere verbo:	Yet a single word is enough to utter the prophecy:
Ille Deus casta nascetur virgine magnus.	That great God will be born of a pure Virgin.

First motet

The motet opens with wonderful serenity on the word "Virgine." The text is set with one note to a syllable until the word "Jucundus" (joyous), which is expanded in a striking manner. The next example of this kind of expansion is less apparent to the ear because it occurs in the inner voices, on the last two words of the next line, "forte diebus" (He, the mighty one, in days to come). Notice the slight quickening of pace on the words "multi multa ferent" (Many will bear), which are repeated for emphasis. The climax comes in reverse—a dramatic descent to lower register on "fata laboris" (heavy burden of labor), as if the voices were literally bowed down by the weight they had to bear. "Solo" is set for a single voice, on a note that makes an effective contrast with what preceded because it is so much higher. F natural and F sharp are contrasted vividly in the setting of "verbo" (word). The two notes are pitted against each other with an even stronger change of harmonic color in the final line of the poem, where the music veers from F to F sharp and back. Lassus repeats the last three words of the poem, thereby underlining the fact that they present the central thought of the prophecy.

His art marks the climax of a century and a half of Flemish polyphony. It is an art that incarnates the verve and splendor of the Renaissance, and well merits the judgment carved on his tomb: "Here lies that Lassus who refreshes the weariness of the world, and whose harmony revolves its discord."

Palestrina and the Catholic Reform

Giovanni Pierluigi da Palestrina.

After the revolt of Martin Luther the desire for a return to true Christian piety brought about a reform movement within the Catholic Church. This movement became part of the Counter-Reformation whereby the Church strove to recapture the minds of men. Among its manifestations were the activities of Franciscans and Dominicans among the poor; the founding of the Society of Jesus (Jesuits) by St. Ignatius Loyola (1491–1556); and the deliberations of the Council of Trent, which extended–with some interruptions–from 1545 to 1563.

In its desire to regulate every aspect of religious discipline, the Council took up the matter of church music. The cardinals were much concerned over the corruption of the traditional chant by the singers, who added all manner of embellishments to the Gregorian melodies. They objected to the use of instruments other than the organ in the religious service, to the practice of incorporating popular songs in Masses, to the secular spirit that was invading sacred music, and to the general irreverent attitude of church musicians. They pointed out that in polyphonic settings of the Mass the sacred text was made unintelligible by the overelaborate contrapuntal texture. Certain zealots advocated abolishing counterpoint altogether and returning to Gregorian chant, but there were many music lovers among the cardinals who opposed so drastic a step. The committee assigned to deal with the problem contented itself with issuing general recommendations for a more dignified service. The authorities favored a pure vocal style that would respect the integrity of the sacred texts, that would avoid virtuosity and encourage piety.

His life

Giovanni Pierluigi, called da Palestrina after his birthplace (c. 1525–94), met the need for a reformed church music in so exemplary a fashion that for posterity he has remained *the* Catholic composer. He served as organist and choirmaster at various churches including that of St. Peter's in Rome. His patron, Pope Julius III, appointed him a member of the Sistine Chapel choir even though, as a married man, he was ineligible for the semi-ecclesiastical post. He was dismissed by a later Pope but ultimately returned to St. Peter's, where he spent the last twenty-three years of his life. Palestrina's music gives voice to the religiosity of the Counter-Reformation, its transports and its visions. He created a universal type of expression ideally suited to moods of mystic exaltation. The contemplative beauty of his music does not exclude intense emotion; but this is emotion directed to an act of faith.

A true Italian, Palestrina was surpassingly sensitive to the needs of the human voice. It was from this vantage point that he viewed his function as a church composer: "I have held nothing more desirable than that what is sung throughout the year, according to the season, should be agreeable to the ear by virtue of its vocal beauty." It was his good fortune to live not only at a time when the art of music had progressed far enough for him to achieve this goal, but also within a historical situation that made it necessary for him to do so.

Missa Ascendo ad Patrem

Mass excerpts
SIDE 2/5 (EI)
SIDE 12/3 (S)

Typical of his style is the *Mass Ascendo ad Patrem* (I ascend to the Father), so called because its basic motive was drawn from an earlier motet of that name. The idea of ascent is dramatized in the music by an upward leap of an octave, which is used in various ways at the beginning of each movement. The work is for five voices–soprano, alto, two tenors, and bass–that interweave mellifluously. In the Sanctus each voice enters in turn with the ascending octave:

The key word "Sanctus" (Holy) is expanded throughout the opening statement, which proceeds at a measured pace. From C as a central tone the music moves to a cadence on G–an anticipation of the Tonic-Dominant relationship that will become so important later on. At the words "Dominus Deus Sabaoth" (Lord God of Hosts), the rate of movement quickens. The music grows in fullness to illustrate the idea "Pleni sunt coeli et terra gloria tua" (Heavens and earth are full of Thy glory). A brief faster section, with a change to triple meter on the words "Hosanna in excelsis" (Praise in the Highest), serves as a codetta that ends affirmatively on what we think of today as a C-major chord.

In the Benedictus two sopranos and an alto are combined with a tenor. The soloistic writing creates a texture of utter transparency. Palestrina bases the opening measures on the sensuous beauty of the women's voices. The vocal lines, lying close together, frequently crisscross as they weave their contrapuntal web. The music flows gently on the words "Benedictus qui venit" (Blessed is He who comes), leading to what sounds like a cadence in A. Palestrina sustains the contemplative mood through the second half of the sentence, "in nomine Domine" (in the name of the Lord). The Hosanna is repeated in an expanded version, giving a well-rounded form (**A-B-C-B**), and the movement ends vigorously on the same C-major cadence as before.

Palestrina's style incarnates the pure a cappella ideal of vocal polyphony, in which the individual voice fulfills its destiny through submergence in the group. His music remains an apt symbol of the greatness art can aspire to when it subserves a profound moral conviction.

The Renaissance Madrigal

In the madrigal the Renaissance found one of its chief forms of secular music. The sixteenth-century *madrigal* was an aristocratic form of poetry-and-music that came to flower at the small Italian courts, where it was a favorite diversion of cultivated amateurs. The text was a short poem of lyric or reflective character, rarely longer than twelve lines, marked by elegance of diction and refinement of sentiment. Conspicuous in it were the affecting words for weeping, sighing, trembling, dying that the Italian madrigalists learned to set with such a wealth of expression. Love and unsatisfied desire were by no means the only topics of the madrigal. Included, too, were humor and satire, political themes, scenes and incidents of city and country life, with the result that the Italian madrigal literature of the sixteenth century presents a vivid panorama of Renaissance thought and feeling.

Instruments participated, duplicating or even substituting for the voices. Sometimes only the top part was sung while the other lines were played on instruments. During the first period of the Renaissance madrigal—the

The madrigal was an aristocratic form that flowered at the Italian courts, where it was a favorite diversion of cultivated amateurs. A painting by Sebastiano Florigerio (c. 1500–45), **Divertissement musical.** (Bruckmann/Art Reference Bureau.)

second quarter of the sixteenth century—the composer's chief concern is to give pleasure to the performers, without much thought to an audience. In the middle phase (c. 1550–80), the Renaissance madrigal becomes a conscious art form directed toward the listener. It takes on the elaborateness of concert music, with much contrapuntal imitation and development of musical ideas. Also, there is a closer relationship between words and music.

The final phase of the Italian madrigal (1580–1620) extends beyond the late Renaissance into the world of the Baroque. The form achieves the height of sophistication both in poetry and music. It becomes the direct expression of the composer's personality and feelings. Certain traits are carried to the point of mannerism: rich chromatic harmony, dramatic declamation, vocal virtuosity, and vivid depiction in music of emotional words.

Arcadelt: Il bianco cigno

A number of Franco-Flemish composers occupied important posts at the Italian courts during the early Renaissance. They came from Burgundy, northern France, and the Netherlands, and constituted a natural link between the French chanson and Italian madrigal. Whether they remained or went back, their art was tempered by the humanistic winds emanating from Italy. We have discussed two members of this group—Dufay and Josquin. A third was Jacob Arcadelt (c. 1505–c. 1560), a Netherlander who came to Rome in his early thirties and for several years was head of the Pope's chapel.

Arcadelt helped establish the Italian madrigal as a chamber-music piece for four solo voices. (Later in the century there was greater emphasis on five- and six-voice settings.) He deftly combined homophonic and contrapuntal elements in a style notable for the expressive power of the harmony. His music blends the old modes with a modern major-like sound and reflects the meaning of the words in an extraordinarily sensitive way.

SIDE 2/6 (E I)

Arcadelt's *Il bianco cigno* is a superb example of pure a cappella writing as it took shape in the madrigal's first phase:

Il bianco e dolce cigno cantando more, ei io piangendo giung'al fin del viver mio; stran'e diversa sorte, ch'ei morte sconsolato, et io moro beato.	The sweet white swan dies singing, While I weep as I reach my life's end. How strange that he dies disconsolate And I die happy.
Morte che nel morire, m'empie di gioia tutt'e di desire; se nel morir'altro dolor non sento, di mille mort'il di sarei contento.	Weary to the point of death, Drained of all joy and desire, I meet death without sorrow, Content to die a thousand deaths a day.

Renaissance humanism, viewing man as the measure of all things, could not but place a new emphasis on his moods and feelings. The kind of despair expressed in the lines above introduced a new romantic-subjective element into poetry and music, immeasurably expanding the expressive capacities of both. Hand in hand with this development went a closer relationship between words and music than had ever existed before. The works we have discussed in the last few chapters revealed an absorbing preoccupation with God and the hereafter. Music henceforth turns more and more to man in the here-and-now.

Arcadelt's setting is profoundly moving. The texture is predominantly homophonic, with clear-cut phrases and cadences. The four voices–soprano, alto, tenor, bass–are given equal importance, in true chamber-music style. The sweetness of this music is established in the gentle flow of the opening phrase:

In setting a poem line by line there was a danger that the piece would take on a sectional, somewhat disjointed character. Arcadelt and his compeers overcame this through overlapping. One voice begins the new phrase even as the other three complete the old. The result is a continuous forward movement that builds inexorably, in this madrigal, to the emotional climax of the words "io moro beato" (I die happy). From there the tension subsides. How poignant is the sound, and how pure as the voices flow gently into the final cadence.

The atmosphere of courtly refinement out of which the madrigal grew is accurately reflected in this music. Many conditions–social, political, literary, and musical–had to flow together to create so subtle an art.

Weelkes: As Vesta Was Descending

As in the case of the sonnet, England took over the madrigal from Italy and developed it into a native art form. All the brilliance of the Elizabethan age is reflected in the school of madrigalists who flourished in the late sixteenth century and on into the reign of James I. Among the most important figures were Thomas Morley (1557–1603), John Wilbye (1574–1638), Thomas Weelkes (c. 1575–1623), and Orlando Gibbons (1583–1625). Weelkes, one of the greatest of the madrigalists, was organist of Chichester Cathedral. He also wrote church music, anthems, and some instrumental works.

In 1601, Morley edited a collection of madrigals in honor of Queen Elizabeth, with the common refrain "Long live fair Oriana." The work, called *The Triumphs of Oriana,* was not published until 1603, by which time the Queen was dead. In the last two madrigals the refrain, accordingly, was changed to "In Heaven lives Oriana."

Weelkes's *As Vesta Was Descending* is one of the masterpieces in the collection. It was written for six voices—two sopranos and alto, two

SIDE 2/7 (E I)
SIDE 12/4 (S)

In this contemporary woodcut, illustrating the month of April for Edmund Spenser's The Shepheardes Calendar, *Queen Elizabeth is surrounded by her musical ladies-in-waiting.*

tenors and bass. The poem, probably by the composer, is a far cry from Shakespeare's beautiful tribute to the Queen:

And the imperial votaress passed on,
In maiden meditation, fancy-free.

But it does have the merit of lending itself to music, whereas Shakespeare's lines would resist the composer since they already are music.

As Vesta was from Latmos hill descending,
She spied a maiden Queen the same ascending,
Attended only by all the shepherds swain,
To whom Diana's darlings came running down amain:

First two by two, then three by three together,
Leaving their Goddess all alone, hasted thither,
And mingling with the shepherds of her train,
With mirthful tunes her presence entertain.

Then sang the shepherds and nymphs of Diana,
Long live fair Oriana.

Word painting

Weelkes takes every opportunity to indulge in the Renaissance fondness for word painting; he makes the music reflect every shade of thought and action in the words. The opening statement—"As Vesta was from Latmos hill descending"—is sung by four of the six voices, with the notes moving downward on "descending." At the first action—"She spied" —the voice parts become individualized, with much imitation among them. On the word "ascending," at the end of the second line, there is upward movement in all the parts. "Attended by all" in the next line brings in the other two voices, Tenor II and Bass.

"Came running down amain" inspires vivacious eighth notes tripping down the scale. "First two by two, then three by three" is illustrated first by two voices, then by three. At "all alone" we hear a brief solo. On the words "And mingling with the shepherds of her train," the six voices mingle very happily. So too, "With mirthful tunes her presence entertain" introduces a mood of jollity. The setting, up to this point, is mostly syllabic —that is, a single syllable to a note—with three important exceptions: the action verbs—"descending," "ascending," and "entertain"—are expanded over several notes. The writing throughout is brilliant, the voices moving over a wide range and frequently crisscrossing. The rhythm has the plasticity we noted in Renaissance music, accommodating itself in the most natural manner to the inflections of our language.

All the voices, fortissimo, announce "Then sang the shepherds and nymphs of Diana." This serves to introduce the refrain, which is the most important line. "Long live fair Oriana" enters on a melodious motive that is imitated by each voice in quick succession:

The rest of the madrigal is an extended fantasy on these four words. Weelkes handles the imitative counterpoint like a virtuoso, the result being a headlong interplay in which all the voices join on an equal basis. Excitement mounts steadily until the basic motive is announced fortissimo in augmentation (longer note values) in the bass:

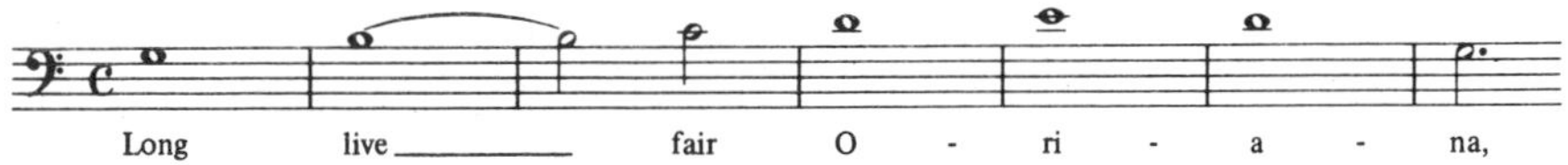

This leads into the final measures, which make a powerful effect at the final cadence. One hopes that Elizabeth at some point heard this brave sound raised in her honor. By all accounts she was musician enough (like her father) to have enjoyed its fine points.

The madrigal, so characteristic of the Renaissance, prepared the way for one of the most innovative and influential forms of Western music, the opera. With this genre, we reach the next great style period, the Baroque.

62

The Baroque

"I do not know what I may appear to the world; but to myself I seem to have been only like a boy playing on the seashore, and diverting myself in now and then finding a smoother pebble or a prettier shell than ordinary, whilst the great ocean of truth lay all undiscovered before me." — SIR ISAAC NEWTON (1642–1727)

The period of the Baroque stretched across a turbulent century and a half of European history. It opened shortly before the year 1600, a convenient signpost that need not be taken too literally; and may be regarded as having come to a close with the death of Bach in 1750.

The term "baroque" was probably derived from the Portuguese *barroco,* a pearl of irregular shape much used in the jewelry of the time. The century and a half of Baroque art divides itself into three fifty-year periods; early, middle, and late Baroque. Since public interest until recently concentrated on the late phase, many came to think of Bach and Handel as the first great composers. Viewed against the total panorama of their era, these masters are seen rather to have been the heirs of an old and surpassingly rich tradition.

The period 1600–1750 was a time of change and adventure. The conquest of the New World stirred the imagination and filled the coffers of the Old. The middle classes gathered wealth and power in their struggle against the aristocracy. Empires clashed for mastery of the world. Ap-

The emergence of the Baroque style–bold, vigorous, decorative–may be seen in this monumental masterpiece. A fresco painting by Michelangelo (1474–1564), **The Creation of Man,** *in the Sistine Chapel, Vatican City.*

The court of Louis XIV at Versailles provided a model of splendor for the rest of Europe. A view of the courtyard.

palling poverty and wasteful luxury, magnificent idealism and savage oppression—against contradictions such as these unfolded the pomp and splendor of Baroque art: an art bold of gesture and conception; vigorous, decorative, monumental.

Baroque art

The transition from the classically minded Renaissance to the Baroque was foreshadowed by Michelangelo (1475–1564). His turbulent figures, their torsos twisted in struggle, reflect the Baroque love of the dramatic. In like fashion the Venetian school of painters—Titian, Tintoretto, Veronese—captured the dynamic spirit of the new age. Their crowded canvases are ablaze with color and movement. They glory in the tension of opposing masses. They dramatize the diagonal.

Politics

The Baroque was the era of absolute monarchy. Princes throughout Europe took as their model the splendor of Versailles. Louis XIV's famous "I am the State!" summed up a way of life in which all art and culture served the cult of the ruler. Courts large and small maintained elaborate musical establishments including opera troupes, chapel choirs, and orchestras. Baroque opera, the favorite diversion of the aristocracy, aimed at a lofty pathos that left no room for the frailties of ordinary men. It centered about the gods and heroes of antiquity, in whom the occupant of the royal box and his courtiers found a flattering likeness of themselves.

Scientific frontiers

The Baroque was also an age of reason. Adventurers more bold than the conquistadors set forth upon the uncharted sea of knowledge. The findings of Kepler, Galileo, and Copernicus in physics and astronomy, of Descartes in mathematics and Spinoza in philosophy were so many milestones in the intellectual history of Europe. Harvey discovered the circulation of the blood. Locke laid the foundation for a scientific study of the workings of the mind. Newton's theory of gravitation revealed a universe based upon law and order. Descartes expressed the confidence of a brave new age when he wrote, "Provided only that we abstain from receiving anything as true which is not so, there can be nothing so remote that we cannot reach it, nor so obscure that we cannot discover it."

Excluded from the salons of the aristocracy, the middle classes created a culture of their own. Their music making centered about the home, the church, and the university group (known as *collegium musicum*). For them came into being the comic opera which, like the prose novel, was filled with keen and witty observation of life. For them painting forsook its grandiose themes and turned to intimate scenes of bourgeois life. The leaders of the Dutch school—Vermeer, Frans Hals, Ruysdael—embodied the vitality of a new burgher art that reached its high point in Rembrandt (1606–69), a master whose insights penetrated the recesses of the soul. Under the leadership of merchant princes and financiers, the culture of the city came to rival that of the palace. These new connoisseurs vied with the court in their love of splendor, responding to the opulence of Baroque art, to the sensuous beauty of brocade and velvet, marble and jewels and precious metals. This aspect of the Baroque finds expression in the art of Titian (c. 1490–1576), whose canvases exude a driving energy, a reveling in life. His voluptuous nudes established the seventeenth-century ideal of feminine beauty.

The Baroque was an intensely devout period. Religion was a rallying cry on some of the bloodiest battlefields in history. The Protestant camp included England, Scandinavia, Holland, and the north German cities, all citadels of the rising middle class. On the Catholic side were the two powerful dynasties, Hapsburg and Bourbon, who fought one another no less fiercely than they did their Protestant foes. After decades of struggle, the might of the Spanish-Hapsburg empire was broken. France emerged as the leading state on the continent; Germany was in ruins; England rose to world power. Europe was ready to advance to the stage of modern industrial society.

Protestant culture was rooted in the Bible. Its emphasis upon the individual promoted a personal tone and strengthened the romantic tendency in the Baroque. Milton (1608–74) in *Paradise Lost* produced the poetic epic of the Protestant world view, even as Dante three and a half centuries earlier had produced that of the Catholic in *The Divine Comedy.* The heroic hymn tunes of the Reformation nourished the profoundly spiritual art of Bach. The oratorios of Handel harnessed Baroque splendor to an ethical ideal. The two composers mark the supreme musical achievement of the Protestant spirit.

The Catholic world for its part tried to retrieve the losses inflicted by Luther's secession. The Counter-Reformation mobilized all the forces of the church militant. The Jesuits, recognizing faith to be a matter of the whole personality, strove to fire the hearts and minds and senses of the faithful. They made music, sculpture, architecture, painting, and even the theater arts tributary to their purpose. The rapturous mysticism of the Counter-Reformation found expression in the canvases of El Greco (1541–1614). His eerie landscapes, bathed in an unearthly light, are creations of a visionary mind that distorts the real in its search for a reality

Left: The art of Jan Vermeer (1632–75) turned to intimate scenes of bourgeois life. **The Artist in His Studio.** (Kunsthistorisches Museum, Vienna.) *Right: The theatricality of the Baroque is brilliantly manifested in this sculpture by Gianlorenzo Bernini (1590–1680),* **Apollo and Daphne.**

beyond. Baroque theatricalism and pathos came to fullness in the sculptor Gianlorenzo Bernini (1598–1680). His famous *Apollo and Daphne* captures in marble all the restlessness and dramatic quality of the Baroque.

Between the conflicting currents of absolute monarchy and rising bourgeois power, Reformation and Counter-Reformation, the Baroque fashioned its grandiose art. Alien to its spirit were restraint and detachment. Rather it achieved its ends through violent opposition of forces, lavish creativity, and abandon. With these went the capacity to organize a thousand details into a monumental, overpowering whole.

The role of the artist

The artist played a variety of roles in Baroque society. He might be an ambassador and intimate of princes, as were Rubens and Van Dyck; or a priest, as was Vivaldi; or a political leader, like Milton. He functioned under royal or princely patronage, as did Corneille and Racine; or, like Bach, was in the employ of a church or free city. To the aristocrats whom he served he might be little more than a purveyor of elegant entertainment. Yet, beneath the obsequious manner and fawning dedications demanded by the age, there was often to be found a spirit that dared to probe all existing knowledge and shape new worlds; a voice addressing itself to those who truly listened—a voice that was indeed "the trumpet of a prophecy."

63

Main Currents in Baroque Music

"The end of all good music is to affect the soul." — CLAUDIO MONTEVERDI

The Emergence of Opera

Monody

With the transition from Renaissance to Baroque came a momentous change: the shifting of interest from a texture of several independent parts of equal importance to music in which a single melody predominated; that is, from polyphonic to homophonic texture. The new style, which originated in vocal music, was named *monody*—literally, "one song," music for one singer with instrumental accompaniment. (Monody is not to be confused with monophony; see p. 295.) The year 1600 is associated with the emergence of the monodic style. Like many such milestones, the date merely indicates the coming to light of a process that was long preparing.

The Camerata

The victory of the monodic style was achieved by a group of Florentine writers, artists, and musicians known as the Camerata, a name derived from the Italian word for "salon." Among their numbers were Vincenzo Galilei, father of the astronomer Galileo, and the composers Jacopo Peri and Giulio Caccini. The men of the Camerata were aristocratic humanists. Their aim was to resurrect the musical-dramatic art of ancient Greece. Since almost nothing was known of the music of the Athenian tragedy, they imagined it in terms of their own needs and desires. Instead of resurrecting something dead the Camerata came forth with an idea that was very much alive.

The stile rappresentativo

This idea was that music must heighten the emotional power of the text. The Florentine humanists dreamed of bringing their music into close relationship with poetry, and through poetry with life itself. "I endeavored," wrote Caccini in 1602, "the imitation of the conceit of the words, seeking out the chords more or less passionate according to the meaning." Thus came into being what its inventors regarded as the *stile rappresentativo* (representational style), consisting of a recitative that moved freely over a foundation of simple chords.

The origins of opera

The Camerata soon realized that the representational style could be applied not only to a poem but to an entire drama. In this way they were led to the invention of opera, considered by many to be the single most important achievement of Baroque music. The first complete opera that has come down to us, *Euridice,* was presented in 1600 at the marriage of Henry IV of France to Maria de' Medici. The libretto was by Ottavio Rinuccini, the music by Peri (with the addition of some passages by Caccini).

The composer Jacopo Peri in the role of Orpheus in the first production of his opera Euridice *(1600).*

The Camerata appeared at a time when it became necessary for music to free itself from the complexities of counterpoint. The year 1600, like the year 1900, bristled with discussions about *le nuove musiche*—"the new music" and what its adherents proudly named "the expressive style." As sometimes happens with inventors, the noble amateurs of the Florentine salon touched off more than they realized.

The Figured Bass

The melody-and-chords of the new music was far removed from the intricate interweaving of voices in the old. Since musicians were familiar with the basic harmony, it was unneccessary to write the chords out in full. Instead the composer put a numeral, indicating the harmony required, above or below the bass note. For example, the figure 6 under a bass note indicated a chord whose root lay a sixth above the note. Thus, a 6 below the note A called for the F-major or F-minor triad. The application of this principle on a large scale resulted in "the most successful system of musical shorthand ever devised"—the *figured bass* or *thorough-bass* (from *basso continuo,* a continuous bass, "thorough" being the old form of "through.") The actual filling in and elaboration of the harmony was left to the performer. A similar practice obtains in jazz music today, where the player

The thorough-bass instrument looming above the harpsichord testifies to the importance of this practice in Baroque performance. A wash drawing by Giuseppe Zocchi (1711–69), **Concerto** *(c. 1720).*

elaborates on the harmonies from the skeletal version on the page or in his head.

Thorough-bass instruments

So important was this practice for a century and a half that the Baroque is often referred to as the period of thorough-bass. The figured bass required at least two players: one to perform the bass line on a sustaining instrument—cello, double bass, or bassoon—and the other to fill in or "realize" the chords on an instrument capable of harmony, such as a harpsichord or organ, a guitar or lute.

The shorthand of figured-bass writing was particularly valuable at a time when printing was an involved and costly process. Since most works were intended for a single occasion or season they were left in manuscript, the parts being copied out by hand. It was a boon to composers to be able to present their music in abbreviated fashion, knowing that the performers would fill in the necessary details. When we read of an old master producing hundreds of cantatas and dozens of operas, we may be sure that "there were giants in the earth in those days." But the thorough-bass helped.

Keyboard Instruments

Baroque organ

The three important keyboard instruments of the Baroque were the organ, the harpsichord, and the clavichord. The Baroque organ had a pure, transparent tone. Its stops did not blend the colors into a symphonic cloudburst, as is the case with the twentieth-century organ, but let the voices stand out clearly so that the ear could follow the counterpoint. The colors of the various stops contrasted sharply; but, although the tone was penetrating, it was not harsh because the wind pressure was low. Through the use of two keyboards it was possible to achieve even levels of soft and loud.

Harpsichord

The *harpsichord* too was capable of producing different sonorities because of its two keyboards. The instrument differed from the piano in two important respects. First, its strings were plucked by quills instead of being struck with hammers. The resultant tone was bright and silvery, but it could not be sustained like the tone of the piano. There had to be continual movement in the sound: trills, embellishments of all kinds, chords broken up into arpeggio patterns, and the like. Second, the pressure of the fingers on the keys varied the tone only slightly on the harpsichord, whereas the piano has a wide range of dynamics. The harpsichord was therefore incapable of the crescendo and decrescendo that became so essential a feature of Classic-Romantic music. But it was an ideal medium for contrapuntal music, for it brought out the inner voices with luminous

The Compenius organ at Frederiksborg Castle, Denmark, dates from about 1610.

This beautifully decorated Italian harpsichord was built by Jerome de Zentis in 1658. (The Metropolitan Museum of Art, The Crosby Brown Collection of Musical Instruments, 1889.)

clarity. It lent itself to a grand manner of playing that on the one hand was elevated and dramatic, on the other, rhythmically precise, refined, and playful. It was immensely popular during the Baroque as a solo instrument. In addition, the harpsichord was indispensable in the realization of the thorough-bass, and was the mainstay of the ensemble in chamber music and at the opera house.

Clavichord

The clavichord, which we first encountered in Chapter 58, continued to be a favorite instrument for the home. By the end of the eighteenth century both clavichord and harpsichord had been supplanted in public favor by the piano. The word *clavier* (or *klavier*) was used in Germany as the general term for keyboard instruments, including harpsichord, clavichord, and organ. Whether a certain piece was intended for one rather than the other must often be gathered from the style rather than the title. In any event, the rendering of Bach's *Wohltemperiertes Clavier* as *Well-Tempered Clavichord* is misleading. Closer to the mark is *Well-Tempered Clavier.*

The Major-Minor System

The Baroque witnessed one of the most significant changes in all music history: the transition from the Medieval church modes to major-minor tonality. As music turned from vocal counterpoint to instrumental harmony, it demanded a simplification of the harmonic system. The various church modes gave way to two standard scales: major and minor. With the establishment of major-minor tonality, the thrust to the keynote or *do* became the most powerful force in music.

Now each chord could assume its function in relation to the key center. Composers of the Baroque soon learned to exploit the opposition between the chord of rest, the I (Tonic), and the active chord, the V (Dominant). So, too, the movement from home key to contrasting key and back became an important element in the shaping of musical structure. Composers developed larger forms of instrumental music than had ever been known before.

Important in this transition was a major technical advance. Due to a curious quirk of nature, keyboard instruments tuned according to the scientific laws of acoustics (first discovered by the ancient Greek philosopher Pythagoras) give a pure sound for keys with signatures of up to three flats or sharps, but the intervals become increasingly out-of-tune as more sharps or flats are added. As instrumental music acquired greater prominence, it became more and more important to be able to play in all the keys. In the seventeenth century, a discovery was made: by slightly mistuning the intervals within the octave—and thereby spreading the discrepancy evenly among all keys—it became possible to play in every major and minor key without unpleasant results. This adjustment is known as *equal temperament.* It increased the range of harmonic possibilities available to the composer, as Johann Sebastian Bach demonstrated in *The Well-Tempered Clavier,* whose two volumes each contain a prelude and fugue in every one of the twelve major and twelve minor keys. Equal temperament transformed the major-minor system at last into a completely flexible medium of expression.

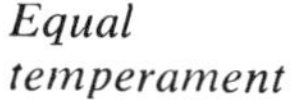

Use of dissonance

The growing harmonic sense brought about a freer handling of dissonance. Baroque musicians used dissonant chords for emotional intensity

A German clavichord by John Christopher Jesse, dated 1765. (The Metropolitan Museum of Art, The Crosby Brown Collection of Musical Instruments, 1889.)

and color. In the setting of poetry the composer heightened the impact of an expressive word through dissonance. Such harmonic freedom could not fail to shock the conservatives. The Italian theorist Artusi, writing in 1600 *On the Imperfections of Modern Music*—an attack on Monteverdi and his fellow innovators—rails against those musicians who "are harsh to the ear, offending rather than delighting it," and who "think it within their power to corrupt, spoil, and ruin the good old rules."

The major-minor system emphasized the distinction between the tones included in the key, that is, the diatonic tones, and the five foreign or chromatic tones. Baroque composers associated moods of well-being with diatonic harmony, anguish with chromatic.

The major-minor system was the collective achievement of several generations of musicians. It expressed a new dynamic culture. By dividing the world of sound into definite areas and regulating the movement from one to the other, it enabled the composer to mirror the exciting interplay of forces in the world about him.

64

Further Aspects of Baroque Music

"Musick hath 2 ends, first to pleas the sence, & that is done by the pure Dulcor of Harmony, & secondly to move ye affections or excite passion."

— ROGER NORTH: *The Musicall Grammarian* (1728)

The Doctrine of the Affections

Now that man was become the measure of all things, there was much speculation concerning the passions and affections, by which were meant the deep-lying forces that determine our emotional life. It was realized that these are peculiarly responsive to music. The *doctrine of the affections* related primarily to the union of music and poetry, where the mental state was made explicit by the text. The Baroque developed an impressive technique of what is known as tone painting, in which the music vividly mirrored the words. Ideas of movement and direction—stepping, running, leaping, ascending, descending—were represented graphically through the movement of the melody and rhythm. Bach exhorted his pupils to "play the chorale according to the meaning of the words." He associated the idea of resurrection with a rising line. The sorrow of the Crucifixion was symbolized by a bass line that might descend stepwise along the chromatic scale. Temptation was allied to a sinuous theme that suggests the serpent.

Tone painting

Rhythm in Baroque music produces the same effect of turbulent, yet controlled motion that animates Baroque painting. Peter Paul Rubens (1577–1640), **The Lion Hunt.**

Once the musical figure is brought into being, it abandons its picture quality and becomes abstract musical material to be developed according to purely musical procedures. In short, the imagination of the pure musician takes over.

Word repetition and melisma

This supremacy of music shows itself in two traits that strike the listener in hearing the vocal literature of the Baroque. We have already encountered both. In the first place, lines, phrases, and individual words are repeated over and over again in order to allow room for the necessary musical expansion. This practice springs from the realization that music communicates more slowly than words and needs more time in which to establish its meaning. In the second place, a single syllable will be extended to accommodate all the notes of an expressive melodic line, so that the word is stretched beyond recognition (the style of setting known as melismatic). Thus, the music born of words ends by swallowing up the element that gave it birth.

In instrumental music the practice took root of building a piece on a single mood—the basic "affection." This was established at the outset by a striking musical subject out of which grew the entire composition. In this way composers discovered the imperious gesture that opens a piece of Baroque music, of a tension and pathos that pervade the whole movement.

Rhythm in Baroque Music

The Baroque, with its fondness for energetic movement, demanded a dynamic rhythm based on the regular recurrence of accent. The bass part became the carrier of the new rhythm. Its relentless beat is an arresting trait in many compositions of the Baroque. This steady pulsation, once under way, never slackens or deviates until the goal is reached. It imparts to Baroque music its unflagging drive, producing the same effect of turbulent yet controlled motion that animates Baroque painting, sculpture, and architecture.

Dance forms

Composers became ever more aware of the capacity of the instruments for rhythm. They found that a striking dance rhythm could serve as the basis for an extended piece, vocal or instrumental. Popular and court dances furnished an invigorating element to musical art. Nor, in that stately age, were the rhythms necessarily lively. Idealized dance rhythms served as the basis for tragic arias and great polyphonic works. In a time when courtiers listened to music primarily for entertainment, composers dressed up a good part of their material in dance rhythms. Many a dance piece served to make palatable a profounder discourse. In effect, rhythm pervaded the musical conception of the Baroque and helped it capture the movement and drive of a vibrant era.

Continuous Melody

The elaborate scrollwork of Baroque architecture bears witness to an abundance of energy that would not leave an inch of space unornamented. Its musical counterpart is to be found in one of the main elements of Baroque style—the principle of continuous expansion. A movement based on a single affection will start off with a striking musical figure that unfolds through a process of ceaseless spinning out. In this regard the music of the Baroque differs from that of the Classical era, with its balanced phrases and cadences. It is constantly in motion, in the act of becoming. When its energy is spent, the work comes to an end.

In vocal music the melody of the Baroque was imbued with the desire always to heighten the impact of the words. Wide leaps and the use of chromatic tones served to emphasize the affections. There resulted a noble melody whose spacious curves outlined a style of grand expressiveness and pathos.

Terraced Dynamics

Baroque music does not know the constant fluctuation of volume that marks the Classic-Romantic style. The music moves at a fairly constant level of sonority. A passage uniformly loud will be followed by one uniformly soft, creating the effect of light and shade. The shift from one level to the other has come to be known as *terraced dynamics* and is a characteristic feature of the Baroque style.

The composer of the Classic-Romantic era who desired greater volume of tone directed each instrument to play louder. The Baroque composer wrote instead for a larger number of players. The Classic-Romantic musician used the crescendo as a means of expression within a passage.

The elaborate scrollwork of Baroque architecture finds its musical counterpart in continuous melody. The High Altar of the Theatiner Church, Munich.

The Baroque composer found his main source of expression in the contrast between a soft passage and a loud—that is, between the two terraces of sound. Each passage became an area of solid color set off against the next. This conception shapes the structure of the music, endowing it with a monumental simplicity. (Probably, in performance, singers and players used the crescendo and decrescendo more than we think.)

It follows that Baroque composers were much more sparing of expression marks than those who came after. The music of the period carries little else than an occasional forte or piano, leaving it to the player to supply whatever else may be necessary.

Two-Part Form

Two-part or binary (**A-B**) form played an important role in Baroque music. This is the question-and-answer type of structure found, in its simplest form, in a tune such as *Frère Jacques.* The principle gave rise to a tightly knit structure in which the **A** part moved from home to contrasting key while the **B** part made the corresponding move back. Both parts used closely related or even identical material. The form was made apparent to the ear by the modulation and a full stop at the end of the first part. As a rule each part was repeated, giving an **A-A-B-B** structure.

In three-part form contrast is injected by the middle section. Binary form, on the other hand, is all of a piece in texture and mood. It embodies a single affection—that is, a single mood for which reason it was favored by a musical style based on continuous expansion. Binary form prevailed in the short harpsichord pieces of dance character that were produced in quantities during the seventeenth and early eighteenth centuries. It was a standard type in the suite, one of the favorite instrumental forms of the Baroque.

The Ground Bass

The principle of unity in variety expressed itself in an important procedure of Baroque music, the *ground bass* or *basso ostinato* (literally, "obstinate bass"). This consisted of a short phrase that was repeated over and over in the bass while the upper voices pursued their independent courses. With each repetition of the bass, some aspect of melody, harmony, and/or rhythm would be changed. The upper voices were frequently improvised. Thus the ostinato supplied a fixed framework within which the composer's imagination disported itself. Baroque musicians developed a masterful technique of variation and embellishment over the ground bass.

The ostinato is extremely effective both as a unifying device and as a means of building tension. Later we shall find it playing an important part in twentieth-century music.

Baroque Instruments

The Baroque was the first period in history in which instrumental music was comparable in importance to vocal. The growing interest in this branch of the art stimulated the development of new instruments and the perfecting of old. Playing techniques grew more fluent, and great virtuosos appeared—Bach and Handel at the organ, Corelli and Tartini on the violin.

On the whole, composers still thought in terms of line, so that a string instrument, a woodwind, and a brass might be assigned to play the same line in the counterpoint. Besides, since a movement was based upon a single affection, the same instrumental color might be allowed to prevail throughout, as opposed to the practice of the Classical and Romantic periods, when color was constantly changed. Much music was still performed by whatever instruments happened to be available at a particular time and place. At the same time, composers—especially in the late Baroque—chose instruments more and more for their color. As their specifications became more precise, the art of orchestration was born.

Later adaptations

Baroque music continued to be played in subsequent eras—but it was often adapted to the new tastes of the time. No less a composer than Mozart reorchestrated the accompaniments to Handel's *Messiah* to make them conform more closely to the Classical style. Later, in the nineteenth and early twentieth centuries, an even more overblown approach was common. The organ works of Bach were thundered out on mammoth

At the Aston Magna Summer Festivals, seventeenth- and eighteenth-century music is performed on authentic instruments. Photographed during a concert at St. James Church, Great Barrington, Massachusetts in 1981.

instruments, instead of the more appropriate Baroque organs. His keyboard works were played on the grand piano rather than on the harpsichord. Full symphonic forces, appropriate for the tone poems of Richard Strauss, played his suites and concertos (and even orchestral transcriptions of his organ works)—and the music of the Classical period was also subject to such inflation.

Authenticity today

Increasingly, in the past few decades, all this began to change. As a result, when our symphony orchestras play Bach or Mozart, they use only part of their full strength. Chamber orchestras have come into existence that specialize in old (and also modern) works for smaller ensembles. Contemporary organ builders have learned to emulate the virtues of the Baroque instrument. The harpsichord is a widely accepted instrument. The choral works of Bach and Handel are sung, not by hundreds of voices, but on a scale approximating that of the composers' own time. More and more concertgoers have come to expect, and appreciate, this concern for authenticity.

In recent years musicians have begun to aspire to still greater authenticity. For one, musicians today try to play eighteenth-century works on instruments that approximate as closely as possible those for which the music was written. It must be remembered that although our instruments are nominally the same as those of the eighteenth century, most of them have evolved in the direction of increased brilliance and volume to help fill the large public halls that did not exist in the time of Bach or Mozart. String instruments were modified to permit greater tension in the strings. In addition, gut strings were often replaced with steel; the bow became heavier, longer, and capable of greater pressure. The key systems added to woodwinds and the valves added to brass enabled the players to achieve greater virtuosity and to manage the new chromatic music. But all these changes had one result: they altered the character of the sound. To cite another example, there is an enormous difference between the *fortepiano* of Mozart's day, an instrument of clear and delicate tone (especially in the bass register), and the modern concert grand, whose metal frame permits high string tensions and the resultant greater volume. Yet there are subtleties possible on the older instrument which are lost on the modern piano.

The new drive for authenticity, therefore, has made the original sounds of eighteenth-century music familiar to us even as it has revived Medieval and Renaissance instruments. Recorders and wooden transverse flutes, restored violins with gut strings, the refractory but mellower-toned valveless brass instruments are heard again, and the Baroque orchestra has recovered not only its scale, but also its transparent tone quality. The gentler voices of the authentic instruments balance more comfortably in counterpoint. Naturally, they are not suitable for our largest concert halls, but they have proved especially effective on recordings, and many versions are now available of Bach's *Brandenburg Concertos*, for example, played on eighteenth-century instruments.

Virtuosity and Improvisation

The interest in instruments went hand in hand with a desire to master their technique. Virtuosity on the organ and harpsichord, violin and trumpet had its counterpart in the opera house in a phenomenal vocal technique that has never been surpassed.

Technical mastery brought a growing awareness of what each instrument could do best, and with it a heightened sense of style. Composers differentiated ever more clearly among the various styles: vocal and instrumental; church, theater, chamber; keyboard, string, woodwind, brass. At the same time they were given to mixing the styles. It was part of the Baroque straining for effect to cause one medium to take over the qualities of another: to make Dresden china imitate the daintiness of lace, wrought iron the curl of leaves and flowers. In like fashion instrumental music copied the brilliant coloratura of the voice, while vocal music emulated the arabesques of the instruments. Church music used to advantage the dramatic style of opera and the rhythms of the dance. The delicate ornamentation of harpsichord music influenced the writing for strings. Organ sonority affected the style of the orchestra. Each nourished the other, to the enrichment of all.

Improvisation played a prominent part in the musical practice of the Baroque. The realizing of the thorough-bass would have been impossible if musicians of the period had not been ready to "think with their fingers." A church organist was expected as a matter of course to be able to improvise an intricate contrapuntal piece. The ability in this regard of great organists such as Bach and Handel was legendary. This abandonment to the inspiration of the moment suited the rhapsodic temper of the

Titian (c. 1477–1576) captured the dynamic spirit of the Baroque age in his canvases, ablaze with color and movement. In ***Bacchanale*** *we sense the tension of opposing masses and the dramatization of the diagonal.* (Scala/Art Resource.)

The rapturous mysticism of the Baroque Counter-Reformation found expression in the canvases of El Greco (1541–1614). His ***View of Toledo*** *is the work of a visionary mind that distorts the real in its search for a reality beyond.* (The Metropolitan Museum of Art, Bequest of Mrs. H. O. Havemeyer, 1929. The H. O. Havemeyer Collection.)

Baroque, and even influenced the art of composition. Many passages in the fantasias and toccatas of the time, with their abrupt changes of mood, bear the mark of extemporaneous speech.

Improvisation functioned in Baroque music also in another way. The singer or player was expected to add his own embellishments to what was written down (as is the custom today in jazz). This was his creative contribution to the work. The practice was so widespread that Baroque music sounded altogether different in performance from what it looked like on paper.

Baroque Opera

The formal or serious opera of the Baroque, the *opera seria,* was attuned to the social order that ended with the French Revolution. This was an opera for princely courts, the favorite diversion of Hapsburgs, Bourbons, Medici, and the rest, embodying the world view of a feudal caste whose gaze was directed to the past, to an imaginary realm where heroes torn between love and honor declaimed to noble music while time stood still in an enchanted grotto out of antiquity or the Medieval age.

This art form was much too stylized and formal to appeal to the nineteenth century. However, in the twentieth a reaction has occurred. The upsurge of interest in the Baroque brought about a revival of some of its operas; and it has become apparent that if these noble works are approached with imagination and adapted to the modern taste, they have much to say to us.

One of the characteristic conventions of Baroque opera was the assignment of heroic roles to the *castrato,* the artificial male soprano or alto who dominated the operatic scene of the early eighteenth century. Such singers submitted–or were subjected by their elders–to an operation during their boyhood that preserved the soprano or alto range of their voices for the rest of their lives. What resulted, after years of training, was an incredibly agile voice that combined the power of the male with the brilliance of the high register and that, strange as it may seem to us, was associated by Baroque audiences with heroic male roles. The great castratos were famous throughout Europe, even though the French philosophers, in the spirit of the Enlightenment, made fun of the Italians for "having Alexander, Caesar, and Pompey settle the destiny of the world with women's voices." The era of the French Revolution saw the decline and eventual abolition of a custom so incompatible with the dignity of man. When castrato roles are revived today they are usually sung in lower register by a tenor or baritone.

Baroque opera was a vital force whose influence extended far beyond the theater. It created the great forms of the lyric drama–recitative and aria, ensemble and chorus–that served as models to every branch of the art. The *da capo aria,* in which the first part is repeated after the middle section, established the ternary form (**A-B-A**) as a basic pattern of

Baroque opera embodied the splendor and monumentality of Baroque art. Scene from an opera performance at the Teatro Regio, in Turin, 1740. From a contemporary engraving.

musical structure. Within its own conventions, Baroque opera taught composers to depict the passions and the affections, the lyric contemplation of nature, the quintessence of love, hate, fear, jealousy, exaltation. In sum, the opera house of the Baroque was the center for new trends and experiments, through which music attained a dramatic-expressive power such as it had never possessed before.

The Composer and His Patron

The Baroque was a period of international culture. National styles existed —without nationalism. Lully, an Italian, created the French lyric tragedy. Handel, a German, gave England the oratorio. There was free interchange among national cultures. The sensuous beauty of Italian melody, the pointed precision of French dance rhythm, the luxuriance of German counterpoint, the freshness of English choral song—these nourished an all-European art that absorbed the best of each.

The Baroque composer was employed by a court, a church, a municipal council, or an opera house. He was in direct contact with his public. As like as not he was his own interpreter, which made the contact even closer. He created his music for a specific occasion—it might be a royal wedding or a religious service—and for immediate use: in a word, for communication. He was an artisan in a handicraft society. He functioned as a religious man fired by the word of God, or as a loyal subject exalting his king. He was not troubled overmuch by concern for self-expression, but because he spoke out of passionate conviction he expressed both himself and his era. He did not discuss esthetics or the nature of inspiration; but, impelled by a lofty moral vision, he united superb mastery of his craft with profound insights into the nature of experience. He began by writing for a particular time and place; he ended by creating for the ages.

65

Claudio Monteverdi

"The modern composer builds upon the foundation of truth."

Claudio Monteverdi.

The innovations of the Florentine Camerata awaited the composer who would infuse life into them and enrich them with the resources of the past. That composer was Claudio Monteverdi (1567–1643), in whom the dramatic spirit of the Baroque found its first spokesman.

His Life and Music

Monteverdi spent twelve fruitful years at the court of the Duke of Mantua. In 1613 he was appointed choirmaster of St. Mark's in Venice, and retained the post until his death thirty years later. Into his operas and ballets, madrigals and religious works he injected an emotional intensity that was new to music. The new-born lyric drama of the Florentines he welded into a coherent musical form and tightened their shapeless recitative into an expressive line imbued with drama. He originated what he called the *stile concitato* (agitated style) to express the hidden tremors of the soul, introducing such novel sound-effects as tremolo and pizzicato as symbols of passion. Monteverdi aspired above all to make his music express the emotional content of poetry. "The text," he declared, "should be the master of the music, not the servant."

Monteverdi used dissonance and instrumental color for dramatic expressiveness, atmosphere, and suspense. He emphasized the contrast between characters by abrupt changes of key. He held that rhythm is bound up with emotion. A master of polyphonic writing, he retained in his choruses the great contrapuntal tradition of the past. There resulted a noble art, full of pathos and rooted in the verities of human nature. The characters in his music dramas were neither puppets nor abstractions, but men and women who gave vent to their joys and sorrows through song. When his patron the Duke of Mantua suggested a libretto on a mythological subject of the kind fashionable at the time—a dialogue of the winds—the composer of *Orfeo* (1607) and of *Arianna* (1608) protested: "How shall I be able to imitate the speaking of winds that do not speak; and how shall I be able to move the affections by such means? Arianna was moving because she was a woman, and likewise Orfeo was moving because he was a man and not a wind. The harmonies imitate human beings, not the noise of winds, the bleating of sheep, the neighing of horses."

Scene from L'Orfeo

SIDE 3/1 (E I)
SIDE 12/5 (S)

The qualities of Monteverdi's art are well exemplified in the recitative from *L'Orfeo* (Orpheus), *Tu se' morta.* Orfeo, the poet-singer of antiquity whose music charmed rocks, trees, and savage beasts, having learned of his wife Eurydice's death, decides to follow her to the nether regions:

Tu se' morta, se' morta, mia vita,	You are dead, dead, my darling,
ed io respiro; tu se' da me partita,	And I live; you have left me,
se' da me partita per mai più,	Left me forevermore,
mai più non tornare, ed io rimango—	Never to return, yet I remain—
no, no, che se i versi alcuna cosa ponno,	No, no, if verses have any power,
n'andrò sicuro al più profondi abissi,	I shall go boldly to the deepest abysses,
e intenerito il cor del re dell'ombre,	And having softened the heart of the king of shadows,
meco trarotti a riverder le stelle,	Will take you with me to see again the stars,
o se ciò negherammi empio destino,	Or if cruel fate will deny me this,
rimarrò teco in compagnia di morte!	I will remain with you in the presence of death!
Addio terra, addio cielo, e sole, addio.	Farewell earth, farewell sky, and sun, farewell.

Recitative

The recitative is accompanied by a small organ and a bass lute that realizes the harmonies. With what economy of means Monteverdi transforms the text into a grandly pathetic declamation! The vocal line is the epitome of simplicity, yet it floods the words with emotion. Notice how the

repetition of key words and phrases heightens the pathos; how the voice descends on the words "profondi abissi" (deepest abysses), and rises again on the phrase "meco trarotti a riverder le stelle" (will take you with me to see again the stars). The harmony is for the most part composed of simple triads, with dissonances used sparingly to generate tension. Chromatic intervals and an occasional wide leap project the tragic mood. Wholly Italian is the sensitivity to the beauty and affective power of the voice. Wholly Monteverdian is the poignancy of the emotion conveyed, a poignancy that music henceforth was never to forget.

Chorus

The chorus offers a majestic commentary on Eurydice's death, addressing itself to the cruelty of fate:

Ahi, caso acerbo, ahi, fat'empio e crudele,
ahi, stelle ingiuriose, ahi, cielo avaro.
Non si fidi uom mortale di ben caduco e frale,
che tosto fugge, e spesso a gran salita il precipizio è presso.

Ah, bitter chance, ah, fate wicked and cruel,
Ah, stars of ill omen, ah, heaven avaricious.
Let not mortal man trust good fortune, short-lived and frail,
Which soon disappears, for often to a bold ascent the precipice is near.

Monteverdi achieves extraordinarily rich sound based on a succession of chords moving at a stately pace. There is a sudden piano as the text reminds mortal man that Fortune is a capricious goddess. The words "che tosto fugge" (which soon disappears), in true madrigal style, bring a quickening of pace and lively imitation among the contrapuntal lines. On the final line, "a gran salita il precipizio è presso" (to a bold ascent the precipice is near), the music returns to the stately chords of the opening.

When an art form genuinely reflects the soul of a nation, its history manifests a striking unity of outlook and achievement. From Monteverdi the heritage descends through two hundred and fifty years of Italian opera to Giuseppe Verdi. In the plaint of Orfeo we hear the throb of passion, the profoundly human quality that echoes in more familiar guise through the measures of *Aïda* and *Otello*.

Zefiro torna

Monteverdi's madrigals span the transition from Renaissance to Baroque. They assimilated the techniques of the new style, such as an instrumental accompaniment with basso continuo, recitative, and the expressive melody of the newly created opera.

The poem of *Zefiro torna* (1632) is by Ottavio Rinuccini, the librettist of *Arianna*. This madrigal is not to be confused with another of the same title that Monteverdi wrote to a sonnet by Petrarch.

SIDE 3/2 (E I)

Zefiro torna e di soavi accenti
L'aer fa grato e'l piè discioglie a l'onde,
E mormorando tra le verdi fronde,
Fa danzar al bel suon su'l prato i fiori;

Inghirlandato il crin Fillide e Clori,
Note temprando amor care e gioconde;
E da monti e da valli ime e profonde,
Raddoppian l'armonia gli antri canori.

Sorge più vaga in ciel l'aurora el Sole,
Sparge più luci d'or, più puro argento,
Fregia di Teti più il bel ceruleo manto.

Sol io per selve abbandonate e sole,

The West Wind returns and with gentle accents
Makes the air pleasant and quickens one's step,
And, murmuring among the green branches,
Makes the meadow flowers dance to its lovely sound.

With garlands in their hair Phyllis and Clorinda
Are sweet and joyous while Love makes music,
And from the mountains and valleys hidden deep,
The echoing caves redouble the harmony.

At dawn the sun rises in the sky more gracefully,
Spreads abroad more golden rays, a purer silver,
Adorns the sea with an even lovelier blue mantle.

Only I am abandoned and alone in the forest,

L'ardor di due begli occhi el mio tormento,	The ardor of two beautiful eyes is my torment:
Come vuol mia ventura hor piango, hor canto.	As my fate may decree, now I weep, now I sing.

Among the works of Monteverdi's mature years, *Zefiro torna* stands out for its lightness of mood and a lyric charm inspired by the nature images in the poem. It is a duet for two tenors (or sopranos), accompanied by a viola da gamba that plays the bass line, and a harpsichord that realizes the harmonies. The bass part consists of a two-bar motive that is repeated fifty-six times in succession, and then recurs five more times toward the end. Over this basso ostinato Monteverdi releases a flow of melody that moves forward in a continuous evolution, each phrase growing inevitably out of the one before.

Basso ostinato

Since only two voices are involved, each takes on greater profile than would be the case in a madrigal for three, four, or more voices. In certain passages Monteverdi distributes the melody between the two voices, so that they seem to be sharing a single melodic line. This occurs in the opening measures:

At times the two voices imitate one another; or they harmonize, sometimes in the mellifluous thirds and sixths that were to become a staple of Italian opera. Characteristic is the repetition of important words and phrases, such as the first two words of the poem. Also the expansion of basic words across a succession of notes (melismatic setting), especially if the meaning justifies this: for example, "l' aer" (the air) in line 2, and "mormorando" (murmuring) in line 3. "Fa danzar al bel suon su'l prato" (makes the meadow flowers dance) inspires the dancelike rhythm in triple meter that pervades the piece.

Tone painting

Striking is the gradual ascent on the repeated word "note" (notes—that is, music) in line 2 of the second stanza, as if Love were slow striking up his lyre. The next line impels the master to tone painting: on "monti" (mountains), the first tenor part leaps upward, on "valli" (valleys), the second as precipitously descends. The image of echoing caves in line 4 is reflected in the alternation of loud and soft. Rather than depend on the performers for this echo effect, Monteverdi wrote the words forte and piano into the score. "Ciel" (sky) and "aurora" (dawn), in the opening line of the third stanza, are set on the highest notes of the phrase. Notice how the melodic line ascends on "Sole," to suggest the rising of the sun.

With the final stanza the personal pronoun enters the picture: "Sol io per selve abbandonate e sole" (Only I am abandoned and alone in the forest). Here the mood changes abruptly; the flowing madrigal style gives way to operatic recitative and a considerably slower tempo. The music passes from G major, which has predominated until this point, to E modal-major, whence it moves through a series of changing harmonies back to the home key. It is amazing how much dramatic power Monteverdi is able to achieve through a simple recitative supported by chords.

Recitative

The recitative continues through the first phrase of the last line: "come vuol mia ventura hor piango" (as my fate may decree, now I weep), sung in succession by the two voices in ascending sequence; the rise in pitch intensifies the emotion, as does the dissonance at the end of each phrase. On "hor canto" (now I sing) the music returns to the home key of G major and to the original meter, tempo, and mood, while the basso ostinato starts up again. This is interrupted once more, by four measures of recitative. The last reference to "piango" (I weep) impels Monteverdi to the kind of affective dissonance he customarily reserved for ideas of passion, sorrow, and death. The final passage is a brilliant fantasy on the last two words of the poem, "hor canto," which are expanded in both voices in a melisma that is altogether operatic in character. The madrigal ends with a quiet cadence in G major.

Claudio Monteverdi was one of the great pioneers in the communication of feeling through tone. He was indeed—as his contemporaries called him—a "Prophet of Music."

66

Henry Purcell

"As Poetry is the harmony of Words, so Musick is that of Notes; and as Poetry is a Rise above Prose and Oratory, so is Musick the exaltation of Poetry."

His Life and Music

Henry Purcell.

Henry Purcell (c. 1659–95) occupies a special niche in the annals of his country. He was last in the illustrious line that, stretching back to pre-Tudor times, won for England a foremost position among the musically creative nations. With his death the ascendancy came to an end. Until the rise of a native school of composers almost two hundred years later, he remained for his countrymen the symbol of an eminence they had lost.

Purcell's brief career unfolded at the court of Charles II, extending through the turbulent reign of James II into the period of William and

Mary. He held various posts as singer, organist, and composer. Purcell's works cover a wide range, from the massive contrapuntal choruses of the religious anthems and the odes in honor of his royal masters, to patriotic songs like ***Britons, Strike Home,*** which stir his countrymen even as do the patriotic speeches that ring through the histories of Shakespeare.

Yet this national artist realized that England's music must be part of the European tradition. It was his historic role to assimilate the achievements of the Continent—the dynamic instrumental style, the movement toward major-minor tonality, the recitative and aria of Italian opera, and the pointed rhythms of the French—and to acclimate these to his native land.

Purcell's odes and anthems hit off the tone of solemn ceremonial in an open-air music of great breadth and power. His instrumental music ranks with the finest achievements of the middle Baroque. His songs display the charm of his lyricism no less than his gift for setting our language. In the domain of the theater he produced, besides a quantity of music for plays, what many of his countrymen still regard as the peak of English opera.

Dido and Aeneas

Presented in 1689 "at Mr. Josias Priest's boarding-school at Chelsy by young Gentlewomen . . . to a select audience of their parents and friends," *Dido and Aeneas* achieved a level of pathos for which there was no precedent in England. A school production imposed obvious limitations, to which Purcell's genius adapted itself in extraordinary fashion. Each character is projected in a few telling strokes. The mood of each scene is established with the utmost economy. The libretto by Nahum Tate, one of the drearier poets laureate of England, provided Purcell—despite some execrable rhymes—with a serviceable framework. As in all school productions, this one had to present ample opportunities for choral singing and dancing. The opera took about an hour. Within that span Purcell created a work of incredible concentration and power. Both he and his librettist could assume that their audience was familiar with Vergil's classic. They could therefore compress the plot and suggest rather than fill in the details.

Overture

The Overture begins with a stately Lento on $\frac{4}{4}$, in C minor. There follows a bright Allegro moderato in contrapuntal style. Purcell wears his learning lightly. The interweaving lines combine in a texture so transparent that it conceals the art behind it.

Act I, Scene 1

The first scene takes place in Dido's palace. The Queen, already in love with Aeneas, cannot bring herself to acknowledge her love. Her confidante Belinda and her courtiers (the chorus) assure her that both she and Carthage will be happier if she marries Aeneas. In Belinda's opening recitative, *Shake the cloud from off your brow,* the expansion of key words such as "shake" and "flowing" is noteworthy. This style of setting text is characteristic of the Baroque. The chorus sustains the mood with *Banish sorrow, banish care, Grief should ne'er approach the fair.*

Dido's first aria, an Andante in 3/4, in C minor, wreathes the Queen in an atmosphere of noble grief: *Ah, Belinda, I am prest with torment not to be confest.* The affecting melody unfolds over a brief ground bass that is repeated over and over:

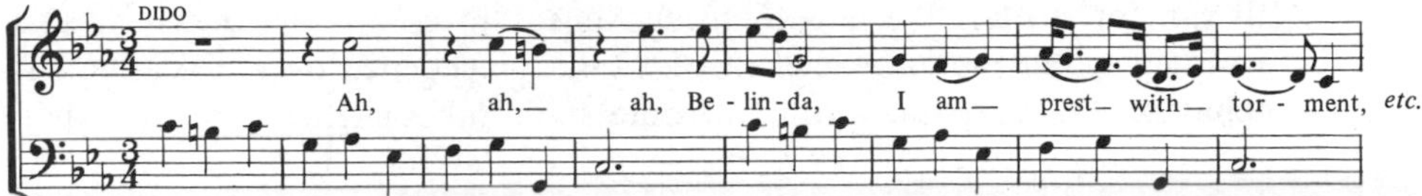

The aria reaches its emotional climax with the expansion of the word "languish," as the Queen confesses her love for Aeneas.

She then expresses pity for the warrior who fled the fall of Troy. Belinda and a lady of the court reassure the Queen in a lovely duet in C, a Vivace in triplet meter: *Fear no danger to ensue, The hero loves as well as you.* The chorus echoes their optimism.

Aeneas enters with his retinue. He declares his devotion and his companions second him: *Cupid only throws the dart that's dreadful to a warrior's heart.* Belinda encourages his suit, Dido yields, and the lovers decide to celebrate their troth with a royal hunt. The scene ends with a sprightly chorus and dance in praise of love and beauty, all this in a joyful C major.

Act I, Scene 2

Scene 2, in the cave of the Sorceress, transports us to a dark F minor, Lento. She summons her sisters in evil and outlines to them her plot to rob Dido of her happiness. The witches respond with gusto. Their *Laughing Chorus,* a Molto Allegro in 3/8, in C minor, makes it plain that Dido has plenty to fear. The Sorceress outlines her plot. One of the witches, disguised as Mercury, will remind Aeneas that the gods desire him to continue his travels and found a new Troy—Rome—on Italy's shore. In Vergil's epic this is Aeneas's manifest destiny. In Tate's less plausible version, the hero will be fooled by the Sorceress.

Two witches undertake to further the plot by conjuring up a storm that will separate Aeneas from his beloved. They outline their intent in an Allegro energico that starts out as a canon: one part repeats the melody of the other a measure later. The scene ends with a sinister chorus of the witches, *In our deep vaulted cell the charm we'll prepare.* Purcell here makes a wonderful use of echo effects. The *Echo Dance of Furies* is an Allegro vivace in 4/4, in F major. In this number musicians behind the scene echo the orchestra in the pit. The dramatic contrast of soft and loud exemplifies the terraced dynamics that were so dear to the Baroque.

Act II

Act II opens with the protagonists resting after the boar hunt in the "hills and dales" outside Carthage. Belinda and chorus set the mood in a rousing number: *So fair the game, so rich the sport, Diana's self might to these woods resort.* The mention of the goddess of the hunt reminds Dido of the sad fate of Actaeon, the great hunter whom Diana caused to be devoured by his own hounds. To entertain Aeneas, Dido's women mime the sad tale in a dance.

Aeneas barely has time to draw attention to the enormous boar he has killed when the storm breaks. Belinda's *Haste, haste to town* sounds more like eighteenth-century London than ancient Carthage. In any case, all run for shelter. We might expect Aeneas to escort the Queen at such a moment, but the exigencies of plot take precedence over a gentleman's behavior. He is separated from the others and takes shelter in a cave where a witch disguised as Mercury, messenger of the gods, reminds him of his divine mission. The faked message from Jove is clear: *Tonight thou must forsake this land, The angry god will brook no longer stay.*

Aeneas is taken in by the hoax. Can it be that the witch is only telling him what he secretly wishes to hear? Be that as it may, he realizes that he has no choice but to depart, much as he hates to hurt the Queen. His lament contains what is probably the worst rhyme in the libretto: *How can so hard a fate be took? One night enjoy'd, the next forsook!* Tate liked it so much that he used it again later on.

Act III

Act III takes place in the harbor. The scene opens with the *Sailors' Chorus and Dance,* an Allegro vivace in $\frac{3}{4}$, in B-flat major. The sailors are as British a bunch as ever set sail from Troy:

> Come away, fellow sailors, your anchors be weighing,
> Time and tide will admit no delaying;
> Take a boozy short leave of your nymphs on the shore,
> And silence their mourning with vows of returning,
> But never intending to visit them more.

The Sorceress and her hags exult: *Our plot has took, the Queen's forsook!* They laugh in triumph, and the Sorceress promises to continue her evil by stirring up another storm once Aeneas is on his way. (In this chorus Dido is referred to by her other name, Elissa.) The witches reveal their motive—sheer joy in hurting others:

> From the ruin of others our pleasures we borrow,
> Elissa bleeds tonight, and Carthage flames tomorrow . . .
> Destruction's our delight, delight our greatest sorrow.

The scene ends with a dance of witches and sailors, its heavy accents appropriate to the business in hand.

Dido's Lament
SIDE 3/3 (E I)
SIDE 12/6 (S)

With the entrance of Dido and her train the music shifts to G minor. The Queen expresses her grief to Belinda. Aeneas tries to defend himself but Dido cuts him short: *Thus on the fatal banks of Nile weeps the crocodile.* Stung by her reproaches, Aeneas offers to disobey the gods and stay. Dido will not accept his reluctant gesture. She sends him away and prepares to meet her fate in the great lament that is the culminating point of the opera: *When I am laid in earth.* This majestic threnody, scored for soprano and strings, unfolds over a ground bass that descends along the chromatic scale.

The aria builds in a continuous line to the searing high G on "Remember me"—one of those strokes of genius that, once heard, is never forgotten. In Vergil's poem the Queen mounts the funeral pyre whose flames light the way for Aeneas's ships as they sail out of the harbor. In Purcell's opera the chorus sings a final lament: *With drooping wings, ye Cupids, come, And scatter roses on her tomb.*

Purcell in this work struck the true tone of lyric drama. He might have established opera in England had he lived twenty years longer. As it was, his masterpiece had no progeny. It remained as unique a phenomenon in history as the wonderful musician whom his contemporaries called "the British Orpheus."

67

Antonio Vivaldi

"Above all, he was possessed by music." — MARC PINCHERLE

For many years interest in the Baroque centered about Bach and Handel to such an extent that other masters were neglected. None suffered more in this regard than Antonio Vivaldi (1678–1741), who has been rediscovered in the twentieth century. He was born in Venice, the son of a

Antonio Vivaldi.

violinist, was ordained in the Church in his twenties, and came to be known as "the red priest," an epithet which in that distant age referred to nothing more than the color of his hair. For the greater part of his career Vivaldi was *maestro de' concerti* at the most important of the four music schools for which Venice was famous. These were attached to charitable institutions of a religious nature that the city maintained for the upbringing of orphaned girls, and they played a vital role in the musical life of the Venetians. Much of Vivaldi's output was written for the concerts at the Conservatorio del'Ospedale della Pietà, which attracted visitors from all over Europe. As one French writer declared, "I swear that nothing is more charming than to see a young and pretty nun, dressed in white, a sprig of pomegranate blossom behind one ear, leading the orchestra and beating time with all the grace and precision imaginable." Judging by the music that Vivaldi wrote for them, the young ladies were expert performers.

In addition to his position in Venice, Vivaldi spent time in other Italian cities, especially in conjunction with his work as an opera composer, and also in Amsterdam, where many of his works were published. A story that has been widely repeated, whether true or not, has it that on one occasion when celebrating Mass, Vivaldi left the altar unattended in order to write down a musical idea that had just occurred to him. For this breach of discipline, the tribunal of the Inquisition suspended him from his duties as a priest. Vivaldi himself explained the incident much more simply, attributing his inability to celebrate Mass to his uncertain health. The end of his life is mysterious; a contemporary Venetian account states that "the Abbé Don Antonio Vivaldi, greatly esteemed for his compositions and concertos, in his day made more than fifty thousand ducats, but as a result of excessive extravagance he died poor in Vienna." He was buried in a pauper's grave, and to save expense his funeral was given "only a small peal of bells."

His music

Vivaldi was amazingly prolific, even for that prolific era. His list includes some three hundred and fifty solo concertos for diverse instruments (over two hundred and thirty of these for violin), forty double concertos, thirty ensemble concertos, and nearly sixty concertos and sinfonias for string orchestra; there are also about ninety sonatas of various kinds. Among the vocal works are oratorios, cantatas, and other church music, and forty operas (a number of them unfortunately lost). Much of this music is still unknown. Only with the publication of his complete works—a project begun in 1947 and still not finished—will it be possible fully to evaluate the achievement of this strikingly original musician.

Vivaldi was active during a period that was of crucial importance in the exploration of the new instrumental style—a style in which the instruments were liberated from their earlier bondage to vocal music. His novel use of rapid scale passages, extended arpeggios, and contrasting registers contributed decisively to the development of violin style and technique. In his love of brilliant color, Vivaldi was a true son of Venice. He also played a leading part in the history of the concerto, exploiting with vast effectiveness the contrast in sonority between large and small groups of players.

A Baroque concert at the Villa Pisani. In this painting from the School of Pietro Longhi, the string players may be seen on either side of the keyboard.

The Baroque Concerto

No less important than the principle of unity in Baroque music was that of contrast. This found expression in the concerto. As we saw, this is a form based on the opposition between two dissimilar masses of sound. (The Latin verb *concertare* means "to contend with," "to vie with." The *concertante* style is based on this principle.)

Baroque composers produced two types of concerto. That for solo instrument and an accompanying group became an important medium for experimentation in sonority and instrumental virtuosity. The violin concerto was the most important variety of solo concerto. It usually consisted of three movements, in the sequence allegro-adagio-allegro, and prepared the way for the violin concerto of the Classic and Romantic periods. The *concerto grosso*—an example of which we will consider in the chapter on Bach—was based on the opposition between a small group of instruments and a larger group.

The concerto embodied what one writer of the time called "the fire and fury of the Italian style." Of the many Italian masters of the concerto, Vivaldi was the greatest and most prolific.

The Four Seasons

Perhaps Vivaldi's best-known work is *The Four Seasons,* a suite of four violin concertos. We have spoken of the propensity for word painting that shows itself in Baroque vocal works, where the music is meant to portray the action described by the words. In *The Four Seasons,* Vivaldi applies this principle to instrumental music. Each of the concertos is accompanied by a poem, presumably written by the composer, describing the joys of that particular season. Each line of the poem is printed above a certain passage in the score; the music at that point mirrors, as graphically as possible, the action described. This of course results in a much more literal connection between words and music than that which occupied composers of program music in the nineteenth century, whose aim was to suggest rather than to depict. However, the attempt to establish a close connection between music and the sights and sounds of the external world could not but stimulate the imagination at a time when composers were exploring new areas of their art. Vivaldi finds ways to depict the pleasures of the hunt and the baying of dogs in *L'Autunno* (Autumn), or teeth chattering from the cold and people slipping on the ice in *L'Inverno* (Winter). When they fall down, the music descends; when they pick themselves up and proceed on their way, it moves upward. Yet, although the pictorial ideal influences the shape of the musical motive, once stated, the motive is treated in a purely musical way. In short, it becomes music.

La Primavera

Of the four concertos, *La Primavera* (Spring) is the least graphic; it evokes mood and atmosphere rather than specific actions. The solo violin is accompanied by an orchestra consisting of first and second violins, violas, and cellos, with the basso continuo realized on harpsichord or organ. The poem is in sonnet form; its first two quatrains are distributed throughout the first movement, an Allegro in E major.

First movement
SIDE 3/4 (E I)

"Spring is here, and the birds salute it festively with their joyous song." The piece opens with the terraced dynamics so dear to the Baroque; a three-measure phrase is played forte and immediately echoed piano. Then we hear a phrase that recurs again and again in the manner of a refrain:

Such a fixed passage is known as *ritornello,* a term related to our word return. It is played by the entire ensemble, alternating with sections assigned to the solo violin.

The first solo section, marked *Canto de Gl'Ucelli* (Song of the Birds), pits the soloist against two solo violins from the orchestra. The image of joyous bird calls takes shape in repeated staccato notes, trills, and running scales in high register. After a brief ritornello, we hear the second contrasting section. "Meanwhile the streams and springs, at the breath of gentle breezes, run their course with a sweet murmur." A murmurous figure takes over the solo part and is echoed in the orchestra. The ritornello reappears in B major.

Now the mood changes. "Thunder and lightning come to announce the season, covering the air with a black mantle." A shuddering of rapid repeated notes seizes the orchestra (thunder), answered by ascending scales (lightning). The soloist emerges with arpeggio figures in the upper register that must have sounded even more exciting to eighteenth-century ears than to ours:

This somber mood is underlined when the ritornello reappears in C-sharp minor, the relative minor of E.

The storm passes very quickly. "When things have quieted down, the little birds return to their melodious warbling." The trills and repeated notes come back in the solo part and are shared with the orchestra. The next passage for orchestra introduces material related to the opening of the movement, and brings us back to the home key of E. A florid passage for solo violin leads to the final ritornello, played with the same echo effects that attended its first appearance.

Second movement
SIDE 3/5 (E I)

The second movement is a Largo in ¾. To achieve a lighter, gentler texture, Vivaldi omits cellos and basso continuo. "On a pleasant field of flowers, the goatherd sleeps, lulled by the sweet murmur of leaves and plants, his faithful dog by his side." Vivaldi added further specifications to the score. These confirm that the droning dotted rhythm of the first and second violins represents the murmuring of the leaves. Over the bass line of the violas, which sound an eighth note followed by a quarter on the second beat of each measure, he wrote, "The dog who barks." This dog clearly has a sense of rhythm. The solo violin unfolds a melody in the noblest style, tender and melancholy; it is marked, "the goatherd sleeps." The movement is in C-sharp minor, with a brief modulation to G-sharp minor. Adagio melody is one of the glories of the Baroque. Shaped to the singing strength of the violin, this one is a masterly example:

Third movement
SIDE 3/6 (E I)

The Finale is an Allegro, marked "Rustic Dance," "To the gay sound of bagpipes, nymphs and shepherds dance in the fields resplendent with spring." Solo and first violins announce a graceful melody that moves in phrases of three rather than four measures:

Pedal points on E and B, the first and fifth steps of the E-major scale, evoke the drone bass sound of bagpipes. Then the violin embarks on a long solo in the upper register. The opening passage, which serves as a ritornello, is heard again, this time in C-sharp minor. Terraced dynamics and echo effects are in evidence throughout. There are several brief modulations, with emphasis on B major and a return to the home key of E. Now, in a vivid contrast, the ritornello shifts from E major to minor. A striking passage for the solo instrument, almost in the nature of a cadenza, unfolds over a long pedal point on B, which prepares for the final appearance of the ritornello in the home key of E.

Vivaldi's music flowered from a noble tradition. His dynamic conceptions pointed to the future. How strange that he had to wait until the middle of the twentieth century to come into his own.

68

Johann Sebastian Bach (Instrumental Music)

"The aim and final reason of all music should be nothing else but the Glory of God and the refreshment of the spirit."

Johann Sebastian Bach (1685–1750) was heir to the polyphonic art of the past. This he vitalized with the passion and humanity of his own spirit. He is the culminating figure of Baroque music and one of the titans in the history of art.

Johann Sebastian Bach.

His Life

He was born at Eisenach in Germany, of a family that had supplied musicians to the churches and town bands of the region for upwards of a century and a half. Left an orphan at the age of ten, he was raised in the town of Ohrdruf by an older brother, an organist who prepared him for the family vocation. From the first he displayed inexhaustible curiosity concerning every aspect of his art. "I had to work hard," he reported in later years, adding with considerably less accuracy, "Anyone who works as hard will get just as far."

Early years

His professional career began when he was eighteen with his appointment as organist at a church in Arnstadt. The certificate of appointment admonishes the young man to be true, faithful, and obedient to "our Noble and Most Gracious Count and Master . . . to conduct yourself in all things toward God, High Authority, and your superiors as befits an honorable servant and organist." High Authority soon had cause to reprove the new organist "for having made many curious *variationes* in the chorale and mingled many strange tones in it, and for the fact that the Congregation has been confused by it." The church elders were inquiring shortly after "by what right he recently caused a strange maiden to be invited into the choir loft and let her make music there." The maiden seems to have been his cousin Maria Barbara, whom he married in 1707.

The Weimar period

After a year at a church in Mühlhausen, Bach—at twenty-three—received his first important post: court organist and chamber musician to the Duke of Weimar. His nine years at the ducal court (1708–17) were spent in the service of a ruler whose leaning toward religious music accorded with his own. The Weimar period saw the rise of his fame as an organ virtuoso and the production of many of his most important works for that instrument.

Disappointed because the Duke had failed to advance him, Bach decided to accept an offer from the Prince of Anhalt-Cöthen. He needed his master's permission to take another post. This the irascible Duke refused to give. The musician stood up for his rights; whereupon, as the court chronicle relates, "on November 6, the former music director and court organist Bach was placed under arrest in the County Judge's place of detention for too stubbornly forcing the issue of his dismissal and finally on December 2 was freed from arrest with notice of his unfavorable discharge."

The Cöthen period

At Cöthen, Bach served a prince partial to chamber music. In his five years there (1717–23) he produced suites, concertos, sonatas for various instruments, and a wealth of clavier music; also the six concerti grossi dedicated to the Margrave of Brandenburg. The Cöthen period was saddened by the death of Maria Barbara in 1720. The composer subsequently married Anna Magdalena, a young singer in whom he found a loyal and understanding mate. Of his twenty children—seven of the first marriage and thirteen of the second—half did not survive infancy. One son died in his twenties, another was mentally deficient. Four others became leading composers of the next generation: Wilhelm Friedemann and Carl Philipp Emanuel, sons of Maria Barbara; and Anna Magdalena's sons Johann Christoph and Johann Christian.

The Leipzig years

Bach was thirty-eight when he was appointed to one of the most important posts in Germany, that of Cantor of St. Thomas's in Leipzig. The cantor taught at the choir school of that name, which trained the choristers of the city's principal churches (he was responsible for nonmusical subjects too); and served as music director, composer, choirmaster and organist of St. Thomas's Church. Several candidates were considered before him, among them the then much more famous composer Telemann, who declined the offer. As one member of the town council reported, "Since

When Bach lived there, Leipzig was an important commercial center and university town of about 25,000 inhabitants. St. Thomas's Church may be seen at the left of the picture.

the best man could not be obtained, lesser ones would have to be accepted." It was in this spirit that Leipzig received the greatest of her cantors.

Bach's twenty-seven years in Leipzig (1723–50) saw the production of stupendous works. The clue to his inner life must be sought in his music. It had no counterpart in an outwardly uneventful existence divided between the cares of a large family, the pleasures of a sober circle of friends, the chores of a busy professional life, and the endless squabbles with a host of officials of town, school, and church who never conceded that they were dealing with anything more than a competent choirmaster. The city fathers were impressed but also disquieted by the dramaticism of his religious music. Besides, like all officials they were out to save money and not averse to lopping off certain rights and fees that Bach felt belonged to him. He fought each issue doggedly, with an expenditure of time and emotion that might have gone to better things. Despite his complaints he remained in Leipzig. With the years the Council learned to put up with their obstinate cantor. After all, he was the greatest organist in Germany.

The routine of his life was enlivened by frequent professional journeys, when he was asked to test and inaugurate new organs. His last and most interesting expedition, in 1747, was to the court of Frederick the Great at Potsdam, where his son Carl Philipp Emanuel served as accompanist to the flute-playing monarch. Frederick on the memorable evening announced to his courtiers with some excitement, "Gentlemen, old Bach has arrived." He led the composer through the palace showing him the new pianos that were beginning to replace the harpsichord. Upon Bach's invitation the King gave him a theme on which he improvised one of his astonishing fugues. After his return to Leipzig he further elaborated on the royal theme, added a trio sonata, and dispatched *The Musical Offering* to "a Monarch whose greatness and power, as in all the sciences of war and peace, so especially in music everyone must admire and revere."

The prodigious labors of a lifetime took their toll; his eyesight failed. After an apoplectic stroke he was stricken with blindness. He persisted in his final task, the revising of eighteen chorale preludes for the organ. The dying master dictated to a son-in-law the last of these, *Before Thy Throne, My God, I Stand.*

His Music

The artist in Bach was driven to conquer all realms of musical thought. His position in history is that of one who consummated existing forms rather than one who originated new ones. Whatever form he touched he brought to its ultimate development. He cut across boundaries, fusing the three great national traditions of his time—German, Italian, French—into a convincing unity. His sheer mastery of the techniques of composition has never been equaled. With this went incomparable profundity of thought and feeling and the capacity to realize to the full all the possibilities inherent in a given musical situation.

Bach was the last of the great religious artists. He considered music to be "a harmonious euphony to the Glory of God." And the glory of God was the central issue of man's existence. His music issued in the first instance from the Lutheran hymn tunes known as chorales. Through these, the most learned composer of the age was united to the living current of popular melody, to become the spokesman of a faith.

Organ music

The prime medium for Bach's poetry was the organ. His imagery was rooted in its keyboard and pedals, his inspiration molded to its majestic sonorities. He created for the instrument what is still the high point of its literature. In his own lifetime he was known primarily as a virtuoso organist, only Handel being placed in his class. When complimented on his playing he would answer disarmingly, "There is nothing remarkable about it. All you have to do is hit the right notes at the right time and the instrument plays itself."

Keyboard music

In the field of keyboard music his most important work is the *Well-Tempered Clavier.* The forty-eight preludes and fugues in these two volumes (1722, 1742) have been called the pianist's Old Testament (the New, it will be recalled, being Beethoven's sonatas). In the suites for clavier the Leipzig cantor dons the grace and elegance of the French style. Two sets of six each, dating from Bach's earlier years, came to be known as the *French* and *English Suites.* Another six from the Leipzig period were named *Partitas* (1726–31). The keyboard music includes a wide variety of pieces. Among the most popular are the *Chromatic Fantasy and Fugue* (c. 1720), the *Italian Concerto* (1735), and the *Goldberg Variations* (1742; so called after a virtuoso of the time).

Of the sonatas for various instruments, a special interest attaches to the six for unaccompanied violin (c. 1720). The master creates for the four strings an intricate polyphonic structure and wrests from the instrument forms and textures of which one would never have suspected it capable. *The Brandenburg Concertos* (1721) present various instrumental combinations pitted against one another. The four *Suites for Orchestra* contain dance forms of appealing lyricism. We will discuss in detail the *Suite No. 3* and the *Brandenburg Concerto No. 2.*

Chamber and orchestral music

Cantatas

The two-hundred-odd cantatas that have come down to us form the centerpiece of Bach's religious music. They constitute a personal document of transcendent spirituality; they project his vision of life and death. The drama of the Crucifixion inspired Bach to plenary eloquence. His Passions are epics of the Protestant faith. That according to St. John (1724) depicts the final events in the life of Christ with almost violent intensity. *The Passion According to St. Matthew* (1727 or 1729) is more contemplative in tone.

B-minor Mass

The *Mass in B minor* occupied Bach for a good part of the Leipzig period. The first two movements, the Kyrie and Gloria, were written in 1733, and were dedicated to Friedrich Augustus, Elector of Saxony. The greatest of Protestant composers turned to a Catholic monarch in the hope of being named composer to the Saxon court, a title that would strengthen him in his squabbles with the Leipzig authorities. The honorary title was eventually granted. To the Kyrie and Gloria originally sent to the Elector "as an insignificant example of that knowledge which I have achieved in musique" he later added the other three movements required by Catholic usage, the Credo, Sanctus, and Agnus Dei. The dimensions of this mightiest of Masses make it unfit for liturgical use. In its mingling of Catholic and Protestant elements the work symbolically unites the two

In May, 1747, Bach visited the court of Frederick the Great in Potsdam. The Musical Offering *was one of the results of this trip*

factions of Christendom. It has found a home in the concert hall, a place of worship to whose creed all that come may subscribe.

Last works

In his final years the master, increasingly withdrawn from the world, fastened his gaze upon the innermost secrets of his art. *The Musical Offering* (1747), in which he elaborated the theme of Frederick the Great, runs the gamut of contrapuntal thinking. The work culminates in an astounding six-voice fugue. Bach's last opus, *The Art of the Fugue* (1745–50), constitutes his final summation of the processes of musical thought. There is symbolism in the fact that he did not live to finish this encyclopedic work; the ultimate question had still to remain unanswered.

The Fugue

From the art and science of counterpoint issued one of the most exciting types of Baroque music, the fugue. The name is derived from *fuga,* the Latin for "flight," implying a flight of fancy, possibly the flight of the theme from one voice to the other. A *fugue* is a contrapuntal composition in which a theme or subject of strongly marked character pervades the entire fabric, entering now in one voice, now in another. The fugue consequently is based on the principle of imitation. The subject constitutes the unifying idea, the focal point of interest in the contrapuntal web.

Fugal voices

A fugue may be written for a group of instruments; for a solo instrument such as organ, harpsichord, or even violin; for several solo voices or for full chorus. Whether the fugue is vocal or instrumental, the several lines are called voices, which indicates the origin of the type. In vocal and orchestral fugues each line is articulated by another performer or group of performers. In fugues for keyboard instruments the ten fingers—on the organ, the feet as well—manage the complex interweaving of the voices.

Subject

Answer

Countersubject

The *subject* or theme is stated alone at the outset in one of the voices—soprano, alto, tenor, or bass. It is then imitated in another voice—this is the *answer*—while the first continues with a *countersubject* or countertheme. Depending on the number of voices in the fugue, the subject will then appear in a third voice and be answered in the fourth, with the other voices usually weaving a free contrapuntal texture against these. (If a fugue is in three voices there is, naturally, no second answer, since there is no fourth voice.) When the theme has been presented in each voice once, the first section of the fugue, the Exposition, is at an end. The Exposition may be restated, in which case the voices will enter in a different order. From there on the fugue alternates between exposition sections that feature the entrance of the subject and less weighty interludes known as *episodes,* which serve as areas of relaxation.

Episodes

Key relationships

The subject of the fugue is stated in the home key, the Tonic. The answer is given in a related key, that of the Dominant, which lies five tones above the Tonic. There may be modulation to foreign keys in the course of the fugue, which builds up tension against the return home. The Baroque fugue thus embodied the contrast between home and contrasting keys that was one of the basic principles of the new major-minor system.

As the fugue unfolds there must be not only a sustaining of interest but the sense of mounting urgency that is proper to an extended art work. The composer throughout strives for continuity and a sense of organic growth. Each recurrence of the theme reveals new facets of its nature. The composer manipulates the subject as pure musical material in the same way that the sculptor molds his clay. Especially effective is the *stretto* (from the Italian *stringere,* "to tighten"), in which the theme is imitated in close succession, with the subject entering in one voice before it has been completed in another. The effect is one of voices crowding upon each other, creating a heightening of tension that brings the fugue to its climax. A frequent feature of the fugue—generally toward the end—is the *pedal point,* by which we mean one tone, usually the Dominant or Tonic, that is sustained in the bass while the harmonies change in the other parts. (The pedal point sometimes occurs in the treble register.) The final statement of the subject, generally in a decisive manner, brings the fugue to an end.

Stretto

Pedal point

The fugue is based on a single affection, or mood—the subject that dominates the piece. Episodes and transitional passages are usually woven from its motives or from those of the countersubject. There results a remarkable unity of texture and atmosphere. Another factor for unity is the unfaltering rhythmic beat (against which, however, the composer may weave a diversity of counterrhythms). The only section of the fugue that follows a set order is the Exposition. Once that is done with, the further course of the fugue is bound only by the composer's fancy. Caprice, exuberance, surprise—all receive free play within the supple framework of this form.

Fugal technique reached unsurpassable heights at the hands of Bach and Handel. In the Classic-Romantic period the fugue was somewhat neglected, although fugal writing became an integral part of the composer's technique. Passages in fugal style occur in many a symphony, quartet, and sonata, often in the Development section. Such an imitative passage inserted in a nonfugal piece is known as a *fugato.* It affords the composer the excitement of fugal writing without the responsibilities.

Fugato

The fugue, then, is a rather free form based on imitative counterpoint, that combined the composer's technical skill with imagination, feeling, and exuberant ornamentation. There resulted a type of musical art that may well be accounted one of the supreme achievements of the Baroque.

Organ Fugue in G minor

SIDE 4/1 (E I)
SIDE 14/1 (S)

The *G-minor Fugue* known as "the Little," to distinguish it from a longer fugue in the same key called "the Great," is one of the most popular of

Bach's works in this form. This organ fugue is in four voices. The subject is announced in the soprano and is answered in the alto. Next it enters in the tenor and is answered in the bass. In accordance with fugal procedure these entries alternate between the home key (G minor) and the contrasting key (D minor). The subject is a sturdy melody that begins by outlining the Tonic chord and flowers into fanciful arabesques.

The Exposition completed, an episode appears in which a striking motive is heard in imitation between alto and soprano. This motive takes on increasing significance as the fugue proceeds.

The piece is marked by compactness of structure and directness of speech. The subject, as is customary in fugues in the minor mode, is presently shifted to the major. After a climactic expansion of the material the theme makes its final appearance on the pedals, in the home key. The work ends brilliantly with a major chord.

The Suite

The *suite* consisted mainly of a series of dance movements, all in the same key. It presented an international galaxy of dance types: the German *allemande,* in duple meter at a moderate tempo; the French *courante,* in triple meter at a moderate tempo; the Spanish *sarabande,* a stately dance in triple meter; and the English *jig* (*gigue*), in a lively 6/8 or 6/4. These had begun as popular dances, but by the time of the late Baroque they had left the ballroom far behind and become abstract types of art music. Between the slow sarabande and fast gigue might be inserted a variety of optional numbers of a graceful song or dance type such as the minuet, the *gavotte,* the lively *bourrée* or *passepied.* These dances of peasant origin introduced a refreshing earthiness into their more formal surroundings. The suite sometimes also incorporated the operatic overture, as well as a variety of short pieces with attractive titles. In short, once a composer passed the formal prelude or overture he had wide choice in the organization of the suite, whether it was for solo instrument or orchestra.

The standard form of the pieces in the suite was the binary structure **(A-B)** consisting of two sections of approximately equal length, each being rounded off by a cadence. The first part, you will recall, usually moved from the home key (Tonic) to a contrasting key (Dominant), while the **B** part made the corresponding move back. Composers might have demurred, a century later, at writing a group of five, six, or seven pieces all in the same key; but at a time when major-minor tonality was still a novelty, the assertion of the home key over and over again had a reassuring effect.

The essential element of the suite was dance rhythm, with its imagery of physical movement. The form met the needs of the age for elegant entertainment music. At the same time it offered composers a wealth of popular rhythms that could be transmuted into art.

Suite No. 3 in D major

Bach wrote four orchestral suites. Two are supposed to have been written during the Cöthen period (1717–23), two more at Leipzig. The *Suite No. 3* is scored for two oboes, three trumpets, drums, first and second violins, violas, and basso continuo.

First movement

1. Overture. The stately opening, in common time, with its dotted rhythms and sweeping gesture, is in the tradition of the French overture. The oboes play along with the first violins. Trumpets, in the upper part of their range, and timpani introduce a note of grandeur that is surprising when one considers the economy of means wherewith it is produced. Bach does not attempt to blend the various instrumental colors. Quite the contrary, the different timbres are individualized throughout, the contrast serving to bring out the lines of the texture.

The massive introduction is followed by a lively fugal section that unfolds in the effortless, self-generating contrapuntal lines of which the old masters had the secret. Bach indicated the tempo with *Vite,* the French

word for "fast." The subject is compact and full of animation. Bach occasionally repeats its motives in sequence, either higher or lower. Based as it is on a "single affection," the movement displays the highest degree of organic unity. The unflagging rhythm, the forward drive of the counterpoint, and the steady building of tension show the Baroque style at its most characteristic.

There follows a return to the slower pace of the opening. Bach places a repeat sign at the end of the first section, another at the end of the movement. These are not always observed in performances of the work.

Second movement
SIDE 4/2 (E I)
SIDE 13/1 (S)

2. Air. Modeled on the operatic aria, this lyric type of movement was introduced into the suite for greater contrast. The Air from Bach's *Suite No. 3,* for strings only, won universal popularity in an arrangement for the violin by the nineteenth-century virtuoso August Wilhelmj, under the title *Air for the G String.* The seamless melody unfolds in a continuous flow,

presented by the first violins over the steady beat of the cellos. The Air is a two-part form. The first part, which is repeated, modulates from the Tonic, D major, to the Dominant, A major. The second part, twice as long as the first, leads back to D major, ending with a strong cadence. This part too is repeated.

Third movement

3. Gavotte. A sprightly dance piece in quick duple time, the Gavotte displays the terraced dynamics of the Baroque style. A phrase for the full ensemble alternates with one scored solely for oboes and strings. This movement really consists of two gavottes. Gavotte I is a two-part structure, each part being repeated; the first modulates from D major to A, the second back to D. The second part opens with an inversion of the basic

motive. Gavotte II serves as the Trio or middle section. It too consists of two sections, each of which is repeated. The terraced dynamics of the orchestration continue to present contrasting areas of light and shade. The key scheme of the Trio parallels that of the Gavotte proper: from D to A in the first part, while the second returns to the home key. Gavotte I is repeated da capo.

Fourth movement

4. Bourrée. A light-hearted dance form in duple meter and two-part structure. The same motive serves as point of departure for both sections. The first section modulates from D to A, the second returns to the home key, D.

Fifth movement
SIDE 4/3 (E I)
SIDE 13/2 (S)

5. Gigue. A sprightly dance piece to which the 6/8 time imparts a most attractive lilt. (The French gigue, it will be recalled, developed from the Irish and English jig.) The formal scheme is similar to that of the other dance numbers: a two-part structure in which each part is repeated. As has been pointed out, not all the repeat signs are likely to be observed in performance. Once again, the first part modulates from D to A major; the second part returns to D. The piece is noteworthy for Bach's use of melodic patterns in sequence.

This *Suite in D,* like its companions, shows the lighter side of Bach's genius. Its courtly gestures and ornate charm evoke a vanished world.

Brandenburg Concerto No. 2

In 1719 Bach had occasion to play before the Margrave Christian Ludwig of Brandenburg, son of the Great Elector. The prince was so impressed that he asked the composer to write some works for his orchestra. Two years later Bach sent him the six pieces that have become known as the *Brandenburg Concertos,* with a dedication in flowery French that beseeched His Royal Highness "not to judge their imperfection by the strictness of that fine and delicate taste which all the world knows You have for musical works; but rather to take into consideration the profound respect and the most humble obedience to which they are meant to bear witness." It is not known how the Margrave responded to the works that have immortalized his name.

In these pieces Bach captured the spirit of the concerto grosso, in which two groups vie with each other, one stimulating the other to sonorous flights of fancy. The second of the set, in F major, has long been a favorite, probably because of the brilliant trumpet part. The solo group—the ***concertino***—consists of trumpet, flute, oboe, and violin, all of them instruments in the high register. The accompanying group—the ***tutti***—includes first and second violins, violas, and double basses. The basso continuo is played by cello and harpsichord.

First movement
SIDE 4/4 (E I)
SIDE 15/1 (S)

The opening movement is a sturdy Allegro, bright and assertive. The broad, simple outlines of its architecture depend on well-defined areas of light and shade—the alternation of the tutti and the solo group. The virile tone of the opening derives from the disposition of the parts. Flute, oboe, and violin play the theme in unison with the first violin of the accompanying group, while the trumpet outlines the Tonic triad. The con-

trapuntal lines unfold in a continuous, seamless texture, powered by a rhythmic drive that never flags from beginning to end. The movement modulates freely from the home key of F major to the neighboring major and minor keys. When its energies have been fully expended it returns to F for a vigorous cadence.

The slow movement is an Andante in D minor, a soulful colloquy among solo violin, oboe, and flute. Each in turn enters with the theme:

Second movement
SIDE 4/5 (E I)
SIDE 15/2 (S)

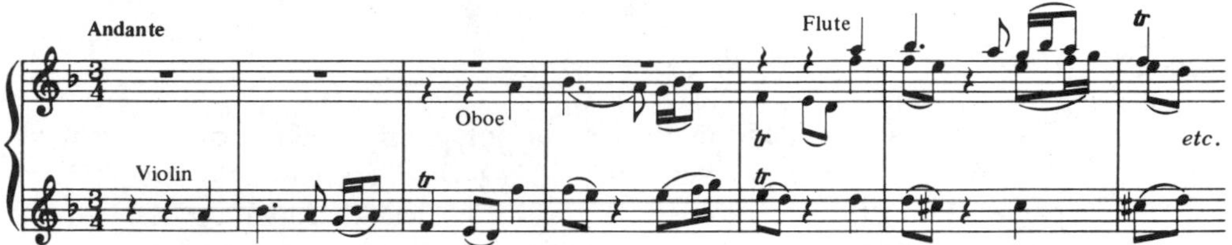

The continuo instruments articulate the affective harmonies of the accompaniment, while the solo instruments trace serenely melodious lines. This moving Andante is informed with all the noble pathos of the Baroque.

Third and last is an Allegro assai (very fast). Trumpet, oboe, violin, and flute enter in turn with the jaunty subject of a four-voiced fugue.

Third movement
SIDE 4/6 (E I)
SIDE 15/3 (S)

The contrapuntal lines are tightly drawn, with much crisscrossing of parts. The lively interchange is in the nature of a gay conversation among four equals, abetted in frothiest fashion by the members of the tutti. The movement reaches its destination with the final pronouncement of the subject by the trumpet.

69

Johann Sebastian Bach (Vocal Music)

"To God alone be the praise."

— BACH'S INSCRIPTION AT THE END OF HIS RELIGIOUS WORKS

Bach's lyricism found its purest expression in the arias distributed throughout his vocal works. These are elaborate movements with ornate vocal lines and expressive instrumental accompaniments. Many are in the da capo aria form of Italian opera, in which the contrasting middle section is followed by an exact repetition of the first part (**A-B-A**). Others follow less clear-cut patterns. The orchestral accompaniments abound in striking motives that combine contrapuntally with the vocal line to create the proper mood for the text and illustrate its meaning. In many cases the aria is conceived as a kind of duet between the voice and a solo instrument—violin, flute, oboe, or the like—so that a single instrumental color is apt to prevail throughout the piece. The aria is introduced by the recitative, which may be either secco ("dry," that is, supported by organ or harpsichord) or accompagnato (accompanied by the orchestra.)

Baroque Vocal Forms

The Baroque inherited the great vocal polyphony of the sixteenth century. At the same time composers pursued a new interest in solo song accompanied by instruments and in dramatic musical declamation. Out of the fusion of all these came two important forms—oratorio and cantata.

Oratorio

The oratorio descended from the religious play-with-music of the Counter-Reformation. It took its name from the Italian word for a place of prayer. The first oratorios were sacred operas, and were produced as opera. However, toward the middle of the seventeenth century, the oratorio shed the trappings of the stage and developed its own characteristics as a large-scale musical work for solo voices, chorus, and orchestra, based as a rule on a biblical story and imbued with religious feeling. It was performed in a church or hall without scenery, costumes, or acting. The action usually unfolded with the help of a Narrator, in a series of recitatives and arias, ensemble numbers such as duets and trios, and choruses. The role of the chorus was often emphasized. Bach's *Passions* represent a special type of the final events of Christ's life. (In the next chapter, we will study an oratorio by Handel, an equally great master of this form.)

Cantata

The *cantata* (from the Italian *cantare*, "to sing"—that is, a piece to be sung) was a work for vocalists, chorus, and instrumentalists based on a poetic narrative of a lyric or dramatic nature but shorter and more intimate in scope than an oratorio. Consisting of several movements such as recitatives, arias, and ensemble numbers, it bore the same relation to the oratorio as a one-act opera would to a full-length one.

Cantatas, however, might be based on either secular or sacred themes. In the Lutheran tradition, to which Bach belonged, the sacred cantata was an integral part of the service, related, along with the sermon and prayers that followed it, to the Gospel for the day. Every Sunday of the church year required its own cantata. With extra works for holidays and special occasions, an annual cycle came to about sixty cantatas. Bach composed four or five such cycles, from which only two hundred works have come down to us. By the time of Bach's Leipzig years, the German cantata had absorbed the recitative, aria, and duet of the opera; the pomp of the French operatic overture; and the dynamic instrumental style of the Italians. These elements were unified by the all-embracing presence of the Lutheran chorale.

The Lutheran Chorale

A *chorale* is a hymn tune, specifically one associated with German Protestantism. The chorales served as the battle hymns of the Reformation. Their sturdy contours bear the stamp of an heroic age.

An illustration from J. G. Walther's Music Dictionary *(1732) showing details of the orchestra used in a cantata performance.*

Martin Luther

As one of his reforms, Martin Luther (1483–1546) established that the congregation participate in the service. To this end, he inaugurated services in German rather than Latin, and allotted an important role to congregational singing. "I wish," he wrote, "to make German psalms for the people, that is to say sacred hymns, so that the word of God may dwell among the people also by means of song."

Luther and his aides created the first chorales. They adapted a number of tunes from Gregorian chant, others from popular sources and from secular art music. Appropriate texts and melodies were drawn, too, from Latin hymns and psalms. In the course of generations there grew up a body of religious folk song that was in the highest sense a national heritage. Originally sung in unison, these hymns soon were written in four-part harmony to be sung by the choir. The melody was put in the soprano, where all could hear it and join in singing it. In this way, the chorales greatly strengthened the trend to clear-cut melody supported by chords (homophonic texture).

In the elaborate vocal works that appeared in the Protestant church service, the chorale served as a unifying thread. When at the close of an extended work the chorale unfolded in simple four-part harmony, its granitic strength reflected the faith of a nation. One may imagine the impact upon a congregation attuned to its message. The chorale nourished centuries of German music and came to full flower in the art of Bach.

Cantata No. 80: Ein feste Burg ist unser Gott

In the cantata *Ein feste Burg ist unser Gott* (A Mighty Fortress is our God), Bach was treading on hallowed ground. Martin Luther's chorale of that name, for which the founder of Lutheranism probably composed the music as well as the words, is a centerpiece of Protestant hymnology. Based in part on an earlier work, as was not infrequently Bach's practice, the cantata was performed on the Feast of the Reformation, probably in 1724. Luther's words and melody are used in the first, second, fifth, and last movements. The rest of the text is by Bach's favorite librettist, Salomo Franck.

The chorale

Luther's chorale is a majestic melody of imposing directness; notice that, except for an occasional leap, the melody moves stepwise:

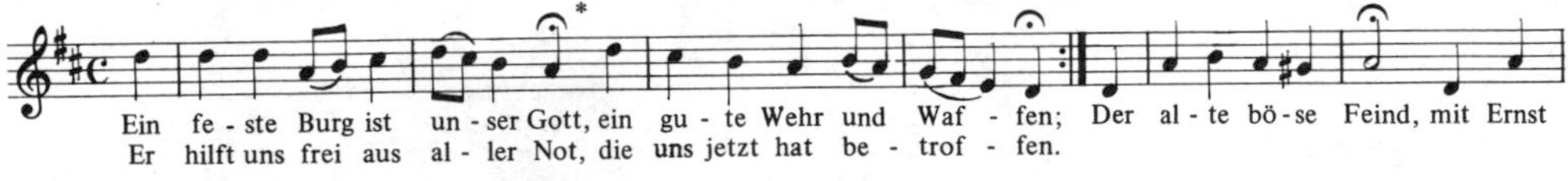

* A curve over a dot is a sign known as a *fermata* or "hold," indicating that the note under it is to be held longer than its value. Like commas in punctuation, these holds mark the ends of phrases of the chorale, and were useful in congregational singing, as they gave the laggards who fell behind a chance to catch up with the group.

First movement
SIDE 5/1 (E I)
SIDE 13/3 (S)

1. Choral fugue, D major, 4/4. 3 trumpets, timpani, 2 oboes, first and second violins, violas, and continuo (cellos, basses, organ).

Ein feste Burg ist unser Gott, ein' gute Wehr und Waffen; er hilft uns frei aus aller Not, die uns jetzt hat betroffen. Der alte böse Feind, mit Ernst er's jetzt meint, gross Macht und viel List sein grausam Rüstung ist, auf Erd' ist nicht seinsgleichen.	A mighty fortress is our God, A good defense and weapon; He helps free us from all the troubles That have now befallen us. Our ever evil foe, In earnest plots against us, With great strength and cunning He prepares his dreadful plans. Earth holds none like him.

Each stanza of Luther's poem has nine lines, his melody nine phrases (the first two phrases are repeated for lines three and four of the poem). Of course Bach took it for granted that the devout congregation of St. Thomas's knew Luther's chorale by heart, and his cantata begins with a dramatic choral expansion of it.

In this elaborate fantasia, each line of the text receives its own fugal entry—that is, the musical phrase is announced by one voice and imitated in turn by the other three. (For purposes of his musical setting, Bach treats the first two lines as a single unit, and then repeats their music exactly for the next two lines.) The opening theme, introduced by the tenors and imitated in turn by altos, sopranos, and basses, is a trenchant musical idea that immediately captures our attention. Yet if you examine it closely, you will find embedded in it the first phrase of the chorale (the notes marked **x**):

When this theme is taken up by the altos, Bach deploys against it as a countertheme the second phrase of the chorale:

As if this were not enough, Bach also treats the chorale melody as the basis of a canon between his outer instrumental parts, whose successive phrases appear at strategic points along the movement's way. The canon presents the tune in augmentation:

As Bach wrote it, the upper voice of this canon was assigned to the oboes, the lower voice to the instrumental basses; after his death, however, his son Wilhelm Friedemann, striving to enhance the pomp and splendor of the sound, added trumpets and drums to the orchestra, and assigned one of the trumpets to the upper voice of the canon. It is in this version that the cantata is usually heard today. (The various fanfares for trumpets and drums in this movement are entirely Wilhelm Friedemann's invention.)

The movement is mostly in major, but at the mention of the foe's "deadly plans" (*grausam Rüstung*), a darker color prevails; that line is set with the utmost severity, in the minor mode. With the final entry on the last line of the poem, tension mounts and flows over into a stretto; the imitating voices, as though too impatient to await their turns, enter before the preceding ones have completed their phrases. In the closing measures, double basses and organ sustain a pedal point on low D and the chorus reaches a powerful cadence on the tonic chord of D major. In this stupendous piece, Bach erects a "mighty fortress" of contrapuntal art with a technical wizardry that is nothing short of dazzling; yet the virtuosity is always subservient to dramatic expressiveness.

Second movement
SIDE 5/2 (E I)
SIDE 13/4 (S)

2. Duet for soprano and bass, D major, 4/4. Oboe, strings (first and second violins, violas) in unison, continuo.

SOPRANO

Mit unsrer Macht ist nichts getan, wir sind gar bald verloren. Es streit't für uns der rechte Mann, den Gott selbst hat erkoren. Fragst du, wer er ist? Er heisst Jesus Christ, der Herre Zebaoth, und ist kein andrer Gott, das Feld muss er behalten.	With our own strength nothing is achieved, we would soon be lost. But on our behalf strives the Mighty One, whom God himself has chosen. Ask you, who is he? He is called Jesus Christ, Lord of Hosts, And there is no other God, He must remain master of the field.

To depict Christ's struggle against the forces of evil, Bach unfolds several elements on his canvas. First is a tumultuous leaping figure set up by the strings in unison over a running bass:

There are two textual elements in this duet. The second stanza of Luther's chorale is given to the soprano in a variant of the original chorale melody. Here is how the notes of the chorale (marked by **x**) are embedded in the new version:

Against this the bass sings a florid counterpoint, to different words. His text, as though in answer to the supplications of the soprano, promises the ultimate victory of good over evil:

BASS

Alles was von Gott geboren, ist zum Siegen auserkoren, Wer bei Christi Blutpanier in der Taufe Treu' geschworen, siegt im Geiste für and für.	Everything born of God has been chosen for victory. He who holds to Christ's banner, Truly sworn in baptism, His spirit will conquer forever and ever.

The combination of the energetic repeated notes of the strings, the vigorous coloratura of the bass, and the assured stride of the great chorale makes one of Bach's most vivid musical pictures.

3. Recitative and arioso for bass in B minor and F-sharp minor, 4/4. Continuo.

Third movement
SIDE 5/3 (E I)

RECITATIVE

Erwäge doch, Kind Gottes,
die so grosse Liebe,
da Jesus sich mit seinem Blute
dir verschriebe,

womit er dich zum Kriege
wider Satan's Heer, und wider Welt
und Sünde geworben hat.
Gib nicht in deiner Seele
dem Satan und den Lastern statt!

Lass nicht dein Herz,
den Himmel Gottes auf der Erden,
zur Wüste werden,
bereue deine Schuld mit Schmerz,

Consider, child of God,
the great love
That Jesus with his sacrifice
showed you,

Whereby he enlisted you
in the fight against Satan's horde
and the sinful world.
Yield no place in your soul
to Satan and wickedness!

Do not let your heart,
God's heaven on earth,
become a wasteland,
repent of your sin with tears,

ARIOSO

dass Christi Geist
mit dir sich fest verbinde.

So that Christ's spirit
may be firmly united with you.

With this recitative, a note of pathos enters the work. The vocal line unfolds over the chromatic harmonies that in Bach's mind were associated with grief. He uses here the most unstable chords in his vocabulary. The pace of the accompaniment picks up in the arioso, based on a three-measure phrase in which stepwise movement soon gives way to wide leaps.

It is immediately repeated a step higher, and this rising sequence gives a sense of intensification. The second half of the phrase is then repeated and expressively extended. Here, concentration of thought goes hand in hand with intensity of feeling.

4. Aria for soprano in B minor, 12/8. Continuo.

Fourth movement
SIDE 5/3 (E I)

Komm in mein Herzenshaus,
Herr Jesu, mein Verlangen.
Treib Welt und Satan aus,
und lass dein Bild in mir
erneuert prangen.
Weg, schnöder Sündengraus!

Come dwell within my heart,
Lord Jesus of my desiring.
Drive out the evil of the world,
And let Thine image shine before me
in renewed splendor.
Begone, base shape of sin.

Highly congenial to the visionary in Bach was the image of the soul in rapturous communion with its Maker. Such is the "affection" behind this aria in a pastoral 12/8 meter. The serenely flowing melody, first announced in the continuo, unwinds in long graceful phrases:

Typical is the enormous expansion of the second syllable of "Verlangen" (desiring). Bach varies the otherwise similar setting of the next line by adding an upward interval at the ends of the phrases. The last sentence of the text ("Weg, schnöder Sündengraus!") is set to new material, after which the opening melody returns, and the continuo rounds the piece off with the same phrase that introduced it.

5. Chorale for unison chorus, D major, 6/8. 3 trumpets, timpani, 2 oboe d'amore, taille, strings, continuo.

Fifth movement
SIDE 5/4 (E I)
SIDE 13/5 (S)

Und wenn die Welt voll Teufel wär
und wollten uns verschlingen,
so fürchten wir uns nicht so sehr,
es soll uns doch gelingen.
Der Fürst dieser Welt,
wie saur er sich stellt,
tut er uns doch nichts,
das macht, er ist gericht't,
ein Wörtlein kann ihm fällen.

Though the world were full of devils
eager to devour us,
We need have no fear,
as we will still prevail.
The Arch-fiend of this world,
No matter how bitter his stand,
cannot harm us,
Indeed he faces judgment,
One Word from God will bring him low.

Bach called for a larger group of oboes in this number. The *oboe d'amore* is a mezzo-soprano instrument, pitched a minor third below the ordinary oboe; it has the pear-shaped bell of the English horn. The "amore" probable refers to its sound, which was sweeter than that of other oboes. It was invented around 1720 and Bach, one of the most progressive musicians of his day, introduced it into his music a few years later. The *taille* is a tenor oboe.

The orchestra creates a proper framework for the battle between the hosts of good and evil. The movement goes at a spanking allegro that intensifies the effect of the running sixteenth notes played in unison by oboes and violins, following an undulating phrase that is yet another transformation of Luther's chorale:

Against this tumult the chorale melody makes its way, not to be deflected from its path. Sung in unison by all the voices, it takes on a quality of unconquerable strength. The basic tune, adapted to 6/8 meter, sounds almost like a marching song:

The nine phrases of the chorale are spaced out with orchestral interludes between them. Since the impetuous sixteenth-note rhythm rarely lets up, the forward drive of the music never falters. (As before, the trumpets and drums were added by Bach's son.)

6. Recitative and arioso for tenor, B minor and D major, 4/4. Continuo.

Sixth movement
SIDE 5/5 (E I)

So stehe denn bei Christi
  blutgefärbter Fahne, O Seele, fest
und glaube dass dein Haupt
  dich nicht verlässt,
ja, dass sein Sieg auch dir
den Weg zu deiner Krone bahne.
	So take your stand firmly
	  By Christ's bloodstained banner, O my soul,
	And believe that God
	  will not forsake you.
	Yea, that His victory will lead you too
	On the path to salvation.

Tritt freudig an den Krieg! Wirst du nur Gottes Wort so hören als bewahren, so wird der Feind gezwungen auszufahren,	Go forth joyfully to do battle! If you but hear God's word and obey it, The Foe will be forced to yield.

ARIOSO

dein Heiland bleibt dein Heil, dein Heiland bleibt dein Hort.	Your Savior remains your salvation, Your Savior remains your refuge.

Where the first recitative had pathos, this one has confidence. Characteristic of Baroque vocal writing are the *roulades,* or groups of rapid notes decorating the vocal line, such as the one depicting joy in the exhortation, "Go forth joyfully to do battle":

The arioso, in the relative major, contains several of these, which are echoed in the final measures by the continuo.

7. Duet for alto and tenor, G major, 3/4. Oboe da caccia, violin, continuo.

Seventh movement
SIDE 5/5 (E I)

Wie selig sind doch die,
  die Gott im Munde tragen,
doch selger ist das Herz,
  das ihn im Glauben trägt.
Es bleibet unbesiegt
  und kann die Feinde schlagen
und wird zuletzt gekrönt,
  wenn es den Tod erlegt.
	How blessed are they
	  whose words praise God,
	Yet more blessed is he
	  who bears Him in his heart.
	He remains unvanquished
	  and can defeat his foes,
	And is finally crowned
	  when Death comes to fetch him.

An *oboe da caccia* was probably an alto oboe, built in the shape of a curved hunting horn (*caccia* is the Italian word for the chase or hunt), with a sound that evoked the outdoors.

We hear a canon, with the violin imitating the oboe da caccia a measure later:

The mood is pastoral, the tonality a bright G major. When the instruments have concluded their canon, the two voices enter, singing a phrase in thirds. Then they take up their own version of the canon, alto leading and tenor following a measure behind, while the instruments engage in a more florid canon—in sum, a double canon.

For the next two lines of text, Bach follows the same procedure: a canonic instrumental prelude followed by a double canon—but this time the roles are reversed (violin and tenor now leading) and the imitation is *two* measures later instead of one. The final lines are treated more vigorously, but no less intricately; near the end the tonality turns briefly to minor at the mention of death. The two instruments repeat the introduction as a postlude. Such is Bach's technical mastery that all his contrapuntal devices perfectly serve his expressive purpose.

Eighth movement
SIDE 5/6 (E I)
SIDE 13/6 (S)

8. Chorale, D major, 4/4. Full chorus and orchestra.

Das Wort, sie sollen lassen stahn	Now let the Word of God abide
und kein Dank dazu haben.	without further thought.
Er ist bei uns wohl auf dem Plan	He is firmly on our side
mit seinem Geist und Gaben.	with His spirit and strength.
Nehmen sie uns den Leib,	Though they deprive us of life,
Gut, Ehr, Kind und Weib,	Wealth, honor, child and wife,
lass fahren dahin,	we will not complain,
sie habens kein Gewinn;	It will avail them nothing
das Reich muss uns doch bleiben.	For God's kingdom must prevail.

To round off the cantata, Luther's chorale is now sung in Bach's own four-part harmonization. Each voice is doubled by instruments of the full ensemble. The great melody stands revealed in all its simplicity and grandeur.

Bach's spirit animated not only the nineteenth century but, in even more fruitful manner, the twentieth. We see him today not only as a consummate artist who brought new meanings to music, but as one of the gigantic figures of Western culture.

70

George Frideric Handel

"Milord, I should be sorry if I only entertained them. I wished to make them better."

George Frideric Handel.

If Bach represents the subjective mysticism of the late Baroque, Handel incarnates its worldly pomp. Born in the same year, the two giants of the age never met. The Cantor of Leipzig had little point of contact with a composer who from the first was cut out for an international career. Handel's natural habitat was the opera house. He was at home amid the intrigues of court life. A magnificent adventurer, he gambled for fame and fortune in a feverish struggle to impose his will upon the world, and dominated the musical life of a nation for a century after his death.

His Life

He was born in 1685 at Halle in Germany, in what was then the kingdom of Saxony, the son of a prosperous barber-surgeon who did not regard music as a suitable profession for a young man of the middle class. His father's death left him free to follow his bent. After a year at the University of Halle the ambitious youth went to Hamburg, where he gravitated to the opera house and entered the orchestra as second violinist. He soon absorbed the Italian operatic style that reigned in Hamburg. His first opera, *Almira,* was written when he was twenty and created a furor.

The early operas

Handel's thoughts turned to Italy. Only there, he felt, would he master the operatic art. He reached Rome shortly before his twenty-second birthday; the three years he spent in Italy unfolded against a splendid background peopled by music-loving princes and cardinals. His opera *Rodrigo* was produced in Florence under the patronage of Prince Ferdinand de' Medici. The libretto of his opera *Agrippina* was written by the Viceroy of Naples, Cardinal Grimani. Presented at Venice in 1709, the work sent the Italians into transports of delight. The theater resounded with cries of "Long live the dear Saxon!"

The move to London

At the age of twenty-five Handel was appointed conductor to the Elector of Hanover. He received the equivalent of fifteen hundred dollars a year at a time when Bach at Weimar was paid eighty. A visit to London in the autumn of 1710 brought him for the first time to the city that was to be his home for well-nigh fifty turbulent years. *Rinaldo,* written in a fortnight, conquered the English public with its fresh, tender melodies. A year later Handel obtained another leave and returned to London, this time for good. With the *Birthday Ode for Queen Anne* and the *Te Deum* (hymn of thanksgiving) for the Peace of Utrecht he entered upon the writing of large-scale works for great public occasions, following in the footsteps of Purcell. Anne rewarded him with a pension, whereupon nothing would make him go back to his Hanoverian master. By an unforeseen turn of events his master came to him. Anne died and the Elector ascended the throne of England as George I. The monarch was vexed with his truant composer; but he loved music more than protocol, and soon restored him to favor.

Opera in London

Handel's opportunity came with the founding in 1720 of the Royal Academy of Music. The enterprise, launched for the purpose of presenting Italian opera, was backed by a group of wealthy peers headed by the King. Handel was appointed one of the musical directors and at thirty-five found himself occupying a key position in the artistic life of England. For the next eight years he was active in producing and directing his operas as well as writing them. His crowded life passed at a far remove from the solitude we have come to associate with the creative process. He produced his works in bursts of inspiration that kept him chained to his desk for days at a time. He would turn out an opera in from two to three weeks.

Hardly less feverish was the struggle for power inseparable from a position such as his. Overbearing, obstinate when crossed, the Saxon was no mean master of the art of making enemies. His fiery temper found much to exercise it. He was at the mercy of the cliques at court, and was viewed with suspicion by the leaders of English thought, who saw in his operas a threat to native music and theater. Addison and Steele, in the pages of the *Spectator* and *Tatler,* missed no opportunity to attack his ventures. It must be said that other men of letters more justly estimated his stature. Pope in the *Dunciad* (1742) thus describes his monumental style:

> Strong in new Arms, lo! Giant HANDEL stands,
> Like bold Briareus, with a hundred hands;
> To stir, to rouze, to shake the Soul he comes,
> And Jove's own Thunders follow Mars's Drums.

Handel functioned in a theater riddled with the worst features of the star system. When the celebrated soprano Cuzzoni refused to sing an aria as he directed, Handel, a giant of a man, seized her around the waist and threatened to drop her out of a window if she would not obey. The rivalry between Cuzzoni and the great singer Faustina Bordoni culminated in a hair-pulling match on the stage, accompanied by the smashing of scenery and fist fights throughout the house. A rivalry no less fierce developed between Handel and his associate in directing the Academy, the composer Giovanni Bononcini. The supposition that genius resided in one or the other, which brought to the arena of art the psychology of the prize-ring, appealed strongly to the fashionable hangers-on of the Royal Academy. Bononcini was the protégé of the Tory Duchess of Marlborough; whereupon Handel, whose interest in British politics was—to say the least—limited, became *the* Whig composer. The feud was immortalized in a jingle that made the rounds of the coffee houses.

Handel's house on Brook Street, London. Watercolor signed "L. M." (Mr. Gerald Coke.)

Some say that Signor Bononcini
Compared to Handel is a ninny;
Whilst others say that to him Handel
Is hardly fit to hold a candle.
Strange that such difference should be
'Twixt Tweedledum and Tweedledee.

It was amid such distractions that Handel's operas—he produced forty in a period of thirty years—came into being. Some were written too hastily, in others he obviously accommodated himself to the needs of the box office; yet all bear the imprint of a genius. Despite his productivity the Royal Academy tottered to its ruin, its treasury depleted by the extravagance of the peers, its morale sapped by mismanagement and dissension. The final blow was administered in 1728 by the sensational success of John Gay's *The Beggar's Opera*. Sung in English, its tunes related to the experience of the audience, this humorous ballad opera was the answer of middle-class England to the gods and heroes of the aristocratic opera seria. Ironically, even a bit of Handel's *Rinaldo* found its way into the score.

The rise of ballad opera

Canaletto (1697–1768), **View of London,** *c. 1750.* (Crown Collections, Copyright reserved to Her Majesty the Queen.)

It should have been apparent to the composer-impresario that a new era had dawned; but, refusing to read the omens, he invested thousands in the New Royal Academy of Music. Again a succession of operas rolled from his pen, among them *Orlando Furioso* (1733), "the boldest of his works." But not even Handel's colossal powers could indefinitely sustain the pace. He was fifty-two when he crashed. "This infernal flesh," as he called it, succumbed to a paralytic stroke. Desperate and grievously ill, he acknowledged defeat and went abroad to recover his health. His enemies gloated: the giant was finished.

They underestimated his powers of recovery. He came back to resume the battle. It needed five more expensive failures to make him realize that opera seria in London was finished. At this lowest point in his fortunes there opened, by chance, the road that was to lead him from opera in Italian to oratorio in English, from ruin to immortality. Many years before, in 1720, he had written a masque entitled *Haman and Mordecai,* on a text by Pope adapted from Racine's *Esther.* He subsequently decided to bring this "sacred opera" before the public. When the Bishop of London forbade the representation of biblical characters in a theater, Handel hit upon a way out. "There will be no acting upon the Stage," he announced in the advertisement, "but the house will be fitted up in a decent manner, for the audience." In this way London heard its first Handelian oratorio.

The Handelian oratorio

He could not remain indifferent to the advantages of a type of entertainment that dispensed with costly foreign singers and lavish scenery. *Deborah* and *Athalia* had been composed in 1733. The next six years witnessed his final struggle on behalf of opera seria. Then, in 1739, there followed two of his greatest oratorios, *Saul* and *Israel in Egypt,* both composed within the space of a little over three months. Many dark moments still lay ahead. He had to find his way to a new middle-class public. That indomitable will never faltered. *Messiah, Samson, Semele,*

Joseph and His Brethren, Hercules, Belshazzar (1742–45), although they did not conquer at once, were received sufficiently well to encourage him to continue on his course. Finally, with *Judas Maccabaeus* (1746), the tide turned. The British public responded to the imagery of the Old Testament. The suppression of the last Stuart rebellion created the proper atmosphere for Handel's heroic tone. He kept largely to biblical subjects in the final group of oratorios (1748–52)—*Alexander Balus, Joshua, Susanna, Solomon, Jephtha*—an astonishing list for a man in his sixties. With these the master brought his work to a close.

Final years

There remained to face the final enemy—blindness. But even this blow did not reduce him to inactivity. Like Milton and Bach, he dictated his last works, which were mainly revisions of earlier ones. He continued to appear in public, conducting the oratorios and displaying his legendary powers on the organ.

In 1759, shortly after his seventy-fourth birthday, Handel began his usual oratorio season, conducting ten major works in little over a month to packed houses. *Messiah* closed the series. He collapsed in the theater at the end of the performance and died some days later. The nation he had served for half a century accorded him its highest honor. "Last night about Eight O'clock the remains of the late great Mr Handel were deposited at the foot of the Duke of Argyll's Monument in Westminster Abbey. . . . There was almost the greatest Concourse of People of all Ranks ever seen upon such, or indeed upon any other Occasion."

His Music

Himself sprung from the middle class, Handel made his career in the land where the middle class first came to power. A vast social change is symbolized by his turning from court opera to oratorio. In so doing he became one of the architects of the new bourgeois culture and a creator of the modern mass public.

The oratorios

The oratorios of Handel are choral dramas of overpowering vitality and grandeur. Vast murals, they are conceived in epic style. Their soaring arias and dramatic recitatives, stupendous fugues and double choruses consummate the splendor of the Baroque. With the instinct of the born leader he gauged the need of his adopted country, and created in the oratorio an art form steeped in the atmosphere of the Old Testament, ideally suited to the taste of England's middle class. In the command of Jehovah to the Chosen People to go forth and conquer the land of Canaan they recognized a clear mandate to go forth and secure the British Empire.

Handel made the chorus—the people—the center of the drama. Freed from the rapid pace imposed by stage action, he expanded to vast dimensions each scene and emotion. The chorus now touches off the action, now reflects upon it. As in Greek tragedy it serves both as protagonist and ideal spectator. The characters are drawn larger than life-size. Saul,

Joshua, Deborah, Judas Maccabaeus, Samson are archetypes of human nature; creatures of destiny, majestic in defeat as in victory.

The Handelian oratorio emerged as England's national art form soon after the master's death. The hundredth anniversary of his birth was marked by a celebration in Westminster Abbey in which over five hundred singers and players participated. This number was enlarged in subsequent Handel festivals until a chorus of three and a half thousand drowned out an orchestra of five hundred, occasioning Horace Walpole's lovely remark: "The Oratorios thrive abundantly; for my part they give me an idea of Heaven, where everybody is to sing whether they have voices or not." Handel, be it remembered, produced his oratorios with a chorus of about thirty singers and a like number of instrumentalists. To increase the size of this group more than fiftyfold meant sacrificing many subtleties of his writing. Yet his art, with its grand outlines and sweeping effects, was able to take such treatment. It was indeed "the music for a great active people," inviting mass participation even as it demanded mass listening.

Handel's rhythm has the powerful drive of the Baroque. One must hear one of his choruses to realize what momentum can be achieved with a simple 4/4 time. He leaned to diatonic harmony even as Bach's more searching idiom favored the chromatic. His melody, rich in mood and feeling, unfolds in great majestic arches. His thinking is based on massive pillars of sound—the chords—within which the voices interweave. Rooted in the world of the theater, Handel made use of tone color for atmosphere and dramatic expression. His wonderful sense of sound comes out in the pieces intended for outdoor performance, the *Water Music* and *Royal Fireworks Music*.

Other works

The operas contain some of the composer's finest measures. In recent years several of these stage works have been revived with success. Handel's big choral pieces were written to celebrate occasions of national rejoicing. Most famous are the *Coronation Anthems* for the accession of George II, one of which—*Zadok the Priest*—has helped crown every subsequent ruler of England. Among the master's vocal pieces are a variety of odes, cantatas, passion music, church music, chamber works, and songs. He also produced an impressive amount of instrumental music. Best known in this category are the twelve concerti grossi, Opus 6, which with Bach's *Brandenburg Concertos* represent the peak of Baroque orchestral music.

Giulio Cesare

Handel's opera about Julius Caesar is one of his finest. The action hinges about Cleopatra's struggle against Ptolemy, her brother and rival for the throne of Egypt, and her love affair with Caesar—a subject that was subsequently treated, in somewhat more intellectual fashion, by George Bernard Shaw. The libretto freely departs from historical fact. This does not seem to have disturbed either Handel or his listeners, but it did give

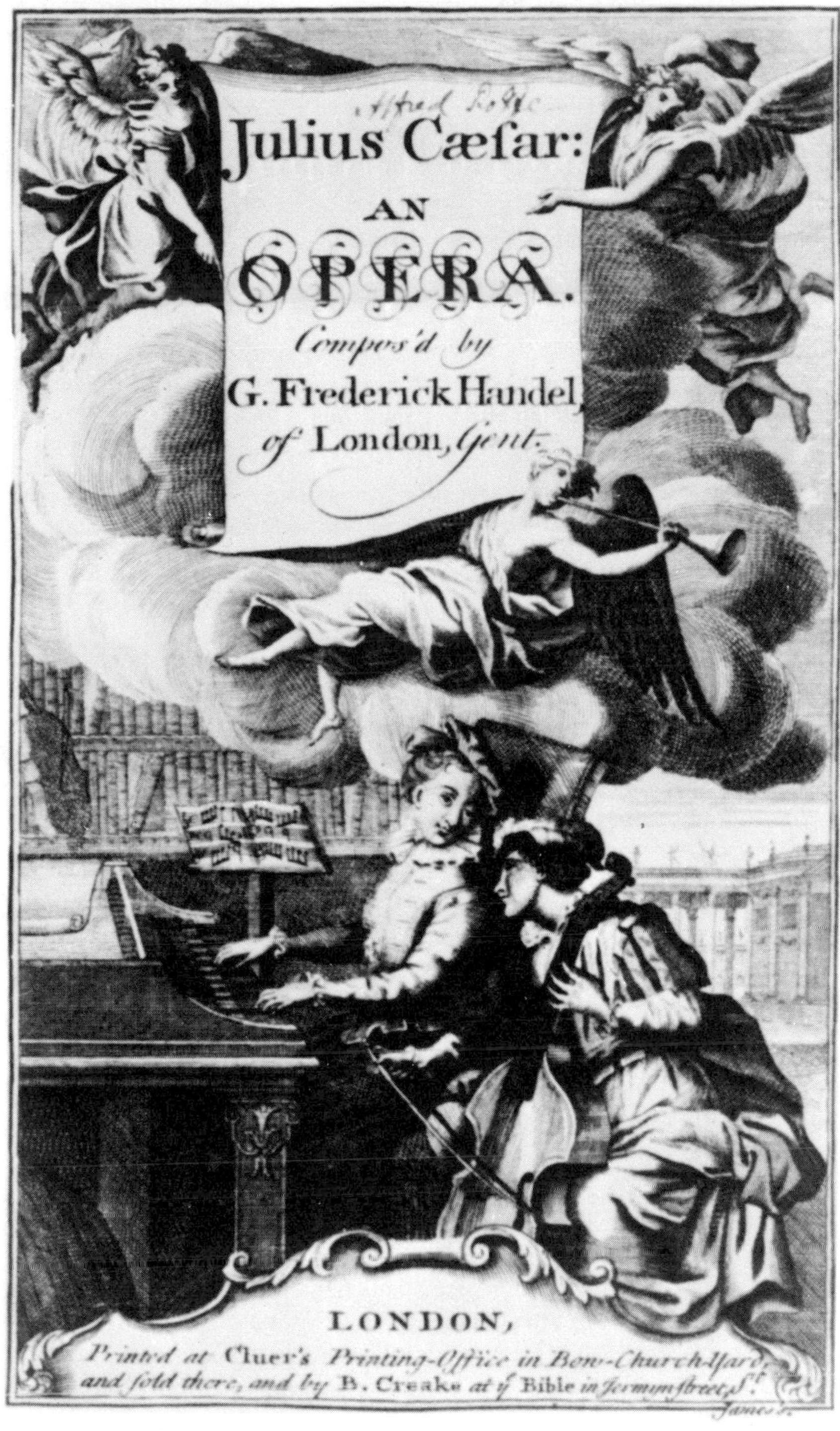
Julius Cæsar:

AN

OPERA.

Compos'd by

G. Frederick Handel,

of London, Gent.

LONDON,

Printed at Cluer's Printing-Office in Bow-Church-Yard,
and sold there, and by B. Creake at ye Bible in Jermyn street, St. James's.

The title page of Julius Caesar, *published in London in 1724.*

him the opportunities he needed for the arias, duets, and ensemble numbers that were his prime concern. Within the conventions of the Baroque lyric theater—the role of Julius Caesar, for example, was written for an alto castrato—he created characters who come alive through the music.

Presti omai

We will discuss three arias that show the scope of the work. The first is Caesar's *Presti omai* (No. 2), in which he exults as the proud conqueror of Egypt.

Presti omai l'Egizia	Let Egypt at last
le sue palme al vincitor!	Offer her palms to the victor!

This aria, today usually sung by a bass, is an Allegro in D in common time. The "basic affection" of vigor and assertiveness is established in the introduction, which is played by strings and continuo. The opening measures set up an unflagging rhythm that gives this number its momentum. The mood is reinforced by the energetic vocal solo, which begins with wide leaps:

The two lines of text are split into phrases that are repeated over and over. Structurally the aria divides into three sections. The first modulates to the key of the Dominant, A major, with a florid expansion on the word "palme," which at this brisk gait demands real virtuosity of the singer. This melisma shows Handel's fondness for the ascending sequence; he presents a motive four times in succession, each a step higher:

The second section returns to the home key, D. It begins like the first but branches off in another direction. Again there is florid expansion of "palme." The third section begins in G major but soon returns to D, again with a melisma on "palme," in the course of which the voice holds a long-sustained A while the harmonies change (pedal point). This time the word "vincitor" (victor) comes in for expansion as well. The forward drive of the music is interrupted, just before the end of the solo, by a *fermata* (a held note or silence of indeterminate length). This gives the singer an opportunity to improvise a cadenza. The introduction is repeated as a postlude and brings the number to an assertive close.

V'adoro
SIDE 4/7 (E I)

Cleopatra, intent upon conquering Caesar with her beauty, arranges in Act II to have him come to her palace. He is enchanted by her love song (No. 17).

V'adoro, pupille, saette d'amore,	I adore you, O eyes, arrows of love,
le vostre faville son grate nel sen.	Your sparks are pleasing to my heart.
Pietose vi brama il mesto mio core,	My sad heart begs for your mercy,
ch'ogn'ora vi chiama l'amato suo ben.	Never ceasing to call you its beloved.

In the hands of the masters the da capo aria was not a set form but was varied to accommodate the most diverse situations. In this case the orchestral introduction that would normally open the aria has been heard earlier as part of the "symphony" that greeted Caesar upon his arrival at the palace. Handel's orchestration creates the atmosphere for a passage of love. It includes, besides the usual oboes, bassoons, and strings, a harp, a viola da gamba, and a bass lute. Cleopatra's aria is a long-breathed Largo in F in ¾ time. Notice how Handel uses the first four notes as a recurrent motive, continually varying the first interval:

He follows this by presenting the motive in an ascending sequence; it is heard five times in a row. Such insistence on a single pattern is unusual. There is the usual repetition of text. The first two lines are presented in the opening section, which ends with a cadence in F. Cleopatra's mention of her sad heart calls for a change of mood; the middle section begins in D minor (the relative minor of F). At the end of the middle section Handel, instead of proceeding immediately with the repetition of the first part, interjects a line of recitative on the part of the enraptured Caesar: "Not even the Thunderer in heaven has a melody to rival so sweet a song!" The repetition of the **A** section gave the soprano an opportunity for embellishing the melody with trills, runs, grace notes, and similar ornaments. These were not written down by Handel but were added by the singer in accordance with the performance practice of the Baroque.

In Act III Cleopatra is taken prisoner by Ptolemy, her brother and rival for the throne. He puts her in chains. She laments her fate in a moving da capo aria, *Piangerò la sorte mia* (No. 32; in the New York City Opera recording of *Giulio Cesare*, this aria is shifted to Act I).

Piangerò

Piangerò la sorte mia,	I shall weep for my fate,
si crudele e tanto ria,	So cruel and so evil,
finchè vita in petto avrò.	As long as I have life in my breast.
Ma poi morta d'ogn'intorno	But then in death, from every side,
il tiranno e notte e giorno	My ghost shall haunt the tyrant
fatta spettro agiterò.	Both night and day.

The text falls into two stanzas, each of three lines, that give rise to the two contrasting sections of this **A-B-A** form. The first is a grandly pathetic slow movement in E with a melody of extraordinary breadth. Notice how the gently descending line in the last two measures balances the upward leaps that precede:

Flutes double the first-violin part, imparting a subtle poignance to the orchestral color. Wide leaps in the second phrase—an octave, a seventh, a ninth—add tension to the melody line. Individual words and phrases are repeated, so that the setting of the first three lines grows into a sizable section that ends with a cadence in E major.

The middle section is an Allegro in 4/4, in the relative minor of E, C-sharp minor. The abrupt change of tempo, meter, key, and mode creates an intensification of emotion. There is florid expansion on the crucial word "agiterò" (shall haunt). The section ends with a cadence in the key of the Dominant, G-sharp minor. The first section is then repeated da capo, with embellishments.

Messiah

"For the Relief of the Prisoners in the several Gaols, and for the Support of Mercer's Hospital in Stephen's-street and of the Charitable Infirmary on the Inn's Quay, on Monday the 12th of April, will be performed at the Musick Hall in Fishamble-Street, *Mr. Handel's new Grand Oratorio, called the Messiah,* in which the Gentlemen of the Choirs of both Cathedrals will assist, with some Concertos on the Organ, by Mr. Handel." In this fashion Dublin was apprised in the spring of 1742 of the launching of one of the world's most widely loved works.

The music was written down in twenty-four days, Handel working as one possessed. His servant found him, after the completion of the *Hallelujah Chorus,* with tears streaming from his eyes. "I did think I did see all Heaven before me, and the Great God Himself!" Upon finishing *Messiah,* the master went on without a pause to *Samson,* the first part of which was ready two weeks later. Truly it was an age of giants.

With its massive choruses, tuneful recitatives, and broadly flowing arias *Messiah* has come to represent the Handelian oratorio in the public mind. Actually it is not typical of the oratorios as a whole. Those are imbued with dramatic conflict, while *Messiah* is cast in a mood of lyric contemplation.

The libretto is a compilation of verses from the Bible. The first part treats of the prophecy of the coming of Christ and His birth; the second of His suffering, death, and the spread of His doctrine; and the third of the

A performance of Handel's Messiah, *1784. From a contemporary engraving.*

redemption of the world through faith. The verses are drawn from various prophets of the Old Testament, especially Isaiah, from the Psalms, the Evangelists, and Paul. Upon this assorted material the music imposes a magnificent unity. The great choruses become the pillars of an architectonic structure in which the recitatives and arias serve as areas of lesser tension.

Handel's original orchestration was extraordinarily modest and clear in texture. He wrote mainly for strings and continuo; oboes and bassoons were employed to strengthen the choral parts. Trumpets and drums were reserved for special numbers. The work was conceived, in terms of Baroque practice, for a small group of players supplemented at the climactic moments by a larger group. In the late eighteenth and nineteenth centuries, when the practice grew common of performing *Messiah* with mammoth choruses, various musicians, Mozart among them, made augmented orchestrations to balance the choral tone. Today, however, Handel's original scoring is being restored to its rightful place.

Part I
SIDE 6/1 (E I)
SIDE 14/2 (S)

The Overture—called "Sinfony" in the score—opens with a Grave (slow, solemn) section, in a somber E minor. The strings project an "affection" of intense pathos. Handel uses the stately dotted rhythm that in the preceding century had been associated with the French operatic overture of Lully:

This section is repeated and leads into a sturdy fugue in three voices, also in E minor, marked Allegro moderato and based on an incisive subject announced by the oboes and first violins:

In Baroque fashion, the brisk rhythm is maintained without a letup until the ritard (and return to the opening dotted rhythm) at the very end.

SIDE 6/2 (E I) SIDE 14/3 (S) The recitative *Comfort ye, my people* underlines the consolatory sense of the words by replacing the E minor of the overture with E major. This tenor arioso unfolds over one of those broadly flowing accompaniments of which Handel knew the secret. It is marked Larghetto e piano (larghetto is not as slow as largo) and is identified in the score as "Accompagnato." Characteristic is the majestic span of the melody. At the end, the arioso style is replaced by simple recitative for "The voice of him that crieth in the wilderness."

SIDE 6/2 (E I) SIDE 14/3 (S) There follows the aria *Ev'ry valley shall be exalted,* still in E major, which contains several examples of Baroque tone painting. First of all, the extraordinary rising expansion of the word *exalted:*

No less striking is the setting of the words "and ev'ry mountain and hill made low," with the phrase leaping to its peak on the word *mountain* and descending graphically on the word *low:*

The thought that the crooked shall be made straight and the rough places plain is vividly mirrored in the vocal line:

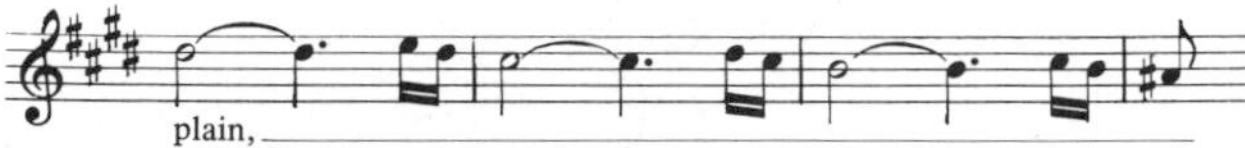

In this and later arias, at the end of the vocal part, there is usually a place for the soloist to improvise a cadenza. Handel broadens the architecture of his arias by orchestral introductions, interludes, and postludes. The music unfolds continuously from the opening figure, embodying that single affection which imparts to each number its sovereign unity of thought and expression.

SIDE 6/3 (E I)

The first chorus, *And the glory of the Lord shall be revealed,* is a vigorous Allegro in A major. The vision of divine glory fires Handel's imagination to a spacious choral fresco in which an exciting contrapuntal texture alternates with towering chords. From the opening motive and

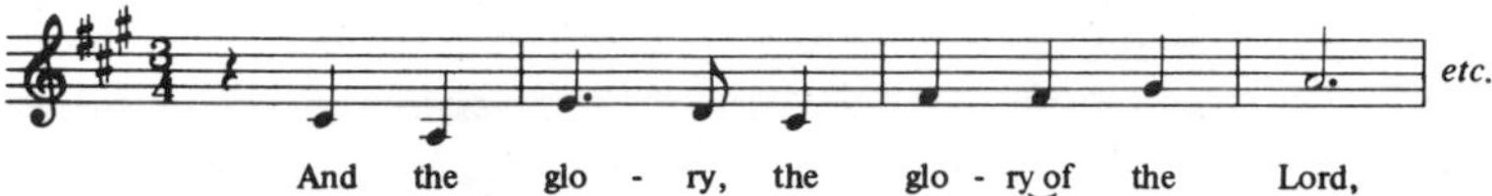

those that follow is fashioned a fabric of continuous imitation and expansion, with much repetition of text. The forward stride of the bass never slackens. Highly dramatic is the grand pause before the end.

The bright A-major sound gives way to a somber D minor in the accompanied recitative for bass, *Thus saith the Lord of Hosts: Yet once a little while, and I will shake the heav'ns and the earth.* The florid expansion on the word "shake" is worthy of note. Handel's operatic background is revealed by the expressive accompaniment with its urgent dotted rhythm and repeated chords. This leads into a bass aria, *But who may abide the day of His coming?* with a dramatic change from larghetto to prestissimo at the words "For He is like a refiner's fire." The fugal chorus in G minor, *And He shall purify the sons of Levi,* is one of four choral numbers in *Messiah* whose themes Handel drew from an earlier work. There follows a gracious group in D major. The recitative for alto, *Behold! a virgin shall conceive,* leads into the aria *O thou that tellest good tidings to Zion.* The expressive melody in flowing 6/8 meter is one of Handel's happiest inspirations. It is taken over, in subtly altered guise, by the chorus: the emotion projected at first through the individual is now experienced by mankind as a whole.

An affecting change from major to minor comes with the arioso for bass, *For behold, darkness shall cover the earth.* The idea of darkness is projected through a sinuously chromatic figure in the following aria, *The people that walked in darkness have seen a great light.* We encounter at this point a memorable example of Handel's sensitivity to key. The movement from darkness to light is marked repeatedly by a modulation from minor to major.

SIDE 6/4 (E I)
SIDE 14/4 (S)

There follows one of the highlights of the score, the chorus *For unto us a Child is born.* The theme, taken from one of the master's Italian duets, is of Handelian sturdiness.

The piece displays the unflagging rhythmic energy of the Baroque. Harmonic and contrapuntal elements are fused into a stalwart unity. There is joyously florid expansion on the word "born." Unforgettable is the pomp and glory at "Wonderful, Counselor . . ." The words peal forth in earth-shaking jubilation; yet with what economy of means the effect is achieved.

The *Pastoral Symphony* is the only orchestral number in *Messiah* outside the Overture. It is cast in the gently flowing, dotted $^{12}/_{8}$ rhythm that recurs throughout the work as a unifying thread. Generally associated with pastoral moods, this is derived from an Italian folk dance and sets the scene for the following recitatives, of which the first is *There were shepherds abiding in the field, keeping watch over the flocks by night.* Wonder and tenderness pervade this music. There follows the chorus *Glory to God* in the key of D major, where for the first time in the work Handel calls for trumpets. This number is often begun in a bright fortissimo, as befits good tidings; yet Handel intended rather a quiet beginning, for he marked the trumpets Da lontano e un poco piano (as from afar and somewhat softly). The soprano aria *Rejoice greatly, O daughter of Zion!* is a brilliant Allegro. The basic affection, an exalted joy, is established at the outset by the leaping figure in the vocal line.

A brief recitative for alto is followed by one of the most beautiful arias of the oratorio, *He shall feed His flock like a shepherd* (shared by alto and soprano), in the pastoral siciliano rhythm. An infinite quietude of spirit informs this promise of rest to the heavy-laden. The chorus *His yoke is easy* is a finely wrought fugal piece marked by lively interplay of the voices. Handel derived the subject from one of his Italian duets. A dramatic pause in the coda interrupts the expansive mood, after which the voices unite in the grandiose chords that bring the first part of *Messiah* to an end.

Part II

The tone of the second part is established by the sorrowful chorus *Behold the Lamb of God,* with its slow dotted rhythm and drooping inflection. The tragic mood continues with the da capo aria for alto, *He was despised and rejected of men.* The affective words "acquainted with grief" inspire chromatic harmony. The vocal declamation takes on dramatic intensity in the middle section, "He gave His back to the smiters," as does the agitated orchestral accompaniment. Personal grief broadens into collective expression in a grandly pathetic chorus in F minor, *Surely*

He hath borne our griefs and carried our sorrows—the first of three consecutive choruses. Plangent discords underline the thought "He was bruised for our iniquities." The tone of anguish is carried into the second chorus, *And with His stripes we are healed.* The subject of this spacious fugue is marked by the downward leap of a diminished seventh—an emotionally charged interval—on the word "stripes." The third chorus, *All we like sheep have gone astray,* completes the majestic fresco. It is marked by driving rhythm, relentless contrapuntal energy, and briskly moving harmonic masses.

Concerts today are considerably shorter than they were in the leisure-class society of Handel's time. It is customary to reduce *Messiah* in length by omitting some numbers, especially from the second and third parts. Rarely omitted is a favorite in Part II, the chorus *Lift up your heads, O ye gates!* The question "Who is the King of Glory?" elicits a reply of Handelian grandeur. Another popular number is the deeply felt soprano aria in G minor, *How beautiful are the feet of them that preach the gospel of peace,* in which we find again the 12/8 siciliano rhythm. Hardly less popular is the bass aria *Why do the nations so furiously rage together?* in which the florid expansion of the word "rage" demands some virtuoso singing.

The climax of the second part is of course the *Hallelujah Chorus.* The musical investiture of the key word is one of those strokes of genius that resound through the ages. The triumphal outburst has been compared to

SIDE 6/5 (E I)
SIDE 14/5 (S)

the finale of Beethoven's *Fifth Symphony.* The drums beat, the trumpets resound. This music sings of a victorious Lord, and His host is an army with banners.

The third part opens with *I know that my Redeemer liveth,* a serene expression of faith that is one of the great Handel arias. When on the crucial statement "For now is Christ risen from the dead" the soprano

Part III
SIDE 6/6 (E I)
SIDE 14/6 (S)

voice ascends stepwise to the climactic G sharp on "risen," there is established unassailably the idea of redemption that is the ultimate message of the work. The thought triumphs with the three final choral sections, *Worthy is the Lamb that was slain, Blessing and honor . . . ,* and the

Amen Chorus. Of the last, one need only say that it meets the supreme challenge of following the *Hallelujah Chorus* without a sense of anticlimax. With this is consummated a work as titanic in conception as in execution.

Messiah today is regarded as a religious work. It was, however, in no way intended for a church service, but was meant to be an Entertainment, as its librettist described it. That is, it was intended for the commercial concert hall by a bankrupt impresario-composer eager to recoup his losses. That so exalted a conception could take shape in such circumstances testifies to the nature of the age whence it issued—and to the stature of the master of whom Beethoven said, "He was the greatest of us all."

71

From Baroque to Classical

"The state of music is quite different from what it was . . . Taste has changed astonishingly, and accordingly the former style of music no longer seems to please our ears."
— JOHANN SEBASTIAN BACH (writing in 1730)

Baroque music developed a number of instrumental forms that we have not discussed. It may be helpful to describe briefly the most important of these.

The Sonata

The sonata was widely cultivated throughout the Baroque. It consisted of either a movement in several sections, or several movements that contrasted in tempo and texture. A distinction was drawn between the *sonata da camera* or *chamber sonata,* which was usually a suite of stylized dances intended for performance in the home, and the *sonata da chiesa* or *church sonata*. This was more serious in tone and more contrapuntal in texture. Its four movements, arranged in the sequence slow-fast-slow-fast, were supposed to make little use of dance rhythms. In practice the two types somewhat overlapped. Many church sonatas ended with one or more dancelike movements, while many chamber sonatas opened with an impressive introductory movement in the church-sonata style. (It should be noted that "sonata," to the Baroque, did not mean the highly structured, three-sectional movement it became in the Classical period.)

Types

Instrumentation

Sonatas were written for from one to six or eight instruments. The favorite combination for such works was two violins and continuo. Because of the three printed staffs in the music, such compositions came to be known as *trio sonatas*. Yet the title is misleading, because it refers to the number of parts rather than to the number of players. As we saw, the basso continuo needed two performers—a cellist (or bass viol player or bassoonist) to play the bass line, and a harpsichordist or organist to realize the harmonies indicated by the figures.

Other Instrumental Forms

Prelude

A *prelude* is a fairly short piece based on the continuous expansion of a melodic or rhythmic figure. The prelude originated in improvisation on the lute and keyboard instruments. In the late Baroque it served to introduce a group of dance pieces or a fugue. Bach's *Well-Tempered Clavier,* we saw, consists of forty-eight Preludes and Fugues.

The prelude achieved great variety and expressiveness during the Baroque. It assimilated the verve of dance rhythm, the lyricism of the aria, and the full resources of instrumental style. Since its texture was for the most part homophonic, it made an effective contrast with the contrapuntal texture of the fugue that followed it.

Toccata

The Baroque *toccata* (from the Italian *toccare,* "to touch," referring to the keys) was a composition for organ or harpsichord that exploited the resources of the keyboard in a glittering display of chords, arpeggios, and scale passages. It was free and rhapsodic in form, marked by passages in a harmonic style alternating with fugal sections. In the hands of the north German organists the toccata became a virtuoso piece of monumental proportions, either as an independent work or as companion piece to a fugue.

Chorale prelude and variations

Church organists, in announcing the chorale to be sung by the congregation, fell into the practice of embellishing the traditional melodies. In so doing they drew upon the wealth of Baroque ornamentation, harmony, and counterpoint. There grew up a magnificent body of instrumental art—*chorale prelude* and *chorale variations*—in which organ virtuosity of the highest level was imbued with the spirit of inspired improvisation.

Passacaglia

One of the most majestic forms of Baroque music is the *passacaglia,* which utilizes the principle of the ground bass. A melody is introduced alone in the bass, usually four or eight bars long, in a stately triple meter. The theme is repeated again and again, serving as the foundation for a set of continuous variations that exploit all the resources of polyphonic art. A related type is the *chaconne,* in which the variations are based not on a melody but on a succession of harmonies repeated over and over. Passacaglia and chaconne exemplify the Baroque urge toward abundant variation and embellishment of a musical idea, and that desire to make much out of a little which is the essence of the creative act.

Chaconne

Overtures, French and Italian

The operatic overture was an important type of large-scale orchestral music. The French overture (of which the overture to Handel's *Messiah* is an example) generally followed the pattern slow-fast-slow. Its middle section was in the loosely fugal style known as fugato. The *Italian overture* consisted of three sections too: fast-slow-fast. The opening section was not in fugal style; the middle section was lyrical; there followed a vivacious, dancelike finale. This pattern, expanded into three separate movements, was later adopted by the concerto grosso and the solo concerto. In addition, the operatic overture of the Baroque was one of the ancestors of the symphony.

Inventions and sinfonias

An *invention*—the word signifies an ingenious idea—is a short piece for the keyboard in contrapuntal style. The title is known to pianists from Bach's collection of fifteen inventions in two voices and a like number in three. Bach called the latter group *Sinfonias,* which shows how flexible was musical terminology in those days. His purpose in the inventions, he wrote, was "upright instruction wherein the lovers of the clavier, and especially those desirous of learning, are shown a clear way not alone to have good *inventiones* but to develop the same well."

The instrumental forms of the Baroque manifest great diversity and venturesomeness. In this they epitomize the spirit of the era that shaped their being.

A Comparison of Styles: Baroque and Classical

In comparing the Baroque and Classical styles, it becomes apparent that the Baroque favored a highly emotional type of expression. Its turbulence is at the opposite end from Classical poise. It had a far greater interest in religious music than did the Classical era. The Baroque gave equal importance to instrumental and vocal forms. During the Classical era the emphasis shifted steadily to the instrumental branch of the art.

Forms

The great instrumental types of the Classical era—solo and duo sonata, trio and quartet, symphony and concerto—traced their ancestry to the Baroque sonata, concerto and concerto grosso, suite and overture. But between the Baroque and Classical eras there interposed a momentous shift of interest from polyphonic to homophonic texture. Baroque music exploited the contrapuntal—that is, the linear-horizontal aspect of music, even as the Classical era developed the harmonic or chordal-vertical aspect. This basic difference affected every aspect of musical style.

Texture

In Baroque music, a movement was usually shaped by a single affection or mood. Thus, the chief instrumental form of the Baroque, the fugue, was based on a single theme presented within a contrapuntal texture. The Classical sonata-allegro, on the other hand, centered about two contrasting themes presented in a homophonic texture. The fugue depended on theme imitation, the sonata form on theme development. The fugue theme basically retains its identity throughout; the sonata themes undergo substantial changes as the material is developed. The fugue presents a continuous texture, while the sonata form consists of three contrasting sections—Exposition, Development, and Recapitulation. As someone has well said, the sonata is sewn together, the fugue is woven together.

Color

The Baroque concept of the "single affection" influenced instrumental color. An oboe will accompany the voice throughout an entire movement of a cantata or Mass. The Classical style, on the other hand, demanded continual changes of tone color. So too, the relentless single rhythm that dominates an entire movement of Baroque music gives way in the Classical era to more flexible patterns. Composers of the Baroque did not mix timbres as the Classical composers did. They used the different instruments to trace the lines of the counterpoint; for this reason they chose single colors that would stand out against the mass.

Improvisation vs. specificity

Improvisation was of the essence in Baroque style; the performer who realized the figured bass participated in creating the music. The Classical era, on the other hand, influenced by the spirit of rationalism, tried to give the composer total control over his material. The Classical composers wrote out all the parts, limiting improvisation to the soloist in opera and concerto. They specified what instruments were to be used in the performance of their scores, as well as the dynamic markings, whereas composers of the Baroque were inclined to leave such matters to the taste and discretion of the performer. Hence it was only in the Classical era that the orchestra was stabilized in the four sections that we know today. Music founded on the thorough-bass emphasized soprano and bass; the Classical composers aimed for a more equable distribution of the parts. Once the figured bass was eliminated, the harpsichord disappeared from the orchestra. Now the other instruments shared in the responsibility of filling in the harmonies, a circumstance that spurred the development of an orchestral style. The terraced dynamics of the Baroque resulted in even levels of soft and loud alternating in areas of light and shade. The Classical era exploited the crescendo and decrescendo, as well as the dramatic surprise inherent in explosive accents, sudden fortissimos and sudden rests.

The Baroque was a period of rhapsodic improvisation. Hence its music, in its massiveness and wealth of ornamentation, its tumultuous piling-up of sonorities and its rapturous outpouring, was far closer to the Romantic spirit than to the Classical. For this reason we are able to trace a certain parallelism in the history of art: from the visionary mysticism of the Middle Ages to the Classicism of the Renaissance; from the pathos and passion of the Baroque to the ordered beauty of late eighteenth-century Classicism; and from the Romanticism of the nineteenth century to the Neoclassicism of the twentieth.

72

Aftermath of the Baroque: The Rococo

"There are harmonies that are sad, languishing, tender, agreeable, gay, and striking. There are also certain successions of harmonies for the expression of these passions."
— JEAN-PHILIPPE RAMEAU (1722)

As famous as Louis XIV's "I am the State" is his successor's "After me, the deluge." In the reigns of the two Louis, which lasted for more than a hundred years, the old regime passed from high noon to twilight. The gilded minority at the top of the social pyramid exchanged the goal of power for that of pleasure. Art moved from the monumentality of the Baroque to the playfulness of the Rococo.

The word derives from the French *rocaille,* a shell, suggesting the decorative scroll- and shell-work characteristic of the style. The Rococo took shape as a reaction from the grandiose gesture of the Baroque. Its elegant prettiness is familiar to us from the Dresden china shepherdesses, the gilt mirrors and graceful curves of the Louis XV style. Out of the disintegrating world of the Baroque came an art of feminine allure centered about the salon and the boudoir–a miniature, ornate art aimed at the enchantment of the senses and predicated upon the attractive doctrine that the first law of life is to enjoy oneself.

Jean Antoine Watteau (1684–1721), with his dream-world of love and gallantry, was the artistic counterpart of François Couperin. **Mezzetin.** (The Metropolitan Museum of Art, Munsey Fund, 1934.)

Watteau and Couperin

The greatest painter of the French Rococo was Jean Antoine Watteau (1684–1721). To the dream-world of love and gallantry that furnished the themes for his art, Watteau brought the insights and the techniques of his Flemish heritage. His counterpart in music was François Couperin (1668–1733), who—although he spoke the language of the Rococo—was rooted in the illustrious past. He was one of a family of distinguished musicians and the greatest of the French school of clavecinists. (The harpsichord is known in France as *clavecin.*) His art crystallizes the miniature world of the Rococo and the attributes of Gallic genius—wit, refinement, pointed rhythm and scintillating ornament, clarity and precision. Its goal is the goal of his nation's music from Lully to Debussy and on down to Milhaud and Poulenc: to charm, to delight, to entertain.

Rameau

The desire to systematize all knowledge that characterized the Enlightenment made itself felt also on the musical scene. Jean-Philippe Rameau (1683–1764), the foremost French composer of the eighteenth century, tried to establish a rational foundation for the harmonic practice of his time. His theoretical works, such as the *Treatise on Harmony Reduced to Its Natural Principles* (1722), set forth concepts that furnished the point of departure for modern musical theory.

Rameau's operas have not maintained themselves on the stage. He is remembered today for his instrumental compositions. In his music for the harpsichord he achieved that union of lucid thinking and refined feeling which is the essence of French sensibility. Listening to his charming miniatures, one understands why the greatest composer of modern France, Claude Debussy, remarked: "French music aims first of all to give pleasure. Couperin, Rameau—these are true Frenchmen!"

The Gallant Style in Germany and Italy

The Rococo witnessed as profound a change in taste as has ever occurred in the history of music. In turning to a polished entertainment music, composers embraced a new ideal of beauty. The learned counterpoint of the past seemed to them heavy and overly serious. Elaborate polyphonic texture yielded to a single melody line with a simple chord accompaniment. This age desired its music above all to be simple and natural.

The change was already apparent in the lifetime of Bach. It manifests itself in the graces and "gallantries," as he called them, of his harpsichord suites. The gallant style reached its apex in Germany in the mid-eighteenth century, a period that saw the activity of Bach's four composer sons—Wilhelm Friedemann, Carl Philipp Emanuel, Johann Christoph, and Johann Christian. They and their contemporaries consummated that revolution in taste which caused Bach's music to be neglected after his death.

Italy in the eighteenth century produced an important group of composers. Among them were Giovanni Battista Sammartini (1701–75), Baldassare Galuppi (1706–85), and Giovanni Battista Pergolesi (1710–36).

A triumph of secular Rococo architecture, the **Zwinger** *(1711–22), by Mathaes Daniel Pöppelmann, aims at the enchantment of the senses.* (Dresden, Germany.)

Certain of their works combine elements of both the Baroque and the Rococo. The towering figure among them was Domenico Scarlatti.

Domenico Scarlatti: Sonata in E major, *K. 46*

His life and music

Born in the same year as Bach and Handel, Domenico Scarlatti (1685–1757) was one of the most original spirits in the history of music. He left Italy in his middle thirties to take a post at the court of Portugal. When his pupil, the Infanta of Portugal, married the heir to the Spanish throne, the composer followed her to Madrid, where he spent the last twenty-eight years of his life.

Scarlatti's genius was as subtly attuned to the harpsichord as was that of Chopin, a century later, to the piano. His art was rooted in Baroque tradition. At the same time it looked forward to the Classical style. Scarlatti's fame rests upon his over five hundred sonatas, of which only thirty were published by the composer himself under the unassuming title of *Esercizi per gravicembalo*—exercises or diversions for harpsichord. The individual pieces in the collection were labeled sonatas. The Scarlattian sonata is a one-movement binary form. The first part modulates from home to related key, the second marks the return. In many of these movements Scarlatti underlines the two key areas by contrasting themes. At the end of the second part, he presents the final section of the first part transposed from the Dominant to the Tonic. His sonatas thus bear the seed of the sonata-allegro form that was about to come into being.

Scarlatti's sonatas are written in an epigrammatic style of great vivacity. They abound in beguiling melody, piquant harmonies, and daring modulations. Characteristic are the abrupt contrasts of polyphonic and homophonic texture, and the equally arresting changes from Rococo playfulness to Baroque drama and intensity. The brilliant runs and scale passages, crossing of hands, contrasts of low and high register, double notes, repeated notes, trills, and arpeggio figures, managed with inimitable grace and ingenuity, established the composer as one of the creators of the true keyboard idiom.

SIDE 7/1 (E I)

A typical work is the *Sonata in E major* (No. 46 in Ralph Kirkpatrick's catalogue of Scarlatti's works). Marked Presto, the music is built up from pointed ideas, with symmetrical two- or four-bar phrases alternating with non-symmetrical ones. Each thought is apt to be repeated either at the same pitch or another, giving the miniature effect so characteristic of Rococo architecture. The piece proceeds meticulously from one thought to the next, avoiding extended development.

Though miniature in scale, this sonata is characteristically prodigal with its musical ideas. First there is an introductory idea that establishes the home key of E, ending in a descending arpeggio. Then another theme follows that will prove to be the most important, in the key of the dominant, B major. A capricious little tune with a syncopated snap, it is followed by figuration from the opening idea.

After a pause comes still another idea, skittish in nature, which is then repeated a step lower. Now the tune with the snap returns in minor, leading to an extended section that eventually settles in B major; notice particularly the repeated trills and wide downward skips in the left hand. The first part ends with the descending arpeggio so characteristic of this sonata, and is then repeated.

In the second part, these materials appear in several keys. Then the entire closing section of the first part returns in the home key, and this scintillating little sonata closes with the familiar arpeggio plunging downward along the tonic chord of E major. The second part, like the first, is repeated. The overall impression is one of effortless movement and charm.

Domenico Scarlatti.

In the past few decades Domenico Scarlatti has come into his own. He stands revealed as one of the great musicians of his time: an artist of boundless imagination whose fastidious taste led him to a superb sense of style.

The Changing Opera

The vast social changes taking shape in the eighteenth century were bound to be reflected in the lyric theater. Baroque opera, geared to an era of absolute monarchy, had no place in the changing scene. Increasingly its pretensions were satirized by men of letters all over Europe. The defeat of opera seria in London by *The Beggar's Opera* in 1728 had its counterpart in Paris a quarter century later. In 1752 a troupe of Italian singers presented in the French capital Pergolesi's famous comic opera *La serva padrona* (The Servant as Mistress). Immediately there ensued the "War of the Buffoons" between those who favored the traditional French court opera and those who saw in the Italian opera buffa a new realistic art. The former camp was headed by the King, Mme. de Pompadour, and the aristocracy; the latter by the Queen and the Encyclopedists—Rousseau, d'Alembert, Diderot—who hailed the comic form for its expressive melody and natural sentiment, and because it had thrown off what they regarded as the outmoded "fetters of counterpoint." In the larger sense, the "War of the Buffoons" was a contest between the rising bourgeois art and a dying aristocratic art (even if Louis XV's Queen, for personal reasons, sided against him and with the Encyclopedists).

Opera buffa

Rousseau's celebrated *Letter on French Music* was an outcome of the controversy. More important, he put theory into practice and composed an opéra-comique, *Le Devin du village* (The Village Soothsayer; 1752), to exemplify his doctrines. The versatile philosopher-humanist was a limited composer. But his little operetta, with its fresh melodies, its pastoral background, and its fund of feeling, gave impetus to the trend toward simplicity and naturalness, qualities that were to take a central place in the new middle-class art.

Opéra-comique

An anonymous eighteenth-century engraving depicting the performance of an opera buffa and showing the full orchestra just below the stage.

Gluck: Orfeo ed Euridice

His life and music

It was a German-born composer trained in Italy and writing for the imperial court in Vienna who brought lyric tragedy into harmony with the thought and feeling of a new era. Christoph Willibald Gluck (1714–87) began his work within the tradition of the Italian opera based on florid vocal virtuosity. From there he found his way to a style that met the new need for dramatic truth and expressiveness. This does not mean that, as it is commonly put—and as Gluck himself expressed it—he made the music subservient to the poetry. A great composer, no matter what he says about his aims, is the last person on earth to make music subservient to anything. What it does mean is that Gluck severely curtailed the purely musical elements that had attached themselves to opera and were thwarting its dramatic purpose. "I have striven to restrict music to its true office of serving poetry by means of expression and by following the situations of the story, without interrupting the action or stifling it with a useless superfluity of ornaments." How well he realized the esthetic needs of the new age: "Simplicity, truth, and naturalness are the great principles of beauty in all forms of art."

This conviction was embodied in three works written for the imperial theater at Vienna: *Orfeo ed Euridice* (Orpheus and Eurydice; 1762), *Alceste* (1767), *Paride ed Elena* (Paris and Helen; 1770). There followed the lyric dramas with which he conquered the Paris Opéra, the most important being the two based on Homeric legend—*Iphigénie en Aulide* (Iphigenia in Aulos; 1774) and *Iphigénie en Tauride* (Iphigenia in Tauros; 1778). In these works he sucessfully fused a number of elements: the monumental choral scenes and dances that had always been a feature of French lyric tragedy, the animated ensembles of comic opera, the verve and dynamism of the new instrumental style in Italy and Germany, and the broadly arching vocal line that was part of Europe's operatic heritage. There resulted a music drama whose dramatic truth and expressiveness profoundly affected the course of operatic history.

Christoph Willibald Gluck.

There can be no better introduction to Gluck's art than to listen, with libretto, to the complete recording of *Orfeo*. In the original version of the opera the male role was sung by a castrato. When Gluck revised the work for the Paris production he altered the role of Orpheus from contralto to tenor (a change much more in line with modern conceptions of music drama). A half century later his great admirer Hector Berlioz prepared a third version. Eager that his friend, the famous Pauline Viardot, sing Orpheus, Berlioz restored the role to the contralto register, but retained other innovations of Gluck's Paris version. It is in this version that the opera is often performed today, although it makes much more sense to have the role of Orpheus sung by a tenor.

Generations of composers—among them, as we have seen, Claudio Monteverdi—had been fascinated by the legend of Orpheus and Eurydice. Overwhelmed with grief at the death of his beloved wife, Orpheus arouses

Orfeo leading Euridice out of the nether regions. Act III in the Metropolitan Opera production of Orfeo ed Euridice. *Orfeo was sung by Marilyn Horne.* (Copyright © Beth Bergman, 1983.)

the pity of the god Amore, who permits him to descend to Hades to find his beloved and lead her back to the land of the living. The god of love imposes only one condition; Orpheus must not turn to look at her until he has recrossed the river Styx.

SIDE 7/2 (E I) In Act III Orpheus leads his wife out of the nether regions. He urges her on, eager to recross the Styx; but she, increasingly agitated by the fact that he has not looked at her, becomes convinced that he no longer loves her. Orpheus naturally cannot disclose the reason for his strange behavior. Finally, unable to bear her reproaches, he impetuously turns around, whereupon the god's decree comes to pass: she dies, and Orpheus sings *Che farò senza Euridice* (I have lost my Eurydice), a lament that became one of the famous arias of the eighteenth century. It displays the serene and mellifluous lyricism that was Gluck's finest vein:

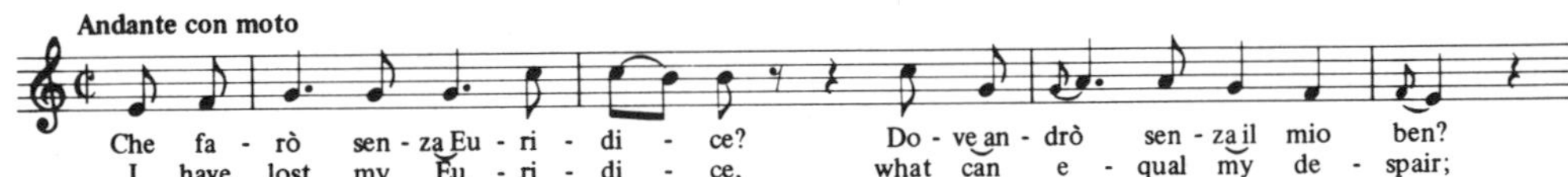

This melody, in C major, is heard three times, alternating with two episodes, the first in G, the second in C minor. It is rounded off by a brief postlude. Orpheus's outpouring of grief moves not only the audience but also the god Amore, who restores Eurydice to life and a happy ending. The opera concludes with a trio (Orpheus, Eurydice, and Amore) in praise of the power of love, and a series of dances; the final number is a stately chaconne.

Gluck issued from the miniature world of the Rococo. He rose above its shortness of breath in the most ingenious way, by combining several units into one well-rounded section. What sustains his work, besides its fund of melody, is his sense of dramatic characterization and that sure intuition for what will go in the theater which makes the true opera composer.

Pre-Classical Sonata and Symphony

The decades that comprised the aftermath of the Baroque were among the most momentous in music history. They witnessed the birth of that whole new manner of thinking which came to fruition in the Classical symphony.

At stake was nothing less than a revolution in musical syntax and structure. In the course of it composers traveled all the way from an idiom rooted in the vocal polphony of the past to the modern language of the orchestra. They gave up the elaborate contrapuntal imitation that was at the heart of the fugue. They enriched the new symphonic style with elements drawn from the operatic aria and overture, from the tunes and rhythms of opera buffa. To the charm of the gallant style they added the emotional urgency of a world in ferment. From all this was born a new thing—the idiom of the Classical sonata-symphony. The new art form was the collective achievement of several generations of musicians who were active in Italy, France, and Germany throughout the pre-Classical period (c. 1740–75).

C. P. E. Bach

One of the outstanding figures of the late Rococo was Carl Philipp Emanuel Bach (1714–88), the second son of Johann Sebastian. He deepened the emotional content of the abstract instrumental forms and played a decisive part in the creation of the modern piano idiom. His dramatic sonata style exerted a powerful influence upon Haydn, Mozart, and Beethoven. Besides more than two hundred clavier works and fifty-two clavier concertos he produced eighteen symphonies, a quantity of chamber and church music, and about two hundred and fifty songs; also a theoretical work, the *Essay on the True Art of Playing Keyboard Instruments,* which throws much light on the musical practice of the mid-eighteenth century.

A number of Carl Philipp Emanuel's works—symphonies, concertos, chamber and piano compositions—have been made available on records. They reveal his singing fluency, the freshness of his thematic material, and the poetic slow movements that endeared him to the masters of the Classical era. In ideas, in expression, and in execution this pre-Classical master rose above the limitations of gallant entertainment music. He could truthfully say, "It seems to me that it is the special province of music to move the heart."

J. C. Bach

Of major importance too was Carl Philipp Emanuel's half-brother Johann Christian Bach (1735–82), the youngest son of the great Cantor. Johann Christian at nineteen went to Italy, where he was converted to Catholicism and to the Italian ideal of suavely beautiful melody. Known as the "London Bach"—a good part of his artistic career unfolded in that city—he was a prolific composer of operas in the Italian manner and of instrumental music, symphonies, overtures, clavier pieces, and chamber music. His tender songfulness and meticulous forms are the essence of Rococo. Johann Christian's influence upon Mozart was as marked as was Carl Philipp Emanuel's upon Beethoven.

It was the historic task of the composers of the mid-eighteenth century to pilot their art through a period of vast change in all branches of life as well as in musical taste. When they had completed their work the stage was set for the emergence of the Classical school, and for the magnificent flowering of the large instrumental forms that we associate with Haydn, Mozart, and Beethoven.

PART SIX

The Twentieth Century

"The century of aeroplanes has a right to its own music. As there are no precedents, I must create anew." — CLAUDE DEBUSSY

73

Transition to a New Age

"I came into a very young world in a very old time." — ERIK SATIE

It became apparent toward the end of the nineteenth century that the Romantic impulse had exhausted itself. The grand style had run its course, to end in the overblown gestures that mark the decline of a tradition. The composers born in the 1860s and '70s, who reached artistic maturity in the final years of the century, could not but feel, as did Satie, that they had come into the world in a "very old time." It was their historic task to bridge the gap between a dying Romanticism and the twentieth century.

The post-Romantic era, overlapping the Romantic period, extended from around 1890 to 1910. This generation of composers included radicals, conservatives, and those in between. Some continued in the traditional path; others struck out in new directions; still others tried to steer a middle course between the old and the new. During these years the national

The Romantic tradition persisted in the work of many artists at the turn of the century. Arnold Böcklin (1827–1901), **The Isle of the Dead.** (The Metropolitan Museum of Art, Reisinger Fund, 1926.)

schools–French, Russian, Bohemian–that had ended the supremacy of German musical culture continued to flourish. This development came to a head with the First World War, when Germany and Austria were cut off from the rest of Europe. In the post-Romantic period several newcomers appeared on the musical horizon. Besides Finland these included England, Spain, and the United States. And there emerged the movement that more than any other ushered in the twentieth century–Impressionism.

We discussed three members of this generation—Puccini, Strauss, and Rachmaninoff—in the section on Romanticism, because their careers were rooted in the nineteenth-century tradition. Yet some of their later works, such as Strauss's *Salome* and Puccini's *Turandot,* unquestionably belong to the new age. In any case, the decades that framed the turn of the nineteenth century are of paramount interest to music lovers. They not only brought the art from the twilight of one epoch to the dawn of another, but also contained the seeds of much that is important to us today.

74

Gustav Mahler

Gustav Mahler in 1907.

"To write a symphony is, for me, to construct a world."

One of the striking phenomena of the mid-century musical scene has been the upsurge of Gustav Mahler's popularity. For whatever reason, his troubled spirit seems to reach our musical public in a most persuasive way. "My time will come," he used to say. It has.

His Life

Gustav Mahler (1860–1911) was born and raised in Bohemia. His father, owner of a small distillery, was not slow in recognizing the boy's talent. Piano lessons began when Gustav was six. He was sent to Vienna and entered the Conservatory at fifteen, the University three years later. His professional career began modestly enough: at the age of twenty, he was engaged to conduct operettas at a third-rate summer theater. A dynamic conductor who found his natural habitat in the opera house, Mahler soon achieved a reputation that brought him ever more important posts, until at twenty-eight he was director of the Royal Opera at Budapest. From Budapest Mahler went to Hamburg. Then, at thirty-seven, he was offered the most important musical position in the Austrian Empire–the directorship, with absolute powers, of the Vienna Opera. His ten years there

(1897–1907) made history. He brought to his duties a fiery temperament, unwavering devotion to ideals, and the inflexible will of the zealot. When he took over, Massenet was the chief drawing card. By the time his rule ended he had taught a frivolous public to revere Mozart, Beethoven, and Gluck, and made them listen to uncut versions of Wagner's operas.

Conversion to Catholicism

Shortly before he was appointed to Vienna, Mahler became a convert to Catholicism. This step was motivated in the first instance by the desire to smooth his way in a city where anti-Semitism was rampant. Beyond that, Mahler belonged to a generation of Jewish intellectuals who had lost identification with their religious heritage and who sought roots in the Austro-German culture of which they felt themselves to be a part. His was the inquiring intellect of the perpetual doubter; yet he yearned for the ecstasy of faith and the wholeness of soul that came with certainty. "I am thrice homeless," he remarked. "As a Bohemian born in Austria. As an Austrian among Germans. And as a Jew throughout the world."

"Humanly I make every concession, artistically–none!" Such intransigence was bound to create powerful enemies. Mahler's final years in Vienna were embittered by the intrigues against him, which flourished despite the fact that he had transformed the Imperial Opera into the premier lyric theatre of Europe. The death of a little daughter left him grief-stricken. A second disaster followed soon after: he was found to have a heart ailment. When he finally was forced to resign his post, the blow was not unexpected. Mahler, now almost forty-eight (he had only three more years to live), accepted an engagement at New York's Metropolitan Opera. He hoped to earn enough to be able to retire at fifty, so that he finally might compose with the peace of mind that had never been granted him. His three years in New York were not free of the storms that his tempestuous personality inevitably provoked. In 1909 he assumed direction of the New York Philharmonic Orchestra. When the ladies of the Board made it plain to Alma Mahler that her husband had flouted their wishes, she expostulated, "But in Vienna the Emperor himself did not dare to interfere!"

New York Philharmonic

In the middle of a taxing concert season with the Philharmonic he fell ill with a streptococcus infection. It was decided to bring him to Paris, where a new serum treatment had been developed. Arrived in Paris, he took a turn for the worse. Thus he set forth on his last journey, back to the scene of his greatest triumphs–the enchanting, exasperating Vienna he both loved and detested. On his deathbed he conducted with one finger on the quilt, uttering a single word: "Mozart. . . ."

He was buried, as he had requested, beside his daughter in a cemetery outside Vienna. At last that unquiet heart was at rest.

His Music

"The act of creation in me is so closely bound up with all my experience that when my mind and spirit are at rest I can compose nothing." In this identification of art with personal emotion Mahler was entirely the Romantic. Music for him was vision, intoxication, fulfillment: "a mysterious language from beyond." The sounds were symbols of states of mind and soul. "What is best in music," he observed, "is not to be found in the notes." In his notes resound the great themes of an age that was drawing to its close: nature, poetry, and folklore, love of man and faith in God, the sorrow of human destiny and the loneliness of death.

Vocal music

The spirit of song permeates Mahler's art. He followed Schubert and Schumann in cultivating the song cycle. *Lieder eines fahrenden Gesellen* (Songs of a Wayfarer), composed in 1883, is a set of four songs suffused with Schubertian longing. Mahler wrote the texts himself, roused by an image that appealed strongly to his imagination: the rejected lover wandering alone over the face of the earth. His next cycle was inspired by a famous collection of German folk poetry, *Des Knaben Wunderhorn* (The Youth's Magic Horn; 1888). The moving *Kindertotenlieder* (Songs on the Death of Children; 1902) is a cycle for voice and orchestra to the grief-laden poems of Rückert. The peak of his achievement in this direction is, of course, the cycle of six songs with orchestra that make up *Das Lied von der Erde* (The Song of the Earth; 1908).

Symphonies

Mahler was the last in the illustrious line of Viennese symphonists that extended from Haydn, Mozart, Beethoven, and Schubert to Bruckner and Brahms. His tone imagery was permeated by the jovial spirit of Austrian popular song and dance. His nine symphonies abound in lyricism, with melodies long of line and richly expressive harmonies. (The *Tenth Symphony* was left unfinished at his death, but recently has been edited and made available for performance.) In his sense of color Mahler ranks with the great masters of the art of orchestration. He contrasts solo instruments in the manner of chamber music, achieving his color effects through clarity of line rather than massed sonorities. It was in the matter of texture that Mahler made his most important contribution to contemporary technique. Basing his orchestral style on counterpoint, he caused two or more melodies to unfold simultaneously, each setting off the other. Mahler never abandoned the principle of tonality; he needed the key as a framework for his vast design.

Symphony No. 4

First movement

The *Fourth Symphony,* completed in 1900, is one of Mahler's least problematical works. The mood of the first movement is one of heartwarming lyricism; its melodies have about them a folklike simplicity. An introduction of three measures is marked Bedächtig, Nicht eilen (moderato, unhurried). It presents a jingling theme adorned with grace notes, as of sleighbells, which recurs as a unifying element both in this and the last movement:

The movement proper is marked Recht gemächlich (comfortable, easy-going). Its principal theme, marked grazioso (graceful), is a songful idea of great charm, presented by the first violins against a pizzicato background, and contains several motives (under the brackets) that will figure actively in the development of the movement:

The lower strings—violas, cellos, double basses—answer with a related idea that is continued by the horns. Notice that the dotted rhythm in the preceding example (measure 3) is now expanded:

Notice also the sixteenth-note triplets followed by three eighths in measure 3, a rhythm that will recur throughout the movement.

This theme group establishes the home key of G major. A vigorous transition leads into the key of the Dominant, D major, which is represented by two melodies in Mahler's most expansive mood. The first, presented by the cellos, must—as Mahler put it—be sung broadly:

The second, too, is introduced by the cellos:

This tune is rounded off by a gesture of Mahlerian impishness:

Before closing his Exposition, Mahler returns to the sleighbells of the opening, and restates the principal theme in the home key—thus, an element of rondo procedure in a sonata-allegro form. The Exposition ends with a beautiful codetta.

The Development opens with another return of the sleighbells, and an imaginative use of the triplet rhythm to which we have alluded. The richness of Mahler's developmental process may be gauged from the variety of forms assumed by his principal theme:

1. Expansion through repetition and sequence:

2. Melody altered through change of intervals, and with dotted figure descending instead of ascending. Notice the change of key:

3. Intensification by use of ascending sequence at climax of phrase:

Also worthy of note, in this intricately textured Development, is the introduction of new elements, such as the following childlike melody in the high register of the flutes, which will take on importance in the final movement:

The Recapitulation is introduced very subtly, without the sleighbells. The two lyric themes are transposed to the Tonic, and Mahler invests the coda with a quality of leave taking that is highly characteristic of his expressive vocabulary.

Second movement

Second is the Scherzo, which Mahler described as "mystical, bewildering, and weird." Here, he wrote in a sketchbook, "Death plays the music." The figure of Death as a fiddler has haunted the imagination of Europe's artists since the Middle Ages. Mahler in this movement heightens the fantastic element by writing a solo for a violin tuned a full step higher than usual, giving it a shriller, tauter sound, and directs that the instrument be played "like a street fiddle" (as opposed to the more elegant violin). The movement, in C minor, is marked to be played "At a comfortable pace; unhurried." Its main theme is a kind of bizarre waltz whose spectral quality is not without an element of parody:

The idea returns again and again, in alternation with contrasting themes in the major of a lighter, more relaxed quality. This is a long movement that follows the pattern scherzo-trio-scherzo-trio-scherzo-coda. It ends in C major.

Third movement

Third is the slow movement, a lyric meditation descended from the serene andantes of Schubert. Marked Poco adagio and Ruhevoll (tranquil), it unfolds in broadly spun arcs of melody. Like the slow movement of Beethoven's *Fifth,* it is cast in the form of a set of variations on two themes. The first, marked espressivo molto cantabile, is played by the cellos: a melody in G major that rises gently above the pizzicato tread of the basses.

Its simplicity leaves room for the variations to come. The second, in E minor, is darker and more intense; Mahler thought of it as klagend (mournful, weeping). It is introduced by the oboe:

The continuation of this theme in the first violins becomes a structural element of great importance in the course of the movement, for it contains within itself the tension of which climaxes are made:

In form this movement is an **A-B-A-B-A-coda,** but instead of repetition we have continual variation, by means of which Mahler alters the character and emotional content of his two themes, building always on the major-minor contrast between them. The main theme runs the gamut from gentle lyricism to impassioned proclamation. The coda contains a fleeting reference to a theme in the first movement and floats into the upper register, serving to prepare the listener for the celestial visions of the fourth movement.

Fourth movement
SIDE 8/3 (E II)
SIDE 15/4 (S)

Like many sophisticated, complex natures, Mahler longed for the innocence and trust of childhood. Something of this he found in the folk poems of *Des Knaben Wunderhorn,* which furnished texts for his songs throughout his career. From this *Youth's Magic Horn* came the poem that inspired the final movement of the *Fourth Symphony,* a child's view of Heaven that he transformed into an enchanting song for soprano and orchestra. The anonymous poet depicts the joys of the celestial abode in artless terms. There is much dancing and singing, encouraged by an endless supply of fresh fruit, vegetables, free wine, and bread baked by the angels. St. John furnishes the lamb, St. Luke slaughters the ox, St. Peter catches fish, St. Martha does the cooking while St. Cecilia and her band make music to which none on earth can compare. The opening clarinet melody recalls the flute theme from the first movement's Development, and the sleighbell motive recurs as a refrain between the stanzas. The opening phrase of the vocal part sets the tone of childlike innocence:

The mood is sustained until the end, when the English horn plays in longer notes the jingling grace-note figure, now becalmed, with which the work began.

Mahler engaged in a gigantic effort to breathe vitality into the Romantic world of thought and feeling that was in process of disintegration. This circumstance imparts to his music its fevered unrest, his nostalgia. His intensely personal vision of life and art has made him one of the major prophets of the twentieth century.

75

Impressionism

For we desire above all—nuance,
Not color but half-shades!
Ah! nuance alone unites
Dream with dream and flute with horn.
— PAUL VERLAINE

The Impressionist Painters

In 1867 Claude Monet, rebuffed by the academic salons, exhibited under less conventional auspices a painting called *Impression: Sun Rising.* Before long "impressionism" had become a term of derision to describe the hazy, luminous paintings of this artist (1840–1926) and his school. A distinctly Parisian style, Impressionism counted among its exponents Camille Pissarro (1830–1903), Edouard Manet (1832–83), Edgar Degas (1834–1917), and Auguste Renoir (1841–1919). Discarding those elements of the Romantic tradition that had hardened into academic formulas, they strove to retain on canvas the freshness of their first impressions. They took painting out of the studio into the open air. What fascinated them was the continuous change in the appearance of things. They painted water lilies, a haystack, or clouds again and again at different hours of the day. Instead of mixing their pigments on the palette they

The Impressionists took painting out of the studio into the open air; their subject was light. Claude Monet (1840–1926), **Impression: Sun Rising** (Giraudon/Art Resource.)

Turning from the grandiose subjects of Romanticism, the Impressionists derived their themes from everyday life. Pierre Auguste Renoir (1841–1919), **A Young Girl with Daisies.** (The Metropolitan Museum of Art, Mr. and Mrs. Henry Ittleson, Jr., Fund, 1959.)

juxtaposed brush-strokes of pure color on the canvas, leaving it to the eye of the beholder to do the mixing. An iridescent sheen bathes their painting. Outlines shimmer and melt in a luminous haze.

The Impressionists abandoned the grandiose subjects of Romanticism. The hero of their painting is not man but light. Not for them the pathos, the drama-packed themes that had inspired centuries of European art. They preferred "unimportant" material: still life, dancing girls, nudes; everyday scenes of middle-class life, picnics, boating and café scenes; nature in all her aspects, Paris in all her moods. Ridiculed at first—"Whoever saw grass that's pink and yellow and blue?"—they ended by imposing their vision upon the age.

The Symbolist Poets

A parallel revolt against traditional modes of expression took place in poetry under the leadership of the Symbolists, who strove for direct poetic experience unspoiled by intellectual elements. They sought to suggest rather than describe, to present the symbol rather than state the thing. Symbolism as a literary movement came to the fore in the work of Charles Baudelaire (1821–67), Stéphane Mallarmé (1842–98), Paul Verlaine (1844–96), and Arthur Rimbaud (1854–91). These poets were strongly influenced by Edgar Allan Poe (1809–49), whose writings were introduced into France by his admirer Baudelaire. They used a word for its color and its music rather than its proper meaning, evoking poetic images "that sooner or later would be accessible to all the senses."

The Symbolists experimented in free verse forms that opened new territories to their art. They achieved in language an indefiniteness that had hitherto been the privilege of music alone. Characteristic was Verlaine's pronouncement: "Music above all!" Like the Impressionist painters, the Symbolists discarded the grand pathos of Romanticism; they glorified the tenuous, the intimate, the subtle. They expressed the moral lassitude of their time, its longing for enchantment of the senses, its need for escape.

The essentially musical approach of the Symbolists was not lost upon the musicians. According to the composer Paul Dukas, it was the writers, not the musicians, who exerted the strongest influence on Debussy.

Impressionism in Music

When young Debussy submitted to the authorities of the Conservatory his cantata *The Blessed Damozel* they stated in their report: "It is much to be desired that he beware of this vague impressionism which is one of the most dangerous enemies of artistic truth." Therewith was transferred to the domain of music a term that was already firmly established in art criticism. Debussy himself never liked the word and expressed himself acidly concerning "what some idiots call impressionism, a term that is altogether misused, especially by the critics." But the label stuck, for it seemed to describe what most people felt about his music.

Impressionism came to the fore at a crucial moment in the history of European music. The major-minor system had served the art since the seventeenth century. Composers were beginning to feel that its possibilities had been exhausted. Debussy's highly individual tone sense was attracted to other scales, such as the Medieval modes that impart an archaic flavor to his music. Debussy emphasized the primary intervals–

Music and ballet furnished Edgar Degas (1834–1917) with many themes, as in this painting, **The Rehearsal Room.** (The Metropolitan Museum of Art, Bequest of Mrs. H. O. Havemeyer, 1929. The H. O. Havemeyer Collection.)

octaves, fourths, and fifths–which he used in parallel motion. Notice the strong resemblance between the opening measures of *La Cathédrale engloutie* (The Sunken Cathedral)–

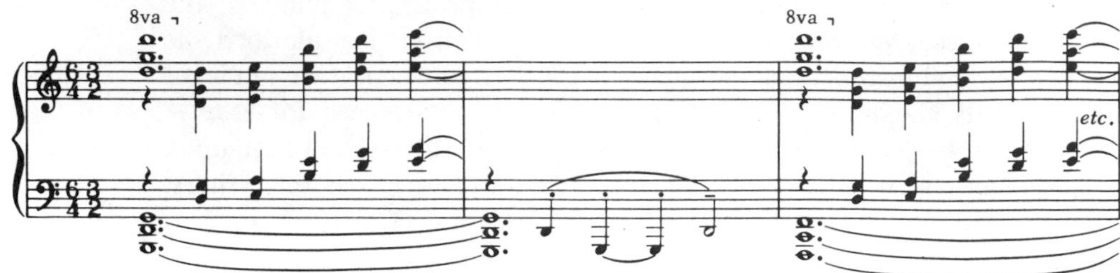

–and the following example of ninth-century organum:

Here Debussy evokes an image of powerful austerity, old and remote things. He was also sympathetic to the novel scales introduced by the Russian and Scandinavian nationalists, and lent a willing ear to the harmonies of Borodin, Musorgsky, Grieg. He responded to the Moorish strain in Spanish music. Especially he was impressed by the Javanese and Chinese orchestras that were heard in Paris during the Exposition of 1889. In their music he found a new world of sonority: rhythms, scales, and colors that offered a bewitching contrast to the stereotyped forms of Western music.

Uses of dissonance

The major-minor system, as we saw, is based on the pull of the active tones to the Tonic or rest tone. Debussy regarded this as a formula that killed spontaneity. We do not hear in his music the triumphal final cadence of the Classic-Romantic period, in which the Dominant chord is resolved to the Tonic with the greatest possible emphasis. His fastidious ear explored subtle harmonic relationships; he demanded new and delicate perceptions on the part of the listener. Classical harmony looked upon dissonance as a momentary disturbance that found its resolution in the consonance. But Debussy used dissonance as a value in itself, freeing it from the need to resolve. In the following example–the closing measures of his piano prelude *Ce qu'a vu le vent d'Ouest* (What the West Wind Saw)–he creates a type of cadence in which the final chord takes on the function of a rest chord not because it is consonant, but because it is less dissonant than what preceded. Through these and kindred procedures Debussy strengthened the drive toward the "emancipation of the dissonance." He thus taught his contemporaries to accept tone combinations that had hitherto been re-

garded as inadmissible, even as the Impressionist painters taught them to see colors in sky, grass, and water that had never been seen there before.

Whole-tone scale

Debussy is popularly associated with the *whole-tone scale.* This is a pattern built entirely of whole-tone intervals, as in the sequence C–D–E–F♯–G♯–A♯–C. The whole-tone scale avoids the semitone distances 3–4 and 7–8 (*mi-fa* and *ti-do*) of the major scale. Thereby it sidesteps the thrust of *ti* to *do* that gives the traditional scale its drive and direction. There results a fluid scale pattern whose charm can be gauged only from hearing it played. Debussy did not invent the whole-tone scale nor did he use it as frequently as many suppose. It lent itself admirably, however, to the nuances of mood and feeling that haunt his music, as in the following magical passage from the third act of *Pelléas et Mélisande:*

Parallel chords

Several other procedures have come to be associated with musical Impressionism. One of the most important is the use of parallel or "gliding" chords, in which a chord built on one tone is duplicated immediately on a higher or lower tone. Here all the voices move in parallel motion, the effect being one of blocks of sound gliding up or down. In the following measures from *Soirée dans Grenade* (Evening in Granada), the entire passage consists of a single chord structure which is duplicated on successive tones.

Such parallel motion was prohibited in the classical system of harmony; but it was precisely these forbidden progressions that fascinated Debussy. Also, he liked to sustain a chord in the bass that suggests a definite key while the chords above it give the impression of having escaped to another key. Such "escaped" chords point the way to twentieth-century harmony. In the following example—the opening of *General Lavine—Eccentric* from the second book of *Preludes*—C-major tonality is established in the first measure, against which is heard a series of triads alien to the tonality:

Ninth chords

The harmonic innovations inseparable from Impressionism led to the formation of daring new tone combinations. Characteristic was the use of the five-tone combination known as *ninth chords* (from the interval of a ninth between the lowest and highest tones of the chord). These played so prominent a part in *Pelléas* that the work came to be known as "the land of ninths." Here is a characteristic sequence of parallel ninth chords from *Pelléas:*

As a result of the procedures just outlined, Impressionist music wavered between major and minor without adhering to either. In this way was abandoned one of the basic contrasts of Classical harmony. Impressionism advanced the disintegration of the major-minor system. It floated in a borderland between keys, creating elusive effects that might be compared to the misty outlines of Impressionist painting.

Orchestral color

These evanescent harmonies demanded colors no less subtle. No room here for the thunderous climaxes of the Romantic orchestra. Instead there was a veiled blending of hues, an impalpable shimmer of pictorial quality: flutes and clarinets in their dark lower register, violins in their lustrous upper range, trumpets and horns discreetly muted; and over the whole a silvery gossamer of harp, celesta, and triangle, glockenspiel, muffled drum, and cymbal brushed with a drumstick.

Rhythmic pulse

So too the metrical patterns of the Classic-Romantic era, marked by an accent on the first beat of the measure, were hardly appropriate for this new dreamlike style. In many a work of the Impressionist school the music glides from one measure to the next in a gentle flow that discreetly veils the pulse of the rhythm.

Small forms

Impressionism inclined toward the miniature. Debussy's turning away from the big forms led him to short lyric pieces: preludes, nocturnes, arabesques—the titles indicate his leaning toward intimate lyricism. The question arises: Was Impressionism a revolt against the Romantic tradition or simply its final manifestation? Beyond question Debussy rebelled against certain aspects of Romanticism, notably the Wagnerian gesture. Yet in a number of ways Impressionism continued the fundamental tendencies of the Romantic movement: in its love of beautiful sound, its emphasis on program music, its tone painting and nature worship, its addiction to lyricism; its striving to unite music, painting, and poetry; and its emphasis on mood and atmosphere. In effect, the Impressionists substituted a thoroughly French brand of Romanticism for the German variety.

Impressionist music enjoyed an enormous vogue during the first three decades of the twentieth century. It attained the proportions of an international school. Yet from our vantage point Impressionism turns out to have been largely a one-man movement. No one else of Debussy's stature found in it the complete expression that he did. In this respect it differed from the Romantic style that allowed room for so many diverse personalities. The procedures of Impressionism worked in a limited area; they became stereotyped and soon lost their novelty. It grew to be practically impossible to write Impressionist music without sounding like Debussy. Composers were consequently forced to seek other idioms. Also, by excluding pathos and the heroic element, Impressionism narrowed its human appeal.

But on its own premises it created a finely wrought, surpassingly decorative art. It opened up to music a world of dream and enchantment. And it captured a vision of fragile beauty in a twilight moment of European culture.

76

Claude Debussy

"I love music passionately. And because I love it I try to free it from barren traditions that stifle it. It is a free art gushing forth, an open-air art boundless as the elements, the wind, the sky, the sea. It must never be shut in and become an academic art."

His Life

The most important French composer of the early twentieth century, Claude Debussy (1862–1918) was born near Paris in the town of St.

Germain-en-Laye, where his parents kept a china shop. He entered the Paris Conservatory when he was eleven. Within a few years he shocked his professors with bizarre harmonies that defied the sacred rules. "What rules then do you observe?" inquired one of his teachers. "None—only my own pleasure!" "That's all very well," retorted the professor, "provided you're a genius." It became increasingly apparent that the daring young man was.

Claude Debussy.

He was twenty-two when his cantata *L'Enfant prodigue* (The Prodigal Son) won the Prix de Rome. Like Berlioz before him, he looked upon his stay in the Italian capital as a dreary exile from the boulevards and cafés that made up his world. Already he discerned his future bent. "The music I desire," he wrote a friend, "must be supple enough to adapt itself to the lyrical effusions of the soul and the fantasy of dreams."

The 1890s, the most productive decade of Debussy's career, culminated in the writing of *Pelléas et Mélisande*. Based on the symbolist drama by the Belgian poet Maurice Maeterlinck, this opera occupied him for the better part of ten years. He continued to revise the score up to the opening night, which took place on April 30, 1902, at the Opéra-Comique. *Pelléas* was attacked as being decadent, precious, lacking in melody, form, and substance. Nevertheless, its quiet intensity and subtlety of nuance made a profound impression upon the musical intelligentsia. It caught on and embarked on an international career.

After *Pelléas* Debussy was famous. He was the acknowledged leader of a new movement in art, the hero of a cult. "The Debussyists," he complained, "are killing me." He appeared in the capitals of Europe as conductor of his works and wrote the articles that established his reputation as one of the most trenchant critics of his time. In the first years of the century he exhausted the Impressionist vein and found his way to a new and tightly controlled idiom, a kind of distillation of Impressionism.

Later years

His energies sapped by the ravages of cancer, he worked on with remarkable fortitude. The outbreak of war in 1914 rendered him for a time incapable of all interest in music. France, he felt, "can neither laugh nor weep while so many of our men heroically face death." After a year of silence he realized that he must contribute to the struggle in the only way he could, "by creating to the best of my ability a little of that beauty which the enemy is attacking with such fury." He was soon able to report to his publisher that he was "writing like a madman, or like one who has to die next morning." To his perturbation over the fate of France were added physical torment and, finally, the realization that he was too ill to compose any longer. His last letters speak of his "life of waiting—my waiting-room existence, I might call it—for I am a poor traveler waiting for a train that will never come any more."

He died in March 1918 during the bombardment of Paris. The funeral procession took its way through deserted streets as the shells of the German guns ripped into his beloved city. It was just eight months before the victory of the nation whose culture found in him one of its most distinguished representatives.

His Music

For Debussy, as for Monet and Verlaine, art was primarily a sensuous experience. The epic themes of Romanticism were distasteful to his temperament both as man and artist. "French music," he declared, "is clearness, elegance, simple and natural declamation. French music aims first of all to give pleasure."

Upholding the genius of his race, he turned against the grand form that was the supreme achievement of the Germans. Exposition-Development-Restatement he regarded as an outmoded formula. At a concert he whispered to a friend, "Let's go—he's beginning to develop!" But the Viennese sonata-symphony was not the only form alien to the Gallic spirit. A greater threat was posed by the Wagnerian music drama, which at that time attracted the intellectuals of France. The French, he points out, are too easily influenced by the "tedious and ponderous Teuton." Wagner's grandiose *Ring* he found especially tedious. "The idea of spreading one drama over four evenings! Is this admissible, especially when in these four evenings you always hear the same thing? . . . My God! how unbearable these people in skins and helmets become by the fourth night." In the end, however, he paid moving tribute to the master whose fascination he had had to shake off before he could find his own way. Wagner "can never quite die," he writes, and calls him "a beautiful sunset that was mistaken for a dawn."

From the Romantic exuberance that left nothing unsaid Debussy sought refuge in an art of indirection, subtle and discreet. He substituted for the sonata structure those short flexible forms that he handled with such distinction. Mood pieces, they evoked the favorite images of Impressionist painting: gardens in the rain, sunlight through the leaves, clouds, moonlight, sea, mist.

Orchestral works

Debussy worked slowly, and his fame rests on a comparatively small output. Among the orchestral compositions the *Prélude à l'après-midi d'un faune* (Prelude to the Afternoon of a Faun) is firmly established in public favor, as are the three *Nocturnes* (1893–99): *Nuages* (Clouds), *Fêtes* (Festivals), *Sirènes* (Sirens); *La Mer* (The Sea; 1905); and *Ibéria* (1908). His handling of the orchestra has the French sensibility. He causes individual instruments to stand out against the mass. In his scores the lines are widely spaced, the texture light and airy.

Piano pieces

One of the important piano composers, he created a distinctive new style of writing for the instrument. The widely spaced chords with their parallel successions of seconds, fourths, and fifths create a sonorous halo. He exploits the resources of the instrument with infinite finesse—the contrast of low and high registers, the blending of sonorities through the use of pedal, the clash of overtones. His piano pieces form an essential part of the modern repertory. Among the best-known are *Clair de lune* (Moonlight; 1890), the most popular piece he ever wrote; *Soirée dans Grenade* (Evening in Granada; 1903); *Reflets dans l'eau* (Reflections in the Water; 1905), and *La Cathédrale engloutie* (The Sunken Cathedral; 1910).

Vocal music

Debussy was one of the most important among the group of composers who established the French song as a national art form independent of the lied. His settings of Baudelaire, Verlaine, and Mallarmé—to mention three poets for whom he had a particular fondness—are marked by exquisite refinement. In chamber music he achieved an unqualified success with his *String Quartet in G minor* (1893). The three sonatas of his last years—for cello and piano; flute, viola, and harp; violin and piano—reveal him as moving toward a more abstract, more concentrated style.

Chamber music

Opera

Finally there is *Pelléas et Mélisande*. This "old and sad tale of the woods" captures the ebb and flow of the interior life. The characters move in a trancelike world where a whisper is eloquence: Mélisande of the golden hair and the habit of saying everything twice; Pelléas, caught in the wonder of a love he does not understand; Golaud, who marries Mélisande but never fathoms her secret, driven by jealousy to the murder of his younger half-brother; and Arkel, the blind king of this shadowy land. Maeterlinck's drama gave Debussy his ideal libretto. The result was a unique lyric drama that justifies Romain Rolland's description of him as "this great painter of dreams."

Prélude à l'après-midi d'un faune

SIDE 9/2 (E II)
SIDE 15/5 (S)

Debussy's best-known orchestral work was inspired by a pastoral of Stéphane Mallarmé that evokes the landscape of pagan antiquity. The poem centers about the mythological creature of the forest, half man, half goat. The faun, "a simple sensuous passionate being," in Edmund Gosse's phrase, awakes in the woods and tries to remember. Was he visited by three lovely nymphs or was this but a dream? He will never know. The sun is warm, the earth fragrant. He curls himself up and falls into a wine-drugged sleep.

Debussy completed the tone poem in 1894 when he was thirty-two. His imagination was attuned to the pagan setting, and his music invokes emotions as voluptuous as they are elusive. It unfolds what he well called his "harmonious harmony."

The piece opens with a flute solo in the velvety lower register. The melody glides along the chromatic scale, narrow in the range, languorous; the tempo is "very moderate":

A photograph of the legendary dancer Nijinsky, as he appeared in the ballet L'après-midi d'un faune *in Paris, 1912.*

Glissandos on the harp usher in a brief dialogue of the horns. Of these sounds it may be said, as of the opening chords of *Tristan,* that their like had never been heard before. The dynamic scheme is discreet; pianissimo and mezzo-piano predominate. There is only one fortissimo. The whole-tone scale is heard. Notable is the limpid coloring. The strings are muted and divided. Flute and oboe, clarinet and horns are used soloistically, standing out against the orchestral texture.

The work is in sections that follow the pattern of statement-departure-return. Yet the movement is fluid, rhapsodic. Debussy here achieves his goal of a music "free from motives and themes, founded in reality on a single continuous theme which nothing would interrupt and which would never return upon itself." This continuity of theme imparts to the piece an extraordinary unity of mood and texture.

Almost every fragment of melody is repeated forthwith, a trait that the composer carries to the length of mannerism. Characteristic is the relaxed rhythm which flows across the barline in a continuous stream. By weakening and even wiping out the accent Debussy achieved that dreamlike fluidity which is a prime trait of Impressionist music.

A more decisive motive emerges, marked En animant (growing lively). It is played by a solo oboe "softly and expressively," and leads into a slight crescendo. Its wider range and more active rhythm contrast with the opening melody:

The third theme is marked Même mouvement et très soutenu (same tempo and very sustained). Played in unison first by woodwinds, then by the strings, it is an ardent melody that carries the composition to its emotional crest.

The first melody returns in altered guise. At the close, antique cymbals are heard, *ppp*. (*Antique cymbals* are small discs of brass, held by the player one in each hand; the rims are struck together gently and allowed to vibrate.) "Blue" chords sound on the muted horns and violins, infinitely remote. The work dissolves in silence. It takes nine minutes to play. Rarely has so much been said so briefly.

Fêtes

That Debussy's music also commands forceful rhythms is made plain by *Fêtes* (Festivals), the second of his *Nocturnes* for orchestra. Debussy used the term "nocturne" in much the same way as did Whistler for his evocative canvases. The composer explained: "The title *Nocturnes* is to be understood here in a general, more especially in a decorative sense. It is not intended to denote the usual form of the nocturne, but rather all that this word suggests of diversified impressions and the special effects of light."

In *Fêtes,* he stated, he tried to capture movement and rhythm "dancing in the atmosphere with sudden bursts of light. There is also the episode of a procession—a dazzling and fantastic vision—which passes through the festive scene and becomes a part of it. But the background remains the same—ever the festival and the music blending with it—luminous dust participating in the rhythm of the universe."

Certainly this music captures the play of light, the "luminous dust" that pervades and envelops Debussy's canvas. The piece opens in 4/4 time, Animé et très rhythmé (lively and very rhythmical). Violins establish the provocative triplet rhythm against which English horn and clarinets trace a gliding figure. An ascending glissando on the harp gives the effect, in this coloristic setting, of nothing less than a shower of sparks. There follows a motive that becomes a structural element in the work.

Debussy here attains his ideal of a music that unfolds freely and flexibly, untrammeled by a preconceived mold: the fluid form of the prelude. Motives emerge out of the orchestral haze, melodious fragments that are stated and immediately repeated. The form has the charm and intimacy of the miniature, proceeding in a kind of mosaic work, step by step, that reminds one of the Rococo and of the master whom Debussy hailed as a true exponent of the French spirit—Couperin. Suddenly the orchestral sonority is hushed. Harps, kettledrum, and the lower strings set up a curtain of sound, *ppp,* against which the muted trumpets whisper a fanfare. The procession sets forth, shadowy and remote but coming ever closer, powered by a rhythmic ostinato based on the underlying triplets, whose ceaseless repetition outlines a steady growth in the volume of sound. This is an orchestral crescendo of irresistible verve and power. The procession arrives on the crest of it; the shadowy shapes and revels deploy before us and, as the music is hushed again, move off in the distance, infinitely mysterious and remote. The pianissimo ending is wonderfully suggestive, with its veiled triplets and flickerings of light: oboe, flutes, bassoons, a stippling of string tone, muted horns and trumpet, and a cymbal ever so lightly brushed by a drumstick. It was Couperin's contemporary, Watteau, who painted *Mezzetin,* that serene canvas bathed in golden light which epitomizes Rococo art (see p. 422). In *Fêtes* Debussy captures the grace and elegance of the great Fleming whose amorous figures so discreetly follow the summons to the pleasure island of the foam-born goddess.

A sensitive tone poet who was relentlessly exacting with himself, Debussy looms as the first major composer of our era. He bridges the gap between Romanticism and the twentieth century. His is a domain limited in scope but replete with beauty. Every note he set down justifies the proud title he assumed in the time of his country's peril: Claude Debussy, *musicien français.*

77

Maurice Ravel

"Any music created by technique and brains alone is not worth the paper it is written on. A composer should feel intensely what he is composing."

Maurice Ravel (1875–1937) may be accounted a post-Impressionist. As in the case of Cézanne, a classical streak in his makeup led him to impose form and order on what, he feared, might otherwise degenerate into amorphous fantasy.

His Life

Maurice Ravel.

Ravel was born in Ciboure, near Saint-Jean-de-Luz, in the Basses-Pyrénées region at the southwestern tip of France. The family moved to Paris shortly after Maurice was born. His father, a mining engineer who had aspired to be a musician, was sympathetic to the son's artistic proclivities. Maurice entered the Conservatory when he was fourteen, and remained there for sixteen years—an unusually long apprenticeship.

Ravel's artistic development was greatly stimulated by his friendship with a group of avant-garde poets, painters, and musicians who believed in his gifts long before those were recognized by the world at large. Youthful enthusiasts, they called themselves the "Apaches." In this rarefied atmosphere the young composer found the necessary intellectual companionship. Ravel's career followed the same course, more or less, as that of almost all the leaders of the modern movement in art. At first his music was hissed by the multitude and cried down by the critics. Only a few discerned the special quality of his work, but their number steadily grew. Ultimately the tide turned, and he found himself famous.

American trip

In the years after the First World War Ravel came into his own. He was acknowledged to be the foremost composer of France and was much in demand to conduct his works throughout Europe. In 1928 he was invited to tour the United States. Before he would consider the offer he had to be assured of a steady supply of his favorite French wines and cigarettes. Ravel and America took to one another, although he tired first. "I am seeing magnificent cities, enchanting country," he wrote home, "but the triumphs are fatiguing. Besides, I was dying of hunger."

Last years

Toward the end of his life Ravel was tormented by restlessness and insomnia. He sought surcease in the hectic atmosphere of the Parisian night clubs, where he would listen for hours to American jazz. As he approached sixty he fell victim to a rare brain disease that left his faculties unimpaired but attacked the centers of speech and motor coordination. It gradually became impossible for him to read notes, to remember tunes, or to write. Once, after a performance of *Daphnis et Chloé,* he began to weep, exclaiming: "I have still so much music in my head!" His companion tried to comfort him by pointing out that he had finished his work. "I have said nothing," he replied in anguish. "I have still everything to say."

So as not to watch himself "go piece by piece," as he put it, he decided to submit to a dangerous operation. This was performed toward the end of 1937. He never regained consciousness.

His Music

Comparison with Debussy

Ravel shared with Debussy an affinity for the scales of medieval and exotic music. Both men were attracted by the same aspects of nature—daybreak, the play of water and light. Both exploited exotic dance rhythms, especially those of Spain. Both loved the fantastic and the antique, and the old French harpsichordists. Both were repelled by the passion of nineteenth-century music, and believed the primary purpose of art to be sensuous delight. Ravel, too, was inspired by the symbolist poets and had a gift for setting the French language to music. Both men in surpassing degree exemplified Gallic sensibility. And both considered themselves rebels against the nineteenth-century spirit, although it is apparent to us now that Romanticism was the soil out of which their music flowered.

The differences between the pair are as pronounced as the similarities. Much of Ravel's music has an enameled brightness that contrasts with the twilight softness of Debussy's. He is less visionary. His rhythms are more incisive and have a verve, a drive that Debussy rarely strives for. He goes beyond Debussy's conception of dissonance. Ravel's sense of key is firmer, the harmonic movement more clearly outlined; he is far less partial to the whole-tone scale than Debussy. He is more conventional in respect to form, and his melodies are broader in span, more direct. His texture is more contrapuntal, often being based on the interplay of lines rather than on the vertical blocks of sound that fascinated Debussy. Ravel's orchestration derives in greater degree from the nineteenth-century masters; he stands in the line of descent from Berlioz, Rimsky-Korsakov, and Richard Strauss. Whereas Debussy aimed to "decongest" sound, Ravel handled the huge post-Romantic orchestra with brilliant virtuosity.

Piano and vocal works

Ravel ranks as one of the outstanding piano composers of the twentieth century. He extended the heritage of Liszt, even as Debussy was the spiritual heir of Chopin. Among his most widely played works for the piano are *Pavane pour une infante défunte* (Pavane for a Dead Infanta; 1899), *Jeux d'eau* (Fountains; 1901), and the *Sonatine* (1905). The French art song found in Ravel one of its masters. Characteristic of his style is *Shéhérazade,* a song cycle for voice and orchestra (1903). *Trois Poèmes de Stéphane Mallarmé* (1913) exemplifies the twentieth-century interest in chamber music with voice, as do the sensuous *Chansons madécasses* (Songs of Madagascar; 1926) for voice, flute, cello, and piano.

Orchestral works

But it was through his orchestral works that Ravel won the international public. The best known of these are *Rapsodie espagnole* (Spanish Rhapsody; 1907); *Ma Mère l'Oye* (Mother Goose; 1912); the ballet *Daphnis et Chloé,* one of his strongest works (1912); *La Valse,* which we will discuss; the ever popular *Boléro* (1928), which exploits the hypnotic power of relentless repetition, unflagging rhythm, steady crescendo, and brilliant orchestration; the classically oriented *Piano Concerto in G* (1931); and the dramatic *Concerto for the Left Hand* (1931), a masterpiece.

Ravel, like Debussy, has always been immensely popular in the United States. His harmonies and orchestration exercised a particular attraction for jazz arrangers and Hollywood composers. As a result his idiom (somewhat watered down, to be sure) become a part of the daily listening experience of millions of Americans.

La Valse, *choreographed by George Balanchine, is a very successful work in the New York City Ballet repertory.* (Photograph by Martha Swope.)

La Valse

The idea of writing a piece to glorify the Viennese waltz came to Ravel as early as 1906. Thirteen years—and a world war—later, Ravel returned to the project. The dance that originally was to have given utterance to his joy in life now returned to his mind in the guise of a *danse macabre.* The external stimulus came from Serge Diaghilev, the famed impresario of the Russian Ballet, who wanted Ravel to do a piece for his company. The work was completed in 1920.

Ravel's conception of this ballet—a scene at the imperial palace, around 1855—is explained in a note that he appended to the score: "Through whirling clouds we catch a glimpse of couples waltzing. The clouds gradually lift, revealing an immense hall filled with dancers. The scene is gradually lit up. There is a burst of light from the chandeliers." It is worthy of note, in view of the pictorial character of Ravel's orchestration, that he closely associated an upsurge in sound with an upsurge of light.

In *La Valse* a number of disparate elements are deftly intertwined. The spirit of Vienna (as evoked by a sensibility that is wholly French) is combined at the beginning with the mistiness of Impressionism, at the end with the dazzling sonorities of the post-Romantic orchestra. The radiant waltz of Johann Strauss becomes a symbol here of a dying world indulging in its last dance. Hence the duality of the emotion, that strange bittersweet quality so characteristic of Ravel. Like *Boléro, La Valse* is a study in orchestral crescendo—but a crescendo more capricious, more subtle.

The piece opens pianissimo with tremolos in the muted strings. Wisps of melody float out of an Impressionist haze; we seem to be on the verge of hearing a waltz tune which, tantalizingly, never emerges. The only thing the ear can make out is Ravel's tempo, Mouvement de Valse viennoise. Finally a melody takes shape in the bassoons and violas:

Then another, a caressing tune on the violins and violas:

At this point the mutes are removed one at a time. From then on the music unfolds one seductive waltz tune after another, now gathering momentum, now returning to the pianissimo sonorities of the opening. Ravel artfully husbands his resources until the frenzied climax, when he unleashes all the clashing dissonances of which the orchestra of his time was capable. It is in these frenetic final measures that his alluring "apotheosis of the waltz" becomes a dance of terror and destruction. The harsh dissonances, *fff,* almost pass beyond what a recording is able to convey. This steep rise in dissonance content, abetted by a crescendo and accelerando, brings the work to an electrifying close.

Between them Debussy and Ravel held up an ideal of sonorous beauty that incarnated the sensibility and *esprit* of their nation. And they opened wide the door to the twentieth century.

78

Main Currents in Twentieth-Century Music

"The entire history of modern music may be said to be a history of the gradual pull-away from the German musical tradition of the past century." — AARON COPLAND

The Reaction Against Romanticism

"Epochs which immediately precede our own," writes Stravinsky, "are temporarily farther away from us than others more remote in time." The

The transition from nineteenth-century Romanticism to twentieth-century fantasy was epitomized in the last great painting of Henri Rousseau (1844–1910), titled **The Dream.** (Collection, The Museum of Modern Art, New York. Gift of Nelson A. Rockefeller.)

first quarter of the twentieth century was impelled before all else to throw off the oppressive heritage of the nineteenth. Composers of the new generation were fighting not only the Romantic past but the Romanticism within themselves.

The turning away from the nineteenth-century spirit was manifest everywhere. Away from the subjective and the grandiose; from pathos and heaven-storming passion; from the Romantic landscape and its picture-book loveliness; from the profound musings on man and fate; from the quest for sensuous beauty of tone—"that accursed euphony," as Richard Strauss called it. The rising generation viewed the Romantic agony as

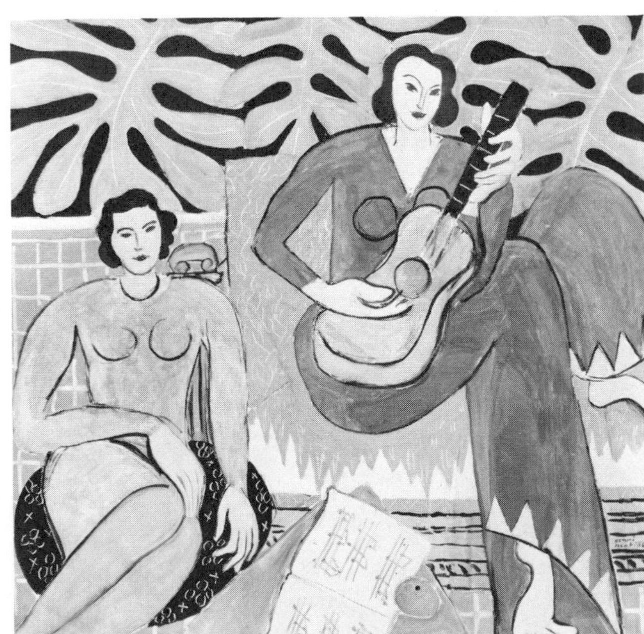

Henri Matisse (1869–1954) turned away from the tumultuous spirit of the nineteenth century and sought an art of balance, purity, and serenity through linear and coloristic freedom. **Music.** (Albright-Knox Art Gallery, Buffalo, New York. Room of Contemporary Art Fund.)

Wagnerian histrionics. It considered itself to be made of sterner stuff. Its goal was a sweeping reversal of values. It aimed for nothing less than "To root out private feelings from art."

Non-Western Influences

The new attitudes took shape just before the First World War. The spiritual exhaustion of Western culture showed itself in an indefinable restlessness. European art sought to escape its overrefinement, to renew itself in a fresh and unspoiled stream of feeling. There was a desire to capture the spontaneity, the freedom from inhibition that was supposed to characterize primitive life. People idealized brute strength and the basic impulses that seemed to have been tamed by an effete civilization. Even as the fine arts discovered the splendid abstraction of African sculpture, music turned to the dynamism of non-Western rhythm. Composers ranged from Africa to Asia and eastern Europe in their search for fresh rhythmic concepts. Out of the unspoiled, vigorous folk music in these areas came powerful rhythms of an elemental fury that tapped fresh sources of feeling and imagination, as in Bartók's *Allegro barbaro* (1911), Stravinsky's *The Rite of Spring* (1913), and Prokofiev's *Scythian Suite* (1914).

The splendid abstraction of African sculpture helped European art escape its overrefinement. An ivory head from Zaire. (The Metropolitan Museum of Art, The Michael C. Rockefeller Memorial Collection, Bequest of Nelson A. Rockefeller, 1979.)

The New Classicism

One way of rejecting the nineteenth century was to return to the eighteenth. The movement "back to Bach" assumed impressive proportions in the early twenties. There was no question here of duplicating the accents of the Leipzig master; the slogan implied rather a reviving of certain principles that appeared to have been best understood in his time. Instead of worshiping at the shrine of Beethoven and Wagner, as the Romantics had done, composers began to emulate the great musicians of the eighteenth century–Handel, Scarlatti, Couperin, Vivaldi–and the detached, objective style that was supposed to characterize their music.

There was a misconception here. Only the social music of the eighteenth century, the concerti grossi, harpsichord pieces, serenades and divertimenti, may be said to embody sweet reasonableness and detachment. In their great works Bach and Handel marshaled all the expressive power of which music in their time was capable. But each age recreates the past in its own image. To the nineteenth century, Bach was a visionary and mystic. For the twentieth he became the model for an amiable counterpoint that jogged along as crisply as ever did a piece of dinner music for a German prince. All this implied a rejection of the intensely personal quality of Romantic art. Where the nineteenth-century artist was as subjective as possible, his twentieth-century counterpart tried to see the world objectively.

Basic to the new esthetic was the notion that the composer's function is

The New Classicism exalted the virtues of order, balance and proportion as exemplified in **Rue de Crimee, Paris** *(c. 1910), by Maurice Utrillo (1885–1955).*

not to express emotions but to manipulate abstract combinations of sound. This view found its spokesman in Stravinsky. "I evoke neither human joy nor human sadness," he declared. "I move toward a greater abstraction." A Classicist by temperament and conviction, he upheld the rule of law and order in art. Music, he maintained, "is given to us with the sole purpose of establishing an order among things." This order, to be realized, requires a construction. "Once the construction is made and the order achieved, everything is said."

Absolute music

The Neoclassicists sought to rid the art of the story-and-picture meanings with which the nineteenth century had endowed it. "People will always insist," Stravinsky points out, "upon looking in music for something that is not there. They never seem to understand that music has an entity of its own apart from anything it may suggest to them." Neoclassicism spelled the end of the symphonic poem and of the Romantic attempt to bring music closer to the other arts. It led composers from programmatic to absolute music.

Neoclassicism focused attention on craftsmanship, elegance, taste. It concentrated on technique rather than content and elevated the *how* over the *what,* as generally happens in periods of experimentation. It strove for the ideal balance between form and emotion. It went even further, proclaiming that form *is* emotion, and it pointed up the intellectual rather than emotional elements in art. Future generations will find it significant that in a period of social, political, and artistic upheaval there should have been affirmed so positively the Classical virtues of objectivity, serenity, and balance.

The New Nationalism

In the twentieth century nationalism pursued different aims than in the nineteenth. The Romantic composers had idealized the life of the people. They fastened on those elements of local color and atmosphere that were picturesque and exportable. The new nationalism went deeper. It approached folk song in the spirit of scientific research, separating genuine peasant music from the watered-down versions of the café musicians. It sought the primeval soul of the nation and encouraged the trend toward authenticity. We find this point of view very much to the fore in the works of such men as Béla Bartók, Manuel de Falla, and Ralph Vaughan Williams. In addition, a new type of nationalism came into being that emanated from the culture of cities rather than the countryside and sought to capture the pulse of modern urban life.

Twentieth-century nationalism uncovered the harsh dissonances, percussive rhythms, and archaic modes that became elements of a new tonal language. Its discoveries enriched the resources of music and encouraged the breaking away from nineteenth-century ideals.

The paintings of Marc Chagall (b. 1889) invariably seek to touch the soul of his native Russia, tinged, however, with the harsh fantasy of his Jewish heritage. **Green Violinist** *(1924–25)*. (The Solomon R. Guggenheim Museum.)

Expressionism

If Paris was the center of the New Classicism, Vienna remained the stronghold of dying Romanticism. From the city of Freud emanated the attempt to capture for art the shadowy terrain of the subconscious.

Expressionism was the German answer to French Impressionism. Whereas the Latin genius rejoiced in luminous impressions of the outer world, the Germanic temperament preferred digging down to the subterranean regions of the soul. Expressionism set up inner experience as the only reality. It enthroned the irrational. Through the symbolism of dreams it released the primitive impulses suppressed by the intellect. "There is only one greatest goal toward which the artist strives," declared Arnold Schoenberg: *"To express himself."* But expression, for the Expressionists, had to take place at the deepest levels of awareness.

Expressionist painters

As with Impressionism, the impulse for the movement came from painting. Wassily Kandinsky (1866–1944), Paul Klee (1879–1940), Oskar Kokoschka (1886–), and Franz Marc (1880–1916) influenced Schoenberg and his disciples even as the Impressionist painters influenced Debussy. The distorted images of their canvases issued from the realm of the unconscious—hallucinated visions that defied conventional notions of beauty in order to achieve the most powerful expression of the artist's inner self. Yet, within a twentieth-century framework, Expressionism retained certain nineteenth-century attitudes. It inherited the Romantic love of overwhelming effect and intensity, of the strange, the macabre, the grotesque. It took over the Romantic interest in the demonic forces hidden deep within the human personality. Like the Romantic movement itself, Expressionism in music triumphed first in the central European area that lies within the orbit of Germanic culture. The movement reached its peak in the period of the Weimar Republic. It is familiar to Americans through the paintings of Kandinsky and Klee, the writings of Franz Kafka (1883–1924), the dancing of Mary Wigman (made familiar in the United States through the art of Martha Graham), the acting of Conrad Veidt, and through such films as *The Cabinet of Dr. Caligari.* Expressionist tendencies entered European opera through Richard Strauss's *Salome* and *Elektra,* and reached their full tide in the dramatic works of Schoenberg and his disciple Alban Berg. Within the orbit of our own culture, Expressionistic elements are to be discerned in the work of such dissimilar artists as James Joyce, William Faulkner, and Tennessee Williams.

The musical language of Expressionism took its point of departure from the ultrachromatic idiom of *Tristan und Isolde.* It favored a hyperexpressive harmonic language linked to inordinately wide leaps in the melody and to the use of instruments in their extreme registers. Composers hitherto had always set texts in accordance with the natural inflections of the language; Expressionist composers deliberately distorted the normal accentuation of words, just as Expressionist actors distorted the normal pattern of gesture, in order to secure a heightening of tension, a reality

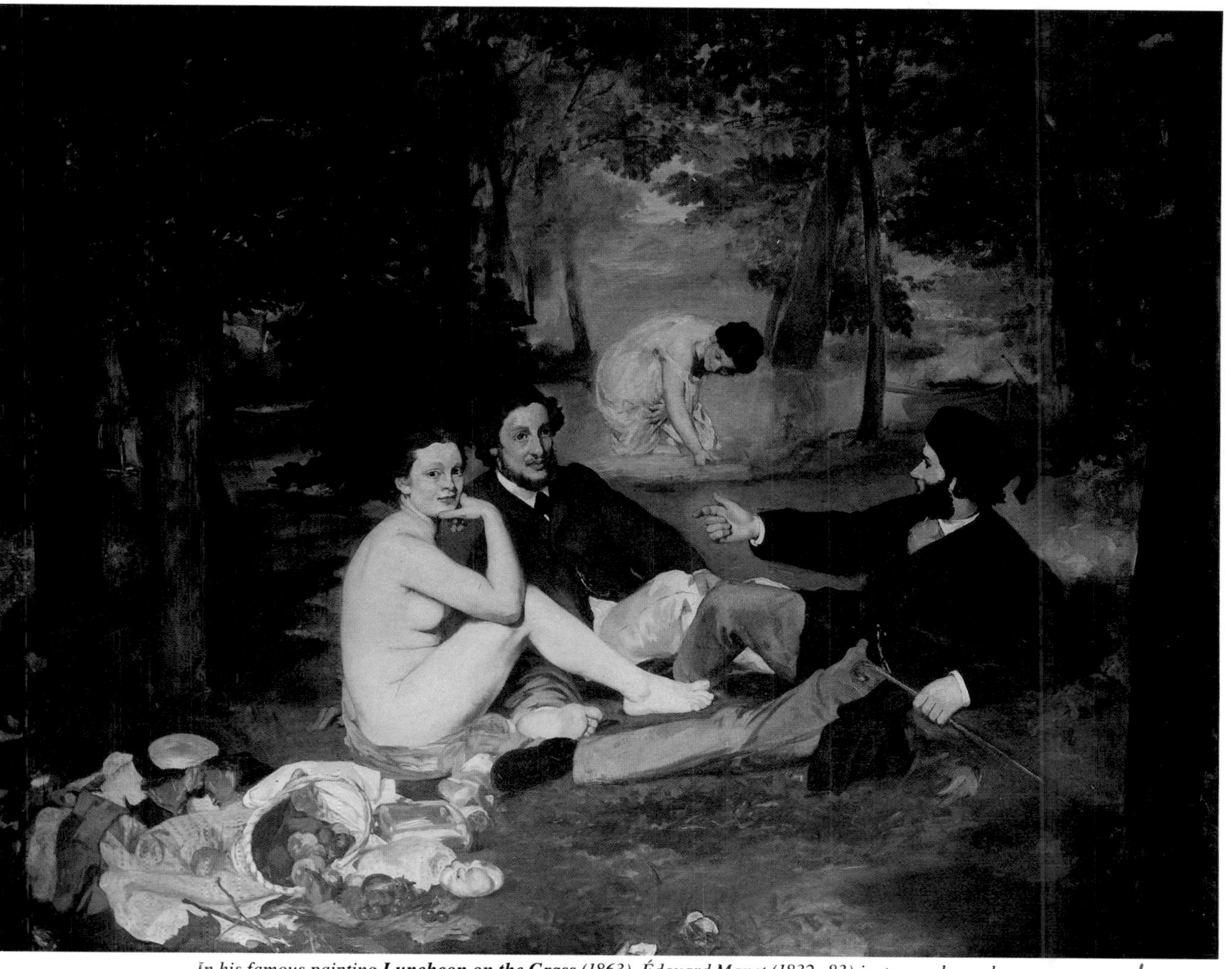

*In his famous painting **Luncheon on the Grass** (1863), Édouard Manet (1832–83) juxtaposed a nude with clothed figures in a picnic setting, thereby asserting the painter's privilege to combine any elements he chose for aesthetic effect.* (Clichés des Musées Nationaux.)

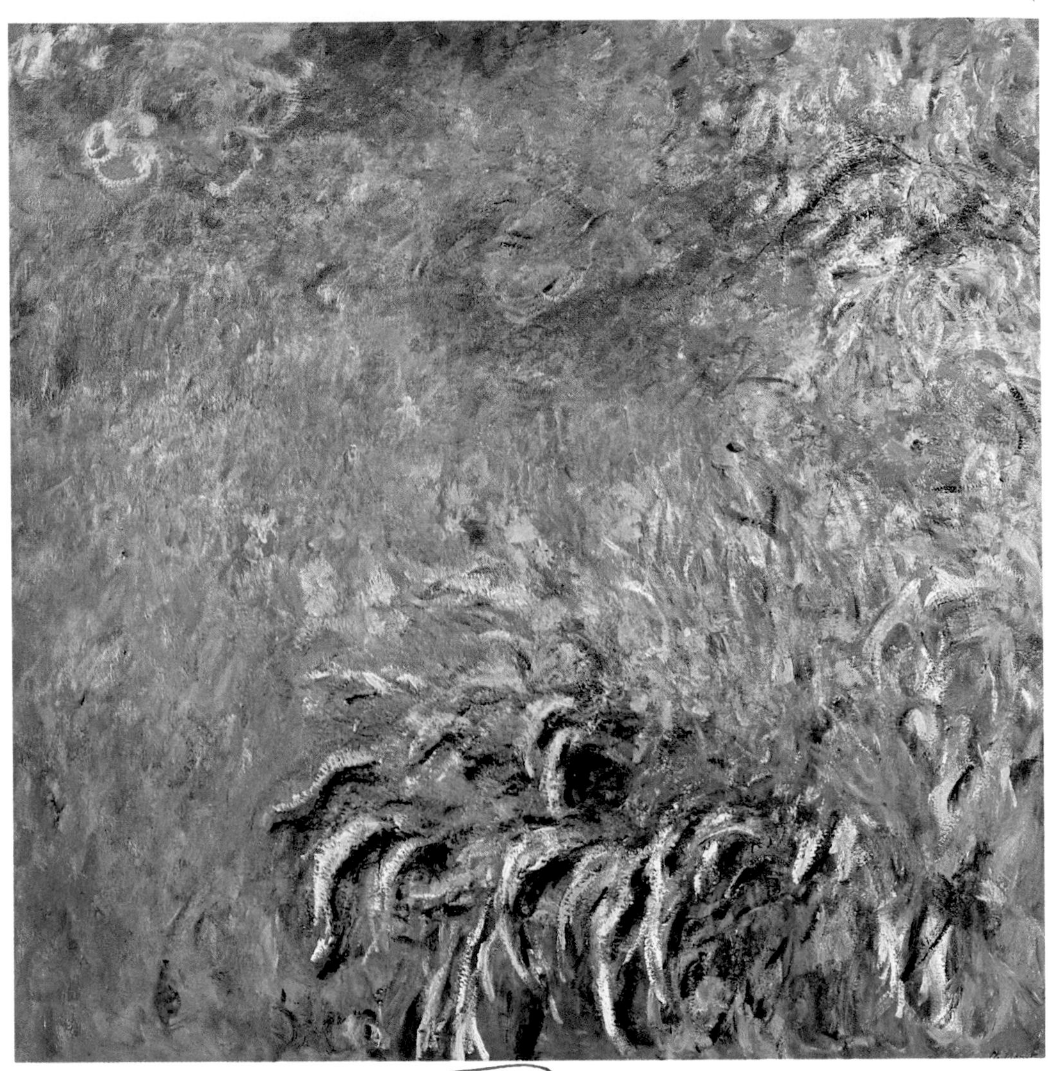

An irridescent sheen bathes Impressionistic painting; outlines shimmer and melt in a luminous haze in this seductive canvas by Claude Monet (1840–1926), ***Iris By the Pond.*** (The Art Institute of Chicago.)

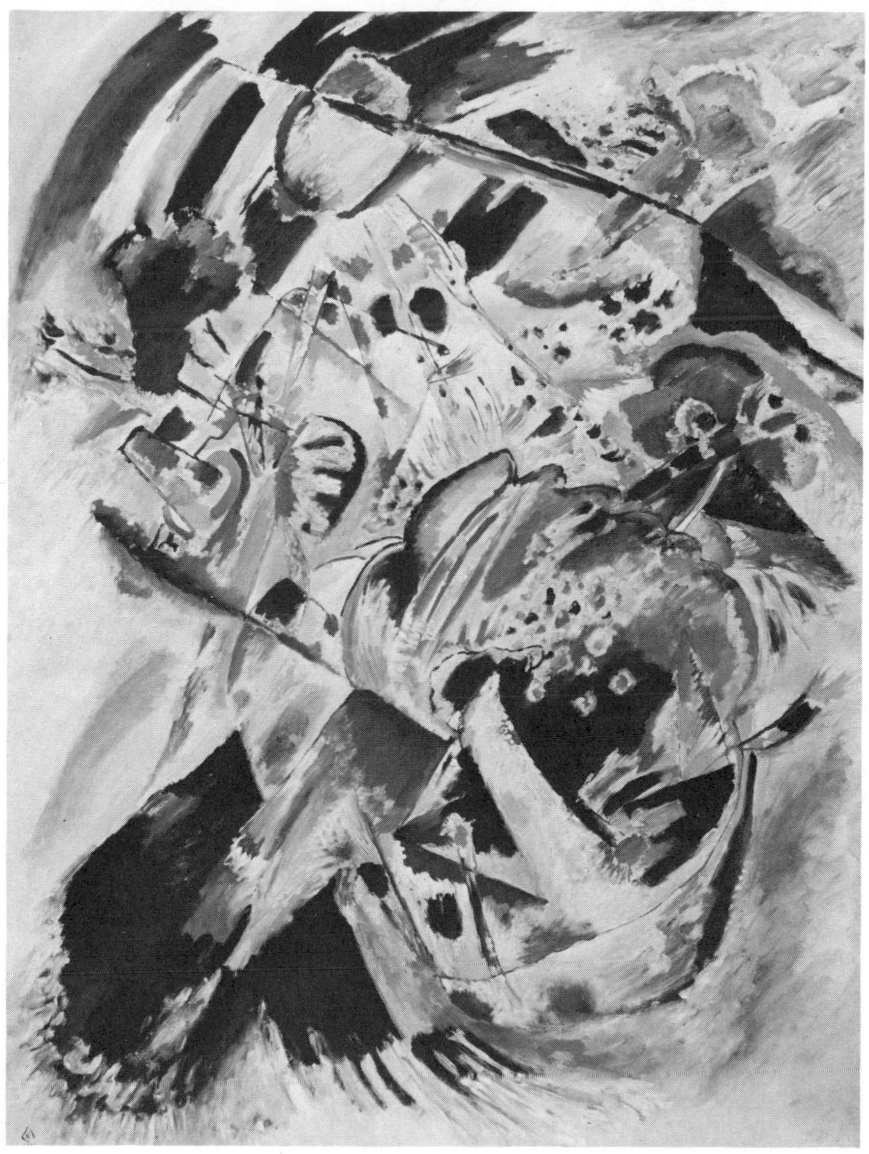

The images on the canvases of Expressionist painters issued from the realm of the unconscious: hallucinated visions that defied the traditional notions of beauty in order to express the artist's inner self. Wassily Kandinsky (1886–1944), **Painting (Winter).** (The Solomon R. Guggenheim Museum.)

transcending the real. Aaron Copland well describes the ambience of Expressionist music when, in discussing Schoenberg's *Pierrot Lunaire,* he speaks of its "curious vocal line, half spoken and half sung, the total lack of any recognizable tonal bearings, the thinly stretched and strained sonorities, the complexities of texture, the almost neurotic atmosphere engendered by the music itself."

In its preoccupation with states of soul, Expressionist music sought ever more powerful means of communicating emotion, and soon reached the boundaries of what was possible within the major-minor system. Inevitably, it had to push beyond.

79

New Elements of Style

"Music is now so foolish that I am amazed. Everything that is wrong is permitted, and no attention is paid to what the old generation wrote as composition."

— SAMUEL SCHEIDT (1651)

The Revitalization of Rhythm

Europe after the First World War found surcease for its shattered nerves in athletics and sports. The body itself came to be viewed as a rhythmic machine. Thus ballet came to provide an important platform for the new music, and some of the foremost composers of the twentieth century won success in this field.

This physicality—along with primitivism, the hectic pace of urban life, the surge and clatter of a highly industrialized society—found a musical outlet in increasingly complex rhythms. Twentieth-century music turned away from the standard patterns of duple, triple, or quadruple meter. Composers explored the possibilities of nonsymmetrical patterns based on odd numbers: five, seven, eleven, thirteen beats to the measure.

In nineteenth-century music a single meter customarily prevailed through an entire movement or section. Now the metrical flow shifted constantly, sometimes with each bar, as in Stravinsky's *The Rite of Spring* (1913; see the example on p. 480. Formerly music presented to the ear one rhythmic pattern at a time, sometimes two. Now composers turned to *polyrhythm*—the use of several rhythmic patterns simultaneously. As a result of these innovations, Western music achieved something of the complexity and suppleness of Asiatic and African rhythms. The music of Stravinsky and Bartók revealed to their contemporaries an explosive, elemental rhythm of enormous force and tension. Both men were partial to the rhythmic ostinato—the use of a striking rhythmic pattern which, by being repeated over and over again, takes on an almost hypnotic power.

Polyrhythm

The twentieth century turned away from metrical rhythms based on the regular recurrence of accent, just as it turned away from metrical poetry to free verse. The new generation of composers preferred freer rhythms. The listener will not respond to these new rhythms as he would to a Strauss waltz or a Sousa march, by tapping his foot or waving his hand with the beat. As compensation, he will find rhythms that are flexible in the highest degree, of an almost physical power and drive. Indeed, the revitalization of rhythm is one of the major achievements of early twentieth-century music.

Melody

Rhythm was not the only element in which symmetrical structure was abandoned. Melody was affected too. In the nineteenth century, melody was often based on regular phrases of four or eight measures set off by evenly spaced cadences. This expansive structure is not congenial to the modern temper.

Composers today do not develop the neatly balanced repetitions that prevailed formerly. Their ideal is a direct forward-driving melody from which all nonessentials have been cut away. They assume a quicker perception on the part of the hearer than did composers in the past. A thing is said once rather than in multiples of four. The result is a taut, angular melody of telegraphic conciseness. A splendid example is the resilient theme from the finale of Bartók's *Concerto for Orchestra* (1943; see the example on p. 493).

Instrumental melody

Nineteenth-century melody was fundamentally vocal in character; composers tried to make the instruments "sing." Twentieth-century melody is based primarily on an instrumental conception. It is neither unvocal nor antivocal; it is simply not conceived in relation to the voice. It abounds in wide leaps and dissonant intervals. The second theme in the opening movement of Shostakovich's *First Symphony* (1925) illustrates the instrumental character of twentieth-century melody.

Twentieth-century composers have enormously expanded our notion of what is a melody. As a result, many a pattern is accepted as a melody today that would hardly have been considered one a century ago.

Harmony

No single factor sets off the music of our time more decisively from that of the past than the new conceptions of harmony that emerged in the twentieth century. Instead of a single generally accepted harmonic language as in the past, the twentieth century has brought into being several, to suit the needs of many different composers. They have given rise to a wealth of new sounds and new harmonies.

The triads of traditional harmony, we saw, were formed by combining three tones, on every other degree of the scale: 1-3-5 (for example, C-E-G), 2-4-6 (D-F-A), and so on. Such chords are built in *thirds* (the interval from step 1 to step 3 is known as a third—that is, a distance of three tones). Traditional harmony also employed four-note combinations, with another third piled on top of the triad, known as *seventh chords* (steps 1-3-5-7), and five-note combinations known as *ninth chords* (steps 1-3-5-7-9). Twentieth-century composers added another "story" or two to such chords, forming highly dissonant combinations of six and seven tones—for instance, chords built from steps 1-3-5-7-9-11 and 1-3-5-7-9-11-13 of the scale. The emergence of these complex "skyscraper" chords brought greater tension to music than had existed before.

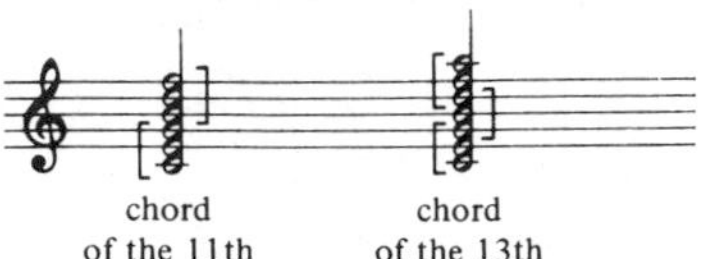

A seven-tone chord, such as the second one shown above, lacks the unity of the Classical triad. In fact, it contains no less than three separate triads: the I chord (steps 1-3-5), the V chord (steps 5-7-9) and the II chord (steps 2-4-6 or 9-11-13). In this formation the Dominant (V) chord is superimposed on the Tonic (I), so that the two poles of Classical harmony are brought together in a kind of montage. What our forebearers were accustomed to hearing in succession is thus sounded simultaneously.

Polychords and polyharmony

A seven-tone "skyscraper" is therefore a kind of *polychord*. A succession of such chords creates, in effect, *polyharmony*, in which the composer plays two or more streams of harmony against each other, exactly as single strands of melody were combined in former times. The interplay of the several independent streams adds a new dimension to the harmonic space. The following is a famous example of polyharmony from Stravinsky's *Petrushka* (1919):

To some composers, the interval of the third was associated with the music of the past. To free themselves from the sound of the eighteenth and nineteenth centuries, they cast about for new methods of chord construction; for example, they began to base chords on the interval of the fourth. This turning from *tertial* to *quartal harmony* constitutes one of the important differences between nineteenth- and twentieth-century music. Chords based on fourths have a pungency that is very much of our century, as the following examples demonstrate:

Quartal harmony

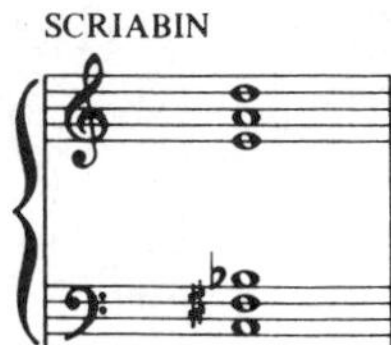

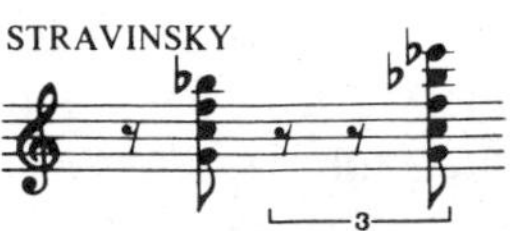

Composers also based their harmonies on other intervals. Here is a chord of piled-up fifths from Stravinsky's *Rite of Spring* (1913), and cluster chords based on seconds from Bartók's *Mikrokosmos* (1926–37).

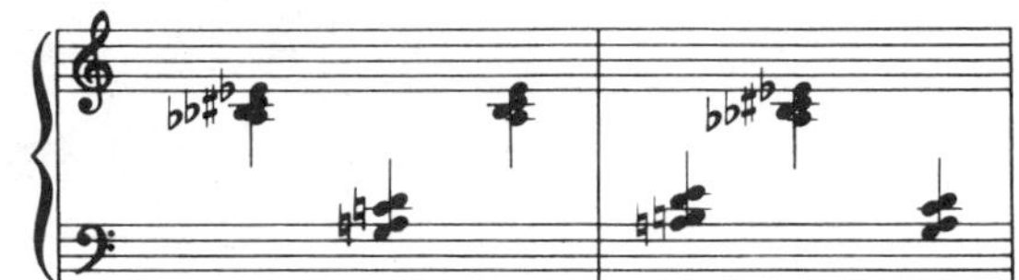

The Emancipation of the Dissonance

The history of music, we have seen, has been the history of a steadily increasing tolerance on the part of listeners. Throughout this long evolution, one factor remained constant: a clear distinction was drawn between dissonance, the element of tension, and consonance, the element of rest. Consonance was the norm, dissonance the temporary disturbance. In many contemporary works, however, tension becomes the norm. The difference between consonance and dissonance is considered nowadays to be only a difference in degree, relative rather than absolute. Therefore, a dissonance can serve as a final cadence, as in the example from Debussy on p. 445, because it is less dissonant than the chord that came before. In relation to the greater dissonance, it is judged to be consonant.

Twentieth-century composers emancipated the dissonance, first, by making it more familiar to the ear; second, by freeing it from the obligation to resolve to consonance. Their music taught listeners to accept tone combinations whose like had never been heard before.

Texture: Dissonant Counterpoint

The nineteenth century was preoccupied with harmony; the early twentieth emphasized counterpoint. Where the Romantics exalted the magic sonority of chords, new generations stressed the fabric of lines. This was part of the movement "back to Bach" and to the earlier masters of polyphony. The substitution of line for mass lightened the swollen sound of the post-Romantic period. The new style swept away both the Romantic cloudburst and Impressionistic haze. In their stead was installed an airy linear texture that fit the Neoclassic ideal of craftsmanship, order, and detachment.

Consonance unites the constituent tones of harmony or counterpoint; dissonance separates them and makes them stand out against each other. Composers began to use dissonance to set off one line against another. Instead of basing their counterpoint on the euphonious intervals of the third and sixth, they turned to astringent seconds and sevenths, as in the following example from Hindemith's *Ludus Tonalis* (1943):

The great architect Le Corbusier (Charles-Edouard Jeanneret, 1887–1965) strove for purity of line and proportion in his early masterpiece the Villa Savoye (1928–30), Poissy, France.

Or the independence of the voices might be heightened by putting them in different keys. Thus came into being a linear texture based on dissonant counterpoint: objective, logical, and marked by solid workmanship as by sober sentiment.

New Conceptions of Tonality

These many new sounds of twentieth-century music necessarily burst the confines of traditional tonality and called for new means of organization, extending or replacing the major-minor system. These approaches, in general, followed three principal paths: 1) expanded tonality; 2) the simultaneous employment of two or more keys; and 3) the rejection of tonality altogether.

Expanded Tonality

In the major-minor system, a key consisted of seven tones chosen from the available twelve. However, the widespread use of chromatic harmony in the later nineteenth century frequently called into play all twelve notes. This eventually led, in the twentieth century, to the free use of all twelve tones around a center. Such an approach, espoused by composers like

Hindemith and Bartók, retained the basic principle of traditional tonality, loyalty to the Tonic; but, by considering the five chromatic tones to be as much a part of the key as the seven diatonic ones, it expanded the borders of tonality.

Such use of all twelve tones around a center not only did away with the distinction between diatonic and chromatic, but also wiped out the distinction between major and minor modes so important to the Classic-Romantic era. Instead of being in either C major or C minor, for example, a twentieth-century piece could be simply "in C"—that is, using all the twelve tones around the center C, rather than either the major or minor group. The resulting ambiguous form of tonality offered expressive possibilities attractive to the modern temper.

In general, a key no longer defined an area in musical space as strongly as it had, and the shift from one key center to another was made with a dispatch that put to shame the most exuberant modulations of the Wagner era. Transitional passages were often dispensed with; one tonality was simply displaced by another, in a way that kept both the music and the listener on the move. An excellent example is the popular theme from *Peter and the Wolf* (1936). Prokofiev was extremely fond of this kind of displacement. (The asterisk indicates the change of tonality.)

Expansion of tonality was encouraged by a number of factors: interest in the exotic scales of Bali, Java, and other Far Eastern cultures; use of scales derived from the folk music of areas more or less outside the major-minor orbit, such as those of Russia, Scandinavia, Spain, Hungary, and other Balkan countries; revival of interest in the Medieval church modes and in composers who wrote long before the major-minor system evolved, such as the masters of fifteenth- and sixteenth-century counterpoint. The twentieth-century composer went far afield both in time and space in order to find new means of expression.

Polytonality

Tonality implied the supremacy of a single key and tonal center. Composers in the past made the most of the contrast between two keys heard in succession. From the development of polyharmony, which we discussed earlier, a further step followed logically: to heighten the contrast of two keys by presenting them simultaneously.

Confronting the ear with two keys at the same time meant a radical departure from the basic principle of traditional harmony, a single central key. *Polytonality*—the use of two or more keys together—came to the fore in the music of Stravinsky and Milhaud, whence it entered the vocabulary of the age. Toward the end of a piece, one key was generally permitted to assert itself over the others. In this way the impression was restored of orderly progression toward a central point.

By putting two or more streams of music in different keys, the friction between them was immeasurably heightened. A famous example is the chord from Stravinsky's *Petrushka* that is associated with the luckless hero of this ballet: a C-major arpeggio superimposed upon one in F-sharp major.

Polytonality was used to bring out the different levels of the harmony or counterpoint. For the clash of keys to be fully effective, each key had to be firmly established. In the following example from Prokofiev's *Sarcasms* for piano (1912), right and left hand play in different keys:

So, too, the daring harmonic combinations of *Petrushka* occur in music that has a surprisingly C-major look—comparatively few sharps or flats; what used to be referred to as "white-key" music. The tendency toward "white-keyness" was one of the characteristics of Parisian Neoclassicism.

By the same token, Vienna, the center of Expressionism, inherited the fondness for chromatic harmony that was at the heart of German Romanticism.

Atonality

Although the time-honored principle of key was variously and ingeniously adjusted to the needs of the new music, there was bound to appear a musician who wondered whether the concept of key had outlived its usefulness altogether. That musician was Arnold Schoenberg.

Schoenberg maintained that as long as the tones of the key, whether seven or twelve, remained subordinate to a central tone, it was impossible to utilize all the resources of the chromatic scale. He advocated doing away with the Tonic by treating the twelve tones as of equal importance. In this way, he believed, music would be freed from a number of procedures that had ceased to be fruitful. Schoenberg pointed out that since the major-minor system had not existed longer than three centuries, there was no reason to suppose that it could not be superseded. "Tonality is not an eternal law of music," he asserted, "but simply a means toward the achievement of musical form." The time had come, according to him, to seek new means.

To the music of Schoenberg and his school, there attached itself the label *atonality*. He disliked the term as strongly as Debussy did the term impressionism. "I regard the expression atonal as meaningless. Atonal can only signify something that does not correspond to the nature of tone." However, the name persisted.

Atonal music was much more of an innovation than polytonal music, for it entirely rejected the framework of key. Consonance, according to Schoenberg, was no longer capable of making an impression; atonal music moved from one level of dissonance to another, functioning always at maximum tension, without areas of relaxation. Dissonance resolving to consonance had been, symbolically, an optimistic act, affirming the triumph of rest over tension, of order over chaos. Atonal music, significantly, appeared at a time in European culture when belief in that triumph was sorely shaken.

Having accepted the necessity of moving beyond the existing tonal system, Schoenberg sought a unifying principle that would take the place of the system of tonality. He found this in a strict technique that he had worked out by the early 1920s. He named it "the method of composing with twelve tones."

The Twelve-Tone Method

"I was always occupied," Schoenberg declared, "with the desire to base the structure of my music *consciously* on a unifying idea." The *twelve-tone method* sprang from his conception of a basic shape (*Grundgestalt* in German) that would be the origin of every element in a work. Each composition that uses Schoenberg's method is based on an arrangement of the twelve chromatic tones that is called a *tone row*—or, as he sometimes called it, a *basic set*. This row or set is the unifying idea for that particular composition, and serves as the source of all the musical events that take place in it. (The term *dodecaphonic,* the Greek equivalent of *twelve-tone,* is sometimes also used for Schoenberg's method, while *serialism,* an allusion to the series of twelve tones, has come to refer, in more recent decades, to postwar extensions of the technique.)

Serialism

The tone row

A tone row differs from a scale in several important respects. First, a scale is a traditional pattern that furnishes the material for hundreds of composers and thousands of compositions, and is thus almost always already familiar to the listener. A tone row, on the other hand, is unique to a particular composition, a configuration of the twelve tones not to be found in any other piece. Second, a scale does not determine the order in which a composer uses its notes; they may appear in whatever sequence he desires. In a row, the order of the twelve notes is fundamental, for it determines the choice and succession of the intervals, and thus shapes the overall sound of the piece. Third, although some notes in a scale (especially the Tonic and Dominant) are more important than others, in a tone-row all twelve notes are of equal standing—in fact, no one of them is allowed to appear more than once in the series, lest it take on the prominence of a Tonic. (A tone may be repeated immediately, but this is regarded as an extension, not a new appearance.)

Forms of the row

Just as a scale is not a theme, neither is a twelve-tone row. What the row does is to establish a series of pitches and—even more important—a series of intervals from which the composer will draw themes, counterpoints, and harmonies. Recognizing that a single form of the tone-row would hardly furnish sufficient variety of material for a major musical work, Schoenberg's method provides for alternative, closely related forms of the row. Thus, its notes and intervals may also be used in reverse sequence (*retrograde*); with the intervals turned in the opposite directions (*inversion*); or in a combination of the two (*retrograde inversion*). The following example shows the four versions of the basic set of Schoenberg's *Piano Concerto*, Opus 42. O stands for the original form, R for retrograde, I for inversion, and RI for retrograde inversion.

Furthermore, any of these four forms—the original row and its three variants—may begin on any of the twelve notes of the scale, yielding a total of forty-eight possibilities. There is, however, no requirement that the composer use all forty-eight possible forms of the row. That will depend, in practice, on the size of the work and on the potential of a particular tone row. In any case, that basic row will pervade the entire fabric of the composition. Its persistence in the melodies and harmonies of an extended composition is intended to result in the closest possible relationship between these two dimensions of the musical tissue—what Schoenberg was fond of calling "the identity of horizontal and vertical musical space."

Schoenberg never intended that the detailed workings of the twelve-tone method should concern the listener, any more than do the intricacies of traditional harmony and counterpoint. Musical composition has always had its "rules of the game," and they have always seemed somewhat arbitrary to laymen. What Schoenberg expected the listener to hear was the themes, developments, textures, and emotional expressivity of his music; he always insisted that he wrote "not *twelve-tone* music, but twelve-tone *music*."

At first, when all the composers using the technique belonged essentially to the Expressionistic school centered around Schoenberg, it was regarded as esthetically limited. Over the music of these first masters of the twelve-tone style brood the troubled visions that agonized the consciousness of Europe in the aftermath of the First World War. In fact, the twelve-tone method is not equivalent to any particular style of composition. In recent years, as Schoenberg's technique has been adopted and developed by many composers of different esthetic persuasions, it has become clear that twelve-tone music can be written in many styles.

The adherents of the twelve-tone method gained world-wide influence in the years following the Second World War. In the 1950s and '60s, serial thinking emerged as the most advanced line of thought in musical esthetics, and profoundly influenced the course of contemporary music.

Orchestration

Orchestral writing followed the same anti-Romantic direction as prevailed in other departments of the art. The rich sonorities of nineteenth-century orchestration were alien to the temper of the 1920s and '30s. The trend was toward a smaller orchestra and a leaner sound, one that was hard, bright, sober. "One is tired," wrote Stravinsky, "of being saturated with timbres."

The decisive factor in the handling of the orchestra was the change to a linear texture—the texture, for example, of Stravinsky's *Symphony of Psalms* or Schoenberg's *Variations for Orchestra*. Color came to be used in the new music not so much for atmosphere or enchantment as for bringing out the lines of counterpoint and of form. Whereas the nineteenth-century orchestrator made his colors swim together, the Neoclassicist desired each to stand out against the mass. Instruments were used in their unusual registers. The emotional crescendo and diminuendo of Romantic music gave way to even levels of soft or loud. This less expressive scheme revived the solid areas of light and shade of the age of Bach. The string section lost its traditional role as the heart of the orchestra. Its tone was felt to be too personal. Attention was focused on the more objective winds. There was a movement away from brilliancy of sound. The darker instruments came to the fore—viola, bassoon, trombone. The emphasis on rhythm brought the percussion group into greater prominence than ever before. The piano, which in the Romantic era was pre-eminently a solo instrument, found a place for itself in the orchestral ensemble. Composers explored the piano's capacity for percussive rhythm, frequently treating it as a kind of xylophone in a mahogany box, and in this way opening up new possibilities for the favored instrument of Chopin and Liszt.

Music in the second quarter of our century revived the Baroque practice of pitting one instrument against another; that is, the concertante style. In many pieces the sound of the orchestra drew closer to the chamber-music ideal. In general, Neoclassicism rejected the Romantic use of timbre as an end in itself. Composers restored color to its Classical function, as the obedient handmaiden of idea, structure, and design.

The Popularity of Absolute Forms

The Neoclassicists took over from their Romantic predecessors the large forms of absolute music–symphony and concerto, solo sonata, string quartet and other types of chamber music–which they adapted to their own esthetic. Their attitude was summed up in Prokofiev's observation, "I want nothing better than sonata form, which contains everything necessary for my needs." In addition, they revived a number of older forms: toccata, fugue, passacaglia and chaconne, concerto grosso, theme and variations, suite, and the social forms of the Viennese period–divertimento and serenade.

Formalism

The tendency to elevate formal above expressive values is known as *formalism*. The second quarter of our century, it goes without saying, was a formalist age. The New Classicism, like the old, strove for purity of line and proportion. Characteristic of this goal was Stravinsky's emphasis on formal beauty rather than emotional expression: "One could not better define the sensation produced by music than by saying that it is identical with that evoked by contemplating the interplay of architectural forms. Goethe thoroughly understood this when he called architecture frozen music."

The Influence of Jazz

Composers through the ages have vitalized their music by the use of forms and materials drawn from popular music. In the twentieth century, a primary source for new inspiration from outside the realm of art music was Afro-American jazz.

Even in the nineteenth century, the music of black Americans had fascinated Europeans—most notably Antonín Dvořák, who heard Negro spirituals during his stay in the United States and encouraged his black student Harry Burleigh to draw inspiration from them. The tours of the Fisk Jubilee Singers carried the sound of spirituals all over the continent.

The title page of Stravinsky's piano arrangement of Ragtime *(J. & W. Chester, London, 1917) was designed by Pablo Picasso (1881–1974).*

Later, the ragtime piano style, with its sprightly syncopations, traveled across the Atlantic. As early as 1905, Debussy's *Golliwog's Cakewalk* borrowed ragtime elements. Later, this same style would fascinate Stravinsky: in addition to *Ragtime* for eleven instruments (1918) and *Piano-Rag-Music* (1920), his *L'Histoire du soldat* (The Soldier's Tale, 1918) includes a sequence of popular dances, beginning with a tango and waltz, that climaxes in a ragtime movement.

An important step in the introduction of new American musical styles into Europe came with America's entry into World War I, when a number of black regiments went abroad with excellent bands. The most famous of these was the 369th Infantry Band, under James Reese Europe, which gave concerts throughout France. Since Europe's band played from printed music, what they produced could not really be called jazz, which was always improvised. But they played with the rhythmic vitality of the new style, and introduced Europeans to a new kind of virtuosity and tone color.

These novel wind and brass sounds, produced with special mutes and with higher wind pressures than were used by classical players, were among the things that fascinated European composers when the first true jazz records crossed the ocean, followed soon thereafter by groups of players from America. The vigorous syncopation of jazz rhythms was welcomed as a vitalizing element. The chamber-music sonority that came from an ensemble of soloists (woodwind and brass) playing against the rhythmic-harmonic background (piano, string bass, banjo, and drums) was stimulat-

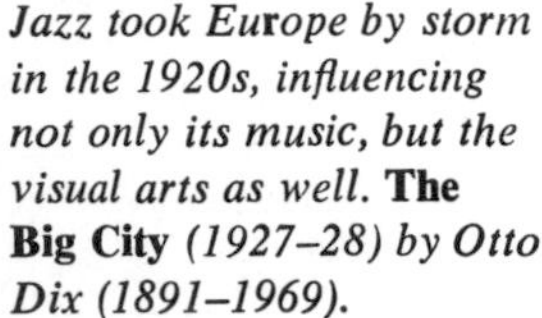

Jazz took Europe by storm in the 1920s, influencing not only its music, but the visual arts as well. **The Big City** *(1927–28) by Otto Dix (1891–1969).*

ing to composers in flight from the overblown orchestra of the Romantic era. So too, the untrammeled counterpoint of group improvisation introduced them to a new kind of texture. The melodic and harmonic inflections of blues musicians intrigued ears accustomed to more "correct" intonation.

Although European composers did not adopt the improvisational procedures that are fundamental to jazz, they did aspire to capture something of its spontaneity, to evoke its sonorities, textures, and rhythmic freedom. And when they came to America, they invariably made a point of visiting Harlem nightclubs to encounter the real thing. Darius Milhaud, for one, incorporated impressions of his visit to Harlem in the ballet *La Création du monde*, as did Maurice Ravel in his *Piano Concerto*. Others learned their jazz without leaving Europe, like Ernst Krenek, whose opera *Jonny spielt auf*, with a jazz violinist as hero, was an international success in the late 1920s. The dry textures and snappy tempos of jazz resound through the operas of Kurt Weill—*The Three-Penny Opera* and *Mahagonny*. Even into the high Expressionism of Alban Berg's concert aria *Der Wein* and his opera *Lulu,* the erotic voice of the saxophone brings an echo of the new trans-Atlantic idiom.

To be sure, jazz assumed some strange shapes as soon as it left American hands. Nevertheless, the New Classicism for a time advanced under the twin banners of Bach and jazz—a formidable combination.

80

Igor Stravinsky

"I hold that it was a mistake to consider me a revolutionary. If one only need break habit in order to be labeled a revolutionary, then every artist who has something to say and who in order to say it steps outside the bounds of established convention could be considered revolutionary."

Igor Stravinsky.

It is granted to certain artists to embody the most significant impulses of their time and to affect its artistic life in the most powerful fashion. Such an artist was Igor Stravinsky (1882–1971), the Russian composer who for half a century gave impetus to the main currents in twentieth-century music.

His Life

Stravinsky was born in Oranienbaum, a summer resort not far from St. Petersburg (Leningrad), where his parents lived. He grew up in a musical environment; his father was the leading bass at the Imperial Opera. Although he was taught to play the piano, his musical education was kept on the amateur level; his parents wanted him to study law. He matriculated at the University of St. Petersburg and embarked on a legal career, meanwhile continuing his musical studies. At twenty he submitted his work to Rimsky-Korsakov, with whom he subsequently worked for three years.

Diaghilev

Success came early to Stravinsky. His music attracted the notice of Serge Diaghilev, the legendary impresario of the Russian Ballet, who commissioned Stravinsky to write the music for *L'Oiseau de feu* (The Firebird), which was produced in 1910. Stravinsky was twenty-eight when he arrived in Paris to attend the rehearsals. Diaghilev pointed him out to the ballerina Tamara Karsavina with the words, "Mark him well—he is a man on the eve of fame."

The Firebird was followed, a year later, by *Petrushka.* Presented with Nijinsky and Karsavina in the leading roles, this production secured Stravinsky's position in the forefront of the modern movement in art. In the spring of 1913 was presented the third and most spectacular of the ballets Stravinsky wrote for Diaghilev, *Le Sacre du printemps* (The Rite of Spring). The opening night was one of the most scandalous in modern musical history; the revolutionary score touched off a near riot. People hooted, screamed, slapped each other, and were persuaded that what they were hearing "constituted a blasphemous attempt to destroy music as an art." A year later the composer was vindicated when the *Sacre,* presented at a symphony concert under Pierre Monteux, was received with enthusiasm and established itself as a masterpiece of new music.

The outbreak of war in 1914 brought to an end the whole way of life on which Diaghilev's sumptuous dance spectacles depended. Stravinsky, with his wife and children, took refuge in Switzerland, their home for the next six years. The difficulty of assembling large bodies of performers during the war worked hand in hand with his inner evolution as an artist: he moved away from the grand scale of the first three ballets to works more intimate in spirit and modest in dimension.

The Russian Revolution had severed Stravinsky's ties with his homeland. In 1920 he settled in France, where he remained until 1939. During these years Stravinsky concertized extensively throughout Europe, performing his own music as pianist and conductor. He also paid two visits to the United States. In 1939 he was invited to deliver the Charles Eliot Norton lectures at Harvard University. He was there when the Second World War broke out, and decided to live in this country. He settled in California, outside Los Angeles, and in 1945 became an American citizen. In his later years, Stravinsky's worldwide concert tours made him the most celebrated figure in twentieth-century music, and his caustically witty books of "conversations" with his disciple Robert Craft are full of musical wisdom and footnotes to history. He died in New York on April 6, 1971.

Later years

His Music

Stravinsky showed a continuous development throughout his career. With inexhaustible avidity he tackled new problems and pressed for new solutions. This evolution led from the post-Impressionism of *The Firebird* and the audacities of *The Rite of Spring* to the austerely controlled classicism of his maturity. In the course of it he laid ever greater emphasis upon tradition and discipline. "The more art is controlled, limited, worked over, the more it is free." He consistently extolled the element of construction as a safeguard against excess of feeling. "Composing for me is putting into an order a certain number of sounds according to certain interval relationships." A piece of music was for him first and foremost a problem. "I cannot compose until I have decided what problem I must solve." The problem was esthetic, not personal. As one of his biographers points out, "We find his musical personality in his works but not his personal joys or sorrows."

Stravinsky, we noted, was a leader in the revitalization of European rhythm. His first success was won as a composer of ballet, where rhythm is allied with body movement and expressive gesture. His is a rhythm of unparalleled dynamic power, furious yet controlled. In harmony Stravinsky reacted against the restless chromaticism of the Romantic period, but no matter how daring his harmony, he retained a robust sense of key. Stravinsky's subtle sense of sound makes him one of the great orchestrators. Unmistakably his is that enameled brightness of sonority, and a texture so clear that, as Diaghilev remarked, "One could see through it with one's ears."

Early works

The national element predominates in his early works, as in *The Firebird* and *Petrushka,* in which he found his personal style. *Le Sacre du printemps* recreates the rites of pagan Russia. The decade of the First World War saw the turn toward simplification of means. *L'Histoire du soldat* (The Soldier's Tale; 1918), a dance-drama for four characters, is an intimate theater work accompanied by a seven-piece band. The most important work of the years that followed is *Les Noces* (The Wedding; final version, 1923), a stylization of a Russian peasant wedding. Four singers and a chorus support the dancers, accompanied by four pianos and a diversified percussion group.

Neoclassical period

The Neoclassical period was ushered in by the *Symphonies of Wind Instruments* (1920), dedicated to the memory of Debussy. The instrumental works that followed incarnate the principle of the old concerto grosso–the pitting against each other of contrasting tone masses. This "return to Bach" crystallized in the *Concerto for Piano and Wind Orchestra* (1924). Stravinsky's Classical period culminated in several major compositions. *Oedipus Rex* (1927) is an "opera-oratorio"; the text is a translation into Latin of Cocteau's adaptation of the Greek tragedy. From the shattering impact of the opening chords, *Oedipus Rex* is an unforgettable experience in the theater. The archaic Greek influence is manifest too in several ballets, of which the most important is *Apollon Musagète* (Apollo, Leader of the Muses; 1928), which marked the beginning of his collaboration with the choreographer George Balanchine.

The *Symphony of Psalms* (1930) is regarded by many as the chief work of Stravinsky's maturity. The *Symphony in C* (1940), a sunny piece of modest dimensions, pays tribute to the spirit of Haydn and Mozart. With the *Symphony in Three Movements* (1945), Stravinsky returns to bigness of form and gesture. In 1950 there followed *The Rake's Progress,* an opera on a libretto by W. H. Auden and Chester Kallman, after Hogarth's celebrated series of engravings. Written as the composer was approaching seventy, this radiantly melodious score, which uses the set forms of the Mozartean opera, is the quintessence of Neoclassicism.

Twelve-tone works

Stravinsky, imperturbably pursuing his own growth as an artist, had still another surprise in store for his public. In the works written after he was seventy, he showed himself increasingly receptive to the serial procedures of the twelve-tone style, which in earlier years he had opposed. This preoccupation came to the fore in a number of works dating from the middle fifties, of which the most important is the *Canticum sacrum ad honorem Sancti Marci nominis* (Sacred Song to Honor the Name of St. Mark; 1956) for tenor, baritone, chorus, and orchestra. There followed the ballet *Agon* (1957) and *Threni–id est Lamentationes Jeremiae Prophetae* (Threnodies: Lamentations of the Prophet Jeremiah; completed 1958). In these works, as in the *Movements* for piano and orchestra (1958–59), *A Sermon, a Narrative and a Prayer* (1960–61), *The Flood* (1961), and the *Requiem Canticles* (1966), Stravinsky assimilated the twelve-tone technique to his personal style and turned it with utter freedom to his own use.

Stravinsky's aphorisms display his gift for trenchant expression. "We have a duty to music, namely, to invent it. . . . Instinct is infallible. If it leads us astray it is no longer instinct. . . . It is not simply inspiration that counts. It is the result of inspiration–that is, the composition. . . ." Speaking of his *Mass:* "The Credo is the longest movement. There is much to believe." When asked to define the difference between *The Rite of Spring* and *Symphony of Psalms:* "The difference is twenty years." Of the innumerable anecdotes to which his ready tongue has given rise it will suffice to quote one. After the out-of-town opening of *Seven Lively Arts,* which included a ballet by Stravinsky, the managers of the show, apprehensive as to how the music would be received on Broadway, wired him: "Great success. Could be sensational if you authorize arranger Mr. X to add some details to orchestration. Mr. X arranges even the works of Cole Porter." To which Stravinsky wired back: "Am satisfied with great success."

Le Sacre du printemps

Le Sacre du printemps (The Rite of Spring; 1913)–"Scenes of Pagan Russia"–not only embodies the cult of primitivism that so startled its first-night audience; it also sets forth the lineaments of a new tonal language–the percussive use of dissonance, polyrhythms, and polytonality. The work is scored for a large orchestra, including an exceptionally varied percussion group.

Part I
SIDE 9/3 (E II)
SIDE 16/1 (S)

Part I. *Adoration of the Earth.* The Introduction is intended to evoke the birth of spring. A long-limbed melody is introduced by the bassoon, taking on a curious remoteness from the circumstance that it lies in the instrument's uppermost register. The narrow range and repetition of fragments gives this theme a primitive character:

The awakening of the earth is suggested in the orchestra. On stage, a group of young girls is discovered before the sacred mound, holding a long garland. The Sage appears and leads them toward the mound. The orchestra erupts into a climax, after which the bassoon melody returns.

Dance of the Adolescents. Dissonant chords in the lower register of the strings exemplify Stravinsky's "elemental pounding"; their percussive quality is heightened by the use of polytonal harmonies. A physical excitement attends the dislocation of the accent, which is underlined by syncopated chords hurled out by eight horns. The ostinato–a favorite rhythmic device of Stravinsky–is repeated with hypnotic insistence. A theme emerges on the bassoons, moving within a narrow range around a central tone, with a suggestion of elemental power.

The main theme of the movement, a more endearing melody in folk style, is introduced by the horns. Stravinsky expands this idea by means of the repetition technique so characteristic of the Russian school.

Game of Abduction. The youths and maidens on the stage form into two phalanxes which in turn approach and withdraw from one another. Fanfares on the woodwinds and brass add a luminous quality to the sound.

Spring Dance. A pastoral melody is played by the high clarinet in E flat and the bass clarinet, two octaves apart, against sustained trills on the

flutes. Modal harmonies create an archaic atmosphere. Four couples are left on stage. Each man lifts a girl on his back and with measured tread executes the Rounds of Spring. The movement is sostenuto e pesante (sustained and heavy) with blocklike harmonies propelled by ostinato rhythms.

Games of the Rival Cities—Entrance of the Sage—Dance of the Earth. The peremptory beating of drums, against the sound of trombones and tubas, summons the braves of the rival tribes to a display of prowess. The main idea is presented by two muted trumpets. Notice that the third measure repeats the melodic curve of the two preceding ones, but with a rhythmic dislocation which causes the notes to fall on different beats within the measure:

The orchestration evokes a neolithic landscape. The score abounds in orchestral "finds," such as the braying sound produced by a simultaneous trill in piccolo and flutes, oboes and English horn, clarinets, horns, trumpets, and trombones over an ostinato in the basses. The entrance of the Sage touches off a powerful crescendo that rises over a persistent figure in the brass. An abrupt silence—a pianissimo chord in the bassoons as the dancers prostrate themselves in mystic adoration of the earth. Then they

Valentine Hugo's sketches of the Danse Sacrale *from the original ballet* Le Sacre du printemps *(1913), choreographed by Nijinsky.*

leap to their feet, and to music of the sheerest physicality perform the *Dance of the Earth.*

Part II

Part II. *The Sacrifice.* The Introduction is a "night piece" that creates a brooding atmosphere. The Sage and the maidens sit motionless, staring into the fire in front of the sacred mound. He must choose the Elect One who will be sacrificed to ensure the fertility of the earth. A poignant melodic idea in Russian folk style, first presented by the muted violins in harmonics, pervades the movement.

The music is desolate, but there is nothing subjective about it. This desolation is of the soil, not the soul.

Mystic Circle of Young Girls. The theme of the preceding movement alternates with a melody presented by the alto flute, which stands out

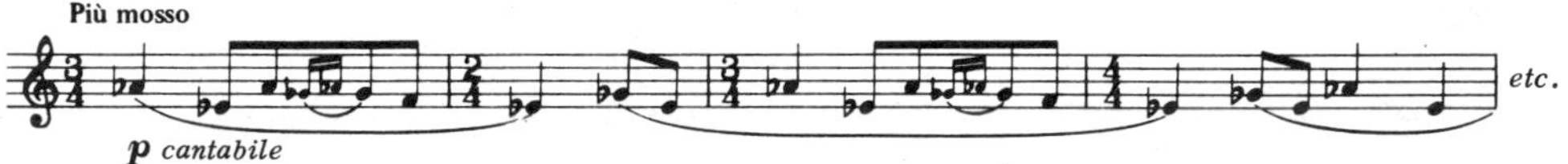

against a dissonant background. The two themes are repeated in various registers with continual changes of color. The major-minor ambiguity goes hand in hand with the soft colors of the orchestration.

The Dance in Adoration of the Chosen Virgin has the Stravinskyan muscularity of rhythm. The eighth note is the metric unit, upon which are projected a series of uneven meters that change continually, sometimes with each bar. The piece develops into a frenzied dance.

Evocation of the Ancestors—Ritual Act of the Old Men. After a violent opening, the movement settles down to a kind of languorous "blues." An English-horn solo presents a sinuously chromatic figure against a background of drums and pizzicato chords in the strings. The music carries a suggestion of swaying bodies and shuffling feet.

Sacrificial Dance of the Chosen Virgin. In this, the climactic number of the ballet, the sacrifice is fulfilled. The music mounts in fury while the chosen maiden dances until she falls dead. The men in wild excitement bear her body to the foot of the mound. There is the scraping sound of the *guiro* (a Latin-American instrument consisting of a serrated gourd scraped with a wooden stick); an ascending run on the flutes and piccolos; and with a fortissimo growl in the orchestra this luminous score comes to an end.

More than half a century has passed since *Le Sacre* was written. It is still an amazing work.

Symphony of Psalms

The *Symphony of Psalms* (1930) was among the works commissioned by the Boston Symphony Orchestra to celebrate its fiftieth anniversary. There resulted one of Stravinsky's grandest works, "composed for the glory of God" and "dedicated to the Boston Symphony Orchestra."

The choice of instruments is unusual. The score omits clarinets, violins, and violas, and calls for two pianos and a mixed chorus. The three movements are performed without a break. The first movement is the shortest. The slow movement is about twice, and the jubilant finale about three times as long.

Psalm XXXVIII (Vulgate)
Verses 13–14

Exaudi orationem meam, Domine,	Hear my prayer, O Lord,
et deprecationem meam:	and my supplication;
auribus percipe lacrimas meas.	give ear to my tears.
Ne sileas, quoniam advena ego sum apud te,	Be not silent; for I am a stranger with Thee,
et peregrinus, sicut omnes patres mei.	and a sojourner, as all my fathers were.
Remitte mihi,	O forgive me,
ut refrigerer prius quam abeam,	that I may be refreshed,
et amplius non ero.	before I go hence, and be no more.

First movement
SIDE 9/4 (E II)
SIDE 16/2 (S)

The symphony opens with a prelude-like section in which flowing arabesques are traced by oboe and bassoon. These are punctuated by an urgent E-minor chord which, spread out across the orchestral gamut, asserts the principal tonality. The altos enter with a chantlike theme consisting of two adjacent notes—the interval of a minor second (semitone) that plays an important role throughout the work.

This idea alternates with the fuller sound of choral passages as the movement builds to its climactic point on the words "Remitte mihi" (O forgive me) over a strong pedal point on E. The modal harmony creates an archaic atmosphere and leans towards the Phrygian (the mode that matches the pattern of the white keys on the piano from E to E). Tension is created by the fact that, although the music seems again and again to be climbing toward the key of C, that tonality will not be reached until the second movement. The sonorous cadence on a G-major triad serves to launch the slow movement.

Psalm XXXIX (Vulgate)
Verses 2, 3, and 4

Expectans expectavi Dominum, et intendit mihi.	With expectation I have waited for the Lord: and He was attentive to me,
Et exaudivit preces meas; et eduxit me de lacu miseriae, et de luto faecis.	And He heard my prayers, and brought me out of the pit of misery and the mire of dregs.
Et statuit super petram pedes meos; et direxit gressus meos.	And He set my feet upon a rock, and directed my steps.
Et immisit in os meum canticum novum, carmen Deo nostro.	And He put a new canticle into my mouth, a song to our God.
Videbunt multi et timebunt: et sperabunt in Domino.	Many shall see and shall fear: and they shall hope in the Lord.

Second movement

The slow movement is a *double fugue*—that is, a fugue with two subjects—for chorus and orchestra. Its flowing counterpoint underlines Stravinsky's affinity with Bach. Each fugue is in four voices. The orchestral subject is announced by the oboe. Wide leaps impart to the melody its assertive character:

After the Exposition in the orchestra, the sopranos enter with the theme of the choral fugue. The interval of a falling fourth lends expressivity to the words "Expectans expectavi:

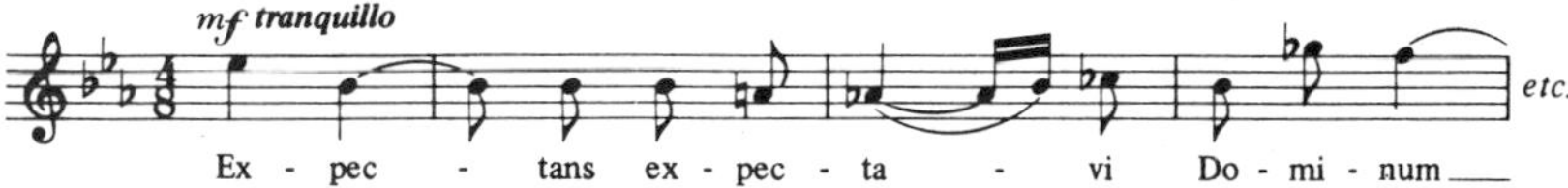

This theme is taken over by altos, tenors, and basses in turn, to be treated in strict fugal fashion, while the orchestra expatiates upon the opening theme. Both the choral fugue and the orchestra build tension through a stretto—a passage, that is, in which the fugue subject enters in one voice before it has been completed in another. The choral stretto comes on the words "Et statuit super petram pedes meos," sung without accompaniment—that is, a cappella. This is followed by a stretto in the orchestral fugue, the impression of mounting tension being underlined by dotted rhythms. In the final measures elements of the two fugal themes are combined in chorus and orchestra. The climax comes through understatement. In a sudden piano the chorus in unison sings "et sperabunt in Domino," while a high trumpet in quarter notes, together with cellos and basses in eighths, reminds us of the subject of the first fugue.

Psalm CL (Vulgate)

Alleluia.
Laudate Dominum in sanctis ejus:
laudate eum in firmamento virtutis ejus.
Laudate eum in virtutibus ejus:
laudate eum secundum multitudinem magnitudinis ejus.
Laudate eum in sono tubae:
laudate eum in psalterio et cithara.
Laudate eum in timpano et choro:
laudate eum in chordis et organo.
Laudate eum in cimbalis benesonantibus:
laudate eum in cimbalis jubilationis:
omnis spiritus laudet Dominum.
Alleluia.

Alleluia.
Praise ye the Lord in His holy places:
praise ye Him in the firmament of His power.
Praise ye Him for his mighty acts:
praise ye Him according to the multitude of His greatness.
Praise Him with sound of trumpet:
praise Him with psaltery and harp.
Praise Him with timbrel and choir:
praise Him with strings and organs.
Praise Him with high sounding cymbals:
praise Him with cymbals of joy:
let every spirit praise the Lord.
Alleluia.

Third movement

The solemn "Alleluia" serves as introduction. The C-minor harmony in the chorus is pitted against a C-major arpeggio figure in the orchestra. The Allegro proper opens with Stravinskyan rhythms that project the spirit of the Psalm in dancelike measures. The music starts out in a bright C major, with the Tonic chord repeated against a driving rhythmic ostinato in the bass, the whole set off by staccato interjections in the orchestra. As so often in Stravinsky's music, the syncopation is underlined by melodic-rhythmic patterns that are shifted from one beat of the measure to another.

The sopranos enter on the "Laudate" with the two-note theme of the opening movement. But these notes are now a major instead of a minor second apart. The music gains steadily in power, its forward momentum reinforced by striking modulations. A sudden interruption brings a return of the opening Alleluia and a resumption of the forward drive. Presently there is a broadening into the slower tempo of the introduction, with a new dotted figure in the vocal parts. Then, subito piano e ben cantabile (suddenly soft and very songful), the peroration gets under way, on the words "Laudate eum in cimbalis benesonantibus," in the key of E flat. This serene coda, which takes up about one-third of the movement, unfolds over a four-note ostinato in the bass in three-four time, so that the bass pattern begins a beat later with each recurrence. The noble melody of the so-

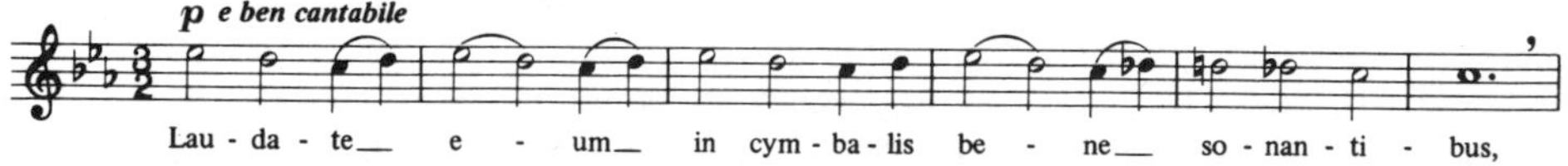

pranos reaffirms the semitone interval that has played a fertilizing role throughout the symphony; and the powerful E-flat major tonality rises at the very last to a major cadence in C major that evokes the "Alleluia" with which the movement opened.

For sheer grandeur of conception there is little in the output of the first half of our century to rival the closing pages of the *Symphony of Psalms*.

81

Béla Bartók

"What is the best way for a composer to reap the full benefits of his studies in peasant music? It is to assimilate the idiom of peasant music so completely that he is able to forget all about it and use it as his musical mother tongue."

Béla Bartók (Photo copyright by G. D. Hackett, New York.)

It was the mission of Béla Bartók (1881–1945) to reconcile the folk melody of his native Hungary with the main currents of European music. In the process he created an entirely personal language and revealed himself as one of the major artists of our century.

His Life

Early contact with folk music

Bartók was born in a small Hungarian town where his father was director of an agricultural school. He studied at the Royal Academy in Budapest, where he came in contact with the nationalist movement that aimed to shake off the domination of German musical culture. His interest in folklore led him to realize that what passed for Hungarian in the eyes of the world—the idiom romanticized by Liszt and Brahms and kept alive by café musicians—was really the music of the Gypsies. The true Hungarian folk idiom, he decided, was to be found only among the peasants. In company with his fellow composer Zoltán Kodály he toured the remote villages of the country, determined to collect the native songs before they died out forever. He became an authority on the songs of the Danubian basin—Slovakian, Romanian, and Bulgarian—and subsequently extended his investigations to include Turkish and Arab folk song.

Personal contact with peasant life brought to the surface the profound humanity that is the essential element of Bartók's art. "Those days I spent in the villages among the peasants were the happiest of my life. In order really to feel the vitality of this music one must, so to speak, have lived it. And this is possible only when one comes to know it by direct contact with the peasants."

In 1907 Bartók was appointed professor of piano at the Royal Academy in Budapest. Together with Kodály he founded a society for the presentation of contemporary music. The project was defeated by the apathy of a public that refused to be weaned from the traditional German repertory. Bartók was sufficiently embittered to give up composing for a time. He resumed his folklore studies and during the First World War devoted himself to a collection of soldier songs.

With the performance at the Budapest Opera of his ballet *The Wooden Prince,* Bartók came into his own. The fall of the Hapsburg monarchy in

1918 released a surge of national fervor that created a favorable climate for his music. In the ensuing decade Bartók became a leading figure in the musical life of his country.

The alliance between Admiral Horthy's regime and Nazi Germany on the eve of the Second World War confronted the composer with issues that he faced squarely. He protested the performances of his music on the Berlin radio and at every opportunity took an anti-Fascist stand. To go into exile meant surrendering the position he enjoyed in Hungary. But he would not compromise. "He who stays on when he could leave may be said to acquiesce tacitly in everything that is happening here." Bartók's friends, fearing for his safety, prevailed upon him to leave the country while there was still time. He came to the United States in 1940 and settled in New York City.

Emigration to the U.S.

The last five years of his life yielded little in the way of happiness. Sensitive and retiring, he felt uprooted, isolated in his new surroundings. He made some public appearances, playing his music for two pianos with his wife and onetime pupil, Ditta Pásztory-Bartók. These did not suffice to relieve his financial straits. To his son he wrote in the fall of 1941, "Concerts are few and far between. If we had to live on those we would really be at the end of our tether."

Last years

In his last years he suffered from leukemia and was no longer able to appear in public. Friends appealed for aid to ASCAP (American Society of Composers, Authors, and Publishers). Funds were made available that provided the composer with proper care in nursing homes and enabled him to continue writing to the end. A series of commissions from various sources spurred him to the composition of his last works. They rank among his finest. He worked feverishly to complete the *Third Piano Concerto* and a concerto for viola and orchestra that had been commissioned by William Primrose. When he realized that he was dying he concentrated on the piano concerto in order to leave his wife "the only inheritance within his power." In his race against time he wishfully wrote *vége*—The End—on his working sketch a few days before he actually finished the piece. The *Viola Concerto,* left unfinished, was brought to completion from his sketches by his friend and disciple Tibor Serly. "The trouble is," he remarked to his doctor shortly before the end, "that I have to go with so much still to say." He died in the West Side Hospital in New York City.

The tale of the composer who spends his last days in poverty and embitterment only to be acclaimed after his death would seem to belong to the Romantic past, to the legend of Mozart, Schubert, Musorgsky. Yet it happened in our time. Bartók had to die in order to make his success in the United States. Almost immediately there was an upsurge of interest in his music that soon assumed the proportions of a boom. As though impelled by a sense of guilt for their previous neglect of his works, conductors, performers, record companies, broadcasting stations, and even his publishers rushed to pay him the homage that might have brought him comfort had it come in time.

His Music

Like Stravinsky, Bartók was careful to disclaim the role of revolutionary. "In art there are only fast or slow developments. Essentially it is a matter of evolution, not revolution." Despite the newness of his language he was rooted in the Classical heritage. "In my youth my ideal was not so much the art of Bach or Mozart as that of Beethoven." He adhered to the logic and beauty of Classical form, and to Beethoven's vision of music as an embodiment of human emotion.

Bartók found authentic Hungarian folk music to be based on ancient modes, unfamiliar scales, and nonsymmetrical rhythms. These freed him from what he called "the tyrannical rule of the major and minor keys," and brought him to new concepts of melody, harmony, and rhythm. "What we had to do," he wrote, "was to divine the spirit of this unknown music and to make this spirit, so difficult to describe in words, the basis of our works."

Melody and harmony

Classic and Romantic elements intermingle in Bartók's art. His Classicism shows itself in his emphasis on construction. Characteristic is a type of melody that, like Stravinsky's, moves in a narrow range and creates an effect of primitive force. His harmony can be bitingly dissonant. Polytonality abounds in his work; but, despite an occasional leaning toward atonality, he never wholly abandoned the principle of key. In the popular *Allegro barbaro,* written in 1911, we find the percussive treatment of dissonant chords that was to come into vogue with Stravinsky's *The Rite of Spring*. Bartók's is one of the great rhythmic imaginations of modern times.

Rhythmic innovation

Bartók recording folk songs in Transylvania. (Photo copyright by G. D. Hackett, New York.)

His pounding, stabbing rhythms constitute the primitive aspect of his art. Passages in his scores have a Stravinskyan look, the meter changing almost at every bar. Like the Russian master, he is fond of syncopation and repeated patterns (ostinatos). Bartók played a major role in the revitalization of European rhythm, infusing it with earthy vitality, with kinetic force and tension.

Form

He was more traditional in respect to form. His model was the sonata of Beethoven. In his middle years he came under the influence of pre-Bach music and turned increasingly from harmony to linear thinking. His complex texture is a masterly example of modern dissonant counterpoint. It sets forth his development toward greater abstraction, tightness of structure, and purity of style.

Orchestration

From the orchestra of Richard Strauss and Debussy Bartók found his way to a palette all his own. His orchestration ranges from brilliant mixtures to threads of pure color that bring out the intertwining melody lines; from a hard, bright glitter to a luminous haze. A virtuoso pianist himself, Bartók is one of the masters of modern piano writing. He typifies the twentieth-century use of the piano as an instrument of percussion and rhythm. The most important work for piano of his later years is *Mikrokosmos* (1926–37), a collection of one hundred and fifty-three pieces ranging from the simplest grade to virtuoso playing.

Chamber music

The six string quartets may very well rank among the finest achievements of our century. These are uncompromising and extraordinarily expressive works, certain of them impregnated with the brooding pessimism that was the aftermath of the First World War. Bartók is best known to the public by the three major works of his last period. The *Music for Strings, Percussion, and Celesta,* written in 1936, is regarded by many as his masterpiece. Tonal opulence and warmth characterize the *Concerto for Orchestra* (1943), a favorite with American audiences. The master's final statement, the *Third Piano Concerto* (1945), is an impassioned and broadly conceived work, its three movements by turn dramatic, contemplative, satanic. The last-named quality connects him with the Hungarian master of the Romantic period, Franz Liszt.

Bartók's music encompasses the diverse trends of his time, polytonality and atonality, Expressionism and Neoclassicism, folk dance and machine music, the lyric and the dynamic. It reaches from the primitive to the intellectual, from program music to the abstract, from nationalism to the universal. Into all these he infused the high aim of a former age: to touch the heart.

Concerto for Orchestra

In the summer of 1943 Bartók was confined in Doctors Hospital in New York City. One day he received a visit from Serge Koussevitzky, who came offering a thousand-dollar commission and a first performance by the Boston Symphony Orchestra for any piece he would write. The knowledge that his music was wanted and that a major orchestra was waiting to perform the as-yet-unwritten score had a beneficent effect on the incurably ill composer. He was able to quit the hospital, and set to work on the *Concerto for Orchestra,* which was completed in October of that year. "The general mood of the work," he wrote, "represents, apart from the jesting second movement, a gradual transition from the sternness of the first movement and the lugubrious death-song of the third to the life-assertion of the last."

Of symphonic dimension, the work is called a concerto because of its tendency, as Bartók explained, "to treat the single instruments in a concertante or soloistic manner." In other words, he used the term as the eighteenth century did. The element of virtuosity prevails, but the virtuoso is the entire orchestra.

First movement
SIDE 10/1 (E II)
SIDE 16/3 (S)

I. *Introduzione.* Andante non troppo—Allegro vivace. The Introduction is spacious of gesture. It prepares the listener for a large work. In the composer's best vein are the sonorities of the opening passage, a solemn statement by cellos and basses set off by tremolos on upper strings and flute. The theme is based on the interval of the fourth (indicated by brackets), which occupies a prominent position in the melodic formations of this composer.

The first subject of the Allegro vivace consists of a vigorously syncopated figure that ascends to a climax and as briskly subsides:

Here too the fourth is prominent. A contrasting idea in folklore style consists mainly of two notes. The Development builds up tension through contrapuntal imitation. The Restatement is abbreviated, as is customary in twentieth-century works. The movement has the quality of inevitable progression that is the essence of symphonic style.

Second movement

II. *Giuoco delle coppie* (Game of Pairs). So called because the wind instruments are paired at specific intervals, bassoons in sixths, oboes in thirds, clarinets in sevenths, flutes in fifths, muted trumpets in seconds. This "jesting second movement," as Bartók called it, is marked Allegretto scherzando. The side drum, without snares, ushers in music of a proces-

sional nature that is filled with teasing ideas. In evidence is the element of the bizarre that appealed to Berlioz and Mahler no less than to Bartók. The form is a "chain" of five little sections, each featuring another pair of instruments. There is a chorale for brass. The five sections are then restated with more elaborate instrumentation.

Third movement

III. *Elegia.* Andante non troppo. This movement is the "lugubrious death song." An oboe traces a long line of lamentation against Bartókian flickerings of clarinet, flute, and harp tone. The music is rhapsodic, visionary; it rises to a tragic climax. This is a heroic canvas in the great line of the hymnic adagios of Beethoven.

Fourth movement

IV. *Intermezzo interrotto* (Interrupted Intermezzo). A plaintive tune in folk-song style is introduced by the oboe and continued by the flute.

The nonsymmetrical rhythm, an alternation of ¾ and ⅝, imparts to the movement a wayward charm. There follows a broadly songful theme on the strings, one of the great melodies of the twentieth century. The mood

is interrupted as the music turns from folk lyricism to the sophisticated tone of the cafés. The return of the lyric theme on muted strings makes a grandly poetic effect. The movement is replete with capriciousness and tender sentiment.

Fifth movement

V. Finale. Pesante–Presto. There is an introduction of seven bars marked pesante (heavily), in which the horns outline the germinal theme. The movement of "life-assertion" gets off to a whirlwind perpetuum mobile (perpetual motion) in the strings. The fugue that follows parades intricate devices of counterpoint; yet so lightly does Bartók wear his learning that there is nothing here to tax the untutored ear. The fugue subject is presented by the second trumpet. Notice again the decisive role played by the interval of a fourth.

The answer, played by the first trumpet, is an inversion of the theme. The folk tune as Bartók uses it here has nothing in common with the prettified peasant dances of the nineteenth century. Its harmonies are acrid, its rhythms imbued with primitive strength. The movement rises to a mood of heroic affirmation.

Music for String Instruments, Percussion, and Celesta

This work (1936) was a landmark in the twentieth-century cultivation of chamber-music textures. Bartók's conception called for two string groups to frame the percussion and celesta. He carefully specified the arrangement of the players on the stage:

	Double Bass I	Double Bass II	
Cello I	Timpani	Bass Drum	Cello II
Viola I	Side Drums	Cymbals	Viola II
Violin II	Celesta	Xylophone	Violin IV
Violin I	Piano	Harp	Violin III

I. Andante tranquillo. The movement is based on a single crescendo that grows inexorably from *pp* to a fortissimo climax and then works back to a *ppp*. We hear a fugue for strings, based on an undulating chromatic theme that includes all the semitones within its range of a fifth, from A to E.

First movement

Each time the subject enters, it appears alternately a fifth higher and lower, growing steadily in power until the climactic point is reached on E flat. Thereupon the subject is inverted and the fugue returns to the central A. Since the entire movement is woven out of the generating theme, this Andante achieves an extraordinary concentration of thought and consistency of texture.

II. Allegro. The main idea of this closely knit sonata form is a taut, imperious subject whose chromatic character relates it to the subject of the preceding movement. The key areas are loosely defined through free use

Second movement

of the twelve chromatic tones around a Tonic (C) and a Dominant (G). The Development section contains an exciting fugato. In the Recapitulation, the main idea returns in a typically Bartókian rhythm—an alternation of groups of two, three, and five beats—before it settles into 3/8. The two groups of strings are used antiphonally, in question-and-answer formation.

Third movement

III. Adagio. This "night piece" reveals Bartók's gift for evoking a magical nocturnal landscape through instrumental color. The movement is in "arch form," proceeding to a high point and then retracing its path back to the beginning. The eerie repetition of the high F on the xylophone ushers in a rhapsodic cantillation on the viola (section **A**). A lyric section (**B**) is presented by celesta and violin, against a background of Bartókian flickerings of sound. The climax of the movement (section **C**) is based on a tense five-note motive that is bandied about among the instruments:

This constitutes the central point of the movement. The material heard earlier then returns, but in reverse order, closing with an abbreviated form of section **A.**

Fourth movement

IV. Allegro molto. The finale combines the passionate abandon of Magyar folk dance and contrapuntal processes that are tossed off with true virtuosity. The movement, an expanded rondo form, opens with plucked chords that conjure up the sound of folk instruments. The central idea is in a Bulgarian dance rhythm of eight eighth notes, written as 2/2 but grouped in the pattern 2-2-3:

In the contrasting sections, Bartók deploys his propulsive rhythms—which at times take on a jazzlike animation—and his powerful cluster chords on the piano. Each recurrence of the rondo theme brings fresh variation. The movement builds to a triumphal return of the germinal theme from the first movement, now purged of its chromaticism and presented with expanded intervals. The coda leads to a clangorous, affirmative climax.

Bartók's prime characteristic both as musician and man was the uncompromising integrity that informed his every act—what a compatriot of his has called "the proud morality of the mind." He was one of the great spirits of our time.

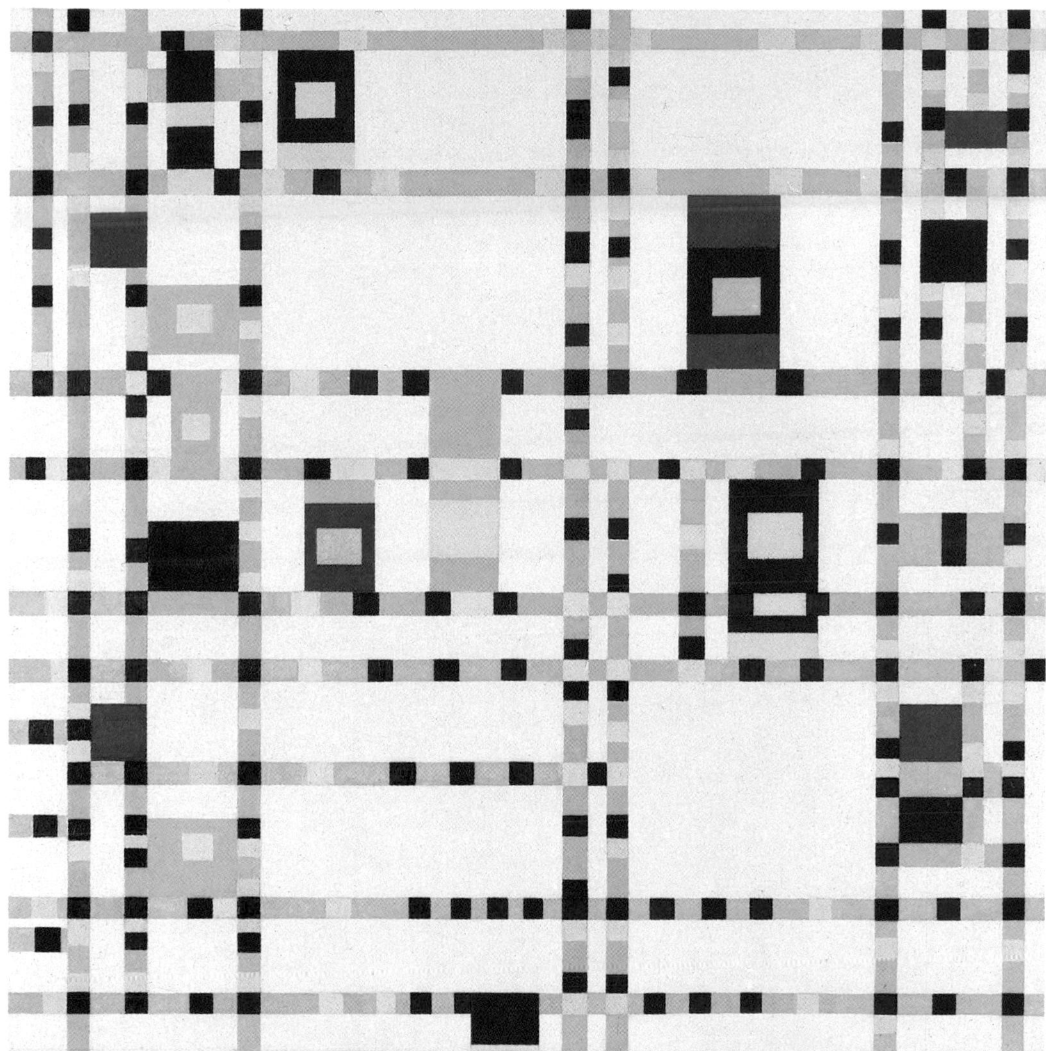

The impact of the city is manifest in ***Broadway Boogie-Woogie*** *(1942–43) by Piet Mondrian (1872–1944), in whose work architectonic unity and economy of means are prime characteristics.* (Collection, The Museum of Modern Art, New York. Given anonymously.)

This late work by the painter Paul Klee (1879–1940), ***Heroic Strokes of the Bow,*** *expresses the artist's intensely personal reactions to music through simple, yet symbolic forms.* (Collection, The Museum of Modern Art, New York. Nelson A. Rockefeller Bequest.)

82

Arnold Schoenberg

"I personally hate to be called a revolutionist, which I am not. What I did was neither revolution nor anarchy."

Arnold Schoenberg.

It is worthy of note that, like Stravinsky and Bartók, the other great innovator of our time disclaimed revolutionary intent. Quite the contrary, his disciples regard him as having brought to its culmination the thousand-year-old tradition of European polyphony.

His Life

Arnold Schoenberg (1874–1951) was born in Vienna. He began to study the violin at the age of eight, and soon afterward made his initial attempts at composing. Having decided to devote his life to music, he left school while in his teens. For a time he earned his living working in a bank, and meanwhile continued to compose, working entirely by himself. Presently he became acquainted with a young musician, Alexander von Zemlinsky, who for a few months gave him lessons in counterpoint. This was the only musical instruction he ever had.

Early years

Through Zemlinsky young Schoenberg was introduced to the advanced musical circles of Vienna, which at that time were under the spell of *Tristan* and *Parsifal*. In 1899, when he was twenty-five, Schoenberg wrote the string sextet *Verklärte Nacht* (Transfigured Night). The following year several of Schoenberg's songs were performed in Vienna and precipitated a scene. "And ever since that day," he once remarked with a smile, "the scandal has never ceased."

It was at this time that Schoenberg began a large-scale work for voices and orchestra, the *Gurre-Lieder* (Songs of Gurre). For the huge forces, choral and instrumental, required for this cantata he needed music paper double the ordinary size. Work on the *Gurre-Lieder* was interrupted by material worries. In 1901, after his marriage to Zemlinsky's sister, he moved to Berlin and obtained a post in a theater, conducting operettas and music-hall songs. Schoenberg's early music already displayed certain traits of his later style. A publisher to whom he brought a quartet observed, "You must think that if the second theme is a retrograde inversion of the first theme, that automatically makes it good!"

Return to Vienna

Upon his return to Vienna Schoenberg became active as a teacher and soon gathered about him a band of disciples, of whom the most gifted were Alban Berg and Anton Webern. The devotion of these advanced young musicians sustained him in the fierce battle for recognition that still lay ahead. With each new work Schoenberg moved closer to as bold a step as any artist has ever taken—the rejection of tonality.

The First World War interrupted Schoenberg's creative activity. Although he was past forty, he was called up for military service in the Vienna garrison. He had reached a critical point in his development. There followed a silence of seven years, between 1915 and 1923, during which he clarified his position in his own mind, and evolved a set of structural procedures to replace tonality. The goal once set, Schoenberg pursued it with that tenacity of purpose without which no prophet can prevail. His "method of composing with twelve tones" caused great bewilderment in the musical world. All the same, he was now firmly established as a leader of contemporary musical thought. On his fiftieth birthday the chorus of the Vienna Opera performed his cantata *Friede auf Erden* (Peace on Earth), which he had written almost two decades before. The next year he was appointed to succeed Ferruccio Busoni as professor of composition at the Berlin Academy of Arts. The uniquely favorable attitude of the Weimar Republic toward experimental art had made it possible for one of the most iconoclastic musicians in history to carry on his work from the vantage point of an official post.

Move to the United States

This period in Schoenberg's life ended with the coming to power of Hitler in 1933. He arrived in the United States in the fall of 1933. After a short period of teaching in Boston, he joined the faculty of the University of Southern California, and shortly afterward was appointed professor of composition at the University of California in Los Angeles. In 1940 he became an American citizen. He taught until his retirement at the age of seventy, and continued his musical activities till his death in 1951. A seeker after truth until the end, to no one more than to himself could be applied the injunction he had written in the text of his cantata *Die Jakobsleiter* (Jacob's Ladder; 1913): "One must go on without asking what lies before or behind."

His Music

Schoenberg stemmed out of the Viennese past. He took his point of departure from the final quartets of Beethoven, the richly wrought piano writing of Brahms, and the orchestral sonority of Bruckner and Mahler—behind whom, of course, loomed the un-Viennese figure of Wagner.

Post-Wagnerian Romanticism

Schoenberg's first period may be described as one of post-Wagnerian Romanticism; he still used key signatures and remained within the boundaries of tonality. The best-known work of this period is *Verklärte Nacht,* Opus 4, which poses no problems to anyone who has listened to *Tristan.* Indeed, the work became something of a popular hit after it was used by Antony Tudor as the accompaniment for his Expressionist ballet *Pillar of Fire.* Schoenberg's second period, the atonal-Expressionist, got under way with the *Three Piano Pieces,* Opus 11 (1909), in which he abolished the distinction between consonance and dissonance as well as the sense

Atonal Expressionism

The emotionally-charged atmosphere of the painting **Gerda, Half-Length Portrait** *(1914) by Ernst Ludwig Kirchner (1880–1938) was characteristic of German Expressionism.* (Solomon R. Guggenheim Museum, Partial Gift, Mr. and Mrs. Mortimer M. Denker.)

of a home key. Concentrated and intense, these short pieces point the way to his later development. The high points of this period are the *Five Pieces for Orchestra,* Opus 16, which we will discuss, and *Pierrot lunaire* (Moonstruck Pierrot, Opus 21; 1912), for female reciter and five instruments–flute, clarinet, violin, cello, and piano (with three alternating instruments–piccolo, bass clarinet, viola). This work, the first that carried Schoenberg's name beyond his immediate circle, introduced an eerily expressive kind of declamation midway between song and speech, known as *Sprechstimme* (speaking voice).

Twelve-tone period

Schoenberg's third period, that of the twelve-tone method, reached its climax in the *Variations for Orchestra,* Opus 31 (1927–28). This is the first twelve-tone composition for orchestra and one of Schoenberg's most powerful works. In the fourth and last period of his career–the American phase–he carried the twelve-tone technique to further stages of refinement. He also modified his doctrine sufficiently to allow tonal elements to coexist with the twelve-tone style, and on occasion wrote "old-fashioned" music with key signatures. In the category of tonal works we find the *Suite for String Orchestra in G major* (1934), intended for the use of students; also the *Kol Nidre* for speaker, chorus, and orchestra, Opus 39 (1939), an impressive setting of the Hebrew prayer. Several among the late works present the twelve-tone style in a manner markedly more accessible than earlier pieces, often with tonal implications. Among those are the

American period

brilliant *Piano Concerto* (1942) and the cantata *A Survivor from Warsaw* (1948), which we will discuss. The strict use of twelve-tone technique is represented by such compositions as the lyrical *String Quartet No. 4,* Opus 37 (1936), his last work in this medium, and the *Violin Concerto,* Opus 36 (1936), which is in Schoenberg's most uncompromising manner. Mention should be made too of the Biblical opera *Moses and Aaron,* a major work. The first two acts were finished by 1932, but the third act was interrupted by his emigration to the United States; he never completed it.

Schoenberg was a tireless propagandist for his ideas, a role for which his verbal gifts and his passion for polemics eminently fitted him. Essays and articles flowed from his pen, conveying his views in a trenchant, aphoristic style which, late in life, he transferred from German to English. The following observations are characteristic: "Genius learns only from itself, talent chiefly from others. . . . One must believe in the infallibility of one's fantasy and the truth of one's inspiration. . . . Creation to an artist should be as natural and inescapable as the growth of apples to an apple tree. . . . The twelve tones will not invent for you. . . . It is said of many an author that he has indeed technique, but no invention. That is wrong: either he also lacks technique or he also has invention. . . . An apostle who does not glow preaches heresy. . . . The laws of nature manifested in a man of genius are but the laws of the future."

Five Pieces for Orchestra, *Opus 16*

The *Five Pieces for Orchestra* (1909) constitute one of the key works of Schoenberg's second period, when his language became atonal. In order to solve the problems of the new idiom, he concentrated on the short lyric forms. In line with the Expressionist point of view, he connected the *Five Orchestral Pieces* with specific emotions and moods and gave them descriptive titles. Forty years later—in 1949—he revised the *Five Pieces,* rescoring them for an orchestra of the usual size instead of the huge ensemble required in the original version.

First piece
SIDE 10/2 (E II)
SIDE 16/4 (S)

I. *Vorgefühle* (Premonitions). The first piece, marked "very fast," shows how well the atonal idiom lends itself to the expression of fear and anxiety. This music evokes a hallucinatory world where agony of soul reigns unrelieved. The basic theme is an ascending motive that is announced at the outset by muted cellos, against descending parallel fifths on clarinets:

This theme reappears throughout the piece in manifold guises, with changes of rhythm (augmentation and diminution) and variation in the size of its intervals. The climb to the final note underlines the continuous sense of climax. Schoenberg exploits striking instrumental effects, such as the frightening rasp of muted horn and trombone, and *fluttertonguing* (a rolling of the tongue, as if pronouncing d-r-r-r, used in playing wind instruments) on the muted trumpet. He intrigues the ear with unwonted contrasts of high and low registers, achieves a remarkable luminosity of texture, and keeps the sound mass in a state of dynamic impulsion.

Second piece
SIDE 10/3 (E II)
SIDE 16/5 (S)

II. *Vergangenes* (Yesteryears). Andante. A lyrical meditation, intensely Romantic in character. The opening harmonies are composites of colors as well as tones: each note of the chord is played by a different instrument. The bare look of the notes on the page shows the line of descent from the fervidly chromatic idiom of *Tristan* (see p. 168). The introductory motive on the cello sets the mood for a music that seems to be suspended in time.

A new section is ushered in by an expressive idea on the muted viola, which emerges as the principal theme of the piece. There enters a hopping figure on the bassoon, against a flowing ostinato on the celesta, which becomes a countersubject for the principal idea. The climax is a whisper: sixteenth-note figures derived from the bassoon motive build up—to a *ppp!* The chief motive dominates the closing pages. The final sounds are extremely rarefied: a splash of color on the celesta, harmonics on strings and harp, against sustained harmonies in woodwinds and muted brass.

Third piece

III. *Sommermorgen an einem See: Farben* (Summer Morning by a Lake: Colors). Moderato. Schoenberg originally called this study in sonority *Der wechselnde Akkord* (The Changing Chord). The piece sprang out of a conversation he had with Mahler, in which he argued that it should be possible to create a melody by sounding a single tone on the different instruments: in other words, the Schoenbergian concept of *Klangfarbenmelodie* (tone-color melody). Mahler disagreed. In the writing, Schoenberg expanded his original notion. The harmonies in the piece do change, but so imperceptibly that the ear is led to concentrate on the continual shifting of color.

When he wrote the piece Schoenberg was much interested in painting. Hence the musical conception connected itself in his mind with a visual image—the shimmer of the morning sun on the calm surface of a lake. The harmonic current flows so slowly that it seems hardly to move, gleaming gently as the various colors play upon it. The opening measure illustrates Schoenberg's method in this essay in pure orchestration. The first chord is played *ppp* by two flutes, clarinet, bassoon, and viola. It is then repeated, with a subtle change of color, by English horn, bassoon, muted horn, muted trumpet, and double bass.

Fourth piece

IV. *Peripetie.* Molto Allegro. The Greek word *peripetia* signifies a sudden crisis or reversal in the events of a drama. We are back in the brooding atmosphere of the first piece. Woodwinds and brass by turns trace impetuous figures. The music shows the rhythmic flexibility, fragmentation of texture, and wide leaps in the melody so characteristic of Schoenberg. He makes dramatic use of the muted brass playing fortissimo. Tension mounts to the end.

Fifth piece

V. *Das obligate Rezitativ* (The Obligatory Recitative). Allegretto. The last of the set is in a vein of impassioned lyricism. The short, breathless phrases communicate intense emotion. Schoenberg here achieves his desire to create a melody that perpetually renews itself, never weakening its tension through repetition. He was increasingly aware of the problem that his intricate polyphonic textures posed to conductor, performer, and student. In *Das obligate Rezitativ* he used for the first time a system of signs to distinguish the principal voice from the other contrapuntal lines—a practice he retained in all his later scores.

A Survivor From Warsaw

The cantata *A Survivor from Warsaw* sprang out of one of the most profound experiences of Schoenberg's life. Like many Austrian-Jewish intellectuals of his generation, he had grown away from his Jewish origins and ultimately became a Catholic. The rise of Hitlerism reminded him that he was a Jew. After he left Germany he found it spiritually necessary to return to the Hebrew faith. He was deeply shaken when, at the end of the war, the world learned how the Nazis had transported millions of Jews from all over Europe into the Warsaw Ghetto and then herded them into the gas chambers of Dachau, Buchenwald, Auschwitz. The world learned too how the final remnant of Jews in the Ghetto decided to die fighting rather than be slaughtered, and organized the first uprising in Occupied Europe. Emotionally involved as he was in these historic events, Schoenberg in *A Survivor from Warsaw* (1947) produced one of his most dramatic works.

We pointed out how well the atonal idiom lent itself to the moods of fear and suspense that were native to German Expressionism. These moods predominate in *A Survivor,* a six-minute cantata marked by the same emotional intensity that we noted in the first of the *Five Pieces for Orchestra* (*Premonitions*). Here the fear and suspense are brought into dramatic focus through the text, which was written by Schoenberg himself in English. He was no literary craftsman, and he was writing in a language that he had learned late in life; yet the blazing sincerity out of which he wrote more than makes up for a certain crudity of style.

The plot

A narrator recounts how a group of Jews were conducted to their death by a detachment of Nazi soldiers. The Germans order the Jews out of the camp and line them up for the final march. They urge them on with blows and curses, shooting those that fall behind. Finally the order comes to count off, so that the sergeant may know how many to deliver to the gas chamber. They begin to count, first slowly, then faster. Finally, as by a common impulse, they begin to sing the *Shema Yisroel*–the ancient prayer that is the central creed of the Hebrew faith.

The grim tale is told by one who survived because he was left among the dead. At two points narration gives way to action. First, when the narrator quotes the sergeant, imitating his brutal manner of barking commands. Here Schoenberg uses the percussion instruments–bass drum, snare drum, xylophone, cymbals–to underscore the text. Second, at the dramatic climax of the piece, the grandiose moment, as Schoenberg called it, when in the face of death the Jews begin to sing. At this point, when the narrator is replaced by male chorus, the full orchestra enters for the first time. (Hitherto the orchestra has played only in groups.)

The music

From the suspenseful fanfare of the trumpets at the outset, the score abounds in remarkable strokes. For example, the high trill on the trombones in the orchestral introduction. Or the unusual effects on the string instruments, produced by tapping the strings with the stick of the bow or by scratching the strings with the stick. In the same category are the high trills on the woodwinds, fluttertonguing on the muted brass, and the snarling sound produced by forcing the tone of muted trumpets and horns. Extraordinary too is the crescendo, accelerando, and breathless intensification of rhythm (based on a pattern of two against three) when the Jews count off, faster and faster, until "it finally sounded like a stampede of wild horses."

The cantata belongs to the final period of Schoenberg's career, when he was using the fully developed twelve-tone method. A few examples will suffice to show how this technique nurtured his sense of logical structure. The piece opens with two urgent trumpet fanfares, each accompanied by a two-note chord in the strings:

The row

Although the twelve-tone row on which the cantata is based does not appear in melodic form until the entrance of the chorus, all the previous material is derived from it. Thus, the four notes of Trumpet I are the first four notes of the row, and the two violin notes are the next two.

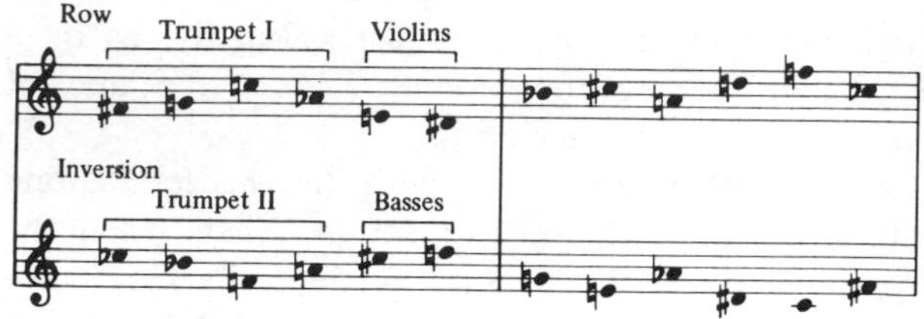

The fanfare, in Trumpet II, and its accompanying notes comprise the beginning of the row's inversion (remember that in twelve-tone composition a pitch may appear in any octave).

Schoenberg uses the elements of the row in diverse ways. It will suffice to cite one further example. When the narrator speaks of "the old prayer they had neglected for so many years," a melody is heard in the muted horn, pianissimo:

This melody consists of the first six notes of the row, transposed to begin on B flat:

Later, this melody returns at the climax, as the opening phrase of the *Shema Yisroel*.

Despite the formal intricacies of his method, Schoenberg maintained again and again that the prime function of a composer was to move the listener. "I write what I feel in my heart–and what finally comes on paper is what first coursed through every fibre of my body. A work of art can achieve no finer effect than when it transmits to the beholder the emotions that raged in the creator, in such a way that they rage and storm also in him." In *A Survivor from Warsaw* Schoenberg fashioned a work of art that fully transmits to us the emotions that raged in him.

His belief in the necessity and rightness of his method sustained him and gave him the strength to carry through his revolution. His doctrines focused attention on basic compositional problems, and decisively affected the course of musical thought in the twentieth century.

83

Alban Berg

Alban Berg.

"When I decided to write an opera, my only intention was to give to the theater what belongs to the theater. The music was to be so formed that at each moment it would fulfill its duty of serving the action."

It was the unique achievement of Alban Berg (1885–1935) to humanize the abstract procedures of the Schoenbergian technique, and to reconcile them with the expression of feeling. Upon a new and difficult idiom he imprinted the stamp of a lyric imagination of the first order.

His Life

Berg was born in Vienna. He came of a well-to-do family and grew up in an environment that fostered his artistic proclivities. At nineteen he made the acquaintance of Arnold Schoenberg, who was sufficiently impressed with the youth's manuscripts to accept him as a pupil. During his six years with Schoenberg (1904–10) he acquired the consummate mastery of technique that characterizes his later work. Schoenberg was not only an exacting master, but also a devoted friend and mentor who shaped Berg's whole outlook on art.

The outbreak of war in 1914 hurled Berg into a period of depression. "The urge 'to be in it,' " he wrote to Schoenberg, "the feeling of helplessness at being unable to serve my country, prevented any concentration on work." A few months later he was called up for military service, despite his uncertain health (he suffered from asthma and attacks of nervous debility). He was presently transferred to the War Ministry in Vienna. Already *Wozzeck* occupied his thoughts; but he could not begin writing the music until the war was over. In December 1925 *Wozzeck* was presented at the Berlin State Opera. At one stroke Berg was lifted from comparative obscurity to international fame.

In the decade that remained to him he produced only a handful of works; but each was a significant contribution to his total output. During these years he was active as a teacher. He also wrote about music, propagandizing tirelessly on behalf of Schoenberg and his school. With the coming to power of Hitler, the works of the twelve-tone composers were banned in Germany as alien to the spirit of the Third Reich. The resulting loss of income was a source of worry to Berg, as was, to a far greater degree, the rapid Nazification of Austria. Schoenberg's enforced emigration to the United States was a bitter blow.

Exhausted and ailing after the completion of the *Violin Concerto,* Berg went to the country for a short rest before resuming work on his opera *Lulu.* An insect bite brought on an abscess that caused infection. Upon his return to Vienna he was striken with blood poisoning. He died on Christmas Eve 1935, seven weeks before his fifty-first birthday.

His Music

Berg's art issued from the world of German Romanticism—the world of Schumann, Brahms, Wagner, Richard Strauss, and Mahler. The Romantic streak in his temperament bound him to this heritage even after he had embraced the dodecaphonic style. Berg's was the imagination of the musical dramatist. For him the musical gesture was bound up with character and action, mood and atmosphere. Yet, like his teacher, he leaned toward the formal patterns of the past—fugue and invention, passacaglia, variations, sonata, and suite.

The list of his published works begins with the *Piano Sonata,* Opus 1 (1908), a highly charged work in a post-Wagnerian idiom. The four songs of Opus 2 (1909) reveal the composer in a period of transition from Mahlerian Romanticism to the Expressionist tendencies of his later years. In the last of the four, the young composer abandons key signatures. The *Three Orchestral Pieces,* Opus 6 (1913–14), consist of a Prelude, Round, and March. With the third piece of this set we find ourselves in the atmosphere of *Wozzeck.* Berg's most widely known composition, after *Wozzeck,* is the *Lyric Suite,* written in 1925–26. The work is in six movements. The first and last follow strictly "the method of composing with twelve tones." Originally written for string quartet, the *Lyric Suite* achieved such popularity that in 1928 the composer arranged the three middle movements for string orchestra.

Berg spent the last seven years of his life on the opera *Lulu.* The work is based on a single twelve-tone row. The composer fashioned the libretto himself from two dramas by Frank Wedekind—*Earth Spirit* (1893) and *Pandora's Box* (1901). Lulu is the eternal type of *femme fatale* "who destroys everyone because she is destroyed by everyone." Berg was in the midst of orchestrating *Lulu* when he interrupted the task to write the *Violin Concerto* (1935). The opera remained unfinished for many years, but recently the orchestration was completed by the Austrian composer Friedrich Cerha, and now *Lulu* has taken its place alongside *Wozzeck* as one of the challenging works of the modern lyric theater.

Alban Berg is probably the most widely admired master of the twelve-tone school. His premature death robbed contemporary music of a major figure.

Wozzeck

In 1914 Berg saw the play that impelled him to the composition of *Wozzeck.* His work was interrupted by the war, and the opera was not completed until 1922. The vocal score was published the following year with the financial help of Alma Mahler, to whom *Wozzeck* was dedicated.

The author of the play, Georg Büchner (1813–37), belonged to the generation of intellectuals who were stifled by the political repressions of Metternich's Europe. His socialist leanings brought him into conflict with the authorities. After his death at twenty-four, the manuscripts of *Danton's Tod* (The Death of Danton) and the unfinished *Woyzeck* (this was the original spelling) were found among his papers. In the stolid infantryman Wozzeck he created an archetype of "the insulted and injured" of the earth.

Libretto

Berg's libretto tightened the original play. He shaped the material into three acts, each containing five scenes. These are linked by brief orchestral interludes whose motivic facture serves to round off what has preceded as well as to introduce what follows. As a result, Berg's "opera of protest and compassion" has astonishing unity of texture and mood.

The action centers around Wozzeck's unhappy love for Marie, by whom he has had an illegitimate child. Wozzeck is the victim of the sadistic Captain and of the Doctor, a coldly scientific gentleman who uses Wozzeck for his experiments—to which the soldier submits because he needs the money. (Wozzeck is given to hallucinations. The Doctor is bent on proving his theory that mental disorder is related to diet.) Marie cannot resist her infatuation with the handsome Drum Major. Wozzeck slowly realizes that she has been unfaithful to him. Ultimately he kills her. Driven back to the death-scene by guilt and remorse, he drowns himself. The tragedy unfolds in three acts. The first is the exposition of the theme: "Wozzeck in relation to his environment." The second is the development of the theme: "Wozzeck becomes more and more convinced of Marie's infidelity." The third act is the catastrophe: "Wozzeck murders Marie and atones by suicide."

The vocal line sensitively portrays characters and situations. Harmonically, the greater part of the opera is cast in an atonal-Expressionist idiom. Berg anticipates certain twelve-tone procedures; he also looks back to the tonal tradition, puts a number of passages in major and minor keys, and uses leitmotifs in the Wagnerian manner. The snatches of popular song in the score create an effective contrast to their atonal surroundings. Appearing in so special a context, they take on a strange wistfulness.

Act I, Scene 1

In the opening scene, Wozzeck is shaving the Captain. From the hysterical Captain's opening remark—"Langsam, Wozzeck, langsam" (Slow, Wozzeck, go slow!)—the jagged vocal line, with its wide leaps and brusque inflections, projects the atmosphere of German Expressionism. Wozzeck's music is more sustained in manner. His reply introduces the chief motive associated with him, on the words "Wir arme Leut! Sehn Sie, Herr Hauptmann, Geld, Geld! Wer kein Geld hat!" (Poor folk like us! You see, Captain, money! Without money . . .).

This motive in various guises underlines the key statement of the scene, beginning with "Ja, wenn ich ein Herr wär": "Yes indeed, if I were a fine gentleman and had a silk hat and watch and an eyeglass, and could talk fancy, I would be virtuous too. But I'm a poor nobody."

Scene 2

Scene 2, in which Wozzeck and his friend Andres are seen cutting branches in a field, is one of several in which Berg conjures up an atmosphere of fear through his handling of the orchestra. Flickerings of sound on piccolos, oboes, and clarinets admirably prepare Wozzeck's "Du, der Platz ist verflucht!" (Man, this place is cursed). In this scene we have the first of the songs, that of Andres: "Das ist die schöne Jägerei" (Hunting is a good sport.) This is in 6/8, a meter traditionally associated with hunting scenes; the song illustrates Berg's way of evoking popular elements, although in a somewhat distorted form. The following scene, which takes place in Marie's room, shows her growing interest in the Drum Major. Berg here uses military music in a most poignant way. Marie's enthusiastic "Soldaten sind schöne Burschen" (Soldiers are handsome fellows!) brings with it a suggestion of A-flat major despite the shifting chromatic harmonies. The lullaby that follows, in 6/8 time—"Mädel was fängst du jetzt an?" (Girl, what song shall you sing? You've a little child but no husband!)—is a hauntingly lovely bit. When the child falls asleep, Marie remains lost in thought. The scene ends with the strings intoning a motive of fifths closely associated with her:

Scene 3

"Their harmonic immobility," Berg wrote, "expresses, as it were, her aimless waiting, which is only terminated with her death."

Scene 4

Scene 4, between Wozzeck and the Doctor, takes places in the latter's study; we return to the atmosphere of obsession. The music takes the shape of a passacaglia. How better to express the Doctor's *idée fixe*—the connection between nutrition and insanity—than by twenty-one variations on a theme? The theme of the passacaglia is a twelve-tone row that is first played by the clarinet at the end of the orchestral interlude. Here it is presented by the cellos and basses, extending over eight bars, and fol-

Scene 5

lowed by the variations. The final scene of Act I, a street in front of Marie's door, brings the climax of the action thus far: Marie yields to the Drum Major.

The first scene of Act II, again in Marie's room, involves another motive of fear, this time felt by the child, when Marie bursts out impatiently "Schlaf, Bub!" (Go to sleep, boy!): a minor second on the xylophone, which returns in various forms throughout the scene.

Act II, Scene 1

When Wozzeck enters, suspicious, this motive (x) reappears in a sudden slow tempo as a canon on the muted trombones:

Scene 2

The second scene takes places on a street where the Captain and the Doctor meet. The Doctor feeds the Captain's neurotic fears about his health. A passage "in slow waltz time" adds an ironic touch to this obsessive dialogue. When Wozzeck appears they torment him with veiled references to Marie's infidelity. The music for this scene is based on two forms of the Baroque: an invention (which, it will be remembered, was associated with Bach's keyboard music); and a fugue based on three themes, each associated earlier in the opera with one of the three men.

The scene culminates in Wozzeck's agonized outcry, "Gott in Himmel! Man könnte Lust bekommen sick aufzuhängen!" (God in Heaven! A man might want to hang himself!). The orchestral interlude that follows is a brooding Largo scored for chamber orchestra. In the third scene, in front of Marie's dwelling, Wozzeck threatens her. When he raises his hand against her, Marie's words point to the tragic outcome: "Rühr mich nicht an"—"Don't touch me. Better a knife in my flesh than a hand on me. My father didn't dare when I was ten." Scene 4, which takes place at the inn, is introduced by a slow *ländler* (an Austrian popular dance in the style of a rustic waltz). Various elements—a song of two young workingmen, a waltz, a chorus, a song by Andres, Wozzeck's rage at seeing Marie dance with the Drum Major, and a mock sermon by a drunken young fellow—are welded into a vivid scene in which Berg skillfully exploits the clash between the band onstage and the orchestra. Noteworthy is the guitar sound that accompanies the waltz of Marie and the Drum Major. Scene 5, which takes place in the guard house, opens with the snores of the sleeping soldiers. The Drum Major boasts of his new conquest. Wozzeck throws himself at the Major, but is beaten down by his burly opponent.

Scene 3 *Scene 4* *Scene 5*

Act III, Scene 1

Act III opens with Marie's reading of the Bible, a profoundly moving scene. She tells her child about a poor orphan who had no one in the world, who was hungry and wept. . . . The passage stands out against its atonal surroundings because it is in F minor. A fugue unfolds as she reads about Mary Magdalen and pleads that the Lord forgive her frailty. The scene of the murder, which takes place along a forest path by a pond, abounds in ominous sonorities, as at Marie's words "Wie der Mond rot aufgeht" (How red the moon is!), where the strings hold a B natural spread out over five octaves against muted trombones and fluttertonguing on muted trumpets. Unforgettable is the repeated stroke on two timpani, going from a whisper to a spine-chilling *fff* as Wozzeck cries "Ich nicht, Marie! Und kein Andrer auch nicht!" (If not me, Marie, then no other!) just before he kills her. The drum strokes become softer and return to a pianissimo. In the interlude that follows, the note B is sustained by the orchestra for thirteen bars in a dramatic crescendo, punctuated by the brutal rhythm that symbolizes the catastrophe.

Scene 2

Scene 3

In Scene 3 Wozzeck returns to the tavern and dances with Marie's friend Margaret, who notices blood on his hands. The scene opens with a wild polka accompanied by an out-of-tune piano.

Scene 4
SIDE 10/4 (E II)
SIDE 17/1 (S)

The haunted atmosphere returns as Wozzeck, in Scene 4, goes back to the pond.

WOZZECK

Das Messer? Wo ist das Messer? Ich hab's dagelassen. Näher, noch näher. Mir graut's . . . da regt sich was. Still! Alles still und tot.	The knife? Where is the knife? I left it there. Around here somewhere. I'm terrified . . . something's moving. Silence. Everything silent and dead.
(shouting)	
Mörder! Mörder!	Murderer! Murderer!
(whispering again)	
Ha! Da ruft's. Nein, ich selbst.	Ah! Someone called. No, it was only me.
(still looking, he staggers a few steps further and stumbles against the corpse)	
Marie! Marie! Was hast Du für eine rote Schnur um den Hals? Hast Dir das rote Halsband verdient, wie die Ohrringlein, mit Deiner Sünde! Was hängen Dir die schwarzen Haare so wild? Mörder! Mörder! Sie werden nach mir suchen. Das Messer verrät mich!	Marie! Marie! What's that red cord round your neck! Was the red necklace payment for your sins, like the ear-rings? Why's your dark hair so wild about you? Murderer! Murderer! They will come and look for me. The knife will betray me!
(looks for it in a frenzy)	
Da, da ist's!	Here! Here it is!
(at the pond)	
So! Da hinunter!	There! Sink to the bottom!
(throws the knife into the pond)	
Es taucht ins dunkle Wasser wie ein Stein.	It plunges into the dark water like a stone.

*(The moon appears, blood-red, from behind the clouds.
Wozzeck looks up.)*

Aber der Mond verrät mich, der Mond ist blutig. Will denn die ganze Welt es ausplaudern? Das Messer, es liegt zu weit vorn, sie finden's beim Baden oder wenn sie nach Muscheln tauchen.	But the moon will betray me: the moon is blood-stained. Is the whole world going to incriminate me? The knife is too near the edge: they'll find it when they're swimming or diving for snails.

(wades into the pond)

Ich find's nicht. Aber ich muss mich waschen. Ich bin blutig. Da ein Fleck—und noch einer. Weh! Weh! Ich wasche mich mit Blut—das Wasser ist Blut . . . Blut . . .	I can't find it. But I must wash myself. There's blood on me. There's a spot here—and there's another. Oh, God! I am washing myself in blood—the water is blood . . . blood . . .

(drowns)

(The doctor appears, followed by the captain.)

CAPTAIN

Halt!	Wait!

DOCTOR *(stops)*

Hören Sie? Dort!	Can you hear? There!

CAPTAIN

Jesus! Das war ein Ton!	Jesus! What a ghastly sound!

(stops as well)

DOCTOR *(pointing to the pond)*

Ja, dort!	Yes, there!

CAPTAIN

Es ist das Wasser im Teich. Das Wasser ruft. Es ist schon lange Niemand ertrunken. Kommen Sie Doktor! Es ist nicht gut zu hören.	It's the water in the pond. The water is calling. It's been a long time since anyone drowned. Come away, Doctor. It's not good for us to be hearing it.

(tries to drag the doctor away)

DOCTOR *(resisting, and continuing to listen)*

Das stöhnt, als stürbe ein Mensch. Da ertrinkt Jemand!	There's a groan, as though someone were dying. Somebody's drowning!

CAPTAIN

Unheimlich! Der Mond rot, und die Nebel grau. Hören Sie? . . . Jetzt wieder das Ächzen.	It's eerie! The moon is red, and the mist is grey. Can you hear? . . . That moaning again.

DOCTOR

Stiller, . . . jetzt ganz still.	It's getting quieter . . . now it's stopped altogether.

CAPTAIN

Kommen Sie! Kommen Sie schnell!	Come! Come quickly!

(He rushes off, pulling the doctor along with him.)

Scene 5

There follows a symphonic meditation in D minor, a passionate lament for the life and death of Wozzeck. This inspired fantasy indicates how richly Berg's art was nourished by the Romanticism of Mahler. The final

The final, heartbreaking moment of Alban Berg's Wozzeck *in the Metropolitan Opera production.* (Copyright © Beth Bergman, 1983.)

scene takes place in the morning in front of Marie's house. Children are playing. Marie's little boy rides a hobbyhorse.

CHILDREN

Ringel, Ringel, Rosenkranz, Ringelreih'n. Ringel, Ringel, Rosenkranz, Ring . . .	Ring-a-ring-a-roses. A pocket full of . . .

(Their song and game are interrupted by other children bursting in.)

ONE OF THE NEWCOMERS

Du, Käthe! Die Marie!	Hey, Katie! Have you heard about Marie?

SECOND CHILD

Was ist?	What's happened?

FIRST CHILD

Weisst' es nit? Sie sind schon Alle 'naus.	Don't you know? They've all gone out there.

THIRD CHILD *(to Marie's little boy)*

Du! Dein' Mutter ist tot!	Hey! Your mother's dead!

MARIE'S SON *(still riding)*

Hopp, hopp! Hopp, hopp! Hopp, hopp!	Hop hop! Hop hop! Hop hop!

SECOND CHILD

Wo ist sie denn?	Where is she then?

FIRST CHILD

Drauss' liegt sie, am Weg, neben dem Teich.	She's lying out there, on the path near the pond.

THIRD CHILD

Kommt, anschaun!	Come and have a look!

(All the children run off.)

MARIE'S SON *(continuing to ride)*

Hopp, hopp! Hopp, hopp! Hopp, hopp!	Hop hop! Hop hop! Hop hop!

(He hesitates for a moment and then rides after the other children.)

For sheer heartbreak the final curtain, with the child riding off on his hobbyhorse to the sound of clarinet, drum, xylophone, and strings *ppp*, has few to equal it in the contemporary lyric theater.

Wozzeck envelops the listener in a hallucinated world in which the hunters are as driven as the hunted. It could have come only out of central Europe in the twenties. But its characters reach out beyond time and place to become eternal symbols of the human condition.

84

Anton Webern

Anton Webern.

"With me, things never turn out as I wish, but only as is ordained for me—as I must."

Anton Webern (1883–1945) is still not very well known to the public at large. All the same his works have shaped the musical thinking of our time in a most decisive fashion.

His Life

Anton von Webern (he dropped the prefix of nobility in later life) was born in Vienna. His musical gifts asserted themselves at an early age. He was twenty-one when he met Schoenberg and, with Alban Berg, formed the nucleus of the band of disciples who gathered around the master. He also studied musicology, and received his doctorate in this field.

After leaving the University, Webern conducted at various German provincial theaters and in Prague. But Vienna was the hub of his world. He directed the Vienna Workers' Symphony Concerts organized by the authorities of the then socialist city, but as the years passed he found public activity less and less congenial to his retiring disposition. After the First World War he settled in Mödling, a suburb of Vienna, where he lived quietly, devoting himself to composition and teaching.

Webern suffered great hardship after Austria became part of the Third Reich. The Nazis regarded his music as *Kulturbolshevismus* (cultural bolshevism), forbade its performance, and burned his writings. He was permitted to teach only a few pupils, and had to give his lectures—in which he expounded the Schoenbergian point of view—in secret. In order to avoid forced labor during the war, he worked as proofreader for a Viennese publisher. To escape the Allied bombings of Vienna, Webern and his wife sought refuge at the home of their son-in-law in Mittersill, a small town near Salzburg. But fate awaited him there. On September 15, 1945, as he stepped out of his house in the evening to smoke a cigarette (the war had ended five months before, but Mittersill was still under a curfew), he failed to understand an order to halt and was shot by a trigger-happy sentry of the American occupying forces. "The day of Anton Webern's death," wrote his most celebrated admirer, Igor Stravinsky, "should be a day of mourning for any receptive musician. We must hail not only this great composer but also a real hero. Doomed to total failure in a deaf world of ignorance and indifference, he inexorably kept on cutting out his diamonds, his dazzling diamonds, of whose mines he had such a perfect knowledge."

His Music

Webern responded to the radical portion of Schoenbergian doctrine, just as Berg exploited its more conservative elements. Of the three masters of the modern Viennese school, he was the one who cut himself off most completely from the tonal past. The Schoenbergians, we saw, favored the short forms. Webern carried this urge for brevity much further than either of his comrades, as is clear from his *Five Orchestral Pieces*. Such conciseness seems to nullify the very notion of time as we have come to understand it in music. Hardly less novel is the musical fabric in which he clothed his ideas. His scores call for the most unusual combinations of instruments. Each tone is assigned its specific function in the overall scheme. The instruments are often used in their extreme registers; they not infrequently play one at a time, and very little. This technique confers upon the individual sound an importance it never had before.

The *Passacaglia for Orchestra,* Opus 1 (1908), was followed by a number of significant works: *Five Movements for String Quartet,* Opus 5

(1909); *Six Orchestral Pieces,* Opus 6 (1910); *Six Bagatelles for String Quartet,* Opus 9 (1913); and *Five Orchestral Pieces,* Opus 10 (1913). These were flanked by the poetic songs—some with piano, others with instrumental accompaniment—in which Webern's essentially lyric gift found a congenial outlet.

With his *Symphony,* Opus 21 (1928) Webern came into his fully matured style. In this and the works that followed, the twelve-tone technique is used with unprecedented strictness. Schoenberg had contented himself with an organization based upon fixed series of pitches. Webern extended this concept to include timbres and rhythms. Therewith he moved toward complete control of the sonorous material—in other words, total serialization. His disciples carried the implications of Webern's music still further. As a result, Webern emerged as the dominant influence in the dodecaphonic thinking of the mid-twentieth century.

Five Pieces for Orchestra, *Opus 10*

The *Five Pieces for Orchestra* (1911–13) show, early in Webern's career, his striving for that rigorous control of the musical material which became so compelling a preoccupation of his later years. These pieces bring to the fore what Webern called "the almost exclusively lyrical nature" of his music. The concentrated lyricism here makes for unprecedented brevity: the set of five numbers lasts about five minutes. The fourth is the shortest piece in the entire orchestral literature; six and one-third bars that take less than half a minute to play.

The work is scored for an orchestral group in which each player is a soloist. Webern includes mandoline and guitar, instruments that have been favored by the Viennese composers because of their bright pointed sound. The pieces belong to the composer's atonal—that is to say, pre-twelve-tone—period, and come out of the Expressionist atmosphere that prevailed in central Europe at that time. However, as in the case of *Wozzeck,* the score shows an occasional foreshadowing of the twelve-tone technique.

First piece

I. Sehr ruhig und zart (very calm and soft). For flute, clarinet; muted trumpet and muted trombone; celesta, harp, glockenspiel; muted violin, viola, and muted cello. In 2/4 time, the piece opens with single tones on muted trumpet and harp followed by a tone on the celesta, harmonics on the viola and harp, and a single tone fluttertongued on the flute. A sparse motivic texture is woven for twelve and one-quarter bars, the dynamic level ranging from *ppp* to *pp*

Second piece

II. Lebhaft und zart bewegt (lively, moving softly). The second piece, the only rapid one of the set, is in triple meter, save for two brief reversions to 2/4 time. It is scored for piccolo, oboe, two clarinets; muted horn, trumpet, and trombone; harmonium, celesta, harp, glockenspiel, cymbals, triangle; muted violin, viola, cello, and double bass. (The *harmonium* is a small type of organ that was developed in the nineteenth century.) Clarinet and violin state their respective motives in the opening measure. A delicate fabric of sound extends for fourteen bars, woven out of motivic cells and single-note sonorities moving from *p* to a *fff* of menacing urgency.

Third piece
SIDE 11/1 (E II)
SIDE 16/6 (S)

III. Sehr langsam und äusserst ruhig (very slow and extremely calm). A true son of Austria, Webern loved the mountains of his native land and their bell sounds. The third piece is almost a study in bell sonorities, evoking as it does the clear open spaces of a mountain scene. It is eleven and one-half measures in length, in 6/4 time (except for a measure of 3/4 and one of 2/4). Harmonium, mandoline, guitar, celesta, harp, glockenspiel, and cowbells play trills and repeated notes against gentle trills on the drums, while clarinet, muted horn and trombone, violin, muted viola and cello trace their brief, tenuous motives.

Fourth piece
SIDE 11/2 (E II)
SIDE 16/7 (S)

IV. Fliessend, äusserst zart (flowing, extremely soft), in 3/4 time. Clarinet, muted trumpet and trombone, mandoline, celesta, harp, snare drum, muted violin, and viola unfold their traceries for precisely six and one-third measures. The first twelve tones are all different ones—in other words, a tone row. Nothing is scored below middle C. A figure on the mandoline, with a chord on the harp, is answered by one on the muted trumpet. The violin finishes with five notes played *ppp,* wie ein Hauch (like a whisper).

Fifth piece

V. Sehr fliessend (flowing), in 3/4 time, with nine measures in 2/4. This movement, consisting of thirty-two bars, is the most elaborately scored, calling for flute, oboe, clarinet, bass clarinet; muted horn and trumpet; harmonium, mandoline, guitar, celesta, harp, glockenspiel, xylophone, bass and snare drum, cymbals; and the four solo strings, muted. The flickering motives work up to a climax with a fortissimo chord on the harmonium in the ninth bar. There is a sudden subsiding; a second dynamic peak is reached with several percussive chords that run the gamut of the orchestra. The last fifteen measures are sparsely scored, with the softest of dynamics. The music trails off into silence.

The creator of this remarkable music was content to go his way, an obscure figure in the musical circles of his time, overshadowed by those who made a bigger noise in the world. He had no way of knowing that little over a decade after his death, many avant-garde musicians in Europe and America would think of themselves as belonging to "the age of Webern."

85

Other Modern Europeans

The French School

Milhaud

Darius Milhaud (1892–1975) was a leading figure in contemporary French music after the death of Ravel. One of this century's most prolific composers, his opus numbers run well past the three-hundred mark. Milhaud was essentially a lyricist. He is associated specifically with polytonality, having explored in greater detail than almost any of his confreres the possibilities of several keys sounding at once. Among his better-known works may be mentioned the ballet *Le Boeuf sur le toit* (named after a famous Parisian cabaret, The Bull on the Roof; 1919); *Saudades do Brasil* (Brazilian Moods; 1921), a suite of piano pieces which the composer also arranged for orchestra; *La Création du monde* (The Creation of the World; 1923); and the popular two-piano suite *Scaramouche* (1937).

Honegger

Arthur Honegger (1892–1955), born in Le Havre of Swiss parents, spent the greater part of his professional life in Paris and was justly regarded as one of the French school. At the same time he was the least Gallic among them. The spacious lines of the Classical sonata and the rhetoric of Wagnerian drama, neither of which flourishes in the Parisian atmosphere, appealed to his imagination. Honegger had a natural affinity for the choral idiom. *King David* (1921), a "symphonic psalm" for chorus and orchestra, and the biblical opera *Judith* (1926) manifest a Handelian bigness of gesture. *Jeanne d'Arc au bûcher* (Joan of Arc at the Stake; 1938) is a kind of oratorio with a speaking part for the heroine amid vivid frescoes for chorus and orchestra. Much publicity accrued to Honegger because of his symphonic movement *Pacific 231* (1923), an orchestral depiction of a locomotive that was the last word in modernism in the twenties. His *Symphony No. 5* (1951), a profoundly felt and powerful work, may be regarded as his finest achievement.

Poulenc

The music of Francis Poulenc (1899–1963) is urbane, Parisian. His piano pieces form a twentieth-century brand of salon music. The *Mouvements perpetuels* for piano, written in 1918 when he was nineteen, are precisely right for what Anatole France called "the intimate conversations of five o'clock." Poulenc's chamber music shows the sympathetic handling of the woodwinds for which French composers are noted. He was one of the outstanding song composers of our time; his choral works too reveal a rich vein of lyricism. His operas—*Dialogues des Carmélites* (Dialogues of the Carmelites, on a libretto by Georges Bernanos; 1953–55) and *La Voix humaine* (The Human Voice, based on a one-act play by Jean Cocteau; 1958)—established him as one of the most important representatives of the trend toward a new Romanticism.

Messiaen

Of a slightly later generation is Olivier Messiaen (1908–), who first attracted attention when, still in his twenties, he declared with romantic exuberance: "Melody first and foremost." Messiaen has tried to revive the religious ideal in art; he has placed his music, as he says, "at the service of the dogmas of Catholic theology." Among the works inspired by religious mysticism may be mentioned *L'Ascension* (Four Symphonic Meditations; 1933–34); the *Quartet for the End of Time,* which we will discuss; and *Vingt Régards sur l'enfant Jésus* (Twenty Glances at the Infant Jesus, for piano; 1944).

Several other influences intermingle in Messiaen's art: the rhythmic freedom of Gregorian chant, the asymmetrical rhythms of Hindu music, and a love of nature that shows itself in his frequent use of bird song as a a melodic source. From this last preoccupation stem such works as *Oiseaux exotiques* (Exotic Birds, for piano and orchestra; 1956), and *Catalogue d'oiseaux* (Catalogue of Birds, for piano; 1956–58). All the strands of Messiaen's style are woven into the colorful tapestry of the *Turangalîla-Symphony* (1948), a massive orchestral work in ten movements.

Messiaen: Quartet for the End of Time

When the Second World War broke out Messiaen, then thirty-one, was organist of the Church of Trinity in Paris. He was drafted into the army. In

June 1940 he was captured by the Germans and transferred to a prisoner-of-war camp, Stalag VIIIA in Saxony. Among the prisoners were three French musicians, a violinist, cellist, and clarinetist. Messiaen began to write a chamber-music piece for them, to which he soon added a piano part. It was a monumental work in eight movements that helped to sustain the composer through this terrible time. When it was finished, Messiaen and his friends decided to organize a performance of the quartet. The violinist and clarinetist had managed to hold on to their instruments. A cello was found in the camp, with one of its strings missing, and an old upright piano "badly out of tune, with some keys sticking periodically." The concert took place on a bitter cold night in January 1941, in front of five thousand prisoners from France, Belgium, Poland, and other countries. Messiaen prepared this polyglot audience of peasants, workers, intellectuals, soldiers, by explaining to them what he had tried to say in the music. In later years he declared that he had never had so attentive and understanding a public.

The work that was given to the world under such dramatic circumstances was the *Quatuor pour la fin du temps* (Quartet for the End of Time). It was inspired by a wonderful passage in the Revelation of St. John, Chapter X: "I saw an angel full of strength descending from the sky, clad with a cloud and having a rainbow over his head. His face was like the sun, his feet like columns of fire. He set his right foot on the sea, his left foot on the earth and, standing on the sea and on the earth, he raised his hand to the sky and swore by Him who lives in the centuries of centuries, saying: *There shall be no more Time,* but on the day of the seventh Angel's trumpet the mystery of God shall be accomplished."

First movement

1. *Liturgy of crystal.* Bien modéré (quite moderate), $\frac{3}{4}$. "Between three and four in the morning, the awakening of the birds: a blackbird or a nightingale improvises, surrounded by a sonorous cloud of dust, by a halo of trills lost high up in the trees." The solo parts–clarinet and violin–are marked "like a bird." Messiaen directs that the chords on the piano, legato and pianissimo, should be "enveloped in pedal." The movement unfolds at a pianissimo, and ends *ppp.*

Second movement

2. *Vocalise for the Angel who announces the end of Time.* "The first and third sections, very short, evoke the power of this mighty angel. . . . On the piano, soft cascades of blue-orange chords envelop in their distant chimes the song of the violin and cello, which is almost like plainchant." The movement, in $\frac{3}{4}$, alternates between Robuste, modéré (vigorous, moderate) and Presque vif, joyeux (fairly lively, joyous). Its "impalpable harmonies" are marked *ppp* and Presque lent (fairly slow). Messiaen compares them to "drops of water in the rainbow." These are surrounded at either end by incisive chords on the piano, *fff.*

Third movement

3. *Abyss of the birds.* "For clarinet solo. The abyss is Time, with its sorrows and lassitudes. The birds are the opposite of Time: our desire for light, for stars, for rainbows and jubilant vocalises!" This movement is marked Lent, expressif et triste (slow, expressive, and sad). A broad

arc of desolate melody alternates with passages that are to be played, according to Messiaen's directions, in a gay, capricious manner, evoking the birds that are "the opposite of Time."

Fourth movement

4. *Interlude.* "A Scherzo, more extrovert than the other movements, but attached to them by several melodic reminiscences." Décidé, moderé, un peu vif (decisive, moderate, somewhat lively), 2/4. This was the first of the movements to be written, before Messiaen decided to add the piano part. The opening passage, which returns toward the end of the movement, has a dancelike character. The middle section, with its rapid runs and trills on the clarinet and a lovely melodic phrase in the upper register of the violin, evokes birds.

Fifth movement

5. *Praise to the Eternity of Jesus.* Infiniment lent, extatique (infinitely slow, ecstatic). "Jesus is here considered as the Word. A long and infinitely slow phrase on the cello magnifies, with love and reverence, the eternity of this powerful and mild Word, 'whose years shall not be consumed.' " This rapturous meditation deploys all the expressive capacities of the cello. The melody is accompanied by soft chords on the piano:

Sixth movement

6. *Dance of fury, for the seven trumpets.* Décidé, vigoureux, granitique, un peu vif (decisive, vigorous, granitic, somewhat fast). "Rhythmically this is the most characteristic movement. The four instruments in unison imitate the charm of bells and trumpets. . . . Listen especially to the terrible fortissimo of the theme in augmentation and changed register toward the end of the movement."

Seventh movement

7. *Glow of rainbows for the Angel who announces the end of Time.* Rêveur, presque lent (dreamily, fairly slow), 3/4. "Certain passages from the second movement return here. . . . In my dreams I hear and see groups of chords and melodies, colors and familiar shapes. Then, after this transitory stage, I pass into the unreal and experience with ecstasy a whirling, a dancing interpenetration of superhuman sounds and colors. These

swords of fire, these streams of blue-orange lava, these sudden stars—this is the glow, these are the rainbows!" Certainly no other composer of the twentieth century has described in such vivid detail the visionary, almost hallucinatory character of the creative act—better, the creative act as he experienced it.

Eighth movement

8. *Praise to the immortality of Jesus.* "This praise is love. Its slow rise towards the climax traces the ascent of men toward God, of the Child of God toward His Father, of the human-made-God toward Paradise." Extrêmement lent et tendre, extatique (extremely slow and tender, ecstatic), 4/4. When the violin soars into the upper regions of its highest string we have a romantic atmosphere, whether the composer is singing of divine or earthly love. Thus the listener can enjoy this music whether or not he shares the theology behind it.

It testifies to the courage of the human spirit that Messiaen was able to rise above the squalor, hunger, and cold of that dreadful winter in Stalag VIIIA to conceive and execute so bold a work. This need to soar above the immediacies of life to a higher plane of experience imparts to all his music its quality of aspiration, its essential spirituality.

The Russians

Prokofiev

The modern Russian school produced a world figure in Serge Prokofiev (1891–1953). His clean, muscular music, bubbling over with wit and whimsy, struck a fresh note. Characteristic of his style are the athletic march rhythms, the harmonies pungently dissonant but rooted in the key, the abrupt modulations, the unexpected turns of phrase, and the orchestral color that manifests all the brilliance we associate with the Russian school.

A greater number of Prokofiev's works have established themselves as "classics" with the international public than those of any of his contemporaries save Stravinsky. Among these are the *Scythian Suite* for orchestra (1914), with its deliberate primitivism; the *Classical Symphony* (1916–17); the *Third Piano Concerto,* which we will discuss; *Lieutenant Kije* (1934), a suite arranged from his music for the film; *Peter and the Wolf* (1936); *Alexander Nevsky* (1938), a cantata arranged from the music for the celebrated Eisenstein film; the ballets *Romeo and Juliet* (1935) and *Cinderella* (1944); the two *Violin Concertos* (1914, 1935); the *Seventh Piano Sonata* (1939–42); and the *Fifth Symphony* (1944). Several of Prokofiev's operas have found favor outside his homeland—*Love for Three Oranges* (1919), *The Flaming Angel* (1922–25), and *War and Peace* (final revision, 1952), after Tolstoi's novel. Prokofiev was one of those fortunate artists who achieve popularity with the masses and at the same time win the admiration of their fellow musicians.

Shostakovich

Dmitri Shostakovich (1906–1975) was the first Russian composer of international repute who was wholly a product of Soviet musical culture. He was trained at the Leningrad Conservatory. His *First Symphony* (1925), written as a graduation piece when he was nineteen, won instant success both at home and abroad. There followed a stream of works in all branches of music, the most important being the *Fifth Symphony* (1937) and the *Seventh,* the *Leningrad Symphony* (1941); the ballet *The Golden Age* (1929–30); the opera *Lady Macbeth of Mzensk* (1930–32); eleven string quartets and the *Quintet for Piano and Strings* (1940); the *Concerto for Piano, Trumpet, and Strings* (1933); and the *Violin Concerto* (1955). His facility made for unevenness of quality, but behind his output stood a vigorous creative personality in command of a big style that caught the attention of the world.

Khatchaturian

The Armenian composer Aram Khatchaturian (1903–78) bases his art on the folklore of his native republic. Khatchaturian's *Piano Concerto* (1936) combines Armenian folk elements with the grand virtuoso tradition of Liszt. Similarly his *Violin Concerto* (1940) displays lavishness of melody, sumptuous color, and the bravura style.

Prokofiev: Piano Concerto No. 3

The *Third Piano Concerto,* completed in 1921, is one of the most widely played works in the current repertory.

First movement

I. Andante–Allegro. "The first movement," Prokofiev wrote, "opens with a short introduction. The theme is announced by an unaccompanied clarinet and is continued by the violins for a few bars.

Soon the tempo changes to Allegro, the strings having a short passage in sixteenths, which leads to the statement of the principal subject by the piano." This driving theme exemplifies—as does the entire work—Prokofiev's skill in achieving rhythmic diversity within the traditional meters. Notice the abrupt change of key, so typical of this composer, at the beginning of the third measure:

"Discussion of this theme is carried on in a lively manner, both the piano and the orchestra having a good deal to say on the matter." Prokofiev exploits the contrast between piano and orchestral sonority with great vigor. "A passage in chords for the piano alone leads to the more expressive second subject, heard in the oboe with a pizzicato accompaniment."

"This is taken up by the piano and developed at some length, eventually giving way to a bravura passage in triplets. At the climax of this section the tempo reverts to Andante and the orchestra gives out the first theme, fortissimo. The piano joins in, and the theme is subjected to an impressively broad treatment." The Allegro returns, the two main ideas are treated with great brilliance, and the movement ends with an exciting crescendo.

Second movement

II. Andantino. The second movement consists of a theme with five variations. The theme, strongly Russian in character, is announced by the orchestra.

"In the first variation," the composer explained, "the piano treats the opening of the theme in quasi-sentimental fashion, and resolves into a chain of trills as the orchestra repeats the closing phrase. The tempo changes to Allegro for the second and third variations, and the piano has brilliant figures, while snatches of the theme are introduced here and there in the orchestra. In Variation 4 the tempo is once again Andante, and the piano and orchestra discourse on the theme in a quiet and meditative fashion. Variation 5 is energetic (Allegro giusto) and leads without pause into a restatement of the theme by the orchestra, with delicate chordal embroidery in the piano."

Third movement

III. Allegro ma non troppo. The Finale displays the gradations that Prokofiev assigned to "scherzo-ness"–jest, laughter, mockery. The mood is established at the outset by a staccato theme for bassoons and pizzicato strings:

This is interrupted by what Prokofiev called the blustering entry of the piano, playing chordal textures of great propulsive force. "The orchestra holds its own with the opening theme and there is a good deal of argument, with frequent differences of opinion as regards key." The solo part carries the first theme to a climax.

The melodist in Prokofiev is represented by the second theme, in his finest vein of lyricism, introduced by the oboes and clarinets. "The piano replies with a theme that is more in keeping with the caustic humor of the work." Then the lyric theme is developed. An exciting coda brings the concerto to a close on a decisive (and dissonant) C-major cadence.

Prokofiev's popularity with the public is due, in part, to his belief that the artist must communicate with his audience. "When I was in the United States and England," he wrote a year before his death, "I often heard discussions on the subject of whom music ought to serve, for whom a composer ought to write, and to whom his music should be addressed. In my view the composer, just as the poet, the sculptor or the painter, is in duty bound to serve man, the people. He must be a citizen first and foremost, so that his art may consciously extol human life and lead man to a radiant future."

Germany and Central Europe

Hindemith

Paul Hindemith (1895–1963) was the most substantial figure among the composers who came into prominence in Germany in the years after the First World War. Hindemith's harmony, based on the free use of twelve tones around a center, never abandoned tonality, which he regarded as an immutable law of music; hence his opposition to the Schoenbergians. Hindemith wrote an enormous quantity of music. His best-known works include the opera *Mathis der Maler* (Mathis the Painter; 1934), from which he developed the symphony of the same name; two ballets—*Nobilissima visione* (Most Noble Vision; 1938) and *The Four Temperaments* (1940); *Das Marienleben* (The Life of Mary; 1923, revised 1948), a song cycle for soprano and piano to poems of Rainer Maria Rilke; and a choral setting of Walt Whitman's *When Lilacs Last in the Dooryard Bloom'd* (1946). Hindemith left Germany when Hitler came to power—his music was banned from the Third Reich as "cultural bolshevism"—and he spent two decades in the United States, during which he taught at Yale University and at the summer school in Tanglewood, Massachusetts, where many young Americans came under his influence.

Kodály

Zoltán Kodály (1882–1967) was associated with Béla Bartók in the collection and study of peasant songs. The folklore element is paramount in his music. Two works of Kodály's have won international success: the *Psalmus Hungaricus* (Fifty-fifth Psalm; 1923) for tenor solo, mixed chorus, children's voices, and orchestra; and *Háry János* (1926), a folk play with music centering about a retired soldier of exuberant imagination.

Orff

Carl Orff (1895–1982) took his point of departure from the clear-cut melody, simple harmonic structure, and vigorous rhythm of Bavarian folk song. Orff's best-known work is the "dramatic cantata" *Carmina burana* (Songs of Beuren; 1936), based on the famous thirteenth-century collection of student songs and poems that were discovered in an ancient

Bavarian monastery. These inspired a work whose lilting melodies and appealing rhythms have made it one of the most popular of twentieth-century compositions.

Krenek

Ernst Krenek was born in Vienna in 1900. In the 1920s he fell under the spell of jazz. He subsequently found his way to the twelve-tone method. When the Nazis took over Austria, Krenek came to the United States, where he has since taught at several colleges. His book *Music Here and Now* reveals an intellect that probes the complexities of contemporary musical thought. Krenck is one of the most prolific composers of our time. Among his works are eleven operas, three ballets, six piano sonatas, five symphonies, four piano concertos, and eight string quartets.

Weill

Kurt Weill (1900–1950) was one of the most arresting figures to emerge in Germany in the 1920s. To the international public his name is indissolubly linked with *Die Dreigroschenoper* (The Three-Penny Opera) that he and the poet Bertolt Brecht adapted from John Gay's celebrated *Beggar's Opera.* Upon the lusty antics of Gay's work, Weill and Brecht superimposed the despair, the agonized outcry of a Germany in the aftermath of the First World War. Launched in 1928, the work was a fabulous success. Repeated revivals have made it one of the century's best-known theater pieces.

England

Britten

Benjamin Britten (1913–76), a musician of great invention, technical mastery, and charm, was the most important English composer of his generation. Besides a quantity of orchestral, choral, and chamber music, Britten wrote several operas, of which the most important is *Peter Grimes* (1945). *Billy Budd* (1951), from the story by Melville, received its American premiere on television in 1952 and made a strong impression. *The Turn of the Screw* (1954) captures the eerie atmosphere of Henry James's famous story. *A Midsummer Night's Dream* (1960), after Shakespeare, and *Death in Venice* (1974) after Thomas Mann, affirm Britten's position as one of the foremost operatic composers of our time. In 1962, Britten was commissioned to compose a work for the opening of the rebuilt Coventry Cathedral in England, which had been destroyed by German bombs; the resulting *War Requiem,* which intermingled the text of the Latin Requiem Mass with the war poems of Wilfred Owen, won instant recognition as a masterpiece.

Britten: Four Sea Interludes *from* Peter Grimes

"In writing *Peter Grimes* I wanted to express my awareness of the perpetual struggle of men and women whose livelihood depends on the sea." Around this struggle revolves the daily life of a fishing village in Suffolk, as depicted in *The Borough,* the eighteenth-century poem by George Crabbe on which Britten and his librettist, Montagu Slater, based their opera. Extraordinary care was taken to build up the various characters who inhabit the village—so much, indeed, that one can aptly say that the true protagonist of the opera is the Borough.

The theme that underlies most of Britten's operas—"the persecution and betrayal of innocence"—is here presented through a powerful symbol: a lonely individual persecuted by a hostile society. The drama, projected through the figure of Peter Grimes, the misunderstood fisherman who hardens into a misanthrope, mounts relentlessly to his suicide. In the original poem, Grimes is a sadistic ruffian, but in Britten's opera he takes on dimension and humanity. He yearns for love, but his pride prevents him from accepting it when Ellen Orford, the village schoolmistress, offers it to him. He dreams of happiness, but the fatal conflict within his nature drives him to destroy whatever happiness he might have hoped to attain. Tragically flawed from the start, Grimes cannot escape his fate.

Interlude I

The scenes of the opera are linked by orchestral interludes that refer back to what has already passed or set the scene for what is about to happen. Britten arranged four of these into a concert suite that has had great success with the public. Interlude I, *Dawn,* marked Lento e tranquillo, is an atmospheric piece in duple meter that portrays daybreak on a cold gray morning in the village; it subsequently serves as background for the opening chorus in the first scene. Britten paints his tone picture with three elements: a melody, arpeggios, and chords. The melody is a plaintive tune in high register that unfolds in delicate traceries on the flutes and violins, in A minor:

The rippling arpeggios, in harp, clarinet, and strings, swell and diminish as they suggest other tonal regions. And in between, mysterious A major chords in the low brass rise in successively broader arches, suggesting the primordial swell of the sea.

Interlude II

Interlude II, *Sunday morning,* is an Allegro spiritoso in 2/2 that begins Act II, evoking "a fine sunny morning, with church bells ringing." The opening measures, depicting the pealing bells of the Borough, are lineally descended from the rather grander chiming of the Coronation Scene in Musorgsky's *Boris Godunov*. Over alternating thirds in the horns, woodwinds play figures that continually change their rhythmic position in the measure, thereby capturing the random charm of bells ringing:

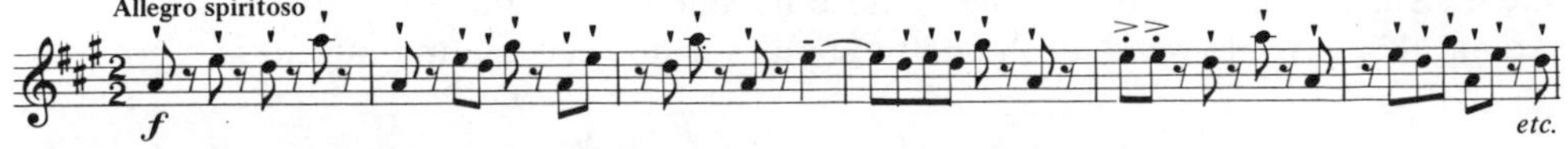

Alternating with an expressive melody in the strings, the bell patterns work up to an *fff* climax, from which the music gradually subsides to the *ppp* ending. Note that the flute figures decorating the string melody are diminutions of the bell tune. In the opera, the string melody becomes the setting of Ellen's opening lines in the second act, "Glitter of waves and glitter of sunlight . . ."

Interlude III

The third interlude, *Moonlight,* an Andante in 2/2, introduces the first scene of the third act, set on the moonlit street between the village and the seashore. Gentle syncopations in the lower strings take shape as a melody; Britten asks for a slight swell on each of these notes:

Flickering octaves in flutes and harp form the other element of this nocturne, which builds to a climax through the gentle movement of the melody against pedal points in the horns.

Interlude IV

Interlude IV, *The Storm,* is marked Presto con fuoco (very fast, with fire); the alternation of duple and triple meter suggests the irrationality of nature's forces. The principal section derives mainly from a short motive:

Britten's storm rages loudly and picturesquely, with evocative use of snarling trombones and trumpets moving in parallel fifths, and angry horns answering in octaves. Near the end, the tumult subsides as unison strings reach up several times in the yearning melody to which Grimes had earlier sung his poignant query, "What harbor shelters peace?" Then the storm boils over again.

In *Peter Grimes* Britten produced a genuinely national work. The opera is suffused with the sights and sounds of an English village; its vocal lines are shaped by the rhythms and inflections of English speech. And its music springs from what one of Britten's countrymen well called "an unusually compassionate and English heart."

PART SEVEN

The American Scene

"A true musical culture never has been and never can be solely based upon the importation of foreign artists and foreign music, and the art of music in America will always be essentially a museum art until we are able to develop a school of composers who can speak directly to the American public in a musical language which expresses fully the deepest reactions of the American consciousness to the American scene."

— AARON COPLAND

86

Music in the United States

"Music . . . the favorite passion of my soul" — THOMAS JEFFERSON

What is American music? The question is more complex than one might suppose. Even the American Indians originally came to this hemisphere from Asia. Consequently no music has its roots solely in this land. It is our nation's great achievement to have created, out of elements inherited from older cultures, entirely new and fresh kinds of music. We all recognize what is American in music, although we might be hard put to it to define exactly what that quality is. Having been shaped by a variety of factors, the American quality is not any single thing.

The Development of American Styles

Until the end of the nineteenth century, the music of the American Indians remained an isolated oral tradition, ignored by those who arrived here later. Other immigrant groups—the Spanish who came to seek gold and preach Catholicism, the Dutch who came to trade, the British and French and Germans who came to escape religious persecution, and the Africans who were brought as slaves—carried their own music with them from their homelands. This was the mélange that provided the initial ingredients for America's musical melting pot.

Colonial times

In the Atlantic colonies, English music dominated. The Puritans of New England sang psalms from their Protestant tradition, and their *Bay Psalm Book* (1638) was the first book printed in the British colonies of North America. The ballads of England and Scotland continued to be sung in colonial America, gradually changing as they were handed down from generation to generation. As cities became more populous in the eighteenth century, theatrical entertainments—primarily successful ballad operas from London—flourished.

Early nineteenth century

The Revolutionary War made little difference to musical life, for in the early nineteenth century American society continued to model itself to a considerable extent on its English counterpart. The Handelian choral tradition soon took root in such organizations as the Boston Handel and Haydn Society, founded in 1815 to perform *Messiah, The Creation,* and other oratorios. Even opera first came to America via London, in the form

Frontispiece of The New England Psalm-Singer *(1770) featuring a canon by William Billings engraved by Paul Revere.*

of English-language adaptations such as *The Libertine,* a version of Mozart's *Don Giovanni* introduced to New York in 1817.

But music from other sources found an audience as well. As early as 1825, Rossini's *The Barber of Seville* was performed in New York in Italian, by a touring company under Manuel García, the Spanish tenor who had sung in the opera's first performance. New Orleans became a center of French opera. The increasing flow of German immigrants, especially after the failure of the 1848 revolutions, included many musicians, and Germans were important figures in the founding of the Philharmonic Society of New York in 1842, America's first permanent orchestra. There were composers among the immigrants as well, who for the most part wrote music indistinguishable from what they would have written had they remained at home.

That, perhaps, is the crucial point in defining American music: when did it become something that could not have happened anywhere else? This first came to pass in areas other than concert music. Already in the eighteenth century, William Billings (1746–1800) of New England composed highly individual hymns, anthems, and "fuging tunes," of an abrasive directness quite unlike the more genteel work of his English forebears. Later and in another style came Stephen Foster (1826–64), whose universally loved songs drew on sources as diverse as Italian opera, English ballads, Irish popular songs, and the music of the minstrel show (a theatrical entertainment performed by whites in blackface). African slaves, taught to sing Protestant hymns when they were converted to Christianity, absorbed this idiom into the traditions they had brought from Africa, developing what came to be known as the "spiritual," with a rhythmic pulse and

Under P. T. Barnum's management, the Swedish soprano Jenny Lind took American audiences by storm. A contemporary engraving depicts her first appearance in America, at Castle Garden on September 11, 1850.

melodic colorings not known in the churches of their masters. All of these were new kinds of music, unique to America, products of her position that inherited and amalgamated many cultures.

By 1850, a substantial concert life had grown up in our major cities, but it continued to be dominated by Europe. German music and musicians ruled the concert halls, while opera was principally supplied by the Italians. The vogue of the visiting virtuoso began. The Norwegian violinist Ole Bull, who came in 1843, was followed some years later by "the Swedish Nightingale," Jenny Lind. What with her gift for song and P. T. Barnum's genius for publicity, Jenny was a sensation. America made her own contribution to the tradition of the touring virtuoso in the person of Louis Moreau Gottschalk (1829–69), a charismatic pianist and composer born in New Orleans and trained in Paris, who made his American debut in 1853. Some of Gottschalk's original compositions, such as *The Banjo* and *Bamboula*, incorporated features of an Afro-American musical idiom.

Later nineteenth century

In the nineteenth century, the European musical tradition was at a flood tide of creativity. Naturally many talented young Americans attracted to concert music—whether as composers or performers—thought it necessary to complete their musical studies abroad. Several generations of American composers went to Germany to sit at the feet of disciples of Beethoven, Mendelssohn, Schumann, Liszt, and Wagner. Only rarely, upon their return, did they succeed in freeing themselves from the shadow of those great masters. So too, American singers who hoped to make a career in opera not only studied in Italy, but found it advantageous to Italianize their names: the famous soprano billed as Nordica was really Lillian Norton from Farmington, Maine.

The romantic adventurousness associated with the westward expansion of the United States is expressed in this famous bronze by Frederic Remington (1861–1909), **The Outlaw.** The Metropolitan Museum of Art, Bequest of Jacob Ruppert, 1939.)

We have seen how Antonín Dvořák, during his stay in the United States (1892–95), urged American composers to draw inspiration from native material and to build a musical tradition on that, as he had done on the songs and dances of his native Bohemia. But Americans did not at first find convincing ways to use such material. The works of early American musical nationalists such as Arthur Farwell (1872–1952) and Henry F. Gilbert (1868–1928) won little favor from concert audiences of their day or since. Edward MacDowell (1861–1908), on the other hand, won a considerable success in his own day. The efforts of these composers and some of their contemporaries foreshadowed the eventual breakdown of the monopoly of the German symphonic style, as did somewhat later the music of Charles Tomlinson Griffes (1884–1920), who began to look for inspiration to

The United States Marine Band with leader John Philip Sousa (1854–1932) during their first Pacific Coast Concert Tour in September 1891.

France and the music of the Impressionists rather than to Germany, where he was trained. Meanwhile an unknown New Englander was working in isolation to find a vital way of expressing the American spirit in music—Charles Ives, whom the perspective of history reveals as the first major prophet of our musical coming of age.

In the meantime, America continued to generate distinctive musical styles outside the classical idiom. The marches of John Philip Sousa (1854–1932) were internationally recognized as a peculiarly American achievement. From roots in spirituals, blues, and ragtime, as we have noted, jazz sprang to worldwide attention. And the lively rhythms of Afro-American music, around the turn of the twentieth century, infused American theater music with a new impulse; the songs of Jerome Kern, Irving Berlin, George Gershwin, Richard Rodgers, Cole Porter, and Harold Arlen made Broadway and Hollywood (after the advent of the sound film) into world musical centers. Since that time, American popular music has been the world standard.

The twentieth century

In this century American composers of art music, beginning with Ives, have found their own voices, drawing upon the many traditions of which, as Americans, they are inheritors–not hewing to any one style, but distilling their own innovative, personal, national syntheses from among the available possibilities. The extraordinary emigration of composers and other musicians from Europe on the eve of the Second World War added a further element to the mix, and their teaching has been assimilated as well. Since World War II, the United States has been the birthplace of many of the most significant new developments in art music. After a long period in search of "American music," we have discovered that there is no single such thing, but many different American musics—every one of them impossible to imagine as the product of any other culture.

87

Charles Ives

"Beauty in music is too often confused with something that lets the ears lie back in an easy chair. Many sounds that we are used to do not bother us, and for that reason we are inclined to call them beautiful. Frequently, when a new or unfamiliar work is accepted as beautiful on its first hearing, its fundamental quality is one that tends to put the mind to sleep."

Charles Edward Ives (1874–1954) waited many years for recognition. Today he stands revealed as the first great American composer of the twentieth century, and one of the most original spirits of his time.

His Life

Charles Ives.

Ives was born in Danbury, Connecticut. His father had been a bandmaster in the Civil War, and continued his calling in civilian life. Charles at thirteen held a job as church organist and already was arranging music for the various ensembles conducted by his father. At twenty he entered Yale, where he studied composition with Horatio Parker. Ives's talent for music asserted itself throughout his four years at Yale; yet when he had to choose a career he decided against a professional life in music. He suspected that society would not pay him for the kind of music he wanted to compose. He was right.

He therefore entered the business world. Two decades later he was head of the largest insurance agency in the country. The years it took him to achieve this success—roughly from the time he was twenty-two to forty-two—were the years when he wrote his music. He composed at night, on weekends, and during vacations, working in isolation, concerned only to set down the sounds he heard in his head.

The few conductors and performers whom he tried to interest in his works pronounced them unplayable. After a number of these rebuffs Ives gave up showing his manuscripts. When he felt the need to hear how his music sounded, he hired a few musicians to run through a work. Save for these rare and quite inadequate performances, Ives heard his music only in his imagination. He pursued his way undeflected and alone, piling up one score after another in his barn in Connecticut. When well-meaning friends suggested that he try to write music that people would like, he could only retort, "I can't do it—I hear something else!"

Ives's double life as a business executive by day and composer by night finally took its toll. In 1918, when he was forty-four, he suffered a physical breakdown that left his heart damaged. The years of unrewarded effort had taken more out of him emotionally than he had suspected. Although he lived almost forty years longer, he produced nothing further of importance.

When he recovered he faced the realization that the world of professional musicians was irrevocably closed to his ideas. He felt that he owed it to his music to make it available to those who might be less hidebound. He therefore had the *Concord Sonata* for piano privately printed, also the *Essays Before a Sonata*—a kind of elaborate program note that presented the essence of his views on life and art. These were followed by the *114 Songs*. The three volumes, which were distributed free of charge to libraries, music critics, and whoever else asked for them, caused not a ripple as far as the public was concerned. But they gained Ives the support of other experimental composers who were struggling to make their way in an unheeding world. The tide finally turned in this country when the American pianist John Kirkpatrick, at a recital in Town Hall in January, 1939, played the *Concord Sonata*. Ives was then sixty-five. The piece was repeated several weeks later by Kirkpatrick and scored a triumph. The next morning Lawrence Gilman hailed the *Concord Sonata* as "the greatest music composed by an American."

Ives had already begun to exert a salutary influence upon the younger generation of composers, who found in his art a realization of their own ideals. Now he was "discovered" by the general public and hailed as the grand old man of American music. In 1947 his *Third Symphony* achieved performance, and won a Pulitzer Prize. This story of belated recognition was an item to capture the imagination, and was carried by newspapers throughout the country. Ives awoke at seventy-three to find himself famous. Four years later the *Second Symphony* was presented to the public by the New York Philharmonic, exactly half a century after it had been composed. The prospect of finally hearing the work agitated the old man; he attended neither the rehearsals nor the performances. He was, however, one of millions who listened to the radio broadcast.

He died in New York City three years later, at the age of eighty.

His Music

Charles Ives, both as man and artist, was rooted in the New England heritage, in the tradition of plain living and high thinking that came to flower in the idealism of Hawthorne and the Alcotts, Emerson and Thoreau. The sources of his tone imagery are to be found in the living music of his childhood: hymn tunes and popular songs, the town band at holiday parades, the fiddlers at Saturday night dances, patriotic songs and sentimental parlor ballads, the melodies of Stephen Foster, and the medleys heard at country fairs and in small theaters.

Ives's polytonality and polyrhythms

This wealth of American music had attracted other musicians besides Ives. But they, subservient to European canons of taste, had proceeded to smooth out and "correct" these popular tunes according to the rules they had absorbed in Leipzig or Munich. Ives was as free from subservience to the European tradition as Walt Whitman. His keen ear caught the sound of untutored voices singing a hymn together, some in their eagerness straining and sharpening the pitch, others just missing it and flatting; so that in place of the single tone there was a cluster of tones that made a deliciously dissonant chord. Some were a trifle ahead of the beat, others lagged behind; consequently the rhythm sagged and turned into a welter of polyrhythms. He heard the pungent clash of dissonance when two bands in a parade, each playing a different tune in a different key, came close enough together to overlap; he heard the effect of quarter tones when fiddlers at a country dance brought excitement into their playing by going a mite off pitch. He remembered the wheezy harmonium at church accompanying the hymns a trifle out of tune. All these, he realized, were not departures from the norm. They *were* the norm of popular American musical speech. Thus he found his way to such conceptions as polytonality, atonality, polyharmony, cluster chords based on intervals of a second, and polyrhythms. All this in the last years of the nineteenth century, when Schoenberg was still writing in a post-Wagner idiom, when neither Stravinsky nor Bartók had yet begun their careers, when Hindemith had just been born. All the more honor, then, to this singular musician who, isolated alike from the public and his fellow composers, was so advanced in his conceptions and so accurate in his forecast of the paths that twentieth-century music would follow.

Orchestral works

The central position in his orchestral music is held by the four symphonies (1896–1916). Among his other orchestral works are *Three Places in New England,* which we will discuss; *Three Outdoor Scenes* (1898–1911), consisting of *Hallowe'en, The Pond,* and *Central Park in the Dark,* the last-named for chamber orchestra; and *The Unanswered Question* (1908). The *Sonata No. 2* for piano—"Concord, Mass., 1840–1860"—which occupied him from 1909 to 1915, reflects various aspects of the flowering of New England; its four movements are entitled *Emerson, Hawthorne, The Alcotts,* and *Thoreau.* Ives also wrote a variety of songs, as well as chamber, choral, and piano compositions.

Three Places in New England

In this work (1903–14) Ives evokes three place-names rich in associations for a New Englander.

The "St. Gaudens" in Boston Common

I. *The "St. Gaudens" in Boston Common: Col. Shaw and his Colored Regiment.* Very slowly. (The reference in the title is to the famous statue by Augustus St. Gaudens.) It will suffice to quote the opening lines of the poem that Ives wrote into the score:

> Moving,—Marching—Faces of Souls!
> Marked with generations of pain.
> Part-freers of a Destiny,
> Slowly, restlessly—swaying us on with you
> Towards other Freedom! . . .

An atmosphere of solemn dedication envelops the opening measures. No familiar tunes are actually quoted in this movement, yet the melodic line unmistakably suggests the world of the Stephen Foster songs and the range of emotions attached to the Civil War. The ostinato patterns in the bass, the urgency of the brass, the complex chord structures on the piano used for their color value, the fluid polyrhythms, and the polytonal effects are all characteristic of the composer, as are the wide-apart instrumental lines and the effect of distance that Ives achieves at the emotional climax by pitting high woodwinds against low brass. The texture is predominantly homophonic. The form is free, in the manner of a prelude or fantasy. The piece ends, as it begins, *ppp.*

Putnam's Camp
SIDE 11/3 (E II)
SIDE 17/2 (S)

II. *Putnam's Camp, Redding, Connecticut.* Allegro (Quick-Step Time). "Near Redding Center," Ives wrote, "is a small park preserved as a Revolutionary Memorial; for here General Israel Putnam's soldiers had their winter quarters in 1778–9. Long rows of stone camp fireplaces still remain to stir a child's imagination." The scene is a "4th of July" picnic held under the auspices of the First Church and the Village Cornet Band. The child wanders into the woods and dreams of the old soldiers, of the hardships they endured, their desire to break camp and abandon their cause, and of how they returned when Putnam came over the hills to lead them. "The little boy awakes, he hears the children's songs and runs down past the monument to 'listen to the band' and join in the games and dances."

In this vivid tone-painting Ives conjures up the frenetic business of having a good time on a holiday picnic in a small American town: the hubbub, the sweating faces, the parade with its two bands that overlap, their harmonies clashing. This section abounds in polytonal, atonal, and polyrhythmic effects. Its main theme is a marching song:

Characteristic is Ives's way of quoting a popular tune and then "dissolving" it in another idea. For example, a fragment of *Yankee Doodle* is "dissolved" into something else, but the four notes of the famous tune have sufficed to release a flood of associations in the listener:

This is followed by a melody, presented as a violin solo, that has all the characteristics of a folk song without being one:

Following is the marching song from the middle section (the dream sequence):

Another marchlike melody in this section illustrates Ives's singular ability to create themes that capture the accents of American popular song:

A deep love of all things American lies at the heart of this movement. There is an exciting passage where two march rhythms clash, four measures of the one equalling three of the other. The intricate polyrhythms in the final measures lead to a daringly dissonant ending, *ffff*. This is one of those works that spring from the soil and soul of a particular place, and could have been conceived nowhere else.

The Housatonic at Stockbridge

III. *The Housatonic at Stockbridge*. Adagio molto (Very slowly). Ives quotes the poem of that name by Robert Underwood Johnson:

> Contented river! in thy dreamy realm—
> The cloudy willow and the plumy elm . . .
> Thou hast grown human laboring with men
> At wheel and spindle; sorrow thou dost ken; . . .
>
> . . . . Wouldst thou away!
> I also of much resting have a fear;
> Let me thy companion be
> By fall and shallow to the adventurous sea!

The muted strings set up a rippling current of sound, *pppp,* as background for the melody that presently emerges, divided between the French horn and English horn. It is a serene, hymnic tune that evokes the prayer

meetings of Ives's boyhood. This contemplative nature piece flows calmly and steadily to the *fff* climax, then subsides to a pianissimo ending.

The music of Charles Ives is now firmly established in our concert halls. Like the writers he admired most, he has become an American classic.

88

Edgard Varèse

"I refuse to submit myself only to sounds that have already been heard."

Edgard Varèse was one of the truly original spirits in the music of our time. The innovations of Stravinsky, Schoenberg, and Bartók unfolded within the frame of the traditional elements of their art, but Varèse went a step further: he rejected certain of those elements altogether.

His Life

Edgard Varèse.

Varèse was born in Paris in 1883, of Italian-French parentage. He studied mathematics and science at school, since his father intended him for an engineering career. But at eighteen he entered the Schola Cantorum, and subsequently studied at the Paris Conservatoire. With the outbreak of war in 1914 Varèse was mobilized into the French army, but was discharged the following year after a serious illness. He came to the United States in December, 1915, when he was thirty-two, and lost no time in making a place for himself in the musical life of his adopted land.

The greater part of Varèse's music was written during the Twenties and early Thirties. He found a champion in Leopold Stokowski, who performed his scores despite the violent opposition they aroused in conventionally minded concertgoers. Then, like his colleague Ives, Varèse fell silent when he should have been at the height of his powers. During the next twenty years he followed the new scientific developments in the field of electronic instruments, and resumed composing in 1949, when he began to work on *Déserts*.

By that time the scene had changed; there existed a public receptive to experimental music. When an enterprising record company made available four of his works, Varèse was enabled to reach an audience that had never before heard his music. He was invited by the State Department to conduct master classes in composition in Darmstadt, Germany. The younger generation of European composers who were experimenting with tape-recorded music suddenly discovered him as one whose work had been prophetic of theirs. The long-neglected master finally came into his own. He died in New York City in 1965.

His Music

The abstract images that brood over Varèse's music are derived from the life of the big city: the rumble of motors, the clang of hammers, the shriek and hiss and shrilling of factory whistles, turbines, steam drills. His stabbing, pounding rhythms conjure up the throb and hum of the metropolis. It follows that his attention is focused on the percussion, which he handles with inexhaustible invention. His music unfolds in geometrical patterns based on the opposition of sonorous planes and volumes—patterns which, in their abstraction, are the counterpart in sound of the designs of cubist painting. Varèse's music was utterly revolutionary in its day. It sounded like nothing that had ever been heard before.

The fanciful names Varèse gave his works indicated the connection in the composer's mind between his music and scientific processes. *Hyperprism* (1923) is for a chamber orchestra of two woodwinds, seven brass, and sixteen percussion instruments. *Arcana* (1927–28), for orchestra, develops a basic idea through melodic, rhythmic, and instrumental varia-

Life in the big city became an important subject in twentieth-century American art. A painting by John Marin (1870–1953), **Lower Manhattan.** (Collection, The Museum of Modern Art, New York. The Philip L. Goodwin Collection.)

tion, somewhat in the manner of a passacaglia. Of Varèse's other compositions for conventional instruments we should mention *Octandre,* a chamber work for eight instruments (1923), and *Intégrales,* for winds and percussion (1925).

"Speed and synthesis are characteristic of our epoch. We need twentieth-century instruments to help us realize those in music." With *Déserts* (1954) Varèse entered the world of electronic sound. The piece is written for orchestra; but at three points in the score there are interpolations of what Varèse called "organized sound"—music on tape. There followed, in 1958, *Poème électronique,* which was commissioned by the Philips Radio Corporation to be played in a pavilion designed by Le Corbusier at the Brussels Fair. This was intended as "a poem of the electronic age." Thus, at the age of seventy-three, the intrepid explorer was still pursuing new paths, bringing back to his less venturesome fellows the shapes and sounds of the music of the future.

Ionisation

SIDE 11/4 (E II)
SIDE 17/3 (S)

Varèse's most celebrated composition is scored for thirty-five different instruments of percussion and friction, played by thirteen performers. *Ionisation* (1931) is an imaginative study in pure sonority and rhythm, in which Varèse frees percussion and bell sounds from their traditional subservience to melody and harmony.

The instruments used fall into three groups. Those of definite pitch include tubular chimes, celesta, and piano. Among those of indefinite pitch are drums of various kinds, cymbals, tam-tam (gong), triangle, slapstick, Chinese blocks, sleighbells, castanets, tambourine, and two anvils. Also a number of exotic instruments, such as *bongos* (West Indian twin drums with parchment heads, played either with small wooden sticks or with the fingers); a *guiro* (a Cuban dried gourd, serrated on the surface and scratched with a wooden stick); *maracas* (Cuban rattles); *claves* (Cuban sticks of hardwood); and a *cencerro* (a cowbell without a clapper, struck with a drumstick). The instruments of continuous pitch include two sirens and a string drum known as a *lion's-roar,* consisting of a medium-size wooden barrel with a parchment head through which a rosined string is drawn, the sound being produced by rubbing the string with a piece of cloth or leather. Varèse directed that a *theremin*—one of the first electronic instruments—might be substituted for the sirens.

The score displays the characteristic traits of Varèse's style, especially his uncanny ability to project masses of tensile sound that generate a sense of space. The ear is teased by complex rhythmic patterns whose subtle texture recalls the rhythms of African and Asian music. Varèse deploys his array of noisemakers on interlocking planes, analogous to the soprano, alto, tenor, and bass levels of the orchestra and choir. Used in this fashion, the percussion instruments create a harmony and counterpoint all their own. The sirens set up a continuous pitch. Their protracted wail, with its mounting sense of urgency, takes shape as a vast shadowy image of our Age of Anxiety. Most adroitly managed is the relaxation that comes toward the end of the piece with the entrance of the chimes and the tone clusters in the low register of the piano. The energy stored up in these sonorous "ions" has been released; the machine comes gently to rest.

Varèse's emphasis on sheer sonority presaged one of the most important trends of our era. In the light of what is happening today, *Ionisation* stands revealed as one of the prophetic scores of the twentieth century.

89

Twentieth-Century Americans (I)

"Music is immediate, it goes on to become." — W. H. AUDEN

The generation of American composers born around the turn of the twentieth century had an easier time than their predecessors. The gradual victory of musical modernism in Europe could not but have repercussions here. Besides, the emergence of a strong native school became a matter of national pride and found support in various quarters. The era of prosperity in the 1920s encouraged private patronage in the form of grants and fellowships. Of great help was the forward-looking policy of conductors like Serge Koussevitzky, Leopold Stokowski, and Dimitri Mitropoulos, who made a point of giving the American composer a hearing. The conservatories too, which had hitherto concentrated on the training of instrumentalists and singers, began to turn their attention to the needs of young composers. The music departments of our colleges and universities also took on new importance as centers of progressive musical activity.

During these years our composers were steadily moving forward professionally. In terms of craftsmanship, their scores began to bear comparison with the best of Europe's. The decade before the Second World War saw this country emerge as the musical center of the world. The presence here of Stravinsky, Schoenberg, Bartók, Hindemith, Milhaud, Krenek, and their confreres had a tremendous impact on our musical life. Many of our younger musicians studied with these masters and came directly under their influence.

Composers Born 1890–1910

Moore

Douglas Moore (Cutchogue, Long Island, 1893–1969 Greenport, Long Island) taught at Columbia University, where he was Edward MacDowell Professor of Music. He was a Romantic at heart and regarded Romanticism as a characteristic American trait. He had his greatest success in his sixties, with the production of his opera *The Ballad of Baby Doe* (1956), on a dramatically compelling libretto by John LaTouche. An earlier opera, *The Devil and Daniel Webster* (1938), with a libretto by Stephen Vincent Benét, also achieved wide popularity.

Piston

Walter Piston (Rockland, Maine, 1894–1976, Belmont, Massachusetts) was a leading representative of the international outlook among American composers. He believed that art limits itself through exclusive preoccupation with native themes. Piston was a Neoclassicist; his music was urbane, polished, witty. He taught at Harvard University from 1926 until his retirement in 1960. Characteristic of his style are the *Concerto for Orchestra* (1934); the *Concertino for Piano and Chamber Orchestra* (1937); and the *Fourth Symphony* (1950).

Thomson

The art of Virgil Thomson (Kansas City, Missouri, 1896–) is rooted in the homespun hymns and songs, many of Civil War vintage, that were the natural inheritance of a boy growing up in the Middle West. On this was superimposed the cultural tradition of Harvard; and upon that, during a fifteen years' residence in Paris, the Gallic approach to art and life whose foremost American spokesman he became. He came into prominence with the production in 1934 of his opera *Four Saints in Three Acts* on a libretto by Gertrude Stein. Among Thomson's varied list of works are the

Symphony on a Hymn Tune (1928); a symphonic sketch, *The Seine at Night* (1947); and several notable film scores, of which the best-known is *Louisiana Story* (1948).

Sessions

The music of Roger Sessions (Brooklyn, New York, 1896–) presents distinguished musical ideas in a distinguished way. Romantic and Neoclassical elements intermingle, in his mature style, with Expressionist and twelve-tone influences. His eight symphonies bear the imprint of profound thought and concentrated emotion so characteristic of this composer. More accessible is his incidental music to *The Black Maskers* (1923), a symbolist play by the Russian dramatist Leonid Andreyev. *The Trial of Lucullus* (1947) is a highly effective opera, based on a play by Bertolt Brecht, in which the celebrated Roman general stands trial after his death, his jury consisting of the little people whose lives were shattered by his triumphs. *Montezuma,* a full-scale opera treating Cortez's conquest of the Aztecs, had its premiere in Berlin in 1964, but had to wait until 1976 for its first American performance in Boston.

Harris

Roy Harris (Lincoln County, Oklahoma, 1898–1979, Santa Monica, California) was hailed in the early 1930s as the great hope of American music. For a decade he was the most played and most publicized composer in the country. Harris's music is American in its buoyancy and momentum. His Neoclassic bent led him to the large instrumental forms. Twelve symphonies form the core of his output; the *Third* (1938) has remained his finest achievement, and is a notable contribution to the repertory of American symphonies.

Howard Hanson (Wahoo, Nebraska, 1896–1981, Rochester, New York) played a crucial role during the 1920s when the battle for American music had still to be won. As director of the Eastman School of Music and conductor of the Rochester Symphony Orchestra, he organized annual festivals of American music at which some of the most important works of the period received their first performance. In his own music Hanson is traditional and eclectic. Of his five symphonies the most important is the *Second,* the *Romantic* (1930).

George Gershwin

"Jazz I regard as an American folk music; not the only one, but a very powerful one, which is probably in the blood and feeling of the American people more than any other style of folk music. I believe that it can be made the basis of serious symphonic works of lasting value."

George Gershwin.

In terms of native endowment, George Gershwin (1898–1937) was without question one of the most gifted musicians that this country has produced. He was born in Brooklyn of Russian-Jewish parents who had immigrated some years before, and grew up on the teeming East Side of New York City. The dynamic, extrovert youngster was about ten when he began to study the piano. Given his intensity and his eagerness to learn, he might have gone on to a conservatory, but his future direction was already clear to him. The sixteen-year-old boy, discussing jazz with his teacher, said, "This is American music. This is the kind of music I want to write."

Gershwin took the three ingredients that went into the folk song of the streets of New York—jazz, ragtime, and the blues—and out of these wove a characteristic popular art. He was able to do this because of his spontaneous lyric gift. His first hit, *Swanee,* was brought to fame by Al Jolson. In the ensuing decade he produced a number of the memorable songs associated with his name, among them *Somebody Loves Me, Oh Lady Be Good, Fascinating Rhythm, The Man I Love,* and *'S Wonderful.*

Songs

In these show tunes we encounter the distinctive profile of the Gershwin song: fresh lyricism; subtle rhythms, now caressing, now driving; chromatic harmony; and sudden modulations. Gershwin's imagination impelled him to transcend the limitations of what was a stereotyped commercial form. He found his lyricist in his brother Ira, whose unconventional word patterns perfectly suited his notes. Together they helped to bring into being a sophisticated type of popular song that caught the pulse of the 1920s.

Musical comedy

His success in musical comedy made him all the more determined to bridge the distance between "popular" and "classical." He achieved this aim in the *Rhapsody in Blue* (1924), which we will discuss. The following year he crossed the hitherto impassable barrier between Tin Pan Alley and Carnegie Hall when he played his *Concerto in F* with Walter Damrosch and the New York Symphony Orchestra. He next tackled the Lisztian tone poem and produced *An American in Paris* (1928). *Porgy and Bess* followed in 1935. With the years, this "folk opera" has taken on the character of a unique work. Gershwin here was guided by the instinct of the musical dramatist. He had, besides, tenderness and compassion, the lyrics of his brother Ira, and the wonderful tunes to go with them. And so he captured, as Lawrence Gilman put it, "the wildness and the pathos and tragic fervor than can so strangely agitate the souls of men."

Opera

Physically attractive and endowed with a magnetic personality, George Gershwin was the center of an adoring circle of friends. He played his own music with enormous flair, and thoroughly enjoyed doing so. The last year and a half of his life was spent in Hollywood, where he wrote the music for two Fred Astaire movies—*Shall We Dance?* and *A Damsel in Distress*. He was not happy working in pictures, for the conventions of Hollywood were even less tractable than those of Broadway; besides, he missed the excitement of New York. But he never returned. After a brief illness, he was found to have a brain tumor. He did not survive the operation.

Film music

Gershwin: Rhapsody in Blue

The *Rhapsody in Blue* had its origin in a fortuitous circumstance—the desire of Paul Whiteman, at that time a leading jazz band leader, to

The original poster for the concert at which Gershwin's Rhapsody in Blue *was first performed.*

prove to the world that jazz was a serious art form. This ambition coincided perfectly with Gershwin's long-standing desire to make jazz the basis of a serious symphonic work. Whiteman decided to present a program of popular music at Aeolian Hall in New York, which at that time was—along with Carnegie Hall and Town Hall—a center of serious music making. He asked Gershwin to write a piece for the occasion. The barrage of press releases in the weeks before the concert referred to a Committee that was to decide "What is American Music?". Since the committee consisted exclusively of musicians born in Europe—Rachmaninoff, Jascha Heifetz, Efrem Zimbalist and the opera singer Alma Gluck—it is obvious that Whiteman was more interested in publicity than in finding an answer to his question. Still, it is significant that he linked his concert to a much larger issue.

Gershwin, busy with putting the finishing touches on his musical comedy *Sweet Little Devil,* set to work only a month before the event. He had originally intended to write an *American Rhapsody,* but at the suggestion of his brother Ira changed the title to *Rhapsody in Blue, for jazz band and piano.* It was during a trip to Boston, where he had to go for the out-of-town tryout of *Sweet Little Devil,* that the plan for the *Rhapsody* took shape, to quote his account, "on the train, with its steely rhythms, its rattle-ty bang that is so stimulating to a composer."

> I frequently hear music in the very heart of noise. And there I suddenly heard—and even saw on paper—the complete construction of the rhapsody, from beginning to end. No new themes came to me, but I worked on the thematic material already in mind and tried to conceive the composition as a whole. I heard it as a sort of musical kaleidoscope of America—of our vast melting pot, of our unduplicated national pep, of our blues, our metropolitan madness. By the time I reached Boston I had a definite *plot* of the piece, as distinguished from its actual substance.

The concert took place on February 12, 1924. Actually the fare that Whiteman offered in the first part of the program was not up to the level of the brilliant audience he had succeeded in luring to Aeolian Hall. Interest was beginning to flag when, toward the end of the long program, Gershwin came out to play his new work. The effect was electrifying. The *Rhapsody* caught on at once and, from that afternoon, embarked on a fantastic career that carried Gershwin's name around the globe. Critics might cavil at its lack of conventional form, but such carping was powerless against the rhythmic verve, infectious high spirits, and wealth of melody that Gershwin poured into the piece.

The word "blue" in the title refers specifically to the use of *blue notes*—the flatted third and seventh (and sometimes fifth) steps of the scale—rather than to the mood of depression characteristic of the blues idiom of black Americans; Gershwin's *Rhapsody* is in fact a buoyantly optimistic work. A rhapsody, as we have seen, was a freely structured work of the Romantic era, and Gershwin alternates sections for solo piano and for orchestra in a loose sequence quite unlike the standard concerto. One can, however, discern the not unfamiliar progression from opening through scherzo and "slow movement" to finale.

The orchestration of Ferde Grofé, especially the use of a "wha-wha" mute on the trumpet, vividly brings to life Gershwin's conception. Because of the pressure of time and the composer's inexperience, the orchestration of the *Rhapsody* was done by Whiteman's gifted arranger, following Gershwin's suggestions. (Today the work is usually played in a later Grofé version for symphony orchestra rather than his original jazz band setting. Gershwin himself orchestrated all his later concert works.) The *Rhapsody in Blue* soon moved beyond its time and place to become, in Virgil Thomson's phrase, "the most successful orchestral piece ever launched by an American composer."

Unforgettable is the exuberant opening in B-flat major, an ascending scale that Russ Gorman, the clarinetist of Whiteman's band, turned into a squealing glissando—the sliding effect familiar on strings but never before heard on a clarinet. The theme that follows mixes eighth notes and triplets in a way characteristic of jazz and of Gershwin's *Rhapsody:*

SIDE 11/6 (E II)
SIDE 18/1 (S)

The piano enters and, after a brief tutti, embarks on a cadenza-like passage combining Lisztian virtuosity with all the ingenuity of jazz pianism. Most striking is Gershwin's use of the jazz style in scintillating passages that range widely over the keyboard, and in pounding repeated chords that build up to the return of the orchestra, playing an up-tempo version of the principal theme. Gershwin relies heavily on syncopation and a continual shifting between eighth notes and triplets, achieving thereby a suppleness of rhythm that gives the *Rhapsody* its wayward charm.

After a cadence in the orchestra, a new theme is introduced, the kind of carefree, syncopated tune of which Gershwin held the secret. Here, too, eighth notes alternate with triplets:

(The orchestral presentation of this theme is sometimes omitted in performance; several cuts were authorized by the composer in the loosely structured *Rhapsody.*) In the course of its next solo, the piano introduces a saucy tune to which grace notes add a mischievous quality. The composer wants it played *scherzando* (playfully):

Then follows a passage (frequently cut) in which the piano decorates a presentation of the opening theme by the winds. A particularly brilliant solo cadenza on the earlier syncopated theme sets the stage for the *Rhapsody*'s climactic moment, the entrance of the broadly flowing lyric theme that is one of Gershwin's great melodies. It is introduced by the strings and woodwinds playing in unison:

After developing this melody, the piano turns to a tricky repeated-note figure, marked *agitato e misterioso*, and the orchestra soon adds to it a spirited transformation of the lyric theme. Excitement builds up steadily to the coda, which is marked *grandioso* and proclaims in triumph several motives heard earlier in the piano. There follows the famous "blue" ending on the flatted seventh step of the scale.

George Gershwin, dead at thirty-nine—when he was on the threshhold of important advances in his art—has remained something of a legend among us. Because he was so close to us we are inclined to view him within the Broadway frame. It is well to remember that so severe a judge as Arnold Schoenberg said of him, "I grieve over the deplorable loss to music, for there is no doubt that he was a great composer."

Aaron Copland

Aaron Copland. (Photo by John Ardoin.)

"I no longer feel the need of seeking out conscious Americanisms. Because we live here and work here, we can be certain that when our music is mature it will also be American in quality."

Aaron Copland (1900–) is generally recognized as the representative figure among present-day American composers. He manifests the serenity, clarity, and sense of balance that we regard as the essence of the Classical temper.

Copland was born "on a street in Brooklyn that can only be described as drab. . . . Music was the last thing anyone would have connected with it." During his early twenties he studied in Paris with Nadia Boulanger, whose first full-time American pupil he was. When Boulanger was invited to give concerts in America, she asked Copland to write a work for her. This was the *Symphony for Organ and Orchestra.* Contemporary American music was still an exotic dish to New York audiences. After the first performance (1925) Walter Damrosch found it necessary to assuage the feelings of his subscribers. "If a young man at the age of twenty-five," he announced from the stage of Carnegie Hall, "can write a symphony like that, in five years he will be ready to commit murder." Damrosch's prophecy, as far as is known, has not been fulfilled.

Jazz idiom

In his growth as a composer Copland has mirrored the dominant trends of his time. After his return from Paris he turned to the jazz idiom, a phase that culminated in his brilliant *Piano Concerto* (1927). There followed a period during which the Neoclassicist experimented with the abstract materials of his art; he produced his *Piano Variations* (1930), *Short Symphony* (1933), and *Statements for Orchestra* (1933–35). "During these years I began to feel an increasing dissatisfaction with the relations of the music-loving public and the living composer. It seemed to me that we composers were in danger of working in a vacuum." He realized that a new public for contemporary music was being created by the radio, phonograph, and film scores. "It made no sense to ignore them and to continue writing as if they did not exist. I felt that it was worth the effort to see if I couldn't say what I had to say in the simplest possible terms." In this fashion Copland was led to what became a most significant development after the Thirties: the attempt to simplify the new music so that it would communicate to a large public.

Neoclassic period

The "new" music

The decade that followed saw the production of the scores that established Copland's popularity. *El Salón México* (1936) is an orchestral piece based on Mexican melodies and rhythms. The three ballets are *Billy the Kid* (1938), *Rodeo* (1942), and *Appalachian Spring* (1944). Copland wrote two works for high-school students—the "play-opera" *Second Hurricane* (1937) and *Outdoor Overture* (1938). Among his film scores are *Quiet City* (1939), *Of Mice and Men* (1939), *Our Town* (1940), *The Red Pony* (1948), and *The Heiress* (1949), which brought him an Academy Award. Two important works written in time of war are *A Lincoln Portrait* (1942), for speaker and chorus, on a text drawn from the Great Emancipator's speeches; and the *Third Symphony* (1944–46). In *Connotations for Orchestra* (1962), Copland showed himself receptive to the serial techniques of the twelve-tone school.

Copland: Four Dance Episodes from Rodeo

The second of Copland's American ballets—it came between *Billy the Kid* and *Appalachian Spring*—boasts one of his freshest scores. *Rodeo* soon established itself as a classic of the American dance repertory, while the suite that the composer arranged from the ballet became a favorite item on concert programs. It consists of four episodes: *Buckaroo Holiday, Corral Nocturne, Saturday Night Waltz,* and *Hoe-Down.*

The choreographer was Agnes de Mille, whose innovations opened a

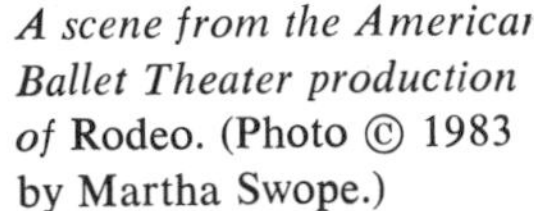

A scene from the American Ballet Theater production of Rodeo. (Photo © 1983 by Martha Swope.)

new era in the American dance theater. It was she who gave Copland the idea for the ballet. "Throughout the American Southwest," Miss de Mille explained, "the Saturday afternoon rodeo is a tradition. On the remote ranches, as well as in the trading centers and the towns, the 'hands' get together to show off their skill in roping, riding, branding, and throwing. Often, on the more isolated ranches, the rodeo is done for an audience that consists only of a handful of fellow-workers, women-folk, and those nearest neighbors who can make the eighty or so mile run-over. The afternoon's exhibition is usually followed by a Saturday night dance at the Ranch House."

The action of the ballet is a cowboy version of the Cinderella/Ugly Duckling story. The Cowgirl, awkward and tomboyish, is in love with the Head Wrangler and tries to impress him by competing with the cowboys; but she makes no headway with the object of her affections, for he has eyes only for the Rancher's daughter. During the afternoon rodeo she is thrown by a bucking bronco and is ridiculed by all. Later, at the Saturday night dance, still dressed in her mannish outfit of pants and shirt, she is very much the wallflower. The sight of the Head Wrangler dancing cheek to cheek with her rival is too much for her. She runs off, disconsolate. When she returns she is completely transformed: the trousers have been replaced by a pretty dress, the boots by slippers, she has a bow in her hair, is the epitome of feminine allure, and quickly becomes the belle of the ball.

Buckaroo Holiday

I. *Buckaroo Holiday* is a zestful Allegro in cut time; Copland creates a sound that fully captures the high spirits of the title. The movement is woven out of three main elements, the first of which is heard in the opening measures: a syncopated version of the C major scale, descending forte and staccato. It is played in unison by woodwinds, trumpets, and strings:

This motive alternates with a complex rhythmic pattern related to the jazz dance known as the Charleston. After a full-bodied expansion of this idea and a more lyrical passage, we hear a "vamp till ready" bass whose rhythms are derived from ragtime. It introduces Copland's version of the cowboy ditty *Sis Joe.*

He punctuates the tune with loud drumbeats that modify the four-beat meter, so that he seems to be looking at the melody in an entirely fresh way. As in *Billy the Kid* and *Appalachian Spring,* Copland does not quote folksongs literally but reshapes the phrases, rearranges motives to suit his fancy, and in general uses the traditional tunes as a point of departure for his own. In short, he assimilates them to his personal style.

The third element is another folk tune, *If he'd be a Buckaroo by trade,* which is introduced by the trombone. Here, too, Copland adds a note here and there that breaks up the four-square symmetry of the phrases. In addition, he inserts measures of silence between the phrases as an element of surprise that heightens the wry humor of the jaunty tune:

These elements are given a genuinely symphonic treatment, into which the composer also introduces a hymnlike idea. Powered by jazzy rhythms, the music races ahead relentlessly, building up tension to the *fff* coda.

Corral Nocturne

II. *Corral Nocturne.* Pianissimo chords on muted brass and strings present the greatest possible contrast to the exuberant finale of the first number. Marked Moderato, the second movement is a gentle landscape piece whose nostalgic mood is akin to the famous Largo (popularly known as *Going Home*) of Dvořák's *New World Symphony.* Eventually broken-chord phrases in the winds form a melody whose first eight notes correspond to the third phrase of *Home Sweet Home,* but because of the difference in rhythm and context, the effect is quite dissimilar:

The *Nocturne* is in **A-B-A** form, but with very little contrast between the sections. Like *Billy the Kid* and *The Tender Land,* it displays Copland's uncanny ability to conjure up the landscape of the West.

Saturday Night Waltz

III. *Saturday Night Waltz.* The introduction suggests violins tuning up. Then an oboe presents one of the loveliest of cowboy songs, *I Ride an Old Paint,* which Copland had already used in *Billy the Kid.* He introduced some changes in order to shape the tune into a slow waltz, but in general preserved its contours.

The piece is in **A-B-A** form. After an atmospheric middle section that is taken a little more slowly, the first section returns. This time the melody is played by oboe and first violins, with a countermelody in the flutes, and leads to a quiet ending.

Hoe-Down
SIDE 12/1 (E II)
SIDE 17/4 (S)

IV. *Hoe-Down.* For this sprightly Allegro, Copland borrowed two square-dance tunes, *Bonyparte* and *McLeod's Reel.* The music vividly suggests the traditional stance—head up, chest out, elbows raised, knees bobbing up and down—that we associate with the more vigorous forms of square dancing:

Copland repeats and alternates the tunes, pits snatches of solo against the full orchestra, contrasts "vamps" in the bass with melodies in the upper register of winds and strings, and manages in an unforgettable way to convey the boundless energy and zest for life that animated the generations who built our country.

Perhaps a psychologist could explain how it happened that the son of Russian-Jewish immigrants, growing up on that drab street in Brooklyn, created the sound by which the cowboy is best known in the ballet houses and concert halls of the world. Whatever the mystery of the artist's imagination, he was able to capture in his music the poetic image of the prairie and in so doing, became the most American of our composers.

Crawford: String Quartet 1931

Ruth Crawford. (Harris and Ewing photograph.)

Ruth Crawford was born in East Liverpool, Ohio in 1901 and grew up "in that traditional cradle of Americanism, a minister's household." She composed along traditional lines until, in her late twenties, she came to New York. There she studied with her future husband, the musicologist Charles Seeger, who along wtih Henry Cowell and others, was active in what was then the avant-garde. Crawford's writing took a boldly experimental turn, and she produced a series of strikingly original works. She was the first woman to hold a Guggenheim fellowship in composition, which made possible a year in Berlin. It was during this year that she wrote her most important work, the *String Quartet 1931*.

There was, however, no audience in America for what she had to say. Like Ives and Ruggles, she gave up composing when she should have been at the height of her creativity. After her marriage to Seeger she collaborated with him in editing collections of American folk songs. This activity played its part in determining the career of her stepson, the talented folk singer Pete Seeger. She died in Chevy Chase, Maryland in 1953, her music practically forgotten. It is only in recent years that she has been recognized as belonging to that small group of innovative American composers who in remarkable fashion anticipated developments that became current only several decades later.

First movement

String Quartet 1931 is a concise, arresting work that displays Crawford's style at its best. The opening movement, in ¾ time and moderate tempo, is marked Rubato assai (very free). The first violin presents a singing line set against the urgent promptings of the cello. This melody has the wide leaps that became increasingly characteristic of twentieth-century music. Notice the dissonant interval of a major seventh at the outset:

Rhapsodical in nature, the movement is unified by motivic-rhythmic cells that pervade the entire work. A favored pattern consists of four sixteenth notes, a triplet and a quintuplet:

Ruth Crawford was much preoccupied with a texture that has been described as *heterophony,* a polyphony in which each line functions as a practically independent entity. Charles Seeger well described it as "together-soundingness in which separate-soundingness predominates." The music is notable for its rhythmic energy, its concentration of thought, and a closely-knit fabric in which one instrument continues the thought of another. As a result, the movement unfolds with boundless momentum in one broad arch, building to a fortissimo climax. The serene coda is interrupted by reminiscences of what has preceded.

The tension in the individual lines is indicated by the following example, in which the first violin moves across a span of three octaves within two measures, only to return to the upper regions:

Second movement

The Scherzo, in 2/4 time, is marked Leggiero (light). It is a snappy movement whose interval relationships and rhythmic patterns are derived from the first but are placed here in so different a context as to sound wholly fresh. Crawford uses an interesting device: each of the instruments contributes a few notes to a continuous ascending or descending line, which becomes more exciting because they all share in it. The principle is most effective in a light, rapid movement. Staccato tones supported by pizzicato underline the whimsical character of this Scherzo. The major-seventh interval that opened the first movement returns here to introduce a lighthearted theme:

Third movement

Third is the slow movement, an Andante in 4/4. Charles Seeger called it "an experiment in dynamic counterpoint. Each part has a different alternation of crescendo and diminuendo, or else the same alternation but beginning and ending at different times." The instruments unite in a continuous flow of sound, so smooth that we do not hear where each instrument enters or drops out. The effect is not unlike that of the third of Schoenberg's *Five Orchestral Pieces, Summer Morning by a Lake.* The composer specified that "the bowing should be as little audible as possible throughout. The crescendi and decrescendi should be equally gradual." The result is an almost static continuum that seems to exist beyond time.

The movement traces a very broad dynamic arch, from a mysterious *ppp* in low register to an *fff* climax in high, then back to low and a *pppp* ending. The four lines are spaced very close together at the beginning, forming tone-clusters of seconds and thirds. They are extremely wide apart at the climax, whose power rests on the dissonance tension inherent in such intervals as major sevenths and minor ninths.

Fourth movement
SIDE 11/5 (E II)
SIDE 17/5 (S)

The finale, an Allegro possibile (as fast as possible) in 2/2, is the most remarkable of the four movements in its anticipation of present-day procedures. The movement consists of two lines that answer one another antiphonally. The upper line is carried by the first violin, the lower by the other three instruments playing in octaves, muted. The upper line begins with a single note that—with each succeeding phrase, one note at a time—grows into a grand unit of twenty notes. This point is reached in the middle of the movement. Then the process is reversed: the music is played backwards (in retrograde), but shifted up a half step, with the units growing progressively shorter until we return to the single note at the end. This goes hand in hand with a rigorous control of dynamics. The violin starts out fortissimo, gradually decreases its volume until it reaches a pianissimo in the middle of the movement, then increases the volume until it returns to fortissimo in the final measures.

The lower part is organized just as rigorously. It is based on an ostinato pattern of ten notes that serves as a tone row, in which—as in the Schoenbergian row—no single pitch is repeated. This is repeated to make a twenty-note pattern that is decreased one note at a time until it reaches a single-note unit in the middle of the movement, whereupon the process is reversed a half tone higher. Each statement of the row begins on the next note of the series and is subject to the kind of permutation that we associate with twelve-tone technique. Here the dynamic scheme is from pianissimo to fortissimo and back to pianissimo.

The opening line of the movement shows how all this works. Notice that the second half of the ostinato (the last ten notes) follows the pattern of the first ten but begins with the second note of the series instead of the first. This entirely changes the disposition of the phrase.

Allegro possibile

ffz *ffz* *ffz*

pp sempre con sordino

What we have here is an attempt to achieve total control over all the elements involved—pitch, rhythm, and phrase structure. In this movement Ruth Crawford foreshadowed in remarkable fashion what became a major preoccupation of composers after the Second World War. One can only conjecture how she might have developed if the time and place had been ready for her.

90

Twentieth-Century Americans (II)

"If music could be translated into human speech, it would no longer need to exist."
— NED ROREM

Composers Born 1910–30

The American composers born in the first quarter of the twentieth century had a much firmer foundation on which to build their careers. Most of them were not only native-born but also native-trained; it was no longer necessary to go to Europe to obtain a superior musical education. The cause of American music was helped too by the rise of radio, long-playing records, and television, which created a much broader audience for music than had ever existed before. Within this new public there were significant minorities who were interested in modern music and, more specifically, in modern American music. A sizable number of works by the new American school found their way onto recordings, thereby taking on a much more viable existence than that afforded by an occasional performance in a concert hall or on the air. From this extremely active generation we name a few representative figures:

Schuman William Schuman (New York City, 1910–) has shown an affinity for the large forms of instrumental music. He combines this classicist esthetic with the robust Americanism of a typically urban mentality. His nine symphonies form the central item in his output; best-known is the *Third* (1941). The *American Festival Overture* (1939) and *New England Triptych* (1956) have also been widely played.

Barber Samuel Barber (West Chester, Pennsylvania, 1910–82, New York) was an avowed romantic. His music is poetic and suffused with feeling; nor is it averse to the grand gestures of the nineteenth-century tradition. Several of his works have achieved wide popularity, among them the light-hearted Overture to *The School for Scandal* (1932), *Adagio for Strings* (1936), and *Essay for Orchestra, No. 1* (1937). Barber's extensive list includes a *Symphony in One Movement* (1936; revised 1942), and two operas: *Vanessa,* on a libretto by Gian-Carlo Menotti (1958); and *Antony and Cleopatra,* on Shakespeare's tragedy, first performed at the inauguration of the new Metropolitan Opera House in 1966 and revised nine years later.

Menotti Gian Carlo Menotti was born in Cadegliano, Italy, in 1911. His inclusion in the American school stretches a point, as he has never renounced his Italian citizenship. But he has spent the greater part of his life in the United States—he came here when he was seventeen—and has won his greatest successes in this country. Besides, his librettos, which he writes himself, are generally in English. Menotti is the most successful opera com-

Paintings such as **Lucky Strike** *by Stuart Davis (1894–1964) are bold commentaries on the modern American scene.* (Collection, The Museum of Modern Art, New York. Gift of The American Tobacco Company, Inc.)

poser of our day. He has created a series of lyric dramas that have spread his name throughout the musical world. The list includes *The Medium* (1946), *The Consul* (1950), *Amahl and the Night Visitors* (1951), *The Saint of Bleecker Street* (1954), *The Last Savage* (1963), and *Help! Help! The Globolinks!* (1968).

Diamond

David Diamond (Rochester, New York, 1915–) projects a vivid personality in music that encompasses violence and tenderness, poetry and a core of strength. Diamond is a prolific composer; eight symphonies occupy the central position on his list. *Rounds for String Orchestra* (1944) has been widely played, as has his suite *Romeo and Juliet* (1947). Diamond's songs and choral music bear witnesss to an exacting literary taste and an evocative handling of text. The stage works include incidental music for *The Tempest* and for Tennessee Williams's *Rose Tattoo.*

Bernstein

Leonard Bernstein (Boston, 1918–) was the first American-born musical director of the New York Philharmonic, and the youngest ever appointed to the post. His serious works include the *Jeremiah Symphony* (1942); *The Age of Anxiety,* for piano and orchestra (1949), based on W. H. Auden's poem of that name; the *Serenade* for violin, strings, and percussion (1954), after Plato's *Symposium;* and the widely-discussed *Mass,* composed for the opening of the John F. Kennedy Center for the Performing Arts in Washington (1971). In his scores for Broadway musicals Bernstein achieves a sophisticated kind of musical theater that explodes with energy. The list includes *On the Town,* a full-length version of his ballet *Fancy Free* (1944); *Wonderful Town* (1953); *Candide* (1956); and the spectacularly successful *West Side Story* (1957).

Mennin

Peter Mennin (Erie, Pennsylvania, 1923–83, New York) was head of the Juilliard School of Music in New York City until his recent death. His music is marked by an easy handling of the large forms, melodious counterpoint, forward-driving rhythms, and an overall sense of bustling energy. His eight symphonies show his steady growth in the manipulation of ideas. The weightiest items on his list, beside the symphonies, are the *Concertato for*

Orchestra (1954); *Sonata Concertante* for violin (1958), which shows him moving toward a simplification of style; and the *Piano Concerto* of 1958.

Rorem

Ned Rorem (Richmond, Indiana, 1923–) is one of the most gifted song writers of his generation. Such songs as *The Lordly Hudson* and *Lullaby of the Mountain Woman* are in the line of descent from the great French art song of the post-Romantic period. Among Rorem's works are three symphonies (1951, 1956, 1958), three piano concertos (1950, 1951, 1969); *Sun*, a suite for soprano and orchestra (1967); *War Scenes,* a powerful song cycle for baritone and piano on texts of Walt Whitman (1969); *Air Music*, a suite for orchestra (1973); *Assembly and Fall,* an orchestral work in one movement (1974); and *Eight Etudes for Piano* (1975).

The United States differs from European countries in one important respect: our people do not come from a single stock. On the contrary, ours is a melting-pot culture in which many national and racial groups are represented. This diversity is reflected in the backgrounds of our composers. For example, Walter Piston, Gian Carlo Menotti, and Peter Mennin are of Italian origin. A number of composers are Jewish, among them George Gershwin, Aaron Copland, William Schuman, David Diamond, and Leonard Bernstein. Varèse came of French-Italian, Howard Hanson of Swedish stock. Among the Black composers of the modern American school may be mentioned William Grant Still (Woodville, Mississippi, 1895–), Ulysses Kay (Tucson, Arizona, 1917–), Howard Swanson (Atlanta, Georgia, 1909–), Julia Perry (Lexington, Kentucky, 1924–), and David Baker (Indianapolis, 1931–).

Schuman: Chester—Overture for Band

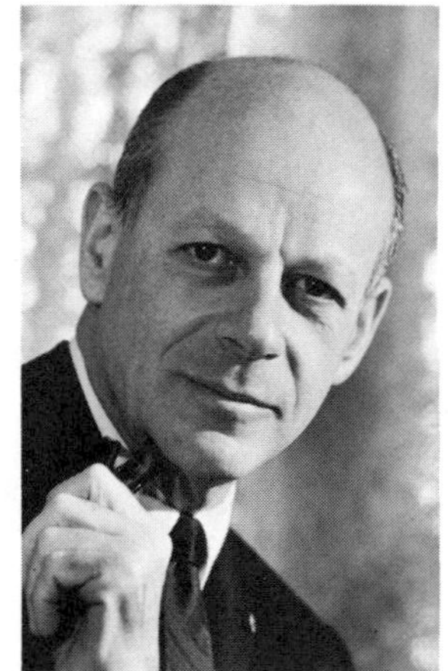

William Schuman. (Photo by Carl Mydans.)

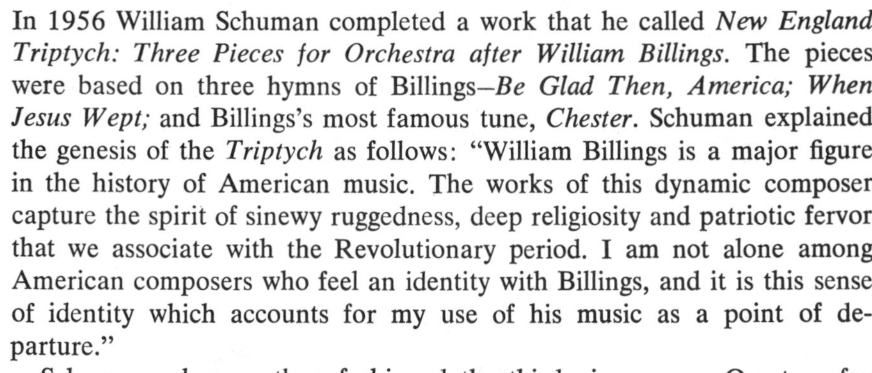

In 1956 William Schuman completed a work that he called *New England Triptych: Three Pieces for Orchestra after William Billings.* The pieces were based on three hymns of Billings—*Be Glad Then, America; When Jesus Wept;* and Billings's most famous tune, *Chester*. Schuman explained the genesis of the *Triptych* as follows: "William Billings is a major figure in the history of American music. The works of this dynamic composer capture the spirit of sinewy ruggedness, deep religiosity and patriotic fervor that we associate with the Revolutionary period. I am not alone among American composers who feel an identity with Billings, and it is this sense of identity which accounts for my use of his music as a point of departure."

Schuman subsequently refashioned the third piece as an Overture for Band. The band version, like the orchestral, explores the dual nature of *Chester*, which began as a church hymn and was subsequently adopted by the Continental Army. It was Schuman's intent, not so much to write a set of variations on a theme, as to fuse the sturdy character of Billings's melody with his own musical language. The opening section is marked Religioso; here the woodwinds present the melody in the upper register, piano, dolce (sweetly), and legato. Then it is taken over by the brass in

The demands of abstract form and color are beginning to overcome representational elements in this painting by Willem de Kooning (b. 1904), titled ***Woman, I.*** (Collection, The Museum of Modern Art, New York.)

The "drip painting" of Jackson Pollock (1912–56) paralleled the interest in chance as an element of musical composition. ***Number 1, 1948.*** (Collection, The Museum of Modern Art, New York.)

middle register, in a majestic forte. Having presented the tune as a hymn, Schuman now explores its potential as a marching song. The mood changes to an Allegro vivo, with the melody in shorter note values. There follow various transformations of the tune through changes in harmony and instrumental color, meter, rhythm, tempo and dynamics, register and key, as well as through the expansion of motives and the adding of contrapuntal lines. A few examples will suffice to show the workings of Schuman's imagination:

1. The melody as it is introduced by woodwinds:

2. The melody in faster tempo and shorter note values (diminution):

3. The melody transformed through the use of staccato and rests:

Schuman's *Chester,* in its band version, has become popular with high-school and college bands throughout the country. Thus Billings's robust tune is reaching a new generation, which is as it should be.

Bernstein: Overture to Candide

Leonard Bernstein. (Photo: Christina Burton.)

Voltaire's *Candide* traces the picaresque adventures of an innocent who, after a series of bizarre mishaps, discovers that all is not for the best in this not-so-best of all possible worlds. He discovers too that happiness consists in staying home and cultivating one's own garden. The attempt to transform Voltaire's satire into a Broadway musical brought together a number of gifted writers. The show, which opened in 1956, had a book by Lillian Hellman, with lyrics by John LaTouche, Dorothy Parker, and Richard Wilbur and music by Leonard Bernstein. For various reasons it failed to please; mainly, one suspects, because the time was not ripe. Almost two decades later *Candide* returned to Broadway, renovated with a new book by Hugh Wheeler and lyrics by Stephen Sondheim. This time the public was ready for it, and Voltaire's hero triumphed.

Bernstein's exuberant Overture sets the scene for the comic tale. The piece, which has become a favorite in the concert hall, is notable for its impetuous rhythm, bright orchestration, and irresistible high spirits. The music leaps off the ground with the opening measure and never loses its drive. The first theme, played by flutes and violins *ff* and brilliante, is an active, upward-leaping melody (of the type that came to be identified, in the symphonies of Haydn and Mozart, as a "rocket theme"):

Against this is balanced the romantic second theme, a melody consisting of two six-measure phrases (more accurately, four three-measure phrases), with a delightful alternation of duple and triple meter:

Several subordinate themes round out the form. The material is restated with increasing tension, leading to a climax through crescendo, accelerando, and a rise to the upper register. This music is thoroughly American in its nervous energy, its freshness and directness of feeling. Bernstein's is a big-city, sophisticated Americanism (what Gershwin, in describing the *Rhapsody in Blue,* called "our metropolitan madness") and he expresses it in a way all his own.

We have mentioned only a handful among three generations of composers whose works reflect important currents in twentieth-century musical thought. To give anywhere near a full account of their work would carry us beyond the limits of this book. Enough has been said, however, to indicate the diversity of these composers and of the tendencies they represent.

PART EIGHT

The New Music

"Composers are now able as never before to satisfy the dictates of that inner ear of the imagination." — EDGARD VARÈSE

91

New Directions

"From Schoenberg I learned that tradition is a home we must love and forgo."
— LUKAS FOSS

We have seen that the term "new music" has been used throughout history. Has not every generation of creative musicians produced sounds and styles that had never been heard before? All the same, the years since World War II have seen such far-reaching innovations in the art that we are perhaps more justified than any previous generation in applying the label to the music of the present. In effect, we have witnessed nothing less than the birth of a new world of sound.

Mid-Century Trends in the Arts

Only rarely does an important movement in art come into being without precursors. It should therefore not surprise us that several elements of avant-garde art can be traced back to earlier developments. For example, in the years immediately before the First World War, the Italian movement known as Futurism attracted musicians who aspired to an "art of noises" that foreshadowed the achievements of Varèse and of electronic music. Another precursor was the Dada movement, which grew up in Zurich during the war and after 1918 spread to other major art centers. The Dadaists, in reaction to the horrors of the bloodbath that engulfed Europe, rejected the concept of Art with a capital A—that is, something to be put on a pedestal and reverently admired; to make their point, they produced works of manifest absurdity. This nose-thumbing spirit of Dadaism was reflected in the music of many composers, especially in France, during the twenties; several decades later it was to influence the American composer John Cage. The Dada group, which included artists like Hans Arp, Marcel Duchamp, and Kurt Schwitters, subsequently merged into the school of Surrealists, who exploited the symbolism of dreams. The best-known Surrealists, such as the writers Guillaume Apollinaire and André Breton, the painters Giorgio de Chirico, Max Ernst, and Salvador Dali, organized the indiscipline of Dada into a visionary art based on the disassociated and distorted images of the world of dreams. Other ele-

Futurism

Dadaism

Surrealism

Left: The spirit of Dadaism is embodied in this Cubist-Surrealist painting, which scandalized the New York Armory Show of 1913. Marcel Duchamp (1887–1968), **Nude Descending a Staircase,** *No. 2.* (Philadelphia Museum of Art: The Louise and Walter Arensberg Colletion.) *Bottom: The Cubist movement encouraged the painter to construct a visual world in terms of geometric patterns.* **Violin and Pipe** *(1920) by Georges Braque (1882–1963).* (Philadelphia Museum of Art: Louise and Walter Arensberg Collection.)

ments entering into the family tree of contemporary art were Cubism, the Paris-based style of painting embodied in the work of Pablo Picasso, Georges Braque, and Juan Gris, which encouraged the painter to construct a visual world in terms of geometric patterns; and Expressionism, which we discussed in Chapter 78.

Cubism

Art since the Second World War has unfolded against a background of unceasing social turmoil. In this regard, of course, the 1950s and '60s have been no different from many decades that preceded them. However, there can be no question that, as the second half of the century wore on, the problems confronting civilization became steadily more severe. The knowledge that man has finally achieved the capacity to wipe himself off the face of the earth broods over our time and feeds its unease. The fixed laws and certainties of Newtonian physics have given way to a relativistic view of the universe in which chance and accident, the probable and unpredictable, are seen to have an increasingly important place. The moral imperatives that we inherited from our forebears are being questioned as never before. This restlessness of spirit is inevitably reflected in the arts, which are passing through a period of violent experimentation with new media, new materials, new techniques. Artists are freeing themselves from every vestige of the past in order to explore new areas of thought and feeling. Some even prefer to reject thought and feeling altogether.

Abstract Expressionism

Since the human eye responds more readily to fresh impressions than does the ear, contemporary painting and sculpture have reached a wider public than has contemporary music. The trend away from objective painting guaranteed the supremacy of Abstract Expressionism in this country during the 1950s and '60s. In the canvases of such men as Robert Motherwell, Jackson Pollock, Willem de Kooning, Franz Kline, and Philip Guston, space, mass, and color are freed from the need to imitate

In Abstract Expressionism, space and mass become independent values, liberated from the need to express reality. A painting by Robert Motherwell (b. 1915), **The Voyage.** (Collection, The Museum of Modern Art, New York. Gift of Mrs. John D. Rockfeller, 3rd.)

The themes and techniques of Pop Art are drawn from modern urban life while incorporating Dada-like incongruities into each work. A construction by Robert Rauschenberg (b. 1925) titled **Monogram.**

objects in the real world; they become values in the autonomous realm of painting. In other words, the Abstract Expressionists strengthened the tradition of "pure" painting–pure, that is, in its independence of external reality. The urge toward abstraction has been felt equally in contemporary sculpture, as is evident in the work of such artists as Henry Moore, Isamu Noguchi, and David Smith.

At the same time, a new kind of realism has come into being in the art of Jasper Johns, Robert Rauschenberg, and their fellows, who owe some of their inspiration to the Dadaists of four decades earlier. Rauschenberg's aim, as he put it, was to work "in the gap between life and art."

Pop Art

This trend culminated in Pop Art, which draws its themes and techniques from modern urban life: machines, advertisements, comic strips, movies, commercial photography, and familiar objects connected with everyday living. The desire to function "in the gap between life and art" motivates Andy Warhol's *Four Campbell Soup Cans* and *Brillo Boxes,* Jim Dine's *Shovel* and *A Nice Pair of Boots,* Claes Oldenburg's monumental *Bacon, Lettuce and Tomato* and *Dual Hamburgers.* Pop Art has absorbed the literal vision of photography and the silk-screen techniques of reproducing photographs on canvas; also the Dada-like inclusion of incongruous objects into art works. For example, Rauschenberg has incorporated into his abstractions a quilt and pillow, a tire, Coke bottles, electric clocks, and fans. These impart to his paintings the three-dimensional quality of sculpture. In this respect he is one of an influential group that is determined to expand the resources of the painter's art.

In a related vein, new styles of art have grown up because of the availability of new materials. The sculptor no longer works simply with traditional marble and bronze, but reaches out to employ wood, new types of concrete, and a variety of plastics—clear or colored, solid, foamlike, or pliable. The flexibility of new materials has suggested new forms, and there is a new genre of Environmental Art that uses all the resources of art and technology to create a world of shapes, sounds, lights, and colors into which the spectator actually steps, to be completely surrounded by the artist's vision.

Environmental Art

Developments in music have paralleled these trends. A number of composers have been strongly influenced by their painter friends. Morton Feldman, to name one, has written: "The new painting made me desirous of a sound world more direct, more immediate, more physical than anything that existed before. To me my score is my canvas, my space. What I do is try to sensitize this area—this time space." The long association between Varèse and the painter Marcel Duchamp engendered a strikingly similar point of view in both artists. A like parallelism exists between Jackson Pollock's attempt to achieve an "indeterminate" kind of painting by allowing the colors to drip freely onto the canvas, and the attempt of John Cage and his followers to achieve an indeterminate music by using procedures based on chance. Like the proponents of Pop Art, Cage has tried to expand resources; he accepts "all audible phenomena as material proper to music." When we examine the new music we find a desire for free forms in which elements of chance and randomness are permitted to operate. Many artists have chosen to loosen their control of

Interaction: art and music

The mobiles of Alexander Calder (1898–1976) achieve an ideal of ever-changing form. **International Mobile,** *1949.* (The Museum of Fine Arts, Houston. Gift of Dominique and John deMenil in memory of Marcel Schlumberger.

the art work by moving away from pre-established forms. A similar desire for freedom inspired the mobiles of Alexander Calder, the component parts of which shift with each current of air to create new relationships. Artists tend more and more to look upon form as the all-pervading element in art that flows directly out of the material, so that each individual work, instead of following a set pattern, must be allowed to create its own form. Significant in this respect is Cage's remark that "Form is what interests everyone and fortunately it is wherever you are and there is no place where it is not."

Dance

Other arts, too, have been subject to wide experimentation. The dance, traditionally chained to specific anecdote and gesture, found itself liberated from storytelling (in the work of George Balanchine) and from traditional patterns of movement (in the work of Martha Graham), and since the Second World War the trend toward abstraction has grown apace. The most important choreographer of the avant-garde, Merce Cunningham, has worked closely throughout his career with John Cage, introducing elements of chance and indeterminacy into his dance compositions. His objective, he states, is "to make a space in which anything can happen."

Poetry

In the field of literature, poetry has, understandably, been the most experimental genre. Many of our poets face the world of today with a profound sense of alienation. They reflect their disjointed epoch in the fragmentation of their syntax and the violence of their imagery. The utmost freedom of verse forms and a sardonic wit tinged with bitterness characterize many of the younger poets, such as the two best-known members of the so-called "New York group": Kenneth Koch and John Ashbery. Contemporary American poetry ranges from the elegant intellectualism of a John Hollander or a Richard Wilbur to the Whitmanesque exuberance of the two leading poets of the "Beat Generation," Allen Ginsberg and Gregory Corso. These poets and their colleagues reveal—as poets have always done—the most profound impulses of their time, but with an energy and passion that are in the great tradition. Even the word-oriented art of poetry, however, has given rise to strong abstract tendencies, most clearly embodied in the idea of "shaped" poems, in which words are arranged in abstract patterns on the page, the visual form taking precedence over the meaning.

Drama

Although the forms of drama and novel are by their very nature based on an imitation of life, they have not remained indifferent to the new trends. The theater has moved away from the social and psychological concerns that permeated the work of Arthur Miller and Tennessee Williams in the 1950s. It has turned instead to the "theater of the absurd," whose leading European proponents—Samuel Beckett, Eugene Ionesco, and Jean Genet—view the world with a vast disillusionment, placing metaphysical absurdity at the core of human existence. No less pervasive has been the influence of the Englishman Harold Pinter, whose plays transform the realities of human relationship into unpredictable patterns. The spirit of the absurd has also penetrated the novel—witness such works as Joseph Heller's *Catch 22* and John Barth's *Giles Goat-Boy,* to name only two of a considerable number of novels that have captured the pulse of our time.

Cinema

Finally, the cinema—of all the arts the one most securely chained to storytelling of a popular kind—has also responded to the twin impulses of experimentation and abstraction. A number of "new wave" directors have opened their films directly onto contemporary experience, mirroring with great eloquence the disjointed patterns of life about them. Among these may be mentioned Michelangelo Antonioni, Jean-Luc Godard, Federico Fellini, and Alain Resnais, in whose *Last Year at Marienbad* the Abstract-Expressionist urge found perhaps its most successful cinematic realization to date.

If the picture of artistic developments in recent decades often seems confused and contradictory, this is inevitable because of our very close vantage point. We have picked out only a few landmarks on the contemporary scene, but these are enough to indicate that art today has become increasingly intellectual, experimental, and abstract.

Toward Greater Organization

When Schoenberg based his twelve-tone method on the use of tone rows, he was obviously moving toward a much stricter organization of the sound material. This desire was even more clearly manifest in the music of Webern. However, it remained for their disciples to extend the implications of the tone-row principle to the elements of music other than pitch. The arrangement of the twelve tones in a series might be paralleled by similar groupings of twelve durations (time values), twelve dynamic values (degrees of loudness), or twelve timbres. Other factors, too, might be brought under serial organization: the disposition of registers and densities, of types of attack, or sizes of intervals. By extending the serial principle in all possible directions, a composer could achieve a totally organized fabric, every dimension of which was derived from and controlled by one basic premise: the generating power of the series.

Total serialism

This move toward *total serialism* resulted in an extremely complex, ultrarational music, marked by the utmost unity among the ideas to be expressed, the means of expressing them, and the structures through which that expression was achieved. In such a conception the series defines all the relationships that operate within a given structure; the act of composition becomes the process whereby those relationships are realized to the fullest degree. Total serialism pushed to the farthermost limits, with the thoroughness of a scientific experiment, some of the new ways of hearing and experiencing music.

Toward Greater Freedom

The urge toward a totally controlled music had its counterpart in the desire for greater–even total–freedom from all predetermined forms and procedures. Music of this type emphasizes the antirational element in artistic experience: intuition, chance, the spur of the moment. Composers who wish to avoid the rational ordering of musical sound may rely on the element of chance and allow, let us say, a throw of dice to determine the selection of their material, or may perhaps build their pieces around a series of random numbers generated by a computer. They may construct a piece from sounds selected at random; arrange it in sections but allow the performer to choose the order in which these are to be played; or indicate the general course of events in regard to pitches, durations, registers, but leave it up to the performer to fill in the details. The performer may shuffle the pages in any sequence he desires; play one fragment rather than another; or react to fellow players in one of several ways (or not at all). In any case, the performance becomes a musical "happening" in the course of which the piece is recreated afresh each time it is played.

Aleatory music

When chance, choice, and the operation of random elements are given a free hand, the things that happen in a piece are dissociated from any pre-existing scheme. Such indeterminate music is known as *aleatory* (from *alea,* the Latin word for "dice," which from ancient times have symbolized the whims of chance). In aleatory music the overall form may be clearly indicated but the details are left to choice or chance. On the other hand, some composers will indicate the details of a composition clearly enough, but leave its overall shape to choice or chance; this type of flexible structure is known as *open form.*

Open form

The composer John Cage has been the leader in this movement. "I try to arrange my composing means," he states, "so that I won't have any knowledge of what might happen." There are, naturally, limits beyond which the aleatory ideal cannot be pursued. At a certain point total freedom in music becomes either total chaos or total silence. All the same, contemporary composers have sought to create musical organisms that would take on a fresh form with each performance, just as Calder's mobiles constantly assume fresh forms. This desire for greater freedom complements the equally strong desire for the tightly organized, ultrarational structures of total serialism.

Related to these tendencies is the increased reliance on improvisation –a technique common enough in music of the Baroque and earlier eras, but so long dormant that it has had to be reintroduced, in the 1950s and '60s, from the domain of jazz. Traditionally improvisation consists of spontaneous invention within a framework and a style that have been clearly established, so that player and listener have fairly well defined ideas of what is "good" and what is "bad." In the more extreme types of aleatory music no such criteria are envisaged, no value judgments called for: anything that happens is acceptable to the composer.

In the past, art has generally striven toward rational, highly organized forms functioning within an ideal universe in which cause gave rise to effect, in which the artist carefully selected what was essential and rigidly excluded what was not. To this ordered view of art, aleatory music and open form oppose an ideal of maximum freedom that mirrors an unpredictable, even irrational world continually in flux. Here art ceases to reflect life; it becomes a part of life, and as uncertain.

Electronic Music

"I have been waiting a long time for electronics to free music from the tempered scale and the limitations of musical instruments. Electronic instruments are the portentous first step toward the liberation of music." — EDGARD VARÈSE

Perhaps the single most important musical development of the 1950s and '60s was the emergence of electronic music. This was foreshadowed, during the earlier part of the century, by the invention of a variety of electronic instruments of limited scope. The most familiar of these is the electronic organ, which was developed primarily as a cheaper substitute for the traditional pipe organ. Others, such as the *Ondes Martenot*—an instrument producing sounds by means of an electronic oscillator and operated by a keyboard—found occasional use in concert music. Although these instruments were not sufficiently flexible to compete successfully with the traditional ones, they did point the way to future developments.

Musique concrète

The post-war emergence of electronic music falls into three stages. The first stage came with the use of magnetic tape recording, which was much more flexible as a medium for storing sounds than the flat disc recording that had been used previously. A group of technicians at the Paris radio station had already begun to experiment with what they called *musique concrète,* a music made up of natural sounds and sound effects recorded on discs and altered by changing the speed of the records. Their activities took on a new impetus when they began to use tape, which gave them a vastly wider range of possibilities in altering the sounds they used as source material, and also enabled them to cut and splice the sounds into new combinations. It was the great achievement of musique concrète to establish firmly the principle that all conceivable sounds and noises could serve as raw material for the creative musician.

There soon presented itself the possibility of using not only natural but also artificially generated sounds. A wide variety of equipment for generating and altering sounds came into use. Significant in this regard were the experiments carried on by Otto Luening and Vladimir Ussachevsky at Columbia University, and by Herbert Eimert and Karlheinz

The RCA Electronic Music Synthesizer at the Columbia Princeton Music Center, New York.

Stockhausen in Cologne. These men began their work in 1951. Within a few years there were studios for the production of tape music in many of the chief musical centers of Europe and America. With the raw sound (either naturally or electronically produced) as a starting point, the composer could isolate its components, alter its pitch, volume, or other dimensions, play it backward, add reverberation (echo), filter out some of the overtones (see Appendix V), or add additional components by splicing and overdubbing. Even though all these operations were laborious and time-consuming—it might take many hours to process only a minute of finished music—composers hastened to avail themselves of the new medium.

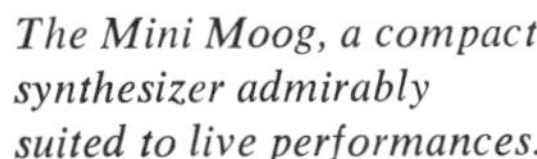

The Mini Moog, a compact synthesizer admirably suited to live performances.

Synthesizers

The second step in the technical revolution came with the evolution of *synthesizers,* which are essentially devices combining sound generators and sound modifiers in one package with a unified control system. The first and most elaborate of these devices was the RCA Electronic Music Synthesizer, first unveiled in 1955; a more sophisticated model was installed four years later at the Columbia-Princeton studio in New York City. This immense and elaborate machine, which today would cost a quarter of a million dollars to build, is capable of generating any imaginable sound or combination of sounds, with an infinite variety of pitches, durations, timbres, dynamics, and rhythmic patterns far beyond the capabilities of conventional instruments. The synthesizer represented an enormous step forward, since the composer was now able to specify all the characteristics of the sound beforehand (by means of a punched paper tape), and thus could bypass most of the time-consuming "hand" techniques associated with tape-recorder music.

Because of its size and cost the RCA machine at Columbia has remained unique; but various smaller synthesizers have been devised that bring most of the resources of electronic music within the reach of a small studio. The best-known of these were the Moog and the Buchla; there is even a portable synthesizer known as the Syn-Ket, designed for the composer John Eaton. The smaller instruments can be played directly (although usually only one note at a time), thus making live performance a possibility.

Computer-generated music

The third stage of electronic development, which is still in progress, involves the use of the electronic computer as a sound generator. The basic principle here is the fact that the shape of any sound wave can be represented by a graph, and this graph can in turn be described by a series of numbers, each of which will represent a point on the graph. Such a series of numbers can be translated, by a device known as a digital-to-analog converter, into a sound tape that can be played on a tape recorder. In theory then, all that a composer has to do is to write down a series of numbers representing the sound wave he wants, feed it into the converter, and play the tape. But composers do not traditionally think in terms of the shape of sound waves, so it was necessary to devise a computer program that would translate musical specifications–pitches, durations, timbres, dynamics, and the like—into numbers. There are now many such programs, and the wide availability of home computers has made them readily accessible. Computer sound-generation is the most flexible of all electronic media, and is likely to dominate the field in years to come.

Electronic music has two aspects of novelty. The most immediately obvious one is the creation of "new sounds," and this has impelled many musicians to use the new medium. Equally important, perhaps, is the fact that the composer of electronic music is able to work directly with the sounds, and can produce a finished work without the help of an intermediary—the performer. We have seen that the serial approach demanded a totally controlled, totally specified music. This requirement found an invaluable ally in electronic music, which freed the composer from the limitations of conventional instruments and performers, leaving only the limitations of the human ear as restrictions upon his thought. An electronic work, once synthesized, was fixed forever in the form that the composer had intended; instead of "music to be performed," it was "music to be reproduced," and no longer needed the concert framework.

However, the combination of electronic sounds with live music has also proved to be a fertile field, especially since many younger composers have been working in both media. Works for soloist and recorded tape have become common, even "concertos" for tape recorder (or live-performance synthesizer) and orchestra. Electronic music has also influenced live music, challenging performers to extend themselves to produce new types of sound, and suggesting to composers new ways of thinking about conventional instruments.

We have used the term *electronic music* in the same way as we would speak of piano music or vocal music—to describe a medium, not a style. Just as piano music or vocal music may be in the Baroque, Classical, or Romantic style, so a piece using electronic sounds may be in one style or another. Naturally, when a composer writes for a particular medium he tries to take advantage of the things that it alone can do. From this point of view it does not make much sense to compose a piece of electronic music in the style of Bach or Beethoven (except, perhaps, as a stunt for the popular market). Electronic music is at its best when it says things that cannot be said in any other medium. All the same, composers of electronic music are free, just as they would be if they were writing for conventional instruments, to compose in any style that suits their fancy.

The New Romanticism

We saw how, after the radical developments in music during the 1910s, composers felt impelled to take stock and consolidate the new advances by returning to styles and procedures of the past, in the movement known as the New Classicism. Similarly, the bewildering variety of trends and movements since World War II has in recent years caused a number of composers to consider simplifying their musical language. For some, this has entailed a reaction similar to the earlier one, but this time turning towards the styles of the nineteenth century.

The *New Romanticism,* as it has been dubbed, takes a variety of forms. Some composers have written in the styles of specific historical figures, while others merely use the generalized language of the Romantic era. Similarly with forms: there are symphonies and concertos and quartets, but also works that find their own, original shapes. Explicit quotation of older works has become a common practice, sometimes for programmatic purposes, sometimes as a structural basis. (Both uses are exemplified by the central movement of Luciano Berio's *Sinfonia:* a movement from Mah-

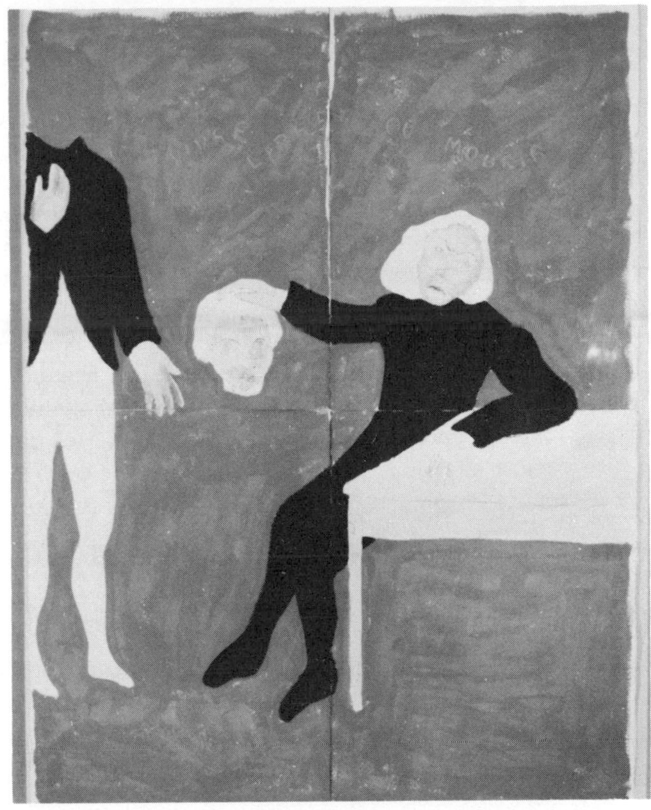

In his painting **Vivre Libre ou Mourir** *(Live Free or Die), Ernesto Tatafiore (b. 1943) evokes the Romantic era by his traditional style of drawing and the passionate nature of his theme.* (Courtesy of the André Emmerich Gallery.)

ler's *Symphony No. 2* acts as a kind of cantus firmus, like a river, in the composer's words, "going through a constantly changing landscape, sometimes going underground and emerging in another, altogether different place," while against it are juxtaposed audible references to other well-known works "chosen . . . for their potential relation to Mahler.") As often in art, there are no clear dividing lines; many works classified as "New Romantic" share techniques with serial and aleatory music, while few composers have been willing to forego the new timbral possibilities opened up in recent decades.

One of the reasons often cited for this resurrection of older styles has been the feeling that contemporary composers need to recapture the general listening audience, which has only slowly accustomed itself to the more radical developments of the twentieth century. By working in a musical language familiar to that audience, a composer hopes to overcome his listeners' initial resistance to something new and strange. At the same time, of course, he may have a more difficult time establishing his own identity and originality, because he risks comparison with the great masters of the last century who used the same language and who still dominate our concert programs. Despite these hazards, a number of today's composers have, to some degree or other, incorporated elements of earlier styles in their music.

Minimalism

In minimal art, the work is a simple object, shorn of suggestions of human receptiveness. One such work is **Signature,** *a sculpture by Anne Truitt (b. 1921).* (Vassar College Art Gallery, Poughkeepsie, New York.

Still others who feel the need to simplify their musical language have turned in another direction. These composers hope to heighten the listener's perception by concentrating it on fewer and fewer details. The urge toward a simple art, which first found expression in painting and sculpture, emerged in the 1970s as a significant force in contemporary music, as certain young composers stripped their music down to the barest essentials.

The salient feature of *minimal music,* as it has come to be known, is the repetition of patterns with very little variation in pitch, speed, volume, or timbre. The music changes so slowly that the listener is forced to focus a maximum of attention upon a minimum of detail. Such concentration can exert a hypnotic effect, and indeed the term "trance music" has attached itself to some works of the minimalists. But it is a label they reject because, as they point out, their material is selected most carefully and worked out in highly disciplined procedures. One can say, however, that in their music—as in the great novel of Marcel Proust—time moves at a different pace than what most of us have been accustomed to.

By simplifying melody, harmony, and rhythm within an unwavering tonality, the minimalists represent a turning away from the complex, highly intellectual style of the serialists. They reject the heritage of Schoenberg and Webern just as they do the intellectual preoccupations of Boulez and Stockhausen. Instead, they open themselves to modes of thought emanating from the Third World, especially India and Africa, as well as from jazz, pop, and rock music. Although influenced by some of the early ideas of John Cage, for the most part they reject his interest in indeterminacy and chance. In the words of one minimalist composer, LaMonte Young, "I'm interested in the most clear and sparse sounds—in control and in knowing what I'm doing." He opts for repetition because "it demonstrates control."

There are many approaches to minimalist music. Some is devoid of pulse, some numbingly regular. Some of it is very busy on the surface, though the harmonies and timbres change very slowly; in other types there is no such distraction. The music of Steve Reich, for example, moves so slowly that listening to it has been compared to watching the minute hand of a clock: "You perceive it moving after you have stayed with it awhile." Reich is concerned with the process of change rather than change itself; as he put it, "I want to be able to hear the process happening through the sounding music." Electronic techniques are naturally highly adaptable to minimalist music, since they facilitate repetition or imitation of patterns, and many minimalists have used electronics as well as live performers. The incessant repetition, indeed, requires a special variety of "new virtuosity" on the part of performers.

Minimalism is not without precedents in Western music: a famous one is the Prelude to Wagner's *Das Rheingold,* which never leaves the E-flat major triad but simply elaborates it with ever-increasing rhythmic and melodic activity. Nevertheless, in its drastic alteration of the time scale at which music happens, minimalism indubitably constitutes a radical break with much of the tradition of Western music. It will be fascinating to observe the directions in which this style develops in the future.

Other Aspects of the New Music

Whether it is serial or aleatory, live or electronic, most new music reflects the conviction that each composition is based upon a set of premises that are unique to it. The function of the piece is to realize fully what is implicit in these premises. Each work is regarded as a self-contained structure independent of all other structures, whose form springs from and is determined by conditions peculiar to itself. Ours obviously is no longer a time when thousands of pieces can be written in sonata, rondo, or **A-B-A** form. These forms ultimately had to degenerate into formulas, in spite of the infinite ingenuity with which the great masters handled them, because their rationale was based on the harmonic system of the Classic-Romantic era. The concept of predetermined form is completely alien to the spirit of the new music. The force that holds a piece together is not superimposed from without but flows directly out of the material. Since the material is unique to the piece, so is the form. It follows that today's composers have introduced infinite variety and flexibility into this aspect of music.

Form

Throughout the eighteenth and nineteenth centuries it was pitch—embodied in melody, harmony, and tonality—that was the dominant structural element of music. In the first half of the twentieth century rhythm in the abstract (as opposed to rhythm embodied in a theme) emerged as a form-generating principle. The new music has elevated dynamics and timbre to equal importance with pitch and rhythm, and these four dimensions may now play an equal role in determining the character of the musical discourse.

Pitch

Contemporary attitudes, it need hardly be said, have liberated all the elements of music from the restrictions of the past. The concept of a music based on the twelve pitches of the chromatic (tempered) scale has obviously been left far behind. Electronic instruments make possible the use of sounds "in the cracks of the piano keys"—the microtonal intervals, such as quarter or third tones, that are smaller than the traditional semitone—and very skilled string and wind players have begun to master these novel scales. In addition, the notion of what is acceptable sonorous material has been broadened to include the domain that lies between music and noise.

Rhythm

Rhythm, too, has been liberated from the shackles of tradition. In the past, musical time was measured according to a system of values that existed only in relation to each other: a whole note was equal to two halves, a half note equalled two quarters, and so on. These values bore no relation to absolute or physical time; they depended on the speed at which the piece was played. But electronic tape brings the composer face to face with the requirements of physical time. An inch of tape is equivalent to so many seconds. For him, therefore, musical time can no longer exist apart from physical time.

Stravinsky, Bartók, Schoenberg, and their disciples developed a musical rhythm no longer based on equal measures and the regular recurrence of accent. Their concepts have been immensely refined in the past quarter century. Music in the past gave the impression of flowing through time in an orderly fashion toward a preordained goal. Many composers today, on the other hand, try to focus the listener's attention on a texture in which each sonority or density stands almost by itself, detached from its surroundings. Their music may unfold as a series of sonorous points, each of which is momentarily suspended in time, surrounded by plenty of "air pockets" of organized silence: great static blocks of sound juxtaposed in musical space, fashioned out of tiny cell-like clusters that spin, whirl, combine, and recombine with a kind of cumulative force.

The new virtuosity

Musical styles so different from all that went before need a new breed of instrumentalists and vocalists to cope with their technical difficulties. One has only to attend a concert of avant-garde music to realize how far the art of piano playing or singing has moved from the world of Chopin and Verdi. The piano keyboard may be brushed or slammed with fingers, palm, or fist; or the player may reach inside to hit, scratch, or pluck the strings directly. A violinist may tap, stroke, and even slap his instrument. Vocal music runs the gamut from whispering to shouting, including all manner of groaning, moaning, or hissing on the way. Wind players have learned to produce a variety of double-stops, subtle changes of color, and microtonal progressions; and the percussion section has been enriched by an astonishing variety of noisemakers and special effects. True, the new performance skills have not yet filtered down to the members of our symphony orchestras. Performances of difficult new works are necessarily limited and, more often than not, unsatisfactory. When, after much effort, a contemporary composer does manage to obtain a hearing, it may be a traumatic experience for him to have his work mauled by players who are unable to cope with its technical problems. Fortunately, in each of the important musical centers groups of young players and singers are springing up who have a genuine affinity with the new music. Singers like Bethany Beardslee, Phyllis Bryn-Julson, and Jan DeGaetani, pianists like David Burge, Robert Helps, Paul Jacobs, Gilbert Kalish, Ursula Oppens, and Charles Rosen, violinists like Matthew Raimondi and Paul Zukofsky, to mention only a few, are masters of a new kind of virtuosity that cannot fail to amaze those who were brought up on the old. They are performing an invaluable service for the new music, and it is an encouraging sign that their numbers are growing.

We mentioned the impact of jazz on serious music during the second quarter of the century. The two genres have grown ever closer together. Serious composers today feel an affinity for the improvisational freedoms of jazz, as well as its cultivation of highly specialized, virtuoso styles of performance. Jazz composers, for their part, are strongly interested in certain avant-garde trends, such as electronics and serialism. The most successful example of this cross-fertilization is Gunther Schuller. He is but one of a number of gifted musicians on either side of the fence who are increasingly influenced by what is happening on the other side.

The Internationalism of the New Music

The advent of tape made it easy to take down a live performance without having to wait until it was recorded, and to send it to any part of the world. This, plus the development of the other media of communication—radio, television, recordings, and the jet plane—brought about an enormous speeding up in the dissemination of musical ideas. Composers in New York, Chicago, or Los Angeles are able to keep abreast of the latest developments in Cologne, Rome, or Paris. Many of the new composers are active on both sides of the Atlantic as performers, conductors, teachers, organizers of musical events, or participants in festivals of the new music. This inevitably has led to an internationalization of the musical scene. The new music is a language shared by European and American composers alike. In this sense music in the mid-twentieth century has recaptured something of the universality it held in the eighteenth century (and lost in the nineteenth as a result of the emphasis upon national schools).

The links between Europe and America were forged before World War II, when such leaders of European music as Stravinsky, Schoenberg, Bartók, Hindemith, and Krenek came to the United States. The war and the events leading up to it disrupted musical life on the Continent much more than in this country, with the result that the United States forged ahead in certain areas. For example, the first composer to apply serial organization to dimensions other than pitch was the American composer Milton Babbitt. The experiments of John Cage anticipated and influenced similar attempts abroad. Earle Brown was the first to use open form, Morton Feldman the first to write works that gave the performer a choice. Once the war was over the Europeans quickly made up for lost time. Intense experimentation went on in Italy, Germany, France, England, Holland, and Scandinavia. This has gradually spread eastward into the Communist world; serial and electronic music have also taken root in Japan, while the music of the East has in turn influenced Western composers.

In the following chapter we will discuss a group of composers—American and European—whose music is representative of the new trends. These men are pushing back boundaries and exploring frontiers; they are actively enlarging the domain of what the rest of us can perceive, experience, and understand. Their music will bring you the excitement of discovering a new world of sound.

92

Composers of Our Time

Krzysztof Penderecki.

"There is no avant-garde. There are only people who are a little late."

— EDGARD VARÈSE

Penderecki: Threnody for the Victims of Hiroshima

"We are at a time of the end of forms. The forms and methods of listening to music will undergo great change in the near future."

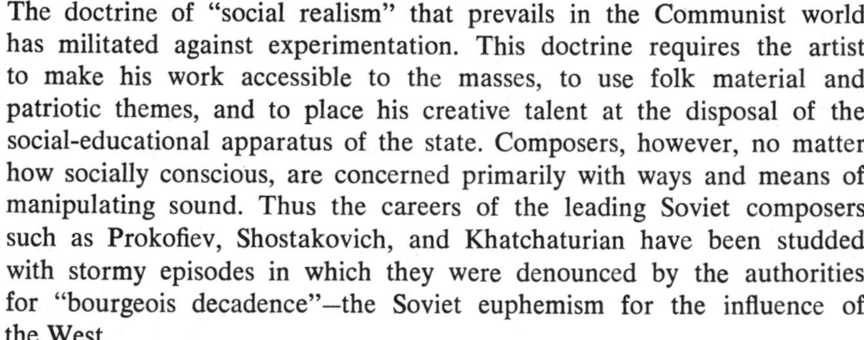

The doctrine of "social realism" that prevails in the Communist world has militated against experimentation. This doctrine requires the artist to make his work accessible to the masses, to use folk material and patriotic themes, and to place his creative talent at the disposal of the social-educational apparatus of the state. Composers, however, no matter how socially conscious, are concerned primarily with ways and means of manipulating sound. Thus the careers of the leading Soviet composers such as Prokofiev, Shostakovich, and Khatchaturian have been studded with stormy episodes in which they were denounced by the authorities for "bourgeois decadence"—the Soviet euphemism for the influence of the West.

The musical isolation of eastern Europe came to an end in the later 1950s. With ever greater momentum contemporary ideas began to infiltrate the Communist world, at first in the satellite countries but ultimately even in the Soviet Union. The leader in this development was Poland, whose musical life now stands in the mainstream of the European avant-garde.

Best-known among the younger Polish composers is Krzysztof Penderecki (1933–). Endowed with a vivid imagination and a strong sense of dramatic effect, he has developed an eclectic style in which elements derived from folksong and Gregorian chant, Bartók and Stravinsky mingle with avant-garde procedures. His popularity stems from his ability to use contemporary techniques in order to project music that makes a strong emotional impact.

Innovative use of strings

A case in point is his *Threnody for the Victims of Hiroshima* (1960), for fifty-two string instruments. The piece exploits a remarkable range of string sonorities. As in so much of the new music, pitch here is made subsidiary to timbre and rhythm, dynamics, textures, and densities; indeed the score of the work uses an elaborate notation to indicate the many unusual effects of bowing, vibrato, mass glissandos, quarter tones, percussive effects (such as those obtained by striking the sounding board of the violin with the wooden part of the bow or with the fingertips), and very rapid tremolos not in precise rhythm. The player is asked to obtain the highest possible tones on his instrument by placing his finger on the string very close to the bowing point, producing sounds that do not have an exact pitch but that contribute a distinctive color to the sonority. Also employed are tone clusters, containing all the pitches within a specified interval; these unfold in bands of sound that expand or contract, divide or merge, almost in the manner of chord progressions.

Original sonorities

The piece opens with high, glassy sonorities that are sustained like a cry of anguish. These are presently heard against percussive noises in the bass and plangent outcries that can hardly be described as dissonant, so far removed is this music from traditional notions of dissonance and consonance. From this torrent of sound emerges an occasional point where the instruments play in a normal manner; these moments stand out in powerful contrast to the cataclysm that surrounds them. Resemblances to electronic sound permeate the changing densities, colors, and continual contrasts of register. In such a context even silence becomes charged with feeling. The somber noise at the end has a density and thrust that are remarkable when one remembers it is produced only by strings. It brings this agonized music to a close as though "seen through a glass darkly."

Ligeti: Atmosphères

György Ligeti.

György Ligeti (Transylvania, 1923–) left his native Hungary while in his early thirties and established himself first in Vienna, then in Stockholm. He also became active in various centers of contemporary music in Germany, such as the electronic studio in Cologne and the famous summer courses at Darmstadt. Strongly influenced by the composers of the modern Viennese school, especially Webern, he has been called "a Viennese by choice." Ligeti belongs to the circle of composers who have tried to broaden the heritage of Schoenberg by making it responsive to more recent currents. He found ways to achieve with traditional instruments the finer gradations of sound made familiar by electronic music. Through tone clusters and amalgams of sound that create a flow of shifting densities and colors, Ligeti has gone beyond focusing on fixed, recognizable pitches to working with large clusters of tones. Influenced by the indeterminacy of John Cage as well as by the minimalists, he has experimented with noise and natural speech elements both in traditional and electronic music.

One of Ligeti's major preoccupations has been the interweaving of many separate strands into a complex polyphonic fabric, deriving the shape and momentum of the music from barely perceptible changes in timbre, dynamics, density, and texture rather than from more easily recognized external events. The result is a shimmering current of sound, to which he applied the term *micro-polyphony*. Instead of using pitch and rhythm as primary elements, he has worked with large blocks of sound, the components of which—pitches and rhythms—have lost their individual identity. This phase of Ligeti's development reached its fullest expression in his works of the early 1960s. He subsequently moved toward a style with more transparent textures and more clearcut melodic, harmonic, and rhythmic contours. The movement toward clarity is apparent in such works as the *Cello Concerto* (1966), *Lontano* for orchestra (1967), and the *Chamber Concerto* for thirteen players of 1970.

Micro-polyphony

Atmosphères (1961), "for large orchestra without percussion," established Ligeti's position as a leader of the European avant-garde. Together with his choral work *Lux aeterna,* it was included in the sound track of the film *2001: A Space Odyssey,* making the composer's name familiar to an international public. In *Atmosphères,* he explored the region that lies between instrumental and electronic music. Although the score interweaves more than sixty individual lines, what the listener hears is a murmurous continuum that exemplifies Ligeti's "micro-polyphony" at its best. As he put it, he was composing with blocks of sound—except that the blocks all merged into a continuous flow. Individual details emerge here and there, yet they are subordinate to the overall sound. The orchestra includes quadruple winds, and the string sections are divided into many parts; at certain points the composer's minutely notated score takes on the appearance of a geometric pattern (see illustration on p. 583).

The overall form of *Atmosphères,* the composer states, is to be realized as a single, wide spanning arch, "the individual sections melting together and subordinate to the great arch." The piece opens with a massive yet gentle cluster chord containing every semitone within a span of nearly five octaves. The winds and violins fade out, leaving only the lower strings, among which individual notes briefly swell and project from the sonic blanket. Wind and string chords alternate, intermix, and then begin to vibrate. Bands of sound creep up and down. Strange rustlings emanate from the strings, played on the fingerboard or the bridge of the instrument, and with the wood of the bow. At the end, everything fades into an amorphous vibration, made by sweeping across the strings of a piano with the brushes used by jazz drummers. Then this, too, evaporates "as it were into nothingness."

There is a dreamlike, other-worldly quality to this piece. It belongs to a group of works that in the 1960s—like those of Varèse forty years earlier—pointed the way to new worlds of sound. As such, it constitutes an important addition to the present-day repertory.

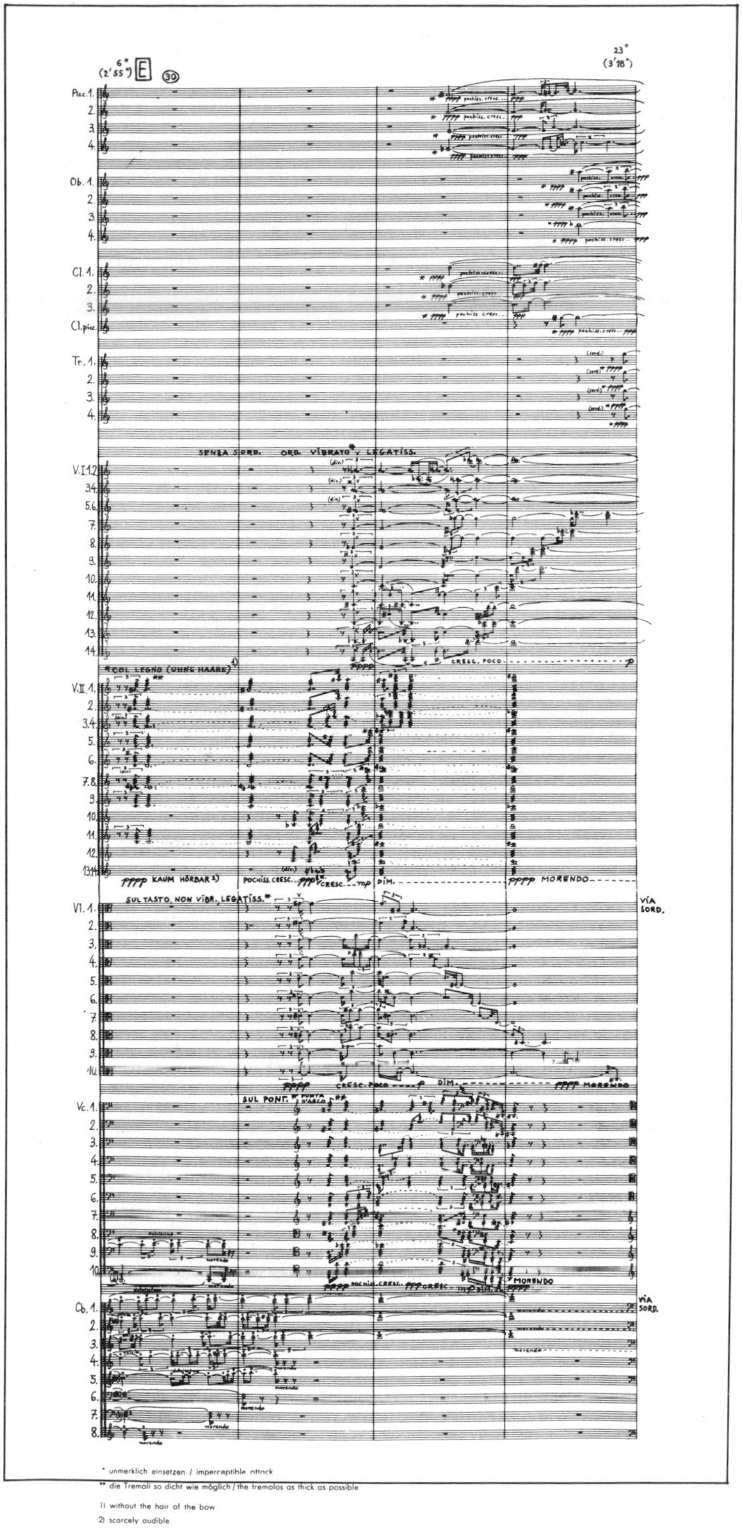
E
Picc. 1.
Ob. 1.
Cl. 1.
Cl. picc.
Tr. 1.
SENZA SORD.
ORD.
VIBRATO
LEGATISS.
V. I 1.2.
CRESC. POCO
COL LEGNO (OHNE HAARE)
V. II 1.
KAUM HÖRBAR
POCHISS. CRESC.
CRESC.
DIM.
MORENDO
SUL TASTO, NON VIBR., LEGATISS.
Vl. 1.
VIA SORD.
SUL PONT.
Vc. 1.
Cb. 1.
* unmerklich einsetzen / imperceptible attack
** die Tremoli so dicht wie möglich / the tremolos as thick as possible
1) without the hair of the bow
2) scarcely audible

A page from the score of Atmosphères *by György Ligeti.*

Crumb: Ancient Voices of Children

George Crumb.

In recent years George Crumb (Charleston, West Virginia, 1929–) has forged ahead to a notable position among the composers of his generation. He owes this preeminence partly to the emotional character of his music, allied to a highly developed sense of the dramatic. His kind of romanticism is most unusual among the advanced composers of his generation. Crumb uses contemporary technique for expressive ends that make an enormous impact in the concert hall. He has won numerous honors and awards, and is currently professor of composition at the University of Pennsylvania.

Crumb has shown an extraordinary affinity for the poetry of Federico García Lorca, the great poet who was killed by the Fascists during the Spanish Civil War. Besides *Ancient Voices of Children* (1970), his Lorca cycle includes four other works: *Night Music I* (1963); four books of madrigals (1965–69); *Songs, Drones, and Refrains of Death* (1968); and *Night of the Four Moons* (1969). "In *Ancient Voices of Children,* as in my earlier Lorca settings," the composer states, "I have sought musical images that enhance and reinforce the powerful yet strangely haunting imagery of Lorca's poetry. I feel that the essential meaning of this poetry is concerned with the most primary things: Life, death, love, the smell of the earth, the sounds of the wind and the sea." These concepts, Crumb goes on to explain, "are embodied in a language which is primitive and stark, but which is capable of infinitely subtle nuance."

Poetry of Lorca

Ancient Voices of Children is a cycle of songs for mezzo-soprano, boy soprano, oboe, mandoline, harp, electric piano, and percussion. The texts are fragments of longer poems which Crumb grouped into a sequence so as to achieve musical continuity. There are two movements for instruments alone. These, and one of the vocal movements as well, are imbued with the spirit of dance. Indeed, the composer suggests that they can be performed by a dancer as well.

Endowed with an aural imagination of remarkable vividness, Crumb tirelessly explores new ways of using voice and instruments. Like many contemporary composers he uses the voice like an instrument, in a vocal style which he describes as ranging "from the virtuosic to the intimately lyrical." He has found his ideal interpreter in the mezzo-soprano Jan De Gaetani, whose recording of the work remains as an example for all other interpreters.

The score abounds in unusual effects. The soprano opens with a fantastic *vocalise* (a wordless melody, in this case based on purely phonetic sounds) which she directs at the strings of an electrically amplified piano, arousing a shimmering cloud of sympathetic vibrations. The pitch is "bent" to produce quarter tones. Included in the score are a toy piano, harmonica, and musical saw. The percussion players use all kinds of drums, gongs and cymbals, Tibetan prayer stones, Japanese temple bells, and tuned tom-toms (high-pitched drums of African origin); also a marimba, vibraphone, sleighbells, glockenspiel plates, and tubular bells.

First song
SIDE 12/2 (E II)
SIDE 17/6 (S)

I. *El niño busca su voz.* Very free and fantastic in character. "The little boy was looking for his voice. (The king of the crickets had it.) In a drop of water the little boy was looking for his voice. I do not want it for speaking with; I will make a ring of it so that he may wear my silence on his little finger." The soprano part offers a virtuoso exhibition of what the voice can do in the way of cries, sighs, whispers, buzzings, trills, and percussive clicks (Crumb specifies *not* a clucking sound). There are even passages marked "fluttertongue"—an effect we have hitherto associated only with instruments. Throughout Crumb captures the rapturous, improvisational spirit of flamenco song. The passion is here, the sense of mystery and wonder—but in a thoroughly twentieth-century setting.

The boy soprano answers, singing offstage through a cardboard speaking tube. His "after-song" should sound "simple and unaffected, even naive." The boy's part ends *pppp,* "timidly."

Dances of the Ancient Earth. Very rhythmic. An ecstatic oboe solo is supposed to sound "raw, primitive, shawm-like." (The shawm, as you will recall, was an early ancestor of the oboe introduced into Europe from Asia Minor around the twelfth century.) The music conjures up the atmosphere of the Near East, of that highly charged, florid melody that entered the Spanish soul through the Moors. "Bended" pitches on mandoline, harp, and oboe produce the quarter-tones that are an integral part of Oriental song. The percussion instruments reinforce the Levantine atmosphere. The piece ends with a joyous outburst on the oboe. Notice throughout the remarkable plasticity of the rhythm.

Second song

II. *Me he perdido muchas veces por el mar.* Musingly. "I have lost myself in the sea many times with my ear full of freshly cut flowers, with my tongue full of love and agony. I have lost myself in the sea many times as I lose myself in the heart of certain children." The soprano whispers the text through a speaking tube, phrase by phrase, against an extraordinary background. A musical saw, played with a cello or double-bass bow, gives forth a haunting sound. No less striking is the glissando produced by moving a chisel along a string of the amplified piano, or the scraping of a fingernail along the metal winding of a harp string, which produces a nasal whistling sound. Each timbre stands out with unusual clarity. All in all, this movement is a tour de force in atmosphere and sonority.

Third song

III. *¿De dónde vienes, amor, mi niño?* Freshly, with dark, primitive energy. In this poem Lorca uses the question-and-answer pattern that is found in folklore throughout the world. A mother questions her unborn child. "From where do you come, my love, my child? From the ridge of hard frost. What do you need, my love, my child? The warm cloth of your dress. . . . When, my child, will you come? When your flesh smells of jasmine-flowers. Let the branches ruffle in the sun and the fountains leap all around!" Lorca here reaches down into what Jung would have called the racial unconscious. The music matches the poet's intention with shattering eloquence. The song opens with birdlike calls to a primitive cry on the words "mi niño" (my child). Now the drums establish an ostinato rhythm: the deliberate, ceremonious pattern of the bolero with which Ravel electrified the world fifty years ago. Crumb adapts it to his own expressive needs in a compact, intense form that avoids the obvious overextension of Ravel's concert piece. The drums beat a powerful crescendo as the mother exuberantly hails her child. A gradual diminuendo extends to the last measure. The final chord, *fff,* is a kind of primal scream.

Fourth song

IV. *Todas las tardes en Granada, todas las tardes se muere un niño.* Hushed, intimate; with a sense of suspended time. "Each afternoon in Granada, a child dies each afternoon." This heart-rending lament has the quality of a primitive mourning ritual. The voice part unfolds in a toneless murmur, supported by harmonica, marimba, and percussion. Then, in the upper register of a toy piano, we heart Bach's *Bist du bei mir*—an echo of life-affirmation triumphant over death. Crumb explains the intrusion, which is wonderfully effective: "In composing *Ancient Voices of Children,* I was intrigued with the idea of juxtaposing the seemingly incongruous: a suggestion of Flamenco with a Baroque quotation (*Bist du bei mir,* from the Notebook of Anna Magdalena Bach), or a reminiscence of Mahler with a breath of the Orient. It later occurred to me that both Bach and Mahler drew upon separate sources in their own music without sacrificing 'stylistic purity.' " What matters, in such cases, is the extent to which the composer absorbs such elements into his personal style. Given a strong creative personality, he is certain to do so.

Ghost Dance. To the accompaniment of maracas and whispered syllables from the percussion players, the mandoline is made to produce an "eerie, spectral" dance with the help of a glass rod and a metal plectrum.

Fifth song

V. *Se ha llenado de luces mi corazón de seda.* Luminous. "My heart of silk is filled with lights, with lost bells, with lilies, and with bees, and I will go very far, farther than those hills, farther than the seas, close to the stars, to ask Christ the Lord to give me back my ancient soul of a child." The metallic clang with which this movement opens is indeed luminous, combining the timbres of metallic plates, antique cymbals, harp, electric piano, tubular bells, vibraphone, and suspended cymbals. A wraithelike passage leads into an ornate Mahlerian melody marked "timidly, with a sense of loneliness." Soprano and oboe alternate, the instrument taking on a remote quality when it moves offstage.

A powerful crescendo leads into the impassioned music for the last line of the poem. This suddenly stands revealed as the climax toward which Crumb has been working from the very beginning (much like the high G on "Remember me" at the climax of Dido's Lament, or the orchestral surge on "höchste Lust" at the end of Isolde's *Liebestod*). "It is sometimes of interest to a composer," Crumb writes, "to recall the original impulse—the 'creative germ'—of a compositional project. In the case of *Ancient Voices* I felt this impulse to be the climactic final words of the last song: '. . . and I will go very far . . . to ask Christ the Lord to give me back my ancient soul of a child.' " The music subsides as soprano and boy soprano remember the birdlike calls of the opening.

In *Ancient Voices* Crumb has found the right music for the dark intimations of Lorca's poetry. The work has justly established itself as a prime example of contemporary imagination and feeling.

Boulez: Le Marteau sans maître

Pierre Boulez.

Pierre Boulez (Montbrison, 1925–) is the most important French composer of the avant-garde. He is also the best known because of his widespread activities as a conductor, in which capacity he has propagandized tirelessly in behalf of contemporary music. The American public grew familiar with his name and work through his five-year stint as music director of the New York Philharmonic.

At the Paris Conservatory Boulez studied with Messiaen, who exerted a powerful influence upon him. He subsequently fell under the spell of Debussy and Stravinsky; and, more significantly, under that of Schoenberg's disciple Anton Webern, whose influence was at its height in the years after the war. Taking his point of departure from Webern's later works, Boulez extended Schoenberg's serial technique to control not only pitch but the other elements of music as well. Despite his total commitment to serial procedures, Boulez became aware that the advances of the modern Viennese school in melody, harmony, and counterpoint had not been equalled by advances in rhythm. He tried to overcome this disequilibrium by taking over the plastic rhythms of his teacher Messian and putting them to his own use within the twelve-tone idiom. Already in his *Sonatine for Flute and Piano,* an early work (1946), he tried, he tells us, "for the first time to articulate independent rhythmic structures, of which Messiaen had revealed to me the possibilities, upon classical serial structures."

The emotional content of Boulez's music extends from a gentle lyricism to a furious Expressionism that ranged him with the "angry young men" of our time. Boulez himself has stated, in an essay on rhythm, "I think that music should be collective magic and hysteria." His violent emotions find their necessary compensation in the mathematical rigor with which his structural schemes are worked out. His writing is marked by extreme concentration of thought, as by the great freedom with which he employs the serial technique. From Messiaen he has taken over a fondness for bell and percussion sounds that evoke the Balinese orchestra known as the *gamelan.* His limpid orchestral texture is based on the clearest possible differentiation of timbres. Because of his extensive activities as a conductor, his output has not been large. Among his chief works we should mention two piano sonatas (1946, 1948) and a still incomplete third; *Le Marteau sans maître* (The Hammer without a Master), which we will discuss; and *Pli selon pli* (Fold upon Fold; 1960), which includes the three *Improvisations on Mallarmé*. In recent years, as director of IRCAM, a research center for new music, Boulez has encouraged investigation into the potential of computers in composition.

Boulez's best known work, *Le Marteau sans maître* (1953–54), presents the chief traits of his style within a compact frame. It is a suite of nine movements based on three short poems of René Char. We will discuss three movements—the setting of the first poem (No. 3), its prelude (No. 1, *Before*) and postlude (No. 7, *After*).

The piece is for contralto and a group of six instruments, of which the alto flute, viola, and guitar are most in evidence. These are supported by a *xylorimba* (an instrument combining the metallic sonority of the xylophone with the gentler wood sound of the marimba) and a vibraphone, which lends a touch of magic to the ensemble. The sixth "instrument" is a varied group of percussion manipulated by a single player. The full group never plays. Instead, each movement presents another combination of instruments from the ensemble.

The overall sound, of the bell and percussion variety, is limpid, brilliant, perhaps evoking the music of the Far East. The transparent texture, rarefied sound, and occasional immobility of this music places it in the line of descent from the late works of Webern. The vocal line shows the wide leaps we associate with twelve-tone music. As might be expected, Boulez does not try to make clear the words of a poem. "If you want to 'understand' the text," says he, "read it!" He believes that music should heighten the meaning of a text rather than set it realistically. This approach establishes a kinship between *Le Marteau sans maître* and Schoenberg's *Pierrot lunaire*. Certainly the later work would have been inconceivable without the earlier.

Char's poetry is thoroughly surrealist in the violence—and disconnectedness—of its images. The reader may find the translation more than a little mystifying. Rest assured, the original is as obscure.

L'Artisanat furieux	*Furious artisans*
La roulotte rouge au bord du clou Et cadavre dans le panier Et chevaux de labours dans le fer à cheval Je rêve la tête sur la pointe de mon couteau le Pérou	The red caravan at the edge of the prison And a corpse in the basket And work horses in the horseshoe I dream, head on the point of my knife, Peru

First movement
SIDE 12/3 (E II)

1. *Before "L'Artisanat furieux."* For alto flute, vibraphone, guitar, and viola. This prelude introduces the attenuated sonority of the post-Webern world. The tempo marking is "rapide"; yet despite the speed of the movement, single notes stand out with extreme clarity. The wide spacing of the instrumental lines contributes to this effect, as do the wide leaps in the flute and viola parts.

The tense plucked-string sound of the guitar here corresponds to the sound of the mandoline in certain works of Schoenberg and Webern. Together with the bell-like sonority of the vibraphone, it forms a backdrop for the gyrations of flute and viola. The dark hue of the viola contrasts ideally with the brighter timbre of the flute. Boulez's serial technique, with its emphasis upon dissonant intervals such as the augmented and diminished octave, makes for a highly integrated texture. Yet the listener is aware not so much of the concentrated thought as of an overall impression of extremely light and luminous sound.

Third movement
SIDE 12/3 (E II)

3. *L'Artisanat furieux* (Furious artisans). This duet between contralto and flute is marked Modéré sans rigueur (moderate, without strictness). The meter changes practically with every measure, resulting in a free rhythmic flow of the utmost plasticity. Hence the music unfolds in that free, improvisational manner, both ornate and rhapsodical, that twentieth-century composers have taken over from the music of the East. One receives an impression of great delicacy and refinement of style.

The words dissolve in music, an effect heightened by the fact that time and again a single vowel is extended for several notes. Here is an example of Boulez's conviction that we should listen not for the words but for what the composer has done with them. In effect, he handles the voice as if it were another instrument. The vocal part therefore becomes pure sonorous material, even as the flute part is. The enormous range of the vocal line and the devilish intervals that the voice has to execute call for a special kind of singer, one preferably with absolute pitch. Voice and instrument complement each other, now echoing, now answering one another. Notice the fluttertonguing on the flute, an effect dear to Mahler, Schoenberg, and Berg. It occurs at three points in the course of the piece, and is especially prominent after the first line of text.

Seventh movement
SIDE 12/3 (E II)

7. *After "L'artisanat furieux."* Rapide. A brief postlude, related to the prelude both in its intervallic structure and sound texture. Boulez here uses three instruments instead of four: flute, vibraphone, and guitar, omitting the viola. Since it does not follow *L'artisanat* in the score, it is a postlude that serves also as a reminiscence.

Boulez has shrewdly assessed the role of his type of composer. "I think that our generation will give itself to synthesizing as much as—if not more so than—discovering: the broadening of techniques, generalising of methods, rationalisation of the procedures of writing—in sum, a synthesis of the great creative currents that have manifested themselves principally since the end of the nineteenth century." To this synthesis he has made a very personal contribution.

Babbitt: Echo Song *from* Philomel

"Anyone who hears well can be educated to appreciate my music. The more you listen to serial music, the better able you are to recognize its grammar, its configurations, its modes of procedure."

Just as composers of the nineteenth century related their music to Romantic poetry and painting, several among the avant-garde composers of

Milton Babbitt.

our time tend to relate their work to the exact sciences, thereby exalting the intellectual-rational element in art over the intuitive-emotional one. A leading proponent of this ultrarational attitude is Milton Babbitt (Philadelphia, 1916–). "Some people say my music is 'too cerebral,'" he states. "Actually, I believe in cerebral music—in the application of intellect to relevant matters. I never choose a note unless I know precisely why I want it there and can give several reasons why it and not another."

Babbitt studied with Roger Sessions. When Sessions was asked to form a graduate department of music at Princeton University he invited his brilliant pupil, then twenty-two, to join its faculty. Babbitt has taught at Princeton ever since, and as professor of composition has had a strong influence on musicians of the younger generation. Given his kind of mind, he was inevitably attracted to the almost scientific logic of the twelve-tone method, which for him represented a revolution in musical thought "whose nature and consequences can be compared only with those of the mid-nineteenth-century revolution in mathematics or the twentieth-century revolution in theoretical physics." He soon realized the possibilities for further development inherent in Schoenberg's system. It became his conviction that "the twelve-tone set must dominate *every* aspect of the piece."

Total serialization

As a result, he led the way toward an ultrarational music in which the composer would control every dimension of the musical fabric. His *Three Compositions for Piano* (1947) and *Composition for Four Instruments* (1948) were the first examples of total serialization. He applied the principle of the series not only to pitch but also to rhythm, dynamics (including not only the soft-loud element but also the attack and decay of the sound), and timbre. Therewith he developed the premises of Schoenberg's method into an all-inclusive system in which the basic row—or set, as Babbitt calls it—totally controlled the relationships and processes within a particular piece.

Works for Synthesizer alone

By the same token Babbitt was one of the first to evaluate the possibilities of electronic music, not because of the new sonorities it made possible—"Nothing," he holds, "becomes old as quickly as a new sound"—but because it offered the composer complete control over the final result. At the Columbia-Princeton Electronic Music Center in New York City he was able to work out his ideas on the RCA Synthesizer. "When you live through as many bad performances of your music as I have, I must confess that I look forward to walking into the electronic studio with my composition in my head and walking out with the performance on the tape in my hand." Out of this "unique and satisfying experience," as he calls it, came two important works in which he explored the possibilities of the new medium: *Composition for Synthesizer* (1960–61) and *Ensembles for Synthesizer* (1962–64).

Works for Synthesizer and performer

All the same, it has never been Babbitt's intention that the Synthesizer should supplant the live musician. "I know of no serious electronic composer who ever asserts that we are supplanting any other form of music or any other form of musical activity. We're interested in increasing the

This painting, ***Chicago 1955,*** *by the American Ben Shahn (1898–1969), reflects the improvisatory technique of its subject matter.* (Scala/Art Resource.)

The Pop Art of Jasper Johns (b. 1930) has absorbed the literal vision of photography, concentrating on familiar objects connected with everyday living. ***Flag*** *(1954–55).* (Collection, The Museum of Modern Art, New York. Gift of Philip Johnson in honor of Alfred H. Barr, Jr.)

resources of music." The next step, Babbitt saw, was to combine electronic music with live performers. This new area he explored in *Vision and Prayer* (1961), for soprano and synthesized accompaniment; *Philomel* (1964), which we will discuss; *Correspondences* (1966–68), for string orchestra and synthesized accompaniment; and *Reflections* (1975), for piano and tape. Nor did he forsake the field of live music: two connected works, *Relata I* (1965) and *Relata II* (1968) are for orchestra, and two string quartets, his *Third* and *Fourth,* date from 1970. Later works for chamber groups include *Arie da Capo* (1974) and *A Solo Requiem* (1977).

Philomel (1964) offers the listener an excellent introduction to the world of electronic sound. The work is for live soprano and tape. The tape contains a synthesized accompaniment and also the recorded voice of a soprano (Bethany Beardslee, for whom the piece was written). The text, by the poet John Hollander, is based on Ovid's version–in the *Metamorphoses*–of an ancient myth concerning the origin of that favorite bird of poets, the nightingale. This indeed is one of those gory Greek myths that impelled Freud to investigate the darker corridors of human nature. Pandion, King of Athens, had two daughters, Procne and Philomel. Procne married Tereus, King of Thrace, by whom she had a son, Itys. After several years she longed to see her younger sister, and prevailed upon her husband to sail to Athens and bring back Philomel. On the return journey Tereus developed a consuming passion for his sister-in-law. When they reached his kingdom he led her into a forest, raped her, and cut out her tongue to silence her. For a year Philomel was held captive; but she managed to communicate her terrible story by weaving it into pictures and sending the tapestry through a servant to Queen Procne. The queen understood the message. She found Philomel and during the annual Bacchic rites brought her back to the palace disguised as one of the celebrants. Aroused to a frenzy by the Bacchanalian celebrations, Procne decided to avenge her sister. She killed her son Itys and cooked his remains, which she served to her husband as a delectable dish. (This theme, interestingly, persists in folklore through the centuries.) When Tereus asked after his son, Philomel took Itys's severed head and hurled it at him. The two sisters fled into the woods, pursued by Tereus. But before he could overtake them the gods transformed him into a hoopoe, an unclean bird that befouls its own nest. Procne was turned into a swallow, and Philomel became a nightingale.

The plot

Babbitt's *Philomel* begins just after the transformation has taken place. The piece falls into three sections. In the first, the newly-created nightingale tries stutteringly to find her voice. She can sing only isolated notes or small groups of notes as she struggles incoherently to express the agony through which she has passed. This section ends with Hollander's felicitous stanza, "Oh, men are sick: The gods are strong . . . What is this humming? I am becoming/ My own song . . ." Second is the *Echo Song*. In a dialogue with the birds of the forest, Philomel accepts her new existence. In the third section, like Keats's nightingale, she pours forth her soul "in full-throated ease."

The live soprano is echoed by the recorded soprano on the tape, who is heard against an electronic background. This recorded voice, which has been modified by electronic devices, represents, in Hollander's words, what Philomel "heard in the woods, what she thought she heard there, what she fancied she heard inside her own head, and so forth." The live sound and the synthesized sound intertwine to become a completely integrated whole. As in other works we will discuss, the combination of a live performer with tape humanizes the electronic sound and gives it another dimension.

The Echo Song

The text of the *Echo Song* recalls a device of seventeenth- and eighteenth-century poetry, in which the echoing voice picks up the final sounds of a question and transforms them into an answer:

Philomel

O thrush in the woods I fly among,
Do you, too, talk with the forest's tongue?

Echo

Stung, stung, stung.
With the sting of becoming
I sing.

Here, the echo attaches the final "s" of "forest's" to the sound of "tongue," thus creating the word "stung." Philomel addresses herself successively to the thrush, the hawk, the owl, the raven, the gull, and finally to the green leaves of the forest. In the dialogue, the urgent lyricism of the live voice contrasts vividly with the distant, electronically dehumanized singing and whispering of the echo voice. The contrast is underlined by the glittering sonority—at times suggesting plucked strings—of the synthesized sounds.

Philomel is based on a series, from which Babbitt derives not only the twelve-tone pitch material of the work but also the layout of rhythms, dynamics, and tone colors. Yet this strict underlying unity clearly does not preclude enormous variety and expressivity. We quoted Stravinsky's remark that "the more art is controlled, limited, worked over, the more it is free." The rules within which an artist works (like the rules within which people play a game such as bridge or poker) do not hamper him. On the contrary, they stimulate his imagination. What Stravinsky is saying, and what artists have learned through the ages, is that you could not have the game without the rules, because then you would have total freedom, which is chaos. This explains why a work like *Philomel,* despite the elaborate structural procedures that control its course, can give the listener a sense of utter buoyancy and freedom.

The significant artist is one who incarnates the significant impulses of his time. Milton Babbitt is such a one. His music embodies important intellectual currents in the contemporary scene.

Carter: Eight Etudes and a Fantasy

"I like music to be beautiful, ordered, and expressive of the more important aspects of life."

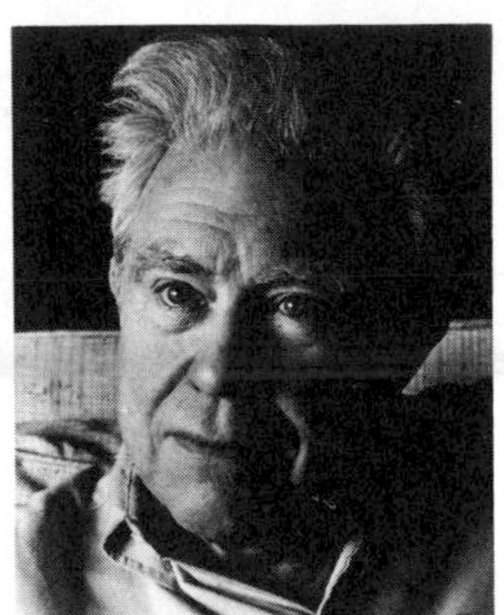
Elliott Carter.

Of the composers who have come into prominence in recent years, none is more widely admired by musicians than Elliott Carter (New York City, 1908–). His works are not of the kind that achieve easy popularity; but their profundity of thought and maturity of workmanship bespeak a musical intellect of the first order.

Carter started out with a musical idiom rooted in diatonic-modal harmony, but gradually assimilated a dissonant chromaticism that places him (if one must attach a label) among the Abstract Expressionists. He employs fluctuating tempo as a form-building element, through the use of a novel technique that he calls "metrical modulation," whereby the speed of the rhythmic pulse is subtly modified. When several instruments are playing together, each with its own pulse and each changing that pulse independently in a different direction, there results an original and powerful kind of texture.

The works of Carter's maturity explore the possibilities of this technique in a variety of ways. The three string quartets (1951, 1959, 1971) are bold, uncompromising works that constitute the most significant contribution to this medium since Bartók; both the *Second* and the *Third* brought the composer Pulitzer Prizes. Beginning with the *Second Quartet,* Carter's music has also sought to throw into relief the characteristics of different instruments and instrumental masses. In the *Double Concerto* (1961), two contrasting keyboard instruments–piano and harpsichord–are placed at opposite sides of the stage, each partnered by its own chamber orchestra, and carry on a sort of musical argument. A similar confrontation pervades the dramatic *Piano Concerto* (1965), the soloist asserting his individuality against the mass. The *Concerto for Orchestra* (1969) exploits the opposition of particular groups and soloists within the orchestra. In the 1970s, Carter turned again to vocal music, which he had not composed for several decades; *A Mirror on Which to Dwell* (1976) sets poems of Elizabeth Bishop, and *Syringa* (1978) combines a poem by John Ashbery with classical Greek quotations.

Carter's impeccable craftsmanship is manifest in *Eight Etudes and a Fantasy* (1950), which offers a fine introduction to his art. The piece grew directly out of his activity as a teacher. He had asked his students to bring in examples illustrating the use of the woodwind instruments, and had invited four woodwind players to the class to perform them. Disappointed in what the class had written, he sketched some passages on the blackboard for the woodwind players to try. These later developed into the *Eight Etudes and a Fantasy,* a work that explores the possibilities of flute, oboe, clarinet, and bassoon in imaginative ways. An etude, it will be recalled, is a study piece that centers around a technical problem. As Chopin did in his etudes, Carter naturally combines the technical problem with an expressive purpose. This series of short pieces reveals an extraordinary command of woodwind writing and an aural imagination of the utmost originality.

Etude 1

1. Maestoso (majestic), 4/4. The opening etude mobilizes the contrasts in color and character inherent in wide leaps from high to low register and back, as well as the dynamic gradations that help to bring such contrasts into focus. Carter treats the four instruments as four equal partners; yet he defines the space that belongs to each. Particularly striking is the flute sound on top, and the hollow voice of the bassoon that serves as the foundation for the sonorous fabric.

Etude 2

2. Quietly, 3/4. In this etude Carter reveals the subtle differences between the four instruments when they are all asked to perform the same material. The flute announces a rippling motive that is taken up on various levels of pitch by each of the others. Sharps and flats abound, so that the very appearance of the theme shows its atonal character:

At the end the motive enters successively in each of the four instruments in ascending order—bassoon, clarinet, oboe, flute. A dissonant chord, *mf,* serves as final cadence.

Etude 3

3. Adagio possibile (as slow as possible), 4/4. Carter here explores the capacity of the woodwinds to sustain tone. The etude is fashioned out of the three tones of the D-major triad: D–F♯–A. This chord continually changes its color, yet we are not aware of the exact moment of change because of "sneak entrances"—that is, one instrument quietly slips in and continues where the other left off, one sound melting into another.

Etude 4
SIDE 12/4 (E II)
SIDE 18/2 (S)

4. Vivace, 3/4. It has been said that the essence of artistic creation is the ability to make much out of little. In this etude Carter makes much out of the littlest—a motivic cell consisting of two notes a semitone apart. This two-note kernal, tossed about among the instruments in diverse ways, flowers into melodies, harmonies, rhythms, colors, counterpoints, and dynamics. Wholly ingenious is Carter's way of having all four instruments, each playing its two tones, combine in a running scale. More important than the ingenuity is the charm of the result.

Etude 5
SIDE 12/4 (E II)
SIDE 18/2 (S)

5. Andante, 4/4. Marked cantando expressivo (singing, expressive), the fifth etude brings a change of mood. The expressive capacities of pure woodwind sound are utilized in this piece to create the kind of emotional lyricism that we generally associate with the string instruments. The music

takes on an almost tragic intensity, and reveals anew how completely the vocabulary of atonality is attuned to the esthetic goals of Expressionism.

Etude 6

6. Allegretto leggero (fairly fast, light), 3/4. In this study Carter explores special effects on the woodwinds—rapid repeated notes, trills, and fluttertonguing. The composer gives instructions in the score for special fingerings to achieve subtle gradations of tone. In short, the piece is a treasure house of ingenious woodwind effects. Notice how the music vanishes at the end.

Etude 7

7. Intensely, 4/4. In our chapter on Schoenberg we referred to his notion that it should be possible to create a melody by sounding the same tone on different instruments. The various colors, according to Schoenberg, ought to hold the listener's attention just as different pitches do in a melody. In this etude Carter implements Schoenberg's idea. The piece consists of a single note which the four instruments play in turn, either alone or in combination. At one point they attack it in succession, at another they overlap. Dynamic gradations between *pp* and *ff* underline the continual changes in timbre. The piece ends pianissimo with the basic tone on the clarinet.

Etude 8
SIDE 12/4 (E II)
SIDE 18/2 (S)

8. Presto, 4/4. This is a *perpetuum mobile* (continuous motion) whose forward drive never lets up. The rapid sixteenth notes are heard against single quarter notes in high or low register that seem to comment on the main action. These quarter notes make an effective contrast, in rhythm as well as register, with the running passages.

Fantasy

Fantasy. Tempo giusto (strict tempo), 4/4. The fantasia of the Baroque was one of its most luxuriant forms. Carter, using the term in that sense, starts off with a fugal texture based on a subject of truly Baroque spaciousness:

Frequent changes of meter show the composer moving toward the ideal of rhythmic flexibility that was to become one of his chief preoccupations. The densely woven texture unfolds in a process of continuous expansion —a process, it will be recalled, that lay at the heart of Baroque music. The Fantasy brings back thematic material and performance devices that were introduced in the etudes, here brought into new focus in the service of artistic expression.

Carter's works, oriented toward the most serious aspects of musical art, offer a continual challenge to the listener. They confirm his position as one of the most important composers in America.

Cage: Fontana Mix

John Cage.

"I am more like a hunter or inventor than a lawmaker."

John Cage (Los Angeles, 1912–) is one of the daring experimenters of his generation. He studied, among others, with Henry Cowell and Schoenberg, each of whom exercised a strong influence upon his thinking. From the beginning of his career he was interested in Oriental philosophy and music, in non-Western scales, and in percussive rhythm as a form-building element. His music for percussion ensembles grew out of this interest. Characteristic are the *Third Construction* of 1940 and the *Construction in Meta*l (1944) for seven percussionists who play bowls, pots, bells, metal bars, tin sheets, and an assortment of gongs. Cage attracted much attention with his music for "prepared piano." The preparation consisted of muffling and altering the piano tone by inserting sundry objects of rubber, felt, or wood, as well as screws, nuts, bolts, and coins between the strings. This transformed the instrument into an ensemble of gentle percussive timbres that vividly conjured up the gongs, drums, and coloration of the Balinese gamelan. His *Sixteen Sonatas and Four Interludes* for prepared piano (1946–48) explored the possibilities of this limited medium. He evolved a vocabulary evocative of Eastern idioms in the subtlety and luminosity of its timbres; he developed rhythm, as Virgil Thomson wrote, "to a point of sophistication unmatched in the technique of any other living composer."

Prepared piano

Cage has rejected the development of themes, the arousal of emotion, and the buildup of architectural forms that constitute the great tradition in Western music. The phrases in his music unfold in fragments, punctuated by dramatic points of silence; this he derived from the twelve-tone composers, especially Webern. He was one of the first to deny the supremacy of pitch as an organizing principle. By freeing himself from the problems of melodic line and harmonic progression, Cage was able to concentrate his attention on rhythm and timbre. This, we have seen, developed into one of the main trends in the new music. He became an eloquent spokesman for the attempt to achieve total freedom in music through dependence on chance and randomness. To quote one of the cardinal tenets of his philosophy, "My purpose is to eliminate purpose." To the ultrarationality of the total serialists Cage opposed the antirationality of total freedom, using dice and kindred procedures to produce an aleatory music that freed the performer—and the musical events—from the composer's control. For

Chance music

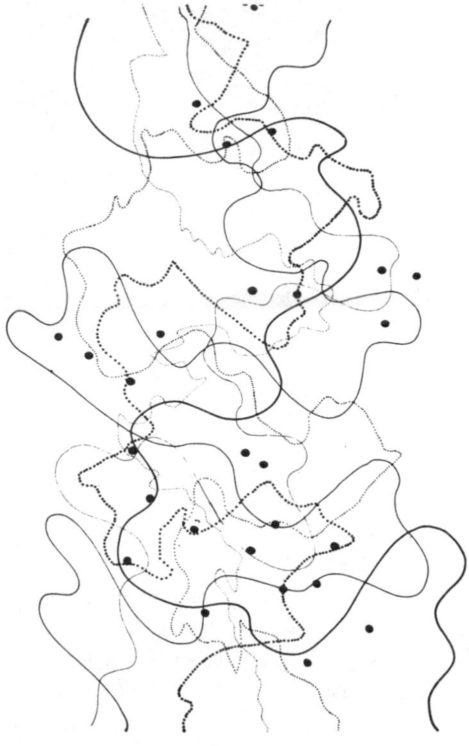

Cage, Fontana Mix: *one of the many possible combinations of a drawing and a transparent sheet. Copyright © 1960 by Henmar Press Inc., 373 Park Avenue South, New York, New York 10016; reprinted with permission of the publisher.*

example, in his famous (according to some, notorious) *Imaginary Landscape* (1951), twelve radios were set going simultaneously, tuned to different stations. The material, consequently, was completely random. The only predetermined element was the time span within which this assemblage of sounds and noises takes place.

Fontana Mix

To set up a framework within which unpredictable events will take place is relatively simple to do in the realm of live performance; but to transfer this indeterminacy to tape—by its nature a fixed medium—requires considerable ingenuity. Cage solved the problem in *Fontana Mix* (1958), the first work on tape to establish conditions whose outcome could not be foreseen. The material consists of a set of drawings and transparent sheets, plus a graph, which can be combined in innumerable ways to produce patterns that suggest specific activities of the performer (or performers). Such a program allows chance to operate, so that *Fontana Mix* sounds different with each performance.

The three recordings that have been made of *Fontana Mix* represent three totally different realizations of the material. The version for magnetic tape alone is very animated, consisting of a montage of disassociated events—hissings, whisperings, groanings, gurglings, twitterings, and rumblings woven into a tapestry of sounds as varied as the free association of ideas when the mind is permitted to wander. These ever-shifting images at times give the same sense of randomness as when one turns the knob of

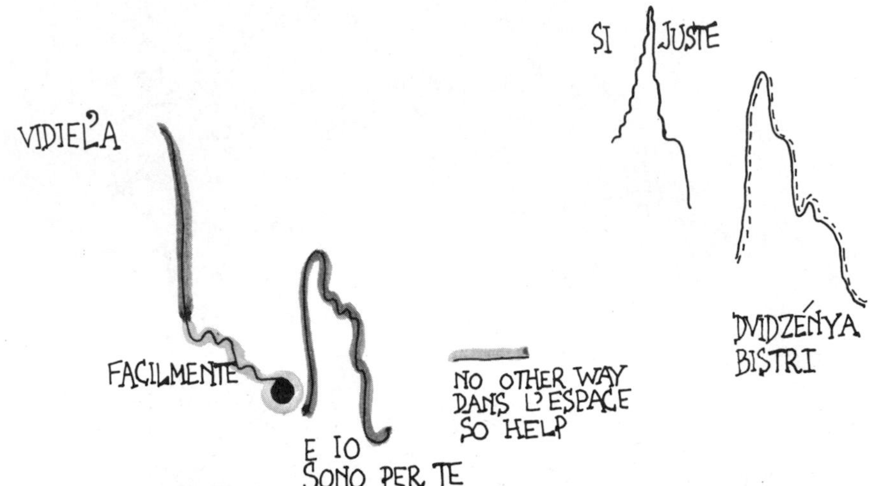

A page from John Cage's Aria.
Copyright © 1960 by Henmar Press Inc., 373 Park Avenue South, New York, New York 10016; reprinted with permission of the publisher.

the radio and hears successive fragments of music or speech from various stations. Here then is a perfect realization of Cage's desire to create "indeterminate music" through discontinuous works that unfold random events within a fixed span of time.

The second, and liveliest, of the three recordings combines *Fontana Mix* with *Aria,* sung by Cathy Berberian. This version focuses interest on Miss Berberian's remarkable performance. The *Aria* is notated in such a manner as to allow the performer to share with the composer in creating the work. "The notation," Cage explains, "represents time horizontally, pitch vertically, roughly suggested rather than accurately described." The vocal line is drawn in black or in one or more of eight colors, each representing another style of singing; jazz, contralto and contralto lyric, sprechstimme, dramatic, Marlene Dietrich, coloratura and coloratura lyric, folk, oriental, baby, and nasal. The text employs vowels and consonants and words from five languages: Armenian, Russian, Italian, French, and English. The composer concludes his instructions by pointing out that all aspects of the performance not notated (such as dynamics, type of attack, and the like) may be freely determined by the singer. Miss Berberian makes the most of this program, the result veering from nonsense singing to satire and parody of a rather delicious kind.

The third recording, by the percussionist Max Neuhaus, represents "the interaction and mixture of feedback channels set up by resting contact microphones on various percussion instruments that stand in front of loudspeakers." (*Feedback* is the acoustical phenomenon that occurs when a microphone picks up the sound from a loudspeaker and "feeds it back" into the same loudspeaker: the result is a howling noise.) This realization consists of a series of signals each of which is sustained for so long a time as to approach—at least for sensitive ears—the threshold of physical pain. The impression of absolute immobility is akin to that in certain yoga exercises which tend to empty the mind of all thought. Toward the middle of the record the sustained noises take on the relentless quality of an electric drill, ending as abruptly as they began.

"I like to think that I'm outside the circle of a known universe, and dealing with things that I don't know anything about." John Cage represents the type of eternally questing artist whose innovations have greater value because of the new domains they open up than because they lead to finished works of art. He has been a seminal influence in the music of our time.

Davidovsky: Synchronisms No. 1

Mario Davidovsky.

The electronic medium all too easily can become austere and rather impersonal. It has been the signal achievement of Mario Davidovsky (Buenos Aires, Argentina, 1934–) to inject into this idiom a high order of wit and imagination. Davidovsky, who teaches composition at City College of the City University of New York and is a director of the Columbia-Princeton Electronic Center, has composed a variety of works for orchestra, ballet, and chamber groups; but he is best known for his lively electronic pieces.

Among those is a series of works that combine electronic sounds with conventional instruments. "The attempt here has been made," he writes, "to preserve the typical characteristics of the conventional instruments and of the electronic medium respectively—yet to achieve integration of both into a coherent musical texture." The first of the series, *Synchronisms No. 1,* is for flute and electronic sounds. The flute, incidentally, plays an outstanding role in the literature of contemporary music. Its special qualities—purity of tone, wide range of dynamics, precision, agility and clear-cut articulation—have recommended it to composers engaged in exploring new kinds of sound. In turn, they have brought the instrument to a level of virtuosity that would have been unthinkable a generation ago.

Rhythm

Davidovsky points out that, in planning his series of *Synchronisms,* "two main problems arise—namely, proper synchronization of rhythm and of pitch. During the shorter episodes, where both electronic and conventional instruments are playing, rather strict timing is adhered to. However, in the more extended episodes of this type, an element of chance is introduced to allow for the inevitable time discrepancies that develop between the live performer(s) and the constant-speed tape recorder."

A basic problem in writing for electronic tape and one or more solo instruments is to reconcile the tempered intonation of the instruments, which is based on the twelve tones of the chromatic scale, and the non-tempered sounds of the electronic medium. Davidovsky achieves this by using, as he explains, "tonal occurrences of very high density"—that is, a high-speed succession of attacks that is possible only in the electronic medium. Given the high speed and short duration of separate tones, as he states, "it is impossible for the ear to perceive the pure pitch value of each separate event; though in reacting, it does trace so to speak a statistical curve of the density." In this context it is the overall impression rather than the individual tone that counts.

SIDE 12/5 (E II)
SIDE 18/3 (S)

Synchronisms No. 1 opens with a single long-sustained tone on the flute that establishes the timbre of the solo instrument. When the accompaniment on tape enters, it hovers about the middle and lower registers. There is a vivacious interplay between the two bodies of sound, the opposition between them underlined through contrasts of timbre, register (high-low), dynamics (loud-soft), rhythm (fast notes-slow notes), quality (legato-staccato), type of attack and decay (percussive-melodic). The pure silvery tone of the flute sets off the guttural sounds of the tape, each maintaining its own character. As the composer expresses it, in the scientific phraseology that has attached itself to electronic composition, "Generally speaking, in the whole series of these pieces, a coherent musical continuum is sought while trying to respect the idiosyncracies of each medium." Noteworthy here is the dramatic tension that can be created through pure sound, the sense of movement and eventful activity, above all the animation, wit and fantasy that Davidovsky is able to infuse into his electronic compositions.

The second generation of electronic composers, by building on the discoveries of their predecessors, have been able greatly to expand the expressive gamut of the medium. In this development Mario Davidovsky has been and continues to be a leader.

Glass: Floe *from* Glassworks

Philip Glass. (Photo copyright by Isabel Carlota Rodriguez.)

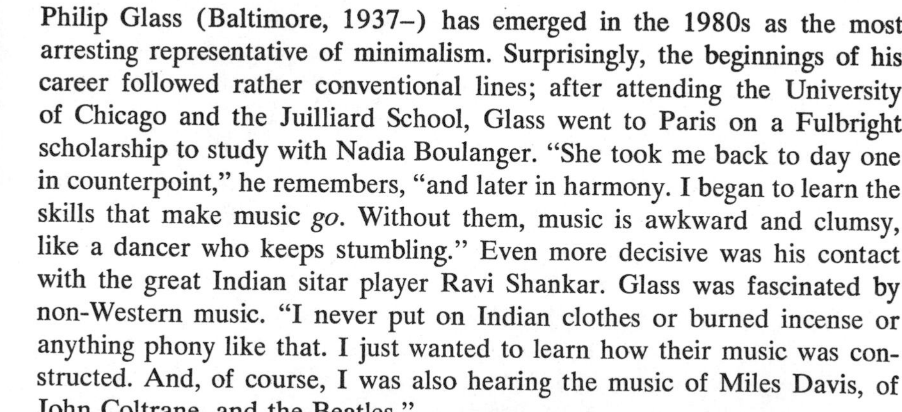

Philip Glass (Baltimore, 1937–) has emerged in the 1980s as the most arresting representative of minimalism. Surprisingly, the beginnings of his career followed rather conventional lines; after attending the University of Chicago and the Juilliard School, Glass went to Paris on a Fulbright scholarship to study with Nadia Boulanger. "She took me back to day one in counterpoint," he remembers, "and later in harmony. I began to learn the skills that make music *go*. Without them, music is awkward and clumsy, like a dancer who keeps stumbling." Even more decisive was his contact with the great Indian sitar player Ravi Shankar. Glass was fascinated by non-Western music. "I never put on Indian clothes or burned incense or anything phony like that. I just wanted to learn how their music was constructed. And, of course, I was also hearing the music of Miles Davis, of John Coltrane, and the Beatles."

He was already embarked on the path that would lead him away from the problems that preoccupied other young composers. "I could not embrace the music of Stockhausen and Boulez, which was the model at that time, and I almost stopped writing. I felt music had come to an impasse, a halt. Modern music had become truly decadent, stagnant, uncommunicative by the 1960s and '70s. Composers were writing for each other and the public didn't seem to care." It was out of this conviction that he evolved his own style, drawing upon the musical traditions of India and Africa, as well as the techniques of rock and progressive jazz.

Upon his return from Europe, Glass settled in New York; the city gave him the artistic stimulation he needed. "It's hard to find cities like New York where you have this terrific density of work and activity—it almost becomes a white heat sometimes." Turning his back on a conventional career, he supported himself through the next decade by driving a taxi and doing odd jobs as a plumber or carpenter. In SoHo he discovered a new generation of sculptors whose stripped-down, minimal style offered an exhilarating parallel to his own aims, and he drew close to three composers —Terry Riley, LaMonte Young, and Steve Reich—who were evolving a similar esthetic. "We saw each other all the time. Two or three nights a week we'd be together pooling all this music. In a way it was a very generative process."

Most important of all, he formed the Philip Glass Ensemble, which began to play his works in the art galleries and lofts of lower Manhattan. The group included two electric organs, at one of which Glass himself presided; four wind players who doubled on amplified flutes, clarinet, and saxophones; and a woman singer who performed a wordless part, the voice being treated as another instrument. At first there weren't many people who would "climb up six flights of stairs" to hear what Glass had to say, but their number steadily increased. "You won't believe," he recalls, "how difficult it was when we started. No one was interested in the music except the art people. We simply began to look for a whole new audience." He found one.

Having his own ensemble was of inestimable value to Glass, not only for the propagation of his music but also for the development of his style. In the next few years he produced the chamber works that formed the basis of the group's repertory, among them *1+1* (1967); *Music in Similar Motion, Music in Fifths, Music in Contrary Motion* (1969); *Music with Changing Parts* (1970); and *Music in Twelve Parts* (1971–74). All were based on the process of "repetition and addition" that became the technical basis of his style. The pieces were built up from a series of melodic fragments, each repeated over and over until Glass signalled his musicians to proceed to the next. Each fragment added a few notes to the preceding one, as the following example from *Music in Fifths* makes clear.

Bar 13 presents a simple four-note figure that ascends and descends along the scale. The next bar adds to this by repeating the first two notes of the ascending group. Bar 15 repeats 14 but adds a repetition of the first two notes of the descending group. Bar 16 adds to that a repetition of the first three ascending notes, to which bar 17 adds the first three descending notes as well—and so on. Through this additive process the original eight-note figure will expand, by the time it reaches bar 35, into a figure of 210 notes.

Glass subsequently branched out into other areas—film, multimedia theater, finally opera. *Einstein on the Beach* (1976) was the first amplified opera to invade the Metropolitan Opera House, where it was presented for two sold-out performances. In 1980 came *Satyagraha,* sung in Sanskrit to a text drawn from the sacred book of the Hindu religion, the *Bhagavad-Gita.* The opera concerns Mohandas Gandhi's struggle against racial discrimination in South Africa between 1893 and 1914. The title, which means "the firmness of truth," refers to the movement based on passive resistance and civil disobedience whereby Gandhi sought, first in South Africa, then in India, to bring spiritual and political freedom to his countrymen. The work is in three acts, each presided over by a revered advocate of nonviolence: Tolstoi, Rabindranath Tagore, and Martin Luther King, Jr. *Satyagraha* established Glass's name on the international scene. His third opera, *Akhnaten* (1983), concerns the Egyptian ruler of the fourteenth century B.C. who made his mark as a religious reformer. The heroes of his three operas—Einstein, Gandhi, and Akhnaten, representing science, political action, and religion—are linked in Glass's mind as "three people who changed history through the force of their inner vision, through simply having an idea. They changed the world completely."

A scene from Glass's opera Einstein on the Beach *(1976).* (Photo copyright by Ken Howard.)

Glassworks, a recording containing six of the composer's pieces, has brought his music to a wide audience. The selection titled *Floe* offers a good introduction to his style. Characteristic is the radiant sonority achieved by a flickering figure in the winds (piccolo, flute, saxophones) and electric organ against the darker hue of the horns. The music unfolds over a repeated figure—an ostinato:

SIDE 12/6 (E II)
SIDE 18/4 (S)

The incessant repetition of these simple harmonies lulls the senses, yet also makes one aware of the minute changes taking place within them. The rhythm of some of the instrumental layers changes as the piece progresses, increasing in intensity. At one point motion almost stops, but the horns resume and a new ascent is begun, during which the ostinato takes on a form that seems to be a veiled allusion to a theme from the last movement of Sibelius's *Fifth Symphony*. *Floe* lasts for a little over five minutes, its materials are of the simplest, and very little actually happens in it; yet the sounds tease the ear with an impression of constant motion and change. Then, having reached its full growth, the music leaves off. It is a rather sudden ending, but one fully in accord with the minimalist style.

The great forms of the Classic-Romantic period, the sonata, symphony, and concerto, imparted to music a direction and goal, a sense of large-scale structure. A piece did not simply stop, it completed itself; the listener was left with a sense of action finished, of tension resolved. Clearly a work such as *Floe* springs out of quite another esthetic, responding to altogether different needs and sensibilities.

Endowed with a vigorous personality and an abundance of creative energy, Philip Glass has responded to the predicament of the contemporary composer by finding his own path—and, in the process, his own audience.

Other Contemporaries (American)

The proponents of the new music in America include composers of several generations, representing a variety of personal styles and esthetic viewpoints.

Wolpe

Stefan Wolpe (Berlin, 1902–71, New York) came to the United States in 1939, and his most important work was done in this country. Such pieces as his *Trio* (1963) for flute, cello, and piano, and the *Chamber Piece No. 1* (1964) are examples of what has aptly been called "cumulative form." They are based on tiny motivic cells that generate increasing energy and tension as the music unfolds, yet retain their character despite the many coloristic, registral, rhythmic, and dynamic changes they undergo. Wolpe's is a single-minded and highly distinctive idiom.

Weisgall

Hugo Weisgall (Ivančice, Czechoslovakia, 1912–) came to the United States when he was eight; he has specialized primarily in opera, writing in an arresting idiom he describes as "pretty much the place where Schoenberg was before his final decisive leap into serialism, and where Berg was in Wozzeck." European dramas have formed the basis for several of his Expressionist-oriented works: *The Tenor* (1950) is derived from a play by Wedekind, *The Stronger* (1952) from a play by Strindberg. Weisgall has also composed a number of song cycles for voice and instruments, such as *End of Summer* (1973).

Perle

George Perle (Bayonne, New Jersey, 1915–) has won a reputation as a theorist as well as a composer; his book *Serial Composition and Atonality* is one of the best studies of the twelve-tone technique. He has sought to combine serial methods with the possibilities for harmonic direction and tension inherent in the major-minor system, and has evolved a technique of *harmonic modes*. This line of thought is fully explored in the eloquent *String Quartet No. 5* (1966). Among Perle's works available on records are *Three Movements for Orchestra* (1963) and a cycle of thirteen songs on poems by Emily Dickinson (1978).

Kirchner

Leon Kirchner (Brooklyn, 1919–) was a student of Schoenberg and Roger Sessions, and has assimilated many of the important traditions of the century into his expressive style. As Aaron Copland has put it, Kirchner's best pages "are charged with an emotional impact and explosive power that is almost frightening in intensity." Two string quartets—*No. 1* (1949), with its Bartókian ancestry, and *No. 3* (1966), which uses electronic sounds—exemplify the range of Kirchner's resources and the development of his personal language. His opera *Lily*, based on Saul Bellow's novel *Henderson the Rain King,* was performed by the New York City Opera in 1977.

Schuller

Gunther Schuller (New York, 1925–), active as a conductor and teacher (from 1968 to 1977 he was head of the New England Conservatory of Music), is self-taught as a composer. His music shows many of the influences to which his generation has been responsive. On the one hand he has been stimulated by the rhythmic freedom and instrumental innovations of experimental jazz, and is a leading exponent of the "third stream" movement, which combines the techniques of contemporary music with those of jazz. On the other hand, he has absorbed serial technique, which he handles in an unorthodox and altogether personal manner. Much of his output is devoted to abstract instrumental works, including the *Symphony for Brass and Percussion* of 1950 and two string quartets (1957 and 1966). Jazz elements figure in *The Visitation* (1966), an opera on Schuller's own libretto after Franz Kafka's *The Trial,* and in his *Seven Studies on Themes of Paul Klee* (1959).

Feldman, Brown, Foss

Among John Cage's important colleagues in the development of indeterminate music have been Morton Feldman (New York, 1926–) and Earle Brown (Lunenberg, Massachusetts, 1926–), who pioneered, respectively, aleatory techniques and open form. A more recent adherent of indeterminacy is Lukas Foss (Berlin, 1922–), who came to America in 1937 and composed first in a Hindemithian Neoclassic style, later developing an interest in group improvisation. More recently, Foss has become fascinated with aleatory procedures and with the use of pre-existing music as a basis for composition. In his *Baroque Variations* (1967), pieces by Handel, Scarlatti, and Bach are modified and distorted as if by a fun-house mirror. A more substantial work is *Time Cycle,* which exists in two versions: the first (1960) for soprano and orchestra, with improvised interludes: the second (1963) for soprano and chamber group. An expert conductor, Foss has been one of the most active performers and propagandists of new musical styles.

Druckman

Jacob Druckman (Philadelphia, 1928–) first won attention for his virtuoso scores combining live performance and prerecorded tapes, such as *Animus II* (1968), for female voice, two percussionists, and tape, which emphasize the theatrical as well as the musical presence of the performers. More recently, his colorful and dramatic works for orchestra—*Windows* (1972), *Lamia* (with mezzo-soprano; 1974), and *Chiaroscuro* (1977)—have been much admired.

Others

Among the many other composers who deserve mention here are: Donald Martino (Plainfield, New Jersey, 1931–), who has stretched the frontiers of instrumental virtuosity in such lucid and elegantly crafted works as the *Parisonatina al'dodecafonia* (1964), composed for the cellist Aldo Parisot, and the *Triple Concerto* for three clarinets and chamber orchestra (1977); John Eaton (Bryn Mawr, Pennsylvania, 1935–), who has worked extensively with sound synthesizers and with microtonal music, and is best known for his operas *Danton and Robespierre* (1978), on a subject from the French Revolution, and *The Cry of Clytemnestra* (1980), after Aeschylus; Steve Reich (New York, 1936–), along with Philip Glass the principal figure in the minimalist movement, who in works such as *Music for 18 Musicians* (1976) has developed a form of canonic imitation in which the parts begin together and gradually, almost imperceptibly, become separated; David del Tredici (Cloverdale, California, 1937–), who has achieved wide celebrity with his continuing series of large and lushly romantic works for soprano and orchestra—including *Final Alice* (1976) and *In Memory of a Summer Day* (1980)—based on Lewis Carroll's *Alice in Wonderland* and *Through the Looking Glass*; Frederic Rzewski (Westfield, Massachusetts, 1938–), himself a virtuoso pianist, whose variations on the Chilean revolutionary song *The People United Will Never Be Defeated!* (1975) and *Four North American Ballads* (1979) vividly combine pianistic imagination with political and social concerns; Charles Wuorinen (New York, 1938–), the brilliant and prolific codirector of the Group for Contemporary Music, whose catalogue ranges from the all-electronic *Time's Encomium* (1969) and the *Percussion Symphony* (1976) for twenty-four players to a series of chamber concertos for various instruments. These are just a few members of the immensely varied and talented community of American composers.

Other Contemporaries (European)

Dallapiccola

Luigi Dallapiccola (Pisino, 1904–75, Florence), like his pupil Berio, unites the age-old tradition of Italian vocal lyricism with the twelve-tone techniques of the Viennese school. Within the serial framework he unfolds his virtuoso handling of contrapuntal and canonic procedures, yet always retains the essentially melodic, vocal character of his lines. A notable choral work is his *Canti di prigionia* (Songs of Captivity; 1938–41), recording a sensitive artist's reaction to the ominous events that led up to the Second World War. Also important are several operas, including *Il prigioniero* (The Prisoner; 1944–48).

Stockhausen

The German counterpart of Pierre Boulez is Karlheinz Stockhausen (Modrath, near Cologne, 1928–), another Messiaen pupil. Beginning from the same Webern-derived point of departure, Stockhausen has nevertheless developed in different directions. He early became interested in the possibilities of electronic music, and has also explored the use of spatial dimensions, as in *Gruppen* (Groups; 1955–57), in which three orchestras, placed on different sides of the audience, play independently, occasionally merging in common rhythm or echoing each other. Both Boulez and Stockhausen have also been influenced by the thinking of John Cage, and the German composer developed a number of elaborate, partially aleatory works using both singers and traditional instruments, plus electronic devices that modify the sounds they produce. Beginning in the 1970s, the influence of Eastern thought directed Stockhausen's interests towards effects of ritual and meditation, as in *Mantra* (1970) and *Sternklang* (1971). For some years now, he has been at work on an immense theater work titled *Licht,* planned to last a week in performance.

Xenakis

Another approach to contemporary composition is exemplified by the Greek composer Iannis Xenakis (Braïla, Romania, 1922–). He was originally trained as an engineer, then studied music in Paris with Messiaen, while also working with the architect Le Corbusier on several projects, including the Philips Pavilion at the 1958 Brussels Fair for which Varèse composed his *Poème électronique.* Xenakis bases his musical theories on the laws of mathematics and physics. Whether his theories are valid or not, Xenakis has developed a distinctive musical idiom, as can be heard in such works as *Pithoprakta* (1955–56)—the title means "action by probabilities"—for forty-six strings, two tenor trombones, xylophone, and wood block. In fact, this work is the source of many of the unusual sound effects heard in Penderecki's *Threnody* and other works of the Polish school.

Berio

Luciano Berio (Oneglia, Italy, 1925–) is a leading figure among the radicals of the post-Webern generation. He was one of the founders of the Milan electronic studio that became a center for the Italian avant-garde. In his earlier works Berio used a very strict serial technique, but injected into these procedures the lyricism that is his birthright as an Italian. In addition, a strong sense of theater pervades his music, especially such works as

Passagio (1965), an opera for solo soprano, two choruses, and orchestra; *Circles* (1960), for soprano, harp, and two percussionists; and the *Sinfonia* (1968), for vocal ensemble and orchestra.

Davies

Since World War II, the renaissance of English musical life has produced a number of gifted composers. Among the most notable is Peter Maxwell Davies (Manchester, 1934–). Beginning from a strong interest in the techniques of Medieval and Renaissance music, Davies has forged an intensely personal style that incorporates elements of parody (of both popular and art music), highly demanding instrumental and vocal virtuosity, and a preoccupation with extreme emotional states. *Eight Songs for a Mad King* (1968) depicts the insanity of England's King George III. The opera *Taverner* (1968) deals with the moral and esthetic conflicts of an English composer of the Reformation. Two symphonies (1976 and 1980) are inspired by the stark landscape of Scotland's Orkney Islands, where Davies now makes his home.

Musgrave, Henze, Reimann

Other important European figures include the Scottish Thea Musgrave (Barnton, Midlothian, 1928–), whose operas *Mary Queen of Scots* (1977) and *A Christmas Carol* (after Dickens; 1979) have been performed and recorded in the United States; the German Hans Werner Henze (Gütersloh, 1926–), who began as an experimentalist of the Stockhausen stamp but has turned toward a more eclectic idiom in an impressive series of orchestral works and operas—among them *Elegy for Young Lovers* (1961) and *The Young Lord* (1965); and his countryman Aribert Reimann (Berlin, 1936–), composer of the operas *Melusine* (1970) and *Lear* (1978), as well as numerous skilful vocal works. There are many others, whose works prove that our time is as rich in gifted composers as was any era of the past.

Postscript

We have included in these pages a variety of facts, historical, biographical, and technical, that have entered into the making of music and that must enter into an intelligent listening to music. For those who desire to explore the subject further we include a list of books that will guide the music lover in his reading. But books belong to the domain of words, and words have no power over the domain of sound. They are helpful only insofar as they lead us to the music.

The enjoyment of music depends upon perceptive listening. And perceptive listening (like perceptive anything) is something that we achieve gradually, with practice and some effort. By acquiring a knowledge of the circumstances out of which a musical work issued, we prepare ourselves for its multiple meanings; we lay ourselves open to that exercise of mind and heart, sensibility and imagination that makes listening to music so unique an experience. But in the building up of our musical perceptions—that is, of our listening enjoyment—let us always remember that the ultimate wisdom resides neither in dates nor in facts. It is to be found in one place only—the sounds themselves.

APPENDIX I

Suggested Reading

The following list is merely a starting point, with emphasis on recent and easily available books. Those desiring to pursue the subject further will find specialized bibliographies in many of the works listed below. An asterisk (*) denotes a book available in a paperback edition.

On the Nature of Art

* Dewey, John. *Art as Experience.* New York: Putnam, 1958.

* Fleming, William. *Arts and Ideas.* New brief ed. New York: Holt, Rinehart & Winston, 1974.

* Meyer, Leonard B. *Music, the Arts and Ideas: Patterns and Predictions in 20th Century Culture.* Chicago: U. of Chicago, 1969.

* ——— *Emotion and Meaning in Music.* Chicago: U. of Chicago, 1956.

* Read, Herbert. *Art and Society.* Rev. ed. New York: Schocken, 1966.

Dictionaries

Apel, Willi. *The Harvard Dictionary of Music.* 2nd rev. ed. Cambridge: Harvard, 1969.

* ———, and Don Michael Randel. *The Harvard Brief Dictionary of Music.* Cambridge: Harvard, 1978.

Baker's Biographical Dictionary of Musicians. 6th ed. (ed. Nicolas Slonimsky). New York: Schirmer, 1978.

The New Grove Dictionary of Music and Musicians (ed. Stanley Sadie), 20 vols. New York: Macmillan, 1980.

Scholes, Percy A. *Concise Oxford Dictionary of Music.* 2nd ed. (ed. J. O. Ward). New York: Oxford, 1964.

Thompson, Oscar. *The International Cyclopedia of Music and Musicians.* 10th rev. ed. (ed. Bruce Bohle). New York: Dodd, Mead, 1975.

Westrup, J. A., and F. Ll. Harrison. *The New College Encyclopedia of Music.* Rev. ed. (ed. Conrad Wilson). New York: Norton, 1977.

The Materials of Music

* Bekker, Paul. *The Orchestra.* New York: Norton, 1963.

* Bernstein, Leonard. *The Joy of Music.* New York: New American Library, 1967.

* Clough, John, and Joyce Conley. *Scales, Intervals, Keys, Triads, Rhythm, and Meter.* New York: Norton, 1964.

* Cooper, Grosvenor W., and Leonard Meyer. *The Rhythmic Structure of Music.* Chicago: U. of Chicago, 1960.

* Copland, Aaron. *What to Listen for in Music.* New York: Mentor, 1964.

* Manoff, Tom. *The Music Kit.* 2nd ed. New York: Norton, 1984.

The New Grove Dictionary of Music and Musicians and *Harvard Dictionary of Music:* articles on melody, harmony, rhythm, meter, tempo, timbre, etc.

Ratner, Leonard G. *Music: The Listener's Art.* 3rd ed. New York: McGraw-Hill, 1977.

* Tovey, Donald F. *The Forms of Music.* New York: Meridian, 1956.

Music History (One-Volume Works)

Abraham, Gerald. *The Concise Oxford History of Music.* New York: Oxford, 1979.

Borroff, Edith. *Music in Europe and the United States: A History.* Englewood Cliffs, N.J.: Prentice-Hall, 1971.

*Einstein, Alfred. *A Short History of Music.* New York: Random House, 1954.

*Gerboth, Walter, *et al.* (eds.). *An Introduction to Music: Selected Readings.* New York: Norton, 1969.

Grout, Donald. *A History of Western Music.* 3rd ed. New York: Norton, 1980.

*Janson, H. W., and Joseph Kerman. *A History of Art and Music.* New York: Abrams, 1968.

Lang, Paul Henry. *Music in Western Civilization.* New York: Norton, 1941.

Rosenstiel, Léonie, *et al.* (eds.). *Schirmer History of Music.* New York: Schirmer, 1982.

*Wiora, Walter. *The Four Ages of Music* (tr. M. D. Herter Norton). New York: Norton, 1967.

Musical Instruments

Baines, Anthony (ed.). *Musical Instruments through the Ages.* New York: Walker, 1975.

*Marcuse, Sybil. *Musical Instruments: A Comprehensive Dictionary.* New York: Norton, 1975.

Sachs, Curt. *History of Musical Instruments.* New York: Norton, 1940.

Styles and Periods

Antiquity and Medieval

Hoppin, Richard H. *Medieval Music.* New York: Norton, 1978.

Reese, Gustave. *Music in the Middle Ages.* New York: Norton, 1940.

*Seay, Albert. *Music in the Medieval World.* 2nd. ed. Englewood Cliffs, N.J.: Prentice-Hall, 1975.

*Strunk, Oliver (ed.). *Source Readings in Music History: Antiquity and the Middle Ages.* New York: Norton, Norton, 1965.

Renaissance and Baroque

*Blume, Friedrich. *Renaissance and Baroque Music* (tr. M. D. Herter Norton). New York: Norton, 1967.

*Brown, Howard M. *Music in the Renaissance.* Englewood Cliffs, N.J.: Prentice-Hall, 1976.

Bukofzer, Manfred F. *Music in the Baroque Era.* New York: Norton, 1947.

*Donington, Robert. *Baroque Music: Style and Performance.* New York: Norton, 1982.

*Palisca, Claude V. *Baroque Music.* Englewood Cliffs, N.J.: Prentice-Hall, 1968.

Reese, Gustave. *Music in the Renaissance.* Rev. ed. New York: Norton, 1959.

*Strunk, Oliver (ed.). *Source Readings in Music History: The Baroque Era.* New York: Norton, 1965.

*——— *Source Readings in Music History: The Renaissance.* New York: Norton, 1965.

Classic and Romantic

*Blume, Friedrich. *Classic and Romantic Music* (tr. M. D. Herter Norton). New York: Norton, 1970.

Einstein, Alfred. *Music in the Romantic Era.* New York: Norton, 1947.

*Longyear, Rey M. *Nineteenth-Century Romanticism in Music.* 2nd ed. Englewood Cliffs, N.J.: Prentice-Hall, 1973.

*Pauly, Reinhard G. *Music in the Classic Period.* 2nd. ed. Englewood Cliffs, N.J.: Prentice-Hall, 1973.

Plantinga, Leon. *Romantic Music.* New York: Norton, 1984.

*Praz, Mario. *The Romantic Agony.* New York: Oxford, 1970.

*Rosen, Charles. *The Classical Style.* New York: Norton, 1972.

*Strunk, Oliver (ed.). *Source Readings in Music History: The Classic Era.* New York: Norton, 1965.

*——— *Source Readings in Music History: The Romantic Era.* New York: Norton, 1965.

Contemporary

Austin, William. *Music in the Twentieth Century.* New York: Norton, 1966.

*Copland, Aaron. *The New Music, 1900–1960.* New York: Norton, 1968.

*Cowell, Henry. *American Composers on American Music.* New York: Ungar, 1962.

Griffiths, Paul. *Modern Music: the Avant-Garde Since 1945.* London: Dent, 1981.

Machlis, Joseph. *Introduction to Contemporary Music.* 2nd ed. New York: Norton, 1979.

*Salzman, Eric. *Twentieth-Century Music: An Introduction.* 2nd ed. Englewood Cliffs, N.J.: Prentice-Hall, 1974.

Slonimsky, Nicolas. *Music Since 1900.* 4th ed. New York: Scribner, 1971.

American Music

Chase, Gilbert. *America's Music, from the Pilgrims to the Present.* 2nd rev. ed. Westport, Conn.: Greenwood, 1981 (repr. of 1966 ed.).

Hamm, Charles. *Music in the New World.* New York: Norton, 1982.

*———. *Yesterdays: Popular Song in America.* New York: Norton, 1979.

*Hitchcock, H. Wiley. *Music in the United States: A Historical Introduction.* 2nd ed. Englewood Cliffs, N.J.: Prentice-Hall, 1974.

Howard, John Tasker. *Our American Music.* 4th ed. New York: Crowell, 1965.

Mellers, Wilfred. *Music in a New Found Land.* New York: Knopf, 1965.

Rockwell, John. *All American Music: Composition in the Late Twentieth Century.* New York: Knopf, 1983.

*Southern, Eileen. *Music of Black Americans.* 2nd ed. New York: Norton, 1983.

*———. *Readings in Black American Music.* 2nd. ed. New York: Norton, 1982.

*Thomson, Virgil. *American Music Since 1910.* New York: Holt, Rinehart & Winston, 1971.

Genres

Griffiths, Paul. *The String Quartet.* London: Thames and Hudson, 1983.

Grout, Donald. *A Short History of Opera.* 2nd ed. New York: Columbia, 1965.

*Kerman, Joseph. *Opera as Drama.* New York: Vintage, 1956.

Meister, Barbara. *An Introduction to the Art Song.* New York: Taplinger, 1980.

Newman, William S. *A History of the Sonata Idea,* 3 vols. Rev. ed. New York: Norton, 1983.

Rosen, Charles. *Sonata Forms.* New York: Norton, 1980.

*Simpson, Robert (ed.). *The Symphony,* 2 vols. London: David and Charles, 1972.

*Stevens, Denis (ed.). *A History of Song.* Rev. ed. New York: Norton, 1970.

Ulrich, Homer. *Chamber Music.* 2nd ed. New York: Columbia, 1966.

*Veinus, Abraham. *The Concerto.* New York: Dover, 1964.

*Weisstein, Ulrich (ed.). *The Essence of Opera.* New York: Norton, 1969.

Composers (By and On)

BACH, J. S.

*David, Hans T., and Arthur Mendel (eds.). *The Bach Reader.* Rev. ed. New York: Norton, 1966.

Geiringer, Karl, with Irene Geiringer. *Johann Sebastian Bach: The Culmination of an Era.* New York: Oxford, 1966.

*Wolff, Christoph, *et al. The New Grove Bach Family.* New York: Norton, 1983.

BARTÓK

*Stevens, Halsey. *The Life and Music of Béla Bartók.* Rev. ed. New York: Oxford, 1967.

BEETHOVEN

*Anderson, Emily (ed. and tr.). *Selected Letters of Beethoven.* Rev. ed. New York: St. Martin's, 1967.

*Forbes, Elliot (ed.). *Thayers' Life of Beethoven.* Rev. ed. Princeton: Princeton U., 1967.

Kerman, Joseph. *The Beethoven Quartets.* New York: Knopf, 1967.

*Schindler, Anton. *Beethoven as I Knew Him.* New York: Norton, 1972.

*Solomon, Maynard. *Beethoven.* New York: Schirmer, 1979.

*Sonneck, O. G. (ed.). *Beethoven: Impressions by His Contemporaries.* New York: Dover, 1967.

*Tyson, Alan, and Joseph Kerman. *The New Grove Beethoven.* New York: Norton, 1983.

BERG

Jarman, Douglas. *The Music of Alban Berg.* Berkeley: U. of California, 1978.

*Perle, George. *Alban Berg* in *The New Grove Second Viennese School.* New York: Norton, 1983.

Reich, Willi. *The Life and Works of Alban Berg.* New York: Da Capo, 1982.

BERLIOZ

*Barzun, Jacques. *Berlioz and His Century: An Introduction to the Age of Romanticism.* Chicago: U. of Chicago, 1982.

———. *Berlioz and the Romantic Century.* 2 vols. 3rd ed. New York: Columbia, 1969.

*Berlioz, Hector. *Memoirs of Hector Berlioz* (ed. and tr. David Cairns). New York: Norton, 1975.

Primmer, Brian. *The Berlioz Style.* New York: Oxford, 1973.

BIZET

Curtiss, Mina. *Bizet and His World.* Westport, Conn.: Greenwood, 1977 (repr. of 1958 ed.).

Boulez

*Boulez, Pierre. *Boulez on Music Today* (tr. Susan Bradshaw and Richard R. Bennett). London: Faber and Faber, 1979.

*Peyser, Joan. *Pierre Boulez.* New York: Schirmer, 1978.

Brahms

Geiringer, Karl. *Brahms: His Life and Works.* 3rd ed. New York: Da Capo, 1981 (repr. of 1948 ed.).

Jacobson, Bernard. *The Music of Johannes Brahms.* London: Tantivy, 1977.

Byrd

Holst, Imogen. *Byrd.* New York: Praeger, 1972.

Cage

*Cage, John. *A Year From Monday; New Lectures and Writings.* Middletown, Conn.: Wesleyan U., 1969.

*———. *Silence.* Middletown, Conn.: Wesleyan U., 1961.

———. *Themes and Variations.* Barrytown, N.Y.: Station Hill, 1982.

Carter

Edwards, Allen. *Flawed Words and Stubborn Sounds: A Conversation with Elliott Carter.* New York: Norton, 1971.

Schiff, Elliott. *The Music of Elliott Carter.* New York: Da Capo, 1983.

Stone, E., and K. Stone (eds.). *The Writings of Elliott Carter: An American Composer Looks at Modern Music.* Bloomington, Ind.: Indiana U., 1977.

Chopin

Abraham, Gerald. *Chopin's Musical Style.* Westport, Conn.: Greenwood, 1980 (repr. of 1939 ed.).

*Huneker, James. *Chopin: The Man and His Music* (ed. H. Weinstock). New York: Dover, 1966.

*Walker, Alan. *The Chopin Companion: Profiles of The Man and the Musician.* New York: Norton, 1973.

Copland

*Copland, Aaron. *Copland on Music.* New York: Norton, 1963.

Couperin

*Mellers, Wilfrid. *François Couperin and the French Classical Tradition.* New York: Dover, 1968.

Debussy

*Debussy, Claude. "Monsieur Croche," in *Three Classics in the Esthetics of Music.* New York: Dover, 1962.

Lockspeiser, Edward. *Debussy.* Rev. 5th ed. London: Dent, 1980.

*Vallas, Leon. *Claude Debussy: His Life and Works.* New York: Dover, 1973.

Dvořák

Clapham, John. *Dvořák.* New York: Norton, 1979.

Gershwin

Jablonski, Edward, and Lawrence Stewart. *The Gershwin Years.* New York: Doubleday, 1973.

Schwartz, Charles. *Gershwin, His Life and Music.* New York: Da Capo, 1979.

Gluck

*Einstein, Alfred. *Gluck.* New York: McGraw-Hill, 1972.

Handel

Abraham, Gerald (ed.). *Handel, A Symposium.* London: Oxford, 1954.

Dean, Winton. *Handel's Dramatic Oratorios and Masques.* London: Oxford, 1959.

*Dean, Winton, with Anthony Hicks. *The New Grove Handel.* New York: Norton, 1983.

*Lang, Paul Henry. *George Frideric Handel.* New York: Norton, 1966.

Haydn

Geiringer, Karl. *Haydn: A Creative Life in Music.* 2nd rev. and exp. ed. Berkeley: U. of California, 1982.

*Larsen, Jens Peter, with Georg Feder. *The New Grove Haydn.* New York: Norton, 1983.

Robbins Landon, H. C. *Haydn: Chronicle and Works,* 5 vols. Bloomington, Ind.: Indiana U., 1977–78.

Ives

Ives, Charles. *Charles E. Ives Memos* (ed. John Kirkpatrick). New York: Norton, 1972.

*Perlis, Vivian. *Charles Ives Remembered: An Oral History.* New York: Norton, 1976.

Rossiter, Frank. *Charles Ives and His America.* New York: Liveright, 1975.

Janáček

Vogel, J. *Leoš Janáček.* Rev. ed. New York: Norton, 1981.

Liszt

Perenyi, Eleanor. *Liszt: The Artist as Romantic Hero.* New York: Little, Brown, 1974.

Walker, Alan. *Franz Liszt: The Virtuoso Years, 1811–47.* New York: Knopf, 1982.

MacDowell

MacDowell, Edward. *Critical and Historical Essays.* New York: Da Capo, 1969.

Mahler

La Grange, Henri-Louis de. *Mahler.* New York: Doubleday, 1973.

*Mahler, Alma Schindler. *Gustav Mahler: Memories and Letters* (ed. Donald Mitchell). Rev. and enlarged. Seattle: U. of Washington, 1971.

*Mitchell, Donald. *Gustav Mahler: The Wunderhorn Years.* Berkeley: U. of California, 1980.

Mendelssohn

Werner, Eric. *Felix Mendelssohn.* New York: Free Press, 1963.

MONTEVERDI

Arnold, Denis. *Monteverdi.* New York: Octagon, 1963.

*Arnold, Denis, and Nigel Fortune (eds.). *The Monteverdi Companion.* New York: Norton, 1972.

Redlich, H. F. *Claudio Monteverdi: Life and Works* (tr. Kathleen Dale). Westport, Conn.: Greenwood, n.d. (repr. of 1952 ed.).

MOZART

Anderson, Emily (ed.). *Letters of Mozart and His Family.* 2 vols. 2nd ed. (ed. A. Hyatt King and Monica Carolan). New York: St. Martin's, 1966.

*Blom, Eric. *Mozart.* New York: Macmillan, 1966.

Deutsch, Otto Erich. *Mozart: A Documentary Biography.* 2nd ed. Stanford, Cal.: Stanford U., 1966.

*Landon, H. C. Robbins, and Donald Mitchell (eds.). *The Mozart Companion.* New York: Norton, 1969.

*Lang, Paul Henry (ed.). *The Creative World of Mozart.* New York: Norton, 1963.

*Sadie, Stanley. *The New Grove Mozart.* New York: Norton, 1983.

MUSORGSKY

*Calvocoressi, M. D. *Mussorgsky.* New York: Collier, 1962.

PROKOFIEV

Nestyev, Israel V. *Prokofiev* (tr. Florence Jonas). Stanford, Cal.: Stanford U., 1960.

PUCCINI

Ashbrook, William. *The Operas of Puccini.* New York: Oxford, 1968.

*Carner, Mosco. *Giacomo Puccini,* in *The New Grove Masters of Italian Opera.* New York: Norton, 1983.

RACHMANINOFF

Bertensson, S., and J. Leyda. *Sergei Rachmaninoff: A Lifetime in Music.* New York: New York U., 1956.

RAMEAU

*Girdlestone, C. M. *Jean-Philippe Rameau: His Life and Work.* New York: Dover, 1970.

RAVEL

Orenstein, Arbie. *Ravel: Man and Musician.* New York: Columbia, 1975.

SCARLATTI, D.

*Kirkpatrick, Ralph. *Domenico Scarlatti.* New York: Apollo, 1968.

SCHOENBERG

*Neighbour, Oliver. *Arnold Schoenberg* in *The New Grove Second Viennese School.* New York: Norton, 1983.

Rosen, Charles. *Arnold Schoenberg.* New York: Viking, 1975.

Schoenberg, Arnold. *Style and Ideas: Selected Writings of Arnold Schoenberg* (ed. Leonard Stein). New York: Faber and Faber, 1982.

SCHUBERT

Brown, Maurice J. E. *Schubert: A Critical Biography.* New York: Da Capo, 1977 (repr. of 1958 ed.).

*Brown, Maurice J. E., with Eric Sams. *The New Grove Schubert.* New York: Norton, 1983.

Deutsch, Otto Erich. *Schubert: Memoirs by His Friends.* New York: Humanities, 1958.

Gál, Hans. *Franz Schubert and the Essence of Melody.* New York: Crescendo, 1977.

SCHUMANN

Abraham, Gerald (ed.). *Schumann: A Symposium.* Westport, Conn.: Greenwood, 1977 (repr. of 1952 ed.).

*Walker, Alan (ed). *Robert Schumann: The Man and His Music.* London: Barrie and Jenkins, 1976.

SESSIONS

*Sessions, Roger. *The Musical Experience of Composer, Performer, Listener.* Princeton: Princeton U., 1971.

*——— *Questions About Music.* New York: Norton, 1971.

SIBELIUS

Layton, Robert. *Sibelius and his World.* New York: Viking, 1970.

Tawaststjerna, Erik. *Sibelius.* Berkeley: U. California, 1976.

STRAUSS, R.

Mann, William S. *Richard Strauss: A Critical Study of the Operas.* New York: Oxford, 1966.

Strauss, Richard. *Recollections and Reflections* (ed. Willi Schuh, tr. L. J. Lawrence). Westport, Conn.: Greenwood, 1974 (repr. of 1953 ed.).

STRAVINSKY

*Lang, Paul Henry (ed.). *Stravinsky: A New Appraisal of His Work.* New York: Norton, 1963.

Libman, Lillian. *And Music at the Close: Stravinsky's Last Years.* New York: Norton, 1972.

*Stravinsky, Igor. *An Autobiography.* New York: Norton, 1962.

*———. *Poetics of Music.* Cambridge: Harvard, 1970.

*———, with Robert Craft. *Conversation with Igor Stravinsky.* Berkeley: U. of California, 1980.

*———, with Robert Craft. *Dialogues.* Berkeley: U. of California, 1980.

*———, with Robert Craft. *Expositions and Developments.* Berkeley: U. of California, 1981.

*———, with Robert Craft. *Memories and Commentaries.* Berkeley: U. of California, 1981.

*———. *Themes and Conclusions.* Berkeley: U. of California, 1982.

White, Eric Walter. *Stravinsky, the Composer and His Works.* 2nd ed. Berkeley: U. of California, 1980.

TCHAIKOVSKY

*Abraham, Gerald. *The Music of Tchaikovsky.* New York: Norton, 1974.

Brown, David. *Tchaikovsky: The Early Years, 1840–1874.* New York: Norton, 1978.

———. *Tchaikovsky: The Crisis Years, 1874–1878.* New York: Norton, 1983.

THOMSON

*Thomson, Virgil. *The Art of Judging Music.* Westport, Conn.: Greenwood, 1969.

———. *A Virgil Thomson Reader.* New York: Houghton Mifflin, 1981.

VARÈSE

Varèse, Louise. *Varèse: A Looking Glass Diary.* New York: Norton, 1972.

VERDI

Osborne, Charles. *The Complete Operas of Verdi.* New York: Knopf, 1970.

*Porter, Andrew. *Giuseppe Verdi,* in *The New Grove Masters of Italian Opera.* New York: Norton, 1983.

VIVALDI

*Pincherle, Marc. *Vivaldi.* New York: Norton, 1962.

WAGNER

Cosima Wagner's Diaries (ed. Martin Gregor-Dellin and Dietrich Mack, tr. Geoffrey Skelton), 2 vols. New York: Harcourt Brace Jovanovich, 1976–77.

*Deathridge, John, and Carl Dahlhaus. *The New Grove Wagner.* New York: Norton, 1983.

*Gutman, Robert. *Richard Wagner: The Man, His Mind, and His Music.* New York: Harcourt Brace Jovanovich, 1974.

*Newman, Ernest. *The Life of Richard Wagner.* 4 vols. New York: Cambridge, 1976.

WEBERN

*Griffiths, Paul. *Anton Webern,* in *The New Grove Second Viennese School.* New York: Norton, 1983.

Kolneder, Walter. *Anton Webern: An Introduction to His Works* (tr. Humphrey Searle). Berkeley: U. of California, 1968.

APPENDIX II

Comparative Ranges of Voices and Instruments

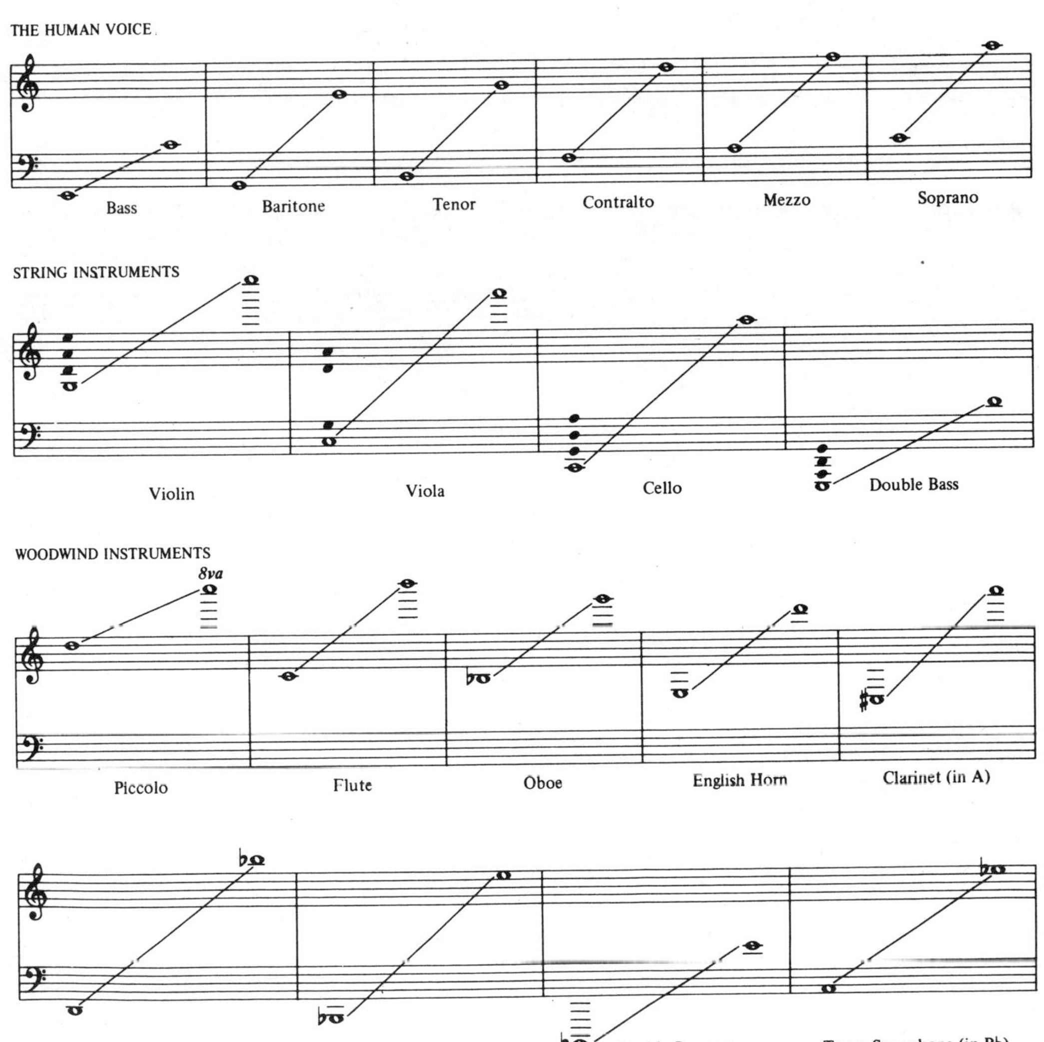

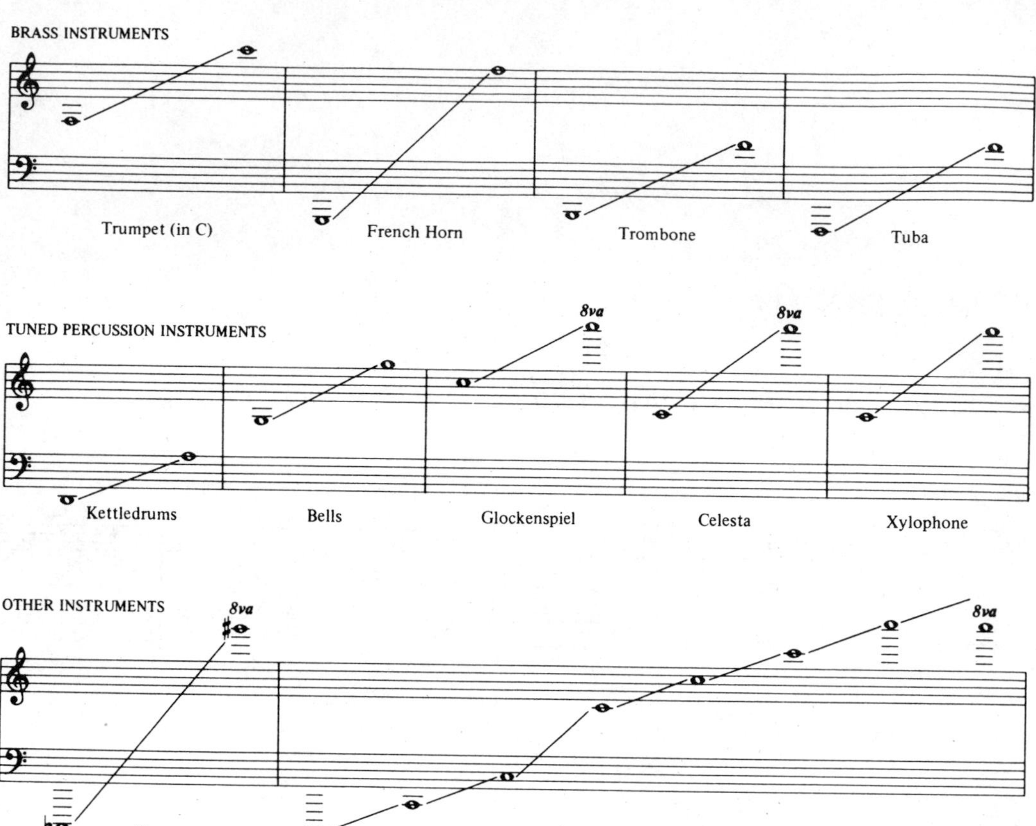
BRASS INSTRUMENTS
Trumpet (in C)
French Horn
Trombone
Tuba
TUNED PERCUSSION INSTRUMENTS
8va
8va
Kettledrums
Bells
Glockenspiel
Celesta
Xylophone
OTHER INSTRUMENTS
8va
8va
Harp
Piano

APPENDIX III

Complete List of Major and Minor Scales

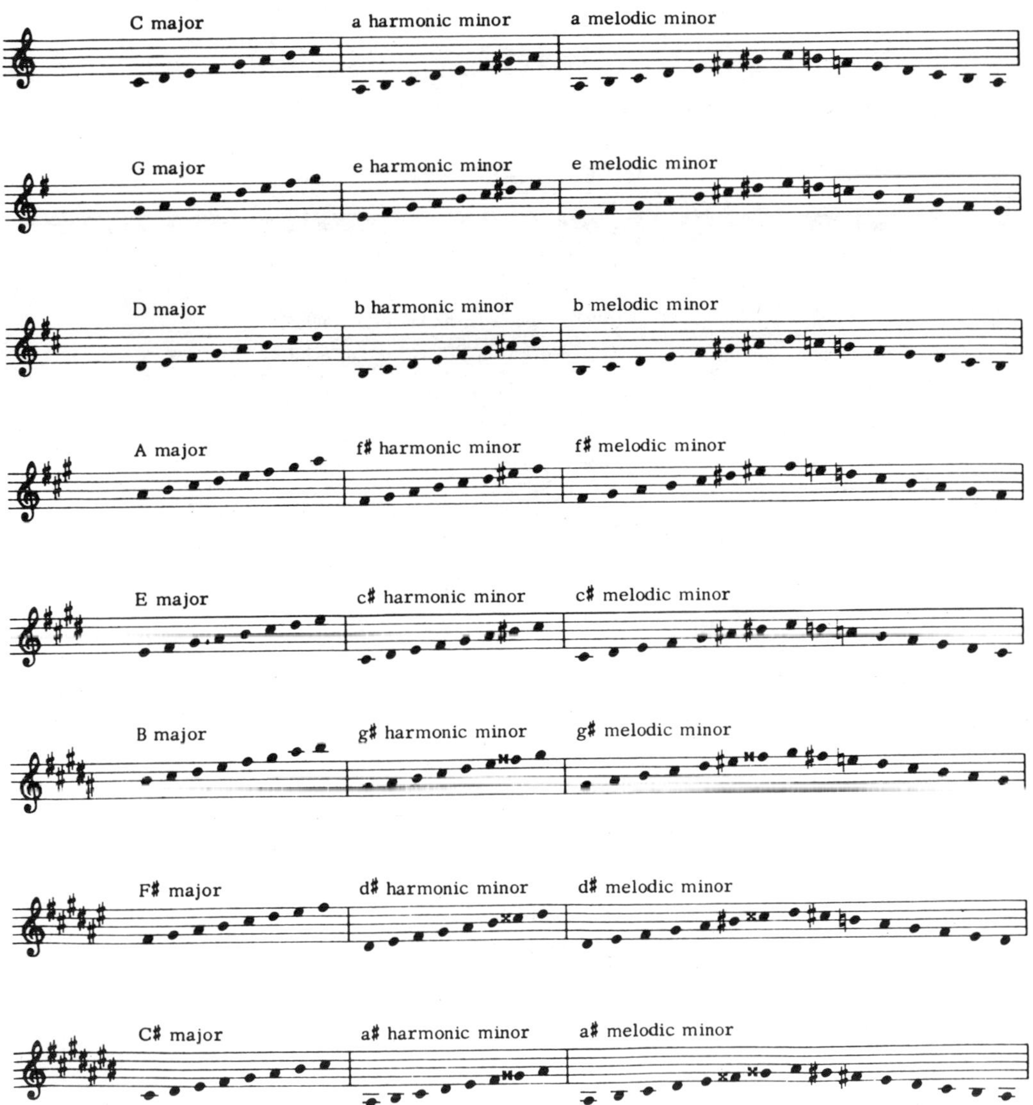

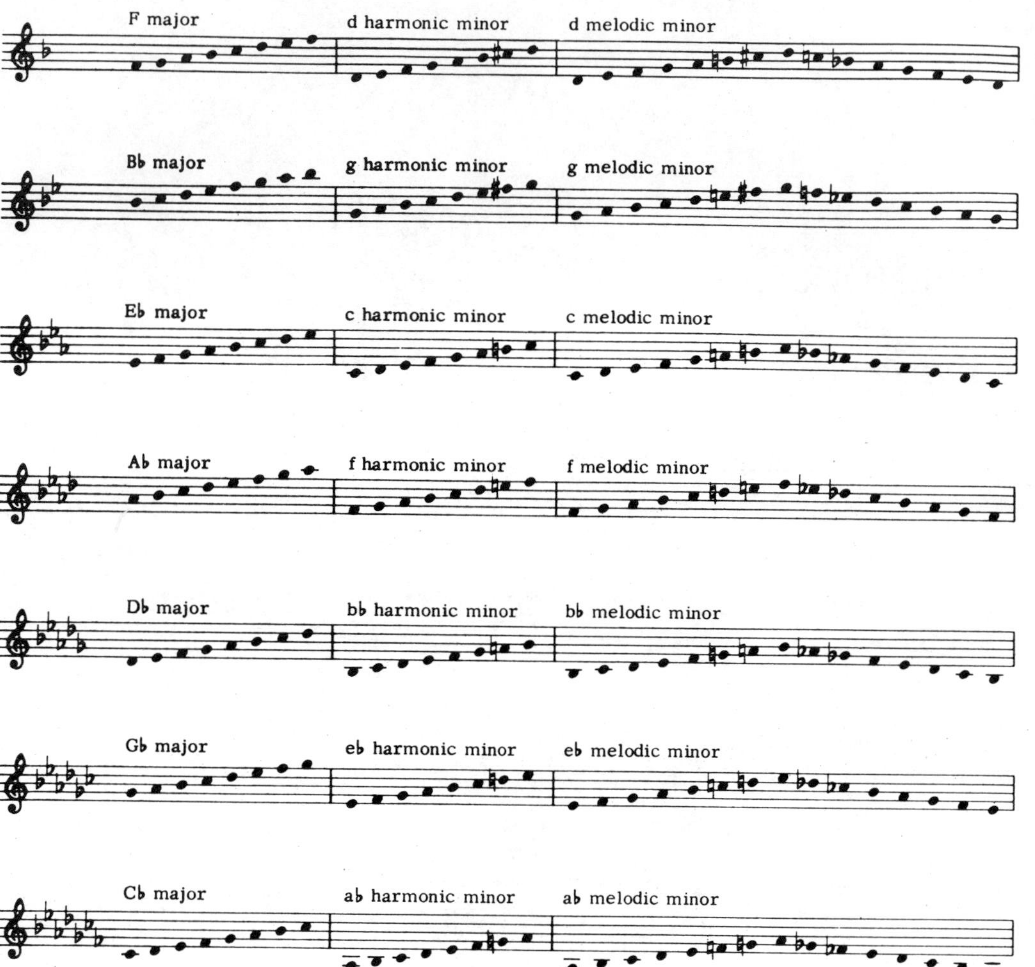
F major
d harmonic minor
d melodic minor
B♭ major
g harmonic minor
g melodic minor
E♭ major
c harmonic minor
c melodic minor
A♭ major
f harmonic minor
f melodic minor
D♭ major
b♭ harmonic minor
b♭ melodic minor
G♭ major
e♭ harmonic minor
e♭ melodic minor
C♭ major
a♭ harmonic minor
a♭ melodic minor

APPENDIX IV

Chronological List of Composers, World Events, and Principal Figures in Literature and the Arts 1300-1983

WORLD EVENTS

1307 *Dante's* Divine Comedy.

1337 *Beginning of the Hundred Years' War between England and France.*

1415 *John Huss burned for heresy. Henry V defeats French at Agincourt.*

1431 *Joan of Arc executed.*

1456 *Gutenberg Bible.*

1492 *Columbus discovers New World.*

1501 *First book of printed music published by Petrucci in Florence.*

1506 *St. Peter's begun by Pope Julius II.*

1509 *Henry VIII becomes King of England.*

1513 *Ponce de Leon discovers Florida. Balboa reaches Pacific.*

1519 *Cortez begins conquest of Mexico.*

1534 *Henry VIII head of Church of England.*

1536 *Anne Boleyn beheaded.*

1541 *De Soto discovers the Mississippi.*

1558 *Elizabeth I becomes Queen of England.*

1572 *St. Bartholomew's Eve Massacre.*

COMPOSERS

GUILLAUME DE MACHAUT (c. 1300–77)

GUILLAUME DUFAY (c. 1400–74)
ANTOINE BUSNOIS (d. 1492)
JOHANNES OCKEGHEM (c. 1420–c. 1495)

JOSQUIN DES PREZ (c. 1450–1521)

THOMAS TALLIS (c. 1505–85)

JACOB ARCADELT (c. 1505–c. 1560)

ANDREA GABRIELI (c. 1520–86)

GIOVANNI DA PALESTRINA (c. 1525–94)

ROLAND DE LASSUS (c. 1532–94)
WILLIAM BYRD (1543–1623)
GIULIO CACCINI (1545–1618)
TOMÁS LUIS DE VICTORIA (c. 1549–1611)

PRINCIPAL FIGURES

Francesco Petrarch (1304–74)

Giovanni Boccaccio (1313–75)

Geoffrey Chaucer (c. 1340–1400)
Luca della Robbia (1400–82)
Giovanni Bellini (1430–1516)
François Villon (1431–c. 1465)
Sandro Botticelli (c. 1444–1510)
Leonardo da Vinci (1452–1519)
Desiderius Erasmus (1466–1536)
Niccolò Machiavelli (1469–1527)
Albrecht Dürer (1471–1528)
Michelangelo (1475–1564)
Titian (1477–1576)
Raphael (1483–1520)
François Rabelais (1400–1553)
Hans Holbein (1497–1543)
Benvenuto Cellini (1500–71)

Pierre de Ronsard (1524–85)
Pieter Brueghel (1525–69)

Michel de Montaigne (1533–92)
El Greco (c. 1541–1614)
Miguel de Cervantes (1547–1616)

Edmund Spenser (1552–99)

WORLD EVENTS

1587 *Mary Queen of Scots executed.*

1588 *Drake defeats Spanish Armada.*

1590 *First three books of Spenser's* Faerie Queene *published.*

1601 *Shakespeare,* Hamlet.

1609 *Henry Hudson explores Hudson River.*

1611 *King James Version of Bible.*

1620 *Mayflower Compact. Plymouth settled. Francis Bacon's* Novum Organum.

1637 *Descartes's* Discourse on Method.

1640 The Bay Psalm Book, *first book printed in the American colonies.*

1642 *Puritan Revolution begins in England.*

1661 *Reign of Louis XIV begins. Absolutism.*

1664 *New Amsterdam becomes New York.*

1667 *Spinoza's* Ethics.

1669 *French Academy of Music founded.*

1682 *Reign of Peter the Great begins.*

1702 *Start of War of the Spanish Succession.*

1714 *Queen Anne succeeded by George I, Handel's patron.*

1715 *First Opéra Comique founded.*

1715 *Reign of Louis XV begins.*

1719 *Herculaneum and Pompeii rediscovered. Classical Revival.*

1732 *Linnaeus's* System of Nature.

1732 *George Washington born.*

1737 *San Carlo Opera, Naples, opened.*

1740 *Age of Enlightened Despots begins, lasting till 1796.*

1743 *Thomas Jefferson born.*

1752 *Franklin's discoveries in electricity.*

1756 *Opening of Seven Years' War (in America, the French and Indian War).*

COMPOSERS

LUCA MARENZIO (c. 1553–99)
GIOVANNI GABRIELI (c. 1557–1612)
THOMAS MORLEY (1557–1603)
CARLO GESUALDO (1560–1613)
JACOPO PERI (1561–1633)
CLAUDIO MONTEVERDI (1567–1643)
JOHN WILBYE (1574–1638)
THOMAS WEELKES (c. 1575–1623)
ORLANDO GIBBONS (1583–1625)
HEINRICH SCHUTZ (1585–1672)
GIACOMO CARISSIMI (1605–74)
JEAN-BAPTISTE LULLY (1632–87)
DIETRICH BUXTEHUDE (1637–1707)
ARCANGELO CORELLI (1653–1713)
HENRY PURCELL (1659–95)
FRANÇOIS COUPERIN (1668–1733)
ANTONIO VIVALDI (1678–1741)
GEORG PHILLIP TELEMANN (1681–1767)
JEAN-PHILIPPE RAMEAU (1683–1764)
JOHANN SEBASTIAN BACH (1685–1750)
DOMENICO SCARLATTI (1685–1757)
GEORGE FRIDERIC HANDEL (1685–1759)
GIOVANNI BATTISTA PERGOLESI (1710–36)
WILHELM FRIEDEMANN BACH (1710–84)
CHRISTOPH WILLIBALD GLUCK (1714–87)
CARL PHILIPP EMANUEL BACH (1714–88)
JOHANN STAMITZ (1717–57)
JOSEPH HAYDN (1732–1809)
JOHANN CHRISTIAN BACH (1735–82)
WILLIAM BILLINGS (1746–1800)
DOMENICO CIMAROSA (1749–1801)

PRINCIPAL FIGURES

William Shakespeare (1564–1616)
John Donne (1573–1631)
Ben Jonson (1573–1637)
Peter Paul Rubens (1577–1640)
Frans Hals (1580?–1666)
Gianlorenzo Bernini (1598–1680)
Anthony Van Dyck (1599–1641)
Diego Velázquez (1599–1660)
Rembrandt (1606–69)
Pierre Corneille (1606–84)
John Milton (1608–74)
Molière (1622–73)
John Bunyan (1628–88)
John Dryden (1631–1700)
Jan Vermeer (1632–75)
Sir Christopher Wren (1632–1723)
Jean Baptiste Racine (1639–99)
Daniel Defoe (1659?–1731)
Jonathan Swift (1667–1745)
Joseph Addison (1672–1719)
Richard Steele (1672–1729)
Jean Antoine Watteau (1684–1721)
Alexander Pope (1688–1744)
Voltaire (1694–1778)
Giovanni Battista Tiepolo (1696–1770)
William Hogarth (1697–1764)
François Boucher (1703–70)
Henry Fielding (1707–54)
Samuel Johnson (1709–84)
Jean Jacques Rousseau (1712–78)
Laurence Sterne (1713–68)
Thomas Gray (1716–71)
Sir Joshua Reynolds (1723–92)
Thomas Gainsborough (1727–88)
Oliver Goldsmith (1728–74)
Pierre Augustin Caron de Beaumarchais (1732–99)
Jean Honoré Fragonard (1732–1809)
Edward Gibbon (1737–94)
Jean Antoine Houdon (1741–1828)
Francisco José de Goya (1746–1828)

ORLD EVENTS	COMPOSERS	PRINCIPAL FIGURES

ORLD EVENTS

1 *Queen Victoria dies, Edward VII succeeds. De Vries's mutation theory.*

3 *Wrights' first successful airplane flight. Ford organizes motor company.*

Opening of Russo-Japanese War. London Symphony founded. The Abbey Theatre opens in Dublin.

Sigmund Freud founds psychoanalysis. Norway separates from Sweden. First Russian Revolution.

Einstein's theory of relativity first published.

San Francisco earthquake and fire.

Second Hague Conference. Triple Entente. William James's Pragmatism.

odel T Ford produced.

eary reaches North Pole.

mundsen reaches South Pole.

ina becomes republic. Titanic *sinks.*

nama Canal completed. World War I gins.

sitania sunk. Einstein presents general ory of relativity.

. enters World War I. Russian Revtion. Prohibition Amendment.

ser abdicates. World War I ends in istice.

ty of Versailles. League of Nations hed: Mussolini founds Italian Fascist y.

teenth Amendment (women's suffrage). nd granted home rule.

very of insulin. Fascist revolution ly. John Dewey's Human Nature onduct.

R. established.

dies.

rg's solo flight across Atlantic. and Vanzetti executed.

COMPOSERS

ALBAN BERG (1885–1935)
JELLY ROLL MORTON (1885–1941)
WALLINGFORD RIEGGER (1885–1961)
HEITOR VILLA-LOBOS (1887–1959)
BOHUSLAV MARTINU (1890–1959)
JACQUES IBERT (1890–1963)
SERGE PROKOFIEV (1891–1952)
ARTHUR HONEGGER (1892–1955)
DARIUS MILHAUD (1892–1974)
DOUGLAS MOORE (1893–1969)
BESSIE SMITH (1894–1937)
WALTER PISTON (1894–76)
KAROL RATHAUS (1895–1954)
PAUL HINDEMITH (1895–1963)
WILLIAM GRANT STILL (1895–1978)
CARL ORFF (1895–1982)
HOWARD HANSON (1896–1981)
ROGER SESSIONS (1896–)
VIRGIL THOMSON (1896–)
HENRY COWELL (1897–1965)
QUINCY PORTER (1897–1966)
GEORGE GERSHWIN (1898–1937)
ROY HARRIS (1898–1979)
E. K. ("DUKE") ELLINGTON (1899–1974)
CARLOS CHAVEZ (1899–1978)
RANDALL THOMPSON (1899–)
FRANCIS POULENC (1899–1963)
AARON COPLAND (1900–)
ERNST KRENEK (1900–)
KURT WEILL (1900–50)
LOUIS ARMSTRONG (1900–71)
RUTH CRAWFORD (1901–53)

PRINCIPAL FIGURES

Amedeo Modigliani (1884–1920)
D. H. Lawrence (1885–1930)
Sinclair Lewis (1885–1951)
François Mauriac (1885–1970)
André Maurois (1885–1967)
Diego Riviera (1886–1957)
Juan Gris (1887–1927)
Marcel Duchamp (1887–1968)
William Zorach (1887–1966)
Georgia O'Keeffe (1887–)
Hans Arp (1887–1966)
Marc Chagall (1887–)
Kurt Schwitters (1887–1948)
Giorgio di Chirico (1888–1978)
T. S. Eliot (1888–1965)
T. E. Lawrence (1888–1935)
Thomas Hart Benton (1889–1975)
Karel Čapek (1890–1938)
Max Ernst (1891–1976)
Grant Wood (1892–1944)
John P. Marquand (1893–1960)
Joan Miro (1893–1983)
Ernst Toller (1893–1939)
e. e. cummings (1894–1962)
Aldous Huxley (1894–1963)
Robert Graves (1895–)
F. Scott Fitzgerald (1896–1940)
Robert Sherwood (1896–1955)
John Dos Passos (1896–1970)
William Faulkner (1897–1962)
Louis Aragon (1897–)
Sergei Eisenstein (1898–1948)
Bertolt Brecht (1898–1956)
Ernest Hemingway (1898–1961)
Alexander Calder (1898–1976)
Henry Moore (1898–)
Hart Crane (1899–1932)
Federico García Lorca (1899–1936)
Thomas Wolfe (1900–38)
Ignazio Silone (1900–78)
André Malraux (1901–76)
John Steinbeck (1902–68)

WORLD EVENTS

1759 *Wolfe captures Quebec.*

1763 *Canada ceded to England.*

1769 *Watt's steam engine.*

c. 1770 *Beginning of the factory system.*

1771 *First edition,* Encyclopaedia Britannica.

1776 *Adam Smith's* The Wealth of Nations.

1778 *La Scala Opera opened in Milan.*

1781 *Kant's* Critique of Pure Reason.

1787 *Constitutional Convention.*

1789 *French Revolution begins.*

1791 *Bill of Rights.*

1793 *Eli Whitney's cotton gin.*

1796 *Jenner introduces vaccination.*

1798 *Malthus's* Essay on Population.

1800 *Laplace's mechanistic view of universe.*

1803 *Louisiana Purchase.*

1807 *Hegel's* Phenomenology of Mind.

1812 *Napoleon invades Russia.*

1815 *Battle of Waterloo. Congress of Vienna.*

1817 *Ricardo's* Political Economy and Taxation.

1819 *First steamship to cross Atlantic.*

1823 *Monroe Doctrine.*

1824 *Bolivar liberates South America.*

1829 *Independence of Greece.*

1830 *First railroad, Liverpool–Manchester. July Revolution in France.*

1832 *Morse invents telegraph.*

1833 *Slavery outlawed in British Empire.*

1834 *McCormick patents mechanical reaper.*

1837 *Queen Victoria ascends the throne.*

COMPOSERS

SUPPLY BELCHER (1751–1836)
MUZIO CLEMENTI (1752–1832)
WOLFGANG AMADEUS MOZART (1756–91)
DANIEL READ (1757–1836)
MARIA LUIGI CHERUBINI (1760–1842)
LUDWIG VAN BEETHOVEN (1770–1827)
GASPARO SPONTINI (1774–1851)
NICCOLO PAGANINI (1782–1840)
TIMOTHY SWAN (1785–1842)
CARL MARIA VON WEBER (1786–1826)
GIACOMO MEYERBEER (1791–1864)
GIOACCHINO ROSSINI (1792–1868)
LOWELL MASON (1792–1872)
GAETANO DONIZETTI (1797–1848)
FRANZ SCHUBERT (1797–1828)
VINCENZO BELLINI (1801–35)
HECTOR BERLIOZ (1803–69)
JOHANN STRAUSS (THE FATHER: 1804–49)
MICHAEL GLINKA (1804–57)
FELIX MENDELSSOHN (1809–47)
FRÉDÉRIC FRANÇOIS CHOPIN (1810–49)
ROBERT SCHUMANN (1810–56)
FRANZ LISZT (1811–86)
RICHARD WAGNER (1813–83)
GIUSEPPE VERDI (1813–1901)
WILLIAM HENRY FRY (1815–64)
CHARLES GOUNOD (1818–93)
JACQUES OFFENBACH (1819–80)
CÉSAR FRANCK (1822–90)
ÉDOUARD LALO (1823–92)
BEDŘICH SMETANA (1824–84)
ANTON BRUCKNER (1824–96)

PRINCIPAL FIGURES

Jacques Louis David (1748–1825)
Johann Wolfgang von Goethe (1749–1832)
William Blake (1757–1827)
Robert Burns (1759–96)
Johann Christoph Friedrich von Schiller (1759–1805)
William Wordsworth (1770–1850)
Sir Walter Scott (1771–1832)
Samuel Taylor Coleridge (1772–1834)
J. M. W. Turner (1775–1851)
John Constable (1776–1837)
Jean Dominique Ingres (1780–1867)
George Gordon Lord Byron (1788–1824)
Alphonse Lamartine (1790–1869)
Jean Louis Géricault (1791–1824)
Percy Bysshe Shelley (1792–1822)
John Keats (1795–1821)
Thomas Carlyle (1795–1881)
John Baptiste Camille Corot (1796–1875)
Eugène Delacroix (1798–1863)
Alexander Pushkin (1799–1837)
Honoré de Balzac (1799–1850)
Alexandre Dumas (1802–70)
Victor Hugo (1802–85)
Ralph Waldo Emerson (1803–82)
Nathaniel Hawthorne (1804–64)
George Sand (1804–76)
Honoré Daumier (1808–79)
Edgar Allan Poe (1809–49)
Nikolai Gogol (1809–52)
Alfred Lord Tennyson (1809–92)
William Makepeace Thackeray (1811–63)
Charles Dickens (1812–70)
Robert Browning (1812–89)
Charlotte Brontë (1816–55)
Henry David Thoreau (1817–62)
Emily Brontë (1818–48)
Ivan Sergeyevich Turgenev (1818–83)
Herman Melville (1819–91)
George Eliot (1819–80)
Walt Whitman (1819–92)
John Ruskin (1819–1900)
Pierre Charles Baudelaire (1821–67)
Gustave Flaubert (1821–80)
Feodor Mikhailovich Dostoevsky (1821–81)

WORLD EVENTS

1839 *Daguerrotype invented, beginnings of photography. N.Y. Philharmonic Society and Vienna Philharmonic founded.*

1846 *Repeal of Corn Laws. Famine in Ireland.*

1848 *Revolutions throughout Europe.*

1848 *Gold Rush in California. Mill's Political* Economy. *Marx's* Communist Manifesto.

1852 *Second Empire under Napoleon III. Stowe's* Uncle Tom's Cabin.

1854 *Commodore Perry opens Japan to West. Crimean War.*

1855 *Charge of the Light Brigade.*

1857 *Dred Scott decision.*

1858 *Covent Garden opened as opera house.*

1859 *Darwin's* Origin of Species. *John Brown raids Harper's Ferry.*

1861 *Serfs emancipated in Russia.*

1861 *American Civil War begins.*

1863 *Emancipation Proclamation.*

1865 *Civil War ends. Lincoln assassinated.*

1866 *Transatlantic cable completed.*

1867 *Marx's* Das Kapital *(first vol.). Alaska purchased.*

1870 *Franco-Prussian War. Vatican Council proclaims papal infallibility.*

1871 *William I of Hohenzollern becomes German Emperor. Paris Commune. Unification of Italy complete; Rome becomes capital. Stanley and Livingston in Africa.*

1873 *Dynamo developed.*

1875 *New Paris Opera House opened.*

1876 *Telephone invented. Internal-combustion engine. Bayreuth theater opened.*

1877 *Phonograph invented.*

1880 *Irish Insurrection.*

COMPOSERS

JOHANN STRAUSS (THE SON: 1825–99)
GEORGE FREDERICK BRISTOW (1825–98)
STEPHEN COLLINS FOSTER (1826–64)
WILLIAM MASON (1829–1908)
LOUIS MOREAU GOTTSCHALK (1829–69)
JOHANNES BRAHMS (1833–97)

ALEXANDER BORODIN (1834–87)
CAMILLE SAINT-SAËNS (1835–1921)
LÉO DELIBES (1836–91)

MILY BALAKIREV (1837–1910)
GEORGES BIZET (1838–75)
MODEST MUSORGSKY (1839–81)
JOHN KNOWLES PAINE (1839–1906)

PETER ILYICH TCHAIKOVSKY (1840–93)

EMMANUEL CHABRIER (1841–94)

ANTONÍN DVOŘÁK (1841–1904)
JULES MASSENET (1842–1912)
EDVARD GRIEG (1843–1907)
NIKOLAI RIMSKY-KORSAKOV (1844–1908)

GABRIEL FAURÉ (1845–1924)
HENRI DUPARC (1848–1933)

VINCENT D'INDY (1851–1931)
ARTHUR FOOTE (1853–1937)
LEOŠ JANÁČEK (1854–1928)

GEORGE CHADWICK (1854–1931)

ERNEST CHAUSSON (1855–99)

SIR EDWARD ELGAR (1857–1934)
RUGGIERO LEONCAVALLO (1858–1919)
GIACOMO PUCCINI (1858–1924)

HUGO WOLF (1860–1903)
ISAAC ALBÉNIZ (1860–1909)
GUSTAV MAHLER (1860–1911)
EDWARD MACDOWELL (1861–1908)
CHARLES MARTIN LOEFFLER (1861–1935)
ARTHUR WHITING (1861–1936)
CLAUDE DEBUSSY (1862–1918)
FREDERICK DELIUS (1862–1934)

PRINCIPAL FIGURES

Dante Gabriel Rossetti (1828–82)

Henrik Ibsen (1828–1906)

George Meredith (1828–1909)
Leo Nikolaevich Tolstoi (1828–1910)
Emily Dickinson (1830–86)
Camille Pissarro (1830–1903)

Edouard Manet (1832–83)

James McNeill Whistler (1834–1903)
Hilaire Germain Edgar Degas (1834–1917)
Mark Twain (1835–1910)
Winslow Homer (1836–1910)
Algernon Charles Swinburne (1837–1909)
William Dean Howells (1837–1920)
H. H. Richardson (1838–86)
Henry Adams (1838–1918)
Paul Cézanne (1839–1906)
Alphonse Daudet (1840–97)
Auguste Rodin (1840–1917)
Claude Monet (1840–1926)
Thomas Hardy (1840–1928)
Emile Zola (1840–1902)
Pierre Auguste Renoir (1841–1919)

Stéphane Mallarmé (1842–98)
Henry James (1843–1916)
Paul Verlaine (1844–96)
Friedrich Wilhelm Nietzsche (1844–1900)
Anatole France (1844–1924)

Paul Gauguin (1848–1903)
Augustus St. Gaudens (1848–1907)
Joris Karl Huysmans (1848–1907)
Guy de Maupassant (1850–93)
Robert Louis Stevenson (1850–94)
Vincent Van Gogh (1853–90)
Arthur Rimbaud (1854–91)

Oscar Wilde (1854–1900)

Louis H. Sullivan (1856–1924)
John Singer Sargent (1856–1925)
George Bernard Shaw (1856–1950)
Joseph Conrad (1857–1924)
Georges Seurat (1859–91)
A. E. Housman (1859–1936)
Anton Chekov (1860–1904)
James M. Barrie (1860–1937)
Aristide Maillol (1861–1945)

Gerhart Hauptmann (1862–1946)
Maurice Maeterlinck (1862–1949)

WORLD EVENTS

1881 *Tsar Alexander II assassinated. President Garfield shot.*

1881 *Panama Canal begun. Boston Symphony founded.*

1882 *Koch discovers tuberculosis germ. Berlin Philharmonic founded.*

1883 *Brooklyn Bridge opened. Nietzsche's* Thus Spake Zarathustra. *Metropolitan Opera opened. Amsterdam Concertgebouw founded.*

1884 *Pasteur discovers inoculation against rabies.*

1886 *Statue of Liberty unveiled in New York Harbor.*

1887 *Daimler patents high-speed internal-combustion engine.*

1889 *Eiffel Tower, Paris World's Fair opened. Brazil becomes republic.*

1890 *Journey around world completed in 72 days.*

1892 *Duryea makes first American gas buggy.*

1893 *World's Columbian Exposition, Chicago.*

1894 *Nicholas II, last Tsar, ascends throne.*

1894 *Beginning of Dreyfus affair, lasting till 1905.*

1895 *Roentgen discovers X-rays. Marconi's wireless telegraphy.*

1896 *Becquerel finds radioactivity in uranium. Olympic games revived. Gold rush in Alaska.*

1897 *Queen Victoria's Diamond Jubilee.*

1898 *Pierre and Marie Curie discover radium. Empress Elizabeth of Austria-Hungary assassinated. Spanish-American War.*

1899 *Boer War. First International Peace Conference at the Hague.*

1900 *Boxer Insurrection in China. Count Zeppelin tests dirigible balloon. Philadelphia Symphony founded.*

COMPOSERS

HORATIO PARKER (1863–1919)
PIETRO MASCAGNI (1863–1945)
RICHARD STRAUSS (1864–1949)
ALEXANDER GRECHANINOV (1864–1956)
PAUL DUKAS (1865–1935)
ALEXANDER GLAZUNOV (1865–1936)
JEAN SIBELIUS (1865–1957)
FERRUCCIO BUSONI (1866–1924)
ERIK SATIE (1866–1925)
ENRIQUE GRANADOS (1867–1916)
MRS. H. H. A. BEACH (1867–1944)
HENRY F. GILBERT (1868–1928)

ALBERT ROUSSEL (1869–1937)

ALEXANDER SCRIABIN (1872–1915)
ARTHUR FARWELL (1872–1951)
RALPH VAUGHAN WILLIAMS (1872–1958)

MAX REGER (1873–1916)
SERGEI RACHMANINOFF (1873–1943)
DANIEL GREGORY MASON (1873–1953)
ARNOLD SCHOENBERG (1874–1951)
CHARLES IVES (1874–1954)
MAURICE RAVEL (1875–1937)
MANUEL DE FALLA (1876–1946)
JOHN ALDEN CARPENTER (1876–1951)
CARL RUGGLES (1876–1971)

OTTORINO RESPIGHI (1879–1936)

ERNEST BLOCH (1880–1959)
ILDEBRANDO PIZZETTI (1880–1968)

BÉLA BARTÓK (1881–1945)
GEORGES ENESCO (1881–1955)
JOHN POWELL (1882–1963)

IGOR STRAVINSKY (1882–1971)
ZOLTAN KODALY (1882–1967)
GIAN FRANCESCO MALIPIERO (1882–1973)
EDGARD VARÈSE (1883–1965)
ANTON WEBERN (1883–1945)

CHARLES T. GRIFFES (1884–1920)

PRINCIPAL FIGURES

Gabriele D'Annunzio (186

Henri de Toulouse-Lautre
Rudyard Kipling (1865–1
William Butler Yeats (18

Romain Rolland (1866–1
Wassily Kandinsky (186
H. G. Wells (1866–194
Arnold Bennett (1867–1
John Galsworthy (1867
Luigi Pirandello (1867-
Edmond Rostand (186
Maxim Gorky (1868–1
Edward Arlington Rob
Henri Matisse (1869–
Frank Lloyd Wright
André Gide (1869–19
John Marin (1870–19
John M. Synge (187
Marcel Proust (1871
Theodore Dreiser (1
Georges Roualt (18
Sergei Diaghilev (1
Piet Mondrian (187
Willa Cather (1873

Robert Frost (187
Hugo Von Hofma
Gertrude Stein (1
W. Somerset Mau
Rainer Maria Ril
Thomas Mann (1
Constantine Bran
Marsden Hartley
Isadora Duncan
John Masefield
Vachel Lindsay
Paul Klee (187
E. M. Forster
Raoul Dufy (1
Guillaume Ap
Jacob Epstein
Fernand Lége
Pablo Picasso
Georges Brac
James Joyce
Jean Giraudo
Virginia Wo

Franz Kafk
Maurice Ut
Jose Ortega

W

19
190
190
1905
1905
1906
1907
1908
1909
1911
1912 C
1914 P
be
1915 L
th
1917 U.
ol
1918 Ka
arn
1919 Tre
for
Par
1920 Nin
Irel
1922 Disc
in It
and
1923 U.S.
1924 Lenin
1927 Lindb
Sacco

WORLD EVENTS

1759 *Wolfe captures Quebec.*

1763 *Canada ceded to England.*

1769 *Watt's steam engine.*

c. 1770 *Beginning of the factory system.*

1771 *First edition,* Encyclopaedia Britannica.

1776 *Adam Smith's* The Wealth of Nations.

1778 *La Scala Opera opened in Milan.*

1781 *Kant's* Critique of Pure Reason.

1787 *Constitutional Convention.*

1789 *French Revolution begins.*

1791 *Bill of Rights.*

1793 *Eli Whitney's cotton gin.*

1796 *Jenner introduces vaccination.*

1798 *Malthus's* Essay on Population.

1800 *Laplace's mechanistic view of universe.*

1803 *Louisiana Purchase.*

1807 *Hegel's* Phenomenology of Mind.

1812 *Napoleon invades Russia.*

1815 *Battle of Waterloo. Congress of Vienna.*

1817 *Ricardo's* Political Economy and Taxation.

1819 *First steamship to cross Atlantic.*

1823 *Monroe Doctrine.*

1824 *Bolivar liberates South America.*

1829 *Independence of Greece.*

1830 *First railroad, Liverpool–Manchester. July Revolution in France.*

1832 *Morse invents telegraph.*

1833 *Slavery outlawed in British Empire.*

1834 *McCormick patents mechanical reaper.*

1837 *Queen Victoria ascends the throne.*

COMPOSERS

SUPPLY BELCHER (1751–1836)
MUZIO CLEMENTI (1752–1832)
WOLFGANG AMADEUS MOZART (1756–91)
DANIEL READ (1757–1836)
MARIA LUIGI CHERUBINI (1760–1842)
LUDWIG VAN BEETHOVEN (1770–1827)
GASPARO SPONTINI (1774–1851)
NICCOLO PAGANINI (1782–1840)
TIMOTHY SWAN (1785–1842)
CARL MARIA VON WEBER (1786–(1826)
GIACOMO MEYERBEER (1791–1864)
GIOACCHINO ROSSINI (1792–1868)
LOWELL MASON (1792–1872)
GAETANO DONIZETTI (1797–1848)
FRANZ SCHUBERT (1797–1828)
VINCENZO BELLINI (1801–35)
HECTOR BERLIOZ (1803–69)
JOHANN STRAUSS (THE FATHER: 1804–49)
MICHAEL GLINKA (1804–57)
FELIX MENDELSSOHN (1809–47)
FRÉDÉRIC FRANÇOIS CHOPIN (1810–49)
ROBERT SCHUMANN (1810–56)
FRANZ LISZT (1811–86)
RICHARD WAGNER (1813–83)
GIUSEPPE VERDI (1813–1901)
WILLIAM HENRY FRY (1815–64)
CHARLES GOUNOD (1818–93)
JACQUES OFFENBACH (1819–80)
CÉSAR FRANCK (1822–90)
ÉDOUARD LALO (1823–92)
BEDŘICH SMETANA (1824–84)
ANTON BRUCKNER (1824–96)

PRINCIPAL FIGURES

Jacques Louis David (1748–1825)
Johann Wolfgang von Goethe (1749–1832)
William Blake (1757–1827)
Robert Burns (1759–96)
Johann Christoph Friedrich von Schiller (1759–1805)
William Wordsworth (1770–1850)
Sir Walter Scott (1771–1832)
Samuel Taylor Coleridge (1772–1834)
J. M. W. Turner (1775–1851)
John Constable (1776–1837)
Jean Dominique Ingres (1780–1867)
George Gordon Lord Byron (1788–1824)
Alphonse Lamartine (1790–1869)
Jean Louis Géricault (1791–1824)
Percy Bysshe Shelley (1792–1822)
John Keats (1795–1821)
Thomas Carlyle (1795–1881)
John Baptiste Camille Corot (1796–1875)
Eugène Delacroix (1798–1863)
Alexander Pushkin (1799–1837)
Honoré de Balzac (1799–1850)
Alexandre Dumas (1802–70)
Victor Hugo (1802–85)
Ralph Waldo Emerson (1803–82)
Nathaniel Hawthorne (1804–64)
George Sand (1804–76)
Honoré Daumier (1808–79)
Edgar Allan Poe (1809–49)
Nikolai Gogol (1809–52)
Alfred Lord Tennyson (1809–92)
William Makepeace Thackeray (1811–63)
Charles Dickens (1812–70)
Robert Browning (1812–89)
Charlotte Brontë (1816–55)
Henry David Thoreau (1817–62)
Emily Brontë (1818–48)
Ivan Sergeyevich Turgenev (1818–83)
Herman Melville (1819–91)
George Eliot (1819–80)
Walt Whitman (1819–92)
John Ruskin (1819–1900)
Pierre Charles Baudelaire (1821–67)
Gustave Flaubert (1821–80)
Feodor Mikhailovich Dostoevsky (1821–81)

WORLD EVENTS

1839 *Daguerrotype invented, beginnings of photography. N.Y. Philharmonic Society and Vienna Philharmonic founded.*

1846 *Repeal of Corn Laws. Famine in Ireland.*

1848 *Revolutions throughout Europe.*

1848 *Gold Rush in California. Mill's Political* Economy. *Marx's* Communist Manifesto.

1852 *Second Empire under Napoleon III. Stowe's* Uncle Tom's Cabin.

1854 *Commodore Perry opens Japan to West. Crimean War.*

1855 *Charge of the Light Brigade.*

1857 *Dred Scott decision.*

1858 *Covent Garden opened as opera house.*

1859 *Darwin's* Origin of Species. *John Brown raids Harper's Ferry.*

1861 *Serfs emancipated in Russia.*

1861 *American Civil War begins.*

1863 *Emancipation Proclamation.*

1865 *Civil War ends. Lincoln assassinated.*

1866 *Transatlantic cable completed.*

1867 *Marx's* Das Kapital *(first vol.). Alaska purchased.*

1870 *Franco-Prussian War. Vatican Council proclaims papal infallibility.*

1871 *William I of Hohenzollern becomes German Emperor. Paris Commune. Unification of Italy complete; Rome becomes capital. Stanley and Livingston in Africa.*

1873 *Dynamo developed.*

1875 *New Paris Opera House opened.*

1876 *Telephone invented. Internal-combustion engine. Bayreuth theater opened.*

1877 *Phonograph invented.*

1880 *Irish Insurrection.*

COMPOSERS

JOHANN STRAUSS (THE SON: 1825–99)
GEORGE FREDERICK BRISTOW (1825–98)
STEPHEN COLLINS FOSTER (1826–64)
WILLIAM MASON (1829–1908)
LOUIS MOREAU GOTTSCHALK (1829–69)
JOHANNES BRAHMS (1833–97)

ALEXANDER BORODIN (1834–87)
CAMILLE SAINT-SAËNS (1835–1921)
LÉO DELIBES (1836–91)

MILY BALAKIREV (1837–1910)
GEORGES BIZET (1838–75)
MODEST MUSORGSKY (1839–81)
JOHN KNOWLES PAINE (1839–1906)

PETER ILYICH TCHAIKOVSKY (1840–93)

EMMANUEL CHABRIER (1841–94)

ANTONÍN DVOŘÁK (1841–1904)
JULES MASSENET (1842–1912)
EDVARD GRIEG (1843–1907)
NIKOLAI RIMSKY-KORSAKOV (1844–1908)

GABRIEL FAURÉ (1845–1924)
HENRI DUPARC (1848–1933)

VINCENT D'INDY (1851–1931)
ARTHUR FOOTE (1853–1937)
LEOŠ JANÁČEK (1854–1928)

GEORGE CHADWICK (1854–1931)

ERNEST CHAUSSON (1855–99)

SIR EDWARD ELGAR (1857–1934)
RUGGIERO LEONCAVALLO (1858–1919)
GIACOMO PUCCINI (1858–1924)

HUGO WOLF (1860–1903)
ISAAC ALBÉNIZ (1860–1909)
GUSTAV MAHLER (1860–1911)
EDWARD MACDOWELL (1861–1908)
CHARLES MARTIN LOEFFLER (1861–1935)
ARTHUR WHITING (1861–1936)
CLAUDE DEBUSSY (1862–1918)
FREDERICK DELIUS (1862–1934)

PRINCIPAL FIGURES

Dante Gabriel Rossetti (1828–82)

Henrik Ibsen (1828–1906)

George Meredith (1828–1909)
Leo Nikolaevich Tolstoi (1828–1910)
Emily Dickinson (1830–86)
Camille Pissarro (1830–1903)

Edouard Manet (1832–83)

James McNeill Whistler (1834–1903)
Hilaire Germain Edgar Degas (1834–1917)
Mark Twain (1835–1910)
Winslow Homer (1836–1910)
Algernon Charles Swinburne (1837–1909)
William Dean Howells (1837–1920)
H. H. Richardson (1838–86)
Henry Adams (1838–1918)
Paul Cézanne (1839–1906)
Alphonse Daudet (1840–97)
Auguste Rodin (1840–1917)
Claude Monet (1840–1926)
Thomas Hardy (1840–1928)
Emile Zola (1840–1902)
Pierre Auguste Renoir (1841–1919)

Stéphane Mallarmé (1842–98)
Henry James (1843–1916)
Paul Verlaine (1844–96)
Friedrich Wilhelm Nietzsche (1844–1900)
Anatole France (1844–1924)

Paul Gauguin (1848–1903)
Augustus St. Gaudens (1848–1907)
Joris Karl Huysmans (1848–1907)
Guy de Maupassant (1850–93)
Robert Louis Stevenson (1850–94)
Vincent Van Gogh (1853–90)
Arthur Rimbaud (1854–91)

Oscar Wilde (1854–1900)

Louis H. Sullivan (1856–1924)
John Singer Sargent (1856–1925)
George Bernard Shaw (1856–1950)
Joseph Conrad (1857–1924)
Georges Seurat (1859–91)
A. E. Housman (1859–1936)
Anton Chekov (1860–1904)
James M. Barrie (1860–1937)
Aristide Maillol (1861–1945)

Gerhart Hauptmann (1862–1946)
Maurice Maeterlinck (1862–1949)

WORLD EVENTS

1881 *Tsar Alexander II assassinated. President Garfield shot.*

1881 *Panama Canal begun. Boston Symphony founded.*

1882 *Koch discovers tuberculosis germ. Berlin Philharmonic founded.*

1883 *Brooklyn Bridge opened. Nietzsche's* Thus Spake Zarathustra. *Metropolitan Opera opened. Amsterdam Concertgebouw founded.*

1884 *Pasteur discovers inoculation against rabies.*

1886 *Statue of Liberty unveiled in New York Harbor.*

1887 *Daimler patents high-speed internal-combustion engine.*

1889 *Eiffel Tower, Paris World's Fair opened. Brazil becomes republic.*

1890 *Journey around world completed in 72 days.*

1892 *Duryea makes first American gas buggy.*

1893 *World's Columbian Exposition, Chicago.*

1894 *Nicholas II, last Tsar, ascends throne.*

1894 *Beginning of Dreyfus affair, lasting till 1905.*

1895 *Roentgen discovers X-rays. Marconi's wireless telegraphy.*

1896 *Becquerel finds radioactivity in uranium. Olympic games revived. Gold rush in Alaska.*

1897 *Queen Victoria's Diamond Jubilee.*

1898 *Pierre and Marie Curie discover radium. Empress Elizabeth of Austria-Hungary assassinated. Spanish-American War.*

1899 *Boer War. First International Peace Conference at the Hague.*

1900 *Boxer Insurrection in China. Count Zeppelin tests dirigible balloon. Philadelphia Symphony founded.*

COMPOSERS

HORATIO PARKER (1863–1919)
PIETRO MASCAGNI (1863–1945)
RICHARD STRAUSS (1864–1949)
ALEXANDER GRECHANINOV (1864–1956)
PAUL DUKAS (1865–1935)
ALEXANDER GLAZUNOV (1865–1936)
JEAN SIBELIUS (1865–1957)
FERRUCCIO BUSONI (1866–1924)
ERIK SATIE (1866–1925)
ENRIQUE GRANADOS (1867–1916)
MRS. H. H. A. BEACH (1867–1944)
HENRY F. GILBERT (1868–1928)

ALBERT ROUSSEL (1869–1937)

ALEXANDER SCRIABIN (1872–1915)
ARTHUR FARWELL (1872–1951)
RALPH VAUGHAN WILLIAMS (1872–1958)

MAX REGER (1873–1916)
SERGEI RACHMANINOFF (1873–1943)
DANIEL GREGORY MASON (1873–1953)
ARNOLD SCHOENBERG (1874–1951)
CHARLES IVES (1874–1954)
MAURICE RAVEL (1875–1937)
MANUEL DE FALLA (1876–1946)
JOHN ALDEN CARPENTER (1876–1951)
CARL RUGGLES (1876–1971)

OTTORINO RESPIGHI (1879–1936)

ERNEST BLOCH (1880–1959)
ILDEBRANDO PIZZETTI (1880–1968)

BÉLA BARTÓK (1881–1945)
GEORGES ENESCO (1881–1955)
JOHN POWELL (1882–1963)

IGOR STRAVINSKY (1882–1971)
ZOLTAN KODALY (1882–1967)
GIAN FRANCESCO MALIPIERO (1882–1973)
EDGARD VARÈSE (1883–1965)
ANTON WEBERN (1883–1945)

CHARLES T. GRIFFES (1884–1920)

PRINCIPAL FIGURES

Gabriele D'Annunzio (1863–1938)

Henri de Toulouse-Lautrec (1864–1901)
Rudyard Kipling (1865–1936)
William Butler Yeats (1865–1939)

Romain Rolland (1866–1943)
Wassily Kandinsky (1866–1944)
H. G. Wells (1866–1946)
Arnold Bennett (1867–1931)
John Galsworthy (1867–1933)
Luigi Pirandello (1867–1936)
Edmond Rostand (1868–1918)
Maxim Gorky (1868–1936)
Edward Arlington Robinson (1869–1935)
Henri Matisse (1869–1954)
Frank Lloyd Wright (1869–1959)
André Gide (1869–1951)
John Marin (1870–1953)
John M. Synge (1871–1909)
Marcel Proust (1871–1922)
Theodore Dreiser (1871–1945)
Georges Roualt (1871–1958)
Sergei Diaghilev (1872–1929)
Piet Mondrian (1872–1946)
Willa Cather (1873–1947)
Robert Frost (1874–1963)
Hugo Von Hofmannsthal (1874–1929)
Gertrude Stein (1874–1946)
W. Somerset Maugham (1874–1965)
Rainer Maria Rilke (1875–1926)
Thomas Mann (1875–1955)
Constantine Brancusi (1876–1958)
Marsden Hartley (1877–1943)
Isadora Duncan (1878–1927)
John Masefield (1878–1967)
Vachel Lindsay (1879–1931)
Paul Klee (1879–1940)
E. M. Forster (1879–1969)
Raoul Dufy (1879–1953)
Guillaume Apollinaire (1880–1918)
Jacob Epstein (1880–1959)
Fernand Léger (1881–1955)
Pablo Picasso (1881–1973)
Georges Braque (1882–1963)
James Joyce (1882–1941)
Jean Giraudoux (1882–1944)
Virginia Woolf (1882–1941)

Franz Kafka (1883–1924)
Maurice Utrillo (1883–1955)
Jose Ortega y Gasset (1883–1955)

WORLD EVENTS

1901 *Queen Victoria dies, Edward VII succeeds. De Vries's mutation theory.*

1903 *Wrights' first successful airplane flight. Ford organizes motor company.*

1904 *Opening of Russo-Japanese War. London Symphony founded. The Abbey Theatre opens in Dublin.*

1905 *Sigmund Freud founds psychoanalysis. Norway separates from Sweden. First Russian Revolution.*

1905 *Einstein's theory of relativity first published.*

1906 *San Francisco earthquake and fire.*

1907 *Second Hague Conference. Triple Entente. William James's* Pragmatism.

1908 *Model T Ford produced.*

1909 *Peary reaches North Pole.*

1911 *Amundsen reaches South Pole.*

1912 *China becomes republic.* Titanic *sinks.*

1914 *Panama Canal completed. World War I begins.*

1915 Lusitania *sunk. Einstein presents general theory of relativity.*

1917 *U.S. enters World War I. Russian Revolution. Prohibition Amendment.*

1918 *Kaiser abdicates. World War I ends in armistice.*

1919 *Treaty of Versailles. League of Nations formed: Mussolini founds Italian Fascist Party.*

1920 *Nineteenth Amendment (women's suffrage). Ireland granted home rule.*

1922 *Discovery of insulin. Fascist revolution in Italy. John Dewey's* Human Nature and Conduct.

1923 *U.S.S.R. established.*

1924 *Lenin dies.*

1927 *Lindberg's solo flight across Atlantic. Sacco and Vanzetti executed.*

COMPOSERS

ALBAN BERG (1885–1935)
JELLY ROLL MORTON (1885–1941)
WALLINGFORD RIEGGER (1885–1961)
HEITOR VILLA-LOBOS (1887–1959)

BOHUSLAV MARTINU (1890–1959)

JACQUES IBERT (1890–1963)

SERGE PROKOFIEV (1891–1952)

ARTHUR HONEGGER (1892–1955)

DARIUS MILHAUD (1892–1974)

DOUGLAS MOORE (1893–1969)

BESSIE SMITH (1894–1937)

WALTER PISTON (1894–76)
KAROL RATHAUS (1895–1954)
PAUL HINDEMITH (1895–1963)
WILLIAM GRANT STILL (1895–1978)
CARL ORFF (1895–1982)

HOWARD HANSON (1896–1981)
ROGER SESSIONS (1896–)
VIRGIL THOMSON (1896–)
HENRY COWELL (1897–1965)
QUINCY PORTER (1897–1966)

GEORGE GERSHWIN (1898–1937)

ROY HARRIS (1898–1979)

E. K. ("DUKE") ELLINGTON (1899–1974)

CARLOS CHAVEZ (1899–1978)

RANDALL THOMPSON (1899–)

FRANCIS POULENC (1899–1963)

AARON COPLAND (1900–)

ERNST KRENEK (1900–)

KURT WEILL (1900–50)

LOUIS ARMSTRONG (1900–71)

RUTH CRAWFORD (1901–53)

PRINCIPAL FIGURES

Amedeo Modigliani (1884–1920)
D. H. Lawrence (1885–1930)
Sinclair Lewis (1885–1951)
François Mauriac (1885–1970)
André Maurois (1885–1967)
Diego Riviera (1886–1957)
Juan Gris (1887–1927)
Marcel Duchamp (1887–1968)
William Zorach (1887–1966)
Georgia O'Keeffe (1887–)
Hans Arp (1887–1966)
Marc Chagall (1887–)
Kurt Schwitters (1887–1948)
Giorgio di Chirico (1888–1978)
T. S. Eliot (1888–1965)
T. E. Lawrence (1888–1935)
Thomas Hart Benton (1889–1975)
Karel Čapek (1890–1938)
Max Ernst (1891–1976)
Grant Wood (1892–1944)
John P. Marquand (1893–1960)
Joan Miro (1893–1983)
Ernst Toller (1893–1939)
e. e. cummings (1894–1962)
Aldous Huxley (1894–1963)
Robert Graves (1895–)

F. Scott Fitzgerald (1896–1940)

Robert Sherwood (1896–1955)
John Dos Passos (1896–1970)

William Faulkner (1897–1962)

Louis Aragon (1897–)

Sergei Eisenstein (1898–1948)

Bertolt Brecht (1898–1956)

Ernest Hemingway (1898–1961)
Alexander Calder (1898–1976)

Henry Moore (1898–)

Hart Crane (1899–1932)

Federico García Lorca (1899–1936)

Thomas Wolfe (1900–38)

Ignazio Silone (1900–78)

André Malraux (1901–76)

John Steinbeck (1902–68)

WORLD EVENTS	COMPOSERS	PRINCIPAL FIGURES
1928 Graf Zeppelin *crosses Atlantic. First radio broadcast of N.Y. Philharmonic Orchestra. Penicillin discovered.*	SIR WILLIAM WALTON (1902–83)	Langston Hughes (1902–67)
	STEFAN WOLPE (1902–71)	George Orwell (1903–50)
1930 *The planet Pluto discovered.*	LUIGI DALLAPICCOLA (1904–75)	Mark Rothko (1903–70) Salvador Dali (1904–)
1931 *Japan invades Manchuria. Empire State Building completed.*	MARC BLITZSTEIN (1905–64)	George Balanchine (1904–83) Christopher Isherwood (1904–) Willem de Kooning (1904–)
1933 *Franklin D. Roosevelt inaugurated. Hitler takes over German government.*	DMITRI SHOSTAKOVICH (1906–75)	Arthur Koestler (1905–83)
	ELLIOTT CARTER (1908–)	Jean-Paul Sartre (1905–1980)
1936 *First sit-down strike. Sulfa drugs introduced in U.S. Spanish Civil War.*	OLIVIER MESSIAEN (1908–)	David Smith (1906–62) Samuel Beckett (1906–)
1937 *Japan invades China.*	HOWARD SWANSON (1909–78)	W. H. Auden (1907–73) Theodore Roethke (1908–63)
1939 *World War II starts: Germany invades Poland, Britain and France declare war on Germany, Russia invades Finland. U.S. revises neutrality stand.*	SAMUEL BARBER (1910–82)	Richard Wright (1908–60)
	WILLIAM SCHUMAN (1910–)	Stephen Spender (1900–)
	GIAN CARLO MENOTTI (1911–)	Franz Kline (1910–62)
1940 *Roosevelt elected to third term. Churchill becomes British prime minister.*	VLADIMIR USSACHEVSKY (1911–)	Philip Guston (1912–)
1941 *U.S. attacked by Japan, declares war on Japan, Germany, Italy.*	ARTHUR BERGER (1912–)	Eugene Ionesco (1912–)
1943 *Germans defeated at Stalingrad and in North Africa. Italy surrenders.*	JOHN CAGE (1912–)	Jackson Pollock (1912–56)
1944 *D-Day. Invasion of France.*	HUGO WEISGALL (1912–)	
1945 *United Nations Conference at San Francisco. Germany surrenders. Atom bomb dropped on Hiroshima. Japan surrenders.*	BENJAMIN BRITTEN (1913–76)	Albert Camus (1913–60)
	BILLIE HOLIDAY (1915–59)	Ralph Ellison (1914–)
1946 *First meeting of U.N. General Assembly.*	DAVID DIAMOND (1915–) GEORGE PERLE (1915–)	Dylan Thomas (1914–53) Tennessee Williams (1914–83)
1948 *Gandhi assassinated.*	MILTON BABBITT (1916–)	Arthur Miller (1915–)
1949 *Communists defeat Chiang Kai-shek in China. U.S.S.R. explodes atomic bomb.*	ALBERTO GINASTERA (1916–83)	Robert Motherwell (1915–)
	ULYSSES KAY (1917–)	Robert Lowell (1917–77)
1950 *North Koreans invade South Korea.*	LEONARD BERNSTEIN (1918–)	Ingmar Bergman (1918–)
1951 *Schuman Plan pools coal and steel markets of six European nations.*	GEORGE ROCHBERG (1918–)	J. D. Salinger (1919–)
1952 *George VI dies; succeeded by Elizabeth II. Eisenhower elected President.*	LEON KIRCHNER (1919–)	Federico Fellini (1920–)
	CHARLIE PARKER (1920–55)	
1954 *First atomic-powered submarine,* Nautilus, *launched. War in Indo-China.*	LUKAS FOSS (1922–)	Richard Wilbur (1921–)
1955 *Warsaw Pact signed. Salk serum for infantile paralysis.*	IANNIS XENAKIS (1922–)	
	GYORGY LIGETI (1923–)	Denise Levertov (1923–)

WORLD EVENTS	COMPOSERS	PRINCIPAL FIGURES
1957 *First underground atomic explosion.*		
	PETER MENNIN (1923–83)	Norman Mailer (1923–)
1958 *Fifth Republic in France under de Gaulle.*	MEL POWELL (1923–)	
1959 *Alaska becomes 49th state. Castro victorious over Batista. Hawaii becomes 50th state.*	NED ROREM (1923–) LUIGI NONO (1924–)	
1960 *Kennedy elected President.*	JULIA PERRY (1924–)	James Baldwin (1924–)
1962 *Cuban missile crisis. Algeria declared independent of France. Opening of Lincoln Center for the Performing Arts in New York.*	LUCIANO BERIO (1925–)	Kenneth Koch (1925–)
	PIERRE BOULEZ (1925–)	Robert Rauschenberg (1925–)
	GUNTHER SCHULLER (1925–)	
1963 *President Kennedy assassinated. Lyndon Johnson becomes 36th President.*	EARLE BROWNE (1926–)	Allen Ginsberg (1926–)
1965 *First walk in space. White minority in Rhodesia proclaims itself independent of Britain. Alabama Civil Rights March.*	MORTON FELDMAN (1926–) BEN JOHNSTON (1926–)	
1966 *France withdraws from NATO alliance.*		
1967 *Israeli-Arab "6-Day War." First successful heart transplant in South Africa.*	HANS WERNER HENZE (1926–)	
1968 *Richard M. Nixon elected President. Soviet occupation of Czechoslovakia. Martin Luther King and Robert F. Kennedy assassinated.*	SALVATORE MARTIRANO (1927–) JACOB DRUCKMAN (1928–)	John Ashbery (1927–) Günter Grass (1927–) John Hollander (1928–)
	THEA MUSGRAVE (1928–)	Edward Albee (1928–)
1969 *Apollo 11: first manned landing on the moon. De Gaulle resigns as French president.*	KARLHEINZ STOCKHAUSEN (1928–)	
1970 *U.S. intervention in Cambodia. Nobel Prize in Literature to Aleksandr Solzhenitsyn.*		Adrienne Rich (1929–)
	GEORGE CRUMB (1929–)	Claes Oldenburg (1929–)
1971 *Publication of the "Pentagon Papers." Peoples Republic of China admitted to the U.N.*	DAVID BAKER (1931–)	John Barth (1930–)
1972 *Richard Nixon re-elected. Attempted assassination of Governor George Wallace.*		Jean-Luc Godard (1930–)
	KRZYSZTOF PENDERECKI (1933–)	Jasper Johns (1930–)
1973 *Vietnam War ends. The "Watergate Affair" begins. Energy crisis. Vice President Agnew resigns.*	MARIO DAVIDOVSKY (1934–)	Harold Pinter (1930–)
1974 *President Nixon resigns.*	PETER MAXWELL DAVIES (1934–)	Andy Warhol (1931–) Yevgeny Yevtushenko (1933–) Imamu Amiri Baraka (Le Roi Jones) (1934–)
1975 *Francisco Franco dies. Civil War in Angola.*		

WORLD EVENTS	COMPOSERS	PRINCIPAL FIGURES
1976 *Viking spacecraft lands on Mars. U.S. celebrates its Bicentennial. Mao Tsetung dies. Jimmy Carter elected president.*	JOHN EATON (1935–)	Frank Stella (1936–) Tom Stoppard (1937–)
1977 *New Panama Canal Treaty signed. Military coup in Pakistan. Menachem Begin named Israeli Prime Minister.*	STEVE REICH (1936–)	
1978 *World's first test-tube baby born in England. First Polish Pope (John Paul II) elected. Accord reached at Camp David talks between Egypt and Israel.*	DAVID DEL TREDICI (1937–) PHILIP GLASS (1937–)	Lanford Wilson (1937–)
1979 *Shah of Iran deposed. Salt II treaty between U.S. and U.S.S.R. Major nuclear accident at Three Mile Island.*	WILLIAM BOLCOM (1938–)	
1980 *Iranian militants seize U.S. Embassy in Teheran. Ronald Reagan elected U.S. President. U.S.S.R. invades Afghanistan.*	ELLEN TAAFFE ZWILICH (1939–)	Sam Shepard (1943–)
1981 *First woman appointed to Supreme Court. Space shuttle Columbia launched. President Sadat of Egypt assassinated. American hostages in Iran freed.*	LAURIE ANDERSON (1947–)	
1982 *Argentina invades Falkland Islands. Summit conference of Western nations in France. New Rockefeller wing opens at Metropolitan Museum of Art.*	TOBIAS PICKER (1954–)	Rainer Werner Fassbinder (1946–82)
1983 *First woman astronaut into space.*		

APPENDIX V

The Harmonic Series

When a string or a column of air vibrates, it does so not only as a whole but also in segments—halves, thirds, fourths, fifths, sixths, sevenths, and so on. These segments produce the *overtones*, which are also known as *partials* or *harmonics*. What we hear as the single tone is really the combination of the fundamental tone and its overtones, just as what we see as white light is the combination of all the colors of the spectrum. Although we may not be conscious of the partials, they play a decisive part in our listening; for the presence or absence of overtones in the sound wave determines the timbre, the color of the tone. Following is the table of the Chord of Nature: the fundamental and its overtones or harmonics. Those marked with an asterisk are not in tune with our tempered scale.

Half the string gives the second member of the series, the octave above the fundamental. This interval is represented by the ratio 1:2; that is to say, the two tones of this interval are produced when one string is half as long as the other and is vibrating twice as fast. The one-third segment of the string produces the third member of the harmonic series, the fifth above the octave. This interval is represented by the ratio 2:3. We hear it when one string is two-thirds as long as the other and is vibrating one and a half times (3/2) as fast. The one-fourth segment of the string produces the fourth member of the series, the fourth above. This interval is represented by the ratio 3:4, for its two tones are produced when one string is three-fourths as long as the other and vibrates one and a third times (4/3) as fast. One fifth of the string produces the fifth member of the harmonic series, the major third, an interval represented by the ratio 4:5. One sixth of the string produces the sixth member of the series, the minor third, represented by the ratio 5:6; and so on. From the seventh to the eleventh partials we find approximate whole tones. Between the eleventh harmonic and its octave, 22, the semitone appears. After partial 22 we enter the realm of microtones (smaller than semitones)—third tones, quarter tones, sixth and eighth tones, and so on.

On the brass instruments, the player goes from one pitch to another not only by lengthening or shortening the column of air within the tube, which he does by means of valves, but also by splitting the column of air into its segments or partials, going from one harmonic to another by varying the pressure of his lips and breath. The bugle does not vary the length of the air column, for it has no valves. The familiar bugle calls consist simply of the different harmonics of the same fundamental.

Index

Definitions of terms appear on the pages indicated in **bold** type.

Romantic

Scott Joplin (1868–1917)

Erik Satie (1866–1925)

Jean Sibelius (1865–1957)

Richard Strauss (1864–1949)

Claude Debussy (1862–1918)

Gustav Mahler (1860–1911)

Giacomo Puccini (1858–1924)

Edvard Grieg (1843–1907)

Antonín Dvořák (1841–1904)

Peter Ilyich Tchaikovsky (1840–93)

Modest Musorgsky (1839–81)

Georges Bizet (1838–75)

Camille Saint-Saëns (1835–1921)

Alexander Borodin (1834–87)

Johannes Brahms (1833–97)

Stephen Foster (1826–64)

Anton Bruckner (1824–96)

Bedřich Smetana (1824–84)

Giuseppe Verdi (1813–1901)

Richard Wagner (1813–83)

Franz Liszt (1811–86)

Robert Schumann (1810–56)

Frédéric François Chopin (1810–49)

Felix Mendelssohn (1809–47)

Hector Berlioz (1803–69)

Franz Schubert (1797–1828)

Gioacchino Rossini (1792–1868)

Carl Maria von Weber (1786–1826)